Lecture Notes in Computer Science 13163

More information about this subseries at https://link.springer.com/bookseries/7409

Giuseppe Nicosia · Varun Ojha ·
Emanuele La Malfa · Gabriele La Malfa ·
Giorgio Jansen · Panos M. Pardalos ·
Giovanni Giuffrida · Renato Umeton (Eds.)

Machine Learning, Optimization, and Data Science

7th International Conference, LOD 2021
Grasmere, UK, October 4–8, 2021
Revised Selected Papers, Part I

 Springer

Editors
Giuseppe Nicosia (ID)
University of Catania
Catania, Italy

Emanuele La Malfa (ID)
Department of Computer Science
University of Oxford
Oxford, UK

Giorgio Jansen (ID)
Department of Biochemistry
University of Cambridge
Cambridge, UK

Giovanni Giuffrida (ID)
University of Catania
Catania, Italy

Varun Ojha (ID)
Department of Computer Science
University of Reading
Reading, UK

Gabriele La Malfa (ID)
Cambridge Judge Business School
University of Cambridge
Cambridge, UK

Panos M. Pardalos (ID)
Department of Industrial and Systems
Engineering
University of Florida
Gainesville, FL, USA

Renato Umeton (ID)
Department of Informatics
Dana-Farber Cancer Institute
Boston, MA, USA

ISSN 0302-9743   ISSN 1611-3349 (electronic)
Lecture Notes in Computer Science
ISBN 978-3-030-95466-6   ISBN 978-3-030-95467-3 (eBook)
https://doi.org/10.1007/978-3-030-95467-3

LNCS Sublibrary: SL3 – Information Systems and Applications, incl. Internet/Web, and HCI

This Springer imprint is published by the registered company Springer Nature Switzerland AG
The registered company address is: Gewerbestrasse 11, 6330 Cham, Switzerland

Preface

LOD is an international conference embracing the fields of machine learning, optimization, and data science. The seventh edition, LOD 2021, took place during October 4–8, 2021, in Grasmere (Lake District), UK. LOD 2021 was held successfully online and onsite to meet challenges posed by the worldwide outbreak of COVID-19. This year the scientific program of the conference was even richer than usual; LOD 2021 hosted the first edition of the Advanced Course and Symposium on Artificial Intelligence & Neuroscience – ACAIN 2021. In fact, this year, in the LOD proceedings we decided to also include the papers of the first edition of the Symposium on Artificial Intelligence and Neuroscience (ACAIN 2021). The symposium was scheduled for 2020, but due to the COVID-19 pandemic until we were forced to postpone it to 2021.

The review process for the papers submitted to ACAIN 2021 was double blind, performed rigorously by an international Program Committee consisting of leading experts in the field. The following three articles in this volume comprise the articles accepted to ACAIN 2021:

- Effect of Geometric Complexity on Intuitive Model Selection by Eugenio Piasini, Vijay Balasubramanian, and Joshua Gold.
- Training Convolutional Neural Networks with Competitive Hebbian Learning Approaches by Gabriele Lagani, Giuseppe Amato, Fabrizio Falchi, and Claudio Gennaro.
- Towards Understanding Neuroscience of Realisation of Information Need in Light of Relevance and Satisfaction Judgement by Sakrapee Paisalnan, Frank Pollick, and Yashar Moshfeghi.

Since 2015, the LOD conference has brought academics, researchers, and industrial researchers together in a unique multidisciplinary community to discuss the state of the art and the latest advances in the integration of machine learning, optimization, and data science to provide and support the scientific and technological foundations for interpretable, explainable, and trustworthy AI. In 2017, LOD adopted the Asilomar AI Principles.

The annual conference on machine Learning, Optimization, and Data science (LOD) is an international conference on machine learning, computational optimization, and big data that includes invited talks, tutorial talks, special sessions, industrial tracks, demonstrations, and oral and poster presentations of refereed papers.

LOD has established itself as a premier multidisciplinary conference in machine learning, computational optimization, and data science. It provides an international forum for presentation of original multidisciplinary research results, as well as exchange and dissemination of innovative and practical development experiences.

The manifesto of the LOD conference is as follows:

"The problem of understanding intelligence is said to be the greatest problem in science today and "the" problem for this century – as deciphering the genetic code was for the second half of the last one. Arguably, the problem of learning represents a gateway to understanding intelligence in brains and machines, to discovering how the human brain works, and to making intelligent machines that learn from experience and improve their competences as children do. In engineering, learning techniques would make it possible to develop software that can be quickly customized to deal with the increasing amount of information and the flood of data around us."

The Mathematics of Learning: Dealing with Data
Tomaso Poggio (MOD 2015 and LOD 2020 Keynote Speaker) and Steve Smale

"Artificial Intelligence has already provided beneficial tools that are used every day by people around the world. Its continued development, guided by the Asilomar principles of AI, will offer amazing opportunities to help and empower people in the decades and centuries ahead."

The Asilomar AI Principles

The Asilomar AI Principles were adopted by the LOD conference following their inception (January 3–5, 2017). Since then these principles have been an integral part of the manifesto of the LOD conferences.

LOD 2021 attracted leading experts from industry and the academic world with the aim of strengthening the connection between these institutions. The 2021 edition of LOD represented a great opportunity for professors, scientists, industry experts, and research students to learn about recent developments in their own research areas and to learn about research in contiguous research areas, with the aim of creating an environment to share ideas and trigger new collaborations.

As chairs, it was an honour to organize a premier conference in these areas and to have received a large variety of innovative and original scientific contributions.

During LOD 2021, 12 plenary talks were presented by leading experts:

LOD 2021 Keynote Speakers:

- Ioannis Antonoglou, DeepMind, UK
- Roberto Cipolla, University of Cambridge, UK
- Panos Pardalos, University of Florida, USA
- Verena Rieser, Heriot Watt University, UK

ACAIN 2021 Keynote Lecturers:

- Timothy Behrens, University of Oxford, UK
- Matthew Botvinick, DeepMind, UK
- Claudia Clopath, Imperial College London, UK
- Ila Fiete, MIT, USA
- Karl Friston, University College London, UK
- Rosalyn Moran, King's College London, UK
- Maneesh Sahani, University College London, UK
- Jane Wang, DeepMind, UK

LOD 2021 received 215 submissions from authors in 68 countries in five continents, and each manuscript was independently reviewed by a committee formed by at least five members. These proceedings contain 86 research articles written by leading scientists in the fields of machine learning, artificial intelligence, reinforcement learning, computational optimization, neuroscience, and data science presenting a substantial array of ideas, technologies, algorithms, methods, and applications.

At LOD 2021, Springer LNCS generously sponsored the LOD Best Paper Award. This year, the paper by Zhijian Li, Bao Wang, and Jack Xin, titled "An Integrated Approach to Produce Robust Deep Neural Network Models with High Efficiency", received the LOD 2021 Best Paper Award.

This conference could not have been organized without the contributions of exceptional researchers and visionary industry experts, so we thank them all for participating. A sincere thank you goes also to the 41 subreviewers and to the Program Committee, comprising more than 250 scientists from academia and industry, for their valuable and essential work of selecting the scientific contributions.

Finally, we would like to express our appreciation to the keynote speakers who accepted our invitation, and to all the authors who submitted their research papers to LOD 2021.

October 2021

Giuseppe Nicosia
Varun Ojha
Emanuele La Malfa
Gabriele La Malfa
Giorgio Jansen
Panos Pardalos
Giovanni Giuffrida
Renato Umeton

Organization

General Chairs

Giorgio Jansen — University of Cambridge, UK
Emanuele La Malfa — University of Oxford, UK
Renato Umeton — Dana-Farber Cancer Institute, MIT, Harvard T.H. Chan School of Public Health and Weill Cornell Medicine, USA

Conference and Technical Program Committee Co-chairs

Giovanni Giuffrida — University of Catania and NeoData Group, Italy
Varun Ojha — University of Reading, UK
Panos Pardalos — University of Florida, USA

Special Sessions Chair

Gabriele La Malfa — University of Cambridge, UK

ACAIN 2021 Chairs

Giuseppe Nicosia — University of Cambridge, UK, and University of Catania, Italy
Varun Ojha — University of Reading, UK
Panos Pardalos — University of Florida, USA

Steering Committee

Giuseppe Nicosia — University of Cambridge, UK, and University of Catania, Italy
Panos Pardalos — University of Florida, USA

Program Committee

Adair, Jason — University of Stirling, UK
Adesina, Opeyemi — University of the Fraser Valley, Canada
Agra, Agostinho — University of Aveiro, Portugal
Allmendinger, Richard — University of Manchester, UK
Alves, Maria Joao — University of Coimbra, Portugal
Amaral, Paula — University Nova de Lisboa, Portugal
Arany, Adam — University of Leuven, Belgium
Archetti, Alberto — Politecnico di Milano, Italy

Aringhieri, Roberto	University of Turin, Italy
Baggio, Rodolfo	Bocconi University, Italy
Baklanov, Artem	International Institute for Applied Systems Analysis, Austria
Bar-Hen, Avner	CNAM, France
Bentley, Peter	University College London, UK
Bernardino, Heder	Universidade Federal de Juiz de Fora, Brazil
Berrar, Daniel	Tokyo Institute of Technology, Japan
Berzins, Martin	University of Utah, USA
Beyer, Hans-Georg	Vorarlberg University of Applied Sciences, Austria
Blekas, Konstantinos	University of Ioannina, Greece
Boldt, Martin	Blekinge Institute of Technology, Sweden
Bonassi, Fabio	Politecnico di Milano, Italy
Borg, Anton	Blekinge Institute of Technology, Sweden
Borrotti, Matteo	University of Milano-Bicocca, Italy
Boscaini, Davide	Fondazione Bruno Kessler, Italy
Braccini, Michele	University of Bologna, Italy
Browne, Will	Queensland University of Technology, Australia
Cagliero, Luca	Politecnico di Torino, Italy
Cagnoni, Stefano	University of Parma, Italy
Campbell, Russell	University of the Fraser Valley, Canada
Canim, Mustafa	IBM, USA
Carletti, Timoteo	University of Namur, Belgium
Carrasquinha, Eunice	Universidade de Lisboa, Portugal
Carta, Salvatore	University of Cagliari, Italy
Castellini, Alberto	Verona University, Italy
Cavicchioli, Roberto	Universita' di Modena e Reggio Emilia, Italy
Ceci, Michelangelo	Universita degli Studi di Bari, Italy
Cerveira, Adelaide	INESC-TEC, Portugal
Chakraborty, Uday	University of Missouri - St. Louis, USA
Chen, Keke	Marquette University, USA
Chen, Ying-Ping	National Yang Ming Chiao Tung University, Taiwan
Chinneck, John	Carleton University, Canada
Chlebik, Miroslav	University of Sussex, UK
Cho, Sung-Bae	Yonsei University, South Korea
Chretien, Stephane	National Physical Laboratory, France
Cire, Andre Augusto	University of Toronto, Canada
Codognet, Philippe	University of Tokyo, Japan
Consoli, Sergio	European Commission, Joint Research Centre, Italy
Costa, Juan Jose	Universitat Politecnica de Catalunya, Spain
Damiani, Chiara	University of Milano-Biocca, Italy
Dandekar, Thomas	University of Wuerzburg, Germany
Daraio, Elena	Politecnico di Torino, Italy
De Brouwer, Edward	Katholieke Universiteit Leuven, Belgium
De Leone, Renato	University of Camerino, Italy
Del Buono, Nicoletta	University of Bari Aldo Moro, Italy

Dell'Amico, Mauro	University of Modena and Reggio Emilia, Italy
Dhaenens, Clarisse	Université Lille 1, France
Di Fatta, Giuseppe	University of Reading, UK
Di Gaspero, Luca	University of Udine, Italy
Dias, Joana	University of Coimbra and INESCC, Portugal
Dionisio, Joao	University of Porto, Portugal
Dobre, Ciprian	University Politehnica of Bucharest, Romania
Doerfel, Stephan	Kiel University of Applied Sciences, Germany
Donaghy, John	University of New Hampshire, USA
Drezewski, Rafal	AGH University of Science and Technology, Poland
Durillo, Juan	Leibniz Supercomputing Centre, Germany
Ebecken, Nelson	COPPE/UFRJ, Brazil
Eftimov, Tome	Jozef Stefan Institute, Slovenia
Engelbrecht, Andries	University of Stellenbosch, South Africa
Esposito, Flavia	University of Bari Aldo Moro, Italy
Esposito, Roberto	University of Torino, Italy
Farinelli, Alessandro	Verona University, Italy
Fasano, Giovanni	University Ca'Foscari of Venice, Italy
Ferrari, Carlo	University of Padova, Italy
Filisetti, Alessandro	Explora Biotech Srl, Italy
Fillatre, Lionel	University of Nice Sophia Antipolis, France
Finck, Steffen	Vorarlberg University of Applied Sciences, Austria
Fliege, Joerg	University of Southampton, UK
Formenti, Enrico	Universite Cote d'Azur, France
Franchini, Giorgia	University of Modena and Reggio Emilia, Italy
Franco, Giuditta	University of Verona, Italy
Frandi, Emanuele	Cogent Labs Inc., Japan
Fraternali, Piero	Politecnico di Milano, Italy
Freschi, Valerio	University of Urbino, Italy
Frohner, Nikolaus	TU Wien, Austria
Gajek, Carola	Augsburg University, Germany
Gallicchio, Claudio	University of Pisa, Italy
Garza, Paolo	Politecnico di Torino, Italy
Gauthier, Bertrand	Cardiff University, UK
Gendreau, Michel	Ecole Polytechnique de Montreal, Canada
Giannakoglou, Kyriakos	National Technical University of Athens, Greece
Gnecco, Giorgio	IMT School for Advanced Studies Lucca, Italy
Goncalves, Teresa	University of Evora, Portugal
Granitzer, Michael	University of Passau, Germany
Grishagin, Vladimir	Nizhni Novgorod State University, Russia
Guidolin, Massimo	Bocconi University, Italy
Gurbani, Vijay	Illinois Institute of Technology, USA
Hanse, Gideon	Leiden University, The Netherlands
Hao, Jin-Kao	University of Angers, France
Heidrich-Meisner, Verena	Kiel University, Germany
Henggeler, Antunes Carlos	University of Coimbra, Portugal

Hernandez-Diaz, Alfredo	Pablo de Olvide University, Spain
Herrmann, Michael	University of Edinburgh, UK
Hoogendoorn, Mark	Vrije Universiteit Amsterdam, The Netherlands
Ianovski, Egor	Higher School of Economics, Russia
Jakaite, Livija	University of Bedfordshire, UK
Johnson, Colin	University of Nottingham, UK
Jourdan, Laetitia	Inria, France
Kalinichenko, Vera	UCLA, USA
Kalyagin, Valeriy	Higher School of Economics, Russia
Karakostas, George	McMaster University, Canada
Kavsek, Branko	University of Primorska, Slovenia
Khachay, Michael	Krasovsky Institute of Mathematics and Mechanics, Russia
Kiani, Shahvandi Mostafa	ETH Zurich, Switzerland
Kiziltan, Zeynep	University of Bologna, Italy
Kochetov, Yury	Sobolev Institute of Mathematics, Russia
Kouchak, Shokoufeh	Arizona State University, USA
Kruger, Hennie	North-West University, South Africa
Kumar, Chauhan Vinod	University of Cambridge, UK
Kvasov, Dmitri	University of Calabria, Italy
La Malfa, Gabriele	University of Cambridge, UK
Landa-Silva, Dario	University of Nottingham, UK
Lanz, Oswald	Fondazione Bruno Kessler, Italy
Le Thi, Hoai An	Universite de Lorraine, France
Lera, Daniela	University of Cagliari, Italy
Lombardo, Gianfranco	University of Parma, Italy
Lu, Yun	Kutztown University of Pennsylvania, USA
Lu, Paul	University of Alberta, Canada
Luukka, Pasi	Lappeenranta University of Technology, Finland
Maalouf, Eliane	University of Neuchatel, Switzerland
Manzoni, Luca	University of Trieste, Italy
Maratea, Marco	University of Genova, Italy
Marinaki, Magdalene	Technical University of Crete, Greece
Marinakis, Yannis	Technical University of Crete, Greece
Martins de Moraes, Rafael	New York University, USA
Matsatsinis, Nikolaos	Technical University of Crete, Greece
Matsuura, Shun	Keio University, Japan
Meyer, Angela	Bern University of Applied Sciences, Switzerland
Meyer-Nieberg, Silja	Universitaet der Bundeswehr Muenchen, Germany
Milani, Federico	Politecnico di Milano, Italy
Milne, Holden	University of the Fraser Valley, Canada
Mongiovi, Misael	Consiglio Nazionale delle Ricerche, Italy
Montanez, George	Harvey Mudd College, USA
Nadif, Mohamed	Université de Paris, France
Nanni, Mirco	ISTI-CNR, Italy
Nicosia, Giuseppe	University of Catania, Italy

Nowaczyk, Slawomir	Halmstad University, Sweden
Nunez-Gonzalez, David	University of the Basque Country, Spain
Ojha, Varun	University of Reading, UK
Orchel, Marcin	AGH University of Science and Technology, Poland
Otero, Beatriz	Polytechnic University of Catalonia, Spain
Pacher, Mathias	Goethe-Universität Frankfurt am Main, Germany
Palar, Pramudita Satria	Bandung Institute of Technology, Indonesia
Papastefanatos, George	ATHENA Research Center, Greece
Paquet, Eric	National Research Council, Canada
Paquete, Luis	University of Coimbra, Portugal
Pardalos, Panos	University of Florida, USA
Parsopoulos, Konstantinos	University of Ioannina, Greece
Patane, Andrea	University of Oxford, UK
Pazhayidam, George Clint	Indian Institute of Technology Goa, India
Pedio, Manuela	University of Bristol, UK
Pedroso, Joao Pedro	University of Porto, Portugal
Peitz, Sebastian	Universität Paderborn, Germany
Pelta, David	University of Granada, Spain
Pereira, Ivo	University Fernando Pessoa, Portugal
Perrin, Dimitri	Queensland University of Technology, Australia
Petkovic, Milena	Zuse Institute Berlin, Germany
Ploskas, Nikolaos	University of Western Macedonia, Greece
Podda, Alessandro Sebastian	University of Cagliari, Italy
Poggioni, Valentina	University of Perugia, Italy
Polyzou, Agoritsa	Florida International University, USA
Pravin, Chandresh	University of Reading, UK
Prestwich, Steve	Insight Centre for Data Analytics, Ireland
Qian, Buyue	Xi'an Jiaotong University, China
Qiao, Ting	University of Auckland, New Zealand
Quadrini, Michela	University of Camerino, Italy
Radzik, Tomasz	King's College London, UK
Raidl, Gunther	Vienna University of Technology, Austria
Rauch, Jan	Prague University of Economics and Business, Czech Republic
Rebennack, Steffen	Karlsruhe Institute of Technology, Germany
Regis, Rommel	Saint Joseph's University, USA
Reif, Wolfgang	University of Augsburg, Germany
Requejo, Cristina	University of Aveiro, Portugal
Rinaldi, Francesco	University of Padua, Italy
Ripamonti, Laura Anna	University of Milan, Italy
Rocha, Humberto	University of Coimbra, Portugal
Rodrigues, Maia Jose Gilvan	Universidade Federal do Ceara, Brazil
Roy, Arnab	Fujitsu Laboratories of America, USA
Ruan, Hang	University of Edinburgh, UK

Yuen, Shiu Yin	City University of Hong Kong, Hong Kong
Zabinsky, Zelda	University of Washington, USA
Zaidi, Moayid Ali	Ostfold University College, Norway
Zese, Riccardo	University of Ferrara, Italy
Zhang, Yongfeng	Rutgers University, USA
Zhigljavsky, Anatoly	Cardiff University, UK

Best Paper Awards

LOD 2021 Best Paper Award

"An Integrated Approach to Produce Robust Deep Neural Network Models with High Efficiency"
Zhijian Li[1], Bao Wang[2], and Jack Xin[1]
[1] University of California, Irvine, USA
[2] University of Utah, USA
Springer sponsored the LOD 2021 Best Paper Award with a cash prize.

Special Mention

"Statistical Estimation of Quantization for Probability Distributions: Best Equivariant Estimator of Principal Points"
Shun Matsuura[1] and Hiroshi Kurata[2]
[1] Keio University, Japan
[2] University of Tokyo, Japan

"Neural Weighted A*: Learning Graph Costs and Heuristics with Differentiable Anytime A*"
Alberto Archetti, Marco Cannici, and Matteo Matteucci
Politecnico di Milano, Italy

LOD 2021 Best Talk

"Go to Youtube and Call me in the Morning: Use of Social Media for Chronic Conditions"
Rema Padman[1], Xiao Liu[2], Anjana Susarla[3], and Bin Zhang[4]
[1] Carnegie Mellon University, USA
[2] Arizona State University, USA
[3] Michigan State University, USA
[4] University of Arizona, USA

Contents – Part I

Contents – Part II

Effect of Geometric Complexity on Intuitive Model Selection

Eugenio Piasini$^{(\boxtimes)}$ (ID), Vijay Balasubramanian, and Joshua I. Gold

Computational Neuroscience Initiative, University of Pennsylvania,
Philadelphia, Pennsylvania, USA
epiasini@sas.upenn.edu

Abstract. Occam's razor is the principle stating that, all else being equal, simpler explanations for a set of observations are to be preferred to more complex ones. This idea can be made precise in the context of statistical inference, where the same quantitative notion of complexity of a statistical model emerges naturally from different approaches based on Bayesian model selection and information theory. The broad applicability of this mathematical formulation suggests a normative model of decision-making under uncertainty: complex explanations should be penalized according to this common measure of complexity. However, little is known about if and how humans intuitively quantify the relative complexity of competing interpretations of noisy data. Here we measure the sensitivity of naive human subjects to statistical model complexity. Our data show that human subjects bias their decisions in favor of simple explanations based not only on the dimensionality of the alternatives (number of model parameters), but also on finer-grained aspects of their geometry. In particular, as predicted by the theory, models intuitively judged as more complex are not only those with more parameters, but also those with larger volume and prominent curvature or boundaries. Our results imply that principled notions of statistical model complexity have direct quantitative relevance to human decision-making.

1 Introduction

Occam's razor is a philosophical prescription to keep our models of the world as simple as possible. But does naive human decision-making under uncertainty follow this prescription, and if it does, how strong is the preference for simple models? To answer these questions we must first provide a normative reference point for human behavior, by understanding from first principles what it means for a model to be simple or complex and how strongly should an optimal decision-making process be affected by a simplicity bias.

Many statistical learning techniques are governed by hyperparameters that can be tuned to control some notion of complexity of the underlying model. For instance, in regression, regularization techniques such as LASSO enforce an adjustable-strength constraint on the space of desired solutions [13]. In unsupervised learning, clustering methods often allow to control the desired level

© Springer Nature Switzerland AG 2022
G. Nicosia et al. (Eds.): LOD 2021, LNCS 13163, pp. 1–24, 2022.
https://doi.org/10.1007/978-3-030-95467-3_1

of granularity by specifying in advance the number of clusters [6]. More generally, in many probabilistic model selection settings, one compares several models with different number of parameters. In this case, the well known Akaike and Bayesian Information Criteria (AIC, BIC) state that the best model for a certain set of observations is the one that maximizes the log likelihood of the data minus some penalty that depends on the complexity of the model, measured by the number of parameters it contains [13]. A common thread among these examples is the idea of trading off some goodness of fit on the training data in exchange for model simplicity. A bias towards simplicity is desirable because it improves the performance of the model on unseen data, or because it makes it more interpretable, instantiating Occam's razor in concrete statistical practice. However, the examples above highlight that there are multiple possible definitions of complexity, some of which may be applicable only in relatively narrow contexts.

To overcome this difficulty, we draw on the theory of Bayesian model selection [3,12,16,20]. This framework offers a principled definition of model complexity that is applicable across multiple settings, and makes complexity commensurable with goodness of fit by placing the two quantities on the same scale. Here, "model" always refers to a parametric family of probability distributions. For instance, the set of all Binomial probability distributions with n fixed to a certain value and p unknown, $0 \leq p \leq 1$, is a one-parameter model. Starting from a set of observations $X = \{x_n\}$ and a (finite) set of models, with a choice of prior probability over models $p(\mathcal{M})$ and over the parameters ϑ characterising each of them $p(\vartheta|\mathcal{M})$, by applying Bayes' theorem and marginalising over model parameters one can invert the likelihood function $p(X|\mathcal{M}, \vartheta)$ to yield a posterior distribution over models given the data, $p(\mathcal{M}|X)$. One can then select the model that maximises the posterior. It can be shown [3] that assuming an uninformative prior for the model parameters ϑ leads to an expression for the model posterior that generalizes the BIC. When the number of data points N is large enough, the (log) posterior probability of a model can be approximated by an expression consisting of the maximum log likelihood of the data under that model, plus a number of penalty factors which posses an elegant geometrical interpretation. The expression, known as Fisher Information Approximation (FIA) is

$$
\begin{aligned}
-\log p(\mathcal{M}|X) = &- \log p(X|\hat{\vartheta}) + \frac{d}{2} \log \frac{N}{2\pi} \\
&+ \log \int d^d \vartheta \sqrt{\det g(\vartheta)} \\
&+ \frac{1}{2} \log \left[\frac{\det h(X; \hat{\vartheta})}{\det g(\hat{\vartheta})} \right] + \dots \\
=: &\, L + D + V + R + \dots
\end{aligned}
\tag{1}
$$

where $\hat{\vartheta}$ is the parameter value that maximises the likelihood of the data under $\mathcal{M}$, d is the dimensionality of $\mathcal{M}$ (number of parameters), g and h are respectively the Fisher Information and the Observed Fisher Information [7], and the remainder (...) collects terms that get smaller when N grows larger. We will call the terms of the FIA *likelihood* (L), *dimensionality* (D), *volume* (V) and *robustness* (R), respectively. It can be shown [3] that the volume term actually measures the volume of the model, seen as a statistical manifold in the sense of information geometry [2]. The robustness term is related to the shape of the statistical manifold in the vicinity of the maximum likelihood point, and more specifically to its embedding curvature in data space [24].

By direct application of the rules of Bayesian statistics, one then arrives at the conclusion that more complex models should be penalized, and the correct measure of complexity and its exchange rate with goodness of fit depends not only on the dimensionality of the model (as in the BIC, which corresponds to only using the first two terms of the FIA), but also on its finer geometrical properties. Interestingly, analogous expressions can be obtained by distinct arguments based on information theory, using the Minimum Description Length principle [11,25] or the Predictive Information framework [5].

The elegance of this result, and the fact that the same prescription emerges from distinct approaches in information theory, make it a good candidate for a general notion of statistical complexity upon which to build a normative model of decision making under uncertainty in rational observers. It is natural to ask if human subjects exhibit a preference for simpler models, and if they do, to quantitatively compare their intuitive measurement of complexity to the prescriptions of the theory.

1.1 Related Work

Some evidence for a simplicity bias in human decision-making can be found in the existing literature. Johnson et al. [17] showed that, in a model selection task, subjects prefer simpler models (characterised as those with fewer parameters) when the likelihood of the data is approximately the same across the models being compared. Genewein and Braun [10] also studied a model selection task, providing more solid theoretical grounding in Bayesian model selection theory. However, that study also focused primarily on qualitative preferences in equal-likelihood conditions (showing that indeed subjects possess a bias towards simple models), stopping short of a quantitative evaluation of the strength of the bias. To our knowledge, our work is the first attempt to: 1) precisely quantify the tradeoff between simplicity and goodness of fit in human decision making; 2) investigate the behavioral relevance of geometrical complexity; and 3) consider the individual impact of the model features captured by the terms of the FIA, including the effect of a novel form of penalty that can emerge for models with boundaries.

2 Methods

2.1 Psychophysics

We designed a visual psychophysics experiment to probe human subjects' sensitivity to statistical model complexity. The experiment is based on a two-alternative forced-choice task designed as described below. Detailed preregistration documents for the experiments, including design, sampling and analysis rationale, code for running the task, experimental stimuli, and a snapshot of the core libraries developed to analyze the data are available at [22, 23].

The subjects were shown two curves and 10 dots on a screen (see examples in Fig. 1). One curve was located in the upper half of the screen, the other in the bottom half. The curves represent two parametric statistical models of the form

$$p(x|t) = \frac{1}{\sqrt{2\pi}} \exp\left[-(x - \mu(t))^2/2\right]$$

where x is a location on the 2D plane visualized on the screen and $\mu(t)$ is a parametrization of the curve. In other words, the curves represent Gaussians of unit isotropic variance whose mean μ can be located at any point along them. The dots shown to the subjects were sampled iid from one of the two models, selected at random with uniform probability. The location of the true mean of the Gaussian generating the dots (i.e., the value of t in the expression above) was randomly sampled from Jeffrey's prior for the selected model [15]. All dots shown within a trial come from the same distribution (same model and same true mean). The subjects had to report which curve (model) the dots are more likely to come from. They did so by pressing the "up" or "down" keys on their keyboard to select the curve in the upper or lower part of the screen.

We designed four variants of the task, each of which asked the subjects to make a selection between two models. The model pairings differed across task variants, and are illustrated in Fig. 1. Each model pairing is designed to study primarily a different term of the FIA: dimensionality for the "point" pairing, boundary for "vertical" (we defer the formal introduction of the boundary term until the next section), volume for "horizontal", and robustness for "rounded". The models in the "point" task variant have different dimensionality ($d = 0$ for

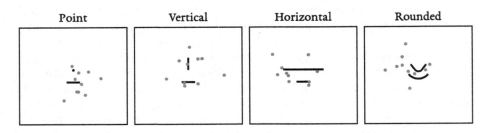

Fig. 1. Task types with corresponding names. Each panel shows an example trial for one of the four task types in the experiment. The model manifolds $\mathcal{M}_1$ and $\mathcal{M}_2$ are drawn in black, and 10 points x sampled from a probability distribution contained in either $\mathcal{M}_1$ or $\mathcal{M}_2$ are shown in red. Given a visual stimulus similar to one of these panels, the subjects have to report which model ($\mathcal{M}_2$ or $\mathcal{M}_2$) is more likely to have generated the data. (Color figure online)

the point and $d = 1$ for the line)[1]. In the "horizontal" variant, the models have the same dimensionality but different volume (length). In the "rounded" variant, the models have the same dimensionality and volume, but their curvature is such that one of them bends away from the region of data space which is more likely to contain ambiguous stimuli, whereas the other bends around it (and therefore the robustness term for these models has opposite sign for data points that fall in that region). Finally, in the "vertical" variant, the models have the same dimensionality and volume, and are both flat so that their robustness terms are always identically zero; however, they are oriented such that the lower endpoint (boundary) of the vertically oriented model is the closest point on the model to the ambiguous (equal-likelihood) region of data space located at the midpoint between the two models. Therefore, if some data falls within that region, assigning that data to the vertically oriented model will incur a penalty due to the boundary effect.

A single run of the task consisted in a brief tutorial followed by 500 trials, divided in 5 blocks of 100 trials each. In each trial, the chosen curve pairing was presented, randomly flipped vertically. At the end of each block, the subject received feedback on their overall performance during that block. Subjects received a fixed compensation for taking part in the experiment.

We ran the experiment on the online platform Pavlovia (https://pavlovia. org). For each task type we collected data from at least 50 subjects who passed a pre-established performance threshold: 60% correct for the "rounded" task variant and 70% correct for the other variants, as reported on the preregistration documents [22, 23]. We discarded the data collected from all other subjects. These exclusion rules led to a final dataset containing 52 subjects for the "rounded" task variant, and exactly 50 subjects for each of the other task variants.

2.2 Penalty Term for Model Boundaries

Most of the models used in the experiments have bounded parameter spaces. For instance, the base model is parametrized by one parameter t that is subject to the constraint $0 \leq t \leq 1$. The conditions $t = 0$ and $t = 1$ are mapped to the endpoints of the segment representing the model in data space in Fig. 1. Having models with such boundaries is an issue for the applicability of the FIA, because one of the hypotheses underlying the derivation of Eq. 1 is that $\hat{\vartheta}$ must be in the interior of the parameter space, and this assumption can easily break down in presence of models with bounded parameter spaces. To solve this issue, we extended the FIA to deal with the simple case of a linear boundary in parameter

---

[1] In a similar way, one could define a two-dimensional model represented by a 2D area on the screen. This approach would be useful to provide an additional evaluation point for the dependence of the simplicity bias on model dimensionality. However, unlike a 0D or 1D model, a 2D model in a 2D data space will always suffer from boundary effects for data falling anywhere outside the model manifold. Therefore, because one primary goal of this study was to disentangle the distinct contributions of the models' different geometrical features to the simplicity bias, we only use 1D models.

space (see Appendix A). When the maximum-likelihood point is on the edge of the parameter space, an additional term, which we indicate with the symbol S, appears in the FIA:

$$S = \frac{1}{2} \log \frac{N}{2\pi} + \log \left[2\pi \|l\|_\Delta \right] \tag{2}$$

where

$$l_a = -\frac{1}{N} \sum_i \frac{\partial}{\partial \vartheta_a} \log p(x_i|\vartheta)$$

is minus the empirical average of the score vector (log-likelihood gradient), and Δ is the inverse of the observed Fisher information:

$$\Delta = h^{-1}, \qquad h_{ab} = -\frac{1}{N} \sum_i \frac{\partial^2}{\partial \vartheta_a \partial \vartheta_b} \log p(x_i|\vartheta)$$

Equation 2 shows that the penalty associated to being at the boundary of parameter space corresponds to increasing the parameter dimensionality by one, plus a term that depends on the norm of the log-likelihood gradient (the gradient is not zero at the maximum likelihood point, precisely because we are on the boundary of the optimization domain). For a broad class of models, the second term can be shown to measure the degree of model misspecification induced by the existence of the boundary [24].

2.3 Comparison Between Subject Behavior and Bayesian Ideal Observer

In our experimental scenario, the theory of Bayesian model selection applies directly. Given two models $\mathcal{M}_1$ and $\mathcal{M}_2$, assuming a flat prior over models $p(\mathcal{M}_1) = p(\mathcal{M}_2) = 1/2$ and an uninformative (Jeffrey's) prior over the parameters of each model, when N is sufficiently large the log posterior ratio for $\mathcal{M}_1$ over $\mathcal{M}_2$ can be written

$$\log \frac{p(\mathcal{M}_1|X)}{p(\mathcal{M}_2|X)} = \log \frac{p(\mathcal{M}_1|X)}{1 - p(\mathcal{M}_1|X)}$$
$$\simeq (L_2 - L_1) + (D_2 - D_1) + (S_2 - S_1) + (V_2 - V_1) + (R_2 - R_1) \tag{3}$$

where L_i, D_i, etc. represent the FIA terms for model i.

This expression suggests a very simple normative model for subject behavior. Equation 3 determines the probability of reporting $\mathcal{M}_1$ for an ideal Bayesian observer performing probability matching. We can then compare subject behavior to the normative prescription by allowing subjects to have distinct sensitivities to the various terms of the FIA:

$$\log \frac{p(\text{report } \mathcal{M}_1|X)}{p(\text{report } \mathcal{M}_2|X)} = \alpha + \beta_L(L_2 - L_1) + \beta_D(D_2 - D_1) +$$
$$+ \beta_S(S_2 - S_1) + \beta_V(V_2 - V_1) + \beta_R(R_2 - R_1) \tag{4}$$

where α and β are free parameters: α captures any fixed bias, β_L the sensitivity to differences in maximum likelihood, β_D the sensitivity to differences in dimensionality, and so on.

2.4 Data Analysis

We fitted the model expressed by Eq. 4 to subject behavior using a hierarchical, Bayesian logistic regression scheme:

$$\nu_\alpha, \nu_L, \ldots, \nu_R \sim 1 + \text{Exponential}(29) \tag{5}$$

$$\mu_\alpha, \mu_L, \ldots, \mu_R \sim \text{Normal}(0, 3) \tag{6}$$

$$\sigma_\alpha, \sigma_L, \ldots, \sigma_R \sim \text{Exponential}(3) \tag{7}$$

$$\alpha_i \sim \text{StudentT}(\nu_\alpha, \mu_\alpha, \sigma_\alpha) \tag{8}$$

$$\beta_{L,i} \sim \text{StudentT}(\nu_L, \mu_L, \sigma_L) \tag{9}$$

$$\vdots \tag{10}$$

$$\beta_{R,i} \sim \text{StudentT}(\nu_R, \mu_R, \sigma_R) \tag{11}$$

$$C_{i,t} \sim \text{Bernoulli}\left(\text{logit}^{-1}\left(\text{lpr}\left(\alpha_i, \beta_{L,i}, \beta_{D,i}, \beta_{S,i}, \beta_{V,i}, \beta_{R,i}, X_{i,t}\right)\right)\right) \tag{12}$$

where $C_{i,t}$ is the choice made by subject i on trial t, $X_{i,t}$ is the sensory stimulus on that same trial, lpr is the log posterior ratio defined by Eq. 4, α_i is the bias for subject i, $\beta_{L,i}$ is the likelihood sensitivity of that same subject, and so on for the other sensitivity parameters. The bias and sensitivity parameters describing each subject are modeled as independent samples from a population-level Student-T probability distribution characterized by a certain shape (ν), location (μ) and scale (σ). The priors assumed over these population-level parameters are standard weakly informative priors [8,18], and broader or flat priors lead to similar results to those presented below. The model was implemented in PyMC3 [26], and inference was performed by sampling from the posterior for the parameters given the experimental data $\{C_{i,t}, X_{i,t}\}$ using the No-U-Turn Sampler algorithm [4,14]. Further technical details on the inference procedure can be found in Appendix B.

3 Results

In our experiment, a simplicity bias would manifest by shifting the psychometric indifference point towards the more complex alternative. In other words, given a sensory stimulus such as those in Fig. 1, a subject with simplicity bias would not always assign the red dots simply to the model that is, on average, closer to the dot cloud. They would instead trade off some of the goodness of fit of the models (in this case the geometrical distance) against some measure of simplicity. For instance, in the "point" task type (Fig. 1, left), for the subject to choose the 1-dimensional model (the line) over the 0-dimensional one (the point), it would not be enough for the dot cloud to be on average closer to the line than to the point, but the difference in distance would have to be larger than a certain nonzero amount. The value of this critical difference is controlled by the exact nature of the tradeoff operated by the subject between simplicity and goodness of fit, or in other words the "exchange rate" between these two desirable objectives.

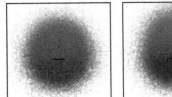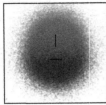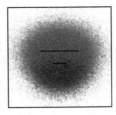

Fig. 2. Overview of experimental data. Each panel overlays all stimuli shown to all subjects that performed a given task type. All 10 dots shown on a given trials are colored red if the subject reported "up" or blue if they reported "down" on that trial. Note that the actual location of the model manifolds and the stimuli were flipped vertically in roughly 50% of trials (see Methods), and have been counter-flipped in this plot for visualization purposes. (Color figure online)

An overview of the experimental data collected is shown in Fig. 2. A qualitative inspection of the figure already suggests the existence of a simplicity bias like the one just described. For instance, in the first panel on the left ("point" task type), the transition from red to blue is located further down than the vertical midpoint between the two models, suggesting that subjects tended to choose the point more often than the line for stimuli that were roughly equidistant from either.

We quantified these effects using the formal framework of Bayesian model selection and compared them to those predicted by the ideal observer. In Fig. 3 we report the mean and standard deviation of the posterior estimates for the sensitivity of individual subjects to the FIA terms (the α_i and β_i parameters in Eq. 4). These estimates show that most subjects possess a bias in favor of simple models, even though the strength of the bias is fairly heterogeneous across the population (this hypothesis was also tested with a formal model comparison procedure, using the Widely Applicable Information Criterion [21]—see Appendix B.3). We also note that the strength of the bias exhibited systematic differences

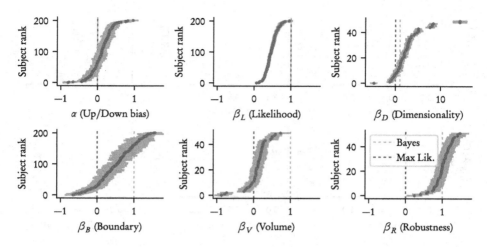

Fig. 3. Subject-level estimates of sensitivity to the terms in Eq. 4. Top left panel, dark gray dots: posterior mean $\mathbb{E}[\alpha_i]_{p(\alpha_i|X,C)}$ for the up/down bias of individual subjects. Light gray bars: standard deviation of the posterior distribution for the same parameters. Subjects are ranked based on the mean posterior. All other panels: same as the top left panel, for the β sensitivity parameters in Eq. 4. Dashed lines: reference value of the parameters for the ideal Bayesian observer described by Eq. 3 (magenta) and a "maximum likelihood" observer that disregards model complexity and selects models only based on distance from the data (purple). Note that number of dots (subjects) differs across panels because three of the regression parameters (β_D, β_V and β_R) can only be estimated for the subjects that performed a specific variant of the task (the "point", "horizontal", and "rounded" variant respectively). By contrast, α, β_L and β_S can be estimated for all subjects. (Color figure online)

in scale between the different terms of the FIA: for instance, the bias towards models with smaller dimensionality (Fig. 3, top right panel) can be much stronger than the bias towards models with a smaller volume (bottom middle panel).

We can get a better idea of these global properties of the estimated parameters by studying the population level parameters μ_α, μ_L, μ_D,... (Eq. 6), which parametrize the location (the mean) of the distributions from which the subject-level sensitivities are sampled. We report the full posterior distribution of the μ parameters in Fig. 4. These analyses indicate that the subjects were sensitive to model complexity in general as well as to all terms of the FIA taken individually, and that some model features contributing to the FIA (dimensionality and shape) seemed to affect subject behavior more strongly than others (volume and presence of boundaries).

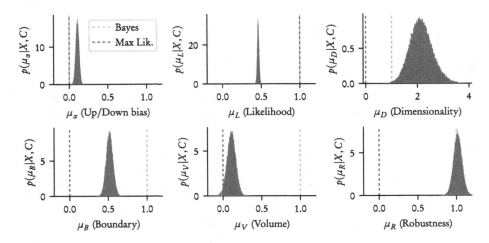

Fig. 4. Population-level estimates of sensitivity to the terms in Eq. 4, reported as the full posterior distribution for the μ_α and μ_β parameters, conditional on the observed experimental data $\{X_{i,t}, C_{i,t}\}$. Dashed magenta and purple lines are the reference values for the ideal Bayesian and maximum-likelihood observers, respectively, as in Fig. 3. (Color figure online)

4   Discussion

Occam's razor is a ubiquitous principle in statistics and learning theory that we can express in a rigorous and elegant way using Bayesian model-selection theory. We sought to build on this solid theoretical grounding by using it to understand if and how Occam's razor applies to human decision-making under uncertainty.

Specifically, we have formulated a class of psychophysical tasks that allowed us to probe this hypothesis directly and quantitatively. A critical technical step in doing so was the extension of the existing theory surrounding the Fisher Information Approximation (Eq. 1) to deal with the case of parametric models with bounded parameter spaces. We have shown that, when the maximum likelihood solution lies on the boundary of the statistical manifold, a novel term appears in the approximation (Eq. 2). This novel boundary term can be seen as describing an aspect of the geometrical complexity of the model [3], but unlike the previously known geometric complexity terms describing the model volume and shape (V and R) it scales logarithmically with the sample size N. This scaling property suggests that, when it is not zero, the boundary term may be the dominant contribution to geometric complexity in all but the most undersampled regimes.

Our experimental data show that naive human subjects are sensitive to model complexity in general, and to each component of the Fisher Information Approximation individually. The sensitivity is different for distinct model features (dimensionality, volume, shape, and presence of boundary), suggesting that perceptual or resource constraints may play an important role in determining the precise pattern of deviation from the ideal observer. Nevertheless, our study shows how to link principled and abstract notions of statistical model complexity to human decision making under uncertainty.

Acknowledgements. We thank Chris Pizzica for help with setting up the web-based version of the experiments, and for managing subject recruitment. We acknowledge support or partial support from R01 NS113241 (EP) and R01 EB026945 (VB and JG).

A Derivation of the Boundary Term in the Fisher Information Approximation

Here we generalize the derivation of the Fisher Information Approximation given by [3] to the case where the maximum likelihood solution for a model lies on the boundary of the parameter space. Apart from the more general assumptions, the following derivation follows closely the original one, with some minor notational changes.

A.1 Set-up and Hypotheses

The problem we consider here is that of selecting between two models (say $\mathcal{M}_1$ and $\mathcal{M}_2$), after observing empirical data $X = \{x_i\}_{i=1}^{N}$. N is the sample size and $\mathcal{M}_1$ is assumed to have d parameters, collectively indexed as ϑ taking values in a compact domain Θ. As a prior over ϑ we take Jeffrey's prior:

$$w(\vartheta) = \frac{\sqrt{\det g(\vartheta)}}{\int d^d\vartheta \sqrt{\det g(\vartheta)}} \tag{13}$$

where g is the (expected) Fisher Information of the model $\mathcal{M}_1$:

$$g_{\mu\nu}(\vartheta) = \mathbb{E}\left[-\frac{\partial^2 \ln p(x|\vartheta)}{\partial \vartheta^\mu \partial \vartheta^\nu}\right]_\vartheta \tag{14}$$

The Bayesian posterior

$$\mathbb{P}(\mathcal{M}_1|X) = \frac{\mathbb{P}(\mathcal{M}_1)}{\mathbb{P}(X)} \int d^d w(\vartheta) \mathbb{P}(X|\vartheta) \tag{15}$$

then becomes, after assuming a flat prior over models and dropping irrelevant terms,

$$\mathbb{P}(\mathcal{M}_1|X) = \frac{\int_\Theta d^d\vartheta \sqrt{\det g} \exp\left[-N(-\frac{1}{N}\ln \mathbb{P}(X|\vartheta))\right]}{\int d^d\vartheta \sqrt{\det g}} \tag{16}$$

Just as in [3], we now make a number of regularity assumptions: 1. $\ln \mathbb{P}(X|\vartheta)$ is smooth; 2. there is a unique global minimum $\hat{\vartheta}$ for $\ln \mathbb{P}(X|\vartheta)$; 3. $g_{\mu\nu}(\vartheta)$ is smooth; 4. $g_{\mu\nu}(\hat{\vartheta})$ is positive definite; 5. $\Theta \subset \mathbb{R}^d$ is compact; and 6. the values of the local minima of $\ln \mathbb{P}(X|\vartheta)$ are bounded away from the global minimum by some $\epsilon > 0$. Importantly, unlike in [3], we don't assume that $\hat{\vartheta}$ is in the interior of Θ.

The Shape of Θ. Because we are specifically interested in understanding what happens at a boundary of the parameter space, we will add a further assumption that, while being not very restrictive in spirit, will allow us to derive a particularly interpretable result. In particular, we will assume that Θ is specified by a single linear constraint of the form

$$D_\mu \vartheta^\mu + d \geq 0 \tag{17}$$

Without loss of generality, we'll also take the constraint to be expressed in Hessian normal form—namely, $\|D_\mu\| = 1$.

For clarity, note this assumption on the shape of Θ is only used from Subsect. A.3 onward.

A.2   Preliminaries

We will now proceed to set up a low-temperature expansion of Eq. 16 around the saddle point $\hat{\vartheta}$. We start by rewriting the numerator in Eq. 16 as

$$\int_\Theta d^l \vartheta \exp\left[-N \left(-\frac{1}{2N} \ln \det g - \frac{1}{N} \ln \mathbb{P}(X|\vartheta) \right) \right] \tag{18}$$

The idea of the Fisher Information Approximation is to expand the integrand in Eq. 18 in powers of N around the maximum likelihood point $\hat{\vartheta}$. To this end, let's define three useful objects:

$$\tilde{I}_{\mu_1 \cdots \mu_i} := -\frac{1}{N} \nabla_{\mu_1} \cdots \nabla_{\mu_i} \ln \mathbb{P}(X|\vartheta)\Big|_{\hat{\vartheta}} = -\frac{1}{N} \sum_{j=1}^N \nabla_{\mu_1} \cdots \nabla_{\mu_i} \ln \mathbb{P}(x_j|\vartheta)\Big|_{\hat{\vartheta}}$$

$$F_{\mu_1 \cdots \mu_i} := \nabla_{\mu_1} \cdots \nabla_{\mu_i} \ln \det g(\vartheta)\Big|_{\hat{\vartheta}}$$

$$\psi := -\frac{1}{2N} \ln \det g - \frac{1}{N} \ln \mathbb{P}(X|\vartheta)$$

We immediately note that

$$\nabla_{\mu_1} \cdots \nabla_{\mu_i} \psi\Big|_{\hat{\vartheta}} = \tilde{I}_{\mu_1 \cdots \mu_i} - \frac{1}{2N} F_{\mu_1 \cdots \mu_i}$$

which is useful in order to compute

$$\psi(\vartheta) = \psi(\hat{\vartheta}) + \nabla_\mu \psi \Big|_{\hat{\vartheta}} (\vartheta^\mu - \hat{\vartheta}^\mu) + \frac{1}{2} \nabla_\mu \nabla_\nu \psi \Big|_{\hat{\vartheta}} (\vartheta^\mu - \hat{\vartheta}^\mu)(\vartheta^\nu - \hat{\vartheta}^\nu) + \dots$$

$$= \sum_{i=0}^{\infty} \frac{1}{i!} \nabla_{\mu_1} \cdots \nabla_{\mu_i} \psi \Big|_{\hat{\vartheta}} (\vartheta^{\mu_1} - \hat{\vartheta}^{\mu_1}) \cdots (\vartheta^{\mu_i} - \hat{\vartheta}^{\mu_i})$$

$$= \sum_{i=0}^{\infty} \frac{1}{i!} \nabla_{\mu_1} \cdots \nabla_{\mu_i} \psi \Big|_{\hat{\vartheta}} \prod_{k=1}^{i} (\vartheta^{\mu_k} - \hat{\vartheta}^{\mu_k})$$

It is also useful to center the integration variables by introducing

$$\phi := \sqrt{N}(\vartheta - \hat{\vartheta}) \tag{19}$$

$$\mathrm{d}^l \phi = N^{d/2} \mathrm{d}^l \vartheta \tag{20}$$

so that

$$\nabla_{\mu_1} \cdots \nabla_{\mu_i} \psi \Big|_{\hat{\vartheta}} \prod_{k=1}^{i} (\vartheta^{\mu_k} - \hat{\vartheta}^{\mu_k}) = N^{-i/2} \left(\tilde{I}_{\mu_1 \cdots \mu_i} - \frac{1}{2N} F_{\mu_1 \cdots \mu_i} \right) \phi^{\mu_1} \cdots \phi^{\mu_i}$$

$$\tag{21}$$

and Eq. 18 becomes

$$\int \mathrm{d}^l \vartheta \exp[-N\psi] = N^{-d/2} \int \mathrm{d}^l \phi \exp\left[-N \sum_{i=0}^{\infty} \frac{1}{i!} N^{-i/2} \left(\tilde{I}_{\mu_1 \cdots \mu_i} - \frac{1}{2N} F_{\mu_1 \cdots \mu_i} \right) \phi^{\mu_1} \cdots \phi^{\mu_i} \right]$$

$$= N^{-d/2} \int \mathrm{d}^l \phi \exp\left\{ -N \left(-\frac{1}{N} \ln \mathbb{P}(X|\hat{\vartheta}) - \frac{1}{2N} \ln \det g(\hat{\vartheta}) \right) + \right.$$

$$\left. -N \left[\sum_{i=1}^{\infty} \frac{1}{i!} N^{-i/2} \left(\tilde{I}_{\mu_1 \cdots \mu_i} - \frac{1}{2N} F_{\mu_1 \cdots \mu_i} \right) \phi^{\mu_1} \cdots \phi^{\mu_i} \right] \right\}$$

$$= N^{-\frac{d}{2}} \exp\left[-\left(-\ln \mathbb{P}(X|\hat{\vartheta}) - \frac{1}{2} \ln \det g(\hat{\vartheta}) \right) \right] \times$$

$$\times \int \mathrm{d}^l \phi \exp\left\{ -N \left[\frac{1}{\sqrt{N}} \tilde{I}_\mu \phi^\mu + \frac{1}{2N} \tilde{I}_{\mu\nu} \phi^\mu \phi^\nu + \right. \right.$$

$$\left. \left. + \frac{1}{N} \sum_{i=1}^{\infty} N^{-\frac{i}{2}} \left(\frac{1}{(i+2)!} \tilde{I}_{\mu_1 \cdots \mu_{i+2}} \phi^{\mu_1} \cdots \phi^{\mu_i+2} - \frac{1}{2i!} F_{\mu_1 \cdots \mu_i} \phi^{\mu_1} \cdots \phi^{\mu_i} \right) \right] \right\}$$

Therefore,

$$
\begin{aligned}
\mathbb{P}(\mathcal{M}_1|X) &= N^{-\frac{d}{2}} \exp\left[-\left(-\ln \mathbb{P}(X|\hat{\vartheta}) - \frac{1}{2}\ln\det g(\hat{\vartheta}) + \ln\int d^d\vartheta\sqrt{\det g}\right)\right] \times \\
&\quad \times \int d^d\phi \exp\left[-\sqrt{N}\tilde{I}_\mu \phi^\mu - \frac{1}{2}\tilde{I}_{\mu\nu}\phi^\mu \phi^\nu + \right. \\
&\quad \left. -\sum_{i=1}^{\infty} N^{-\frac{i}{2}}\left(\frac{1}{(i+2)!}\tilde{I}_{\mu_1\cdots\mu_{i+2}}\phi^{\mu_1}\cdots\phi^{\mu_{i+2}} - \frac{1}{2i!}F_{\mu_1\cdots\mu_i}\phi^{\mu_1}\cdots\phi^{\mu_i}\right)\right] \\
&= N^{-\frac{d}{2}} \exp\left[-\left(-\ln \mathbb{P}(X|\hat{\vartheta}) - \frac{1}{2}\ln\det g(\hat{\vartheta}) + \ln\int_\Theta d^d\vartheta\sqrt{\det g}\right)\right] \cdot Q
\end{aligned}
\tag{22}
$$

where

$$
Q = \int_\Phi d^d\phi \exp\left[-\sqrt{N}\tilde{I}_\mu\phi^\mu - \frac{1}{2}\tilde{I}_{\mu\nu}\phi^\mu\phi^\nu - G(\phi)\right]
\tag{23}
$$

and

$$
G(\phi) = \sum_{i=1}^{\infty} N^{-\frac{i}{2}}\left(\frac{1}{(i+2)!}\tilde{I}_{\mu_1\cdots\mu_{i+2}}\phi^{\mu_1}\cdots\phi^{\mu_{i+2}} - \frac{1}{2i!}F_{\mu_1\cdots\mu_i}\phi^{\mu_1}\cdots\phi^{\mu_i}\right)
\tag{24}
$$

where $G(\phi)$ collects the terms that are suppressed by powers of N.

Our problem has been now reduced to computing Q by performing the integral in Eq. 23. Now our assumptions come into play for the key approximation step. For the sake of simplicity, assuming that N is large we drop $G(\phi)$ from the expression above, so that Q becomes a simple Gaussian integral with a linear term:

$$
Q = \int_\Phi d^d\phi \exp\left[-\sqrt{N}\tilde{I}_\mu\phi^\mu - \frac{1}{2}\phi^\mu\tilde{I}_{\mu\nu}\phi^\nu\right]
\tag{25}
$$

A.3   Choosing a Good System of Coordinates

Consider now the Observed Fisher Information at maximum likelihood, $\tilde{I}_{\mu\nu}$. As long as it is not singular, we can define its inverse $\Delta^{\mu\nu} = (\tilde{I}_{\mu\nu})^{-1}$. If $\tilde{I}_{\mu\nu}$ is positive definite, then the matrix representation of $\tilde{I}_{\mu\nu}$ will have a set of d positive eigenvalues which we will denote by $\{\sigma_{(1)}^{-2}, \sigma_{(2)}^{-2}, \ldots, \sigma_{(d)}^{-2}\}$. The matrix representation of $\Delta^{\mu\nu}$ will have eigenvalues $\{\sigma_{(1)}^2, \sigma_{(2)}^2, \ldots, \sigma_{(d)}^2\}$, and will be diagonal in the same choice of coordinates as $\tilde{I}_{\mu\nu}$. Denote by U the (orthogonal) diagonalizing matrix, i.e., U is such that

$$
U\Delta U^\intercal = \begin{bmatrix} \sigma_{(1)}^2 & 0 & \cdots & 0 \\ 0 & \sigma_{(2)}^2 & & \vdots \\ \vdots & & \ddots & 0 \\ 0 & \cdots & 0 & \sigma_{(d)}^2 \end{bmatrix} \quad , \quad U^\intercal U = UU^\intercal = \mathbb{I}
\tag{26}
$$

Define also the matrix K as the product of the diagonal matrix with elements $1/\sigma_{(k)}$ along the diagonal and U:

$$K = \begin{bmatrix} 1/\sigma_{(1)} & 0 & \cdots & 0 \\ 0 & 1/\sigma_{(2)} & & \vdots \\ \vdots & & \ddots & 0 \\ 0 & \cdots & 0 & 1/\sigma_{(d)} \end{bmatrix} U \qquad (27)$$

Note that

$$\det K = (\det \Delta^{\mu\nu})^{-1/2} = \sqrt{\det \tilde{I}_{\mu\nu}}$$

and that K corresponds to a sphering transformation, in the sense that

$$K\Delta K^{\mathsf{T}} = \mathbb{I} \quad \text{or} \quad K^{\mu}{}_{\kappa}\Delta^{\kappa\lambda}K^{\nu}{}_{\lambda} = \delta^{\mu\nu} \qquad (28)$$

and therefore, if we define the inverse

$$P = K^{-1}$$

we have

$$P^{\mathsf{T}}(\tilde{I}_{\mu\nu})P = \mathbb{I} \quad \text{or} \quad P^{\kappa}{}_{\mu}\tilde{I}_{\kappa\lambda}P^{\lambda}{}_{\nu} = \delta_{\mu\nu} \qquad (29)$$

We can now define a new set of coordinates by centering and sphering, as follows:

$$\xi^{\mu} = K^{\mu}{}_{\nu}\left(\phi^{\nu} + \sqrt{N}\Delta^{\nu\kappa}\tilde{I}_{\kappa}\right) \qquad (30)$$

Then,

$$\mathrm{d}^{d}\xi = \sqrt{\det \tilde{I}_{\mu\nu}}\,\mathrm{d}^{d}\phi \qquad (31)$$

and

$$\phi^{\mu} = P^{\mu}{}_{\nu}\xi^{\nu} - \sqrt{N}\Delta^{\mu\nu}\tilde{I}_{\nu} \qquad (32)$$

In this new set of coordinates,

$$-\sqrt{N}\tilde{I}_{\nu}\phi^{\nu} - \frac{1}{2}\phi^{\mu}\tilde{I}_{\mu\nu}\phi^{\nu} =$$

$$= -\left(\sqrt{N}\tilde{I}_{\nu} + \frac{1}{2}\phi^{\mu}\tilde{I}_{\mu\nu}\right)\phi^{\nu}$$

$$= -\left(\sqrt{N}\tilde{I}_{\nu} + \frac{1}{2}P^{\mu}{}_{\kappa}\xi^{\kappa}\tilde{I}_{\mu\nu}\frac{1}{2}\sqrt{N}\Delta^{\mu\kappa}\tilde{I}_{\kappa}\tilde{I}_{\mu\nu}\right)\phi^{\nu}$$

$$= -\sqrt{N}\tilde{I}_{\nu}P^{\nu}{}_{\lambda}\xi^{\lambda} + N\Delta^{\nu\lambda}\tilde{I}_{\lambda}\tilde{I}_{\nu} - \frac{1}{2}P^{\mu}{}_{\kappa}\xi^{\kappa}\tilde{I}_{\mu\nu}P^{\nu}{}_{\lambda}\xi^{\lambda} + \frac{\sqrt{N}}{2}P^{\mu}{}_{\kappa}\xi^{\kappa}\tilde{I}_{\mu\nu}\Delta^{\nu\lambda}\tilde{I}_{\lambda} +$$

$$+ \frac{\sqrt{N}}{2}\Delta^{\mu\kappa}\tilde{I}_{\kappa}\tilde{I}_{\mu\nu}P^{\nu}{}_{\lambda}\xi^{\lambda} - \frac{N}{2}\Delta^{\mu\kappa}\tilde{I}_{\kappa}\tilde{I}_{\mu\nu}\Delta^{\nu\lambda}\tilde{I}_{\lambda}$$

$$= \frac{N}{2}\tilde{I}_{\nu}\Delta^{\nu\lambda}\tilde{I}_{\lambda} - \frac{1}{2}\xi^{\kappa}\delta_{\kappa\lambda}\xi^{\lambda} \qquad (33)$$

where we have used Eq. 29 as well as the fact that $\Delta^{\mu\nu} = \Delta^{\nu\mu}$ and that $\Delta^{\mu\kappa}\tilde{I}_{\kappa\nu} = \delta^{\mu}{}_{\nu}$ by definition.

Therefore, putting Eq. 31 and Eq. 33 together, Eq. 25 becomes

$$Q = \frac{\exp\left[\frac{N}{2}\tilde{I}_{\mu}\Delta^{\mu\nu}\tilde{I}_{\nu}\right]}{\sqrt{\det\tilde{I}_{\mu\nu}}} \int_{\Xi} d^{l}\xi \exp\left[-\frac{1}{2}\xi_{\mu}\delta^{\mu\nu}\xi_{\nu}\right] \tag{34}$$

The problem is reduced to a (truncated) spherical gaussian integral, where the domain of integration Ξ will depend on the original domain Θ but also on $\tilde{I}_{\mu}$, $\tilde{I}_{\mu\nu}$ and $\hat{\vartheta}$. To complete the calculation, we now need to make this dependence explicit.

A.4   Determining the Domain of Integration

We start by combining Eq. 19 and Eq. 32 to yield

$$\vartheta^{\mu} = \frac{1}{\sqrt{N}}P^{\mu}{}_{\nu}\xi^{\nu} - \Delta^{\mu\nu}\tilde{I}_{\nu} + \hat{\vartheta}^{\mu} \tag{35}$$

By substituting Eq. 35 into Eq. 17 we get

$$D_{\mu}\left(\frac{P^{\mu}{}_{\nu}\xi^{\nu}}{\sqrt{N}} - \Delta^{\mu\nu}\tilde{I}_{\nu} + \hat{\vartheta}^{\mu}\right) + d \geq 0$$

which we can rewrite as

$$\tilde{D}_{\mu}\xi^{\mu} + \tilde{d} \geq 0 \tag{36}$$

with

$$\tilde{D}_{\mu} := \frac{1}{\sqrt{N}}D_{\nu}P^{\nu}{}_{\mu} \tag{37}$$

and

$$\begin{aligned} \tilde{d} &:= d + D_{\mu}\hat{\vartheta}^{\mu} - D_{\mu}\Delta^{\mu\nu}\tilde{I}_{\nu} \\ &= d + D_{\mu}\hat{\vartheta}^{\mu} - \langle D_{\mu}, \tilde{I}_{\mu}\rangle_{\Delta} \end{aligned} \tag{38}$$

where by $\langle \cdot, \cdot \rangle_{\Delta}$ we mean the inner product in the inverse observed Fisher information metric. Now, note that whenever $\tilde{I}_{\mu}$ is not zero it will be parallel to D_{μ}. Indeed, by construction of the maximum likelihood point $\hat{\vartheta}$, the gradient of the log likelihood can only be orthogonal to the boundary at $\hat{\vartheta}$, and pointing towards the outside of the domain; therefore $\tilde{I}_{\mu}$, which is defined as minus the gradient, will point inward. At the same time, D_{μ} will also always point toward the interior of the domain because of the form of the constraint we have chosen in Eq. 17. Because by assumption $\|D_{\mu}\| = 1$, we have that

$$\tilde{I}_{\mu} = \|\tilde{I}_{\nu}\|D_{\mu}$$

and

$$\langle D_{\mu}, \tilde{I}_{\mu}\rangle_{\Delta} = \|D_{\nu}\|_{\Delta} \cdot \|\tilde{I}_{\nu}\|_{\Delta}$$

so that

$$\tilde{d} = d + D_\mu \hat{\vartheta}^\mu - \|D_\mu\|_\Delta \cdot \|\tilde{I}_\mu\|_\Delta \tag{39}$$

Now, the signed distance of the boundary to the origin in ξ-space is

$$l = -\frac{\tilde{d}}{\|\tilde{D}_\mu\|}$$

where the sign is taken such that l is negative when the origin is included in the integration domain. But noting that

$$K^\mu{}_\kappa \Delta^{\kappa\lambda} K^\nu{}_\lambda = \delta^{\mu\nu} \quad \Rightarrow \quad \Delta^{\mu\nu} = P^\mu{}_\kappa \delta^{\kappa\lambda} P^\nu{}_\lambda$$

we have

$$\|\tilde{D}_\mu\| = \sqrt{\tilde{D}_\mu \delta^{\mu\nu} \tilde{D}_\nu} = \sqrt{\frac{1}{N} D_\kappa \left(P^\kappa{}_\mu \delta^{\mu\nu} P^\lambda{}_\nu\right) D_\lambda}$$

$$= \sqrt{\frac{1}{N} D_\kappa \Delta^{\kappa\lambda} D_\lambda} = \frac{\|D_\mu\|_\Delta}{\sqrt{N}}$$

and therefore

$$l = -\sqrt{N} \frac{\tilde{d}}{\|D_\mu\|} \tag{40}$$

Finally, by plugging Eq. 39 into Eq. 40 we obtain

$$l = -\sqrt{N} \left[\frac{d + D_\mu \hat{\vartheta}^\mu}{\|D_\mu\|_\Delta} - \|\tilde{I}_\mu\|_\Delta\right] \tag{41}$$

$$=: \sqrt{2}\,(s - m)$$

where m and s are defined for convenience like so:

$$m := \sqrt{\frac{N}{2}} \frac{d + D_\mu \hat{\vartheta}^\mu}{\|D_\mu\|_\Delta} \quad (\geq 0) \tag{42}$$

$$s := \sqrt{\frac{N}{2}} \|\tilde{I}_\mu\|_\Delta \quad (\geq 0) \tag{43}$$

We note that m is a rescaled version of the margin defined by the constraint on the parameters (and therefore is never negative by assumption), and s is a rescaled version of the norm of the gradient of the log likelihood in the inverse observed Fisher metric (and therefore is nonnegative by construction).

A.5   Computing the Penalty

We can now perform a final change of variables in the integral in Eq. 34. We rotate our coordinates to align them to the boundary, so that

$$\tilde{D}_\mu = (\|\tilde{D}_\mu\|, 0, 0, \ldots, 0)$$

Note that we can always do this as our integrand is invariant under rotation. In this coordinate system, Eq. 34 factorizes:

$$
\begin{aligned}
Q &= \frac{\exp\left[\frac{N}{2}\tilde{I}_\mu \Delta^{\mu\nu}\tilde{I}_\nu\right]}{\sqrt{\det \tilde{I}_{\mu\nu}}} \int_{\mathbb{R}^{d-1}} d^{d-1}\xi \exp\left[-\frac{\xi_\mu \delta^{\mu\nu}\xi_\nu}{2}\right] \int_l^\infty d\zeta \exp\left[-\frac{\zeta^2}{2}\right] \\
&= \sqrt{\frac{(2\pi)^d}{\det \tilde{I}_{\mu\nu}}} \exp\left[\frac{N}{2}\|\tilde{I}\|_\Delta^2\right] \frac{1}{\sqrt{\pi}} \int_l^\infty \frac{d\zeta}{\sqrt{2}} \exp\left[-\frac{\zeta^2}{2}\right] \\
&= \sqrt{\frac{(2\pi)^d}{\det \tilde{I}_{\mu\nu}}} \exp\left(s^2\right) \frac{1}{\sqrt{\pi}} \int_{l/\sqrt{2}}^\infty d\zeta \exp\left[-\zeta^2\right] \\
&= \sqrt{\frac{(2\pi)^d}{\det \tilde{I}_{\mu\nu}}} \exp\left(s^2\right) \frac{\mathrm{erfc}(s-m)}{2}
\end{aligned}
\tag{44}
$$

where $\mathrm{erfc}(\cdot)$ is the complementary error function ([1], [Section 7.1.2]).

Finally, plugging Eq. 44 into Eq. 22 and taking the log, we obtain the extended FIA:

$$
-\ln \mathbb{P}(\mathcal{M}_1|E) \simeq \ln \mathbb{P}(E|\hat{\vartheta}) + \frac{d}{2}\ln \frac{N}{2\pi} + \ln \int_\Theta d^d\vartheta \sqrt{\det g} + \frac{1}{2}\ln\left[\frac{\det \tilde{I}_{\mu\nu}}{\det g_{\mu\nu}}\right] + S \tag{45}
$$

where

$$
S := \ln(2) - \ln\left[\exp\left(s^2\right)\mathrm{erfc}(s-m)\right] \tag{46}
$$

can be interpreted as a penalty arising from the presence of the boundary in parameter space.

A.6   Interpreting the Penalty

We will now take a closer look at Eq. 46. To do this, one key observation we will use is that, by construction, at most one of m and s is ever nonzero. This is because in the interior of the manifold, $m > 0$ by definition, but $s = 0$ because the gradient of the likelihood is zero at $\hat{\vartheta}$; and on the boundary, $m = 0$ by definition, and s can be either zero or positive.

Interior of the Manifold. When $\hat{\vartheta}$ is in the interior of the parameter space Θ, then $\tilde{I}_\mu = 0 \Rightarrow s = 0$ and Eq. 46 simplifies to

$$
S = \ln(2) - \ln\left(\mathrm{erfc}(-m)\right) \tag{47}
$$

but since N is large we have $m \gg 0$, $\mathrm{erfc}(-m) \to 2$ and $S \to 0$, so our result passes the first sanity check: we recover the expression in [3].

Boundary of the Manifold. When $\hat{\vartheta}$ is on the boundary of Θ, $m = 0$ and $s \geq 0$. Equation 46 becomes

$$S = \ln(2) - \ln\left[\exp\left(s^2\right)\mathrm{erfc}(s)\right] = \ln(2) - \ln\left(w(is)\right) \qquad (48)$$

where w is the Feddeeva function ([1], [Section 7.1.3]):

$$w(z) = e^{-z^2}\mathrm{erfc}(-iz)$$

This function is tabulated and can be computed efficiently. However, it is interesting to analyze its limiting behavior.

As a consistency check, when s is small we have at fixed N, to first order:

$$S \simeq \ln(2) - \ln\left(1 - \frac{2s}{\sqrt{\pi}}\right)$$

$$\simeq \ln(2) + \frac{2s}{\sqrt{\pi}} = \ln(2) + \sqrt{\frac{2N}{\pi}}\|\tilde{I}_\mu\|_\Delta \qquad (49)$$

and $S = \ln(2)$ when $\tilde{I}_\mu = 0$, as expected.

However, the real case of interest is the behavior of the penalty when N is assumed to be large, as this is consistent with the fact that we derived Eq. 44 as an asymptotic expansion of Eq. 23. In this case, using the asymptotic expansion for the Feddeeva function ([1], [Section 7.1.23]):

$$\exp\left[s^2\right]\mathrm{erfc}(s) \sim \frac{1}{s\sqrt{\pi}}\left[1 + \sum_{m=1}^{\infty}(-1)^m\frac{1 \cdot 3 \cdots (2m - 1)}{(2s^2)^m}\right]$$

To leading order we obtain

$$S \simeq \ln(2) + \ln\left(s\sqrt{\pi}\right)$$

$$= \ln(2) + \ln\left(\sqrt{\frac{N\pi}{2}}\|\tilde{I}_\mu\|_\Delta\right)$$

which we can rewrite as

$$\boxed{S \simeq \frac{1}{2}\ln\frac{N}{2\pi} + \ln\left[2\pi\|\tilde{I}_\mu\|_\Delta\right]} \qquad (50)$$

We can summarize the above by saying that a new penalty term of order $\ln N$ arose due to the presence of the boundary. Interestingly, comparing Eq. 50 with Eq. 45 we see that the first term in Eq. 50 is analogous to counting an extra parameter dimension in the original Fisher Information Approximation.

A.7   Numerical Comparison of the Extended FIA vs Exact Bayes

Figure 5 shows that the FIA computed with the expressions given above provides a very good approximation to the exact Bayesian log posterior ratio (LPR) for the model pairs used in the psychophysics experiments, and for the chosen sample size ($N = 10$). As highlighted in the panels in the rightmost column, the discrepancies between the exact and the approximated LPR are generally small in relative terms, and therefore are not very important for the purpose of model fitting and interpretation. Note that here, as well as for the results in the main text, the S term in the FIA is computed using Eq. 46 rather than Eq. 50 in order to avoid infinities (that for finite N can arise when the likelihood gradient is very small) and discontinuities (that for finite N can arise on the interior of the manifold, in proximity to the boundary, where the value of S goes from zero when $\hat{\vartheta}$ is in the interior to $\log(2)$ when $\hat{\vartheta}$ is exactly on the boundary).

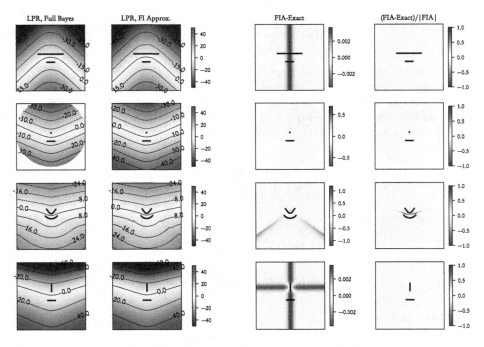

Fig. 5. Comparison of Fisher Information Approximation and full Bayes computation of the log posterior ratio (LPR) for the model pairs used in our psychophysics tasks ($N = 10$). Each row corresponds to one task type (from top to bottom, "horizontal", "point", "rounded", "vertical"). First column from the left: full Bayesian LPR, computed by numerical integration. Second column: LPR computed with the Fisher Information Approximation. Third column: difference between FIA and exact LPR. Fourth column: relative difference (difference divided by the absolute value of the FIA LPR).

Even though overall the agreement between the approximation is good, it is interesting to look more closely at where it is the least so. The task type for which the discrepancies are the largest (both in absolute and relative terms) is the "rounded" type (third row in Fig. 5). This is because the FIA hypotheses are not fully satisfied everywhere for one of the models. More specifically, the models in that task variant are a circular arc (the bottom model in Fig. 5, third row) and a smaller circular arc, concentric with the first, with a straight segment attached to either side (the top model). The log-likelihood function for this second model is only smooth to first order, but its second derivative (and therefore its Fisher Information and its observed Fisher Information) are not continuous at the points where the circular arc is joined with the straight segments, locally breaking hypothesis number 3 in Subsect. A.1. Geometrically, this is analogous to saying that the curvature of the manifold changes abruptly at the joints. It is likely that the FIA for a model with a smoother transition between the circular arc and the straight arms would have been even closer to the exact value for all points on the 2D plane (the data space). More generally, this line of reasoning suggests that it would be interesting to investigate the features of a model that affect the quality of the Fisher Information Approximation.

B   Supplementary Information on the Analysis of the Psychophysics Data

B.1   Technical Details of the Inference Procedure

Table 1. $\hat{R}$ statistic and effective sample size (ESS) for 8 Markov Chain traces run as described in the main text. See [8] (Sections 11.4–11.5) and [27] for in-depth discussion of chain quality diagnostics. Briefly, $\hat{R}$ depends on the relationship between the variance of the draws estimated within and between contiguous draw sequences. $\hat{R}$ is close to 1 when the chains have successfully converged. The effective sample size estimates how many independent samples one would need to extract the same amount of information as that contained in the (correlated) MCMC draws. Note that here, for computational convenience, we report diagnostics for 8 chains with 1000 draws each, while the results reported in the main text have been obtained with 10 times as many draws (8 chains × 10000 draws per chain), run with identical settings.

Parameter	ESS	$\hat{R}$
μ_α	3214	1.00
μ_L	1068	1.01
μ_S	2017	1.00
μ_D	2047	1.00
μ_V	3737	1.00
μ_R	6181	1.00

Posterior sampling was performed with PyMC3 [26] version 3.9.3, using the NUTS Hamiltonian Monte Carlo algorithm [14], with target acceptance probability set to 0.9. The posterior distributions reported in the main text are built by sampling 8 independent Markov chains for 10000 draws each. No divergence occurred in any of the chains. Effective sample size and $\hat{R}$ diagnostics for some of the key parameters are given in table Table 1 for a shorter run of the same procedure.

B.2   Posterior Predictive Checks

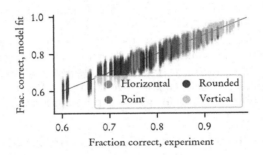

Fig. 6. Simple posterior predictive check, looking at subject performance. A random sample of all subject-level parameters (α_i and β_i) is taken at random from the MCMC chains used for model inference. Using those parameter values, a simulation of the experiment is run using the actual stimuli shown to the subjects, and the resulting performance of all 202 simulated subjects is recorded. This procedure is repeated 2000 times, yielding 2000 samples of the joint posterior-predictive distribution of task performance over all experimental subjects. To visualize this distribution, for each subject we plotted a cloud of 2000 dots where the y coordinate of each dot is the simulated performance of that subject in one of the simulations, and the x coordinate is the true performance of that subject in the experiment plus a small random jitter (for ease of visualization). The gray line is the identity, showing that our inference procedure captures well the behavioral patterns in the experimental data. (Color figure online)

We performed a simple posterior predictive check [18] to ensure that the Bayesian hierarchical model described in the main text captures the main pattern of behavior across our subjects. In Fig. 6, the behavioral performance of the subjects is compared with its posterior predictive distribution under the model. As can be seen from the figure, the performance of each subject is correctly captured by the model, across systematic differences between task types (with subjects performing better in the "vertical" task than the "rounded" task, for instance) as well as individual differences between subjects that performed the same task variant.

B.3   Formal Model Comparison

We compared the Bayesian hierarchical model described in the main text to a simpler model, where subjects were assumed to only be sensitive to likelihood differences, or in other words to choose $\mathcal{M}_1$ over $\mathcal{M}_2$ only based on which model was on average closer to the dot cloud constituting the stimulus on a given trial. Mathematically, this "likelihood only" model was equivalent to fixing all β parameters to zero except for β_L in the model described in the main text. All other details of the model were the same, and in particular the model still had a hierarchical structure with adaptive shrinkage (the subject-level parameters α and β_L were modeled as coming from Student T distributions controlled by population-level parameters). We compared the full model and the likelihood-only using the Widely Applicable Information Criterion [9]. This comparison, shown in Table 2, reveals strong evidence in favor of the full model.

Table 2. WAIC comparison of the full model and the likelihood-only model for the experimental data, reported in the standard format used by [21] (Section 6.4.2). Briefly, WAIC is the value of the criterion (log-score scale—higher is better); pWAIC is the estimated effective number of parameters; dWAIC is the difference between the WAIC of the given model and the highest-ranked one; SE is the standard error of the WAIC estimate; and dSE is the standard error of the difference in WAIC. These estimates were produced with the `compare` function provided by ArviZ [19], using 8 MCMC chains with 1000 samples each for each model (in total, 8000 samples for each model).

Model	Rank	WAIC	pWAIC	dWAIC	SE	dSE
Full	0	−34823.9	640.856	0	188.421	0
Likelihood only	1	−37524.2	369.713	2700.3	190.453	69.3959

References

1. Abramowitz, M., Stegun, I.A.: Handbook of Mathematical Functions: With Formulas, Graphs, and Mathematical Tables. Dover, New York (1972)
2. Amari, S.I., Nagaoka, H.: Methods of information geometry. Translations of Mathematical Monographs. American Mathematical Society (2000)
3. Balasubramanian, V.: Statistical inference, occam's razor, and statistical mechanics on the space of probability distributions. Neural Comput. 9(2), 349–368 (1997). https://doi.org/10.1162/neco.1997.9.2.349
4. Betancourt, M.: A conceptual introduction to hamiltonian monte carlo (2018). https://arxiv.org/abs/1701.02434
5. Bialek, W., Nemenman, I., Tishby, N.: Predictability, complexity and learning. Neural Comput. 13, 2409–2463 (2001). https://doi.org/10.1162/089976601753195969
6. Bishop, C.M.: Pattern Recognition and Machine Learning. Springer, Heidelberg (2006). https://doi.org/10.1007/978-1-4615-7566-5

7. Efron, B., Hinkley, D.L.: Assessing the accuracy of the maximum likelihood estimator: observed versus expected fisher information. Biometrika **65**(3), 457–483 (1978). https://doi.org/10.1093/biomet/65.3.457
8. Gelman, A., Carlin, J.B., Stern, H.S., Dunson, D.B., Vehtari, A., Rubin, D.B.: Bayesian Data Analysis, 3rd edn. CRC Press, Boca Raton (2014)
9. Gelman, A., Hwang, J., Vehtari, A.: Understanding predictive information criteria for Bayesian models. Stat. Comput. **24**(6), 997–1016 (2013). https://doi.org/10.1007/s11222-013-9416-2
10. Genewein, T., Braun, D.A.: Occam's razor in sensorimotor learning. Proc. Roy. Soc. B Biol. Sci. **281**(1783), 20132952 (2014). https://doi.org/10.1098/rspb.2013.2952
11. Grünwald, P.D.: The Minimum Description Length Principle. MIT press, Cambridge (2007)
12. Gull, S.F.: Bayesian inductive inference and maximum entropy. In: Erickson, G.J., Smith, C.R. (eds.) Maximum-Entropy and Bayesian Methods in Science and Engineering, pp. 53–74. Springer, Netherlands (1988). https://doi.org/10.1007/978-94-009-3049-0_4
13. Hastie, T., Tibshirani, R., Friedman, J.: The Elements of Statistical Learning, 2nd edn. Springer, Heidelberg (2009)
14. Hoffman, M.D., Gelman, A.: The No-U-Turn sampler: adaptively setting path lengths in hamiltonian monte carlo. J. Mach. Learn. Res. **15**(47), 1593–1623 (2014). http://jmlr.org/papers/v15/hoffman14a.html
15. Jaynes, E.T.: Probability Theory: The Logic of Science. Cambridge University Press, Cambridge (2003)
16. Jeffreys, H.: Theory of Probability. Clarendon Press, Oxford (1939)
17. Johnson, S., Jin, A., Keil, F.: Simplicity and goodness-of-fit in explanation: the case of intuitive curve-fitting. In: Proceedings of the Annual Meeting of the Cognitive Science Society, vol. 36, no. 36 (2014)
18. Kruschke, J.K.: Doing Bayesian Data Analysis, 2nd edn. Academic Press, Cambridge (2015)
19. Kumar, R., Carroll, C., Hartikainen, A., Martin, O.: Arviz a unified library for exploratory analysis of bayesian models in python. J. Open Source Softw. **4**(33), 1143 (2019). https://doi.org/10.21105/joss.01143
20. MacKay, D.J.C.: Bayesian interpolation. Neural Comput. **4**(3), 415–447 (1992). https://doi.org/10.1162/neco.1992.4.3.415
21. McElreath, R.: Statistical Rethinking. CRC Press, Boca Raton (2016)
22. Piasini, E., Balasubramanian, V., Gold, J.I.: Preregistration document (2016). https://doi.org/10.17605/OSF.IO/2X9H6
23. Piasini, E., Balasubramanian, V., Gold, J.I.: Preregistration document addendum. https://doi.org/10.17605/OSF.IO/5HDQZ
24. Piasini, E., Gold, J.I., Balasubramanian, V.: Information geometry of bayesian model selection (2021, unpublished)
25. Rissanen, J.: Stochastic complexity and modeling. Ann. Stat. **14**(3), 1080–1100 (1986). https://www.jstor.org/stable/3035559
26. Salvatier, J., Wiecki, T.V., Fonnesbeck, C.: Probabilistic programming in python using PyMC3. PeerJ Comput. Sci. **2**, e55 (2016). https://doi.org/10.7717/peerj-cs.55
27. Vehtari, A., Gelman, A., Simpson, D., Carpenter, B., Bürkner, P.C.: Rank-normalization, folding, and localization: an improved $\hat{R}$ for assessing convergence of MCMC. Bayesian Analysis (2020). https://doi.org/10.1214/20-ba1221

Training Convolutional Neural Networks with Competitive Hebbian Learning Approaches

Gabriele Lagani[1]([⊠]), Fabrizio Falchi[2], Claudio Gennaro[2], and Giuseppe Amato[2]

[1] Computer Science Department, University of Pisa, 56127 Pisa, Italy
gabriele.lagani@phd.unipi.it
[2] ISTI-CNR Pisa, 56124 Pisa, Italy
{fabrizio.falchi,claudio.gennaro,giuseppe.amato}@cnr.it

Abstract. We explore competitive Hebbian learning strategies to train feature detectors in Convolutional Neural Networks (CNNs), without supervision. We consider variants of the Winner-Takes-All (WTA) strategy explored in previous works, i.e. k-WTA, e-soft-WTA and p-soft-WTA, performing experiments on different object recognition datasets. Results suggest that the Hebbian approaches are effective to train early feature extraction layers, or to re-train higher layers of a pre-trained network, with soft competition generally performing better than other Hebbian approaches explored in this work. Our findings encourage a path of cooperation between neuroscience and computer science towards a deeper investigation of biologically inspired learning principles.

Keywords: Neural networks · Machine learning · Hebbian learning · Competitive learning · Computer vision · Biologically inspired

1 Introduction

While deep learning has achieved outstanding results in a variety of domains, ranging from computer vision [9] to language processing [4], and reinforcement learning [24], there are still doubts about the biological plausibility of the learning algorithms in use, that are based on supervised end-to-end training with error backpropagation (*backprop*). This strategy lacks biological plausibility, according to neuroscientists [21]. This motivates investigation into different learning approaches, inspired by mammalian plasticity, which might eventually lead to improvements in machine learning models, as well as to a better understanding of how the brain works.

In this article, we consider the biologically plausible Hebbian learning principle [6,8], coupled with different *competitive* learning strategies [7,17,18]. Specifically, we consider variants of the Winner-Takes-All (WTA) strategy, namely

This work was partially supported by the H2020 project AI4EU under GA 825619 and by the H2020 project AI4Media under GA 951911.

G. Nicosia et al. (Eds.): LOD 2021, LNCS 13163, pp. 25–40, 2022.
https://doi.org/10.1007/978-3-030-95467-3_2

k-WTA, e-soft-WTA, and p-soft-WTA. In particular, the latter two strategies are novel variants of the soft-WTA approach [18], that we introduce in order to make soft competition suitable in practical scenarios. The respective learning rules and details are described in the following sections. We provide an experimental evaluation of the proposed strategies in the context of Deep Neural Network (DNN) training on popular computer vision datasets, namely MNIST [16], CIFAR10, and CIFAR100 [12]

Hebbian learning was explored in previous works, to train network layers for computer vision tasks [2,14,22,25]. Nonetheless, only relatively shallow networks were considered. Deeper network architectures were also considered in [1], but still, a thorough investigation of the various competitive learning strategies is missing. Our experiments on different object recognition datasets show that the Hebbian approaches are effective to train early feature extraction layers, or to re-train higher layers of a pre-trained network, when compared to supervised backprop. Comparison with a popular unsupervised approach, the Variational Auto-Encoder (VAE), also based on backprop, suggests that Hebbian learning might represent a better unsupervised feature extraction strategy. Moreover, *soft* competition strategies (e-soft-WTA and p-soft-WTA) perform generally better than *sharp* variants (WTA and k-WTA).

Our work is the results of a cooperation between neuroscience and computer science, suggesting that the collaboration between these two fields might bring a promising potential. Our contributions can be summarized as follows:

- We explore the different competitive learning strategies (WTA, k-WTA, e-soft-WTA, p-soft-WTA), to train Convolutional Neural Networks (CNNs) for feature extraction and classification;
- Among the approaches that we explore, we propose two novel strategies, namely e-soft-WTA and p-soft-WTA, inspired by the soft-WTA approach, but aiming to make soft competition suitable for practical tasks.
- Experimental evaluation of the various approaches on different object recognition datasets is performed.

The remainder of this paper is structured as follows: Sect. 2 presents some related work on this field; Sect. 3 introduces the various competitive Hebbian learning strategies that we explored; Sect. 4 describes the scenarios in which we applied the above mentioned strategies; Sect. 5 goes into the details of our experiments; Sect. 6 provides the results of our evaluation; Finally, in Sect. 7, we present our conclusions and hints for future directions.

2   Related Work

In previous work, Hebbian learning was used together with k-WTA competition on computer vision tasks, but only on relatively shallow networks [14,25]. Nonetheless, results were comparable to those achieved by backprop on networks with similar structure, thus motivating further interest. In [2,22], a different approach based on Hebbian/anti-Hebbian learning was explored, which minimized

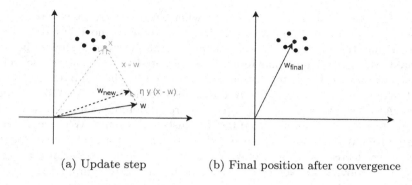

(a) Update step   (b) Final position after convergence

Fig. 1. Hebbian updates with weight decay.

an unsupervised similarity matching objective, equivalent to Principal Component Analysis (PCA) in the linear case. Hebbian PCA rules have also been widely studied in literature [3,23]. Still, the experiments are limited to relatively shallow networks. Deeper networks trained by Hebbian WTA were considered in [1], were it was confirmed that the WTA approach was effective for training early feature extraction layers, thus being suitable for relatively shallow networks, but also to retrain higher layers of a pre-trained network (including the final classifier, by a supervised Hebbian learning variant [15]), while requiring fewer training epochs than backprop, thus suggesting potential applications in the context of transfer learning [26]. Nonetheless, the results of this latter work were preliminary, and involved a single approach (WTA) and a single dataset for testing (CIFAR10).

3 Competitive Hebbian Learning Strategies

Consider a single neuron with weight vector $\mathbf{w}$ and input $\mathbf{x}$. Call $y = \mathbf{w}^T \mathbf{x}$ the neuron output. A learning rule defines a weight update as follows:

$$\mathbf{w}_{new} = \mathbf{w}_{old} + \Delta\mathbf{w} \tag{1}$$

where $\mathbf{w}_{new}$ is the updated weight vector, $\mathbf{w}_{old}$ is the old weight vector, and $\Delta\mathbf{w}$ is the weight update. According to the Hebbian principle, in its most basic form, the latter term is computed as

$$\Delta\mathbf{w} = \eta\, y\, \mathbf{x} \tag{2}$$

where η is the learning rate. Basically, this rule states that the weight on a given synapse is potentiated when the input on that synapse and the output of the neuron are simultaneously high, thus reinforcing connections between neurons whose activations are correlated.

To prevent weights from growing unbounded, a weight decay term is generally added. In the context of competitive learning [7], this is obtained as follows:

$$\Delta\mathbf{w} = \eta\, y\, \mathbf{x} - \eta\, y\, \mathbf{w} = \eta\, y\, (\mathbf{x} - \mathbf{w}) \tag{3}$$

This rule has an intuitive interpretation: when an input vector is presented to the neuron, its vector of weights is updated in order to move it closer to the input, so that the neuron will respond more strongly when a similar input is presented. When several similar inputs are presented to the neuron, the weight vector converges to the center of the cluster formed by these inputs (Fig. 1).

When multiple neurons are involved in a complex network, the Winner-Takes-All (WTA) [7] strategy can be adopted to force different neurons to learn different patterns, corresponding to different clusters of inputs. When an input is presented to a WTA layer, the neuron whose weight vector is closest to the current input is elected as winner. Only the winner is allowed to perform a weight update, thus moving its weight vector closer to the current input (Fig. 2). If a similar input will be presented again in the future, the same neuron will be more likely to win again. This strategy allows a group of neurons to perform clustering on a set of data points (Fig. 2).

WTA enforces a kind of *quantized* information encoding in layers of neural network. Only one neuron activates to encode the presence of a given pattern in the input. On the other hand, actual neural codes exhibit a *sparse, distributed* representation, where multiple neurons activate combinatorially to encode different properties of the input, resulting in an improved coding power. The importance of sparse, distributed representations was also highlighted in [5,20].

A more distributed coding scheme could be obtained by choosing more than one winner at a time. In the k-WTA strategy [17], the k top-activating neurons are selected as winners and allowed to perform the weight update. A *soft* form of competition was also proposed in literature [18]. In this soft-WTA approach, a reward is attributed to each neuron depending on the value of its activation, so that neurons with higher activation also receive a higher reward. Neurons perform update steps whose length is proportional to their reward. The reward r_i for neuron i is computed as follows:

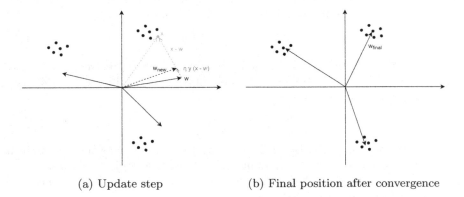

(a) Update step   (b) Final position after convergence

Fig. 2. Hebbian updates with Winner-Takes All competition.

$$r_i = \frac{y_i}{\sum_j y_j} \tag{4}$$

So, basically, the reward is obtained as an L_1 normalization of the activations. We found that this formulation actually worked poorly in practice, because there is no tunable parameter to cope with the variance of activations. For this reason, we introduce a variant of this approach that uses a *softmax* operation in order to distribute the reward:

$$r_i = \frac{e^{y_i/T}}{\sum_j e^{y_j/T}} \tag{5}$$

where T is the *temperature* hyperparameter. The advantage of this formulation is that we can tune the temperature in order to obtain the best performance on a given task, depending on the distribution of the activations. We refer to this *exponential* form of soft competition simply as e-soft-WTA. We also explore a different formulation, based on L_p normalization, in which the reward is computed as:

$$r_i = \frac{y_i^p}{\sum_j y_j^p} \tag{6}$$

In this case, the value p acts as (inverse) temperature parameter. We refer to this *power* form of soft competition as p-soft-WTA.

4   Deep Competitive Hebbian Learning

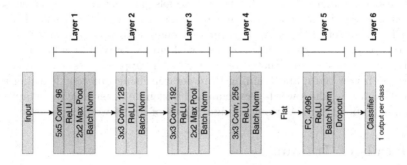

Fig. 3. The neural network used for the experiments.

The core part of our experiments consisted in training the deep layers of a neural network consisting of six layers: five deep layers plus a final linear classifier. The various layers were interleaved with other processing stages (such as ReLU nonlinearities, max pooling, etc.), as shown in Fig. 3. The architecture was inspired by AlexNet [13], but one of the fully connected layers was removed and, in general, the number of neurons was slightly modified, in order to reduce the computational cost of the experiments. The network was trained using the k-WTA, e-soft-WTA and p-soft-WTA approaches, as well as backprop, in order to compare the results.

Since the comparisons mentioned so far involve supervised models (backprop-based) and unsupervised models (Hebbian), we also deemed interesting to compare the Hebbian models with other unsupervised (but still backprop-based) methods. Specifically, we considered a Variational Auto-Encoder (VAE) [11]: the network model in Fig. 3, up to layer 5, acted as encoder, with a fully connected layer mapping the output feature map to a 256 gaussian latent variable representation, while a specular network branch acted as decoder.

In order to evaluate the quality of the features extracted from the various layers of the trained models for the image classification tasks, we placed a linear classifier on top of each already trained layer , and we evaluated the accuracy achieved by classifying the corresponding features. This was done both for the backprop trained network, for the Hebbian trained networks, and for the VAE network. The linear classifier was trained with Stochastic Gradient Descent (SGD) in all cases. Notice that this does not raise biological plausibility issues, because backpropagation is not required when SGD is used to train a single layer. Even if the Hebbian approach is unsupervised, it is also possible to apply a supervised variant [1,15] for training the linear classifier, although, at this stage, we preferred to use SGD in all cases, in order to make comparisons on equal footings. Indeed, the SGD weight update can be considered as a form of supervised Hebbian update, modulated by a teacher signal. Later, we also present a comparison of trained with SGD and with the supervised Hebbian variant, placed on top of features extracted from various network layers, and evaluated on different datasets.

We also implemented hybrid network models, i.e. networks in which some layers were trained with backprop and other layers were trained with Hebbian approach , in order to asses up to which extent backprop layers in our model could be replaced with Hebbian equivalent without excessive impact on the accuracy. The models were constructed by replacing the upper layers of a pre-trained network with new ones, and training from scratch using different learning algorithms. Meanwhile, the lower layers remained frozen, in order to avoid adaptation to the new upper layers. Various configurations of layers were considered.

5   Details of Training

We implemented our experiments using PyTorch.[1] We used the network architecture shown in Fig. 3. The model was fed with RGB images of size 32×32 pixels as inputs. The network was trained using Stochastic Gradient Descent (SGD) with error backpropagation and cross-entropy loss, and with the competitive Hebbian rules, in order to compare the results. For VAE training, we used a network model with 256 gaussian latent variables and a specular decoder structure w.r.t. the encoder. The decoder part was removed at test time and the

---

[1] The code to reproduce the experiments is available at: https://github.com/GabrieleLagani/HebbianPCA/tree/hebbpca.

features extracted from encoder layers were used for classification. Training was performed in 20 epochs (although, for the Hebbian approach, convergence was typically achieved in much fewer epochs) using mini-batches of size 64.

For SGD training, the initial learning rate was set to 10^{-3} and kept constant for the first ten epochs, while it was halved every two epochs for the remaining ten epochs. We also used momentum coefficient 0.9, Nesterov correction, and dropout rate 0.5. An L2 penalty was also used to improve regularization, with weight decay coefficient set to $5 \cdot 10^{-2}$ for MNIST and CIFAR10, and to 10^{-2} for CIFAR100. The VAE was trained in the same fashion but, obviously, in an unsupervised image encoding-decoding task, and no L2 penalty nor dropout was used in this case.

During Hebbian training, the learning rate was set to 10^{-3}. No L2 regularization or dropout was used in this case, since the learning method did not present overfitting issues. Images were preprocessed by a whitening transformation as described in [1,15], although this step didn't have any significant effect for back-prop training. A hyperparameter k is defined to control the behavior of k-WTA, e-soft-WTA, and p-soft-WTA. For the k-WTA approach, the parameter k is simply the number of neurons selected as winners. In e-soft-WTA, the parameter k is defined as the softmax temperature, i.e. $k = T$. For the p-soft-WTA approach, the parameter k is defined as the inverse of the exponent p used to compute the L_p normalization, i.e. $k = \frac{1}{p}$. In this way, a common parameter k controls how reward is distributed: roughly speaking, higher k corresponds to a reward distributed among more neurons, while lower k corresponds to reward distributed among fewer neurons, up to the special case of a single neuron being the only winner, corresponding to simple WTA. In our experiments, we set $k = 5$ for k-WTA, $k = 0.02$ for e-soft-WTA, $k = 0.05$ for p-soft-WTA.

The linear classifiers placed on top of the various network layers were trained with supervision using SGD in the same way as we described above for training the whole network, with learning rate set to 10^{-3}, but the L2 penalty term was reduced to $5 \cdot 10^{-4}$.

All the above mentioned hyperparameters resulted from a parameter search to maximize the accuracy in the respective scenarios.

Concerning the datasets that we used, the MNIST dataset contains 60,000 training samples and 10,000 test samples, divided in 10 classes representing hand-written digits from 0 to 9. In our experiments, we further divided the training samples into 50,000 samples that were actually used for training, and 10,000 for validation. The CIFAR10 and CIFAR100 datasets contain 50,000 training samples and 10,000 test samples, divided in 10 and 100 classes, respectively, representing natural images. In our experiments, we further divided the training samples into 40,000 samples that were actually used for training, and 10,000 for validation. In order to obtain the best possible generalization, *early stopping* was used in each training session, i.e. we chose as final trained model the state of the network at the epoch when the highest validation accuracy was recorded.

Table 1. MNIST accuracy (top-1) and 95% confidence intervals on features extracted from convolutional network layers.

Layer	BP	.	WTA	5-WTA	e-soft-WTA	p-soft-WTA
1	95.80 ± 0.02	**98.67 ± 0.03**	98.16 ± 0.05	98.19 ± 0.08	98.15 ± 0.06	98.20 ± 0.05
2	97.26 ± 0.01	**98.90 ± 0.03**	98.52 ± 0.06	98.45 ± 0.07	98.47 ± 0.08	98.47 ± 0.08
3	98.77 ± 0.01	98.30 ± 0.02	98.55 ± 0.02	98.38 ± 0.08	**98.56 ± 0.02**	98.51 ± 0.04
4	99.56 ± 0.01	94.68 ± 0.04	96.56 ± 0.04	96.45 ± 0.07	96.89 ± 0.10	**97.07 ± 0.04**
5	99.59 ± 0.02	90.32 ± 0.06	**97.15 ± 0.01**	96.18 ±0.08	96.92 ± 0.06	97.09 ± 0.08

6   Results

In the following subsections, we present the experimental results on MNIST, CIFAR10, and CIFAR100 datasets. We performed five independent iterations of each experiment, using different seeds, averaging the results and computing 95% confidence intervals.

6.1   MNIST

In this sub-section we analyze the behavior of Hebbian learning approaches in a simple scenario of digit recognition on the MNIST dataset.

In Table 1, we report the MNIST test accuracy obtained by classifiers placed on top of the various layers of the network. We compare the results obtained on the network trained with supervised backprop (BP), VAE, and competitive Hebbian approaches. We can observe that the Hebbian approaches reach higher performance w.r.t. backprop for the features extracted from the first two layers, suggesting possible applications of Hebbian learning for training relatively shallow networks.

Moreover, the Hebbian approaches seem to perform comparably to each other. They also perform comparably or better w.r.t. the unsupervised VAE approach, especially when higher level features are considered, with an improvement of almost 7% points on the fifth layer.

In Table 2, we report the results obtained on the MNIST test set with hybrid networks. In each row, we reported the results for a network with a different combination of Hebbian and backprop layers (the first row below the header represent the baseline fully trained with backprop). We used the letter "H" to denote layers trained using the Hebbian approach, and the letter "B" for layers trained using backprop. The letter "G" is used for the final classifier (corresponding to the sixth layer) trained with gradient descent. The final classifier (corresponding to the sixth layer) was trained with SGD in all the cases, in order to make comparisons on equal footings.

Table 2 allows us to understand what is the effect of switching a specific layer (or group of layers) in a network from backprop to Hebbian training. The first row represents our baseline for comparison, i.e. the network fully trained with

Table 2. MNIST accuracy (top-1) and 95% confidence intervals of hybrid network models.

L1	L2	L3	L4	L5	L6	Accuracy (%)			
B	B	B	B	B	G	99.59 ± 0.02			
WTA approach						WTA	5-WTA	e-soft-WTA	p-soft-WTA
H	B	B	B	B	G	99.48 ± 0.03	**99.53 ± 0.05**	99.45 ± 0.03	99.49 ± 0.04
B	H	B	B	B	G	99.48 ±0.05	99.42 ± 0.02	99.52 ± 0.03	**99.53 ± 0.03**
B	B	H	B	B	G	**99.55 ± 0.02**	99.54 ± 0.03	**99.55 ± 0.02**	99.54 ± 0.04
B	B	B	H	B	G	**99.61 ± 0.02**	99.59 ± 0.02	99.58 ± 0.03	99.58 ± 0.02
B	B	B	B	H	G	**99.66 ± 0.02**	99.61 ± 0.01	99.65 ± 0.03	99.64 ± 0.04
H	H	B	B	B	G	99.35 ± 0.02	99.30 ± 0.03	**99.36 ± 0.03**	99.34 ± 0.03
B	H	H	B	B	G	99.29 ± 0.02	99.28 ± 0.09	99.31 ± 0.05	**99.34 ± 0.03**
B	B	H	H	B	G	**99.42 ± 0.02**	99.34 ± 0.02	99.37 ± 0.07	99.35 ± 0.04
B	B	B	H	H	G	99.51 ± 0.01	99.37 ± 0.02	**99.58 ±0.02**	**99.58 ± 0.02**
H	H	H	B	B	G	**99.22 ± 0.05**	99.12 ± 0.03	99.20 ± 0.04	99.19 ± 0.02
B	H	H	H	B	G	98.99 ± 0.03	98.92 ± 0.03	99.04 ± 0.05	**99.07 ± 0.02**
B	B	H	H	H	G	99.08 ± 0.02	98.51 ± 0.03	**99.25 ± 0.01**	98.98 ± 0.02
H	H	H	H	B	G	98.45 ± 0.04	98.27 ± 0.08	98.45 ± 0.07	**98.47 ± 0.06**
B	H	H	H	H	G	98.25 ± 0.06	97.28 ± 0.05	98.43 ± 0.07	**98.46 ± 0.04**
H	H	H	H	H	G	**97.15 ± 0.01**	96.18 ± 0.08	96.92 ± 0.06	97.09 ± 0.08

backprop. In the next rows we can observe the results of a network in which a single layer was switched. The Hebbian approaches exhibit comparable results w.r.t. the baseline. A result slightly higher than the baseline is observed when layer 5 is replaced, suggesting that some combinations of layers might actually be helpful. In the successive rows, more layers are switched from backprop to Hebbian training, and a slight performance drop is observed. The Hebbian approaches appear to perform comparably to each other, although it seems that soft approaches (e-soft-WTA and p-soft-WTA) tend to behave better when applied to higher layers, while sharp approaches (WTA and 5-WTA)) seem to be preferable for lower layers.

Table 3 aims to show that it is possible to replace the last two network layers (including the final classifier) with new ones, and re-train them with Hebbian approach (in this case, the supervised Hebbian algorithm [1,15] is used to train the final classifier), achieving accuracy comparable to backprop, but requiring fewer training epochs (1 vs 15, respectively). This suggests potential applications in the context of transfer learning [26].

6.2   CIFAR10

In the previous sub-section, we considered a relatively simple image recognition task involving digits. In this section, we aim at analysing Hebbian learning

Table 3. MNIST accuracy (top-1), 95% confidence intervals, and convergence epochs obtained by retraining higher layers of a pre-trained network.

L1	L2	L3	L4	L5	L6	Method	Acc. (%)	Num. epochs
B	B	B	B	B	G	BP	99.59 ± 0.02	15
B	B	B	B	B	H	SHC	**99.62 ± 0.01**	1
B	B	B	B	H	H	WTA	99.55 ± 0.02	1
						5-WTA	99.54 ± 0.03	1
						e-soft-WTA	99.53 ± 0.03	1
						p-soft-WTA	99.53 ± 0.02	1

Table 4. CIFAR10 accuracy (top-1) and 95% confidence intervals on features extracted from convolutional network layers.

Layer	BP	VAE	WTA	5-WTA	e-soft-WTA	p-soft-WTA
1	61.59 ± 0.08	60.71 ± 0.16	64.79 ± 0.34	63.36 ± 0.20	**65.08 ± 0.41**	65.00 ± 0.43
2	67.67 ± 0.11	56.32 ± 0.31	64.35 ± 0.35	60.88 ± 0.16	**66.27 ± 0.42**	66.20 ± 0.43
3	73.87 ± 0.15	41.31 ± 0.16	59.69 ± 0.16	55.28 ± 0.10	**63.94 ± 0.11**	63.50 ± 0.29
4	83.88 ± 0.04	29.58 ± 0.07	48.56 ± 0.17	43.51 ± 0.26	54.94 ± 0.15	**54.99 ± 0.17**
5	84.95 ± 0.25	26.95 ± 0.12	46.88 ± 0.23	42.40 ± 0.11	**52.31 ± 0.15**	51.99 ± 0.28

approaches in a slightly more complex task involving natural image recognition on the CIFAR10 dataset.

In Table 4, we report the CIFAR10 test accuracy obtained by classifiers placed on top of the various convolutional layers of the network. We compare the results obtained on the network trained with supervised backprop (BP), VAE, and competitive Hebbian approaches. We can observe that the Hebbian approaches reach comparable performance w.r.t. backprop for the features extracted from the first two layers, suggesting possible applications of Hebbian learning for training relatively shallow networks.

Moreover, soft Hebbian approaches seem to perform comparably to each other, and better than sharp approaches. The most prominent difference appears on layer 4, where soft Hebbian approaches reach an improvement of almost 7% points over sharp approaches. Still, further research is needed in order to close the gap with backprop also when more layers are added, in order to make the Hebbian approach suitable as a biologically plausible alternative to backprop for training deep networks. In fact, Hebbian approaches seem to suffer from a decrease in performance when going further on with the number of layers. The same holds also for the unsupervised VAE approach, although Hebbian features appear to behave better than unsupervised VAE features, especially on higher layers, with an improvement up to 25% points on the fifth layer.

In Table 5, we report the results obtained on the CIFAR10 test set with hybrid networks. The table, which has the same structure as that of the previous subsection, allows us to understand what is the effect of switching a specific layer (or group of layers) in a network from backprop to Hebbian training. The first

Table 5. CIFAR10 accuracy (top-1) and 95% confidence intervals of hybrid network models.

L1	L2	L3	L4	L5	L6	Accuracy (%)			
B	B	B	B	B	G	84.95 ± 0.25			
WTA approach						WTA	5-WTA	e-soft-WTA	p-soft-WTA
H	B	B	B	B	G	**84.30** ± 0.26	82.75 ± 0.22	84.07 ± 0.32	84.07 ± 0.31
B	H	B	B	B	G	**81.40** ± 0.14	81.02 ± 0.15	80.74 ± 0.40	81.07 ± 0.21
B	B	H	B	B	G	**80.88** ± 0.02	79.39 ± 0.17	78.30 ± 0.35	78.36 ± 0.49
B	B	B	H	B	G	**81.09** ± 0.16	80.61 ± 0.24	76.92 ± 0.25	76.98 ± 0.17
B	B	B	B	H	G	**84.46** ± 0.07	84.42 ± 0.09	84.36 ± 0.07	84.32 ± 0.15
H	H	B	B	B	G	**79.97** ± 0.46	77.75 ± 0.40	78.87 ± 0.19	79.04 ± 0.29
B	H	H	B	B	G	68.13 ± 0.19	66.26 ± 0.30	74.20 ± 0.26	**74.41** ± 0.15
B	B	H	H	B	G	73.43 ± 0.17	71.39 ± 0.22	**74.10** ± 0.21	73.85 ± 0.25
B	B	B	H	H	G	**78.53** ± 0.12	76.29 ± 0.22	74.88 ± 0.26	74.92 ± 0.24
H	H	H	B	B	G	68.71 ± 0.18	64.50 ± 0.21	**71.75** ± 0.20	**71.75** ± 0.23
B	H	H	H	B	G	49.22 ± 0.21	50.53 ± 0.21	61.45 ± 0.22	**62.65** ± 0.31
B	B	H	H	H	G	68.26 ± 0.14	64.72 ± 0.21	67.96 ± 0.18	**68.57** ± 0.21
H	H	H	H	B	G	52.53 ± 0.18	48.64 ± 0.35	**59.48** ± 0.29	59.27 ± 0.16
B	H	H	H	H	G	45.29 ± 0.05	44.47 ± 0.28	54.91 ± 0.13	**55.87** ± 0.19
H	H	H	H	H	G	46.88 ± 0.23	42.40 ± 0.11	**52.31** ± 0.15	51.99 ± 0.28

row represents our baseline for comparison, i.e. the network fully trained with backprop. In the next rows we can observe the results of a network in which a single layer was switched. Hebbian approaches exhibit comparable results w.r.t. the baseline when they are used to train the first or the fifth network layer. A small, but more significant drop is observed when inner layers are switched from backprop to Hebbian learning. In the successive rows, more layers are switched from backprop to Hebbian training, and a higher performance drop is observed. Still, sharp approaches seem to be preferable when few layers are switched, but soft approaches seem to perform better when more Hebbian layers are involved. The most prominent difference appears when layers 2 to 4 are replaced with Hebbian equivalent, in which case soft approaches show an increase of almost 12% points over sharp approaches.

Table 6 aims to show that it is possible to replace the last two network layers (including the final classifier) with new ones, and re-train them with Hebbian approach (in this case, the supervised Hebbian algorithm [1,15] is used to train the final classifier), achieving accuracy comparable to backprop, but requiring fewer training epochs (1 vs 12, respectively). This suggests potential applications in the context of transfer learning [26].

Table 6. CIFAR10 accuracy (top-1), 95% confidence intervals, and convergence epochs obtained by retraining higher layers of a pre-trained network.

L1	L2	L3	L4	L5	L6	Method	Acc. (%)	Num. epochs
B	B	B	B	B	G	BP	**84.95** ± 0.25	12
B	B	B	B	B	H	SHC	84.59 ± 0.01	1
B	B	B	B	H	H	WTA	82.48 ± 0.14	1
						5-WTA	82.42 ± 0.11	1
						e-soft-WTA	82.67 ± 0.16	1
						p-soft-WTA	82.65 ± 0.14	1

6.3 CIFAR100

In this sub-section, we want to further analyse the scalability of Hebbian learning to a more complex task of natural image recognition involving more classes, namely CIFAR100. In this case, we evaluated the top-5 accuracy, given that CIFAR100 contains a much larger number of classes than the previous datasets.

Table 7. CIFAR100 accuracy (top-5) and 95% confidence intervals on features extracted from convolutional network layers.

Layer	BP	VAE	WTA	5-WTA	e-soft-WTA	p-soft-WTA
1	66.57 ± 0.06	58.46 ± 0.12	59.56 ± 0.13	59.01 ± 0.25	**60.77** ± 0.26	60.46 ± 0.22
2	71.75 ± 0.19	54.63 ± 0.20	58.49 ± 0.20	57.08 ± 0.28	**62.98** ± 0.16	62.65 ± 0.30
3	75.05 ± 0.28	39.46 ± 0.15	52.97 ± 0.22	52.07 ± 0.12	57.89 ± 0.25	**59.05** ± 0.30
4	78.84 ± 0.18	26.42 ± 0.21	37.38 ± 0.12	38.20 ± 0.14	44.02 ± 0.29	**45.98** ± 0.13
5	78.53 ± 0.38	23.03 ± 0.12	37.87 ± 0.21	34.33 ± 0.18	43.45 ± 0.26	**44.89** ± 0.19

In Table 7, we report the CIFAR100 top-5 test accuracy obtained by classifiers placed on top of the various convolutional layers of the network. We compare the results obtained on the network trained with supervised backprop (BP), VAE, and competitive Hebbian approaches. We can observe that Hebbian approaches reach competitive performance w.r.t. backprop for the features extracted from the first two layers, suggesting possible applications of Hebbian learning for training relatively shallow networks.

Moreover, soft Hebbian approaches seem to perform comparably to each other, and better than sharp approaches. The most prominent difference appears on layer 4, where soft Hebbian approaches reach an improvement of almost 8% points over sharp approaches. Still, Hebbian approaches seem to suffer from a decrease in performance when going further on with the number of layers. The same holds also for the unsupervised VAE approach, although Hebbian features appear to behave better than unsupervised VAE features, especially on higher layers, with an improvement up to 21% points on the fifth layer.

Table 8. CIFAR100 accuracy (top-5) and 95% confidence intervals of hybrid network models.

L1	L2	L3	L4	L5	L6	Accuracy (%)			
B	B	B	B	B	G	78.53 ± 0.38			
WTA approach						WTA	5-WTA	e-soft-WTA	p-soft-WTA
H	B	B	B	B	G	76.84 ± 0.41	76.58 ± 0.27	**77.81 ± 0.25**	77.07 ± 0.37
B	H	B	B	B	G	**75.80 ± 0.31**	73.82 ± 0.22	75.30 ± 0.34	75.36 ± 0.53
B	B	H	B	B	G	**77.29 ± 0.27**	76.15 ± 0.35	76.68 ± 0.23	76.50 ± 0.28
B	B	B	H	B	G	**74.42 ± 0.12**	73.36 ± 0.21	70.68 ± 0.38	71.56 ± 0.20
B	B	B	B	H	G	77.42 ± 0.07	**77.77 ± 0.19**	76.99 ± 0.18	77.01 ± 0.15
H	H	B	B	B	G	72.81 ± 0.28	72.22 ± 0.26	**74.50 ± 0.33**	73.98 ± 0.43
B	H	H	B	B	G	**77.10 ± 0.24**	65.15 ± 0.19	71.79 ± 0.17	71.67 ± 0.22
B	B	H	H	B	G	65.89 ± 0.05	63.16 ± 0.17	67.71 ± 0.33	**67.90 ± 0.20**
B	B	B	H	H	G	**70.09 ± 0.13**	65.61 ± 0.15	68.90 ± 0.17	69.77 ± 0.20
H	H	H	B	B	G	66.49 ± 0.42	62.99 ± 0.30	69.21 ± 0.24	**70.16 ± 0.30**
B	H	H	H	B	G	51.85 ± 0.24	51.10 ± 0.24	**58.80 ± 0.12**	58.61 ± 0.13
B	B	H	H	H	G	57.61 ± 0.29	53.80 ± 0.33	60.71 ± 0.20	**60.77 ± 0.10**
H	H	H	H	B	G	42.88 ± 0.32	43.72 ± 0.28	52.49 ± 0.31	**55.09 ± 0.32**
B	H	H	H	H	G	41.42 ± 0.13	40.13 ± 0.14	**51.63 ± 0.26**	51.21 ± 0.17
H	H	H	H	H	G	37.87 ± 0.21	34.33 ± 0.18	43.45 ± 0.26	**44.89 ± 0.19**

In Table 8, we report the results obtained on the CIFAR100 test set with hybrid networks. The table, which has the same structure as those of the previous sub-sections, allows us to understand what is the effect of switching a specific layer (or group of layers) in a network from backprop to Hebbian training. The first row represents our baseline for comparison, i.e. the network fully trained with backprop. In the next rows we can observe the results of a network in which a single layer was switched. The Hebbian approaches exhibit comparable results with the baseline when they are used used to train the first, third, or fifth network layer. A small, but more significant drop is observed when other layers are switched from backprop to Hebbian learning. In the successive rows, more layers are switched from backprop to Hebbian training, and a higher performance drop is observed. Still, sharp approaches seem to be preferable when few layers are switched, but soft approaches seem to perform better when more Hebbian layers are involved. The most prominent difference appears when layers 1 to 4 are replaced with Hebbian equivalent, in which case soft approaches show an increase of almost 13% points over sharp approaches.

Table 9 aims to show that it is possible to replace the last two network layers (including the final classifier) with new ones, and re-train them with Hebbian approach (in this case, the supervised Hebbian algorithm [1,15] is used to train the final classifier), achieving accuracy comparable to backprop, but requiring fewer training epochs (1 vs 7, respectively). This suggests potential applications in the context of transfer learning [26].

Table 9. CIFAR100 accuracy (top-5), 95% confidence intervals, and convergence epochs obtained by retraining higher layers of a pre-trained network.

L1	L2	L3	L4	L5	L6	Method	Acc. (%)	Num. epochs
B	B	B	B	B	G	BP	78.53 ± 0.38	7
B	B	B	B	B	H	SHC	**79.45 ± 0.02**	1
B	B	B	B	H	H	WTA	63.62 ± 0.27	1
						5-WTA	59.76 ± 0.38	1
						e-soft-WTA	70.44 ± 0.23	1
						p-soft-WTA	70.36 ± 0.26	2

7 Conclusions and Future Work

In conclusion, our results suggest that competitive learning approaches are effective for training early feature extraction layers, or to re-train higher layers of a pre-trained network, while requiring fewer training epochs than backprop, suggesting potential applications in transfer learning [26]. In particular, Hebbian approaches seem to produce better features than unsupervised VAE training for the classification tasks, with soft competitive approaches (e-soft-WTA and p-soft-WTA) generally performing better than sharp competitive learning variants (WTA and k-WTA).

In future works, we plan to explore other Hebbian approaches that are based on sparse coding [19,20] and Independent Component Analysis (ICA) [10]. It is also interesting to investigate strategies to combine Hebbian updates with gradient descent updates, in a semi-supervised fashion, in order to combine the task-specific knowledge given by supervised backprop training with the general knowledge extracted by unsupervised Hebbian learning. Finally, an exploration of competitive approaches w.r.t. adversarial examples also deserves attention.

We hope that our work can stimulate further interest and cooperation between the computer science and neuroscience communities towards this field.

References

1. Amato, G., Carrara, F., Falchi, F., Gennaro, C., Lagani, G.: Hebbian learning meets deep convolutional neural networks. In: Ricci, E., Rota Bulò, S., Snoek, C., Lanz, O., Messelodi, S., Sebe, N. (eds.) ICIAP 2019. LNCS, vol. 11751, pp. 324–334. Springer, Cham (2019). https://doi.org/10.1007/978-3-030-30642-7_29

2. Bahroun, Y., Soltoggio, A.: Online representation learning with single and multi-layer hebbian networks for image classification. In: Lintas, A., Rovetta, S., Verschure, P.F.M.J., Villa, A.E.P. (eds.) ICANN 2017. LNCS, vol. 10613, pp. 354–363. Springer, Cham (2017). https://doi.org/10.1007/978-3-319-68600-4_41

3. Becker, S., Plumbley, M.: Unsupervised neural network learning procedures for feature extraction and classification. Appl. Intell. **6**(3), 185–203 (1996)

4. Devlin, J., Chang, M.W., Lee, K., Toutanova, K.: Bert: pre-training of deep bidirectional transformers for language understanding. arXiv preprint arXiv:1810.04805 (2018)
5. Földiak, P.: Adaptive network for optimal linear feature extraction. In: Proceedings of IEEE/INNS International Joint Conference on Neural Networks, vol. 1, pp. 401–405 (1989)
6. Gerstner, W., Kistler, W.M.: Spiking Neuron Models: Single Neurons, Populations, Plasticity. Cambridge University Press, Cambrridge (2002)
7. Grossberg, S.: Adaptive pattern classification and universal recoding: I. parallel development and coding of neural feature detectors. Biol. Cybern. **23**(3), 121–134 (1976)
8. Haykin, S.: Neural Networks and Learning Machines, 3rd edn. Pearson, Boston (2009)
9. He, K., Zhang, X., Ren, S., Sun, J.: Deep residual learning for image recognition. In: Proceedings of the IEEE Conference on Computer Vision and Pattern Recognition, pp. 770–778 (2016)
10. Hyvarinen, A., Karhunen, J., Oja, E.: Independent component analysis. Stud. Inf. Control **11**(2), 205–207 (2002)
11. Kingma, D.P., Welling, M.: Auto-encoding variational bayes. arXiv preprint arXiv:1312.6114 (2013)
12. Krizhevsky, A., Hinton, G.: Learning multiple layers of features from tiny images (2009)
13. Krizhevsky, A., Sutskever, I., Hinton, G.E.: Imagenet classification with deep convolutional neural networks. In: Advances in Neural Information Processing Systems (2012)
14. Krotov, D., Hopfield, J.J.: Unsupervised learning by competing hidden units. Proc. Natl. Acad. Sci. **116**(16), 7723–7731 (2019)
15. Lagani, G.: Hebbian learning algorithms for training convolutional neural networks. Master's thesis, School of Engineering, University of Pisa, Italy (2019). https://etd.adm.unipi.it/theses/available/etd-03292019-220853/
16. LeCun, Y., Bottou, L., Bengio, Y., Haffner, P., et al.: Gradient-based learning applied to document recognition. Proc. IEEE **86**(11), 2278–2324 (1998)
17. Majani, E., Erlanson, R., Abu-Mostafa, Y.S.: On the k-winners-take-all network. In: Advances in Neural Information Processing Systems, pp. 634–642 (1989)
18. Nowlan, S.J.: Maximum likelihood competitive learning. In: Advances in Neural Information Processing Systems, pp. 574–582 (1990)
19. Olshausen, B.A.: Learning linear, sparse, factorial codes. Massachusetts Institute of Technology, AIM-1580 (1996)
20. Olshausen, B.A., Field, D.J.: Emergence of simple-cell receptive field properties by learning a sparse code for natural images. Nature **381**(6583), 607 (1996)
21. O'Reilly, R.C., Munakata, Y.: Computational Explorations in Cognitive Neuroscience: Understanding the Mind by Simulating the Brain. MIT Press, Cambridge (2000)
22. Pehlevan, C., Chklovskii, D.B.: Optimization theory of hebbian/anti-hebbian networks for PCA and whitening. In: 2015 53rd Annual Allerton Conference on Communication, Control, and Computing (Allerton), pp. 1458–1465. IEEE (2015)
23. Sanger, T.D.: Optimal unsupervised learning in a single-layer linear feedforward neural network. Neural Netw. **2**(6), 459–473 (1989)
24. Silver, D., et al.: Mastering the game of go with deep neural networks and tree search. Nature **529**(7587), 484 (2016)

25. Wadhwa, A., Madhow, U.: Bottom-up deep learning using the hebbian principle (2016)
26. Yosinski, J., Clune, J., Bengio, Y., Lipson, H.: How transferable are features in deep neural networks? arXiv preprint arXiv:1411.1792 (2014)

Towards Understanding Neuroscience of Realisation of Information Need in Light of Relevance and Satisfaction Judgement

Sakrapee Paisalnan[1]([✉]), Frank Pollick[1], and Yashar Moshfeghi[2]

[1] University of Glasgow, Glasgow, UK
s.paisalnan.1@research.gla.ac.uk, frank.pollick@gla.ac.uk
[2] University of Strathclyde, Glasgow, UK
yashar.moshfeghi@strath.ac.uk

Abstract. Understanding how to satisfy searchers' information need (IN) is the main goal of Information Retrieval (IR) systems. In this study, we investigate the relationships between information need and the two key concepts of relevance and satisfaction from the perspective of neuroscience. We utilise functional Magnetic Resonance Imaging (fMRI) to measure the brain activity of twenty-four participants during performing a Question Answering (Q/A) task that, following the realisation of an information need, included the opportunity to initiate searches and evaluate returned documents. We contrast brain activity between the time of realisation of information need (IN) and two other periods, relevance judgement (RJ), i.e. IN vs RJ, and satisfaction judgement (SJ), i.e. IN vs SJ. To interpret these results, we use meta-analytic techniques of reverse inference to identify the functional significance of the discovered brain regions. The results provide consistent evidence of the involvement of several cognitive functions, including imagery, attention, planning, calculation and working memory. Our findings lead us to obtain a better understanding associated with the characteristic of information need and its relationships to relevance and satisfaction.

Keywords: Neuroscience · fMRI · Information retrieval · Information need · Relevance · Satisfaction

1 Introduction

One of the most important goals in Information Retrieval (IR) is to satisfy a searcher's Information Need (IN). To understand how this is achieved, researchers in IR have investigated IN as well as its relationship with relevance and satisfaction [17]. A fundamental question has been what are the psychological processes engaged when the state of IN is transformed by a relevant search result and then further transformed when the IN is satisfied. Previous research

© Springer Nature Switzerland AG 2022
G. Nicosia et al. (Eds.): LOD 2021, LNCS 13163, pp. 41–56, 2022.
https://doi.org/10.1007/978-3-030-95467-3_3

addressing this question, and establishing the foundations of modern IR systems, has primarily used behavioural data obtained from searchers when performing a search process [18, 20].

However, a growing number of studies have recently employed a different approach, instead using neuroimaging techniques such as functional Magnetic Resonance Imaging (fMRI) and Electroencephalography (EEG) to better understand key concepts in IR, including relevance [7, 11, 16, 23, 29] and the realisation of IN [12, 25–27]. For example, brain imaging research into the search process by Moshfeghi and Pollick [24] divided the entire search process into a set of individual time periods that reflect processes involving the realisation of IN, query formulation, query submission, relevance, and satisfaction. They then compared brain activity between adjacent time periods of the search process as it progressed from start to finish. Comparison across adjacent time periods showed evidence for an evolution of brain activity and respective cognitive functions across the different stages of search. However, they did not investigate how the brain activity involved in IN compared to brain activity during times when relevance and satisfaction were judged. This is a critical point, as the realisation of IN is arguably the most important event in initiating search and comparison between a realisation of IN and the times of RJ and SJ has the potential to inform how an IN is resolved.

Therefore, in this paper, we would like to address two main research questions: **RQ1:** What are the differences in brain activity between the times of a realisation of IN and a relevance judgment (RJ), and what cognitive functions relate to these differences in brain activity? **RQ2:** What are the differences in brain activity between the times of a realisation of IN and a satisfaction judgment (SJ), and what cognitive functions relate to these differences in brain activity?

To investigate our RQs, we examined brain activity while twenty-four participants performed search tasks that were based on a Question Answering (Q/A) task. We used a Q/A dataset derived from the TREC-8 and TREC-2001 Question Answering Tracks - Main Task. The dataset contained 40 questions that could generate expected search scenarios [27]. In order to examine the functional basis of changes in brain activity among the different search conditions, we used a formal framework for reverse inference to infer psychological processes from brain activity. Reverse inference represents the probability of possible psychological processes by a given pattern of brain activity [6, 32] and can be a useful tool to estimate the likelihood of the engagement of a psychological process given the measurement of brain activity [6, 30, 32]. In this work, we used NeuroSynth[1] [41] to perform reverse inference on fMRI brain data resulting from the comparison of brain activity between the states of IN and RJ as well as IN and SJ.

2   Related Work

Essential Concepts in IR: Information Need is considered to be an essential concept of IR and can also be seen as a core component in the search process.

---

[1] https://www.neurosynth.org.

Several cognitive models in IR showed that the need of information would occur at the early stage during a search process [15,19,40]. Another fundamental concept in IR is Relevance. It is a multidimensional concept, which is influenced by both internal factors (also termed as cognitive), such as the user's background knowledge, and external factors like system effectiveness [34,35]. Relevance is also considered as another measure used for evaluating retrieval systems, especially the effectiveness of the system. The concept of relevance is classified into two fundamental categories consisting of objective relevance and subject relevance [5]. The subjective relevance, also known as user-based relevance or pertinence, has been defined as any documents justified to be relevant as a response of the searcher [5,37]. On the other hand, the objective relevance, or system-based relevance, is the information considered to have a relation to the task or topic [5,34]. Satisfaction is another fundamental concept in IR that closely relates to both prior concepts (i.e. information need and relevance). It is the phenomenon when searchers have gathered relevant information and fulfilled their IN [10,22].

Neuroscience and IR: Recent years has seen the field of IR take an increasing interest in neuroscience [13]. This interest has focused on gaining an understanding of how the different components of IR emerge from measurable activity in the brain. These studies have employed a wide range of brain imaging techniques to probe brain activity related to brain states involved in processing relevance and information need. For example, Moshfeghi et al. [23,25,27] conducted a series of studies using fMRI to understand brain regions activated during relevance judgement and information need. Another study by Moshfeghi et al. [24] revealed how transitions between different segments of an information search task were reflected in activity changes in large scale brain networks. Apart from the fMRI brain imaging technique, several studies have applied other techniques to investigate the concept of IR, especially relevance. For example, a technique called "Electroencephalography" (EEG) that measures electrical signals generated by the brain has been applied in several studies to investigate the concept of relevance to the text information [1,7,11,29]. Another technique called "Magnetoencephalography" (MEG), which can detect the small magnetic fields generated by the brain, was used to understand the concept of relevance of visual information [16]. These previous studies were able to provide clear evidence of neural correlates of the concept of IR. However, they have matched brain activity to function without the benefit of formal meta-analytical tools. The current study benefits from identifying the functions of brain regions activated during a particular activity by using meta-analysis from a large-scale database.

Neuroimaging Meta-analysis Inference: A common objective of neuroscience studies is to discover the brain regions associated with a particular psychological function. The fundamental challenge of the studies is to interpret the noisy imaging data to infer the brain region(s) responsible for the specific psychological process. Most fMRI studies commonly employ a type of inference called "forward inference" [6]. Such studies typically manipulate a specific psychological process and measure the patterns of brain activity associated with the process [14]. Thus, forward inference reflects the probability of observing brain activity in a region by performing a given psychological process. Reverse inference, on the other hand, refers to psychological processes inferred from the given patterns of brain activity. In other words, reverse inference represents the probability of possible psychological processes by a given pattern of brain activity [6,32]. It is generally used to estimate the likelihood of a psychological process engagement given the brain activity measurement. Also, it is suggested to be another strategy that assists the interpretation of neuro-imaging results rather than informally inferring psychological processes from the literature [30]. A number of studies showed that employing this technique can successfully reveal the brain regions underlying a particular psychological process [6,32].

3   Experimental Methodology

Design: A "within-subjects" design was used in this study. We defined three time periods (epochs) during the search process as (1) The realisation of Information Need (IN), (2) Relevance Judgment (RJ), and (3) Satisfaction Judgment (SJ). We considered these three epochs as the independent variables in this study. The dependent variable was brain activity revealed by the Blood Oxygen Level Dependent (BOLD) signal. According to the design, we only analysed brain activity for the cases when, after the initial query, a participant indicated an information need. Only these data and the subsequent search process were considered in our analysis.

Task: Each participant was asked to engage in the search task that could stimulate their IN. At the beginning of the task, they were presented with a fixation screen for 4–6 s before being presented with a question for 4 s. Then, four possible responses were presented for 4 s while the question was still being displayed on the screen. There was always one response indicating the correct answer and another one of them indicating "need to search". Also, the position of all responses was randomised for each question. Participants were not allowed to make a response when observing the question and its responses because we wished to prevent brain activity related to the motor response of pressing the button in the model of brain activity. Next, the participants were asked to make a response by pressing one of the four buttons indicated on the button box on their right-hand side. The time to respond was not restricted so that participants were not under time pressure to respond. The order of the questions was randomised for each participant. After the participants gave a response, if they responded with an answer, the experiment would directly proceed to the next question. Note that we would not consider this case because it indicated that they had no information need for this trial. On the other hand, if the answer "need to search" was chosen, then we labelled this epoch as IN and participants were progressed to the next stage of the search task. In this stage, participants were asked to formulate a query for 4 s before moving to the next stage. After formulating a query, they were required to submit their query within 4 s. Then, a fixation cross was presented on the screen for 4 s before leading to a document obtained from the query. The document was chosen randomly from the four possible documents (two relevant and two non-relevant). The participants had to evaluate the document as a result of their search for 16 s. This 16-s epoch was labelled as the relevance judgment (RJ). Then, they were returned to the original question with the responses. If they selected any response except "need to search", then they were given 4 s to rate their satisfaction with the search. This 4-s epoch was labelled as the satisfaction judgment (SJ). Otherwise, they were returned to another cycle of being presented with another document in response to their query. For each question, they were provided with a maximum of two opportunities to answer the question. An illustration of this task is provided in Fig. 1.

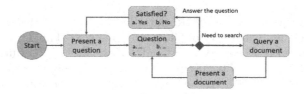

Fig. 1. The figure illustrates the flowchart of the experimental procedure

Procedure: This section describes the flow of the study, from start to finish. Ethical permission was obtained from the Ethics Committee of the College of Science and Engineering, University of Glasgow. A pilot study was conducted before running the actual experiment in order to confirm that the experimental procedure worked as expected. Participants were instructed of the duration of the experiment, which included approximately 50 min to perform all functional brain imaging tasks examining search processes, and approximately 10 min to obtain an anatomical scan of brain structure. Participants were informed that they could leave at any point during the experiment and would still receive payment (the payment rate was £6/hr). They were then asked to sign a consent form. Before beginning, the experiment participants underwent a safety check to guarantee that they did not possess any metal items inside or outside of their body or had any contraindications for scanning, such as certain tattoo inks. They were then provided with gear (similar to a training suit) to wear for the duration of the experiment to avoid potential interference with the fMRI signal from any metal objects in their clothes.

Before starting the experiment, they were given a training session in order to become familiar with the experimental procedure. In the session, a sample task containing a corresponding set of example questions was presented to the participants. After successful completion of their training task, participants entered the fMRI scanner, and the settings of the machine were adjusted to optimise their comfort and vision. While being scanned, each participant engaged in two separate runs of the task, with each run comprised of 20 questions. Two runs were chosen to give the participants a break to relax during the scanning and to prevent fatigue on the task, which could extend in time if a participant often needed to search. After the functional runs were complete, the anatomical data of each participant were obtained.

After completion of scanning, participants filled out an exit questionnaire that provided demographic and qualitative descriptions of their experience during the experiment. They also completed the Edinburgh handedness questionnaire [28] that evaluated whether the participant was right-, left-, or mixed-handed. Handedness information was obtained since lateralisation of brain function is influenced by handedness, and we wished to ensure that our sample of participants approximated the general population.

fMRI Data Acquisition: All fMRI data were collected at the Centre for Cognitive Neuroimaging, University of Glasgow, using a 3T Tim Trio Siemens scanner and 32-channel head coil. A functional T2*-weighted MRI run was acquired for two runs of the task (TR 2000 ms; TE 30 ms; 32 Slices; $3\,mm^3$ voxel; FOV 210. A matrix of 70 × 70). An anatomical scan was performed at the session end, which comprised a high-resolution T1-weighted anatomical scan using a 3D magnetisation prepared rapid acquisition gradient echo (ADNI-MPRAGE) T1-weighted sequence (192 slices; $1\,mm^3$ voxel; Sagittal Slice; TR 1900 ms; TE 2.52; 256 × 256 image resolution).

fMRI Data Preprocessing: The fMRI data were analysed using Brain Voyager QX. A standard pipeline of pre-processing of the data was performed for each participant [9]. This involved slice scan time correction using trilinear interpolation based on information about the TR and the order of slice scanning. Three-dimensional motion correction was performed to correct for small head movements by spatial alignment of all volumes of a participant to the first volume by rigid-body transformations. Also, linear trends in the data were removed, and high pass filtering with a cutoff of 0.0025 Hz was performed to reduce artefact from low-frequency physiological noise. Functional data were then co-registered with the anatomic data and spatially normalised into the common Talairach space. Finally, the functional data of each individual underwent spatial smoothing using a Gaussian kernel of 6mm to facilitate the analysis of group data.

General Linear Model (GLM) Analysis: Analysis began with a first-level analysis of the data of individual participants using a general linear model of the Blood Oxygen Level Dependent (BOLD) response time course in every voxel that modelled the two epochs to be contrasted, including IN vs RJ and IN vs SJ. Predictors' time courses were adjusted for the hemodynamic response delay by convolution with a hemodynamic response function. Group data were statistically tested with a second-level analysis using a random-effects analysis of variance using search epoch as a within-participants factor. Two contrasts were performed between brain activity at different time epoch of the search process, including IN vs RJ and IN vs SJ. To address the issue of multiple statistical comparisons across all voxels, activations are reported using False Discovery Rate (FDR) at a threshold of q < 0.01 [3]. Using FDR, we control for the number of false-positive voxels among the subset of voxels labelled as significant. The brain regions corresponding to the contrasts were identified using Talairach Client version 2.4.3[2].

Psychological Function Inference: NeuroSynth was used to infer the psychological function of brain locations revealed by the GLM analysis [41]. As our goal was to identify psychological functions that are associated with the different brain regions [30,31] we began with a topic set of 50 distinct keyword topics extracted with Latent Dirichlet Allocation (LDA) from the abstracts of all articles in the NeuroSynth database as of July 2018 (507891 activation peaks over 14371 studies) [4,32]. However, since 23 of the 50 were not related to psychological function, we were left with 27 main keywords that best represented their topics in a topic set. For clarity of presentation, these 27 were further reduced to 16 keywords that produced the greatest level of response.

Using the coordinates of each location revealed by the GLM, we applied the reverse inference technique on the selected topics using NeuroSynth (version 0.7, released July 2018) [6,39,41]. NeuroSynth analysis was performed based on the Core NeuroSynth Tools developed on Python[3]. Because all activations in the NeuroSynth database are in MNI152 coordinate space, to perform the analysis, we needed to first transform the results of the GLM from Talairach to MNI152 space. This conversion was achieved using the Yale BioImage Suite Package [21]. Each neural activation was represented by a 10 mm sphere around the coordinate to obtain its co-activation map [32,38]. The co-activation maps of each contrast were used to identify their association with the terms, and the results were displayed as radar plots of the Pearson correlation.

Large-scale Functional Brain Network Analysis: One approach in understanding brain function is to consider the brain activity at individual locations to be part of the activity within large-scale brain networks that subserve different functions. With this approach, the individual locations of activation revealed by the GLM analysis can be mapped onto a standard set of large-scale brain networks [33] and the function of these networks considered (see Table 1 for a summary of the networks). Using the methods described by [24] we found, for each activation revealed by the GLM analysis, which of the ten large-scale networks it most closely belonged to. This analysis provides further insight into potential functions of the brain activations, and because it is derived differently

---

[2] http://www.talairach.org.
[3] https://github.com/neurosynth/neurosynth.

from the inference analysis based on NeuroSynth, it provides an additional check to the proposed function of brain activation.

4 Results

Participant Demographics: Twenty-four healthy participants were recruited to participate in the experiment, consisting of 11 males and 13 females. All participants were under the age of 44, with the largest group between the ages of 18–23 (54.1%), followed by a group between the age of 30–35 (20.8%). The handedness survey indicated that the majority of participants (79.1%) were right-handed, 12.5% of them were left-handed, and 8.33% were mixed-handed. The educational level of the participants indicated that 20.8% of the participants had a postgraduate degree, 33.33% of them had a bachelor degree, and the rest of them (45.8%) had another qualification. The majority of the participants were students, while other individuals were self-employed (20.8%), not employed (4.16%), and employed by a company/organisation (20.8%). Participants were primarily native speakers (79.1%), while the rest were advanced in English language skills. Lastly, all participants had experience in searching an average of 11.66 years with SD 3.58.

Table 1. Summary of the function of ten large-scale brain networks.

Network	Function
Dorsal attention	Top-down attention, visuospatial
Ventral attention	Bottom-up reorienting or shifting of attention
Fronto-parietal task Control	Initiation and adjustment for rapid adaptive control
Cingulo-opercular task control	Stable set control for task maintenance
Salience	Identify relevant items, integrate sensation, cognition and emotion
Default mode	Self-referential thinking, mind-wandering
Visual	Processing of visual information
Auditory	Processing of auditory information
Sensory/somatomotor	Processing of touch and control of action
Memory retrieval	Access to memory

Log Analysis: The fMRI analysis relied upon a participant's response to the question to code whether a trial was IN or No-IN. If the trial was No-IN, then there was no further analysis of that trial since we focused on the search process, starting from initiation of information need to the satisfaction of information need. Because the question set was designed to contain both easy and difficult questions in the same amount, the average number of IN responses and No-IN responses was expected to be equal. In the actual experiment, the average number of IN responses was 17.5 with SD 5.91, and the average number of No-IN responses was 22.5 with SD 5.91. A paired t-test was performed and revealed a marginal difference between the types of responses ($p = 0.05$).

Contrasts of Brain Activity, IN vs RJ and IN vs SJ: The contrasts of brain activity address our two research questions. Answers to the first parts of **RQ1** and **RQ2** can be seen in the results of the GLM analysis, which indicate any differences in brain activity between the time periods contrasted. Answers to the second part of **RQ1** and **RQ2** are led by the use of inference and network analysis techniques to interpret the psychological functions of the brain regions identified by the GLM.

Contrast of IN vs RJ: The condition IN occurs when participants were presented with a question and possible responses, and they decided that they would

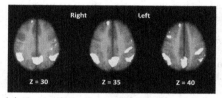

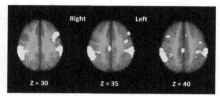

(a) Activation clusters from the contrast of IN and RJ.

(b) Activation clusters from the contrast of IN and SJ.

Fig. 2. Activation clusters from both the a) IN vs RJ contrast and the b) IN vs SJ contrast are shown in yellow, and are projected onto the average anatomical structure for four transverse sections. Note that the brains are in a radiological format where the left side of the brain is on the right side of the image. (Color figure online)

Table 2. Details of activation for the contrast of IN vs RJ, including their hemisphere (H), anatomic label, location (Talairach coordinates), Brodmann Area (BA), effect size as indicated by F statistic, p-value, volume of cluster and large-scale network to which it belongs.

	Brain area	H	Talairach coordinates				Effect size		Voxels	Network
			X	Y	Z	BA	$F(1,21)$	p-value	mm^3	
IN < RJ	Supramarginal gyrus	R	45.0	−46.0	34.0	40	54.29	$<1.0 \times 10^{-6}$	6155	Default mode
	Middle frontal gyrus	R	42.0	11.0	46.0	6	43.58	2.0×10^{-6}	1329	Salience
	Medial frontal gyrus	R	24.0	50.0	10.0	10	28.64	2.6×10^{-6}	909	Salience
	Precuneus	L	−6.0	−64.0	34.0	7	51.30	$<1.0 \times 10^{-6}$	5046	Memory retrieval
	Supramarginal gyrus	L	−48.0	−52.0	28.0	40	66.40	$<1.0 \times 10^{-6}$	5175	Default mode
	Superior temporal gyrus	L	−48.0	−28.0	1.0	22	30.23	1.9×10^{-6}	302	Default mode
	Middle temporal gyrus	L	−54.0	−10.0	−8.0	21	23.82	8.0×10^{-5}	121	Default mode
IN > RJ	Culmen	R	15.0	−43.0	−17.0	*	39.00	3.0×10^{-6}	1579	Visual
	Inferior parietal lobule	L	−42.0	−31.0	43.0	40	39.74	3.0×10^{-6}	3867	Sensory/somatomotor

Table 3. Details of activation for the contrast of IN vs RJ, including their hemisphere (H), anatomic label, location (Talairach coordinates), Brodmann Area (BA), effect size as indicated by F statistic, p-value, volume of cluster and large-scale network to which it belongs.

	Brain area	H	Talairach coordinates				Effect size		Voxels	Network
			X	Y	Z	BA	F(1,21)	p-value	mm^3	
IN < SJ	Supramarginal gyrus	R	57.0	−37.0	37.0	40	104.70	$<1.0 \times 10^{-6}$	32337	Salience
	Insula	R	39.0	2.0	1.0	13	44.94	1.0×10^{-6}	10310	Cingulo-opercular
	Middle frontal gyrus	R	39.0	14.0	43.0	6	28.25	2.9×10^{-5}	795	Fronto-parietal
	Culmen	R	24.0	−46.0	−17.0	*	27.07	3.7×10^{-5}	968	Cerebellar
	Cingulate gyrus	R	3.0	−22.0	37.0	24	29.93	2.0×10^{-5}	1371	Memory retrieval
	Precuneus	L	0.0	−58.0	59.0	7	33.14	1.0×10^{-5}	1467	Dorsal attention
	Postcentral gyrus	L	−60.0	−22.0	37.0	2	57.34	$<1.0 \times 10^{-6}$	20586	Sensory/somatomotor
	Inferior parietal lobule	L	−33.0	−43.0	43.0	40	19.76	2.2×10^{-4}	144	Dorsal attention
IN > SJ	Lingual gyrus	R	12.0	−79.0	−5.0	18	146.20	$<1.0 \times 10^{-6}$	36003	Visual
	Medial dorsal nuclues	L	0.0	−22.0	4.0	*	74.58	$<1.0 \times 10^{-6}$	10313	Subcortical
	Caudate body	R	9.0	5.0	10.0	48	40.41	3.0×10^{-6}	1798	Subcortical
	Culmen	R	0.0	−49.0	−23.0	*	21.71	1.4×10^{-4}	434	Cerebellar
	Cingulate gyrus	L	−6.0	14.0	43.0	32	47.79	1.0×10^{-6}	836	Salience
	Superior frontal gyrus	L	−24.0	11.0	49.0	6	26.34	4.4×10^{-5}	1365	Fronto-parietal
	Precuneus	L	−30.0	−70.0	31.0	19	18.07	3.6×10^{-4}	155	Dorsal attention
	Inferior frontal gyrus	L	−51.0	20.0	22.0	9	88.53	$<1.0 \times 10^{-6}$	9355	Fronto-parietal
	Superior temporal gyrus	L	−57.0	−28.0	4.0	22	21.89	1.3×10^{-4}	722	Default mode

need to search. The other condition, RJ, is when participants viewed and evaluated a provided document, which could be either relevant or non-relevant to the question. Results of the contrast are shown in Fig. 2(a) and Table 2. These results showed seven of nine clusters had higher activation for RJ over IN, while two clusters had higher activation for IN over RJ. The inference approach of NeuroSynth identified several psychological functions in the seven areas where brain activity was greater for RJ than IN (Fig. 3(a) and 3(b)). These functions included working memory, semantic and language processing, social processing, and auditory processing. The finding of default mode activity would likely indicate access of internal information or could possibly arise from mind wandering. The large-scale functional brain network analysis was broadly consistent with the NeuroSynth analysis. Here we found four of the seven clusters in the default mode and two of the seven clusters in the salience network, while one involved memory retrieval. The networks of salience, memory retrieval, and default mode are consistent with internal access of information for the evaluation of a document. Thus, this evidence points to RJ, compared to IN being involved more in the internal processing and evaluation of information.

The inference approach of NeuroSynth identified several psychological functions in the two areas where brain activity was greater for IN than RJ (Fig. 3(c)). This included imagery, attention, planning, calculation, somatosensory, action, working memory [2] and motor. This diverse set of functions would support a view that the regions associated with both cognition and motor function. The large-scale functional brain network analysis was broadly consistent with the NeuroSynth analysis in regards to motor control, though the Neurosynth results indicated more complex cognition at work.

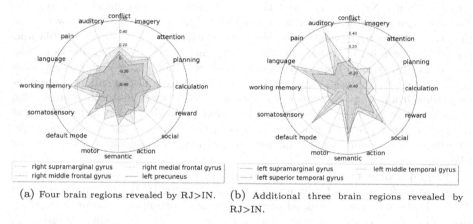

(a) Four brain regions revealed by RJ>IN.

(b) Additional three brain regions revealed by RJ>IN.

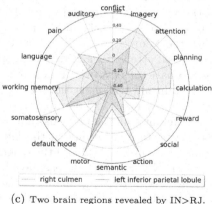

(c) Two brain regions revealed by IN>RJ.

Fig. 3. Three radar charts to illustrate, for each brain region revealed by the IN-RJ contrast, the results of reverse inference for the given brain function terms.

Contrast of IN vs SJ: The condition IN occurs when participants were presented with a question and possible responses, and they decided that they would need to search. The other condition, SJ, is when they were presented with a question of whether they were satisfied with the search and answered the question to provide a satisfaction judgment. The results are shown in Fig. 2(b) and Table 3. These results showed that eight of seventeen clusters had higher activation for SJ over IN. The other nine clusters had higher activation for IN over SJ. The inference approach of NeuroSynth identified several psychological functions arising from when brain activity was greater for SJ than IN (Fig. 4(a) and 4(b)). These functions included somatosensory, motor, action and pain. The finding of pain is somewhat surprising and might show a known limitation of reverse inference using NeuroSynth; that the existing literature influences the results. Namely, pain research is an extremely active field, and the insula is known to be involved in pain processing, and thus this relationship between the insula and pain might overshadow other affective processing aspects of insula function. The large-scale functional brain network analysis was not entirely consistent with the NeuroSynth analysis. Here we found single clusters in the salience, cingulo-opercular, fronto-parietal, memory retrieval and sensory/somatomotor networks, as well as two clusters in the dorsal attention network. It is possible that due to the fact that the SJ comes at the end of the trial, we also see brain activity related to the end of the trial and the switching of tasks and related motor planning.

The inference approach of NeuroSynth identified several psychological functions arising from when brain activity was greater for IN than SJ (Fig. 4(c) and 4(d)). These functions included conflict, imagery, attention, planning, calculation, semantic, working memory, auditory and language processing. These functions are consistent with the view that compared to SJ, IN involves a complex interplay of cognitive faculties. The large-scale functional brain network analysis was broadly consistent with the NeuroSynth analysis. Here we found individual clusters in visual, salience, dorsal attention, and default mode networks, as well as two clusters in the fronto-parietal network. Taken together with the NeuroSynth results indicates that during the realisation of IN, participants require dynamic allocation of cognitive resources to generate an information need.

Generalising across the different contrasts reveals that, compared to RJ and SJ, IN shows a characteristic pattern of results in the left hemisphere, which includes the inferior parietal lobule in IN > RJ and the cingulate gyrus, superior frontal gyrus and precuneus in IN > SJ. These areas have in common the functions of working memory, imagery, attention, planning and calculation. Moreover, these regions also belong to a variety of large-scale networks, including sensory/somatomotor, salience, frontoparietal and dorsal attention networks.

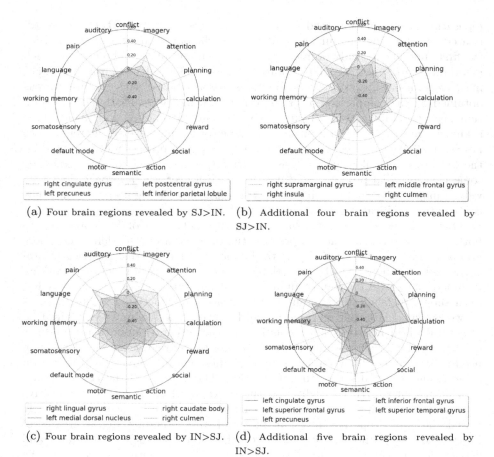

(a) Four brain regions revealed by SJ>IN.

(b) Additional four brain regions revealed by SJ>IN.

(c) Four brain regions revealed by IN>SJ.

(d) Additional five brain regions revealed by IN>SJ.

Fig. 4. Four radar charts to illustrate, for each brain region revealed by the IN-RJ contrast, the results of reverse inference for the given brain function terms.

5   Discussion and Conclusion

As more becomes known about the neuroscience of IR and the realisation of information need, the evidence points towards it being a complex activity that involves a variety of neural processes, spanning many psychological functions [24, 27]. In our experiment, participants engaged in an experimental task imitating a search process. The participants were asked to respond to a set of questions gathered from the TREC-8 and TREC 2001 Q/A Tracks. Contrasts of brain activity were obtained between the period of realisation of information need and two other periods - relevance judgment and satisfaction judgment. These contrasts revealed the different brain regions that were identified to be more active during the different periods, and this answered the first parts of **RQ1** and **RQ2** regarding the identification of the physical manifestation of the realisation of information need. To address the second parts of **RQ1** and **RQ2**, related to informing our understanding of psychological functions, we used for the first time in the study of information need an automatic inference approach based on NeuroSynth [41]. This approach enabled us to identify from the existing psychological literature what functions are associated with the brain areas obtained by the comparison of brain activity during the realisation of information need to brain activity during relevance and satisfaction judgments. It is acknowledged that such an automatic framework using reverse inference does not by itself crucially test causality of a psychological process and is limited by the literature available for analysis, which might be biased towards exploring some psychological processes and not others. However, the approach does provide a quantitative tool to coherently synthesise the existing literature and thus contributes significantly to our understanding.

Our findings demonstrate that during the realisation of IN, compared to both relevance and satisfaction periods, there was a lateralised left hemisphere group of brain areas (inferior parietal lobule, cingulate gyrus, superior frontal gyrus and precuneus) which were related to a common set of functions (working memory, imagery, attention, planning and calculation). As working memory has been shown to facilitate dynamic reconfiguration of functional brain networks [8] we can speculate that representing an IN involves a dynamic reconfiguration of several brain networks [36]. This interpretation contributes to the findings of [27], which showed the multi-faceted nature of the realisation of information need as it balances between accessing available internal sources of information or accessing external sources of information. The findings of the current study provide us with further insight into the concepts of IR from the perspective of neuroscience. This knowledge will stimulate future research to more clearly reveal the core properties of IR in terms of understanding characteristics of information need and how it relates to other concepts such as relevance and satisfaction. In turn, these insights will assist us to understand more about the searcher's behaviour during a search process which could help us in designing IR systems that integrate more closely with human capabilities to produce improved search systems. The current results point towards a left lateralised brain network involved in the realisation of IN. Future brain imaging research should examine in more detail the dynamic processes by which this network is formed and how it might be reconfigured according to other cognitive demands.

References

1. Allegretti, M., Moshfeghi, Y., Hadjigeorgieva, M., Pollick, F.E., Jose, J.M., Pasi, G.: When relevance judgement is happening?: an eeg-based study. In: Proceedings of the 38th International ACM SIGIR Conference on Research and Development in Information Retrieval, pp. 719–722. ACM (2015)
2. Baddeley, A.: Working memory: looking back and looking forward. Nature Rev. Neurosci. **4**(10), 829 (2003)
3. Benjamini, Y., Hochberg, Y.: Controlling the false discovery rate: a practical and powerful approach to multiple testing. J. Roy. Stat. Soc. Ser. B (Methodol.) **57**, 289–300 (1995)

4. Blei, D.M., Ng, A.Y., Jordan, M.I.: Latent Dirichlet allocation. J. Mach. Learn. Res. **3**(Jan), 993–1022 (2003)
5. Borlund, P.: The concept of relevance in IR. J. Am. Soc. Inf. Sci. Technol **54**(10), 913–925 (2003)
6. Chang, L.J., Yarkoni, T., Khaw, M.W., Sanfey, A.G.: Decoding the role of the insula in human cognition: functional parcellation and large-scale reverse inference. Cereb. Cortex **23**(3), 739–749 (2012)
7. Eugster, M.J., et al.: Predicting term-relevance from brain signals. In: Proceedings of the 37th International ACM SIGIR Conference on Research & Development in Information Retrieval, pp. 425–434. ACM (2014)
8. Finc, K., Bonna, K., He, X., Lydon-Staley, D.M., Kühn, S., Duch, W., Bassett, D.S.: Dynamic reconfiguration of functional brain networks during working memory training. Nature Commun. **11**(1), 1–15 (2020)
9. Goebel, R.: Brainvoyager qx, vers. 2.1. Brain Innovation BV, Maastricht, Netherlands (2017)
10. Griffiths, J.R., Johnson, F., Hartley, R.J.: User satisfaction as a measure of system performance. J. Librarianship Inf. Sci. **39**(3), 142–152 (2007)
11. Gwizdka, J., Hosseini, R., Cole, M., Wang, S.: Temporal dynamics of eye-tracking and EEG during reading and relevance decisions. J. Assoc. Inf. Sci. Technol. **68**(10), 2299–2312 (2017)
12. Gwizdka, J., Moshfeghi, Y., Wilson, M.L., et al.: Introduction to the special issue on neuro-information science. J. Assoc. Inf. Sci. Technol. **70**(9), 911–916 (2019)
13. Gwizdka, J., Mostafa, J.: Neuroir 2015: Sigir 2015 workshop on neuro-physiological methods in IR research. In: ACM Sigir Forum, vol. 49, pp. 83–88. ACM, New York (2016)
14. Henson, R.: Forward inference using functional neuroimaging: dissociations versus associations. Trends Cogn. Sci. **10**(2), 64–69 (2006)
15. Jansen, B.J., Booth, D., Smith, B.: Using the taxonomy of cognitive learning to model online searching. Inf. Process. Manag. **45**(6), 643–663 (2009)
16. Kauppi, J.P., et al.: Towards brain-activity-controlled information retrieval: decoding image relevance from meg signals. NeuroImage **112**, 288–298 (2015)
17. Kelly, D.: Methods for evaluating interactive information retrieval systems with users. Found. Trends Inf. Retrieval **3**(1–2), 1–224 (2009)
18. Kelly, D., Fu, X.: Eliciting better information need descriptions from users of information search systems. Inf. Process. Manag. **43**(1), 30–46 (2007)
19. Kuhlthau, C.C.: Inside the search process: information seeking from the user's perspective. J. Am. Soc. Inf. Sci. **42**(5), 361–371 (1991)
20. Kuhlthau, C.C.: A principle of uncertainty for information seeking. J. Documentation **49**(4), 339–355 (1993)
21. Lacadie, C.M., Fulbright, R.K., Rajeevan, N., Constable, R.T., Papademetris, X.: More accurate talairach coordinates for neuroimaging using non-linear registration. Neuroimage **42**(2), 717–725 (2008)
22. Liu, M., Liu, Y., Mao, J., Luo, C., Zhang, M., Ma, S.: "Satisfaction with failure" or "unsatisfied success": investigating the relationship between search success and user satisfaction (2018)
23. Moshfeghi, Y., Pinto, L.R., Pollick, F.E., Jose, J.M.: Understanding relevance: an fMRI study. In: Serdyukov, P., et al. (eds.) ECIR 2013. LNCS, vol. 7814, pp. 14–25. Springer, Heidelberg (2013). https://doi.org/10.1007/978-3-642-36973-5_2
24. Moshfeghi, Y., Pollick, F.E.: Search process as transitions between neural states. In: Proceedings of the 2018 World Wide Web Conference, pp. 1683–1692 (2018)

25. Moshfeghi, Y., Pollick, F.E.: Neuropsychological model of the realization of information need. J. Assoc. Inf. Sci. Technol **70**(9), 954–967 (2019)
26. Moshfeghi, Y., Triantafillou, P., Pollick, F.: Towards predicting a realisation of an information need based on brain signals. In: The World Wide Web Conference, pp. 1300–1309 (2019)
27. Moshfeghi, Y., Triantafillou, P., Pollick, F.E.: Understanding information need: an fMRI study. In: Proceedings of the 39th International ACM SIGIR conference on Research and Development in Information Retrieval, pp. 335–344. ACM (2016)
28. Oldfield, R.C.: The assessment and analysis of handedness: the Edinburgh inventory. Neuropsychologia **9**(1), 97–113 (1971)
29. Pinkosova, Z., McGeown, W.J., Moshfeghi, Y.: The cortical activity of graded relevance. In: Proceedings of the 43rd International ACM SIGIR Conference on Research and Development in Information Retrieval, pp. 299–308 (2020)
30. Poldrack, R.A.: Inferring mental states from neuroimaging data: from reverse inference to large-scale decoding. Neuron **72**(5), 692–697 (2011)
31. Poldrack, R.A.: The future of fMRI in cognitive neuroscience. Neuroimage **62**(2), 1216–1220 (2012)
32. Poldrack, R.A., Mumford, J.A., Schonberg, T., Kalar, D., Barman, B., Yarkoni, T.: Discovering relations between mind, brain, and mental disorders using topic mapping. PLoS Comput. Biol. **8**(10), e1002707 (2012)
33. Power, J.D., et al.: Functional network organization of the human brain. Neuron **72**(4), 665–678 (2011)
34. Saracevic, T.: Relevance: a review of and a framework for the thinking on the notion in information science. J. Assoc. Inf. Sci. Technol **26**(6), 321–343 (1975)
35. Schamber, L., Eisenberg, M.B., Nilan, M.S.: A re-examination of relevance: toward a dynamic, situational definition. Inf. Process. Manag. **26**(6), 755–776 (1990)
36. Shine, J., Poldrack, R.: Principles of dynamic network reconfiguration across diverse brain states. Neuroimage **180**(part b), 396–405 (2018)
37. Swanson, D.R.: Subjective versus objective relevance in bibliographic retrieval systems. Libr. Q. **56**(4), 389–398 (1986)
38. de la Vega, A., Chang, L.J., Banich, M.T., Wager, T.D., Yarkoni, T.: Large-scale meta-analysis of human medial frontal cortex reveals tripartite functional organization. J. Neurosci **36**(24), 6553–6562 (2016)
39. Wendelken, C.: Meta-analysis: how does posterior parietal cortex contribute to reasoning? Front. Hum. Neurosci. **8**, 1042 (2015)
40. Wilson, T.D.: Models in information behaviour research. J. Documentation **55**(3), 249–270 (1999)
41. Yarkoni, T., Poldrack, R.A., Nichols, T.E., Van Essen, D.C., Wager, T.D.: Large-scale automated synthesis of human functional neuroimaging data. Nat. Methods **8**(8), 665 (2011)

New Optimization Approaches in Malware Traffic Analysis

Ivan Letteri[1]([✉])[ID], Antonio Di Cecco[2][ID], and Giuseppe Della Penna[1][ID]

[1] Department of Information Engineering, Computer Science and Mathematics,
University of L'Aquila, L'Aquila, Italy
{ivan.letteri,giuseppe.dellapenna}@univaq.it
[2] School of AI, Rome, Italy

Abstract. Machine learning is rapidly becoming one of the most important technology for malware traffic detection, since the continuous evolution of malware requires a constant adaptation and the ability to generalize [20]. However, network traffic datasets are usually oversized and contain redundant and irrelevant information, and this may dramatically increase the computational cost and decrease the accuracy of most classifiers, with the risk to introduce further noise.

We propose two novel dataset optimization strategies which exploit and combine several state-of-the-art approaches in order to achieve an effective optimization of the network traffic datasets used to train malware detectors. The first approach is a feature selection technique based on mutual information measures and sensibility enhancement. The second is a dimensional reduction technique based autoencoders. Both these approaches have been experimentally applied on the MTA-KDD'19 dataset, and the optimized results evaluated and compared using a Multi Layer Perceptron as machine learning model for malware detection.

Keywords: Malware traffic detection · Malware analysis · Network traffic · Machine learning · Dataset optimization · Dimensional reduction · Feature selection · Mutual information

1 Introduction

Machine learning (as well as any statistical methodology) faces a formidable problem when dealing with high-dimensional data. Indeed, redundant information and variables that are not relevant for a specific classification task can dramatically increase the computational cost and decrease the accuracy of most classifiers [15]. Therefore, typically the number of input variables needs to be decreased before such methodologies can be successfully applied [28]. This operation, that we shall refer to as *dataset optimization* in the rest of the paper, has three important advantages: to prevent the so called "curse of dimensionality" [16], to increase the computational efficiency of the classifiers [25], also reducing the overfitting probability [9] and eases the analysis and visualization of the data [5].

© Springer Nature Switzerland AG 2022
G. Nicosia et al. (Eds.): LOD 2021, LNCS 13163, pp. 57–68, 2022.
https://doi.org/10.1007/978-3-030-95467-3_4

Generally speaking, dataset optimization can be accomplished in two different ways: by selecting only the most relevant variables from the original dataset (*Feature Selection*, FS), or by deriving a smaller set of *new* variables, as a combination of the original ones [29]. Researchers have proposed many algorithms to measure the feature relevance and perform feature selection. Among them, the most promising ones seems to be based on Mutual Information (MI) [19], but MI can be exploited in many different ways with different results. As an example, Balagani and Phoha [2] present an analysis of three well-known algorithms, namely mRMR [13], MIFS [3] and CIFE [1], concluding that they make highly restrictive assumptions on the underlying data distributions. However, Brown et al. [6] after comparing a number of different algorithms, suggest that JMI [4] and mRMR should be an optimal choice for feature selection. On the other hand, recently, autoencoders (AE) have shown promising results in extracting effective features from high-dimensional datasets. As an example, Shuyang et al. [32] propose a new algorithm for autoencoder-guided feature selection which tries to distinguish the task-relevant and task-irrelevant features. Kai et al. [12] exploit AEs to choose the highly-representable features commonly used in a neural network for unsupervised learning.

In this paper we define and compare two novel dataset optimization strategies which exploit and combine several of the state-of-the-art approaches described above in order to achieve an effective optimization of the network traffic datasets used to train malware detectors. In particular, we first develop an *hybrid wrapper-filter* FS strategy that tries to find the best possible subset of features with respect to a target classifier performance choosen as predictor. The naive approach to such kind of so-called *wrapper* strategy is to perform an exhaustive search (i.e., experiment all the possible variables subsets), thus it tends to be computationally expensive, and often impractical when the number of variables to take into account is large. On the other hand, the proposed solution limits the subset space to explore by ranking the features through classifier-independent metrics, in particular mutual information (MI), as common in *filter* strategies, to strongly limit the computation complexity.

The second optimization approach presented performs *Dimensional Reduction* (DR) in order to remove inconsistent and irrelevant information from the dataset [23]. DR techniques are related to FS in that both methods aim at feeding fewer input variables to the predictive model. The difference is that FS selects features to keep or remove from the dataset, whereas DR creates a projection of the data resulting in entirely new variables. In particular, our approach makes use of an *autoencoder* (AE) [14] which maps (compresses) the original variables in a smaller space through nonlinear combinations, and this allows us to remove a certain amount of useless information while, at the same time, generating derived, more informative variables. Indeed, it is well known that the learning performances of any classification algorithm are more positively influenced by the expressiveness of the features rather than by their number.

We use the public dataset MTA-KDD'19 dataset [22] as a benchmark for the FS and the DR approaches, since it has a sufficiently large number of features (33) and it has already obtained excellent classification results (99.73%). Moreover, as far as we are aware, the MTA-KDD'19 is the only public dataset aimed solely at determining malware traffic based on statistical flow analysis and which offers a constantly updated traffic collection. Most of the other public datasets are very specific to, e.g., Android or IoT malware, and sometimes based on the static analysis of executable payloads.

2 Feature Selection Through Mutual Information

Feature Selection methods can be grouped into two broad categories: classifier-independent (*filters*) and classifier-dependent (*wrappers* and *embedded* methods).

Filter methods are based upon classifier-independent metrics such as distance, correlation, mutual information and consistency, which are used to rank each feature and remove the least ones. These methods are effective in term of time computation and give robustness to the overfitting phenomenon [11].

Wrapper methods search the space of feature subsets, using the accuracy of a particular classifier as the measure of feasibility of a candidate subset. Such an approach allows to detect the possible interactions between variables [26] and select only the most relevant, non-redundant subset. However, it also has the disadvantage of a considerable computational cost.

Embedded methods exploit the structure of specific classes of learning models to guide the feature selection process [10]. In particular, the most common embedded methods make use of decision tree algorithms [19]. Actually, building a good decision tree implies making a good feature selection, since a good decision tree puts the most relevant features near to the root. Therefore, even if these methods are less computationally expensive and less prone to overfitting than wrappers, they are still tightly coupled with a specific learning model.

To sum up, filters are faster than embedded methods, and embedded methods are in turn faster than wrappers. In terms of overfitting, wrappers have higher learning capacity so they are more likely to overfit than embedded methods, which in turn are more likely to overfit than filter methods [6]. Furthermore, the defining component of an embedded method is a criterion derived from the deep knowledge of a specific classification function, while the defining component of a wrapper method is simply the search procedure. In contrast, filter methods define a heuristic ranking criterion to act as a proxy measure of the classification accuracy and are independent from any particular classifier, thereby the selected features will be more generic, having incorporated less assumptions.

In this work we will develop a multivariate feature ranking methodology [31], by enhancing the filtering procedure shown in [22], where the Pearson correlation coefficient is used to measure feature dependency. Here, we exploit the mutual information as a more general correlation coefficient.

The mutual information algorithms employed in our FS strategy are all well-known. Thus, for sake of brevity, here we only list them, giving references to address the interested reader.

1. *minimum Redundancy Maximum Relevance* (mRMR) [13]
2. *Joint Mutual Information* (JMI) [4]

3. *Double Input Symmetrical Relevance* (DISR)
4. *Mutual Information-based Feature Selection* (MIFS) [3]
5. *Conditional Mutual Information Maximization* (CMIM) [8,30]
6. *Conditional Information Feature Extraction* (CIFE) [1]

The FS process we developed starts with a **Dataset tampering** step, where we add to the dataset three new random variables, with different distributions and independent from the target variable. Then, we use the six MI algorithms to rank the dataset variables in order of relevance. If any of these algorithms gives to one of the random variables an high ranking (with respect to a suitable threshold), it is removed from our algorithm suite. The first and second variables are generated using the *make_gaussian_quantiles* and *make_blobs* Scikit-Learn library [27] functions, respectively, while the third is generated using the numpy *uniform* library function [24]. The distributions of such random variables are very different from the ones of the real MTA-KDD'19 dataset, so we expect them to be easily identified as *useless* for the traffic classification.

Table 1. Random feature rankings.

Algorithm	1st RandFeat	2nd RandFeat	3rd RandFeat
mRMR	29th	35th	36th
MIFS	21st	35th	36th
CIFE	22nd	33rd	34th
JMI	19th	2nd	3rd
CMIM	25th	8th	9th
DISR	6th	1st	2nd

To make our experimentation more robust, we apply a 5-fold cross validation, so we split our extended dataset in five parts, run the mutual information FS algorithms suite on each part and generate the final ranking by averaging the ranks obtained in the five experiments. In Table 1 we show the results relative to the three random variables. The mRMR and MIFS algorithms responded well to the tampering, giving to such random features a low ranking in all the five experiments. Then we have the CIFE algorithm, which in some experiments gives to the random variables an higher ranking. We discard the other algorithms, which performed worse than CIFE.

Then, we perform a **Backward Feature Elimination**. Back to the original dataset, for each algorithm left in our suite after the first step, i.e., mRMR, MIFS and CIFE, we generate the feature ranking on the current dataset features, then we remove the lowest-ranked feature from the dataset and evaluate the accuracy, precision and recall metrics obtained using a linear SVM on the resulting reduced dataset. If at least one of the three metrics goes below the threshold γ we stop the process, otherwise the process is repeated.

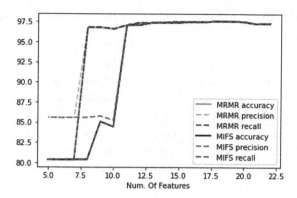

Fig. 1. SVM metrics during backward feature elimination with the mRMR and MIFS rankings.

Note that we considered these metrics as quality/stopping criteria as they give valuable information also on unbalanced datasets as the MTA-KDD'19 [17] that, being constantly fed with up-to-date malware traces, is likely to contain more malware than regular traffic (at the time of our experiments, the dataset was however only slightly unbalanced: 46% vs. 54%). In our experiments, we set $\gamma = 97\%$ which is a reasonable threshold given the number of samples and the specific ML model adopted to calculate the metrics. Figure 1 shows the accuracy, precision and recall metrics calculated during the elimination process from 23 to 5 features, using the mRMR and MIFS rankings. All the performance indicators remain stable above 97% for subsets composed by 23 or more features, even if MIFS appears slightly less accurate than mRMR. From 23 to 11 features the metrics start lowering slowly, and finally they quickly move below 97% when the dataset is reduced to less than 11 features. Therefore, we may conclude that 11 is the minimum number of features that allows us to preserve a reasonable classification accuracy. In the remaining part of this paper, we will refer to this threshold as the *Maximum Dimension Restriction threshold* (MDRt). The CIFE metrics (not shown here) also show this quick decay at the MDRt, but are significantly (about 10%) lower. Therefore, we removed also CIFE from our algorithms suite.

Looking in detail at the top-11 feature rankings given by mRMR and MIFS and reported in Table 2, we can see that they contain the same features. In particular, the top-four features are exactly the same, whereas the remaining seven are the same but in a slightly different order. Therefore, we extract dataset composed by the above *MDRt* features, calling it the *Optimized MTA-KDD'19 dataset*.

2.1 Rank-Relevance Weight and Sensibility Enhancement

To further refine the Optimized MTA-KDD'19 dataset, we assign each feature f a *Rank Relevance-weighted* (RRw) score derived as follows:

Table 2. Ranking of mRMR and MIFS on the 11 most relevant features.

	mRMR		MIFS	
	Feature	Score	Feature	Score
1st	StartFlow	0.3710	StartFlow	0.3516
2nd	NumIPdst	0.3417	NumIPdst	0.3193
3rd	NumCon	0.3392	NumCon	0.3218
4th	NumPorts	0.3101	NumPorts	0.2909
5th	MinLenrx	0.2931	FirstPktLen	0.2179
6th	FirstPktLen	0.2516	MinLen	0.2134
7th	MinLen	0.1327	TCPoverIP	0.0983
8th	UDPoverIP	0.1253	MinLenrx	0.0857
9th	TCPoverIP	0.0972	DNSoverIP	0.0738
10th	DNSoverIP	0.0895	RstFlagDist	0.0615
11th	RstFlagDist	0.0687	UDPoverIP	0.0423

$RRw(f) = \left\| \frac{\sum_{i=1}^{n} s_i(f) \cdot avgF1^k(i)}{n} \right\|$ where $s_i(f)$ is the score given to f by algorithm i (in our case we have $n = 2$ algorithms), whereas the $avgF1_i^k$ is the average F1-score (i.e., the weighted harmonic mean of precision and recall) derived by the $k = 5$ cross folder validation on the 11-features dataset obtained with the i-th algorithm ranking. The final results are normalized in the range $(0,1]$ using a *MinMax* normalization.

We scale the sample values by multiplying each by the corresponding feature RRw score, calling the resulting dataset *RRw-Optimized MTA-KDD'19 dataset*. Such RRw-based scaling acts as a *sensibility enhancing criterion*. Indeed, the most important features are scaled up (having a higher RRw), making them more relevant to the classifier. From the optimizer point of view, the gradient will be higher in the directions given by the upscaled features, allowing it to more quickly reach the minimum classification loss. More formally, in general the sensibility R_i of a model $f(x)$ relative to a feature x_i can be written as $R_i = \left(\frac{\partial f}{\partial x_i} \right)^2$; using the chain rule, we can show that for a function which is locally differentiable the sensibility for the new transformed dataset will be:

$$R_i^w = \left(\frac{\partial f(w_1 x_1, ..., w_i x_i, ... w_N x_N)}{\partial x_i} \right)^2 = \left(w_i \frac{\partial f}{\partial x_i} \right)^2 = w_i^2 R_i$$

Therefore, weighting a feature *enhances the model sensibility to such feature quadratically to its assigned weight.*

3   Dimensional Reduction Through Autoencoder

Our second dataset optimization approach makes use of the ability of AE to encode data into lower-dimensional codes. Indeed, AE are optimized to learn, during their training, an efficient, compressed representation of the input data (obtained by nonlinearly combining such data with different weights) in their internal *bottleneck layer*. Then, if we minimize the reconstruction error (i.e., the error introduced when decompressing data from the bottleneck layer to the output layer), we can extract from the bottleneck layer a new, smaller set of features which preserves the intrinsic information of the original data. To this aim, our AE has 33 input and output neurons (as the total number of features) and, for the bottleneck layer, we choose a size equal to the MDRt derived with the FS methodology (11), which seems to be a reasonable compression threshold.

The current MTA-KDD'19 dataset contains 64554 samples. We split it in an 85% training set (54870 samples) and a 15% *validation set* (9684 samples). Moreover, the training set is further split into a 15% (8231 samples) *testing set* and a 85% *learning set* (46639 samples). The AE training will be performed using the learning and validation sets, whereas the testing set (which is never fed to the network during training) will be used for the final performance tests. The AE is trained for 10 epochs as done in [22] but, from Fig. 2, it is possible to see that the model loss (i.e., the data decompression/reconstruction error) converges nicely and the error becomes acceptable from the fourth epoch.

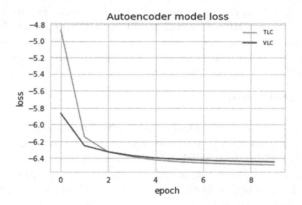

Fig. 2. Autoencoder reconstruction error.

Once the training is completed with satisfying results, use the AE as a "feature compressor". To this aim, we feed it with a 33-feature sample and read its corresponding 11-dimensional latent representation from the bottleneck layer.

Figure 3 shows a scatter plot matrix of both the RRw-Optimized (on the left) and the AE (on the right) MTA-KDD'19 features. This kind of drawing shows the relation between the features and their density distribution (on the diagonals). In the plots, blue dots represent legitimate traffic samples whereas red dots represent malware samples.

The plots clearly show that that the new set of features is actually different from the original one where the separation between classes is particularly clear

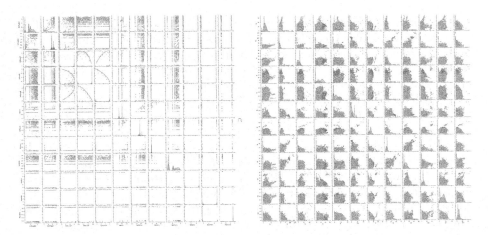

Fig. 3. Scatter plot matrices of the RRw Optimized (left) and AE (right) MTA-KDD'19 datasets. (Color figure online)

especially in three features. The AE mixed the distribution of the samples and changed the range of values, creating only sporadic small clusters and less outliers with respect to the RRw-Optimized MTA-KDD'19 dataset. Moreover, it is worth noting that the spikes relative to the malware traffic have been preserved, whereas legitimate traffic has a Gaussian-like distribution skewed to the left.

4   Experimentation

To measure the accuracy of the Optimized, RRw-Optimized, and AE-generated MTA-KDD'19 datasets we repeated the experiments performed in [22], using its results on the full 33-features MTA-KDD'19 dataset as our baseline. Therefore, we reuse the same MLP described in [22], i.e., a rectangle-shaped fully connected MLP with two hidden layers, both with $2f$ neurons (where f which is the number of features in the dataset), and a single-neuron output layer with sigmoid activation function. Here, obviously, we set $f = 11$ in order to shrink the MLP according to the new dataset features size. The MLP is trained for 10 epochs with batch size equal to 10. The datasets to evaluate are split following the same criteria introduced in the AE experiments, that is, 85% train set, further split in a 15% (8231 samples) test set and a 85% learning set (46639 samples), and a 15% validation set (9684 samples).

To evaluate the model performances we consider its Train Learning Curve (TLC, showing the loss evolution during the training phase of each epoch, i.e., of how well the model is learning) and its Validation Learning Curve (VLC, showing the loss evolution during the validation phase at the end of each epoch, i.e., how well the model is generalizing).

Figure 4(a) shows the learning curves of the MLP trained with the Optimized MTA-KDD'19 dataset. We can see that the model underfits: the loss continues

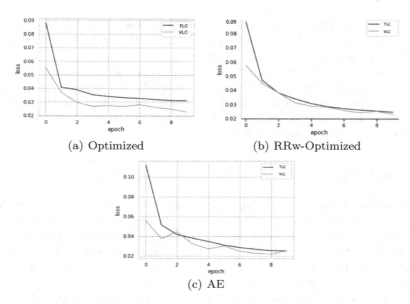

(a) Optimized   (b) RRw-Optimized

(c) AE

Fig. 4. TLC and VLC of the Optimized, RRw-Optimized and AE MTA-KDD'19 datasets.

to decrease at the end of the plot, indicating that the model is capable of further learning and therefore that the training process was halted prematurely. With further experiments (not shown here), we determined that the loss stabilizes after 100 epochs. On the other hand, the learning curves of the MLP trained with the RRw-Optimized MTA-KDD'19 dataset, shown in Fig. 4(b), evolve similarly and the neural network loss stabilizes earlier at an acceptable level. Thus, as expected, re-weighting the dataset helped the classifier.

Finally, Fig. 4(c) shows that, with the AE-Generated dataset, the error reduction is slower than with the RRw-Optimized one, but at the tenth epoch the loss is almost stable.

Table 3. Final metrics on the testing set with the Optimized, RRw-Optimized and AE MTA-KDD'19 datasets.

	Precision	Recall	TPR	TNR	FPR	FNR	FDR	Accuracy
Optimized	99.40	99.95	99.48	99.31	0.069	0.052	0.060	99.40
RRw-Optimized	99.63	99.96	99.61	99.59	0.041	0.039	0.037	99.60
AE	98.78	99.96	99.61	98.60	0.14	0.039	0.12	99.14

Table 3 shows the performance metrics measured after the tenth epoch on the testing set with the three datasets. In particular, the *True Positive Rate* (TPR)/*True Negative Rate* (TNR), and the *False Positive Rate* (FPR)/*False*

Negative Rate (FNR) measure the proportion of positives/negatives that are correctly/wrongly identified, respectively. The *False Discovery Rate* (FDR) indicates the rejection rate of the false positives [7].

We can see that the RRw-Optimization improves *all* the metrics. Furthermore, with the RRw-Optimized dataset, the *generalization gap* (i.e., the distance between training and validation loss) is minimal. The AE-Generated dataset results in a triple false positive rate, but its the overall performance metrics, even if slightly lower, remain acceptable.

5   Conclusions

In the context of machine learning-assisted malware traffic analysis, selecting a small set of meaningful features to train the classifier is a crucial task [21]. In this paper we present two optimization strategies specifically tailored to (malware) traffic datasets, and in particular to the newly presented MTA-KDD'19 dataset [17], which exploit and combine the most promising state-of-the art feature selection and dimensional reduction approaches.

The experiments show that the first, FS-based optimization approach exploiting MI is expensive when calculating the feature relevance and the MDRt, but the corresponding *RRw-optimized* dataset achieves the highest accuracy. On the other hand, the second, AE-based optimization reveals a good compromise between pre-processing time and accuracy of the derived dataset. Therefore, both approaches may be a good choice in specific usage scenarios, possibly integrated in an anti-virus (AV) or in combination with an intrusion detection system (IDS). An offline-trained classifier may profitably exploit the RRw-optimized dataset because it requires more computational time in the pre-processing step but it is more efficient with its 99,60% of accuracy. On the other hand, advanced approaches such as using a MLP as an online-training for a sort of *near real-time* detection, and *dynamic-training* AV and/or IDS, as proposed in the MTA-KDD'19 project [22], requires the model to be *small* and *fast*. Indeed, the dynamic training requires the model to receive, at regular intervals, new input samples to train with and thus update its classification capabilities. Such periodic training must thus be as quick as possible and at the same time preserve the highest possible accuracy. In this case, the AE-Generated dataset would be a better choice with the right compromise between accuracy detection and time training. Both the RRw-Optimized and AE-Generated MTA-KDD'19 datasets will be made publicly available as a fork of GitHub repository [18] of the authors. As a future work, we plan to apply more complex balancing techniques to these datasets in order to further improve the classification accuracy.

References

1. Akadi, A.E., Ouardighi, A.E., Aboutajdine, D.: A powerful feature selection approach based on mutual information (2008)

2. Balagani, K.S., Phoha, V.V.: On the feature selection criterion based on an approximation of multidimensional mutual information. IEEE Trans. Pattern Anal. Mach. Intell. **32**(7), 1342–1343 (2010)
3. Battiti, R.: Using mutual information for selecting features in supervised neural net learning. IEEE Trans. Neural Netw. **5**, 537–550 (1994). https://doi.org/10.1109/72.298224
4. Bennasar, M., Hicks, Y., Setchi, R.: Feature selection using joint mutual information maximisation. Expert Syst. Appl. **42**(22), 8520–8532 (2015). https://doi.org/10.1016/j.eswa.2015.07.007
5. Borges, H.B., Nievola, J.C.: Comparing the dimensionality reduction methods in gene expression databases. Expert Syst. Appl. **39**(12), 10780–10795 (2012)
6. Brown, G., Pocock, A., Zhao, M.J., Luján, M.: Conditional likelihood maximisation: a unifying framework for information theoretic feature selection. J. Mach. Learn. Res. **13**, 27–66 (2012)
7. Colquhoun, D.: An investigation of the false discovery rate and the misinterpretation of p-values. Roy. Soc. Open Sci. **1**(3) (2014). https://doi.org/10.1098/rsos.140216
8. Fleuret, F.: Fast binary feature selection with conditional mutual information. J. Mach. Learn. Res. **5**, 1531–1555 (2004)
9. James, G., Witten, D., Hastie, T., Tibshirani, R.: An Introduction to Statistical Learning. STS, vol. 103. Springer, New York (2013). https://doi.org/10.1007/978-1-4614-7138-7
10. Guyon, I., Gunn, S., Nikravesh, M., Zadeh, L.: Feature extraction: foundations and applications (2006)
11. Hamon, J.: Optimisation combinatoire pour la sélection de variables en régression en grande dimension : Application en génétique animale. (combinatorial optimization for variable selection in high dimensional regression: Application in animal genetic) (2013)
12. Han, K., Li, C., Shi, X.: Autoencoder feature selector. ArXiv abs/1710.08310 (2017)
13. Peng, H., Long, F., Ding, C.: Feature selection based on mutual information criteria of max-dependency, max-relevance, and min-redundancy. IEEE Trans. Pattern Anal. Mach. Intell. **27**(8), 1226–1238 (2005)
14. Hinton, G.E., Zemel, R.S.: Autoencoders, minimum description length and helmholtz free energy. In: Proceedings of the 6th International Conference on Neural Information Processing Systems, pp. 3–10. Morgan Kaufmann Publishers Inc., San Francisco (1993)
15. Huang, Y., Xu, D., Nie, F.: Semi-supervised dimension reduction using trace ratio criterion. IEEE Trans. Neural Netw. Learn. Syst. **23**(3), 519–526 (2012). https://doi.org/10.1109/TNNLS.2011.2178037
16. Hughes, G.: On the mean accuracy of statistical pattern recognizers. IEEE Trans. Inf. Theory **14**, 55–63 (1968). https://doi.org/10.1109/TIT.1968.1054102
17. Letteri, I.: MTA-KDD'19 dataset (2019). https://github.com/IvanLetteri/MTA-KDD-19
18. Letteri, I., Di Cecco, A., Della Penna, G.: Optimized MTA-KDD'19 datasets (2020). https://github.com/IvanLetteri/RRwOptimizedMTAKDD19
19. Letteri, I., Della Penna, G., Caianiello, P.: Feature selection strategies for HTTP botnet traffic detection. In: 2019 IEEE European Symposium on Security and Privacy Workshops, EuroS&P Workshops 2019, Stockholm, Sweden, 17–19 June 2019, pp. 202–210. IEEE (2019). https://doi.org/10.1109/EuroSPW.2019.00029

20. Letteri, I., Della Penna, G., De Gasperis, G.: Botnet detection in software defined networks by deep learning techniques. In: Castiglione, A., Pop, F., Ficco, M., Palmieri, F. (eds.) CSS 2018. LNCS, vol. 11161, pp. 49–62. Springer, Cham (2018). https://doi.org/10.1007/978-3-030-01689-0_4

21. Letteri, I., Della Penna, G., De Gasperis, G.: Security in the internet of things: botnet detection in software-defined networks by deep learning techniques. Int. J. High Perf. Comput. Netw. **15**(3–4), 170–182 (2020). https://doi.org/10.1504/IJHPCN.2019.106095

22. Letteri, I., Della Penna, G., Di Vita, L., Grifa, M.T.: Mta-kdd'19: a dataset for malware traffic detection. In: Loreti, M., Spalazzi, L. (eds.) Proceedings of the Fourth Italian Conference on Cyber Security, Ancona, Italy, 4–7 February 2020, CEUR Workshop Proceedings, vol. 2597, pp. 153–165. CEUR-WS.org (2020). http://ceur-ws.org/Vol-2597/paper-14.pdf

23. Lu, Q., Qiao, X.: Sparse fisher's linear discriminant analysis for partially labeled data. Stat. Anal. Data Min. **11**, 17–31 (2018)

24. Numpy: numpy.random.uniform. https://numpy.org/numpy.random.uniform.html

25. Pasunuri, R., Venkaiah, V.C.: A computationally efficient data-dependent projection for dimensionality reduction. In: Bansal, J.C., Gupta, M.K., Sharma, H., Agarwal, B. (eds.) ICCIS 2019. LNNS, vol. 120, pp. 339–352. Springer, Singapore (2020). https://doi.org/10.1007/978-981-15-3325-9_26

26. Phuong, T.M., Lin, Z., Altman, R.B.: Choosing SNPs using feature selection. In: Proceedings, IEEE Computational Systems Bioinformatics Conference, pp. 301–309 (2005). https://doi.org/10.1109/csb.2005.22

27. Scikit-Learn https://scikit-learn.org

28. Shahana, A.H., Preeja, V.: Survey on feature subset selection for high dimensional data. In: 2016 International Conference on Circuit, Power and Computing Technologies (ICCPCT), pp. 1–4 (2016)

29. Sorzano, C.O.S., Vargas, J., Pascual-Montano, A.D.: A survey of dimensionality reduction techniques. ArXiv abs/1403.2877 (2014)

30. Wang, G., Lochovsky, F.: Feature selection with conditional mutual information maximin in text categorization, pp. 342–349 (2004). https://doi.org/10.1145/1031171.1031241

31. Wang, L., Lei, Y., Zeng, Y., Tong, l., Yan, B.: Principal feature analysis: a multivariate feature selection method for fMRI data. Comput. Math. Methods Med. **2013**, 645921 (2013). https://doi.org/10.1155/2013/645921

32. Wang, S., Ding, Z., Fu, Y.: Feature selection guided auto-encoder. In: Proceedings of the Thirty-First AAAI Conference on Artificial Intelligence, AAAI'17, pp. 2725–2731. AAAI Press (2017)

Topological Properties of Mouse Neuronal Populations in Fluorescence Microscopy Images

Margarita Zaleshina[1]([⊠]) [iD] and Alexander Zaleshin[2] [iD]

[1] Moscow Institute of Physics and Technology, Moscow, Russia
[2] Institute of Higher Nervous Activity and Neurophysiology, Moscow, Russia

Abstract. In this work, we processed sets of images obtained by the light-sheet fluorescence microscopy method. We selected different cell groups and determined areas occupied by ensembles of cell groups in mouse brain tissue. Recognition of mouse neuronal populations was performed on the basis of visual properties of fluorescence-activated cells. Individual elements were selected based on their brightness in grayscale mode. Methods of spatial data processing were applied to identify border areas between ensembles and to calculate topological characteristics of cell groups. By applying cell statistics operations, we obtained the localization of the regions of interest, for subsequent identification of samples with specified topological characteristics. Based on the topological properties of the cell groups, we constructed training samples, and then used these to detect typical sets of ensembles in multi-page TIFF files with optogenetics datasets.

Keywords: Mouse brain · Optogenetics · Pattern recognition · Brain mapping

1 Introduction

The brain can be represented as a spatially distributed multi-scale and multi-level structure in which continuous dynamic processes occur. Neuroimaging techniques are applied to visualize internal characteristics of the brain based on electronic medical records, including the diagnosis of tumors or injuries. Radiologists and neurophysiologists process a series of brain images as two-dimensional slices and develop three-dimensional models based on tomography and microscopy data. With improvements in measuring equipment and increases in the accuracy of data processing, researchers receive data that were unclear when applying of previous methods, and therefore were excluded as noise.

The identification of individual ensembles and the principles of their interaction, and the correlation of activity of ensembles, are considered by many authors. Segmentation of a large set of neurons involves grouping them into neural ensembles, which are usually formed as populations of cells (or cultured neurons) with similar properties.

In this work we applied spatial data processing methods for pattern recognition and comparative analysis of fluorescence microscopy records. Based on the identified topological properties of the images, we performed operations such as contouring and segmentation, and identification of areas of interest. Next, we built a set of training samples and classified the data in optogenetics multi-page TIFF files.

© Springer Nature Switzerland AG 2022
G. Nicosia et al. (Eds.): LOD 2021, LNCS 13163, pp. 69–80, 2022.
https://doi.org/10.1007/978-3-030-95467-3_5

2   Background and Related Works

2.1   Brain Imaging Components

Characteristic sizes of individual elements, distances between elements, and distribution of densities for groups of elements can be used to create typical training samples when processing of brain imaging components.

An analysis of spatially distributed brain structure and activity should include the following main components: choice of coordinate systems and scales; recognition and classification of experimental results; segmentation and calculation of connectivity of brain regions.

Novel developments in biomedical physics support coverage of a wide range of spatio-temporal resolution and sensitivity [1]. A methodology for building computational models based on two-dimensional histological images usually uses visual characteristics to perform image filtering and segmentation, as well as to link neighboring slices [2]. To select neurons of various types, other approaches can also be used, including chemical and genetic ones, which make it possible to present a computational model in a visual form [3]. But many effects have not been considered in detail for cases of intermediate scales and borderline areas.

For individual slices, basic parameters can be calculated for further spatial data processing. At the scale of individual cells, the following spatial characteristics of cells can be used: sizes of individual cells, and distances between cells (including those normalized by cell size). At the scale of cell populations, the following spatial characteristics of areas can be used:

- density of cells inside the area sections, which is equal to the number of cells divided by the areal size of sections;
- coverage coefficient, which is equal to the area occupied by cells divided by total areal size (in sections, or in the total slice);
- density distribution for individual sections within the entire slice.

2.2   Intermediate Scales

It is noticeable that all images of the brain contain data that strongly differ from each other in size, i.e., in fact, such data belong to two different scales. In many studies, data at a different scale is very often cut out as "noise". The proper selection of scale and timeline makes it possible to reduce errors and to use flexible settings for the integration of heterogeneous data.

The scale is determined primarily by the resolution of the measuring device. When resolution is improved, noise typically increases. Scale selection makes it possible to define filters for noise reduction. The ability to distinguish between noise and the true signal can affect the amount of data included in the final analysis. Moreover, noise can be a phenomenon associated with different scales.

Data obtained at intermediate scales affects the identification of single image segments during their processing [4].

Figure 1 shows how final segment contours can be formed in different ways, depending on initial scales:

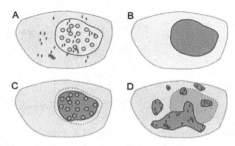

Fig. 1. Selection of segments at different scales (see text for details).

- Figure 3A shows the original set of elements schematically: scale 1 is represented by lilac ovals; scale 2 contains lilac circles; scale 3 contains orange strokes.
- Figure 3B shows a set of segments highlighted for scale 1 in light green.
- Figure 3C shows the set of segments highlighted for scale 2 in light green, with the dotted line showing the outline highlighted for scale 1.
- Figure 3D shows the set of segments selected for scale 3 in light green, while the dotted line and orange color shows the outline area selected for scale 1. It is noticeable that the overlay of such a selection can form its own set of outlines, with new borders.

As illumination typically penetrates the tissue area from one side, obstacles lying in the way of the light-sheet can disturb its quality by scattering and/or absorbing light. This typically leads to dark and bright stripes in the images. If parts of the samples have a significantly higher refractive index (e.g. lipid vesicles in cells), they can also lead to a focusing effect resulting in bright stripes behind these structures. To overcome this artifact, it is possible to change the scale of objects to be recognized.

In addition, the scale can be varied to identify places where dynamically unstable and fuzzy ensembles are formed from cells with similar characteristics.

2.3 Stable Ensembles and Their Surroundings

Extended regions, which are defined as stable ensembles, are composed of elements with similar functional properties. Similar processes, long in time and space, ensure the formation of such dynamically stable large ensembles with a self-sustaining configuration of their parameters. Elements of stable ensembles, as a rule, remain in place for a long time.

However, not all areas that are distinct after segmentation can be attributed to stable ensembles. Usually a region that has the properties of both ensembles appears on the border between two ensembles. This border area is unstable in its temporal and spatial characteristics; its stable elements migrate from place to place over time.

Figure 2 shows two ensembles and the boundary area between them. Elements of the boundary area have different functional properties.

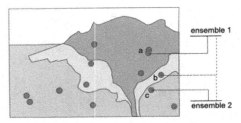

Fig. 2. Ensembles and their surroundings. The area of ensemble 1 (a) is shown in lilac, the intermediate area (b) is shown in beige, and the area of ensemble 2 (c) is shown in pear color. Elements of ensembles are shown in blue circles. (color figure online)

2.4 Formation of Unstable Ensembles Depending on the Porosity of Brain Tissue

A geometric configuration of individual ensembles inside brain tissue depends largely on the porosity of this tissue. In a sparse environment, extended diffuse agglomerations from mixed sets of cells are often found; conversely, within a dense environment, the boundaries of agglomerations become more pronounced, and the ensembles themselves acquire a compact shape.

A nucleus of the brain is an example of stable agglomerations, which are composed of cells that differ in their functional properties. According to functional properties and cytoarchitectonics, groups with hundreds and thousands of cells of a similar type can be distinguished. Thus, individual regions of the reticular formation consist of tens of thousands of cells, and they can be classified by type into groups of tens or hundreds of different types of cells [5].

Fig. 3. Spatial separation of unstable ensembles. Areas of ensembles are shown in lilac, blue and light yellow. (color figure online)

Both within stable ensembles and in border areas between them, unstable ensembles can form. Such unstable ensembles consist of fewer cells, and more often change their configuration over time.

Individual ensembles, consisting of cells of the same type, can be located, not side by side, but separated from each other in space. The scheme of such a division is shown in

Fig. 3. In this figure, the zones to which the connections of the cells of individual ensembles extend are marked with different colors. Ensembles of type 1 cells are represented twice, and do not have a direct connection with each other.

2.5 Brain Imaging Methods and Tools

Many modern studies are devoted to the classification of individual elements in pattern recognition of brain tissue images. The relationships between brain areas have a significant impact on information processing in the brain. The curved surface of the brain directly affects the overall measurement of the activity of ensembles from different segments. The convergence of curved surfaces could modify a possible connection. Spatial analysis makes it possible to understand the relationship between the shape of the brain and brain functions. Brain mapping is the next step towards representing the results of neurobiological observations in the form of multi-layer maps.

The large value of these datasets contributes to the success of machine learning methods [6]. Linking experimental results to spatial and temporal reference points is necessary for comparative analysis of multiple heterogeneous data sets of brain structure and activity, obtained from different sources, with different resolutions, and in different coordinate systems. Evaluation of automatic labeling detection is investigated by Papp et al. [7], who propose a new workflow for spatial analysis of labeling in microscopic sections. This was presented as an automatic method for the segmentation, internal classification, and follow-up of optic pathway gliomas from multi-sequence MRI datasets [8]. Tudorascu et al. evaluated the performance of two popular platforms, Statistical Parametric Mapping and the FMRIB Software Library for brain segmentation [9]. Training models using sub-image stacks composed of channels sampled from larger makes it possible to directly compare a variety of labeling strategies and training approaches on identical cells. This approach revealed that fluorescence-based strategies generally provided higher segmentation accuracy but were less accurate than label-free models when labeling was inconsistent [10].

3 Materials

In this work typical samples of cell groups in the brain were studied. Spatial analysis of the distribution of cells according to fluorescence microscopy datasets was performed based on data packages published in an open repository (https://ebrains.eu). Each dataset comes from a transgenic animal where interneurons of a selected type – parvalbumin (PV), somatostatin (SST), or vasoactive-intestinal peptide (VIP) – express the fluorescent protein. The spatial distribution of different cell types (PV interneurons, SST interneurons, VIP interneurons and pyramidal cells) was calculated across the entire brain.

As raw material, we used fluorescence microscopy datasets obtained from 23 mice *ex vivo*. The data are all from male animals, on post-natal day 56. After perfusion-fixation, the brain was extracted and cleared using CLARITY/TDE [11]. These sets consisted of multi-page TIFF files. Each multi-page TIFF file included separate images - slices with dorsal or ventral projection of the whole volume brain. We used the Allen Mouse Common Coordinate Framework [12] to map data to spatial coordinates. Calculations were performed for the ranges of 10–100 nm. These ranges are typical for cells, ensembles, and agglomerations of cells [13].

Set 1 [14]: We studied whole-brain datasets from transgenic animals with different interneuron populations (PV, SST and VIP positive cells) which are labeled with fluorescent proteins. These datasets were obtained from 11 mice *ex vivo*. The data was represented in 45 multi-page TIFF files. Each multi-page TIFF included 288 slices with dorsal or ventral projections of the mouse brain. The data resolution is 10.4 × 10.4 × 10 microns.

Set 2 [15]: We studied whole-brain datasets obtained using light-sheet microscopy in combination with tissue clearing. These datasets were obtained from 12 mice *ex vivo*. The data was represented in 12 multi-page TIFF files. Each multi-page TIFF included 800 slices with dorsal or ventral projections of the mice brain. The data resolution is 10 × 10 × 10 microns.

4   Methods

Based on data from the light-sheet microscopy datasets, we identified the visual characteristics of elements in multi-page TIFF files, such as the density of surface fill and its distribution over the study area, the boundaries of distinct objects and object groups, and the boundaries between homogeneous areas. Individual elements were selected based on their brightness in grayscale mode. Frequently occurring patterns formed by individual elements were classified and found in other sets of images.

4.1   Step 1. Pre-calculation of Object Parameters

Operations: Selection of the boundaries of the individual elements and areas. Identification of characteristic dimensions of elements, characteristic distances between elements, and characteristic sizes of areas

Input: single pages from multi-page TIFF files.

Output: *i)* selected elements (in the form of point objects) and areas (in the form of polygon objects) on pages (slices), *ii)* calculated typical sizes of elements and preliminary typical sizes of areas.

Individual "cell-like" elements were selected with the Extracts contour lines algorithm (see Sect. 4.5) by their characteristic sizes, distances between cells, and intensities of elements normalized to the background intensity. The interval between contour lines was set as 10 nm. A point was set at the location of the centroid of each identified cell. Long strips of noise were then cleared using a spatial query.

Based on a layer of individual cells, layers with the distribution of cells on the slices were built, and the density of distribution of elements on the slices was calculated. Distinct homogeneous areas were selected using the calculation of the average density of the texture elements of the areas. Between selected areas with different textures, boundaries were constructed in the form of isolines. With the same applied average density parameters, typical "cell-agglomeration" objects were recognized as independent areal elements.

4.2 Step 2. Generalized Processing of Multi-page TIFF Files, Localization of Areas with Intense Activity

Operations: Generalized operations on all pages of multi-page TIFF files. Identification of characteristic distributions of density and intensity for zones.

Input: sets of multi-page TIFF files.

Output: summary layer with generalized zoning for each multi-page TIFF file (such a total output was done for each of the 45 + 12 sets of mice brain images).

The summary sheet generation and calculation of generalized indicators for all multi-page TIFF slices were performed using cell statistics (see Sect. 4.5).

The division of data into separate "intensity zones" was based on the following features:

- intensity of individual "cells" within a slice,
- boundaries of "intensity zones" (by intensity ranges) inside a slice,
- number and density of cells within the border of the "intensity zones".

Additional verification was performed using the Identifies segments tool (see Sect. 4.5). The result of segmentation is to obtain "slot areas", i.e. sets of points and areas, buffers which can be used for subsequent zonal operations.

4.3 Step 3. Calculation of Characteristics for Image Patterns

Operations: Calculation of ranges of values for selection of "samples" in images.

Input: zoned generalized layers.

Output: set of typical samples.

The selection of "samples" was based on the following features:

- shape and size of the "intensity zones",
- distribution of activity within "intensity zones", based on density of luminous elements,
- distribution of activity near the boundaries of "intensity zones",
- calculation of the "intensity zones" offset from slice to slice. As neighbors, sets of 20 slices were considered (this follows from the thickness of the slices and from the typical length).

Figure 4 shows an example of the location of the identified typical sample on adjacent slices of PV-23-ventral multi-page TIFF file (A is a part of PV-23-ventral_page_0198, B is a part of PV-23-ventral_page_0202, ..., D is a part of PV-23-ventral_page_0218). The orange dots show the sample centroids of all slices from page_0198 to page_0218.

4.4 Step 4. Classification with Calculated Training Data Features

Operations: Selection of "samples" according to the specified parameters in the images, and counting of "samples". Overlay of results on the atlas of the mouse brain [12], in order to determine into which zones "samples" most often fall.

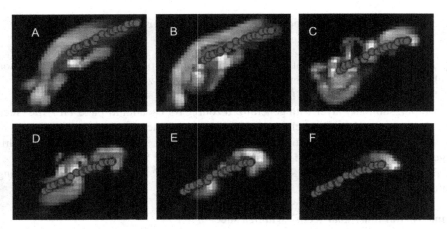

Fig. 4. An example of the location of the identified typical sample on neighboring slices of the multi-page TIFF file. The orange dots show the sample centroids of 21 neighboring slices.

Input: sets of typical samples.

Output: relation of samples to zones and to the coordinates of the mouse brain atlas.

The completed sets of samples, i.e. "ensembles-of-interest", make it possible to perform an analysis of activity, including:

- determining how the localization of a certain "sample" shifts from slice to slice within a single multi-page TIFF file,
- determining the location of a set of cells from a sample to the area of a specific structure of the mouse brain.

4.5   Applications for Spatial Analysis

In this work the data were processed using QGIS geoalgorithms (http://qgis.org); see Table 1 for details.

To create a reference layer, an image calculated as an average over a set of all slices was taken. Cell statistics were performed either on a set of all slices, or on a "test set" consisting of 20 slices. The reference layer parameter specifies an existing raster layer to use as a reference when creating the output raster.

5   Results

As a result of the calculations performed in Step 3, we selected and constructed six sets of typical samples for Set 1 and Set 2 with certain topological properties, on the basis of the density at the boundaries, the density inside the boundaries, and the shape type ("Areal Spot" or "MultiCurve").

The combined indicators typical for parameters of a certain type of area were revealed. The resulting Table 2 shows the ranges of parameters for configuring training samples. One unit means one centroid highlighted in step 1.

Table 1. Spatial data processing applications.

Plugin	Description
Extracts contour lines https://docs.qgis.org/3.16/en/docs/user_manual/processing_algs/gdal/rasterextraction.html#gdalcontour	Generate a vector contour from the input raster by joining points with the same parameters. Extracts contour lines from any GDAL-supported elevation raster
Nearest neighbor analysis https://docs.qgis.org/3.16/en/docs/user_manual/processing_algs/qgis/vectoranalysis.html#qgisnearestneighbouranalysis	Performs nearest neighbor analysis for a point layer. The output tells how data are distributed (clustered, randomly or distributed)
Cell statistics https://docs.qgis.org/3.16/en/docs/user_manual/processing_algs/qgis/rasteranalysis.html#qgiscellstatistics	Computes per-cell statistics based on input raster layers and for each cell writes the resulting statistics to an output raster. At each cell location, the output value is defined as a function of all overlaid cell values of the input rasters.*
Heatmap https://docs.qgis.org/3.16/en/docs/user_manual/processing_algs/qgis/interpolation.html#qgisheatmapkerneldensityestimation	Creates a density (heatmap) raster of an input point vector layer using kernel density estimation The density is calculated based on the number of points in a location, with larger numbers of clustered points resulting in larger values
Identifies segments https://grass.osgeo.org/grass78/manuals/i.segment.html	i.segment - Identifies segments (objects) from imagery data
EnMAP-Box Classification https://enmap-box.readthedocs.io	Classification with training data features

* In this work, the calculation of cell statistics for groups of slices was performed by operations: Majority, Minority, Standard deviation, Variance. The following parameters were used for the calculation: *i)* brightness values in the cell (normalized to the average brightness for all other cells in the slice); *ii)* presence of brightness in the cell above the average threshold (0 - if lower, 1 - if higher).

Table 2. The ranges of parameters for configuring training samples (p < .05)

	Density inside (units per 100 square nanometers)	Boundary density (units per 100 square nanometers)	Linearity (as ratio of length to width)
areal spot A	0.50 ± 0.05	0.60 ± 0.04	0.51 ± 0.05
areal spot B	0.72 ± 0.07	0.59 ± 0.03	0.56 ± 0.05
areal spot C	0.14 ± 0.01	0.44 ± 0.03	0.45 ± 0.05
set of lines D	0.07 ± 0.02	n/a	0.18 ± 0.01
set of lines E	0.10 ± 0.01	n/a	0.14 ± 0.01
set of lines F	0.77 ± 0.05	n/a	0.07 ± 0.01

Using the methods of multi-factor analysis, it was found that the percent ratio differs significantly for different types of parameters considered in Table 2. All factors were checked in pairs against each other in the full record for the absence of dependence (p < .05).

The patterns that are most consistently obtained are represented in Fig. 5:

A – areal spot with high density at the boundaries, B – areal spot with high density inside the boundaries, C – areal spot with low density inside the boundaries, D – fork lines, E – multiset of short lines, and F – single line.

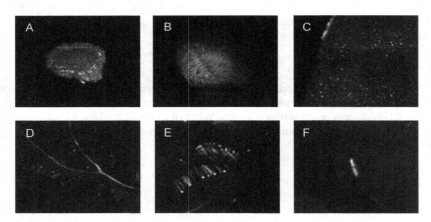

Fig. 5. Typical samples A – F in multi-page TIFF files (see text for details).

The presence of training samples (Fig. 5) was tested for different types of fluorescence microscopy images. The resulting Table 3 shows the result of the analysis of the number of occurrences of typical patterns in multi-page TIFF files (the same sample on a number of adjacent slices is considered as one unit).

Table 3. Availability of samples for different types of fluorescence microscopy, units

	PV	SST	VIP
areal spot A	3	4	3
areal spot B	5	3	5
areal spot C	8	12	7
set of lines D	6	n/a	n/a
set of lines E	4	n/a	n/a
set of lines F	16	18	15

6 Conclusion

In this work we demonstrated the usability of spatial data processing methods for pattern recognition and comparative analysis of fluorescence microscopy records. Geoinformation applications provide sets of options for processing topological properties of images, such as contouring and segmentation, identification of regions of interest, data classification, and training sample construction. We have shown that the application of the procedure for combining a group of cells into typical ensembles enriches the possibilities of brain image processing.

Such applied algorithms and methods can be used for data processing at an "intermediate scale" and in describing the specific characteristics of the distinctive regions formed near the borderlines of stable ensembles. In addition, for unstable ensembles, the effect of porosity of regions near borderlines can be shown.

Methods developed on the basis of the typical characteristics of structures, locations, and typical sizes of brain cells can be used in detection of different types of cells and their ensembles. Training samples can be applied to improve the accuracy of determining the spatial localization of elements in the brain.

References

1. Townsend, D., Cheng, Z., Georg, D., Drexler, W., Moser, E.: Grand challenges in biomedical physics. Front. Phys. **1** (2013)
2. Azevedo, L., Faustino, A.M.R., Tavares, J.M.R.S.: Segmentation and 3D reconstruction of animal tissues in histological images. In: João Manuel, R.S., Tavares, R.M., Jorge, Natal (eds.) Computational and Experimental Biomedical Sciences: Methods and Applications. LNCVB, vol. 21, pp. 193–207. Springer, Cham (2015). https://doi.org/10.1007/978-3-319-15799-3_14
3. Falcucci, R.M., Wertz, R., Green, J.L., Meucci, O., Salvino, J., Fontana, A.C.K.: Novel positive allosteric modulators of glutamate transport have neuroprotective properties in an in vitro excitotoxic model. ACS Chem. Neurosci. **10**, 3437–3453 (2019)
4. Xia, G.-S., Liu, G., Bai, X., Zhang, L.: Texture characterization using shape co-occurrence patterns. IEEE Trans. Image Process. **26**, 5005–5018 (2017)
5. Holmes, C.J., Mainville, L.S., Jones, B.E.: Distribution of cholinergic, GABAergic and serotonergic neurons in the medial medullary reticular formation and their projections studied by cytotoxic lesions in the cat. Neuroscience **62**, 1155–1178 (1994)

6. Menze, B.H., Jakab, A., Bauer, S., Kalpathy-Cramer, J., Farahani, K., Kirby, J., et al.: The multimodal brain tumor image segmentation benchmark (BRATS). IEEE Trans. Med. Imaging. **34**(10), 1993–2024 (2015)

7. Papp, E.A., Leergaard, T.B., Csucs, G., Bjaalie, J.G.: Brain-wide mapping of axonal connections: workflow for automated detection and spatial analysis of labeling in microscopic sections. Front. Neuroinform. **10**(11) (2016)

8. Weizman, L., Ben Sira, L., Joskowicz, L., Constantini, S., Precel, R., Shofty, B., et al.: Automatic segmentation, internal classification, and follow-up of optic pathway gliomas in MRI. Med. Image Anal. **16**(1), 177–188 (2012)

9. Tudorascu, D.L., Karim, H.T., Maronge, J.M., Alhilali, L., Fakhran, S., Aizenstein, H.J., et al.: Reproducibility and bias in healthy brain segmentation: comparison of two popular neuroimaging platforms. Front. Neurosci. **10**, 503 (2016)

10. Cameron, W.D., Bennett, A.M., Bui, C.V., Chang, H.H., Rocheleau, J.V.: Leveraging multimodal microscopy to optimize deep learning models for cell segmentation. APL Bioeng. Am. Inst. Phys. **5**, 016101 (2021)

11. Costantini, I., Ghobril, J.-P., Di Giovanna, A.P., Mascaro, A.L.A., Silvestri, L., Müllenbroich, M.C., et al.: A versatile clearing agent for multi-modal brain imaging. Sci. Rep. **5**, 9808 (2015)

12. Wang, Q., Ding, S.L., Li, Y., Royall, J., Feng, D., Lesnar, P., et al.: The allen mouse brain common coordinate framework: a 3D reference atlas. Cell **181**, 936–953 (2020)

13. Bonsi, P., Ponterio, G., Vanni, V., Tassone, A., Sciamanna, G., Migliarini, S., et al.: RGS 9–2 rescues dopamine D2 receptor levels and signaling in DYT 1 dystonia mouse models. EMBO Mol. Med. **11**(1), e9283 (2019)

14. Silvestri, L., et al.: Whole brain images of selected neuronal types. Human Brain Project Neuroinformatics Platform (2019). https://doi.org/10.25493/68S1-9R1

15. Silvestri, L., Di Giovanna, A.P., Mazzamuto, G.: Whole-brain images of different neuronal markers. Human Brain Project Neuroinformatics Platform (2020). https://doi.org/10.25493/A0XN-XC1

Employing an Adjusted Stability Measure for Multi-criteria Model Fitting on Data Sets with Similar Features

Andrea Bommert$^{(\boxtimes)}$, Jörg Rahnenführer , and Michel Lang

Department of Statistics, TU Dortmund University, 44221 Dortmund, Germany
{bommert,rahnenfuehrer,lang}@statistik.tu-dortmund.de

Abstract. Fitting models with high predictive accuracy that include all relevant but no irrelevant or redundant features is a challenging task on data sets with similar (e.g. highly correlated) features. We propose the approach of tuning the hyperparameters of a predictive model in a multi-criteria fashion with respect to predictive accuracy and feature selection stability. We evaluate this approach based on both simulated and real data sets and we compare it to the standard approach of single-criteria tuning of the hyperparameters as well as to the state-of-the-art technique "stability selection". We conclude that our approach achieves the same or better predictive performance compared to the two established approaches. Considering the stability during tuning does not decrease the predictive accuracy of the resulting models. Our approach succeeds at selecting the relevant features while avoiding irrelevant or redundant features. The single-criteria approach fails at avoiding irrelevant or redundant features and the stability selection approach fails at selecting enough relevant features for achieving acceptable predictive accuracy. For our approach, for data sets with many similar features, the feature selection stability must be evaluated with an adjusted stability measure, that is, a measure that considers similarities between features. For data sets with only few similar features, an unadjusted stability measure suffices and is faster to compute.

Keywords: Feature selection stability · Multi-criteria model fitting · Similar features · Correlated features

1 Introduction

Feature selection and model fitting are some of the most fundamental problems in data analysis, machine learning, and data mining. Especially for high-dimensional data sets, it is often advantageous with respect to predictive performance, run time, and interpretability to disregard the irrelevant and redundant features. This can be achieved by choosing a suitable subset of features that are

---

The R source code for all analyses presented in this paper is publicly available at https://github.com/bommert/model-fitting-similar-features.

© Springer Nature Switzerland AG 2022
G. Nicosia et al. (Eds.): LOD 2021, LNCS 13163, pp. 81–92, 2022.
https://doi.org/10.1007/978-3-030-95467-3_6

relevant for target prediction. The standard approach for fitting predictive models is tuning their hyperparameters only with respect to predictive accuracy. However, multi-criteria tuning approaches have been applied successufully for obtaining models that do not only achieve high predictive accuracy but that are also sparse and have a stable feature selection [3]. The stability of a feature selection algorithm is defined as the robustness of the set of selected features towards different data sets from the same data generating distribution [8]. Stability quantifies how different training data sets affect the sets of selected features.

Many high-dimensional data sets contain similar features. An example are gene expression data sets with genes of the same biological processes often being highly positively correlated. For continuous features, the Pearson correlation is often used to quantify the similarity between features. But other criteria, possibly also measuring non-linear associations, can be considered as well. For categorical features, information theoretic quantities like mutual information can be employed. For data sets with highly similar features, feature selection is very challenging, because it is more difficult to avoid the selection of relevant but redundant features. For such data sets, also the evaluation of feature selection stability is more difficult. Unadjusted stability measures see features with different identifiers as different features. Consider a situation with one set containing a feature X_A and another set not including X_A but instead an almost identical feature X_B. Even though X_A and X_B provide almost the same information, unadjusted measures consider the selection of X_B instead of X_A (or vice versa) as a lack of stability. Adjusted stability measures on the other hand take into account the similarities between the features but require more time for calculation [2].

Performing feature selection on data sets with similar features is not a prominent issue in the literature. Some benchmark studies include scenarios with similar features, see for example [5,6]. Also, feature selection methods for selecting relevant and avoiding redundant features have been defined, for example in [4,13]. These methods are greedy forward search algorithms that measure the redundancy of features by their similarity to the already selected features. Such sequential search methods, however, are infeasible for high-dimensional data sets. In accordance with [4] and [13], we find it desirable to have only one feature per group of relevant and similar features included in the model. This allows an easier interpretation because the model is more sparse. In preliminary studies on data sets with highly similar features, we have observed that established feature selection methods, such as lasso regression or random forest, are not able to select only one feature out of a group of similar features. Instead, they select several features out of groups of relevant and similar features, that is, they select many redundant features. A method that is able to select only one feature per group of relevant and similar features is L_0-regularized regression. For recent work on efficient computation of L_0-regularized regression see for example [7].

In this paper, our goal is finding models with high predictive accuracy that include all relevant information for target prediction but no irrelevant or redundant features. For achieving this for data sets with similar features, we propose considering both the predictive accuracy and the feature selection stability during hyperparameter tuning. This idea has also been described in the first author's dissertation [1]. Configurations with a stable feature selection select almost the same features for all data sets (here: cross-validation splits). If the same features are selected for slightly varying data sets, these features are presumably relevant and not redundant. If the feature selection stability is low, many features are only included in some of the models. In this case, it is likely that these features are either redundant or do not carry much information for target prediction. Therefore, considering the feature selection stability during hyperparameter tuning should lead to models that include neither irrelevant nor redundant features. For data sets with similar features, it is expected that the selected features vary such that features with different identifiers but almost identical information are selected. This is taken into account when employing an adjusted stability measure. We compare our approach to competing approaches based on both simulated data and real data. The aim of the analyses on simulated data is finding out whether the proposed approach allows fitting models that include all features that were used for target generation and no irrelevant or redundant features. On real data, the features that generate the target variable are unknown, but the performance of the models with respect to predictive accuracy and number of selected features can be examined.

The remainder of the paper is organized as follows: In Sect. 2, the proposed approach and competing approaches are explained in detail. Comparative experiments based on simulated and on real data are conducted in Sects. 3 and 4, respectively. Section 5 contains a summary and concluding remarks.

2   Methods

In Subsect. 2.1, three building blocks for the approaches presented in Subsect. 2.2 are described.

2.1   Building Blocks

Stability Measures: Let $V_1, \ldots, V_m$ denote m sets of selected features, $|V_i|$ the cardinality of set V_i, and $E\left[\cdot\right]$ the expected value for a random feature selection. The unadjusted stability measure SMU and the adjusted stability measure SMA (originally called SMA-Count in [2]) are defined as

$$\text{SMU} = \frac{2}{m(m-1)} \sum_{i=1}^{m-1} \sum_{j=i+1}^{m} \frac{|V_i \cap V_j| - E\left[|V_i \cap V_j|\right]}{\sqrt{|V_i| \cdot |V_j|} - E\left[|V_i \cap V_j|\right]},$$

$$\text{SMA} = \frac{2}{m(m-1)} \sum_{i=1}^{m-1} \sum_{j=i+1}^{m} \frac{|V_i \cap V_j| + \text{Adj}(V_i, V_j) - E\left[|V_i \cap V_j| + \text{Adj}(V_i, V_j)\right]}{\sqrt{|V_i| \cdot |V_j|} - E\left[|V_i \cap V_j| + \text{Adj}(V_i, V_j)\right]},$$

$$\text{Adj}(V_i, V_j) = \min\{A(V_i, V_j), A(V_j, V_i)\},$$

$$A(V_i, V_j) = |\{x \in (V_i \setminus V_j) : \exists y \in (V_j \setminus V_i) \text{ with similarity}(x, y) \geq \theta\}|.$$

The two stability measures show a desirable behavior both on artificial and on real feature sets. For details on the computation of the stability measures and a thorough comparative study see [2].

Stability Selection: Stability selection [9,11] is a framework for selecting a stable subset of features. It can be combined with any feature selection algorithm for which the number of features to choose can be set. It repeatedly applies the feature selection algorithm on subsamples of a given data set and finally selects the features that have been selected for sufficiently many subsamples.

ε-Constraint Selection: Having obtained a Pareto front, it often is desirable to choose one point from the front, that provides a good compromise between the objectives, in an automated way. In the following, we present the algorithm "ε-constraint selection" for choosing such a point for the bi-objective maximization problem of finding a configuration with maximal predictive accuracy and maximal feature selection stability. It implements an a posteriori ε-constraint scalarization method [10]. (1) Determine maximal accuracy *acc.max* among all configurations. (2) Remove all configurations with accuracy < *acc.max − acc.const*. (3) Among the remaining configurations, determine the maximal stability *stab.max*. (4) Remove all configurations with stability < *stab.max − stab.const*. (5) Among the remaining configurations, determine the maximal accuracy *acc.end*. (6) Remove all configurations with accuracy < *acc.end*. (7) If more than one configuration is left, then determine the maximal stability *s.end* among the remaining configurations. (8) Remove all configurations with stability < *s.end*. (9) If more than one configuration is left, then randomly choose one of the remaining ones.

2.2 Proposed Approach and Competing Approaches

Our goal is finding models with high predictive accuracy that include all relevant information for target prediction but no irrelevant or redundant features. For classification data sets with similar features, we propose the approach "adj". We compare it to the three competing approaches "unadj", "acc", and "stabs".

"adj": Use L_0-regularized logistic regression as predictive method. L_0-regularized logistic regression has one hyperparameter that balances the goodness of the fit and the sparsity of the model. Tune this hyperparameter with respect to predictive accuracy and to feature selection stability. This way, a set of Pareto optimal configurations is obtained. Choose the best configuration with ε-constraint selection. For assessing the stability of the feature selection during hyperparameter tuning, employ an adjusted stability measure.

"unadj": Proceed as in "adj", but employ an unadjusted stability measure instead of an adjusted measure.

"acc": L_0-regularized logistic regression with hyperparameter tuning only w.r.t. predictive accuracy. Single-criteria hyperparameter tuning w.r.t. predictive accuracy is the standard approach and serves as baseline. Either a single best configuration or a set of configurations with the same predictive accuracy on the training data is obtained. In the latter case, one of these configurations is chosen at random.

"stabs": Perform feature selection with stability selection. Then fit an unregularized logistic regression model including the selected features. For stability selection, employ L_0-regularized logistic regression as feature selection method and tune the hyperparameters of stability selection with respect to predictive accuracy. With this approach, either a single best configuration or a set of configurations with the same predictive accuracy on the training data is obtained. In the latter case, one of these configurations is chosen at random.

3 Experimental Results on Simulated Data

First, the approaches are compared on simulated data. On simulated data, it is known which features have been used for creating the target variable and therefore should be selected and included in a predictive model.

3.1 Experimental Setup

Data Sets: For data set creation, a covariance matrix Σ is defined and then, the data is drawn from the multivariate normal distribution $\mathcal{N}(0, \Sigma)$. The covariance matrices considered in this analysis have a block structure. The features within a block all have Pearson correlation 0.95 to each other and 0.1 to features that are not in this block. All features have unit variance, making the covariance matrices equal to the respective correlation matrices. The features within a block are interpreted as similar to each other. Given the data, five features $X_1, \ldots, X_5$ from different blocks are chosen as explanatory variables. Then, the class variable Y_i is sampled from a Bernoulli distribution with probability $P(Y_i = 1) = \frac{\exp(\eta_i)}{1+\exp(\eta_i)}$ with $\eta_i = x_{1,i} + x_{2,i} + x_{3,i} + x_{4,i} + x_{5,i}$, for $i = 1, \ldots, n$. We consider 12 simulation scenarios defined by all possible combinations of number of observations $n = 100$, number of features $p \in \{200, 2\,000, 10\,000\}$, and block size $\in \{1, 5, 15, 25\}$.

Setup for Hyperparameter Tuning: For L_0-regularized logistic regression the hyperparameter indicating the (maximum) number of features to be included in the model needs to be tuned. Because in the implementation in the R package *L0Learn* this hyperparameter is of type integer, a grid search for the best value is performed. To evaluate the performance of each hyperparameter value, 10-fold cross-validation is conducted. For "acc", the mean classification accuracy of the 10 models on the respective left-out observations for the 10 cross-validation iterations is assessed. For "adj" and "unadj", the mean classification accuracy and the feature selection stability are evaluated. The feature selection stability is quantified based on the 10 sets of features that are included in the 10 models. In the "adj" approach, the adjusted stability measure SMA is employed for stability assessment. SMA interprets features from the same block as exchangeable. In the "unadj" approach, the unadjusted stability measure SMU is used. The values of the stability measures are calculated with the R package *stabm*. Based on the performance values, the best configuration is selected. For ϵ-constraint selection, the cutoff values, *acc.const* = 0.025 and *stab.const* = 0.1 are used. These values have been determined in preliminary studies. For "stabs", the implementation of stability selection from the R package *stabs* is used with 50 complementary subsamples. Two real-valued hyperparameters are tuned with a random search. To determine the quality of hyperparameter values, the classification accuracy of an unregularized logistic regression model with the selected features is evaluated using 10-fold cross-validation.

Evaluation: For each approach, a final model is built based on the entire data set. For "adj", "unadj", and "acc", a L_0-regularized logistic regression model with the best hyperparameter value is fitted. For "stabs", stability selection is conducted with the best hyperparameter values. Then, an unregularized logistic regression model is built with the selected features. Additionally, an unregularized logistic regression model with the five features that were used for generating the target variable is fitted. This provides an upper bound for the predictive accuracy that can be achieved and will be denoted by "truth". Based on the final models, three performance measures are calculated: the classification accuracy on new test data, the number of false positive features, and the number of false negative features. The number of false positive features is the number of irrelevant or redundant features that have been selected for the final model. The number of false negative features is the number of relevant and not redundant features that have not been selected for the final model. For the assessment of the number of false positive and false negative features, features from the same block are interpreted as exchangeable. So, if instead of a feature that was used for generating the target variable, an other feature from the same block is selected, this other feature is accepted as well. For evaluating the test accuracy, a new test data set of the same size is created in the same way as the training data set. Then, the classification accuracy of the final models is assessed. To ensure a fair comparison, all approaches use the same training and test data sets as well as the same cross-validation splits. For each simulation scenario, 50 training and test data sets are created.

3.2   Results

The results of the simulation study are shown in Fig. 1. First, the scenarios with similar features are analyzed. In these scenarios, the predictive performances of the models obtained with "adj", "unadj", and "acc" are very similar. In the scenarios with $p = 200$, the classification accuracies are quite close to the upper bound: the classification accuracy of a model that employs exactly the five features used for target generation. In the scenarios with $p = 2\,000$ and $p = 10\,000$, the predictive performances of the models resulting from the three approaches are noticeably lower than the upper bound. But, the more similar features there are, the closer are the predictive performance values to the upper bound.

Using the adjusted stability measure during tuning leads to much fewer false positive features compared to single-criteria tuning and to tuning using the unadjusted stability measure. So, the models obtained with "adj" contain fewer irrelevant or redundant features than the models resulting from "unadj" and "acc". This advantage comes at the small drawback of a slightly increased number of

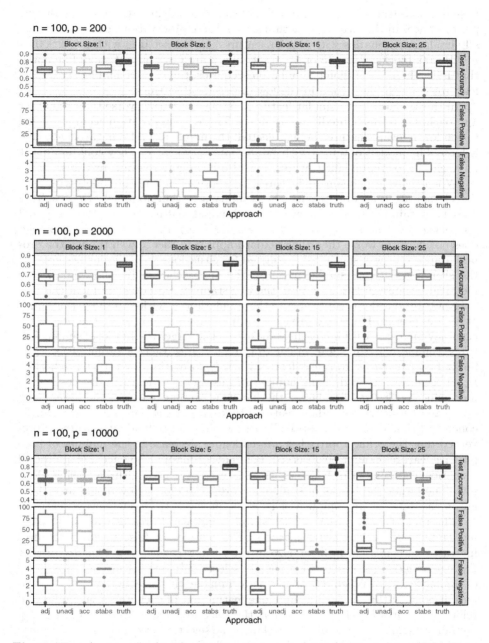

Fig. 1. "Test Accuracy": classification accuracy on independent test data. "False Positive": number of irrelevant or redundant features that have been selected. "False Negative": number of relevant and not redundant features that have not been selected.

false negative features which, however, does not result in a decreased predictive performance. In the situations with $p = 200$, these observations can be made for all simulation scenarios with similar features. In the settings with $p = 2\,000$ or $p = 10\,000$, blocks of size 15 or 25, respectively, are necessary. It should be noted that in the high-dimensional simulation scenarios, the relative number of similar features is much lower than in the low-dimensional settings.

In the scenarios with similar features, "stabs" performs worse than the other approaches in terms of predictive accuracy. The low classification accuracy is due to too few relevant features being selected: the number of false negative features is high. The models obtained with "stabs" are very sparse. They contain almost no irrelevant or redundant features, but also not many relevant features.

When there are no similar features, all approaches lead to models with similar classification accuracy. With the stability selection approach, the resulting models contain the fewest irrelevant or redundant features among the compared approaches. In the scenarios without similar features, the proposed approach does not perform worse than the standard approach "acc", even though the proposed approach was specifically designed for situations with similar features. In the situation with no similar features, the approaches "adj" and "unadj" are identical because in this situation, the two stability measures are identical.

Now, we consider the influence of the simulation scenarios on the performance of each approach. For the approaches "adj", "unadj", and "acc", the predictive accuracy increases with increasing block size. The larger the blocks of similar features, the more features are similar to the 5 features used for target generation. So, it becomes easier to select features with information for target prediction. In all scenarios, for "adj", the number of false positive features decreases with increasing block size. The larger the blocks of similar features, the fewer irrelevant and the more redundant features there are in the data set. So, it can be concluded that with "adj", especially the selection of redundant features is prevented. For the other approaches, an analogous decrease in the number of false positive features cannot be observed. For "adj", "unadj", and "acc", in almost all scenarios, the number of false negative features decreases with increasing block size. The larger the blocks of similar features, the more relevant features there are in the data set, making it easier for the methods to select relevant features.

The prediction accuracy of the "stabs" approach decreases with an increasing number of false negative features. The number of false negative features increases with increasing block size in the scenarios with $p = 200$. Recall that L_0-regularized logistic regression usually selects only one feature out of a group of similar features. When repeatedly performing feature selection on the subsamples, it is likely that each time, only one feature out of each group of similar and relevant features is selected and that the selection frequencies within a group are fairly equal. So, if the blocks are large, the selection frequencies become very small. If the highest of the selection frequencies is below any reasonable value of the inclusion threshold, none of the features is included in the final model. In the scenarios with $p = 2\,000$ and $p = 10\,000$, the number of false negative features is almost constant with respect to the number of similar features. Comparably many relevant and not redundant features are not included in the final models.

4 Experimental Results on Real Data

Now, the approaches are compared based on 12 real data sets from the platform *OpenML* [12] and the R package *datamicroarray*. The data sets come from various domains and differ in dimensions and in feature similarity structures.

4.1 Experimental Setup

In this study, whenever possible, tuning and evaluation are performed in the same way as in Sect. 3. Because it is not possible here to generate independent test data sets, nested cross-validation with 10 inner and 10 outer iterations is used. The inner iterations are used to determine the best configurations and the left-out observations of the outer iterations are used to evaluate the predictive accuracy. So, for each approach and each data set, 10 predictive performance values are obtained. The number of false positive and false negative features cannot be assessed. Instead, the number of features included in the 10 models, whose predictive accuracy is evaluated on the left-out test data, is recorded.

4.2 Results

The top plot in Fig. 2 shows the classification accuracy of the best configurations. The bottom plot displays the number of features that are selected for these configurations. For data sets *sonar, tecator, har, dilbert, lsvt, christensen, arcene*, and *chiaretti*, it is beneficial to perform multi-criteria tuning with respect to both classification accuracy and stability and choosing the best configuration based on ε-constraint selection, compared to single-criteria tuning only with respect to classification accuracy. A comparable or even better predictive performance is achieved with multi-criteria tuning and the fitted models include fewer features. Among these data sets, for *tecator, har, dilbert, lsvt*, and *arcene*, it is necessary to use the adjusted stability measure to achieve this benefit. These data sets contain many similar features. For data sets *sonar, christensen*, and *chiaretti*, which contain only few similar features, the unadjusted stability measure is sufficient. For data sets *kc1-binary, gina_agnostic, gravier*, and *eating*, multi-criteria tuning does not provide a benefit over single-criteria tuning. Still, for these data sets considering the feature selection stability during tuning does not decrease the predictive performance or increase the number of selected features of the resulting models in comparison to single-criteria tuning.

Comparing the results of the proposed approach and "stabs", the proposed approach performs better on the majority of data sets. For data sets *sonar, har, gina_agnostic, lsvt, gravier, eating*, and *arcene*, stability selection leads to a worse predictive accuracy than the other approaches. For data sets *christensen* and *chiaretti*, it fails at excluding irrelevant or redundant features. Only for data

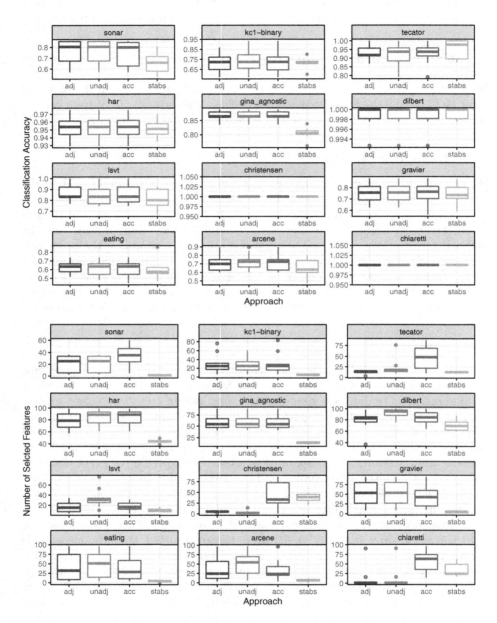

Fig. 2. Top: Classification accuracy of the best configurations on the left-out test data of the outer cross-validation iterations. Bottom: Number of selected features of the best configurations per outer cross-validation iteration.

set *tecator*, models with higher predictive accuracy are obtained with stability selection compared to the other approaches. For *kc1-binary* and *dilbert*, more sparse models with the same predictive quality can be fitted with the stability selection approach. On most data sets, the stability selection approach leads to comparably sparse models, often at the expense of a comparably low predictive accuracy. This has been observed on simulated data as well.

5   Conclusions

Fitting models with high predictive accuracy that include all relevant but no irrelevant or redundant features is particularly challenging for data sets with similar features. We have proposed the approach of tuning the hyperparameters of a predictive model in a multi-criteria fashion with respect to predictive accuracy and feature selection stability. We have used L_0-regularized logistic regression as classification method in our analysis because it performs embedded feature selection and – in contrast to many state-of-the-art feature selection methods – is able to select only one feature out of a group of similar features in a data set. We have evaluated the approach of multi-criteria-tuning its hyperparameter based on simulated and on real data. We have compared it to the standard approach of single-criteria tuning of the hyperparameter as well as to the state-of-the-art technique stability selection.

On simulated data, especially in the scenarios with many similar features, tuning the hyperparameter of L_0-regularized logistic regression with respect to both predictive accuracy and stability is beneficial for avoiding the selection of irrelevant or redundant features compared to single-criteria tuning. To obtain this benefit, the feature selection stability must be assessed with an adjusted stability measure, that is, a stability measure that considers similarities between features. Measuring the stability with an unadjusted measure does not outperform single-criteria tuning in most scenarios. Also, considering the stability during tuning does not decrease the predictive accuracy of the resulting models.

On real data, performing hyperparameter tuning with respect to both predictive accuracy and feature selection stability can be beneficial for fitting models with fewer features without losing predictive accuracy. For data sets with many similar features, an adjusted measure must be used while for data sets with only few similar features, an unadjusted measure is sufficient. For all data sets, almost no predictive accuracy is lost by additionally considering the stability.

Compared to the stability selection approach, models with higher predictive accuracy are fitted with the proposed approach, especially in simulation scenarios with many similar features. On real data sets, the proposed approach outperforms stability selection on many of the data sets. Both on simulated data and on real data, with the stability selection approach, comparably sparse models are fitted. These models, however, often do not include enough relevant features and therefore obtain a comparably low predictive accuracy. Also, the stability selection approach takes much more time for computing. For larger data sets, it is infeasible without a high performance compute cluster.

The proposed approach is not only applicable to classification data but also to regression or survival data by using the respective L_0-regularized methods. Also, other feature selection methods that are able to select only one feature out of a group of similar features can be used instead of L_0-regularized methods.

Acknowledgments. This work was supported by German Research Foundation (DFG), Project RA 870/7-1 and Collaborative Research Center SFB 876, A3. We acknowledge the computing time provided on the Linux HPC cluster at TU Dortmund University (LiDO3), partially funded in the course of the Large-Scale Equipment Initiative by the German Research Foundation (DFG) as Project 271512359.

References

1. Bommert, A.: Integration of Feature Selection Stability in Model Fitting. Ph.D. thesis, TU Dortmund University, Germany (2020)
2. Bommert, A., Rahnenführer, J.: Adjusted measures for feature selection stability for data sets with similar features. In: Nicosia, G., et al. (eds.) LOD 2020. LNCS, vol. 12565, pp. 203–214. Springer, Cham (2020). https://doi.org/10.1007/978-3-030-64583-0_19
3. Bommert, A., Rahnenführer, J., Lang, M.: A multicriteria approach to find predictive and sparse models with stable feature selection for high-dimensional data. Comput. Math. Methods Med. **2017**, 7907163 (2017)
4. Brown, G., Pocock, A., Zhao, M.J., Luján, M.: Conditional likelihood maximisation: a unifying framework for information theoretic feature selection. J. Mach. Learn. Res. **13**, 27–66 (2012)
5. Dash, M., Liu, H.: Feature selection for classification. Intell. Data Anal. **1**, 131–156 (1997)
6. Hall, M.A.: Correlation-based feature selection for machine learning. Ph.D. thesis, University of Waikato, Hamilton, New Zealand (1999)
7. Hazimeh, H., Mazumder, R.: Fast best subset selection: coordinate descent and local combinatorial optimization algorithms. Oper. Res. Art. Adv. **68**, 1526–5463 (2020)
8. Kalousis, A., Prados, J., Hilario, M.: Stability of feature selection algorithms: a study on high-dimensional spaces. Knowl. Inf. Syst. **12**(1), 95–116 (2007)
9. Meinshausen, N., Bühlmann, P.: Stability selection. J. Roy. Stat. Soc. Ser. B (Stat. Methodol.) **72**(4), 417–473 (2010)
10. Miettinen, K.: Introduction to multiobjective optimization: noninteractive approaches. In: Branke, J., Deb, K., Miettinen, K., Słowiński, R. (eds.) Multiobjective Optimization. LNCS, vol. 5252, pp. 1–26. Springer, Heidelberg (2008). https://doi.org/10.1007/978-3-540-88908-3_1
11. Shah, R.D., Samworth, R.J.: Variable selection with error control: another look at stability selection. J. Roy. Stat. Soc. Ser. B (Stat. Methodol.) **75**(1), 55–80 (2013)
12. Vanschoren, J., Van Rijn, J.N., Bischl, B., Torgo, L.: OpenML: networked science in machine learning. ACM SIGKDD Explor. Newsl. **15**(2), 49–60 (2013)
13. Yu, L., Liu, H.: Efficient feature selection via analysis of relevance and redundancy. J. Mach. Learn. Res. **5**, 1205–1224 (2004)

A Study on Relevant Features for Intraday S&P 500 Prediction Using a Hybrid Feature Selection Approach

Mahinda Mailagaha Kumbure[✉] , Christoph Lohrmann ,
and Pasi Luukka

School of Business and Management, LUT University, 53850 Lappeenranta, Finland
{mahinda.mailagaha.kumbure,christoph.lohrmann,pasi.luukka}@lut.fi

Abstract. This paper investigates relevant features for the prediction of intraday S&P 500 returns. In contrast to most previous research, the problem is approached as a four class classification problem to account for the magnitude of the returns and not only the direction of price movements. A novel framework for feature selection using a hybrid approach is developed that combines correlation as a fast filter method, with the wrapper method differential evolution feature selection (DEFS) that deploys distance-based classifiers (k-nearest neighbor, fuzzy k-nearest neighbor, and multi-local power mean fuzzy k-nearest neighbor) as evaluation criterion. The experimental results show that feature selection successfully discarded features for this application to improve the test set accuracies or, at a minimum, lead to similar accuracies than using the entire feature subset. Moreover, all setups in this study ranked technical indicators such as 5-day simple moving average as the most relevant features in this application. In contrast, the features based on other stock indices, commodities, and simple price and volume information were a minority within the top 10 and top 50 features. The prediction accuracies for the positive return class considerably higher than the negative class predictions with over 70% accuracy compared to 30%.

Keywords: Classification · Financial market · Machine learning · K-nearest neighbor · Supervised feature selection

1 Introduction

Forecasting future stock prices or returns is considered an essential subject in finance research, but it has been a challenging task due to the non-linear and non-stationary behavior of the stock market [1]. Having representative and informative input features is crucial for attempting to predict movements of the stock market in the prediction [2]. Many studies in the stock market literature have attempted to determine which features can be used to forecast the market (see e.g., [2–4]). However, most of those studies have been limited to a small number of features. In this study, we focus on examining possibly relevant features from a

© Springer Nature Switzerland AG 2022
G. Nicosia et al. (Eds.): LOD 2021, LNCS 13163, pp. 93–104, 2022.
https://doi.org/10.1007/978-3-030-95467-3_7

large set of input features, including areas such as the macro-economy, technical indicators, commodities, exchange rates and the stocks as well as stock indices. To address the case of dimensionality associated with fitting machine learning models to high-dimensional data, this paper develops an approach based on feature selection to identify a subset of relevant features for the stock market forecasting. Supervised "feature selection" refers to the process of selecting a subset of the relevant features from the set of the existing features [5], which will improve the classification accuracy or, at a minimum, not deteriorate it considerably [6]. Feature selection methods can be categorized into filter methods, which are used for pre-processing, wrapper methods that use a classifier for the selection, and embedded methods, which include feature selection already in the classifier itself [7]. Within this study, a hybrid approach is pursued where initially a filter method is applied to discard linearly associated features before a computationally more expensive wrapper method is provided with this subset to obtain a final feature subset.

Among the various classification methods in machine learning, k-nearest neighbor classifiers are adopted for this investigation due to their simplicity, easy implementation [8], and remarkable achievements in some stock market prediction applications [9,10]. We selected k-nearest neighbor (KNN) [11], fuzzy k-nearest neighbor (FKNN) [12], and also the multi-local power mean fuzzy k-nearest neighbor (MLPM-FKNN) [8] classifier, which was introduced recently [8]. We used this new FKNN method (MLPM-FKNN) since it has shown more robust to outliers and random variables than original ones according to [8]. Distance-based classifiers generally account for all features equally when calculating the distances between points. Thus, we combine the KNN classifiers with a hybrid feature selection approach to address the potentially detrimental impact of irrelevant features on this type of classification.

The remainder of the paper is organized as follows. Section 2 shortly discusses the theoretical concepts applied in this research. A detailed description of the data set used and the empirical process developed are provided in Sect. 3. The empirical results of the feature selection and stock return prediction are presented in Sect. 4 and the concluding remarks on our study are presented in Sect. 5.

2   Preliminaries

2.1   Differential Evolution Feature Selection

Differential evolution (DE) was originally proposed in [13] and is a well-known population-based heuristic optimization method [14]. It has been applied in many disciplines due to its simplicity in implementation, fast convergence, and robustness [15,16]. In the DE method, optimal solutions are searched across four main steps: initialization, mutation, crossover, and evaluation of objective function [17]. To make DE more reliable as a wrapper method for feature selection (FS), the study in [15] has introduced several modifications to its search strategy, referring to the enhanced version as DEFS. This method is applied and implemented in our study, and the complete feature selection process can be found in [15].

2.2   K-Nearest Neighbor Classifier

The idea behind the k-nearest neighbor methods is simple and is based on measuring the distance of a query sample (the sample to be classified) to the labeled samples in the training data. Formally speaking, it starts with computing distances from the query sample (y) to the training set X that is composed of N samples $X = x_1, x_2, ..., x_N$ that belong to C classes. Also each sample $x_i = \{x_i^1, x_i^2, ..., x_i^M\}$, x_i^c is characterized by M feature values and one class label c ($c \in C$). Several distance functions are available to be used for this step, but the one that is often used is the Euclidean distance metric. Next, a set of k nearest neighbors of y together with corresponding class labels is found. In the final step, the class for y is predicted by assigning the most common class among the set of k nearest neighbors.

2.3   Fuzzy K-Nearest Neighbor Classifier

In the FKNN, for the query sample y, a membership degree for each class is assigned, and the class decision is made based on the highest membership degree [12]. In particular, the allocated membership degree of y for each class indicated by the k nearest neighbors is calculated using the following membership function:

$$u_i(y) = \frac{\sum_{j=1}^{k} u_{ij}(1/\|y - x_j\|^{2/(m-1)})}{\sum_{j=1}^{k} (1/\|y - x_j\|^{2/(m-1)})} \tag{1}$$

where, $m \in (1, +\infty)$ is a fuzzy strength parameter and u_{ij} is the membership of the jth sample in the ith class of the training set X. To compute u_{ij}, we used a crisp labeling approach [12] in which full membership is assigned to a known class of each labeled sample and zero membership for all other classes. The fuzzy strength parameter m influences the membership degree by providing relative importance to the distance from y to k nearest neighbors to be weighted. For this parameter a common choice is a value of 2.

2.4   MLPM-FKNN Classifier

As another variant of the KNN, the multi-local power mean fuzzy k-nearest neighbor (MLPM-FKNN) classifier that was introduced in [8] is particularly preferable to the standard KNN and FKNN methods in situations where highly imbalanced classes are present (i.e., there are only a few samples in some classes). In the MLPM-FKNN, the obtained set of k nearest neighbors of y is further grouped into each of the classes they belong to, and then r ($\leq C$) number of multi-local power mean vectors ($M_{t=1}^r$) are computed (r is the number of classes presented in the set of nearest neighbors) using following formula:

$$M_t = \begin{cases} \prod_{i=1}^n x_i^{1/n}, & \text{if } p = 0 \\ (\frac{1}{n}\sum_{i=1}^n x_i^p)^{1/p}, & \text{if } p \neq 0 \end{cases} \tag{2}$$

where, p is a real-valued parameter.

In the next step, the distances of y to multi-local power mean vectors are measured using a suitable distance function (e.g., Euclidean distance). These distances are then used to find the class memberships for y, utilizing Eq. (1), and a decision on the class is made according to the highest membership degree. In this study, however, we slightly updated the learning part of the MLPM-FKNN algorithm before applying it. First, the training data is grouped into classes, and then the sets of k nearest neighbors of y are found from each class. After this, for each k nearest neighbor set in each class, the multi-local power mean vectors are computed. The next steps are the same as in the MLPM-FKNN algorithm. We noticed that the updated version[1] of the MLPM-FKNN outperforms the original one in the classification of the intraday return of the S&P 500—thus, we report the results only for the updated classifier together with the benchmark algorithms in this study.

3   Data and Hybrid Feature Selection

3.1   Data Description

The data set employed in this study contains daily S&P 500 stock index prices and a set of expanding variables that are assumed to be relevant for the prediction of this index. Similar types of variables based on commodity prices, exchange rates, technical indicators, and other stock indices have also been used in previous studies [4,18,19]. Historical time series with 4182 samples were obtained from Yahoo Finance [20] and FRED Economic Data [21] during the period from January 10th, 2007 to October 10th, 2020.

Input Features. We considered and collected 302 features summarized by [22] as frequently used for stock market predictions in previous studies. These selected 302 features were at the top of the list concerning the frequency of usage in stock market forecasting applications according to the study of [22]. The list of features across their categories and the corresponding number of input features used in this study are summarized in Table 1. Technical indicators (TIs) are further categorized into "Basic TIs," which refers to Open, High, Low, and Close prices and Volume of the S&P 500 index and "Other TIs" refers to all other TIs that had to be computed based on the Closing price of the S&P 500,

---

[1] The MATLAB code of the updated MLPM-FKNN algorithm can be found from https://github.com/MahindaMK/Multi-local-Power-means-based-fuzzy-k-nearest-neighbor-algorithm-MLPM-FKNN.

and their variants. From [22], one can find the definitions of commonly known abbreviated forms of the features in Table 1. The different variants of TIs were created by changing the time-period (n in days) and other parameters (n_1, n_2 for EMA, high(H), low(L), middle(M) for Bollinger bands, $slow, fast, sign$ in MACD). For the other time series where it was possible we collected all their basic TIs. Also, % changes of the selected TIs (e.g., Williams R, Stochastic K) and other time series were used.

Table 1. Information of the input features.

Category	Feature list	No. of features
Basic TIs	Open, High, Low, Close, Volume (n)	14
Other TIs	RSI(n), MACD($slow, fast, sign$), EMA(n), Bias (n), SMA(n), Disparity(n), OBV, Return(n), Williams %R(n), CCI(n), Momentum(n), MFI(n), Stochastic %K(n), Stochastic %D(n), TMA(n), Bollinger bands ($H/M/$ L), Chaikin Volatility, Price oscillator (n_1, n_2), Typical price, TRIX	140
Macro-economy	Treasury Bills, Term Spread, AAA Corporate Bond, Treasury Constant Maturity Rate, BAA Corporate Bond, Treasury Yields, Default Spread	27
Commodities	Crude Oil, Gold, Silver	18
Exchange rates	USD/NTD, USD/JPY, USD/GBP, USD/CAD, USD/CNY	25
Other stocks/stock indices	Hang Seng, SSE, CAC40, DJIA, NASDAQ Microsoft, Amazon, JPM, General Electric, JNJ, Apple Inc., Wells Fargo, Exxon Mobil	78

In the data, other technical indicators ("Other TIs") were generated using closing prices of the S&P 500 stock index—for some indicators, high, low, and open prices were also used. Since some indicators require initial data before their value can be calculated, we started our data after such a period (e.g., 5-day moving average MA(5)). Next, the missing values that occurred when the time series data of the S&P 500 was concatenated with other time series were replaced using linear interpolation. All features in the data were scaled into the interval [0, 1]. Technical indicators are commonly used to infer trading signals for when a stock or market is overbought or oversold, and corresponding selling and buying decision may be profitable. Therefore, the continuous data of technical indicators was converted into discrete data (trading signals) to represent actual trading signals rather than the numeric values for the technical indicators they can be inferred from. For the relative strength index (RSI) and commodity channel index (CCI), we followed the techniques presented in [19] to convert them into trading signals. To create the signals from other technical indicators, a quartile-based approach was applied. That is, if the TI > $Q3$ then set to 1, if $Q3 >=$ TI > $Q2$ then set to +0.33, if $Q2 >=$ TI > $Q1$ then set to −0.33, and if the

TI $=< Q1$ then set to -1. Thus, four discrete equally-spaced categories were created, which corresponds to the number of classes.

Output Variable. As in [4], in this paper, the intraday (open-to-close) return of the S&P 500 index was selected as target and set up as a multi-class variable within four classes ("1", "2", "3" and "4") according to daily magnitude of the return. In this variable, class label "4" represents the intraday returns that are smaller than -0.5% (i.e., strong negative), "3" between -0.5% and 0.0% (i.e., slightly negative), "2" between 0.0% and 0.5% (i.e., slightly positive) and "1" larger than 0.5% (i.e., strong positive). The cut-off using $+/-0.5\%$ was selected since it results in quite balanced classes (class 1: 27.42%, class 2: 28.08%, class 3: 23.92%, and class 4: 20.58%) and was also deployed in [4].

3.2 Hybrid Feature Selection

We first split the data set into two data sets, one for training (from January 10th, 2007 to January 18th, 2018) and the other for testing (from January 19th, 2018 to October 10th, 2020). The training sample was further repeatedly divided into 80% for the training and 20% for the validation sets, and these subsets were used in the feature selection and parameter optimization processes. The test sample was kept to evaluate the predictive performance of the trained classifiers with the selected features and optimized parameters in the last phase.

Feature Removal by Pearson Correlation Coefficients. Wrapper methods, especially those including optimization such as the DEFS, require comparably high computational time since they use an iterative process including a classifier for feature selection. Thus, the methodology in this paper includes Pearson correlation, which is used as a filter method before DEFS. The aim is to efficiently remove linearly dependent features initially in order to reduce the number of features and the computational complexity for the DEFS wrapper method.

The Pearson correlation coefficient is a simple filter method that is used in the context of feature selection to measure the linear dependence between a variable and the target (class label) [7], where higher (absolute) correlation is a sign of the relevance of a variable for the target. In contrast to that, a high (absolute) correlation between different explanatory variables may indicate that keeping both variables instead of a single one may not add information, thus potentially being redundant. Here, we followed the second approach and calculated the Pearson correlation coefficient between pairs of features f_i, f_j for $i, j \in \{1, .., 302\}$ to measure how much information they potentially have in common. A threshold of 0.95 for the absolute correlation between two features f_i and f_j was set so that for two variables that have a very high absolute correlation, one of these two variables can be removed. If $corr(f_i, y) > corr(f_j, y)$ then remove f_j, else remove f_i, where y is the class variable.

Parameter Settings and Exploring Relevant Features with DEFS. In this step, the DEFS with each selected classifier was deployed to find the most relevant features for forecasting the intraday return of the S&P 500 index. As parameters in the DEFS, we set both population size and the number of iterations to 50 and the crossover rate to 0.5. Also, we provided $5, 10, 15, ..., 50$ as the desired number of features to be selected (i.e., number of the features in the resulting feature subset). Other parameters involved in the DEFS algorithm were specified according to the previous study in [15]. For the nearest neighbor classification methods, the number of nearest neighbors k was kept constant at 20, the fuzzy strength parameter m was set to 2, and the power mean parameter p was 1.5, as in the previous studies [8,12,23]. We received the selected feature subsets (i.e., feature indices) and classification error rates across the different iterations as outputs from the DE function. This process was cross-validated using the holdout method where the training and the validation sets were generated 10 times randomly.

4 Experiment Results

4.1 Results in the Correlation Analysis

The evidence from the correlation coefficients based analysis suggests eliminating some features due to linear dependence effects. Some pairs of features, such as the low price of the Hang Seng and of the SSE composite index were even perfectly correlated. Overall, in this analysis, the dimensionality of the data set was reduced by discarding potentially redundant features, keeping 207 out of the 302 original features for the subsequent DEFS and classifier training.

4.2 Results in the DEFS

The wrapper DEFS that is the second component in the hybrid feature selection (filter+wrapper) was applied together with each nearest neighbor classifier. Figure 1 illustrates the frequency of the top 50 features according to the DEFS algorithm in combination with each of the classifiers during the holdout cross-validation.

At first glance, it is apparent that for each of the classifiers, the majority of selected features are technical indicators in the list of the top 50 features. The most important features across all these classifiers appear to be the 5-day moving average (SMA (5)) and the Silver low price both being consistently within the top 10 higher ranked features. Other features that were at least contained twice in the top 10 include technical indicators representing model classification of the last 5–15 days such as the SMA (15), Williams R(10), Disparity(10), RSI(6), Chaikin Volatility(10). Finally, it is noteworthy that no macro-economic or exchange rate variations are contained in any of the top 50 features.

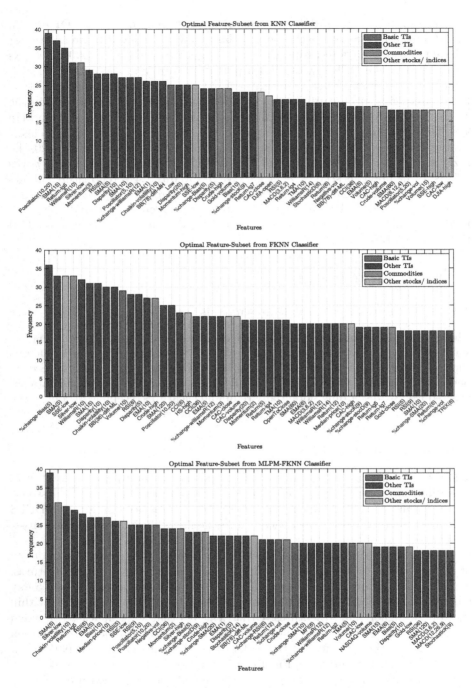

Fig. 1. The frequency of the 50 best features (descending order) based on the DE feature selection with each classifier.

4.3   Prediction Performance

In the training and validation step, the parameters of the classification models were optimized by using 30 runs of cross-validation with the holdout method. The best value for k was searched from the range $\{1, 2, ..., 30\}$ during the training & validation. The value for the parameter p in power means was chosen and optimized from the set $\{0, 0.5, 1, ..., 5\}$ for the MLPM-FKNN model. Accordingly, the optimal parameter values selected were those corresponding to the maximum validation accuracy. Figure 2 illustrates the mean classification errors (%) of each model in the DEFS for each feature subset size.

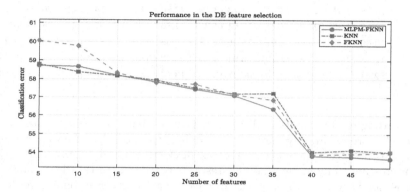

Fig. 2. Mean classification error (%) across ten runs of cross-validation for each feature subset size.

According to the results in Fig. 2, we can see that when the size of the optimal feature subsets with DEFS increases, the MLPM-FKNN model achieves better performance than the KNN and FKNN classifiers. This can be expected because the samples with more features make local power mean vectors more robust (and representative) in the learning. Looking at the classification performance, the mean errors appear quite high compared to other classification tasks with the real accuracies for each model only being in the mid-thirty accuracies. However, it should be kept in mind that this task is a four class problem and that low classification accuracies do not necessarily mean that a trading strategy based on these results would not be able to generate excess returns [4, 24]. When aggregating the four-class prediction (1: strong positive, 2: slightly positive, 3: slightly negative, and 4: strong negative) to a binary class level by counting class 1 and class 2 prediction as "positive" and class 3 and class 4 prediction as "negative", the results become clear and can more easily be compared with other binary studies.

Table 2 presents the aggregated test accuracies on the positive and negative classes by classifier on subset size.

Table 2. Prediction performance (%) on positive and negative classes with test sample for all classifiers and for each feature subset.

Subset	MLPM-KNN		KNN		FKNN	
	Positive	Negative	Positive	Negative	Positive	Negative
5	70.55 (4.99)	30.14 (4.4)	79.18 (3.89)	21.71 (5.3)	67.87 (2.78)	35.49 (3.02)
10	68.71 (4.9)	32.42 (3.76)	77.53 (3.96)	21.45 (4.56)	75.97 (3.57)	29.48 (3.55)
15	73.35 (4.41)	28.08 (4.04)	80.23 (3.73)	24.56 (3.4)	76.64 (4.04)	25.77 (4.12)
20	73.78 (3.24)	26.48 (3.02)	73.78 (2.96)	27.77 (3.12)	77.59 (4.01)	26.38 (4.49)
25	78.00 (3.85)	20.16 (3.3)	78.22 (3.15)	25.98 (3.45)	74.85 (4.2)	28.48 (4.2)
30	75.31 (3.86)	21.05 (4.34)	73.71 (3.45)	27.77 (3.55)	71.95 (3.37)	30.73 (3.47)
35	74.38 (3.31)	23.12 (3.51)	74.73 (3.19)	27.80 (3.82)	77.14 (3.2)	26.90 (4.05)
40	73.00 (4.35)	25.02 (4.3)	77.01 (4.35)	24.86 (4.43)	75.97 (3.49)	28.66 (3.64)
45	70.60 (3.68)	26.60 (4.07)	77.26 (4.48)	24.56 (4.75)	73.83 (4.27)	28.15 (4.2)
50	72.08 (3.82)	24.81 (3.72)	76.91 (4.25)	26.43 (5.25)	73.06 (3.88)	27.02 (3.68)
302	82.24 (3.92)	16.64 (4.15)	90.18 (3.55)	13.17 (4.28)	88.38 (4.08)	14.63 (4.16)

According to the results in Table 2, it is clear that the positive class can be predicted more accurately (around 70%) than the negative class (around 20–30%). This pattern appears consisted for all classifiers and feature subset rises. It is interesting to highlight that this result is not based on the class imbalance, which is not very high (57% positive, 43% negative observations). This result suggests that negative predictions are more challenging and, thus, less accurate for each of the KNN classifiers. This finding that the prediction of "negative" direction of the S&P 500 with less accuracy than "positive" upward movement appears consistent with the prediction results presented by the study of [4], which investigated the intraday S&P 500 return during the period (Oct 2010 to March 2018) using a different classifier (Random Forest).

Furthermore, we can see from Table 2, the last row that shows the test set accuracies with all features are the highest on the positive return but the lowest on the negative return for all classifiers. This indicates that the predictors with all features preferred more to predict positive return but not much on the negative return. This verifies the effectiveness of using relevant features with DEFS since it improves, or at a minimum, does not deteriorate the classification accuracy on the negative return of the intraday return of the S&P 500 even when a substantial amount of the input features is removed.

5   Conclusion

This paper examined potentially relevant features for the prediction of the intraday S&P 500 return in a four-class classification problem. A hybrid feature selection approach consisting of Pearson correlation (filter) and a DEFS algorithm (wrapper) was deployed to select only relevant features for the classification. Three distance-based classifiers (KNN, FKNN, and MLPM-KNN) were used as an evaluation criterion for the DEFS, and all three classifiers almost exclusively ranked technical indicators among the most relevant features for the intraday return S&P 500 predictions. The 5-day simple moving average (SMA (5)) and the Silver low price appear particularly relevant in this study given that all three classifiers include them in their top 10 features out of the more than 207 features included in the DE feature selection. Moreover, macro-economic features are weakly correlated to many technical indicators - however, those features do not appear in the top 50 feature subsets for all classifiers. This remains an open question in our study and is required for further investigations. The aggregated results in this study highlighted that prediction for "negative" movements was much less accurate than for "positive" movements of the S&P 500. This may suggest that the features in this study are related for the prediction of "positive" but other additional features, may be relevant for the predicting "negative" development in the S&P 500. In the future, this finding can be further investigated for the S&P 500 index with different time horizons and classifiers and on different global stock markets.

Acknowledgment. This research was supported by the Finnish Foundation for Share Promotion (Pörssisäätiö).

References

1. Kazem, A., Sharifia, E., Hussainb, F.K., Saberic, M., Hussain, O.K.: Support vector regression with chaos-based firefly algorithm for stock market price forecasting. Appl. Soft Comput. **13**, 947–958 (2013). https://doi.org/10.1016/j.asoc.2012.09.024
2. Zhang, X., Hu, Y., Xie, K., Wang, S., Ngai, E.W.T., Liu, M.: A causal feature selection algorithm for stock prediction modeling. Neurocomputing **142**, 48–59 (2014). https://doi.org/10.1016/j.neucom.2014.01.057
3. Tsai, C.F., Hsiao, Y.C.: Combining multiple feature selection methods for stock prediction: union, intersection, and multi-intersection approaches. Decis. Support Syst. **50**(1), 258–269 (2010). https://doi.org/10.1016/j.dss.2010.08.028
4. Lohrmann, C., Luukka, P.: Classification of intraday S&P500 returns with a random forest. Int. J. Forecast. **35**, 390–407 (2019). https://doi.org/10.1016/j.ijforecast.2018.08.004
5. Kittler, J., Mardia, K.V.: Statistical pattern recognition in image analysis. J. Appl. Stat. **21**, 61–75 (1994)
6. Liang, J., Yang, S., Winstanley, A.: Invariant optimal feature selection: a distance discriminant and feature ranking based solution. Pattern Recogn. **41**, 1429–1439 (2008). https://doi.org/10.1016/j.patcog.2007.10.018
7. Chandrashekar, G., Sahin, F.: A survey on feature selection methods. Comput. Electr. Eng. **40**, 16–28 (2014)
8. Kumbure, M.M., Luukka, P., Collan, M.: An enhancement of fuzzy K-nearest neighbor classifier using multi-local power means. In: Proceeding of the 11th Conference of the European Society for Fuzzy Logic and Technology (EUSFLAT), pp. 83–90, Atlantis Press (2019)

9. Zhang, N., Lin, A., Shang, P.: Multidimensional k-nearest neighbor model based on EEMD for financial time series forecasting. IPhysica A Stat. Mech. Appl. **477**, 161–173 (2017)
10. Cao, H., Lin, T., Li, Y., Zhang, H.: Stock price pattern prediction based on complex network and machine learning. Complexity **2019** (2019)
11. Cover, T., Hart, P.: Nearest neighbor pattern classification. IEEE Trans. Inf. Theor. **13**(1), 21–27 (1967). https://doi.org/10.1109/TIT.1967.1053964
12. Keller, J.M., Gray, M.R., Givens, J.A.: A fuzzy k-nearest neighbor algorithm. IEEE Trans. Syst. Man Cybern. **15**(4), 580–585 (1985). https://doi.org/10.1109/TSMC.1985.6313426
13. Price, K., Storn, R.M., Lampinen, J.A.: Differential Evolution - a Practical Approach to Global Optimization. Springer, Heidelberg (2005)
14. Yang, F., Chen, Z., Li, J., Tang, L.: A novel hybrid stock selection method with stock prediction. Appl. Soft Comput. J. **142**, 820–831 (2019)
15. Khushaba, R.N., Al-Ani, A., Al-Jumaily, A.: Feature subset selection using differential evolution and a statistical repair mechanism. Expert Syst. Appl. **38**, 11515–11526 (2011). https://doi.org/10.1016/j.eswa.2011.03.028
16. Bisoi, R., Dash, P.K., Parida, A.K.: Hybrid variational mode decomposition and evolutionary robust kernel extreme learning machine for stock price and movement prediction on daily basis. Appl. Soft Comput. **74**, 652–676 (2019)
17. Yang, F., Chen, Z., Li, J., Tang, L.: A novel hybrid stock selection method with stock prediction. Appl. Soft Comput. **80**, 820–831 (2019)
18. Nabipour, M., Nayyeri, P., Jabani, H., Shahab, S., Mosavi, A.: Predicting stock market trends using machine learning and deep learning algorithms via continuous and binary data; a comparative analysis. IEEE Access **8**, 150199–150212 (2020). https://doi.org/10.1109/ACCESS.2020.3015966
19. Patel, J., Shah, S., Thakkar, P., Kotecha, K.: Predicting stock market index using fusion of machine learning techniques. Expert Syst. Appl. **42**(4), 2162–2172 (2015). https://doi.org/10.1016/j.eswa.2014.10.031
20. Yahoo Finance. https://finance.yahoo.com/. Accessed 22 Oct 2020
21. FRED Economic Data. https://fred.stlouisfed.org. Accessed 25 Oct 2020
22. Kumbure, M. M., Lohrmann, C., Luukka, P., Porras, J.: Machine learning techniques and data for stock market forecasting: a literature review. Expert Syst. Appl. (2021, Submitted)
23. Kumbure, M.M., Luukka, P., Collan, M.: A new fuzzy k-nearest neighbor classifier based on the Bonferroni mean. Pattern Recogn. Lett. **140**, 172–178 (2020). https://doi.org/10.1016/j.patrec.2020.10.005
24. Teixeira, L.A., De Oliveira, A.L.I.: A method for automatic stock trading combining technical analysis and nearest neighbor classification. Expert Syst. Appl. **37**(10), 6885–6890 (2010). https://doi.org/10.1016/j.eswa.2010.03.033

ViT - Inception - GAN for Image Colourisation

Tejas Bana[1]([envelope]) [iD], Jatan Loya[2][iD], and Siddhant Kulkarni[3][iD]

[1] D.Y Patil College of Engineering, Pune, India
[2] Vishwakarma Institute of Technology, Pune, India
[3] BITS Pilani, Hyderabad, India

Abstract. Studies involving image colourisation have been garnering researchers' keen attention over time, assisted by significant advances in various Machine Learning techniques and compute power availability. Traditionally, image colourisation has been an intricate task that gave a substantial degree of freedom during the assignment of chromatic information. In our proposed method, we attempt to colourise images using Vision Transformer - Inception - Generative Adversarial Network (ViT-I-GAN), which has an Inception-v3 fusion embedding in the generator. Vision Transformer (ViT) is used as the discriminator for a stable and robust network. The model was trained on the Unsplash and the COCO dataset for demonstrating the improvement made by the Inception-v3 embedding. We have compared the results between ViT-GANs with and without Inception-v3 embedding.

Keywords: Image colourising · GAN · Vision Transformer · Deep learning · Inception-v3

1 Introduction

Colourisation is a technique that adds chromatic information to grayscale images. Chromaticity is the quality of colour irrespective of its luminance. Grayscale images often referred to as "black and white" images are commonly present in older multimedia. Accurately adding chromatic data to grayscale images has become a popular focus for research.

With the recent advances in machine learning, researchers have developed multiple sophisticated networks most prominent of them known as Convolutional Neural Networks (CNNs) [1], which have surpassed traditional machine learning techniques that involved feature engineering. CNN's have a large scope of application some of them include image recognition, autonomous driving, video analysis, drug discovery.

Generative Adversarial Network (GAN) [2] by Goodfellow et.al is a framework where the generator is put in competition against the discriminator, this enables generation of new data with the same statistics and distribution as the

© Springer Nature Switzerland AG 2022
G. Nicosia et al. (Eds.): LOD 2021, LNCS 13163, pp. 105–118, 2022.
https://doi.org/10.1007/978-3-030-95467-3_8

training data. Applications of GANs can range from generating art to recon-structing 3D models of objects from images [3]. GAN, more precisely, Style-GAN [4], which Nvidia developed, has been used to create indistinguishable fake human faces. Some researchers have also used StyleGAN for other applications like colouring images.

Since then, many colourisation methods have been proposed, including but not limited to new model architectures [5–10]. Though making seemingly promis-ing progress in colourising, these methods still have some drawbacks including requirement of extensive computational resources and a large dataset for train-ing. Hence, we aim to improve the model performance on a smaller dataset while requiring less computational resources.

Our main contributions in this research work are:

1. Proposed two novel GAN architectures Vision Transformer - Inception - Gen-erative Adversarial Network (ViT-I-GAN) and Vision Transformer - Genera-tive Adversarial Network (ViT-GAN)
2. Proposed Vision Transformers as a discriminator for the training of GANs
3. Demonstrating improvement in GAN performance where dataset is limited by fusing Inception-v3 [12] embedding into the generator.

2   Background

Researchers have undertaken extensive work to improve on the task of colourising grayscale images. Earlier, this involved laborious work since images had to be colourised manually using tools like Adobe Photoshop, which would take up to months to colourise a single image. Colourising a face could take up to 20 layers of green, blue and pink to bring out a satisfactory result. This time has been cut down dramatically with modern machine learning models, which can outperform manual colourising.

The idea of Deep Convolutional Generative Adversarial Networks (DCGANs) [13], StyleGAN [4], Pix2Pix GAN [8] is to have a generator that is trained for an image to image translation to generate desired images from input data and a discriminator which is trained to discriminate between original and generated images. The generator and discriminator compete with each other, eventually improving the generator's capability for generating authentic looking images. The input to GAN can be changed in multiple ways for various tasks including image colourisation. Training GANs is a volatile task that is sensitive to model architecture, specific implementation and hyper-parameter tuning.

Traditionally in GANs, noise is sent as the input to the generator of the network, and then it generates required data from the given noise. Whereas, for image to image translation, the noise is replaced by the features extracted from an image through a CNN encoder which is sent as the input to the decoder, which consequently gives the desired output.

Vision Transformer (ViT) [14], proposed by Dosovitskiy et al., is a self-attention based architecture. Transformers were the top choice for natural lan-guage processing (NLP) as they have enabled a high degree of efficiency, scalabil-ity and speed, which allows us to train models over a huge number of parameters.

Conventionally, CNNs have been the go-to for most computer vision tasks. Inspired by the immense success of Transformers in NLP, researchers have implemented transformers for image classification. For doing this, images are split into patches, and a sequence of linear embeddings is sent as an input to the Transformer. They've also concluded that large scale training outperforms inductive bias, which CNNs are known to have. ViT is on-par or beats state-of-the-art CNNs while using fewer parameters and compute resources.

3   Proposed Method

Conventionally, images are represented in Red-Green-Blue (RGB), where there is one layer for each colour. Images are represented in a grid of pixels, where the pixel value ranges from 0 (black) - 255 (white). We have considered the CIE L*a*b* colour space, where L stands for Lightness, and a* & b* for the colour spectra green-red and blue-yellow. The RGB input image of size $H \times W$ firstly converted to L*a*b* colour space, and the L (Luminance) layer is the input for the model; this gives the semantic information of the image to the model, including but not limited to the objects and their textures. The task is to predict the other two colour channels, rather than the 3 channels in the RGB color space, which significantly reduces the prediction space, leading to better colorization. By coalescing luminance and predicted colour channels, the model warrants a high level of detail in the final colourised images. For colourising images, the neural network creates a correlation between grayscale input images and coloured output images. Our goal is to determine this link as accurately as possible and observe the effect of additional features produced by InceptionNet-v3.

3.1   Preprocessing

In the CIE L*a*b* colour space, the value of L* generally ranges from 0 to 100, and a* & b* range from –127 to 128. As a result of using vision transformers in our model, the input image's size to the classifier must be fixed. We have resized input images to 256 × 256 for the encoder and discriminator. The input size for our network is not restricted to the input size of the pre-trained Inception-v3. Therefore, we have triplicated the luminance channel L to create a three channel grayscale image and have resized it to 299 × 299 for Inception-v3. We have normalised the pixel values for the generator between [–1, 1] and input values for the Inception-v3 model within the interval of [0, 1].

3.2   Architecture

The architecture of proposed model is inspired by U-Net architecture [24] and the usage of fusion layer which was proposed by S. Iizuka et al. [26] in the autoencoder network. Given the luminance information of an image, the model gives its best estimation of alpha and beta components and merges them to give the final colourised output image. We have fetched an embedding of the grayscale image from the last layer of Inception-v3. The architecture of the generator consists of Encoder, Feature Extractor, Fusion, Decoder. The Luminance channel of the image is given to the Encoder and Feature Extractor; their outputs are merged in Fusion Layer; this information is passed to the Decoder, which outputs a* and b* colour channels of the CIE L*a*b* colour scheme. Then, a* and b* colour channels are merged with the image's Luminance channel to produce a colourised image (Fig. 1, 2 and 3).

3.3   Encoder

The encoder processes H x W grayscale images and gives $H/32 \times W/32 \times 512$ feature representation as the output. The encoder consists of 10 convolutional layers with 5×5 kernel, and padding of 2px is applied on each side to maintain the layer's input size. Furthermore, for downsampling, we have used Average Pooling instead of MaxPooling as it smooths the output image, which halves the dimension of their output and hence reduces required computation.

3.4   Feature Extractor

We have used a pre-trained Inception-v3 model for extracting image embedding. Firstly, the input image is scaled to 299×299 px, and normalised input values are received within the interval of [0,1]. Then we pile up these images on themselves to get a three channel image for Inception-v3 dimension criteria. Consequently, the resulting image is fed to the network and the last layer's output before the softmax function is extracted. This gives us a $1000 \times 1 \times 1$ embedding.

3.5   Fusion Layer

The fusion layer takes the feature vector from Inception-v3, then replicates it $(H \times W)/(32 \times 32)$ times and attaches it to the encoder's feature volume along the depth axis. This gives a single volume of the encoded image and the mid-level features of shape $H/32 \times W/32 \times 1512$. By replicating the feature vector and concatenating it repeatedly, we ensure that the feature vector's semantic information is uniformly distributed among all spatial regions of the image [27]. Finally, we apply 512 convolutional kernels of size 1×1, generating a feature volume of dimension $H/32 \times W/32 \times 512$.

3.6   Decoder

The decoder takes $H/32 \times W/32 \times 512$ volume and applies convolution and upsampling layers, which produces a final layer of dimension $H \times W \times 2$. Upsampling is performed using Nearest Neighbour Interpolation to ensure the output dimension is twice the input dimension. We use 5 ConvTranspose layers with 3×3 kernels followed by LeakyReLU with a negative slope of 0.2.

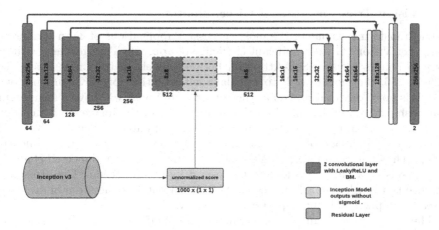

Fig. 1. ViT-I-GAN generator

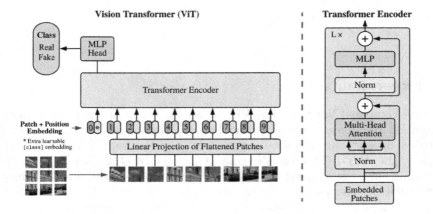

Fig. 2. ViT-GAN generator

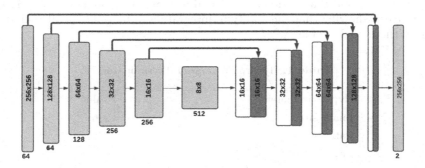

Fig. 3. ViT[14] as discriminator

3.7   Vision Transformer as a Discriminator

Vision transformer is one of the most successful applications of Transformer for Computer Vision [11]. A significant challenge of applying Transformers without CNN to images is using Self-Attention between pixels. If the input image size is 256 × 256, the model needs to calculate self-attention for 65K combinations. Also, it is not likely that a pixel at the corner of an image will have a meaningful relationship with another pixel on the other corner of the image. ViT has overcome this problem by segmenting images into small patches (like 32 × 32). ViT breaks an input image of 256 × 256 into a sequence of patches. Consequently, each patch is flattened into a single vector in a series of interconnected channels of all pixels in a patch, projecting to desired input dimension. The atom of a sentence is a word, similarly in the case of ViT, a patch is the atom of an image instead of a pixel to identify patterns efficiently.

The crux of the Transformer architecture is Self Attention. It enables the model to understand the connection between inputs. ViT combines information across the entire image, even in the lowest layers in Transformers. As quoted in the paper, "We find that some heads attend to most of the image already in the lowest layers, showing that the ability to integrate information globally is indeed used by the model (Table 1)."

Table 1. Hyperparameter of discriminator

Hyperparameter	Value
Image size	256
Patch size	32
Transformer blocks	6
Heads in multi-head attention layer	16
Dimension of the MLP (FeedForward) layer	2048
Dropout rate	0.1
Embedding dropout rate	0.1

4   Experiments

We have compared ViT GAN and ViT-I-GAN on a small dataset due to limited computing resources. For comparison between the models, we have used the Unsplash dataset, and for fine-tuning, we have used Natural-Color Dataset (NCD dataset) [29]. VIT-I-GAN was also trained on the COCO dataset [18] to test its limits and have a generalised model which can colourise a wide variety of images. COCO dataset encapsulates almost every common object since it covers 172 classes, making the model generalise better. We cannot compare our model with state-of-the-art models because their models are trained on 1.4 million images which is far more than what we could train on.

4.1   Dataset

We have used 10,500 images from the Unsplash dataset, which is publicly available. Both models are trained on 10,000 images and are validated and compared on 500 images and NCD dataset, which comprises 723 images of fruits and vegetables. For Fréchet Inception Distance (FID) [30] comparison, we have used 12,000 validation images from the COCO dataset.

4.2   Training

We have trained both models for 50 epochs with a batch size of 16 and a total of 31k steps used for training. Inception-v3 model is initialised with pre-trained weights for ImageNet. Adam optimiser is used with learning rate 0.0002 and momentum parameters $\beta_1 = 0.5$ and $\beta_2 = 0.9$. Adam optimiser is used because it converges faster than other common optimisers, which is favourable for training GANs.

The model utilizes a hybrid loss function, developed by combining the pixel-level L1 loss with the adversarial loss. L1 Loss function is the Least Absolute Deviations (LAD). LAD is used to minimize the error, which creates a criterion that measures the mean absolute error (MAE) between each element in the input y_t and target y_p.

$$\text{L1 Loss Function} = \sum_{i=1}^{n} |y_t - y_p|$$

The adversarial loss is calculated by Binary Cross Entropy between the real and generated images.

$$\text{BCE Loss} = -(\tfrac{1}{N}) \sum_{i=1}^{N} y_i \cdot log(\hat{y_i}) + (1 - y_i) \cdot log(1 - \hat{y_i})$$

5   Results

Why Fusion Layer Helps: just by adding more parameters to the generator or making the generator model deeper by adding more layers to it does not improve the generator's performance and ability to generalise on a limited dataset; hence a parallel network is required, which gives some kind of advantage to the generator, using a pre-trained classifier does work for this purpose since it does not need training for feature extraction hence saving the computational resources, and also the extracted features from the classifier boosts the generator's ability to perform the task. Empirically it was observed that the addition of the fusion layer to the generator helps when training is done for a long period of time.

We have compared the results of our models using both quantitative & qualitative evaluation methods.

5.1   Quantitative Evaluation

The metric used for evaluation is Fréchet Inception Distance (FID) metric which is used to evaluate quality of the images produced by the generator in a GAN. FID is a measure used to calculate the similarities between images of two datasets, hence compares the distribution of generated images with distribution of real images. Lower FID means better quality of the image and hence a better model.

It is calculated using the formula (Table 2 and 3):

$$FID = |\mu - \mu_w|^2 + Tr(\Sigma + \Sigma_w - 2(\Sigma \Sigma_w)^{1/2})$$

μ and μ_w represents the feature wise mean of real and generated images. Σ and Σ_w are covariance matrix for real and generated feature vectors. "Tr" is the trace linear algebra operation.

Table 2. FID comparison on 10 k images from unsplash dataset

	Epochs	ViT-GAN	ViT-I-GAN
Unsplash	25	22.73	23.06
Unsplash	50	24.89	18.16

Table 3. FID comparison on 10 k images from COCO dataset

	Epochs	ViT-GAN	ViT-I-GAN
COCO	50	31.2	26

It was observed that ViT-GAN was performing similar to ViT-I-GAN in terms of FID up till 25 epochs but after that ViT-I-GAN performed much better. This shows that after 25 epochs ViT-GAN stopped improving due to training on limited data whereas the ViT-I-GAN kept on improving demonstrating the usefulness of Inception-v3 embedding in the generator.

5.2   Comparison on Test Images

The test images are from Unsplash dataset and consist of various classes of gray scale images. These are more representative of real world examples where a single image is composed of several objects which makes colourising rather intricate than an image containing just a single object.

Grayscale   ViT-GAN   ViT-I-GAN

Fig. 4. Comparing performance of ViT-GAN and ViT-I-GAN (Color figure online)

As observed in Fig. 4, results produced by ViT-GAN are not able to colour sky and water which are prominent in those images. It attempts to colourise faces but smears red/orange colour in the process. It faintly colours those images having multiple objects.

In the results produced by ViT-I-GAN, it can be clearly observed that this model colours water and sky appropriately. It also colours faces with much better natural tone without smearing any colour. Additionally, it is able to distinguish between multiple objects and colour them properly.

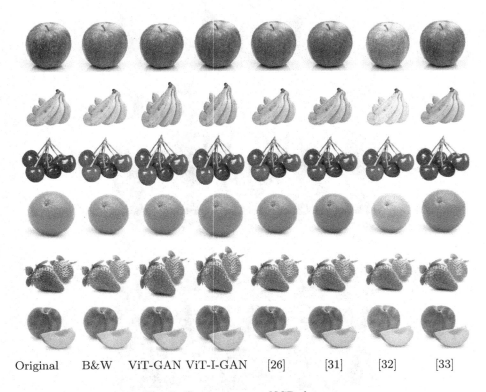

Original   B&W   ViT-GAN ViT-I-GAN   [26]   [31]   [32]   [33]

Fig. 5. Comparison on NCD dataset

5.3 Comparison on NCD Dataset

This comparison is based on the Natural-Color Dataset (NCD). These images were chosen for the dataset because they are true to their colour, a banana will most likely be yellowish or greenish whereas colour of sky can range from blue to orangish. The NCD comprises 723 images over 20 different categories. Our models are trained on 400 images and are tested on 323 images.

We have compared the results of our models with models of various researchers on NCD dataset. In Fig. 5, the first column has original coloured images followed by it's corresponding Black & White image, the next two columns have the output of our models named as ViT-GAN and ViT-I-GAN respectively. The following columns have the output of the similar colourisation work.

The ViT-GAN model is not able to colour the image of strawberry satisfactorily and colours it green. And it also splashes patches of green colour over all images, which is also unwanted. ViT-I-GAN model colourises much better in comparison with the ViT-GAN model. It accurately coloured all fruits with their respective colours and reduced random splashes of colour which were previously observed.

5.4   Additional Results

ViT-I-GAN was trained on the COCO dataset which is a more appropriate dataset for ubiquitous validation. The COCO dataset consists of 118k training images and 40k test images. We have used Adam optimiser with the $\beta_1 = 0.5$ and $\beta_2 = 0.999$. The model was trained for 59k steps with learning rate 2e–4 and then it was trained for 118k steps at a learning rate of 2e–5.

FID for ViT-I-GAN on COCO test data of 40k images is 23. The model properly colours different objects with their respective colours. It is able to differentiate between zebra, giraffe and cow and colours them appropriately. Hence, training on a dataset like COCO generalises the model which enables it to accurately colour a wide variety of images (Fig. 6).

Fig. 6. Performance of ViT-I-GAN on COCO test images

6 Limitation

Almost 20% of the test images were left uncoloured or barely coloured, due to limited resources on small dataset making the model not able to generalize well on complex images. The model was trained to colourize 256×256 images. The models were not validated on the Imagenet dataset.

7 Conclusion and Future Work

Our experiments conclude that by fusing InceptionNet-v3 with the generator, the network gets better intuition of various objects in an image. The network correlates object representation with colouring schema, especially when the training data is limited. This correlation shows significant improvement over generators not having fusion embedding. This improvement is very noticeable while it colours skies and water and refrains from smearing colours. ViT-I-GAN shows FID improvement of 27% on train data and 16% on test data in comparison to ViT-GAN.

Black and White images like historical images, videos and sketches can be colourised better and at scale. Further training of ViT-I-GAN on COCO dataset [18] resulted in better generalization. This improvement can be further enhanced by using a much larger dataset like ImageNet which contains 1.4M images over 1000 classes which will generalise the model for colouring a wide variety of images and by increasing the number of steps for training the model.

References

1. LeCun, Y., Bengio, Y., Hinton, G.: Deep learning. Nature **521**(7553), 436–444 (2015)
2. Goodfellow, I.J., et al.: Generative adversarial networks. arXiv preprint arXiv:1406.2661 (2014)
3. Wu, J., Zhang, C., Xue, T., Freeman, W.T., Tenenbaum, J.B.: Learning a probabilistic latent space of object shapes via 3d generative-adversarial modeling. arXiv preprint arXiv:1610.07584 (2016)
4. Karras, T., Laine, S., Aila, T.: A style-based generator architecture for generative adversarial networks. In: Proceedings of the IEEE/CVF Conference on Computer Vision and Pattern Recognition, pp. 4401–4410 (2019)
5. Vitoria, P., Raad, L., Ballester, C.: ChromaGAN: adversarial picture colorization with semantic class distribution. In: Proceedings of the IEEE/CVF Winter Conference on Applications of Computer Vision, pp. 2445–2454 (2020)
6. Manjunatha, V., Iyyer, M., Boyd-Graber, J., Davis, L.: Learning to color from language. arXiv preprint arXiv:1804.06026 (2018)
7. Bahng, H., et al.: Coloring with words: guiding image colorization through text-based palette generation. In: Proceedings of the European conference on computer vision (ECCV), pp. 431–447 (2018)
8. Zhao, J., Han, J., Shao, L., Snoek, C.G.: Pixelated semantic colorization. Int. J. Comput. Vis. 1–17 (2019)

9. Wang, P., Patel, V.M.: Generating high quality visible images from SAR images using CNNs. In: 2018 IEEE Radar Conference (RadarConf18), pp. 0570–0575. IEEE, April 2018

10. He, M., Chen, D., Liao, J., Sander, P.V., Yuan, L.: Deep exemplar-based colorization. ACM Trans. Graph. (TOG) **37**(4), 1–16 (2018)

11. Jiang, Y., Chang, S., Wang, Z.: TransGAN: Two Pure Transformers Can Make One Strong GAN, and That Can Scale Up Preprint (2021)

12. Szegedy, C., et al.: Going deeper with convolutions. In: Proceedings of the IEEE Conference on Computer Vision and Pattern Recognition, pp. 1–9 (2015)

13. Radford, A., Metz, L., Chintala, S.: Unsupervised Representation Learning with Deep Convolutional Generative Adversarial Networks. CoRR, abs/1511.06434 (2016)

14. Dosovitskiy, A., et al.: An image is worth 16x16 words: Transformers for image recognition at scale. arXiv preprint arXiv:2010.11929 (2020)

15. Deng, J., Dong, W., Socher, R., Li, L.J., Li, K., Fei-Fei, L.: Imagenet: a large-scale hierarchical image database. In: 2009 IEEE Conference on Computer Vision and Pattern Recognition, pp. 248–255. IEEE, June 2009

16. Reed, S., Akata, Z., Mohan, S., Tenka, S., Schiele, B., Lee, H.: Learning what and where to draw. In: Advances in Neural Information Processing Systems. Curran Associates Inc (2016)

17. Perez, E., Strub, F., De Vries, H., Dumoulin, V., Courville, A.: Film: visual reasoning with a general conditioning layer. In: Proceedings of the AAAI Conference on Artificial Intelligence, vol. 32, no. 1, April 2018

18. Lin, Tsung-Yi., et al.: Microsoft coco: common objects in context. In: Fleet, David, Pajdla, Tomas, Schiele, Bernt, Tuytelaars, Tinne (eds.) ECCV 2014. LNCS, vol. 8693, pp. 740–755. Springer, Cham (2014). https://doi.org/10.1007/978-3-319-10602-1_48

19. Wah, C., Branson, S., Welinder, P., Perona, P., Belongie, S.: The caltech-ucsd birds-200-2011 dataset (2011)

20. Russakovsky, O., et al.: Imagenet large scale visual recognition challenge. Int. J. Comput. Vis. **115**(3), 211–252 (2015)

21. Everingham, M., Van Gool, L., Williams, C.K., Winn, J., Zisserman, A.: The pascal visual object classes (VOC) challenge. Int. J. Comput. Vis. **88**(2), 303–338 (2010)

22. Liao, J., Yao, Y., Yuan, L., Hua, G., Kang, S.B.: Visual attribute transfer through deep image analogy. arXiv preprint arXiv:1705.01088 (2017)

23. Simonyan, K., Zisserman, A.: Very deep convolutional networks for large-scale image recognition. arXiv preprint arXiv:1409.1556 (2014)

24. Ronneberger, Olaf, Fischer, Philipp, Brox, Thomas: U-Net: convolutional networks for biomedical image segmentation. In: Navab, Nassir, Hornegger, Joachim, Wells, William M.., Frangi, Alejandro F.. (eds.) MICCAI 2015. LNCS, vol. 9351, pp. 234–241. Springer, Cham (2015). https://doi.org/10.1007/978-3-319-24574-4_28

25. Jia, Y., et al.: Caffe: convolutional architecture for fast feature embedding. In: Proceedings of the 22nd ACM International Conference on Multimedia, pp. 675–678, November 2014

26. Iizuka, S., Simo-Serra, E., Ishikawa, H.: Let there be color! Joint end-to-end learning of global and local image priors for automatic image colorization with simultaneous classification. ACM Trans. Graph. (TOG) **35**(4), 1–11 (2016)

27. Baldassarre, F., Morín, D.G., Rodés-Guirao, L.: Deep Koalarization: image colorization using CNNs and Inception-Resnet-v2. arXiv preprint arXiv:1712.03400 (2017)

28. Ioffe, S., Szegedy, C.: Batch normalization: accelerating deep network training by reducing internal covariate shift. In: International Conference on Machine Learning, pp. 448–456. PMLR, June 2015
29. Anwar, S., et al.: Image colorization: a survey and dataset. arXiv preprint arXiv:2008.10774 (2020)
30. Heusel, M., Ramsauer, H., Unterthiner, T., Nessler, B., Hochreiter, S.: GANs trained by a two time-scale update rule converge to a local Nash equilibrium. In: Proceedings of the 31st International Conference on Neural Information Processing Systems, pp. 6629–6640. Curran Associates Inc (2017)
31. Zhang, Richard, Isola, Phillip, Efros, Alexei A..: Colorful image colorization. In: Leibe, Bastian, Matas, Jiri, Sebe, Nicu, Welling, Max (eds.) ECCV 2016. LNCS, vol. 9907, pp. 649–666. Springer, Cham (2016). https://doi.org/10.1007/978-3-319-46487-9_40
32. Larsson, Gustav, Maire, Michael, Shakhnarovich, Gregory: Learning representations for automatic colorization. In: Leibe, Bastian, Matas, Jiri, Sebe, Nicu, Welling, Max (eds.) ECCV 2016. LNCS, vol. 9908, pp. 577–593. Springer, Cham (2016). https://doi.org/10.1007/978-3-319-46493-0_35
33. Zhang, R., et al.: Real-time user-guided image colorization with learned deep priors. ACM Trans. Graph. **36**(4) (2017)

On Principal Component Analysis of the Convex Combination of Two Data Matrices and Its Application to Acoustic Metamaterial Filters

Giorgio Gnecco[1(✉)] and Andrea Bacigalupo[2]

[1] IMT School for Advanced Studies, Lucca, Italy
giorgio.gnecco@imtlucca.it
[2] University of Genoa, Genoa, Italy
andrea.bacigalupo@unige.it

Abstract. In this short paper, a matrix perturbation bound on the eigenvalues found by principal component analysis is investigated, for the case in which the data matrix on which principal component analysis is performed is a convex combination of two data matrices. The application of the theoretical analysis to multi-objective optimization problems (e.g., those arising in the design of acoustic metamaterial filters) is briefly discussed, together with possible extensions.

Keywords: Principal component analysis · Matrix perturbation · Singular value decomposition · Multi-objective optimization · Acoustic metamaterial filters

1 Introduction

Principal Component Analysis (PCA) is a well-known data dimensionality reduction technique [7]. It works by projecting a dataset of m vectors $\mathbf{x}_j \in \mathbb{R}^n$, $j = 1, \ldots, m$ (represented by a data matrix $\mathbf{X} \in \mathbb{R}^{m \times n}$, whose rows are such vectors) onto a reduced d-dimensional subspace of $\mathbb{R}^n$, which is generated by the first $d < n$ so-called principal directions. These are orthonormal eigenvectors of the symmetric matrix $\mathbf{C} \doteq \frac{1}{m}\mathbf{X}'\mathbf{X} \in \mathbb{R}^{n \times n}$, associated with its d largest positive eigenvalues. The latter are proportional (via the multiplicative factor $\frac{1}{m}$) to the d largest positive eigenvalues of the related Gram matrix $\mathbf{G} \doteq \mathbf{X}\mathbf{X}' \in \mathbb{R}^{m \times m}$, whose element in position (i, j) is the inner product between the vectors $\mathbf{x}_i$ and $\mathbf{x}_j$. Focusing on such eigenvalues is important because the eigenvalues corresponding to discarded principal directions (the ones associated with the successive eigenvalues, not selected by PCA) provide information about the mean squared error of approximation of the dataset when only the first d principal directions are kept to construct that approximation (as a consequence, knowing these eigenvalues is useful also to select a suitable value for d). Moreover, when the dataset has zero mean, each such eigenvalue represents the empirical variance of the projection of the dataset onto the corresponding principal direction.

© Springer Nature Switzerland AG 2022
G. Nicosia et al. (Eds.): LOD 2021, LNCS 13163, pp. 119–123, 2022.
https://doi.org/10.1007/978-3-030-95467-3_9

Given this framework, the goal of this short work is to get a matrix perturbation bound on the eigenvalues of the Gram matrix $\mathbf{G}$, for the case in which the data matrix $\mathbf{X}$ is a convex combination of other two data matrices. According to the authors' experience, this is a non-standard but potentially quite interesting way of using PCA. The application of the theoretical analysis to multi-objective optimization (a framework in which a convex combination of two data matrices can arise) is discussed in the last section, together with possible extensions.

2   Theoretical Analysis

In this section, a matrix perturbation bound on the eigenvalues of the Gram matrix of a dataset is provided, for the case in which its data matrix $\mathbf{X}(\alpha)$ is a convex combination of two data matrices $\mathbf{X}_1$ and $\mathbf{X}_2$, with varying weights $\alpha \in [0,1]$ and $1 - \alpha$.

Proposition. *Let* $\mathbf{X}_1, \mathbf{X}_2 \in \mathbb{R}^{m \times n}$ *be two data matrices,* $\alpha \in [0,1]$, $\mathbf{G}(\alpha) \doteq \mathbf{X}(\alpha)\mathbf{X}'(\alpha) \in \mathbb{R}^{m \times m}$ *be the Gram matrix of their convex combination* $\mathbf{X}(\alpha) \doteq \alpha \mathbf{X}_1 + (1 - \alpha)\mathbf{X}_2$ *with weights* α *and* $1 - \alpha$, $K \in \mathbb{N}$ *and, for* $k = 0, 1, \dots, K$, $\alpha_k \doteq \frac{k}{K}$. *Let the non-negative eigenvalues of* $\mathbf{G}(\alpha)$ *and* $\mathbf{G}(\alpha_k)$ *be ordered, respectively, as* $\lambda_1(\mathbf{G}(\alpha)) \geq \lambda_2(\mathbf{G}(\alpha)) \geq \dots \geq \lambda_m(\mathbf{G}(\alpha))$ *and* $\lambda_1(\mathbf{G}(\alpha_k)) \geq \lambda_2(\mathbf{G}(\alpha_k)) \geq \dots \geq \lambda_m(\mathbf{G}(\alpha_k))$. *Finally, let* $\sigma_1(\mathbf{X}(\alpha))$ *and* $\sigma_1(\mathbf{X}(\alpha_k))$ *be the largest singular values of* $\mathbf{X}(\alpha)$ *and* $\mathbf{X}(\alpha_k)$, *respectively. Then, for any* $k = 0, 1, \dots, K-1$ *and* $\alpha \in [\alpha_k, \alpha_{k+1}]$, *the following holds, for all* $i = 1, \dots, m$:

$$|\lambda_i(\mathbf{G}(\alpha)) - \lambda_i(\mathbf{G}(\alpha_k))| \leq \frac{2}{K} \left(\sigma_1(\mathbf{X}_1) + \sigma_1(\mathbf{X}_2) \right)^2 . \tag{1}$$

Proof. Using the singular value decomposition of $\mathbf{X}(\alpha) = \mathbf{U}(\alpha)\mathbf{\Sigma}(\alpha)\mathbf{V}'(\alpha)$ (being $\mathbf{U}(\alpha) \in \mathbb{R}^{m \times m}$ and $\mathbf{V}(\alpha) \in \mathbb{R}^{n \times n}$ orthogonal matrices, and $\mathbf{\Sigma}(\alpha) \in \mathbb{R}^{m \times n}$ a rectangular matrix whose $q \doteq \min\{m, n\}$ elements on its main diagonal are the singular values $\sigma_i(\mathbf{X}(\alpha))$, ordered from the largest singular value to the smallest one), one gets

$$\begin{aligned} \mathbf{G}(\alpha) &= \mathbf{X}(\alpha)\mathbf{X}'(\alpha) = \mathbf{U}(\alpha)\mathbf{\Sigma}(\alpha)\mathbf{V}'(\alpha) \left(\mathbf{U}(\alpha)\mathbf{\Sigma}(\alpha)\mathbf{V}'(\alpha) \right)' \\ &= \mathbf{U}(\alpha)\mathbf{\Sigma}(\alpha)\mathbf{V}'(\alpha)\mathbf{V}(\alpha)\mathbf{\Sigma}'(\alpha)\mathbf{U}'(\alpha) = \mathbf{U}(\alpha)\mathbf{\Lambda}(\alpha)\mathbf{U}'(\alpha), \end{aligned} \tag{2}$$

where, denoting by $\mathbf{I}_{n \times n} \in \mathbb{R}^{n \times n}$ the identity matrix, the property $\mathbf{V}'(\alpha)\mathbf{V}(\alpha) = \mathbf{I}_{n \times n}$ has been used, and $\mathbf{\Lambda}(\alpha) \doteq \mathbf{\Sigma}(\alpha)\mathbf{\Sigma}'(\alpha) \in \mathbb{R}^{m \times m}$ is a diagonal matrix whose elements on its main diagonal are the squares $\sigma_i^2(\mathbf{X}(\alpha))$ of the singular values $\sigma_i(\mathbf{X}(\alpha))$ of $\mathbf{X}(\alpha)$, plus $m - n$ additional zeros (if and only if $m > n$). The $\sigma_i^2(\mathbf{X}(\alpha))$ and the possible $m - n$ additional zeros are also the eigenvalues $\lambda_i(\mathbf{G}(\alpha))$ of $\mathbf{G}(\alpha)$, since this is a symmetric and positive semi-definite matrix. We consider first the case $m \leq n$, then the case $m > n$.

- Case 1: $m \leq n$. We exploit the matrix perturbation bound on singular values provided in [6, Theorem 3.3.16 (c)], according to which, given any two matrices $\mathbf{A}, \mathbf{B} \in \mathbb{R}^{m \times n}$, one has, for all $i = 1, \dots, \min\{m, n\} = m$,

$$|\sigma_i(\mathbf{A}) - \sigma_i(\mathbf{A} + \mathbf{B})| \leq \sigma_1(\mathbf{B}) . \tag{3}$$

Denoting by $\Delta\alpha$ a variation of α, we apply Eq. (3) with $\mathbf{A} = \mathbf{X}(\alpha)$ and $\mathbf{B} = \mathbf{X}(\alpha + \Delta\alpha) - \mathbf{X}(\alpha) = \Delta\alpha\,(\mathbf{X}_1 - \mathbf{X}_2)$. Recalling the relation $\lambda_i(\mathbf{G}(\alpha)) = \sigma_i^2(\mathbf{X}(\alpha))$ valid for all $i = 1, \ldots, m$, and the fact that $\sigma_i(\mathbf{X}(\alpha)) \geq 0$, we get

$$|\lambda_i(\mathbf{G}(\alpha + \Delta\alpha)) - \lambda_i(\mathbf{G}(\alpha))| = |\sigma_i^2(\mathbf{X}(\alpha + \Delta\alpha)) - \sigma_i^2(\mathbf{X}(\alpha))|$$
$$\leq |\Delta\alpha|\,\sigma_1(\mathbf{X}_1 - \mathbf{X}_2)\,(\sigma_i(\mathbf{X}(\alpha + \Delta\alpha)) + \sigma_i(\mathbf{X}(\alpha))). \tag{4}$$

Moreover, $0 \leq \sigma_1(\mathbf{X}_1 - \mathbf{X}_2) \leq \sigma_1(\mathbf{X}_1) + \sigma_1(\mathbf{X}_2)$ by Eq. (3) with $\mathbf{A} = \mathbf{X}_1$ and $\mathbf{B} = -\mathbf{X}_2$, whereas $0 \leq \sigma_i(\alpha\mathbf{X}_1 + (1 - \alpha)\mathbf{X}_2) \leq \alpha\sigma_i(\mathbf{X}_1) + (1 - \alpha)\sigma_1(\mathbf{X}_2) \leq \sigma_1(\mathbf{X}_1) + \sigma_1(\mathbf{X}_2)$, where the second last inequality is obtained again by Eq. (3) with $\mathbf{A} = \alpha\mathbf{X}_1$ and $\mathbf{B} = (1 - \alpha)\mathbf{X}_2$. Combining all the above, one gets

$$|\lambda_i(\mathbf{G}(\alpha + \Delta\alpha)) - \lambda_i(\mathbf{G}(\alpha))| \leq 2|\Delta\alpha|\,(\sigma_1(\mathbf{X}_1) + \sigma_1(\mathbf{X}_2))^2, \tag{5}$$

from which one obtains Eq. (1) for $|\Delta\alpha| = |\alpha_k - \alpha| \leq \frac{1}{K}$.

- Case 2: $m > n$. The proof is the same as above for all but the last (smallest) $m - n$ eigenvalues of $\mathbf{G}(\alpha)$ and $\mathbf{G}(\alpha_k)$. However, the latter eigenvalues are all equal to 0, and the bound (1) still holds trivially for them.

The bound expressed by Eq. (1), whose proof shows the Lipschitz continuity of the eigenvalues of $\mathbf{G}(\alpha)$ with respect to α, can be used in the following way. First, one finds the sets of eigenvalues of the matrices $\mathbf{G}(\alpha_k)$, for $k = 1, \ldots, K$. Then, for each $\alpha \in [0, 1]$, one finds its nearest α_k, then applies Eq. (1) to locate approximately the eigenvalues of the new matrix $\mathbf{G}(\alpha)$.

3   Discussion and Possible Extensions

The theoretical framework considered in Sect. 2 has application, e.g., in the combination of PCA with the so-called weighted sum method, which is used in the context of multi-objective optimization [3]. In the case of two objective functions, this method approximates the Pareto frontier of a multi-objective optimization problem by minimizing, for $\mathbf{p} \in P \subseteq \mathbb{R}^n$, the trade-off $J_\alpha(\mathbf{p}) \doteq \alpha J_1(\mathbf{p}) + (1 - \alpha)J_2(\mathbf{p})$ between the two objective functions $J_1(\mathbf{p})$ and $J_2(\mathbf{p})$, for different values of the parameter $\alpha \in [0, 1]$ (an adaptive version of the method can be applied in cases for which the classical weighted sum method fails, e.g., when the Pareto frontier is nonconvex [8]). Assuming that both $J_1(\mathbf{p})$ and $J_2(\mathbf{p})$ are differentiable and the optimization problem is unconstrained (i.e., $P = \mathbb{R}^n$) or that it can be reduced to an unconstrained optimization problem by using a suitable penalization approach, one could perform the optimization numerically by applying the classical gradient method, possibly combined with a multi-start approach. In order to reduce the computational effort needed for the exact computation of the gradient at each iteration of the gradient method, one could replace it with its approximation obtained by applying PCA to the gradient field $\nabla J_\alpha(\mathbf{p})$ evaluated on a subset of points $\mathbf{p}_j \in P$ (for $j = 1, \ldots, m$), then projecting the exact gradient onto the subspace generated by the average of the gradients $\nabla J_\alpha(\mathbf{p}_j)$, and by the first principal directions found by PCA, when this is applied to the dataset $\{\nabla J_\alpha(\mathbf{p}_j)\}_{j=1}^m$, after a pre-processing step, which makes it centered[1]. Due to the structure of the objective function $J_\alpha(\mathbf{p})$, such dataset (represented by a data matrix $\mathbf{X}_\alpha$) would be made of the convex combination (with coefficients α and $1 - \alpha$) of the two datasets $\{\nabla J_1(\mathbf{p}_j)\}_{j=1}^m$ and $\{\nabla J_2(\mathbf{p}_j)\}_{j=1}^m$, represented respectively by the two data matrices $\mathbf{X}_1$ and $\mathbf{X}_2$. In this context, the results of our theoretical analysis could be useful to restrict the application of the weighted sum method to a coarse grid of values α_k for $\alpha \in [0, 1]$, from which one could infer, for other values of α, the empirical variances of the projections of the (de-meaned) data matrices $\mathbf{X}^{(c)}(\alpha)$ onto the principal directions either selected or discarded by PCA, when PCA is applied to each such data matrix $\mathbf{X}^{(c)}(\alpha)$. Moreover, in view of this application to multi-objective optimization, the theoretical analysis of this work could be extended by finding upper bounds on the Jordan canonical angles[2] between the subspaces found by PCA applied to the data matrices $\mathbf{X}(\alpha)$ generated from $\mathbf{X}_1$ and $\mathbf{X}_2$ for two different values of $\alpha \in [0, 1]$. Such an extension could be derived by applying a variation (proved in [11]) of the well-known Davis-Kahan theorem in matrix perturbation theory [9, Theorem 3.4]. A second extension of the analysis to the case of nonlinear versions of PCA, such as kernel PCA [5], seems also possible (e.g., via the kernel trick).

We conclude mentioning that, in our related work [4] about the design of acoustic metamaterial filters according to a single-objective optimization framework[3] (see [10] for a physical-mathematical model similar to the one considered in [4]), we have successfully applied PCA to the sampled gradient field of the objective function, achieving numerical results comparable with those obtained by using the exact gradient, but with a much smaller computational effort (e.g., with a reduction of the dimension by a factor 4). A similar outcome is expected when moving to a multi-objective optimization framework[4]. So, for this kind of optimization problems, the application of PCA to the approximation of the

---

[1] It is common practice to apply PCA to centered (also called de-meaned) data matrices $\mathbf{X}^{(c)}$, i.e., having the form $\mathbf{X}^{(c)} \doteq \mathbf{X} - \mathbf{1}_m \bar{\mathbf{x}}'$, where $\mathbf{1}_m \in \mathbf{R}^m$ denotes a column vector made of m ones, and $\bar{\mathbf{x}} \in \mathbf{R}^n$ is a column vector whose elements are the averages of the corresponding columns of $\mathbf{X}$. This does not change the quality of the results of the theoretical analysis, because, by linearity, the centered convex combination of two data matrices $\mathbf{X}_1$ and $\mathbf{X}_2$ is equal to the convex combination of the two respective centered data matrices $\mathbf{X}_1^{(c)}$ and $\mathbf{X}_2^{(c)}$.

[2] These, loosely speaking, represent the *smallest angles* between corresponding elements of the orthonormal bases of two subspaces of $\mathbb{R}^n$, being the bases chosen to minimize such angles. For rigorous definitions, see [11, 12] and the references therein.

[3] Such optimization problems are typically characterized by a high computational effort needed for an exact evaluation of the gradient of their objective functions, which is motivated by the fact that each such evaluation requires solving the physical-mathematical model associated with the specific choice of the vector of parameters of the model, which is also the vector of optimization variables.

[4] The reader is referred to [1] for examples of both single-objective and multi-objective optimal design problems for acoustic metamaterial filters (possible objective functions being the *band gap* and the *band amplitude*).

sampled gradient field of the objective function can be a valid alternative to the use of surrogate optimization methods (which replace the original objective function with a surrogate function, learned either offline or online [2]), in case a gradient-based optimization algorithm is used to solve the optimization problem.

Acknowledgment. A. Bacigalupo and G. Gnecco are members of INdAM. The authors acknowledge financial support from INdAM-GNAMPA (project Trade-off between Number of Examples and Precision in Variations of the Fixed-Effects Panel Data Model), from INdAM-GNFM, from the Università Italo Francese (projects GALILEO 2019 no. G19-48 and GALILEO 2021 no. G21_89), from the Compagnia di San Paolo (project MINIERA no. I34I20000380007), and from the University of Trento (project UNMASKED 2020).

References

1. Bacigalupo, A., Gnecco, G., Lepidi, M., Gambarotta, L.: Design of acoustic meta-materials through nonlinear programming. In: Pardalos, P.M., Conca, P., Giuffrida, G., Nicosia, G. (eds.) MOD 2016. LNCS, vol. 10122, pp. 170–181. Springer, Cham (2016). https://doi.org/10.1007/978-3-319-51469-7_14
2. Bacigalupo, A., Gnecco, G., Lepidi, M., Gambarotta, L.: Computational design of innovative mechanical metafilters via adaptive surrogate-based optimization. Comput. Methods Appl. Mech. Eng. **375**, 113623 (2021)
3. Collette, Y., Siarry, P.: Multiobjective Optimization: Principles and Case Studies, Springer (2003)
4. Gnecco, G., Bacigalupo, A., Fantoni, F., Selvi, D.: Principal component analysis applied to gradient fields in band gap optimization problems for metamaterials. In: Proceedings of the 6th International Conference on Metamaterials and Nanophotonics (METANANO) (2021). J. Phys. Conf. Ser., vol. 2015. https://iopscience.iop.org/article/10.1088/1742-6596/2015/1/012047
5. Gnecco, G., Sanguineti, M.: Accuracy of suboptimal solutions to kernel principal component analysis. Comput. Optim. Appl. **42**, 265–287 (2009)
6. Horn, R.A., Johnson, C.R.: Topics in Matrix Analysis, Cambridge University Press, Cambridge(1991)
7. Jolliffe, I.T.: Principal Component Analysis, Springer, New York (2002). https://doi.org/10.1007/b98835
8. Kim, I.Y., de Weck, O.L.: Adaptive weighted-sum method for bi-objective optimization: pareto front generation. Struct. Multi. Optim. **29**, 149–158 (2005)
9. Stewart, G. W., Sun, J.-G.: Matrix Perturbation Theory, Academic Press, Cambridge (1990)
10. Vadalà, F., Bacigalupo, A., Lepidi, M., Gambarotta, L.: Free and forced wave propagation in beam lattice metamaterials with viscoelastic resonators. Int. J. Mech. Sci. **193**, 106129 (2021)
11. Wedin, P.Å.: Perturbation bounds in connection with singular value decomposition. BIT **12**, 99–111 (1972)
12. Zhu, P., Knyazev, A.V.: Angles between subspaces and their tangents. J. Numer. Math. **21**, 325–340 (2013)

Mixing Consistent Deep Clustering

Daniel Lutscher[1(✉)], Ali el Hassouni[1], Maarten Stol[2], and Mark Hoogendoorn[1]

[1] Vrije Universiteit Amsterdam, Amsterdam, The Netherlands
{a.el.hassouni,m.hoogendoorn}@vu.nl
[2] BrainCreators B.V., Amsterdam, The Netherlands
maarten.stol@braincreators.com

Abstract. Finding well-defined clusters in data represents a fundamental challenge for many data-driven applications, and largely depends on good data representation. Drawing on literature regarding representation learning, studies suggest that one key characteristic of good latent representations is the ability to produce semantically mixed outputs when decoding linear interpolations of two latent representations. We propose the Mixing Consistent Deep Clustering (MCDC) method which encourages interpolations to appear realistic while adding the constraint that interpolations of two data points must look like one of the two inputs. By applying this training method to various clustering (non-)specific autoencoder models we found that using the proposed training method systematically changed the structure of learned representations of a model and it improved clustering performance for the tested ACAI, IDEC, and VAE models on the MNIST, SVHN, and CIFAR-10 datasets. These outcomes have practical implications for numerous real-world clustering tasks, as it shows that the proposed method can be added to existing autoencoders to further improve clustering performance.

Keywords: Adversarial training · Autoencoder · Clustering

1 Introduction

Clustering is the process of assigning data points to groups based on similarity. It constitutes a fundamental part of many data-driven applications and over the past decades a large variety of clustering techniques have been studied [1,24,25]. When applying these techniques to high-dimensional data, they are typically preceded by dimensionality reduction techniques such as Principal Component Analysis (PCA) [32] and spectral methods [22] to overcome the often prevalent limitation of data sparsity. Through recent advances in Deep Learning [18,26], deep neural networks have since also been used as dimensionality reduction techniques. Among existing approaches, autoencoders [11] have widely been used to achieve this task by learning latent representations in an unsupervised setting. In the context of clustering, the successfully trained encoder can then be used to transform the input data into a lower-dimensional latent representation, which in turn serves as the input for clustering techniques. This combination of Deep Learning and clustering is called *Deep Clustering*. Nowadays, several novel architectures emerged from this new research field, mostly by combining an autoencoder and a clustering algorithm through simultaneous optimization [10,12,20].

© Springer Nature Switzerland AG 2022
G. Nicosia et al. (Eds.): LOD 2021, LNCS 13163, pp. 124–137, 2022.
https://doi.org/10.1007/978-3-030-95467-3_10

While the end-to-end optimization shows promising results, a limitation of this approach is that the models are solely trained towards creating non-ambiguous clusters. In other words, they maximize the distance between already existing clusters by minimizing a data point's distance to its assigned cluster centroid. However, they do not change the learned position of latent representations in a way that it would create more *disentangled* clusters. Disentanglement refers to how well the underlying factors of variation are separated [4]. One relevant characteristic of disentanglement in the context of clustering is the occurrence of natural clusters. It is suggested that natural clusters may occur because the local variations on a manifold tend to reflect a single category, and a linear interpolation between data points of different classes involves going through a low density region [4] (see Fig. 1 for a schematic illustration). Thus, while traversing the linearly interpolated path between instances of two clusters, one should not encounter instances of a third cluster. Since the positions of the lower-dimensional feature representations are learned, this interpolation characteristic can be learned as well. This training method, often referred to as *interpolation training*, has been used in supervised settings to increase the robustness of a classifier [9,29] as well as in a semi-supervised setting to achieve comparable performance with fewer class instances [5,30].

This paper makes use of this interpolation training technique in an unsupervised setting. We use a mixing function that linearly interpolates two latent representations using an α coefficient drawn from a uniform distribution. To ensure that the output of mixed latent representations look like stemming from the data distribution at pixel level, we make use of adversarial training [8] by training a discriminator to predict the α coefficient used for the mixing function. Here, the goal of the autoencoder is to fool the discriminator that the outputs of mixed representations are real by always predicting an α coefficient of 0. Furthermore, the autoencoder's loss function includes an additional 'mixing consistency' loss term. The motivation for this term is to enforce the desideratum of linear dependencies between clusters in the latent space, which realizes a structure that is better suited for downstream clustering tasks (see Sect. 3 for an illustration).

This new framework, called MCDC, can be applied to preexisting convolution-based autoencoder models to further improve clustering performance. In summary, the contributions of this work are as follows:

- We combine the approaches of interpolation training and adversarial learning with the explicit enforcement of a desired structure in the latent space.
- Experimentally, we show that MCDC outperforms all other tested models with regard to clustering results on the MNIST, SVHN and CIFAR-10 datasets (Sect. 5).
- We empirically show that this improved framework can be added to various autoencoder architectures to improve clustering performance.

2   Related Work

2.1   Deep Clustering

Recent work in Deep Clustering started to focus on creating a clustering-friendly feature space through the simultaneous minimization of reconstruction and clustering loss. As one of the first to combine both steps into an end-to-end framework, Guo and colleagues [10] published the *Improved Deep Embedded Clustering* (IDEC) model which simultaneously learns feature representations and cluster assignments using an autoencoder. It first pretrains the autoencoder by using a reconstruction loss and then fine-tunes the network by adding a cluster assignment hardening loss, where each point is assigned a probability of belonging to a given cluster. This simultaneous optimization approach significantly increased clustering accuracy compared to separate autoencoder and clustering optimization [10]. Nowadays, the architecture of the IDEC model has been extended to generative models such as variational autoencoders (VAE) [14] and generative adversarial networks (GAN) [8]. For example, Jiang et al. [12] developed the *variational deep embedding* (VaDE) framework, which simultaneously optimizes a Variational Autoencoder and a clustering-specific Gaussian Mixture Model (GMM). This resulted in a significant improvement in clustering accuracy and they outperformed the standard GMM clustering method, VAE and GMM networks with separate optimization as well as other deep clustering methods [12].

2.2 Interpolation Training

Learning good representations is an active field of research that primarily investigates how to learn representations that are *disentangled* [4,28,31]. A disentangled representation unravels the underlying structure and displays several attributes that are useful in the context of clustering, most importantly lower dimensional manifolds, naturally occurring clusters, and a simplicity of factor dependencies (for a list of attributes, see [4]). One common denominator across these attributes is the ability to linearly interpolate between clusters or data points of classes while traversing low density regions. Since the representations of data points in the latent space are learned, it is possible to enforce this interpolation characteristic through training. For example, recent work [3,29] applied an interpolation training method called *Manifold Mixup* in a supervised setting to learn robust features. By interpolating two data points' hidden layer activations, the learned class-representations were more discriminative, compact, and had fewer directions of variance, suggesting that the model learned more disentangled representations.

In an unsupervised setting, a method called *Adversarially Constrained Autoencoder Interpolation* (ACAI) [6] was proposed which uses interpolations of latent representations and an adversarial regularizer to train an autoencoder. Without a clustering-specific loss, this training technique created a latent space structure that is on-par with current state-of-the-art deep clustering models with regard to clustering accuracy.

3   Mixing Consistent Deep Clustering (MCDC)

Let us consider an autoencoder $F(\cdot)$, consisting of the encoder part $f_\phi(x)$ and the decoder $g_\theta(f_\phi(x))$. To train this model, we minimize the following reconstruction loss:

$$L_{f,g} = ||x - g_\theta(f_\phi(x))||^2 \tag{1}$$

where ϕ and θ denote the learned parameters of the autoencoder. Given a pair of inputs, $\{x^{(i)}, x^{(j)}\} \in X$, we would like to encode them into lower dimensional latent representations $z^{(i)} = f_\phi(x^{(i)})$ and $z^{(j)} = f_\phi(x^{(j)})$ where $\{z^{(i)}, z^{(j)}\} \in Z$. Next, we mix them using a convex combination and a mixing coefficient α:

$$z_\alpha^{(i)} = (1 - \alpha) \cdot f_\phi(x^{(i)}) + \alpha \cdot f_\phi(x^{(j)}) \tag{2}$$

for some $\alpha \in [0, 1]$ where $z_\alpha^{(i)} \in Z_\alpha$. Then, we run $z_\alpha^{(i)}$ through the decoder $g_\theta(z_\alpha^{(i)})$. To ensure that the reconstruction $\hat{x}_\alpha^{(i)} = g_\theta(z_\alpha^{(i)})$ resembles realistic and non-blurry samples from the data distribution, we train a discriminator $D_\omega(x)$ on real and mixed sets of reconstructions to predict the α coefficient that was used for the mixing function in Eq. 2. Then, the discriminator D_ω is trained to minimize the following loss:

$$L_D = \underbrace{||D_\omega(\hat{x}_\alpha) - \alpha||^2}_{\text{predict } \alpha \text{ coefficient}} + \underbrace{||D_\omega(\gamma x + (1 - \gamma)\hat{x}||^2}_{\text{improves training stability}} \tag{3}$$

where γ is a scalar hyperparameter.

To produce a latent space structure with low-density regions between clusters and the ability to linearly interpolate between them, the reconstruction $\hat{x}_\alpha$ of a mixed representation z_α must look like a realistic data point from the same cluster. Since we do not have this information in an unsupervised setting, we enforce that the construction $\hat{x}_\alpha$ of a given pair of two inputs $\{x^{(i)}, x^{(j)}\} \in X$ must look like one of the input data points:

$$\hat{x}_\alpha = \begin{cases} x^{(i)} & \alpha \in [0, 0.5] \\ x^{(j)} & \alpha \in [0.5, 1] \\ 0 & otherwise. \end{cases} \tag{4}$$

Consequently, we propose *Mixing Consistent Deep Clustering* (MCDC), where part of the autoencoder's objective is to produce realistic mixed reconstructions that look like coming from the respective data points that were used for the mixing operation. To achieve this, the autoencoder minimizes the following *mixing consistency loss*:

$$L_{mix} = ||x^{(i)} - g_\theta((1 - \alpha)f_\phi(x^{(i)}) + \alpha f_\phi(x^{(j)}))||^2 \tag{5}$$

where $\alpha \in [0, 0.5]$. The overall loss function of MCDC is therefore defined as follows:

$$L_{MCDC} = L_{f,g} + L_{mix} + \lambda||d_\omega(\hat{x}_\alpha)||^2 \tag{6}$$

where λ is a scalar hyperparameter.

To illustrate MCDC in the context of clustering, we first discuss an example of linear interpolations between four clusters without a mixing consistency loss, depicted in Fig. 1. Given two clusters $B = \{x_B^{(1)}, ..., x_B^{(i)}\}$ and $C = \{x_C^{(1)}, ..., x_C^{(j)}\}$, mixing the latent representations of two data points from these clusters:

$$z_\alpha^{(i)} = (1 - \alpha) \cdot f_\phi(x_C^{(i)}) + \alpha \cdot f_\phi(x_B^{(j)}) \tag{7}$$

results in mixed reconstructions that resemble realistic data points of cluster C for $\alpha \approx 0$ and become more semantically similar to data points from cluster B while traversing the space between the clusters as a function of increasing α. In Fig. 1, these mixed latent representations are visualized as blurred versions of the cluster's datapoints.

Algorithm 1. Stochastic gradient descent training of MCDC.

---

for all number of training iterations **do**
    for all k steps **do**
        • Sample batch of m input data points $\{x^{(1)}, ..., x^{(m)}\}$ from the dataset.
        • Run the batch of m samples through the encoder $f_\phi(x)$ to obtain the set of m latent representations $Z_k = \{z^{(1)}, ..., z^{(m)}\}$.
        • create a copy of the set Z_k and reverse the indices such that we receive the set $Z_{\hat{k}} = \{z^{(m)}, ..., z^{(1)}\}$.
        • Mix the two sets Z_k and $Z_{\hat{k}}$ using linear interpolation and a uniformly drawn α-coefficient such that, for the two latent representations $z^{(1)} \in Z_k, z^{(m)} \in Z_{\hat{k}}$ the resulting mixing function is: $z_\alpha^{(1)} = (1 - \alpha) \cdot z^{(1)} + \alpha \cdot z^{(m)}$. This results in a new set of latent representations $Z_\alpha = \{z_\alpha^{(1)}, ..., z_\alpha^{(m)}\}$.
        • Run the two sets of latent representations Z_k and Z_α through the decoder $g_\theta(z)$ to obtain two sets of reconstructions $\hat{X}_k = \{\hat{x}^{(1)}, ..., \hat{x}^{(m)}\}$ and $\hat{X}_\alpha = \{\hat{x}_\alpha^{(1)}, ..., \hat{x}_\alpha^{(m)}\}$.
        • Run the two reconstruction sets $\hat{X}_k$ and $\hat{X}_\alpha$ through the discriminator $D_\omega(\hat{x})$.
        • Update the discriminator and autoencoder by descending their respective stochastic gradient based on the loss function in Eq. (3) and Eq. (6), respectively.
    end for
end for

Let us now consider the outlier $x_B^{(j)} \in B$, at the right end of the coordinate system. If we would mix this data point with $x_C^{(i)} \in C$ to obtain $z_\alpha^{(j)}$, then the reconstruction $\hat{x}_\alpha^{(j)}$ for $\alpha \approx 0.5$ will not necessarily resemble reconstructions of data points of cluster B nor cluster C. This is because the vector $z_\alpha^{(j)}$ would lie in the area where most latent representations are decoded to resemble data points from cluster $D = \{x_D^{(1)}, ..., x_D^{(m)}\}$ (bottom right quadrant in Fig. 1).

Since the mixed reconstruction $\hat{x}_\alpha^{(j)}$ will look like a realistic data point, the discriminator $D_\omega(\hat{x}_\alpha^{(j)})$ will output $\hat{\alpha} = 0$. However, this behaviour would not explicitly enforce linear dependencies between clusters, which is an important characteristic of disentangled representations [4]. Additionally, this also means that the network would not necessarily need to create more disentangled clusters because the described behaviour would not enforce the creation of low density regions between clusters. In the above scenario, the outlier from cluster B does not have any 'incentive' to move towards the cluster centroid but can stay at its position. Instead, we would like the data point to move towards the centroid position to enforce lower density regions between clusters.

To create this incentive of lower density regions between clusters, we introduce a mixing consistency loss to the overall autoencoder loss (Eq. 6) which enforces that all mixed reconstructions look like coming from the respective data points that were used for the interpolation. Hence, in the example of mixing $x_B^{(j)}$ and $x_C^{(i)}$, where $\hat{x}_\alpha^{(j)}$ would resemble $\{x_D^{(1)}, ..., x_D^{(m)}\} \in D$, the overall autoencoder loss would increase as we add the mixing consistency loss (Eq. 5).

Since every position in the coordinate system can only store a single representation (i.e. the vector z_α of mixed latent representations in the coordinate system can only be decoded deterministically as a data point coming from one of the clusters B, C, or D),

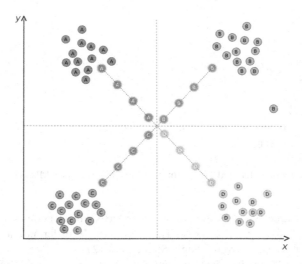

Fig. 1. Illustration of linear interpolations and low-density regions between four clusters.

there will be a conflict of assigning different representations to the same position. As the data point locations are learned through training, it is expected that the pressure to decode consistent representations at positions of mixed latent representations causes the outlier from cluster B to move towards the centroid position of cluster B. Eventually, this would lead to more disentangled clusters and lower-density regions between the clusters as illustrated in Fig. 2.

4   Experiments

In this section, we demonstrate the effectiveness and validation of the proposed method on three benchmark datasets. We provide quantitative results by comparing MCDC against the following models: a convolutional VAE model to see if the MCDC framework can be combined with generative models, the IDEC model to find out if the MCDC framework can further improve on clustering-specific autoencoder models, and the ACAI framework to investigate if the added mixing consistency loss improves clustering performance. The first two models were trained twice, with and without the MCDC framework, and all models are based on the same autoencoder architecture. The code is available at www.github.com/MCDC-autoencoder/MCDC.

4.1   Datasets

The following datasets were used in the experiments:

- **MNIST**: The "Modified National Institute of Standards and Technology" (MNIST) dataset consists of 70,000 greyscale, handwritten digits representing 10 classes [17]. To keep the same input dimensions for all datasets, the original images of size 28×28 pixels were resized to 32×32 pixels using bilinear interpolation.

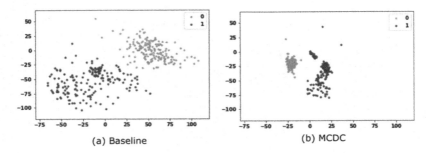

Fig. 2. The models' learned data point positions in a two-class MNIST example.

- **SVHN**: The "Street View House Numbers" (SVHN) dataset consists of 99,289 colored images of size 32 × 32 pixels. They represent 10 different classes and depict house numbers cropped from Google Street View [21].
- **CIFAR10**: The "Canadian Institute For Advanced Research" (CIFAR) developed two datasets of different sizes. For the present paper, we used the CIFAR-10 dataset consisting of 60,000 colored images of 32 × 32 pixels and 10 classes representing various objects including frogs, planes, and cars [15].

4.2   Experimental Setup

General Autoencoder Architecture The overall structure of the encoder includes blocks of two consecutive 3 × 3 convolutional layers where the number of channels is doubled between the first and second layer of a given block. All convolutions are zero-padded to keep equal input and output shapes. Also, every block, except the last one, is followed by 2 × 2 average pooling. The final layer is used as the latent representation and therefore does not use an activation function while all previous layers use a leaky ReLU nonlinearity [19] with a negative slope of $a = 0.2$. The above-described blocks are repeated 3 times, resulting in a latent dimensionality of 256.

The decoder is created symmetrically to the encoder with respect to layer architecture, however, the average pooling function is substituted by 2 × 2 nearest neighbour upsampling [23]. All parameters are initialized as zero-mean Gaussian random variables with the standard deviation:

$$std = \sqrt{2/((1 + a^2) * \text{fan\_in})} \tag{8}$$

where a is the negative slope of the rectifier and fan_in represents the number of incoming neurons from the previous layer. All models are trained with a batch size of 64 and parameters are optimized using Adam [13] with a learning rate of 0.0001 and default values for β_1, β_2, and ϵ. Across all datasets, every model is trained for 400 epochs (Table 1).

Baseline Autoencoder (AE). The baseline AE is the simplest model and is used as a baseline that other models are compared against. The encoder and decoder use the layer

Table 1. Overview of the different autoencoder models

Model	AE Loss	Clustering loss
ACAI	MSE	–
MCDC	MSE	–
IDEC	MSE	KLD on SCA
MCDC+IDEC	MSE	KLD on SCA
VAE	ELBO	–
MCDC+VAE	ELBO	–

Notes. SCA = Soft Cluster Assignment

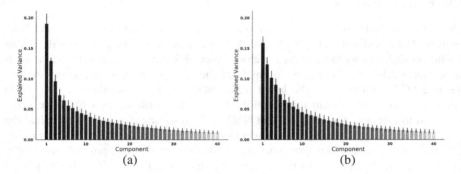

(a)   (b)

Fig. 3. PCA across classes. The left panel (a) shows the PCA for the baseline model and the right panel (b) depicts the principal components for the MCDC model.

architecture and training procedure described above. In our experiments, the network tries to minimize the mean-squared error loss between the input x and reconstruction $\hat{x}$.

Improved Deep Embedded Clustering (IDEC). The IDEC architecture [10] and pre-training procedure are based on the baseline AE. During the fine-tuning phase an additional clustering loss is added to the overall loss of the autoencoder. This clustering loss, called "cluster assignment hardening loss", consists of the KL-divergence loss of the soft cluster assignments [10].

Variational Autoencoder (VAE). The VAE [14] imposes a probabilistic prior distribution $p(z)$ and it trains an encoder $f_\phi(x)$ to approximate the posterior distribution $p(z|x)$ while the decoder $g_\theta(z)$ learns to reconstruct x by parametrizing the likelihood $p(x|z)$. It is trained using a KL-divergence (KLD) loss and the "reparametrization trick" that replaces $z \sim \mathcal{N}(\mu, \sigma I)$ with $\epsilon \sim \mathcal{N}(0, I)$ and $z = \mu + \sigma * \epsilon$ where $\mu, \sigma \in \mathbf{R}^{d_z}$ are the predicted mean and standard deviation produced by $f_\phi(x)$.

Adversarially Constrained Interpolation (ACAI). The ACAI model consists of two networks: the first network is a baseline autoencoder as described above. The second network is a critic that has the same layers as the baseline encoder. It receives real and interpolated reconstructions and tries to predict the α value used for the interpolated reconstructions. The last layer of the critic is flattened and the mean value is taken as the scalar prediction value.

MCDC + IDEC and MCDC+VAE. To address the question if the MCDC method can be combined with generative-, and clustering-specific autoencoder models, the IDEC and VAE were also trained with the MCDC framework, resulting in the MCDC+IDEC and MCDC+VAE models.

4.3 Evaluation Metrics

Clustering methods are commonly evaluated by clustering accuracy (ACC) and Normalized Mutal Information (NMI) [10,20]. We used the K-means algorithm with Euclidean distance as the distance metric. Since this algorithm is sensitive to each dimension's relative variance, we normalized the variance prior to clustering by performing PCA whitening on the latent representations. The algorithm was run 1000 times with different random initializations and the run with the best objective value was used to calculate the accuracy and NMI of the resulting clusters. To calculate the clustering accuracy, a dataset's labels were used, as they were not used in the training process. The accuracy corresponds to the optimal one-to-one mapping of cluster IDs to classes as determined by the Hungarian algorithm [16]. This results in the following equation:

$$ACC = \max_{m} \frac{\sum_{i=1}^{n} 1(y_i = m(c_i))}{n} \tag{9}$$

where c_i is the model's cluster assignment, m is a mapping function that covers all possible one-to-one mappings between assignments and labels, and y_i is the label.

The second metric used in the cluster evaluation is *Normalized Mutual Information (NMI)* [7] which is a way of calculating cluster purity. The NMI calculates the mutual information score $I(Y, C)$ and then normalizes it by the amount of entropy H to account for the total number of clusters. This results in the overall function:

$$NMI(Y, C) = \frac{I(Y, C)}{\frac{1}{2}[H(Y) + H(C)]} \tag{10}$$

where Y represents the class labels and C represents the cluster labels.

5   Results

The results section is structured as follows: we start by quantifying the intuition we presented in Sect. 3 of how adding the mixing consistency loss in MCDC affects the shape and structure of learned latent representations. Then, we show the latent embeddings learned by the models and how they performed on clustering the various datasets.

Table 2. Average clustering accuracy as measured by ACC and NMI (higher is better).

Model	MNIST	SVHN	CIFAR-10
ACAI	90.08/88.60	22.00/15.17	20.30/09.29
MCDC	96.39/92.39	**35.00/43.28**	**25.99/16.41**
IDEC	66.03/72.77	17.97/05.65	21.75 / 09.74
MCDC+IDEC	**97.61/93.80**	18.36/09.74	22.17/10.73
VAE	82.44/88.68	11.64/00.47	20.86 / 10.61
MCDC+VAE	84.95 / 89.63	15.24/01.47	20.85/09.81

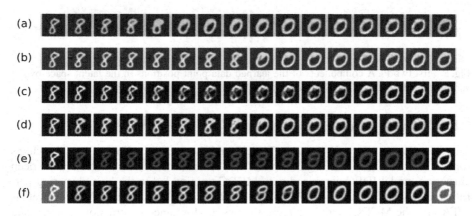

Fig. 4. Interpolations on the MNIST dataset. The panels (a)–(f) show interpolations of the various autoencoders as follows: (a) ACAI, (b) MCDC, (c) IDEC, (d) MCDC+IDEC, (e) VAE, (f) MCDC+VAE.

5.1   Learned Latent Representations

To investigate if the earlier presented intuition can be confirmed in high-dimensional latent spaces, we quantified the shape of the learned embeddings through Principal Component Analysis (PCA). To do this, we trained a baseline autoencoder as well as MCDC on the MNIST dataset. Then, we sub-selected all data points of a given class and encoded the images to receive latent vectors for all images of that class. Subsequently, we performed a PCA on these latent vectors with a self-selected cutoff of 40 in order to obtain the most relevant principal components. After doing this for every class, the components of all classes were normalized and averaged.

The result of this procedure is shown in Fig. 3. In the left panel, the principal components of the baseline model are presented, while the results for the MCDC model are illustrated in the right panel. The first component of the MCDC model explains a visibly smaller amount of variance compared to the first component of the baseline model. Additionally, The differences between the individual components for the MCDC model are in general smaller than for the baseline model. This difference is in line with the intuition outlined in Sect. 3 and we will discuss this finding and its implications about the clusters' shapes in Sect. 6.

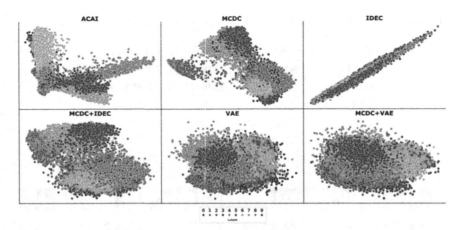

Fig. 5. First two PCA components of the learned data point positions in the latent space by the various models on the MNIST dataset.

5.2 Clustering Performance

The clustering results are shown in Table 2 and the corresponding PCA embeddings for MNIST are depicted in Fig. 5. On the MNIST dataset, the combination of the deep clustering model IDEC combined with MCDC training led to the best clustering performance with an accuracy of 97.61% and an NMI of 93.80%. On the SVHN as well as CIFAR10, the MCDC model achieved the best performance in terms of accuracy and NMI. Across all datasets, the MCDC model performed better than the ACAI model, suggesting that the mixing consistency loss (Eq. 6) indeed improves clustering performance. Additionally, the models that were trained without and with MCDC (i.e. IDEC and VAE) improved in clustering performance when the MCDC training method was added. This empirical result is present across all datasets, suggesting that adding MCDC to an existing autoencoder model further improves its clustering performance.

6 Discussion

As mentioned in Sect. 5.1, the PCA of the MCDC model is characterized by a smaller contribution of the first component and overall smaller differences between the individual components compared to the baseline model. This suggests that the learned data points of each class need more dimensions to be explained well, which can be interpreted as a more spherical shape. This interpretation is supported by the PCA visualization in Fig. 5. The top right panel of the figure shows the learned positions of the embeddings of the MCDC model projected onto the first two principal components. It becomes apparent that the learned embeddings of the classes appear less elongated as opposed to other models like IDEC and ACAI.

The interpolation and clustering results further support these interpretations. The interpolations in Fig. 4 illustrate that MCDC based models, especially MCDC and MCDC + IDEC, decode latent representations to look like the first input image for

$\alpha \geq 0.5$ while they look like the second input image for $\alpha < 0.5$. This result confirms the effect of the mixing consistency loss as illustrated on the toy dataset in Sect. 3. Finally, the clustering results suggest that the more spherical shape learned by MCDC may make it easier for the k-Means algorithm to correctly group the data points.

While MCDC improved clustering performance across different models and datasets in our experiments, some questions remain unanswered. For example, we used datasets containing several balanced classes from which we uniformly sampled data points for interpolations. Future research is needed to investigate whether the results obtained in the experiments generalize to datasets with class imbalances or very few classes (e.g. two classes). In these two scenarios, randomly sampling data points for interpolations may lead to substantially more interpolations of the majority classes or, in the case of very few classes, within-class interpolations. Furthermore, recent work in geometric deep learning suggests that the latent representations may lie on a curved manifold [2] and, consequently, Euclidean distance may not be the most appropriate distance measure. Instead, it was proposed to calculate the curvature of the manifold and use the geodesic distance as a distance metric. Doing this, deep clustering performance have been reported to significantly increase [27,33]. Since the aim of the paper was to introduce MCDC and show its positive impact on adding it to existing methods, combining MCDC with geodesic distance measures was beyond the scope of this paper. Hence, a potential line of research for future work would be to investigate how the MCDC method performs when evaluating the clustering performance using geodesic distance.

7 Conclusion

In the present paper, we proposed Mixing Consistent Deep Clustering (MCDC) and applied it to various clustering (non-)specific autoencoder models. We investigated how interpolation and adversarial training influences the learned positions of latent representations in a model's latent space and, eventually, clustering performance. We measured the models' clustering abilities and found that adding MCDC to a model systematically changed the structure of learned representations of a model, leading to systematic increases in clustering accuracy.

Since the improvement in clustering seems to be robust across autoencoder models, existing autoencoder models can further improve in performance by adding this training method to their training pipeline. In practice, this could lead to better customer segmentation, resulting in individual recommendations based on a person's shopping behaviour. It could also improve the detection of credit card fraud since an anomaly could appear more strongly as an outlier among the normal groups of customer's behaviour. All in all, adding the MCDC training method to existing deep clustering models could yield a great benefit for people's lives and businesses.

References

1. Arthur, D., Vassilvitskii, S.: K-means++: the advantages of careful seeding. In: Proceedings of the Eighteenth Annual ACM-SIAM Symposium on Discrete Algorithms, pp. 1027–1035. Society for Industrial and Applied Mathematics (2007)

2. Arvanitidis, G., Hansen, L.K., Hauberg, S.: Latent space oddity: on the curvature of deep generative models. In: International Conference on Learning Representations (ICLR) (2018)
3. Beckham, C., et al.: On adversarial mixup resynthesis. In: Advances in Neural Information Processing Systems, pp. 4346–4357 (2019)
4. Bengio, Y., Courville, A., Vincent, P.: Representation learning: a review and new perspectives. IEEE Trans. Pattern Anal. Mach. Intell. **35**(8), 1798–1828 (2013)
5. Berthelot, D., Carlini, N., Goodfellow, I., Papernot, N., Oliver, A., Raffel, C.A.: Mixmatch: a holistic approach to semi-supervised learning. In: Advances in Neural Information Processing Systems, pp. 5050–5060 (2019)
6. Berthelot, D., Raffel, C., Roy, A., Goodfellow, I.: Understanding and improving interpolation in autoencoders via an adversarial regularizer. In: International Conference on Learning Representations (ICLR) (2019)
7. Estévez, P.A., Tesmer, M., Perez, C.A., Zurada, J.M.: Normalized mutual information feature selection. IEEE Trans. Neural Networks **20**(2), 189–201 (2009)
8. Goodfellow, I., et al.: Generative adversarial nets. In: Advances in Neural Information Processing Systems, pp. 2672–2680 (2014)
9. Guo, H., Mao, Y., Zhang, R.: Mixup as locally linear out-of-manifold regularization. In: Proceedings of the AAAI Conference on Artificial Intelligence, vol. 33, pp. 3714–3722 (2019)
10. Guo, X., Gao, L., Liu, X., Yin, J.: Improved deep embedded clustering with local structure preservation. In: International Joint Conference on Artificial Intelligence (IJCAI-17), pp. 1753–1759 (2017)
11. Hinton, G.E., Salakhutdinov, R.R.: Reducing the dimensionality of data with neural networks. Science **313**(5786), 504–507 (2006)
12. Jiang, Z., Zheng, Y., Tan, H., Tang, B., Zhou, H.: Variational deep embedding: an unsupervised and generative approach to clustering, pp. 1965–1972, August 2017. https://doi.org/10.24963/ijcai.2017/273
13. Kingma, D.P., Ba, J.: Adam: a method for stochastic optimization. In: International Conference on Learning Representations, pp. 1965–1978, May 2015
14. Kingma, D.P., Welling, M.: Adam: a method for stochastic optimization. In: Conference Proceedings: Papers Accepted to the International Conference on Learning Representations (ICLR) (2014)
15. Krizhevsky, A., Hinton, G.: Learning multiple layers of features from tiny images. Technical Report 4, University of Toronto (2009)
16. Kuhn, H.W.: The Hungarian method for the assignment problem. Naval Res. Logistics (NRL) **52**(1), 7–21 (2005)
17. LeCun, Y.: The mnist database of handwritten digits. http://yann.lecun.com/exdb/mnist/ (1998)
18. LeCun, Y., Bengio, Y., Hinton, G.: Deep learning. Nature **521**(7553), 436 (2015)
19. Maas, A.L., Hannun, A.Y., Ng, A.Y.: Rectifier nonlinearities improve neural network acoustic models. In: Proceedings of ICML, p. 3. no. 1 (2013)
20. Min, E., Guo, X., Liu, Q., Zhang, G., Cui, J., Long, J.: A survey of clustering with deep learning: from the perspective of network architecture. IEEE Access **6**, 39501–39514 (2018)
21. Netzer, Y., Wang, T., Coates, A., Bissacco, A., Wu, B., Ng, A.Y.: Reading digits in natural images with unsupervised feature learning (2011)
22. Ng, A.Y., Jordan, M.I., Weiss, Y.: On spectral clustering: analysis and an algorithm. In: Advances in Neural Information Processing Systems, pp. 849–856 (2002)
23. Odena, A., Dumoulin, V., Olah, C.: Deconvolution and checkerboard artifacts. Distill **1**(10), e3 (2016)
24. Paparrizos, J., Gravano, L.: k-shape: efficient and accurate clustering of time series. In: Proceedings of the 2015 ACM SIGMOD International Conference on Management of Data, pp. 1855–1870. ACM (2015)

25. Rokach, L., Maimon, O.: Clustering methods. In: Maimon, O., Rokach, L. (eds.) Data Mining and Knowledge Discovery Handbook, pp. 321–352. Springer, Boston (2005). https://doi.org/10.1007/0-387-25465-X_15

26. Schmidhuber, J.: Deep learning in neural networks: an overview. Neural Netw. **61**, 85–117 (2015)

27. Shukla, A., Uppal, S., Bhagat, S., Anand, S., Turaga, P.: Geometry of deep generative models for disentangled representations. arXiv preprint arXiv:1902.06964 (2019)

28. Van Den Oord, A., Vinyals, O., et al.: Neural discrete representation learning. In: Advances in Neural Information Processing Systems, pp. 6306–6315 (2017)

29. Verma, V., Lamb, A., Beckham, C., Courville, A., Mitliagkis, I., Bengio, Y.: Manifold mixup: encouraging meaningful on-manifold interpolation as a regularizer. arXiv preprint arXiv:1806.05236 (2018)

30. Verma, V., Lamb, A., Kannala, J., Bengio, Y., Lopez-Paz, D.: Interpolation consistency training for semi-supervised learning. arXiv preprint arXiv:1903.03825 (2019)

31. Wang, D., Cui, P., Zhu, W.: Structural deep network embedding. In: Proceedings of the 22nd ACM SIGKDD International Conference on Knowledge Discovery and Data Mining, pp. 1225–1234 (2016)

32. Wold, S., Esbensen, K., Geladi, P.: Principal component analysis. Chemom. Intell. Lab. Syst. **2**(1–3), 37–52 (1987)

33. Yang, T., Arvanitidis, G., Fu, D., Li, X., Hauberg, S.: Geodesic clustering in deep generative models. arXiv preprint arXiv:1809.04747 (2018)

Utilizing Predictive Models to Identify the Influence of Full Prior Distribution in Hypothesis Testing Problems

Yuval Ben-David and Gail Gilboa-Freedman[(⊠)]

The Inter Disciplinary Center, Herzliya, Israel
gail.gilboa@idc.ac.il

Abstract. We consider a context where (a) statistician publishes results of his study for a hypothesis testing problem, and (b) an observer with a full prior distribution reads the results. The observer may agree or disagree with the results, based on his prior. We provide a framework for classifying possible situations with a similar tendency to demonstrate agreement or contradiction. The framework includes two steps, running computations for many combinations of parameters, and then training a machine learning model to automatically classify the simulations by their behavior.

1 Introduction

In which situations the Bayesian and frequentist approaches give different conclusions? This situation is referred to as Lindley's Paradox [3] and it is interesting in our eyes to explore this paradox in the context of Bayesian observer with a full prior distribution. Bayesians believe that it is usually meaningful to consider the probability of a hypothesis [4]. However, there is often uncertainty regarding this probability [6]. In this work, the observer holds a full prior distribution, rather than a single prior value.

Example: Skeptical Reading of Statistics Results. We exemplify our approach in relation to a burning question arising from the COVID-19 crisis: what is the proportion of people that have been exposed to the virus? Consider a researcher that aims to answer this question for a specific population (e.g. people in a specific region, or a group of kids in a specific school). The researcher follows the common significance testing approach. She raises a hypothesis regarding the proportion of people in the population that have been exposed to the virus and then tests the hypotheses by an experiment. The experiment is an antibody seroprevalence study that samples people from the population and uses serological tests to identify the proportion of people with COVID-19 antibodies in their blood. Assume that the researcher rejects the hypothesis with high significance publishes the results in a scientific paper. Should a reader accept the result? The answer depends on the distribution of his prior.

The current analysis proposes two steps method. The first step involves running simulations for many situations (combinations of values for the prior distribution parameters,

© Springer Nature Switzerland AG 2022
G. Nicosia et al. (Eds.): LOD 2021, LNCS 13163, pp. 138–143, 2022.
https://doi.org/10.1007/978-3-030-95467-3_11

and experiment results). In the second step, the results of the first step are used for training a machine-learning model (decision tree [12, 13]). We design the algorithm to be informative with respect to a target variable: the existence of Lindley's paradox. The algorithm generates a decision tree model that predicts the value of the target based on the input variables (combinations of values of the situation).

2 Methods

We consider a variety of experiments; each is a series of independent identical Binary lotteries. We also consider a variety of hypotheses regarding the probability of success, and a variety of possible prior distributions. A combination of all the parameters just described represents a situation where we explore the following: Will an observer who holds a given prior distribution agree or disagree with the statistician's decision regarding the hypothesis on the probability of success? We label each situation with *agreement/contradiction* and then use the labeled dataset to train a decision-tree algorithm for generating a descriptive model [12, 13].

We define an experiment with a series of N independent Binary lotteries, considering two perspectives: that of an observer raises a hypothesis regarding the probability of success, desires significance p_{value}, and holds full prior distribution, specifically Kumaraswamy distribution (see below) with parameters A, B, being particularly useful to describe many natural phenomena [9, 11]; and that of a statistician who raises hypothesis in association with a fixed value.

The statistician may raise a both-side, a left-hand-side, or a right-hand-side hypothesis. Our study considered all three types of hypotheses, but in this short paper, we only cover the latter as all three reached similar results and as the practical implications of the results covered here are representative of all three hypotheses types. The right-hand side hypothesis assumes that the probability value that is estimated by the experiment is not greater than a fixed value. This value is uniquely defined by its deviation from the mean of the prior distribution, normalized by the std of the distribution. The normalized deviation is denoted as a *gap*.

For recreation purposes, the experiments generated, and the python code can be found on Mendeley [7].

Simulations
We run computational simulations for a variety of parameter combinations.

We fix $N = 100$ *and* $p\_value = 0.05$, parameters that are common in many articles.

We consider the following range for (both) A, B: 0.5–8 (steps of 0.5).

We consider the following range for *gap*:

[0, 0.01, 0.1, 0.25, 0.5, 0.75, 1.0, 1.5, 2.0, −0.01, −0.1, −0.25, −0.5, −0.75, −1.0, −1.5, −2.0]

Kumaraswamy Distribution
The Kumaraswamy double bounded distribution is a family of continuous probability distributions with 2 parameters defined on the interval (0,1). It is similar to the Beta distribution but has advantages in terms of tractability and is simpler to use in simulation-based studies due to the simple closed-form of both its PDF and CDF [9, 10]. This

distribution was originally proposed by Poondi Kumaraswamy for variables that are lower and upper bounded. It has particularly straightforward distribution and quantile functions which do not depend on any special functions [1, 2]. Another reason we chose the Kumaraswamy distribution is that its parameters can be relatively easy to estimate [8, 11].

The Kumaraswamy probability density function (PDF) and cumulative distribution function (CDF) are (Fig. 1):

$$PDF(x) = ABx^{A-1}\left(1 - x^A\right)^{B-1},$$

$$CDF(x) = 1 - \left(1 - x^A\right)^B,$$

where $x \in (0, 1); A > 0, B > 0$.

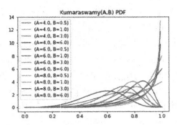

Fig. 1. Kumaraswamy probability density functions (PDFs) of various values of A, B

The Probability that the Bayesian Observer Accepts the Hypothesis

We compute the probability that an observer who holds prior distribution accepts hypothesis H_0, given that the result is at the right tail of the gaussian (the tail is defined by p_{value}). Let's consider two events:

$$Q = \text{experiment result is at the right tail of the gaussian}$$
$$H = H_0 \text{ holds}$$

We aim to compute $P(H|Q) = \frac{P(Q|H)*P(H)}{P(Q)}$.

Each term on the right-hand side of the last equation is computed as follows:

$P(Q|H)$: we define a Gaussian by the mean value p and $std = \sqrt{(\frac{p(1-p)}{N})}$, and compute the complementary probability of the CDF of this gaussian in the value Q.

$P(H)$: computed using N bins and the CDF of the prior:

$$P(H) = CDF\left(\min\left\{p + \frac{1}{2N}, 1\right\}\right) - CDF\left(\max\left\{p - \frac{1}{2N}, 0\right\}\right)$$

$P(Q)$: computed using the complete probability formula, considering N values of $p \in [0, 1]$:

$$P(Q) = \sum_{i=0}^{N-1} P(p_i) * P(Q|p_i)$$

$$where : p_i = \frac{1}{2N} + \frac{i}{N}$$

Decision Trees

The features used for the learning process are $[A, B, gap]$, as those are the features that are not fixed in the simulations. We generate a decision tree [5] that identifies the features of the samples resulting in "contradiction".

The tree can be of use for the reader of the paper in Example 1: first, the reader shall characterize the prior distribution known to him with appropriate values of $Kum(A, B)$. Next, he can follow the tree path to identify, whether the tree predicts that the researcher's conclusion is not valid under the prior.

3   Results

The machine learning process results in a set of rules organized in the hierarchical structure of a decision tree (see Fig. 2). For each leaf (a node with no arrow coming out of it), the tree specifies:

- The Gini index [5]: a measure of impurity, or a criterion to minimize the probability of misclassification. This is a technical detail used by the algorithm itself;
- Samples: the number of epidemic model simulations that are sorted into this leaf;
- A value: a distribution of the samples in terms of how many fall into each class [agreement, contradiction];
- A class: the prediction assigned to this node based on the majority of the sample. For each internal node (not a leaf), the graph also specifies
- A splitting criterion: a logical term that is either True or False.

Observations. We created decision trees [Fig. 2] to identify the cases where we expect a contradiction between the conclusions when taking or not taking into consideration the distribution of the prior. Our first observation, in this case, was that the first split is according to **gap** value, immediately isolating 90.3% of the samples. Also, notice that splitting according to B values was not considered relevant. In addition, notice the node that is labeled with "contradiction". The splits that lead to this node are $gap > 1.25$ *and* $A > 3.75$. This node consists of 172 samples and includes all possible values of B. We also noticed that the distribution of values of A was uniform among those samples, receiving all the values possible ≥ 4.

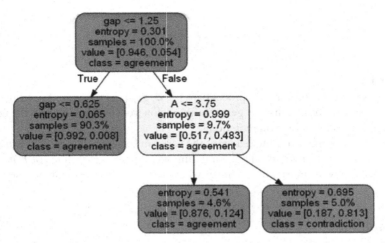

Fig. 2. Machine learning model: Predicting a contradiction in statisticians conclusions

4 Summary

The present research develops a general technique for analyzing the influence of holding full prior distribution when reading the results of someone's statistical research. We consider a huge space of situations (in terms of prior distribution parameters and experimental results) to produce a dataset with the properties of those situations. Then, we use this dataset to train a machine-learning algorithm that identifies classes of situations - whether they induce agreement or contradiction between the Bayesian and the Frequentists.

References

1. Kumaraswamy, P.: A generalized probability density function for double-bounded random processes. J. Hydrol. **46**(1–2), 79–88 (1980)
2. Jones, M.C.: Kumaraswamy's distribution: A beta-type distribution with some tractability advantages. Stat. Methodol. **6**(1), 70–81 (2009)
3. Lindley, D.V.: A statistical paradox. Biometrika **44**(1/2), 187–192 (1957). https://doi.org/10.2307/2333251
4. Good, I.J.: 46656 varieties of Bayesians. Am. Stat. 25(5), 62 (1971)
5. Tangirala, S.: Evaluating the impact of GINI index and information gain on classification using decision tree classifier algorithm. Int. J. Adv. Comput. Sci. Appl. **11**(2), 612–619 (2020)
6. Felix, W.L. Evidence on alternative means of assessing prior probability distributions for audit decision making. Account. Rev. **51**(4), 800–807 (1976). http://www.jstor.org/stable/246127. Accessed 8 July 2021
7. Ben-David, Y., Gilboa-Freedman, G.: Utilizing predictive models to identify the influence of full prior distribution in hypothesis testing problems - Simulation Data. Mendeley Data, V1 (2021). https://doi.org/10.17632/m4dptw3yg7.1
8. Dey, S., Mazucheli, J., Nadarajah, S.: Kumaraswamy distribution: different methods of estimation. Comput. Appl. Math. **37**(2), 2094–2111 (2017). https://doi.org/10.1007/s40314-017-0441-1

9. Bing, X.W., Xiu, K.W., Keming, Y.: Inference on the Kumaraswamy distribution. Commun. Stat. Theory Methods **46**(5), 2079–2090 (2017). https://doi.org/10.1080/03610926.2015.1032425

10. Pablo, A.M.: New Properties of the Kumaraswamy Distribution. Commun. Stat. Theory Methods **42**(5), 741–755 (2013). https://doi.org/10.1080/03610926.2011.581782

11. De Pascoa, M.A.R., Edwin, M.M.O., Gauss, M.C.: The Kumaraswamy generalized gamma distribution with application in survival analysis. Stat. Methodol. **8**(5), 411–433 (2011)

12. Vaibhav, B., Ramesh, C.P., Pankaj, N., Sandeep, K., Vijander, S., Linesh, R., Pranav, D.: Descriptive analysis of COVID-19 patients in the context of India. J. Interdisc. Math. **24**(3), 489–504 (2021). https://doi.org/10.1080/09720502.2020.1761635

13. Lai, K.X., Phung, B.T., Blackburn, T.R.: Descriptive data mining of partial discharge using decision tree with genetic algorithm. Aust. J. Electr. Electron. Eng. **6**(3), 249–259 (2009). https://doi.org/10.1080/1448837X.2009.11464243

Optimally Weighted Ensembles
for Efficient Multi-objective Optimization

Gideon Hanse[(✉)], Roy de Winter, Bas van Stein, and Thomas Bäck

Leiden Institute of Advanced Computer Science, Leiden, The Netherlands
i.j.g.hanse@umail.leidenuniv.nl,
{r.de.winter,b.van.stein,t.h.w.baeck}@liacs.leidenuniv.nl

Abstract. The process of industrial design engineering is often involved
with the simultaneous optimization of multiple expensive objectives. The
surrogate assisted multi-objective S-Metric Selection – Efficient Global
Optimization (SMS-EGO) algorithm is one of the most popular algorithms to solve these kind of problems. We propose an extension of the
SMS-EGO algorithm with optimally weighted, linearly combined ensembles of regression models to improve its objective modelling capabilities.
Multiple (different) surrogates are combined into one optimally weighted
ensemble per objective using a model agnostic uncertainty quantification
method to balance between exploration and exploitation. The performance of the proposed algorithm is evaluated on a diverse set of benchmark problems with a small initial sample and an additional budget of
25 evaluations of the real objective functions. The results show that the
proposed Ensemble-based – S-Metric Selection – Efficient Global Optimization (E-SMS-EGO) algorithm outperforms the state-of-the-art algorithms in terms of efficiency, robustness and spread across the objective
space.

Keywords: Multi-objective optimization · Efficient global
optimization · Surrogate models · Ensemble models · Uncertainty
quantification · S-metric selection · Industrial design

1 Introduction

The process of industrial design engineering is often involved with the optimization of multiple very costly objective functions [17], which can be formulated as
a Multi-objective Optimization Problem (MOP):

$$\min_{\vec{x}} \vec{f}(\vec{x}) \text{ , where } \vec{f}(\vec{x}) = [f_1(\vec{x}), \dots, f_m(\vec{x})] \tag{1}$$

in which $\vec{f}$ is a collection of m objective functions, where $\vec{x} = [x_1, \dots, x_n]$ is a
solution on n independent variables in the feasible region $\Omega \subseteq \mathbb{R}^n$. In a multi-
objective optimization setting, different objectives are commonly conflicting with
each other, where one objective cannot be improved without deteriorating on
another objective function. Consequently, instead of finding one single solution,
the goal is to find a collection of Pareto-optimal solutions $\mathcal{P}$ [13]:

© Springer Nature Switzerland AG 2022
G. Nicosia et al. (Eds.): LOD 2021, LNCS 13163, pp. 144–156, 2022.
https://doi.org/10.1007/978-3-030-95467-3_12

$$\mathcal{P} := \{\vec{x} \in \Omega \mid \nexists \vec{x}' \in \Omega : \vec{f}(\vec{x}') \preceq \vec{f}(\vec{x})\} \tag{2}$$

where $\preceq$ indicates Pareto-dominance. A solution $\vec{x}$ dominates another solution $\vec{x}'$ if and only if

$$\forall_i (f_i(\vec{x}) \leq f_i(\vec{x}')) \text{ and } \exists f_i(\vec{x}) < f_i(\vec{x}'), \quad i = 1, \ldots, m \tag{3}$$

The set of solutions $\mathcal{P}$ together form a *Pareto-front* in the m-dimensional objective landscape. Objective functions in industrial design are often unknown, requiring an iterative evaluation process of proposed design configurations by running simulations [14, 32] or by building prototypes [19]. Such evaluations are often extremely costly and time-consuming, even though more and more computational power becomes available [17].

To avoid spending an excessive amount of time and resources at design evaluation, a widely used method is to approximate real objective functions using surrogate models [19]. In particular, ensembles of multiple surrogate models have been successfully applied to approximate costly objective functions and they were shown to yield great performance in optimization tasks [19, 30].

Unfortunately, existing techniques for multi-objective optimization often still depend on domain-specific prior knowledge about the given optimization tasks [18]. To eliminate this need for prior understanding of MOP landscapes, we propose the *Ensemble-based S-Metric Selection Efficient Global Optimization* (E-SMS-EGO) algorithm, which combines surrogate models into adaptive ensembles to solve computationally very expensive multi-objective optimization problems in an efficient manner.

2   Related Work

A large body of academic work has already been dedicated to study ensembles of surrogates, as well as multi-objective optimization problems. In the following, we cover the most relevant approaches that lie at the foundation of the proposed algorithm.

2.1   Ensembles of Surrogate Models

Combining the output of multiple surrogate models into an ensemble has repeatedly been shown to be beneficial to optimization processes in both practical applications and artificial test settings. For instance, ensembles of surrogate models have improved the optimization of wind turbine allocation [38], the minimization of car crash impact in car designs [2] and more [19, 36].

Aside from classical ensemble techniques, e.g., Ranking, Bagging and Boosting [19], a well-proven method to generate ensembles is by computing the weighted average of multiple surrogate models [16]. Multiple frameworks to find optimal weights have been proposed so far, for which the performance depends heavily on the nature of the given optimization tasks [19].

When generating such weighted ensembles, weights are mainly assigned based on the contributions of individual models [15]. In general, surrogate models that perform better are given higher weights, and the weights for the worst performing models are reduced to zero. As the weights are based on the individual model performance, the composition of the found ensembles strongly depends on the choice of performance metric [15,34].

In the literature, weighted ensemble methods are roughly divided into two categories: Globally weighted averaging, and locally weighted averaging of models [19].

In globally weighted averaging methods, the complete design space is considered altogether in the calculation of individual model performances, and the outputs of the models are combined using the same weight across the whole input space. As a first attempt at weighted model combination, Goel et al. [16] combined several regression models into ensembles by globally weighting the models based on their performances to approximate expensive objective functions. Since then, the main framework from this study has been improved upon in multiple ways, e.g., improving efficiency by clustering the design space [37], introducing an optimization procedure for finding optimal weights [2], and by using a covariance matrix of prediction errors to efficiently find weights [30,34].

Friese et al. [15] showed that a convex, linearly weighted ensemble with positive weights, in terms of measured error cannot perform worse than its worst performing base model and has a chance to perform better than any of the individual base models due to the convex nature of the weight combination. Moreover, they proposed to perform an evolutionary search over model weights to scale up the number of included base models.

In addition, more sophisticated approaches have been studied to generate ensembles based on local accuracy measures. For example, Acar [1] used the cross-validated prediction variance as a local accuracy measure to indicate individual model performance, while still providing fixed weights over the entire input space. Other approaches also assign model weights differently across the input space [19]. By doing so, ensembles are better capable of capturing local trends in specified regions of the design space [38].

2.2 Efficient Global Optimization

In general, a small number of initial evaluated data points is not sufficient to obtain a good representation of the overall objective landscape. Therefore, new points have to be sampled to increase the predictive accuracy of the surrogate models.

A widely used algorithm for the sequential optimization of expensive black-box functions is the *Efficient Global Optimization* (EGO) algorithm as introduced by Jones et al. [20]. The EGO algorithm heavily exploits the proposed surrogate model by sequentially choosing new candidate points for evaluation. These points are chosen based on the prediction of the model, as well as the uncertainty about the prediction at that point by introducing an *infill-criterion*. By addressing both the prediction as well as the uncertainty, the EGO algorithm autonomously balances between exploration and exploitation of the search space.

2.3   Uncertainty Quantification

In the EGO framework, the uncertainty of point predictions has to be taken into account when predicting objective functions, e.g. in terms of variances, standard deviations, or confidence intervals. In such cases, an infill criterion is used as a combined metric of the predicted value and the uncertainty of the prediction, e.g., *Expected Improvement* [20], *Lower Confidence Bound* [8], and *Probability of Improvement* [33].

Some regression models automatically address the confidence of predictions as they also provide an estimation of the prediction variance [19,22].

However, the majority of regression models is not equipped with such built-in variance estimation properties, which calls for an external *uncertainty quantification* (UQ) measure in order to be adopted to the EGO framework. Van Stein et al. [31] provide a fine UQ measure as such that is independent of surrogate modeling assumptions by addressing the empirical prediction error at a given point, as well as the variability of the k nearest neighbours based on the euclidean distance to these neighbouring points. This allows for combining different surrogate models in the EGO framework.

2.4   Model-Based Multi-objective Optimization

In the multi-objective optimization setting, surrogate models have been used for a wide variety of tasks [3]. For example, Loshchilov et al. [25], Bandara et al. [5] trained surrogate models to distinguish dominated solutions from non-dominated solutions. Additionaly, surrogate models have been used to approximate the increase in hypervolume of new proposed individuals [4]. However, as described earlier, the focus of the present study is to apply surrogate models for the approximation of multiple objective functions. Methods that do so are generally scalarization-based [21,27,39], Pareto-based [9,10,24] or Direct Indicator-based [29,35]. A very well known Direct Indicator-based method is the model-assisted *S*-Metric selection approach by Ponweiser et al. [29], which accurately identifies promising data points by optimizing the amount of added hypervolume. Even though the literature about surrogate ensembles and model-based multi-objective optimization is quite extensive, the question on how to combine the two topics in a knowledgeable manner has, to the best of our knowledge, rarely been addressed so far.

3   E-SMS-EGO

In this paper, we propose the *E-SMS-EGO* algorithm, extending the *SMS-EGO* algorithm [29] with optimally weighted ensembles, combined with uncertainty quantification in order to efficiently solve MOPs.

3.1   Initial Sampling

An initial set of data points is obtained with the Latin Hypercube Sampling (LHS) method [26], which provides an equally distributed sample of data points across the search domain. LHS ensures that the amount of information that the surrogate models can derive from the sample is maximized. The initial data points are evaluated on the objective functions to obtain the corresponding objective values for the initial data set.

3.2   Finding Optimal Ensemble Weights

Subsequently, a well-performing and robust ensemble is generated for every objective function by finding the optimal linear combination of weights per objective function. Currently, ensembles are created by calculating the weighted average of five base models, i.e. a kriging model, radial basis function, decision tree, support vector machine and a multivariate adaptive regression spline. In our experiments, we used these five base models with default parameters as implemented in the scikit-learn Python package [28]. However, as the method is model-agnostic, note that it can be used with varying a number of regression models.

In *E-SMS-EGO*, the optimal weights are found per objective by means of 10-fold cross validation, largely based on the linear combination method proposed by Friese et al. [15]. First, all possible weight combinations are obtained by calculating p possible integer partitions with size k (the amount of base models) out of the integer 10. Dividing these partitions by 10 results in weight matrix W:

$$
W_{p,k} = \begin{pmatrix}
1 & 0 & 0 & \cdots & 0 & 0_{1,k} \\
0.9 & 0.1 & 0 & \cdots & 0 & 0_{2,k} \\
0.8 & 0.1 & 0.1 & \cdots & 0 & 0_{3,k} \\
\vdots & \vdots & \vdots & \ddots & \vdots & \vdots \\
0 & 0 & 0 & \cdots & 0.1 & 0.9_{p-1,k} \\
0_{p,1} & 0_{p,2} & 0_{p,3} & \cdots & 0_{p,k-1} & 1_{p,k}
\end{pmatrix}
$$

where: p: number of possible weight combinations. k: amount of base models.

Out of this collection of possible weight combinations, the optimal weights are found separately for all of the objective functions by executing the following steps according to the 10-fold cross validation procedure:

1. First, the base models are trained on the training partition of the cross-validation fold.
2. Subsequently, the trained models are fitted separately to predict the objective value of the configurations in the test partition, resulting in a prediction matrix of size k times the amount of test points in the fold.
3. Next, an ensemble prediction is determined by calculating the weighted average using every possible weight combination, i.e., the rows in matrix W, as in Eq. 5.
4. Finally, the prediction errors of the ensemble predictions are calculated.

This results in ten MSE scores for all of the possible weight combinations, which are averaged to get the cross-validated MSE score per weight vector. As a result, the combination of weights with the minimal corresponding cross-validated MSE value is selected as optimal weight vector $\vec{w}^*_{obj}$ to create the ensemble for approximating the objective function in question.

3.3   Minimizing Ensemble Predictions

Subsequently, a set of potential solutions is found by optimizing the k-NN Ensemble Prediction (KPV) infill criterion per objective:

$$KPV = EPV(\vec{x}) - \widehat{U}_{k-NN} \tag{4}$$

consisting of the Ensemble Predicted Value (EPV):

$$EPV(\vec{x}) = \sum_{i=0}^{N} \vec{w}_i \cdot \hat{f}_i(\vec{x})^T, \text{with} \tag{5}$$

$\hat{f}_i$: an individual base model.
$\vec{w}_i$: the vector of best weights of the corresponding objective function.
N: the number of objective functions.

and the U_{k-NN} measure for the uncertainty about the prediction as introduced by van Stein et al. [31]:

$$\widehat{U}_{k-NN} = \frac{\sum\limits_{i \in N(\vec{x})} w_i^k \left|EPV(\vec{x}) - y_i\right|}{\sum\limits_{i \in N(\vec{x})} w_i^k} + \frac{\min\limits_{i \in N(\vec{x})} d(\vec{x}_i, \vec{x})}{\max\limits_{\vec{x}_i, \vec{x}_j \in \chi} d(\vec{x}_i, \vec{x})}\hat{\sigma}, \text{with} \tag{6}$$

$$w_i = 1 - \frac{d(\vec{x}_i, \vec{x})}{\sum\limits_{i \in N(\vec{x})} d(\vec{x}_i, \vec{x})}, \hat{\sigma} = \sqrt{\text{Var}\left[\{y_i\}_{i \in N(\vec{x})} \cup \{\hat{f}(\vec{x})\}\right]}.$$

Here, $N(\vec{x})$ holds the indices of k nearest neighbours to $\vec{x}$ and $d(\cdot, \cdot)$ denotes the Euclidean distance metric. $\hat{\sigma}$ denotes the standard deviation of the observations in the neighbourhood with the prediction $\hat{f}(\vec{x})$.

Multiple experiments were conducted to investigate the efficacy of using optimally weighted ensembles in combination with uncertainty quantification, which led to the implementation of the $k - NN$ infill criterion, for which the supplementary material can be found on Github[1].

3.4   *S*-Metric Selection

The minimization process in step 3.3 is repeated multiple times, such that a collection of potential points in the search domain is obtained for all of the objectives

---

[1] https://github.com/Gitdeon/E-SMS-EGO.

in parallel. These points are evaluated on all of the composed ensembles, resulting in multiple predictions which can be used to estimate a Hypervolume score for all potential points. The greatest contributor is then found and selected for evaluation with the S-Metric selection approach as described in Sect. 2.4. After evaluation, the optimal point is included in the collection of evaluated data points, such that it is also used for ensemble generation in subsequent iterations. This ensures improvement of the predictions as more iterations have passed.

4   Experiments and Results

The E-SMS-EGO algorithm is compared to state-of-the-art algorithms in terms of Hypervolume and spread of generated solutions. Source code of the proposed solution and experiments can be found on GitHub[2].

The competing algorithms are *NSGA-II* [10], *MOEA/D* [39] and *C-TAEA* [24], as implemented in the Python Multi-Objective Optimization package [6]. To ensure a fair comparison, we used LHS to obtain the same initial sample for all of the algorithms, with a size of $5 \times n$, with n : number of input variables. As the goal is to acquire a well-spread Pareto-front in as little function evaluations as possible, the iteration budget on top of the initial sample was limited to 25 evaluations. Since the competing algorithms make use of populations instead of a single point per iteration, the population sizes and number of generations were both set to 5, also resulting in a budget of 25 evaluations. The shown results for the different algorithms are averages over ten runs with different initial samples and random seeds, guaranteeing reliability of the results. Apart from these parameters, default settings without any further tuning were used for all of the algorithms, including the proposed method.

In order to compare the algorithms, a diverse collection of multi-objective optimization problems was composed, including some artificially designed two-objective problems and real-world like problems. An overview of the test problems is provided in Table 1, showing input dimension (n), Lower Bounds (LB) and Upper Bounds (UB) of the input variables, number of objectives (m) and hypervolume reference point (ref). Problems are artificially designed (AD) or real-world like (RWL). The testbed was limited to these functions as they were implemented in the pymoo package, thus being compatible with the competing algorithm implementations.

4.1   Results

As becomes clear in Table 2, E-SMS-EGO significantly outperforms NSGA-II, MOEA/D and C-TAEA in terms of the Hypervolume scores of the obtained Pareto-fronts. Also, in most cases, the standard deviation in Hypervolume score is lower for E-SMS-EGO, suggesting that the proposed method is more robust and stable than the competing algorithms. On some functions, e.g. TNK, WB,

---

[2] https://github.com/Gitdeon/E-SMS-EGO.

Table 1. Artificially designed and real world Like multi-objective optimization problems as implemented in the *pymoo* package [6].

Problem	Type	m	n	LB	UB	Ref
BNH [7]	AD	2	2	[0, 0]	[5, 3]	[140, 50]
TNK [12]	AD	2	2	[0, 0]	$[\pi, \pi]$	[2, 2]
CTP1 [11]	AD	2	2	[0, 0]	[1, 1]	[1, 2]
ZDT4 [12]	AD	2	10	$[0, -5, \ldots, -5]^n$	$[1, 5, \ldots, 5]^n$	[1,260]
KSW [23]	AD	2	3	$[-5, -5, -5]$	[5, 5, 5]	[−10, 2]
WB [17]	RWL	2	4	[0.125, 0.1, 0.1, 0.125]	[5, 10, 10, 5]	[350,1]
CSI [9]	RWL	3	7	[0.5, 0.45, 0.5, 0.5, 0.875, 0.4, 0.4]	[1.5, 1.35, 1.5, 1.5, 2.625, 1.2, 1.2]	[42, 4.5, 13]

some of the competing algorithms show very poor results in terms of Hypervolume, with abnormally high standard deviations. In these cases, the algorithms did not succeed to find enough feasible, Pareto-optimal solutions below the reference point, therefore receiving a Hypervolume score of 0 in some of the runs. On some problems, especially MOEA/D seemed to perform poorly with a small evaluation budget. However, E-SMS-EGO did not seem to suffer from this issue and was well able to find a Pareto-front in all of the runs.

Table 2. Mean hypervolume score with respect to the reference point for each test function. The best result per test function is shown in boldface if they were significantly higher according to Welch's t-test with $\alpha : 0.05$.

Problem	Measure	NSGA-II	MOAE/D	C-TAEA	E-SMS-EGO
BNH	HV	4760	4617	4723	**5035**
	Std.	134.4	209.8	157.7	35.85
TNK	HV	1.849	0.000	1.015	**3.926**
	Std.	0.597	0.000	1.134	0.116
CTP1	HV	1.115	1.136	1.103	**1.261**
	Std.	0.088	0.061	0.085	0.016
ZDT4	HV	162.1	116.5	161.0	**176.0**
	Std.	18.90	43.16	17.71	14.62
KSW	HV	41.47	43.04	42.01	**56.09**
	Std.	15.05	19.35	12.97	9.923
WB	HV	32.90	1.217	32.49	33.63
	Std.	1.298	5.969	4.690	1.797
CSI	HV	11.14	10.56	16.67	**19.41**
	Std.	3.205	2.092	1.101	0.260

In addition, Figs. 1 and 2 show the Pareto-frontiers obtained by the four algorithms on five of the test functions. Here, it is observed that E-SMS-EGO in general succeeds to find the best Pareto-fronts compared to the competing algorithms, as the solutions are located more towards the minimal values on all objectives. In addition to finding more Pareto-optimal solutions, the solutions found by E-SMS-EGO are well-spread across the objective space, which is demonstrated nicely, especially for the BNH, CTP1, KSW and CSI problems.

Furthermore, it is shown that, for some problems, only a small number of Pareto-optimal solutions could be found, which is most likely explained by the limited number of allowed function evaluations. Especially for NSGA-II and MOEA/D, which were only allowed small population sizes, this explains why so little Pareto-optimal solutions were found. However, the vast majority of solutions that were found by the competing algorithms are still inferior to the solutions found by E-SMS-EGO, verifying that the proposed method beats the competing algorithms altogether in terms of efficacy in multi-objective optimization.

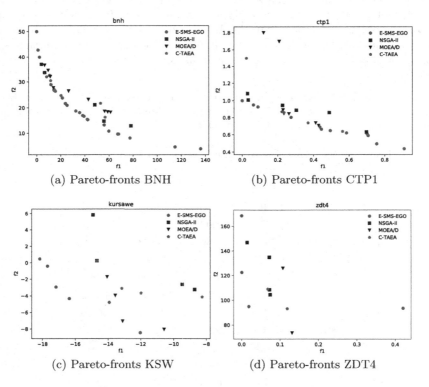

(a) Pareto-fronts BNH   (b) Pareto-fronts CTP1

(c) Pareto-fronts KSW   (d) Pareto-fronts ZDT4

Fig. 1. Pareto frontiers obtained by the four algorithms on four of the test functions.

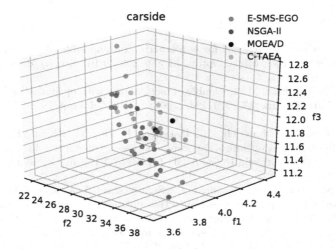

Fig. 2. Pareto frontiers obtained by the four algorithms on the three-objective CSI problem.

5   Conclusions and Future Work

In this paper, the novel Ensemble-based Efficient Global Optimization $S-$Metric Selection (E-SMS-EGO) algorithm is proposed, and has been shown to be successful in finding well-performing, Pareto-optimal solutions to multi-objective optimization problems with a limited evaluation budget. By heavily exploiting already known data points, E-SMS-EGO has been shown to outperform comparable state-of-the art multi-objective optimization algorithms, i.e., NSGA-II, MOEA/D and C-TAEA on a diverse collection of artificially designed and real world like test problems. Multiple experiments were performed with different techniques to compose the proposed algorithm. This resulted in an algorithm that improves upon the SMS-EGO algorithm by using optimally weighted ensembles of regression models as surrogates. By further extending the algorithm with the k-NN variance measure as a method of uncertainty quantification, E-SMS-EGO was able to find minimal solutions that were nicely spread across the objective space, with just a small number of function evaluations. The algorithm can be adapted in several ways which might boost the performance in the future. Local ensemble weighting methods might improve performance, more than five base models could be incorporated into the ensembles and hyper-parameter optimization of the base models can still be performed. Other multi-objective infill criteria can be considered for comparison and finally a constraint handling mechanism could be incorporated to make the algorithm more widely applicable.

References

1. Acar, E.: Various approaches for constructing an ensemble of metamodels using local measures. Struct. Multi. Optim. 42, 879–896 (2010). https://doi.org/10.1007/s00158-010-0520-z

2. Acar, E., Rais-Rohani, M.: Ensemble of metamodels with optimized weight factors. Struct. Multi. Optim. **37**, 279–294 (2008). https://doi.org/10.1007/s00158-008-0230-y

3. Allmendinger, R., Emmerich, M., Hakanen, J., Jin, Y., Rigoni, E.: Surrogate-assisted multicriteria optimization: complexities, prospective solutions, and business case. J. Multi-Criteria Decis. Anal. **24**, 5–24 (2016). https://doi.org/10.1002/mcda.1605

4. Azzouz, N., Bechikh, S., Ben Said, L.: Steady state ibea assisted by MLP neural networks for expensive multi-objective optimization problems. In: Proceedings of the 2014 Annual Conference on Genetic and Evolutionary Computation, GECCO 2014, pp. 581–588. Association for Computing Machinery, New York (2014). https://doi.org/10.1145/2576768.2598271

5. Bandaru, S., Ng, A.H.C., Deb, K.: On the performance of classification algorithms for learning pareto-dominance relations. In: 2014 IEEE Congress on Evolutionary Computation (CEC), pp. 1139–1146 (2014). https://doi.org/10.1109/CEC.2014.6900641

6. Blank, J., Deb, K.: Pymoo: multi-objective optimization in python. IEEE Access **8**, 89497–89509 (2020)

7. Coello, C.A.C., Lamont, G.B., Veldhuizen, D.A.V.: Evolutionary Algorithms for Solving Multi-Objective Problems. Genetic and Evolutionary Computation, Springer, Heidelberg (2006). https://doi.org/10.1007/978-0-387-36797-2

8. Cox, D.D., John, S.: Sdo: a statistical method for global optimization. In: Multidisciplinary Design Optimization: State-of-the-Art, pp. 315–329 (1997)

9. Deb, K., Jain, H.: An evolutionary many-objective optimization algorithm using reference-point-based nondominated sorting approach, part i: solving problems with box constraints. IEEE Trans. Evol. Comput. **18**(4), 577–601 (2014)

10. Deb, K., Pratap, A., Agarwal, S., Meyarivan, T.: A fast and elitist multiobjective genetic algorithm: Nsga-ii. IEEE Trans. Evol. Comput. **6**(2), 182–197 (2002)

11. Deb, K.: Multiobjective Optimization Using Evolutionary Algorithms. Wiley, New York, January 2001

12. Deb, K., Pratap, A., Meyarivan, T.: Constrained test problems for multi-objective evolutionary optimization. vol. 1993, pp. 284–298, March 2001. https://doi.org/10.1007/3-540-44719-9_20

13. Ehrgott, M.: Vilfredo Pareto and multi-objective optimization, pp. 447–453. Documenta mathematica (2012)

14. Fletcher, C.A.J.: Computational Fluid Dynamics: An Introduction. Springer, Heidelberg (1988). https://doi.org/10.1007/978-3-642-97035-1_1

15. Friese, M., Bartz-Beielstein, T., Emmerich, M.: Building ensembles of surrogates by optimal convex combination. In: Bioinspired Optimization Methods and their Applications, pp. 131–143, May 2016

16. Goel, T., Haftka, R., Shyy, W., Queipo, N.: Ensemble of surrogates. Struct. Multi. Optim. **33**, 199–216 (2007). https://doi.org/10.1007/s00158-006-0051-9

17. Gong, W., Cai, Z., Zhu, L.: An efficient multiobjective differential evolution algorithm for engineering design. Struct. Multi. Optim. **38**, 137–157 (2009). https://doi.org/10.1007/s00158-008-0269-9

18. Horn, D., Wagner, T., Biermann, D., Weihs, C., Bischl, B.: Model-based multi-objective optimization: taxonomy, multi-point proposal, toolbox and benchmark. In: Gaspar-Cunha, A., Henggeler Antunes, C., Coello, C.C. (eds.) EMO 2015. LNCS, vol. 9018, pp. 64–78. Springer, Cham (2015). https://doi.org/10.1007/978-3-319-15934-8_5

19. Jiang, P., Zhou, Q., Shao, X.: Surrogate-model-based design and optimization, January 2020. https://doi.org/10.1007/978-981-15-0731-1_7

20. Jones, D., Schonlau, M., Welch, W.: Efficient global optimization of expensive black-box functions. J. Global Optim. **13**, 455–492 (1998). https://doi.org/10.1023/A:1008306431147

21. Knowles, J.: Parego: a hybrid algorithm with on-line landscape approximation for expensive multiobjective optimization problems. IEEE Trans. Evol. Comput. **10**(1), 50–66 (2006)

22. Krige, D.: A statistical approach to some basic mine valuation problems on the witwatersrand. J. South. Afr. Inst. Min. Metall. **52**(9), 201–203 (1952). https://doi.org/10.10520/AJA0038223X_4858

23. Kursawe, F.: A variant of evolution strategies for vector optimization. In: Schwefel, H.-P., Männer, R. (eds.) PPSN 1990. LNCS, vol. 496, pp. 193–197. Springer, Heidelberg (1991). https://doi.org/10.1007/BFb0029752

24. Li, K., Chen, R., Fu, G., Yao, X.: Two-archive evolutionary algorithm for constrained multiobjective optimization. IEEE Trans. Evol. Comput. **23**(2), 303–315 (2019)

25. Loshchilov, I., Schoenauer, M., Sebag, M.: Comparison-based optimizers need comparison-based surrogates. In: Schaefer, R., Cotta, C., Kołodziej, J., Rudolph, G. (eds.) PPSN 2010. LNCS, vol. 6238, pp. 364–373. Springer, Heidelberg (2010). https://doi.org/10.1007/978-3-642-15844-5_37

26. Mckay, M., Beckman, R., Conover, W.: A comparison of three methods for selecting vales of input variables in the analysis of output from a computer code. Technometrics **21**, 239–245 (1979). https://doi.org/10.1080/00401706.1979.10489755

27. Miettinen, K., Mäkelä, M.: On scalarizing functions in multiobjective optimization. OR Spectrum **24**, 193–213 (2002). https://doi.org/10.1007/s00291-001-0092-9

28. Pedregosa, F., et al.: Scikit-learn: machine learning in python. J. Mach. Learn. Res. **12**, 2825–2830 (2011)

29. Ponweiser, W., Wagner, T., Biermann, D., Vincze, M.: Multiobjective optimization on a limited budget of evaluations using model-assisted S-metric selection. In: Rudolph, G., Jansen, T., Beume, N., Lucas, S., Poloni, C. (eds.) PPSN 2008. LNCS, vol. 5199, pp. 784–794. Springer, Heidelberg (2008). https://doi.org/10.1007/978-3-540-87700-4_78

30. Shi, R., Liu, L., Long, T., Liu, J.: An efficient ensemble of radial basis functions method based on quadratic programming. Eng. Optim. **48**(7), 1202–1225 (2016). https://doi.org/10.1080/0305215X.2015.1100470

31. van Stein, B., Wang, H., Kowalczyk, W., Bäck, T.: A novel uncertainty quantification method for efficient global optimization. In: Medina, J., Ojeda-Aciego, M., Verdegay, J.L., Perfilieva, I., Bouchon-Meunier, B., Yager, R.R. (eds.) IPMU 2018. CCIS, vol. 855, pp. 480–491. Springer, Cham (2018). https://doi.org/10.1007/978-3-319-91479-4_40

32. Szabó, B., Babuška, I.: Introduction to Finite Element Analysis: Formulation, Verification and Validation. Wiley Series in Computational Mechanics, Wiley (2011). https://books.google.nl/books?id=bbi7cQAACAAJ

33. Ulmer, H., Streichert, F., Zell, A.: Evolution strategies assisted by gaussian processes with improved preselection criterion. In: The 2003 Congress on Evolutionary Computation, 2003, CEC 2003. vol. 1, pp. 692–699(2003). https://doi.org/10.1109/CEC.2003.1299643
34. Viana, F., Haftka, R., Steffen, Jr, V.: Multiple surrogates: how cross-validation errors can help us to obtain the best predictor. Struct. Multi. Optim. **39**, 439–457 (2009). https://doi.org/10.1007/s00158-008-0338-0
35. Wagner, T.: Planning and Multi-Objective Optimization of Manufacturing Processes by Means of Empirical Surrogate Models. Vulkan Verlag, Essen (2013)
36. Ye, P.: A review on surrogate-based global optimization methods for computationally expensive functions. Softw. Eng. **7**, 68–84 (2019)
37. Ye, P., Pan, G.: Global optimization method using ensemble of metamodels based on fuzzy clustering for design space reduction. Eng. Comput. **33**(3), 573–585 (2016). https://doi.org/10.1007/s00366-016-0490-x
38. Zhang, J., Chowdhury, S., Messac, A.: An adaptive hybrid surrogate model. Struct. Multidiscip. Optim. **46**(2), 223–238 (2012). https://doi.org/10.1007/s00158-012-0764-x
39. Zhang, Q., Liu, W., Tsang, E., Virginas, B.: Expensive multiobjective optimization by moea/d with gaussian process model. IEEE Trans. Evol. Comput. **14**(3), 456–474 (2009)

Anomaly Detection in Smart Grid Network Using FC-Based Blockchain Model and Linear SVM

Saurabh Shukla$^{(\boxtimes)}$ ⓘ, Subhasis Thakur ⓘ, and John G. Breslin ⓘ

National University of Ireland Galway, Galway, Ireland
{saurabh.shukla,subhasis.thakur,john.breslin}@nuigalway.ie

Abstract. Traditional grid network has played a major role in society by distributing and transmitting electric supply to consumers. However, with the advancement in technology in Industry 4.0 has evolved the role of the Smart Grid (SG) network. SG network is a two-way bi-directional communication Cyber-Physical System (CPS). Whereas traditional grid network is a one-way directional physical system. SG is a part of the most revolutionary application of Internet-of-Things (IoT). The information related to power consumption and supplies can be transmitted and recorded in real-time. The connection of SG with the internet has also created a lot of space for different types of anomalies injection and cyber-physical attacks. SG network is open and vulnerable to an outside hacker. The detection of an anomaly in real-time is of utmost importance otherwise it may lead to huge power loss, security, and monetary loss to the consumer, producer, and smart city society. In this paper, we have proposed a private blockchain system model for anomaly detection in SG along with a novel Linear Support Vector Machine Anomaly Detection (LSVMAD) algorithm in a fog computing (FC) environment. Here FC nodes will act as miners to support and make real-time decisions for anomaly detection in an SG network. The anomaly detection accuracy of the LSVMAD algorithm in the FC environment is 89% and in the cloud is 78%. The proposed LSVMAD algorithm easily outperforms the existing techniques and algorithms when compared for anomaly detection accuracy percentage. The simulation tool used in the implementation of works is iFogSim, Anaconda (Python), Geth version 1.9.25, Ganache, Truffle (Compile) and ATOM as a text editor for creating smart contracts.

Keywords: Smart grid · Fog computing · Linear SVM · Internet-of-Things · Smart meter · Cyber-physical system · Machine learning

1 Introduction

Smart Grid (SG) network majorly works on the three components; i.e. physical system, distributed computation, and the communication system [1]. This makes the SG network a complete system for power generation, distribution, transmission, and consumption. SG network is connected with data connectors and smart meters with Home Area Network (HAN), Building Area Network (BAN), and Neighbor Area Network (NAN). SG has

© Springer Nature Switzerland AG 2022
G. Nicosia et al. (Eds.): LOD 2021, LNCS 13163, pp. 157–171, 2022.
https://doi.org/10.1007/978-3-030-95467-3_13

played a major role in smart cities where they were able to provide bi-directional real-time information [2]. The main characteristic of the SG network is to make a clear balance between the generation of power and its consumption over the channel or network. However, the SG network has some major challenges when it comes to avoiding cyber-physical attacks and anomaly detection [3].

The main drawback of the SG network is its open communication channel which makes it's vulnerable for outside attackers to manipulate the electric data consumption, along with an addition of erroneous value in sensor readings, inaccurate electricity bills, and short-circuits in smart meters [4]. All this could be possible by injecting various anomalies during transmission and communication over the SG network [1]. Cyber intruders can further overload and degrade the performance of different sub-station over the SG network. This may lead to continuous consumption of electricity by changing the paraments over the smart meter which is also one of the major neglected issues. The security over the SG network for electric data transmission and consumption is related to three factors or IACC goals; Integrity, Authentication, Availability, and Confidentiality [5]. All these factors are major aspects and concern while working for anomaly detection, classification and avoiding Cyber-Physical System (CPS) attacks.

SG networks work in a distributed open environment; where blockchain can play a major role to secure the electric data from manipulation by outside hackers and attackers [2]. Blockchain operates in a decentralized manner where every transaction is secured using hash functions, encryption techniques, cryptographic operations, and the use of public and private keys. Furthermore, there is a record of every transaction that occurred between various distributed units [6]. On a similar note, fog computing (FC) nodes act as miners close to the edge of SG networks and connect over LAN, BAN, NAN, and WAN [7]. FC is a kind of distributed network where the information is shared between the different nodes at LAN. These FC nodes work at the edge of networks close to the smart grid network and smart meters [8]. The data is processed and filtered for anomalies in FC nodes to make decisions in real-time mode by transmitting the data over a single hop count to consumers and producers. Classification of data and outliers using supervised machine learning techniques such as K-Nearest Neighbors (KNN) and Linear-SVM (Linear-Support Vector Machine) with Principal Component Analysis (PCA) are used to identify the irregular pattern of movement in the data set [9]. These algorithms are used for regression and classification.

In this paper, we have proposed a blockchain-based advanced system model, and a novel Linear Support Vector Machine Anomaly Detection (LSVMAD) algorithm in an FC environment; where FC nodes will act as miners to overcome and identify the different anomalies and malicious data injected by CPS attackers. The proposed system is expected to act promptly to respond to various anomalies occurring in an SG network. Furthermore, the proposed algorithm meets the Quality-of-Service (QoS) requirement for SG network electrical theft and anomaly detection. The main objective of the proposed research work is to detect and classify the anomalies along with malicious data for secure electric data transmission in an SG networks.

2 Background and Related Work

In this section, recent research work has been discussed related to anomaly detection and False Data Injection (FDI) in an SG network. Many of the researchers have highlighted the issue of cyber-physical attacks with the involvement of outside intruders to insert malicious data on the network infrastructure of the SG [10–12]. Some of the works related to the security of communication and computation are mentioned here.

In [5], the authors proposed an advanced novel system model to monitor the anomalies in an SG network promptly. The anomaly detection techniques are facing challenges due to the large transmission of data. Therefore, they further presented a framework to detect electricity consumption anomalies accurately with timely usage of sensor and meter readings. In [13], the authors proposed a framework for anomaly detection. The data is further integrated when collected from smart meters for pattern classification and matching. This classification helps in detecting the values. The system was able to identify and detect one type of anomaly at a time.

In [14], the authors proposed a scheme to detect anomalies in an SG network. They use the unsupervised machine learning technique to identify the irregular pattern in the observed data. The data used for identification was time-series data. The classified data was presented in a hierarchical form. Their proposed approach was based on pattern and cluster-based techniques. Similarly, in [15], the authors proposed a novel approach to identify the anomalies in SG electricity consumption. They used large data sets for training and testing smart meter network data. The proposed scheme has two phases first one is consumption prediction and the second one is anomaly detection. They further used a hybrid Neural Network (NN) approach for the prediction of electricity consumption in a real-time environment. At last, the anomalies are identified by measuring the difference between predicted and real values in consumption.

In [16], the authors proposed a novel approach to cope with external and internal threats. The approach was targeted to detect malicious activities. It was an anomaly detection system to analyze the monitoring data and identify the possible cyber-physical attacks. It was a novel system for ICS/SCADA (Industrial Communication System)/ (Supervisory Control and Data Acquisition) protocols to enable real-time monitoring of power consumption and anomaly detection. In [17], the authors conducted a comprehensive survey analysis of the existing cybersecurity solutions for the SG network with the FC approach. They discussed the role of FC placed at the edges of the network of the smart grid network. Furthermore, they discussed various architectures for SG network and fog-based SCADA systems. The authors classified the security requirements into four major categories i.e., authentication, data privacy, preservation, identification, key management, and intrusion detection solutions. Next, they provide a taxonomy of cyber-physical attacks where they highlight the nine categories of Intruders Detection (ID) and their types of attacks.

In [18], the authors discussed the role of the blockchain model for secure communication on an SG network. A complete in-depth analysis was conducted to elaborate on the benefits of blockchain for SG security solutions. Blockchain worked here in a decentralized manner to secure and close various open entry points of an SG network. In [19], the authors developed and presented a Smart Analyzer tool for security analysis in Advanced Metering Infrastructure (AMI). AMI is a core component in the SG network. The authors mainly focused on the development of the formal model to represent the behaviour of AMI for various types of cyber-attacks. The model works on the device configuration, network topology and interconnected components with LAN, BAN, NAN, and HAN. The system was tested for scalability and reliability on the AMI testbed. The proposed system model and LSVMAD algorithm are designed to detect and identify anomalies along with malicious data for SG networks using blockchain and machine learning (ML) techniques in FC environment. The model further provides a secure communication channel for energy transaction between prosumers and smart meters. Whereas the other state-of-the-art techniques lacks the real-world implementation and development. The existing models and techniques are still in infancy when compares with the proposed novel model and algorithm. Hence, the current algorithms and techniques such as Anomaly Detection Framework (ADF), Cluster-Based Technique (CBT), Hybrid Neural Network (HNN), and Fog-based SCADA (F-SCADA) are not optimized for secure electric data transmission and could not address the above-mentioned issue of anomaly injection and malicious data detection.

3   System Model for Smart Grid

In this section, we discussed the difference between the conventional system model and the proposed advanced system model for the SG. Furthermore, we discussed the advanced system for secure communication in an SG network which enables the identification of anomalies and malicious data during data transmission. See Fig. 1 for the conventional system model.

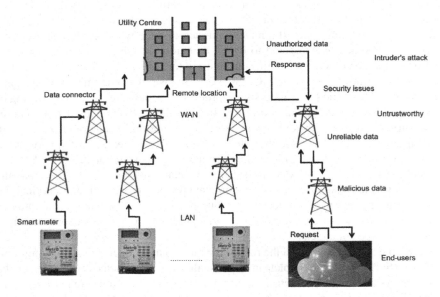

Fig. 1. Conventional system model for data communication flow in the SG network

Figure 1 shows the basic conventional system model for the electric data transmission in the SG network. The model consists of smart meters, data connectors, and a utility centre. All these components in the SG network are connected via LAN and WAN to a remote location. The conventional system model lacks advanced security features such as cryptographic operations and blockchain techniques for secure data transmission. It does not consist of an intelligent system to operate or monitor the electrical data flow status. The conventional model is an open network for outside intruders and CPS attackers to manipulate the smart meter readings and insert false data during electric data transmission. The model lacks the real-time decision-making capability to identify and detect anomalies and malicious data.

See Fig. 2 shows the novel system model for SG network communication, identification of anomalies, and classification of malicious data using fog nodes. Where the classification of outliers is conducted using a supervised machine learning approach. Linear SVM with the 2-PCA technique is used for reducing the number of parameters involve and can easily classify by distinguishing the outliers and similar patterns. In this concept, the fog node serves as a small sub-cloud server with limited storage and processing capabilities. Furthermore, the FC approach is employed in the SG to bring all of the advanced features of the cloud, such as resource sharing and server virtualization, closer to the SG network. As a result, unlike the cloud, the FC has no single point of failure.

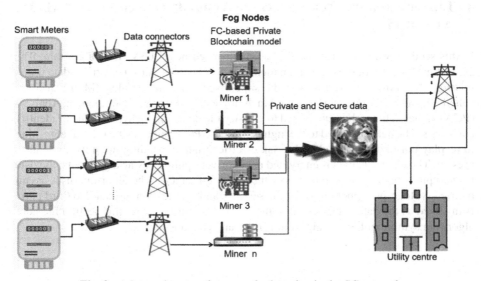

Fig. 2. Advanced system for anomaly detection in the SG network

Figure 2 shows the advanced system model for anomaly and malicious data detection in the SG network. The model consists of smart meters, Wi-Fi routers, data connectors, fog nodes, and a utility centre. The model works in an FC environment where the fog nodes play the role of miners by keeping the data transaction record in the SG network. The novel Linear Support Vector Machine Anomaly Detection (LSVMAD) algorithm works in coordination with fog nodes where the classification of malicious data is conducted inside the fog nodes. FC plays a key role here, utilizing blockchain technology to provide a distributed, scalable network at the smart meter's edge. Distributed FC nodes serve as miners, collecting transaction data in blocks and verifying its correctness. Fog nodes in our proposed work are responsible for handling all possible communication between smart meter devices to provide secure transactions between nodes, devices, and end-users. The proposed advanced system model for the SG network is smart enough to link with a decentralized blockchain model and distributed FC servers placed at the edge of the SG network. Therefore, this decision-making ability makes the advanced SG network an intelligent system when compared with the conventional system model and has an upper hand over it related to the security of the electrical data transmission from outside intruders and cyber-physical attackers. Only the secured encrypted data is transferred to consumers i.e., the smart meter users. The data is further decrypted by the utility office and the trusted authorities by the public-private key arrangement.

4   Linear Support Vector Machine Anomaly Detection (LSVMAD) Algorithm

In this section, we discussed the proposed advanced novel LSVMAD algorithm. The algorithm works to identify the anomalies in an SG network during electrical data transmission. The novel algorithm used the supervised machine learning (ML) algorithm called Linear SVM (Support Vector Machine) with 2-Principal Component Analysis (PCA) values. This technique is used to classify the data along a hyper-plane to identify classifiers. The data classified to the highest varied 2-PCA values using the ML algorithm to display not-under-risk and under-risk electrical data depending upon the anomalies present. The electrical data is encrypted using private-public key arrangements; the data is encrypted and then decrypted as per the user requirement. The algorithm uses asymmetric cryptographic operations for the security and verification of data. No third party is involved as the data is processed in the FC nodes. Furthermore, this section includes algorithm symbol notations, algorithm steps, and pseudocode.

LSVMAD Algorithm Symbol Notations

A_L: The list of electrical data packets having anomalies

A : Anomalies

$ASYM_{EC}$: Asymmetric encryption

C_s: Cloud server

CE_{ds} : The list of classified electrical data

C_T: Ciphertext

C_K : Cipher key

$dist$: distance

D_F : Data format

Db : Decision boundary

$Decryption_{Asym}$: Asymmetric decryption

E_{dp} : Electric data packet

E_{ds} : Electrical data set

E_{dpa}: Electric data packet allocation

$Encrypt_{sym}$: Symmetric encryption

$Encrypt_{Asym}$: Asymmetric encryption

FC_nPUB_K : Public key of the fog node

FC_n: Fog computing node

FC_nPRVT_K : Fog node private key

H_c : Hash code

K_{sym} : Symmetric key

k: Key

L_{SVM} : Linear SVM classifier

M : Miners

MG_w : Marginal width

np: Array for NumPy library package

$PRVT_K$: Private key

PUB_K : Public key

$2 - PCA$: Principal component analysis

Sm_u : Smart meter users

ST_m : Smart Meters

S_mD: Smart meter data

$SPARK$: Real-time analyzer

T_s : Timestamp

U_O : Utility Office

w: Weight vector

X: Input vectors

y: Input vectors

LSVMAD Algorithm Steps

Requirement: FC_n and ST_m devices.

Step 1: Classification of E_{ds} using L_{SVM}

Step 2: Next E_{dpa} at FC_n using private blockchain.

Step 3: FC_n are used to store the E_{dp}

Step 4: A timestamp T_s is attached to the block of E_{dp}

Step 5: ST_m send the E_{dp} to F_n using ledgers and making decisions on A_L

Step 6: FC_n allocates the E_{dp}

Step 7: Applying $2 - PCA$ and predicting the anomalies.

Step 8: Next to perform E_{dpa} and mining at the individual FC_n

Step 9: ST_m sends a key K and E_{dp} to the FC_n

Step 10: Start of encryption process.

Step 11: FC_n verifies the key K

Step 12: Generate the H_C

Step 13 Next, to send the H_C to FC_n acting as miners.

Step 14: Checking of A_L

Step 15: Checking of CE_{ds}

Step 16: FC_n status is checked.

Step 17: Start of decryption process.

Step 18: Verification of ST_m and FC_n

Step 19: Consumers and meter management system can use their own $PRVT_K$ to retrieve the CE_{ds}

LSVMAD Algorithm:

Input: E_{dp} is the electric data packet, K_{sym} Symmetric key, FC_nPRVT_K Fog node private key, S_mD, and E_{ds} Electrical data set.

Output: Decrypted E_{dp} and A_L the list of electrical data packets having anomalies and CE_{ds}.

1: START

2: (FC-based blockchain system is created for anomalies identification)

3: E_{DS} classification using L_{SVM} $2 - PCA$

4: if $(S_m D == A_L)$ then

5: get geo-location and send the data for verification to FC_n using $SPARK$

6: else if $(S_m D == non - A_L)$

7: then

8: $S_m D$ send to FC_n to C_s

9: E_{dp} is allocated to FC_n

10: for each E_{dp} do ($ST_m < - C_T$)

11:   $C_T + T_s < - E_{dp}$

12:   if $FC_n ==$ Available

13:     allocate the E_{dp}

14:       else no allocation

15:   end if

16: end

17: While $(iter \leq \text{maximum iteration})$ do

18: function def distance (self, w, with_lagrange =True):

19: $dist = self.y * (np.dot(self.X, w)) - 1$

20: get $dist$ from Db from the current Db

21:   if $MG_w == 1$

22:     get $dist$ from Db

23: generate CE_{ds} and A_L

24: else if $MG_w == 0$

25:     then $dist$ not retrieve

26:   end if

27:   end if

28: end function

29: $iter \leftarrow iter + 1$

30: function Encrypt (E_{dp})

31:   if ST_m confirms E_{dp} storage over blockchain then

32:       Generate a K_{sym}

33:       $C_T < - Encrypt_{sym}(E_{dp}, K_{sym})$

34:       $C_K < - Encrypt_{Asym}(K_{sym}, FC_n PUB_K)$

35:   else

36:     do no operation

37:   end if

38: end function

39: function $Decrypt$ $(C_T, C_K, FC_n PRVT_K, K_{sym})$

40:   $K_{sym} <- Decryption_{Asym}(C_k, FC_n PRVT_K)$

41:     $E_{dp} <- Decryption$ (C_T, K_{sym})

42: end function

43: END

5   Results and Discussion

This section discusses the results and simulation of the LSVMAD algorithm in the iFogSim Simulator. Next, we have used Anaconda (Python), Geth version 1.9.25, Truffle (Compile) and ATOM as a text editor for creating smart contracts. The algorithm usage the Linear SVM-2-PCA for the classification of data where anomalies are identified and classified by reducing the number of variables across a hyperplane. Moreover, the time complexity of the proposed LSVMAD algorithm for encryption function is $O(N)^2$ and for decryption function is $O(N)^3$. The combined time complexity for both functions used in the LSVMAD algorithm is $T(C) = O(N)^2 + O(N)^3$.

Next, it is necessary to remove the missing values and outliers and then fill the values with a mean data value. The missing values are removed using a Kalman filter. The 2-PCA values are considered to show the highest variation in the classified electrical data. The Geth version 1.9.25 is used to show the block receipts and block headers with new entries while executing the simulation. The algorithm is to be implemented using NetBeans and python with several main packages, modules, and classes. See Table 1 for hardware and software specifications.

Table 1. The hardware and software used for the implementation of the proposed algorithm

Hardware and software	Specification
Processor	Inter® Core^{TM} i9-8750H
CPU	5.30 GHz
RAM	32 GB
System Type	64-bit Windows 10
Platform	iFogSim, SimBlock, and Spyder
Language	Java and Python

See Fig. 3 represent the physical topology configuration consisting of fog devices, master fog controller, cloud server and smart meter devices acting at the edge of the networks. This configuration will help in the future to get the preliminary idea of real-world implementation and deployment of the smart meter-FC-cloud system with sensors and actuators.

Figure 3 shows the physical topology for configuration built-in in the iFogSim simulator. The configuration is solely based on the concept of a proposed system.

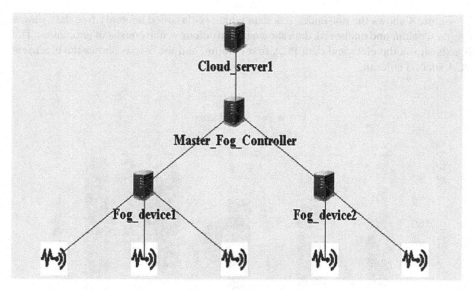

Fig. 3. GUI configuration using iFogSim

Whereas Fig. 4 shows the electrical data is classified for anomaly detection to the highest varied 2-PCA values using the linear SVM.

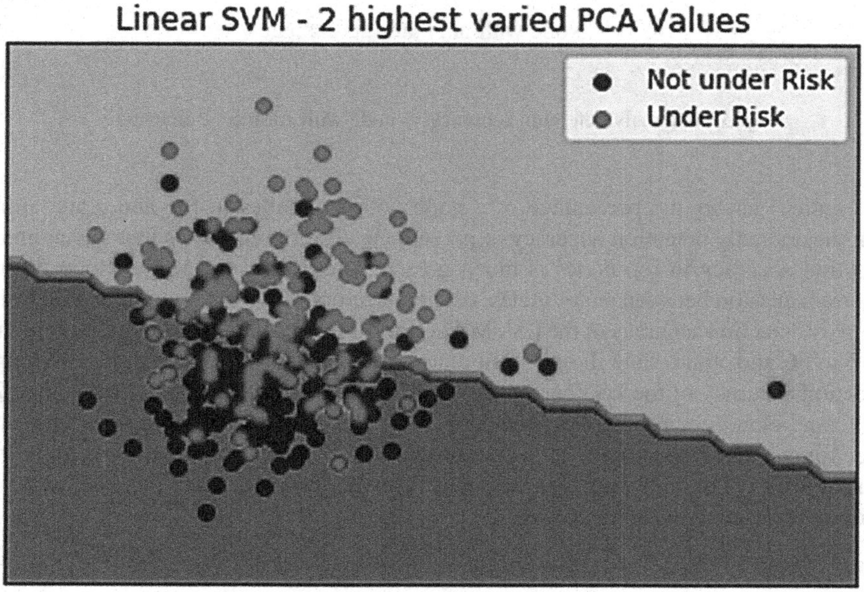

Linear SVM - 2 highest varied PCA Values

Fig. 4. Electrical data classification using Linear SVM-2-PCA for anomalies detection (Color figure online)

Figure 4 shows the not-under-risk data which is classified anomaly free data shown by green colour and under-risk data shown by red colour which consist of anomalies. The X-axis shows the electrical data PCA first column, and the Y-axis shows the electrical PCA second column.

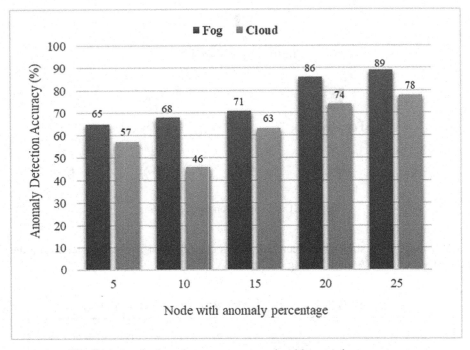

Fig. 5. Anomaly detection accuracy vs node with anomaly percentage

Figure 5 shows the percentage of a node with anomalies in fog and cloud along with the anomaly detection accuracy in percentage. The figure shows that the anomaly detection accuracy in fog nodes is much greater when compared to the cloud during data transmission between smart metes, data connectors, and consumers. The minimum anomaly detection accuracy of the LSVMAD algorithm for a node with anomaly percentage 5 in FC and cloud using iFogSim simulator is 65% and 57%. Whereas the maximum detection accuracy of the LSVMAD algorithm for a node with anomaly percentage 25 in FC and cloud environment is 89% and 78%. The proposed algorithm for anomaly detection accuracy percentage is tested on five different physical topology configurations at different anomaly node percentages. The detection accuracy increases with an increase in anomaly node percentage.

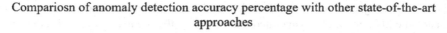

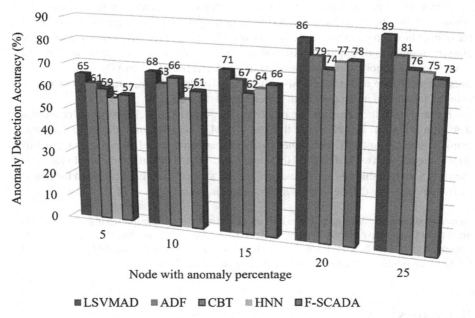

Fig. 6. Anomaly detection accuracy vs node with anomaly percentage performance evaluation

Figure 6 shows the comparison of a node with anomaly percentage vs anomaly detection accuracy for performance evaluation of the proposed LSVMAD algorithm with the other existing state-of-the-art techniques. Different existing algorithms are considered for benchmarking using the iFogSim simulator in five different physical topology configurations. The minimum detection accuracy is 55% for HNN at anomaly node percentage 5. Whereas the minimum detection accuracy for the LSVMAD algorithm is 65% at anomaly node percentage 5. Similarly, the maximum detection accuracy is 81% for ADF at anomaly node percentage 25. Whereas the maximum detection accuracy for the proposed LSVMAD algorithm is 89% at anomaly node percentage 25. The LSVMAD algorithm easily outperforms the other techniques. From Fig. 6 for the anomaly detection accuracy percentage, the proposed algorithm yields marked improvement over the other techniques.

6 Conclusion

SG network has a major role to play in smart cities. They can provide bi-directional information from consumers to the meter-management system and vice-versa. The energy and power are generated, transmitted, distributed, and at last, consumed at the site of smart meter users. However, with the advancement in technology and Industrial Revolution 4.0 (IR 4.0); the SG network becomes vulnerable to outside hackers and cyber-physical attacks. The injection of anomalies, electrical theft, malicious data insertion, and FDI inside the SG network has generated a large risk to the SG network and its consumers.

Hence to overcome this issue we have proposed an advanced system model which consists of distributed fog nodes working as miners at the edge of the SG network with the help of blockchain technology. These fog nodes are intelligent enough to identify and classify anomalies during the transmission of electrical data. Next, we have proposed a novel Linear Support Vector Machine Anomaly Detection (LSVMAD) algorithm which uses the technique of Linear SVM with 2-PCA for data classification. The model was able to classify the anomalies from the electrical data set.

By analyzing the generated results from the proposed novel algorithm for anomaly detection accuracy; it is observed that the LSVMAD algorithm in the FC environment using blockchain and ML techniques easily outperforms the other existing state-of-the-art techniques such as ADF, CBT, HNN, and F-SCADA. The future work includes testing the algorithm to reduce the complexity of the SG system with the increase in the number of IoT devices, fog devices, smart meters, and end-users.

Acknowledgements. This publication has emanated from research supported in part by a research grant from Cooperative Energy Trading System (CENTS) under Grant Number REI1633, and by a research grant from Science Foundation Ireland (SFI) under Grant Number SFI 12/RC/2289_P2 (Insight), co-funded by the European Regional Development Fund.

References

1. Mollah, M.B., et al.: Blockchain for future smart grid: a comprehensive survey. IEEE Internet Things J. **8**(1), 18–43 (2020)
2. Musleh, A.S., Yao, G., Muyeen, S.: Blockchain applications in smart grid–review and frameworks. IEEE Access **7**, 86746–86757 (2019)
3. Gilbert, G.M., Naiman, S., Kimaro, H., Bagile, B.A.: critical review of edge and fog computing for smart grid applications. In: International Conference on Social Implications of Computers in Developing Countries, pp. 763–775. Springer (2019)
4. Drayer, E., Routtenberg, T.: Detection of false data injection attacks in smart grids based on graph signal processing. IEEE Systems Journal (2019)
5. Li, M., Zhang, K., Liu, J., Gong, H., Zhang, Z.: Blockchain-based anomaly detection of electricity consumption in smart grids. Pattern Recogn. Lett. **138**, 476–482 (2020)
6. Yang, Y., Liu, M., Zhou, Q., Zhou, H., Wang, R.: A blockchain based data monitoring and sharing approach for smart grids. IEEE Access **99**, 1 (2019)
7. Hussain, M., Beg, M.: Fog computing for internet of things (IoT)-aided smart grid architectures. Big Data Cogn. Comput. **3**(1), 8 (2019)
8. Jamil, B., Shojafar, M., Ahmed, I., Ullah, A., Munir, K., Ijaz, H.: A job scheduling algorithm for delay and performance optimization in fog computing. Concurrency Comput. Pract. Experience **32**(7), e5581 (2020)
9. Hashmani, M.A., Jameel, S.M., Ibrahim, A.M., Zaffar, M., Raza, K.: An ensemble approach to big data security (cyber security). Int. J. Adv. Comput. Sci. Appl. **9**(9), 75–77 (2018)
10. Gavriluta, C., Boudinet, C., Kupzog, F., Gomez-Exposito, A., Caire, R.: Cyber-physical framework for emulating distributed control systems in smart grids. Int. J. Electr. Power Energy Syst. **114**, 105375 (2020)

11. Zou, T., Bretas, A.S., Ruben, C., Dhulipala, S.C., Bretas, N.: Smart grids cyber-physical security: Parameter correction model against unbalanced false data injection attacks. Electric Power Syst. Res. **187**, 106490 (2020)
12. Wu, K., Cheng, R., Cui, W., Li, W.: A lightweight SM2-based security authentication scheme for smart grids. Alexandria Eng. J. **60**(1), 435–446 (2021)
13. Moghaddass, R., Wang, J.: A hierarchical framework for smart grid anomaly detection using large-scale smart meter data. IEEE Trans. Smart Grid **9**(6), 5820–5830 (2017)
14. Janetzko, H., Stoffel, F., Mittelstädt, S., Keim, D.A.: Anomaly detection for visual analytics of power consumption data. Comput. Graph. **38**, 27–37 (2014)
15. Chou, J.-S., Telaga, A.S.: Real-time detection of anomalous power consumption. Renew. Sustain. Energy Rev. **33**, 400–411 (2014)
16. Matoušek, P., Ryšavý, O., Grégr, M., Havlena, V.: Flow based monitoring of ICS communication in the smart grid. J. Inform. Secur. Appl. **54**, 102535 (2020)
17. Gunduz, M.Z., Das, R.: Cyber-security on smart grid: Threats and potential solutions. Comput. Networks **169**, 107094 (2020)
18. Priyadharshini, N., Gomathy, S., Sabarimuthu, M.: A review on microgrid architecture, cyber security threats and standards. Mater. Today Proc. (2020)
19. Rahman, M.A., Al-Shaer, E., Bera, P.: A noninvasive threat analyzer for advanced metering infrastructure in smart grid. IEEE Trans. Smart Grid **4**(1), 273–287 (2012)

Unsupervised PulseNet: Automated Pruning of Convolutional Neural Networks by K-Means Clustering

David Browne[1][(✉)], Michael Giering[2], and Steven Prestwich[1]

[1] University College Cork, Cork, Ireland
david.browne@insight-centre.org
[2] United Technologies Research Centre, Penrose Quay, Cork, Ireland

Abstract. Convolutional Neural Networks (CNNs) achieve state-of-the-art results in many application areas, including image classification. For some applications it would be useful but impractical to deploy them on mobile devices with limited memory and power. A currently active area of research is the compression of deep networks while maintaining accuracy, with the aim of reducing memory usage, energy consumption and processing time. Several network compression methods have been proposed and have achieved good results, but they usually require the specification of parameters and are computationally expensive. We propose a new fast automated method called *Unsupervised PulseNet* that uses unsupervised k-means clustering to detect clusters of similar filters, and nodes in fully-connected layers, and prunes those that are redundant. We evaluate it on the CIFAR10, CIFAR100 and Tiny-Imagenet datasets using Alexnet, VGG16 and a 2-layer CNN called CifarNet suggested by the Tensorflow group. Compared to other methods in the literature we achieve the greatest compression, in shorter times, and with negligible loss in classification accuracy. In particular, we reduced Alexnet down to less than 0.7% of its original size, while not losing more than 2% classification accuracy.

Keywords: Pruning networks · Network compression · Convolutional Neural Network · Image Recognition · Classification

1 Introduction

In computer vision tasks, such as image recognition and object detection, CNNs have taken the field by storm and set new standards of accuracy [5,7]. However, these results come at a cost: large storage overhead, energy inefficiency, and longer inference times than necessary. This is due to networks often being highly over-parameterized during training, with many redundant parameters. For example, two well-known computer vision network, VGG16 and AlexNet, have over 130 million and 62 million parameters respectively. VGG16 needs more than 500MB for storage and uses over 19 billion floating-point operations (FLOPs)

© Springer Nature Switzerland AG 2022
G. Nicosia et al. (Eds.): LOD 2021, LNCS 13163, pp. 172–184, 2022.
https://doi.org/10.1007/978-3-030-95467-3_14

to classify a single test image, while AlexNet needs over 200MB of storage and uses 1.5 billion FLOPs per image.

A number of approaches have been suggested to help reduce the computational overheads of CNNs, including sparsity [15,20], weight binarization [2,18] and network quantization [6]. Although these methods have achieved good results they usually need additional software and/or hardware, thus increasing problem complexity and making them impractical for real-world applications. [19] presented a student-teacher approach called FitNets, based on the idea of knowledge distillation. Network pruning has shown significant promise in this research area, which includes the pruning of weights [13], filters [8,10,14] and channels [17]. It has the added bonus of being implementable on current software without requiring additional support. Specially designed networks can also improve CNN efficiency [11].

CNNs have additional fully-connected layers, and most work on network pruning focuses on reducing either the convolutional or the fully-connected layers. We decided to prune both convolutional filters and fully-connected layer nodes, thus aiming for high compression. This pruning is independent of several other compression methods mentioned above (sparsity, weight binarization and network quantization) and can potentially be combined with them. It also does not require additional software or hardware so it is easy to deploy in the field. To achieve this pruning we propose a new iterative algorithm called *Unsupervised PulseNet* that finds optimal clusters within the filters or nodes of each layer, selecting only those nearest to the centroids (approximate *medoids*), along with all their associated parameters, and discarding the rest of each cluster. Retraining the reduced network usually recovers any loss in accuracy, and reiterating this process until the accuracy cannot be improved further achieves a high degree of compression with little loss in accuracy. If the network has been pruned beyond recovery, we can easily revert back to the best state found so far, and either prune less aggressively [1] or move onto the next layer for pruning.

Extensive experiments were performed on various datasets and different neural networks, to evaluate the performance and robustness of *Unsupervised PulseNet*. The results show that *Unsupervised PulseNet* is significantly better than other methods, achieving the best compression rate in the literature: it compresses VGG16 by 21× with 2.5% loss of accuracy; AlexNet by 147× with 1.7% loss of accuracy; and CifarNet by 5.4× with 2.5% loss of accuracy. The following are our main contributions. We introduce a novel approach, called *Unsupervised PulseNet*, that automatically selects redundant filters/nodes in a CNN, removes them and compresses the model. The method is the first to use an unsupervised algorithm (K-means clustering) to automatically cluster similar filters and nodes, greatly reducing training computation times. *Unsupervised PulseNet* achieves state-of-the-art results on various CNNs and common benchmark datasets. The rest of the paper is organised as follows. Section 2 discusses related work on CNN pruning and compression. Section 3 explains our proposed method, with its results and discussion given in Sect. 4. Section 5 concludes the paper.

2   Related Work

The authors of [21] formulated their pruning method using a binary integer programming problem and gave a closed-form approximate solution. Their solution took into account not only a singular weight, but also the inputs and other nodes in the network. Their work differed to ours mainly in that they measured the value of the nodes across the network, while we evaluated them layer-by-layer. The authors of [2] quantized the weights in the network with binary values. The authors of [18] proposed using XNOR and bitcount operations, which performed quantization on their weights in a network model called XNOR networks. Han et al. [6] also exploited pruning, quantization and Huffman coding to compress CNNs. Courbariaux et al. [2] proposed using the gradient with respect to the quantized parameters together with randomized rounding method when training a model from scratch. It should be noted that these methods can complement filter pruning, and therefore can be performed in conjunction with *Unsupervised PulseNet* for compression rate improvement.

The authors of [14] focused on pruning entire convolutional filters. The pruning metric used was the L1 norm of all the weights within the filter. The filters were then ranked according to their L1 value, and the n lowest ranked filters layerwise were pruned. The value n was chosen to be a predetermined value at each iteration to prune the network. The network was then fine-tuned to regain accuracy, and the whole process was repeated until the loss in accuracy was too great to recover from. One of their experiments was an analysis of VGG16 using CIFAR-10, which can be directly compared to our results. They reduced the network to 64% of the original size, whereas we reduced it to 4.7% while maintaining similar accuracy.

The authors of [1, 24] use a simple pruning method that analyzes the networks feature maps. When the network is fully trained [1] used the L1 magnitude of each feature map to rank their corresponding filters, removing a predefined number of the lowest ranking ones. While Zou et al. [24] also used feature maps, their pruning decision was based on linear discriminant analysis. Both methods retrained the pruned networks to retrieve as much accuracy as possible. The experimental results of [1] can be directly compared to this work, as can those of [24] on VGG16 using CIFAR10. He et al. [9] argued that the geometric median would be a more appropriate metric than L1 for pruning purposes. The geometric median is a well-known robust estimator of centrality in Euclidean space, and according to its characteristics, filters close to the median, can be represented by the remaining filters, hence chosen to be pruned. Luo et al. [17] proposed ThiNet that used a greedy approach to prune channels with the least effect on the following layer's activation values. He et al. [8], on the other hand, pruned channels by looking at the next network layer's feature maps and minimizing their reconstruction error using LASSO regression. Both found that training the pruned network from scratch caused a reduction in accuracy. Liu et al. [16] implement both their methods, and when they allowed the network to train from scratch but for a longer period, they found that it was possible to achieve slightly better accuracy than the fine-tuning approach.

Lee et al. [13] introduced a single-shot network pruning approach that created an extremely sparse network. Their method identifies the structurally important connections in the network, based on their influence on the loss function at initialization prior to training, namely connection sensitivity, and prune the redundant connections. This means that, instead of taking a pretrained network; pruning it followed by fine-tuning, their method prunes the network and then trains it, hence the name "single-shot pruning". Their approach prunes individual connections and not filters or nodes, and therefore needs additional software to see any actual speed up at inference time, whereas we prune the network and to obtain with a slim version of the original network. The authors of [4] adopted a layer-wise pruning approach. They removed parameters in each layer using a second order derivative metric of the layer's error function. A benefit of this approach is that the network required only limited fine-tuning, although performing a layer-wise reduction can be computationally expensive. To help improve efficiency they suggest a simplified way of calculating the Hessian matrix, thus speeding up the computation of its inverse. Their experiments include the CIFAR-10 dataset and the same networks we used (VGG-16, AlexNet and CIFAR-Net) so we can compare pruning rates achieved between both algorithms.

We believe our proposed algorithm takes the pruning of CNNs a step forward by allowing another machine learning method to determine the redundant filters within each layer in an unsupervised manner. The idea is to let the network evolve by itself to an optimal state. Our results show that not only does *Unsupervised PulseNet* greatly compress state-of-the-art CNNs, but maintains competitive accuracy in doing so.

3   Unsupervised PulseNet

The experimental design for our paper followed the same setup as [1], using the same train/test splits in the datasets. *Unsupervised PulseNet* was evaluated on 3 benchmark datasets CIFAR10, CIFAR100 and Tiny-Imagenet where the robustness and performance of it was demonstrated using two state-of-the-art CNNs AlexNet and VGG16 and a CNN called CifarNet.

Unsupervised PulseNet is a CNN compression algorithm that takes a trained network and iteratively, using a k-means based approach, prunes filters and nodes throughout the network, then fine-tunes the model to regain accuracy. The algorithm continues this process on all layers until the loss in accuracy reaches a threshold (we chose 2% for this work as we want to keep the pruned network accuracy similar to the original network accuracy for direct comparisons), then the network reverts back to its best previous state. At this point, instead of trying to prune all layers in one iteration, the network is pruned in sections, starting with the fully-connected layers as these contain the majority of the network parameters. Again, once the accuracy threshold is exceeded these layers revert to their best previous state, then the convolutional layers are pruned (these are the most computationally expensive part of the network). Finally, for the last section of pruning when the accuracy threshold is exceeded again, each layer is individually pruned, iteratively.

Algorithm 1. Unsupervised PulseNet Algorithm

Define γ and ρ as the network's convolutional and fully-connected layers
Define λ as the classification accuracy of the validation set
Initialize $i = 0$ & $\beta = 2\%$ & $L = \gamma + \rho$
While $i \neq \text{len}(\gamma) + \text{len}(\rho)$
   initialize $p_{in} = \langle 0, 1, 2 \rangle$
   $\forall \ \ l \in L$
      if $l =$ convolution layer
         given filter F represented by w, x, y, z
         Remove rows in y not in p_{in}
         Transpose $(w, x, y, z) \rightarrow (z, w * x * y)$
         $p_{out} =$ Get optimal k clusters of $(z, w * x * y)$ (Algorithm. 2)
         Remove rows in z not in p_{in}
         Transpose $(z, w * x * y) \rightarrow (w, x, y, z)$
      elif $l =$ fully connected layer
         given node N represented by (m, n)
         Remove rows in m not in p_{in}
         Transpose $(m, n) \rightarrow (n, m)$
         $p_{out} =$ Get optimal k clusters of (n, m) (Algorithm. 2)
         Remove rows in n not in p_{in}
         Transpose $(n, m) \rightarrow (m, n)$
   $p_{in} \leftarrow p_{out}$
Calculate $\delta =$ new validation accuracy
if $(\lambda - \delta) > \beta$
   if $[L = (\gamma + \rho)]$
      $L = \rho$
   elif $[L = \rho]$
      $L = \gamma$
   else $[L = \gamma]$
      if $i = \text{len}(\gamma + \rho)$
         $Halt$
      else
         $L = i^{th}$ layer of the full network
         $i = i + 1$

This type of pruning approach can be thought of as coarse (entire network), then medium (each section; convolutional and fully-connected), then fine pruning (individual layers): we believe that this incremental approach helps us to achieve state-of-the-art compression results for the different datasets, as shown in Sect. 4. We show that by using a more intelligent way of selecting the filters or nodes considered to be redundant, which are then pruned from the network, we can achieve an extremely efficient CNN. *Unsupervised PulseNet* uses an unsupervised k-means clustering algorithm, and a maximum pruning factor of 25% was imposed: although k-means automatically determines the number of clusters in the data, it was limited to only looking at a quarter of the layer at a time.

This helped to reduce the probability of the network suffering unrecoverable *brain-damage*, and allowing Unsupervised PulseNet to compress the network even further.

Algorithm 2. Get optimal k clusters

Set $\alpha = 0.25$
given input M
$s = \alpha \times \text{len}(M)$
for k in $s \rightarrow \text{len}(M)$
    k random vectors V as initial clusters centers (ICC)
    Repeat
        (re)assign each V to C to ICC to which it is most similar,
                based on mean value of V within ICC
        update ICC means
    Until *no change*
    store sum of squares within clusters (WCSS)
$D1 = WCSS_{i+1} - WCSS_i, \quad \forall \quad i \in 1 \rightarrow \text{len}(WCSS) - 1$
$D2 = D1_{i+1} - D1_i, \quad \forall \quad i \in 1 \rightarrow \text{len}(D1) - 1$
$\sigma = D2 - D1$
P $\rightarrow$
for u in σ
    if $u > 0$
        P.insert(u)
$C = $ index of max(P)
Y $\rightarrow$
for centre in C
    $v = $ index of vector closest to centre
    Y.insert(v)
return Y

The convolutional layer's parameters are represented by w, x, y, z, where w and x are the filter sizes, y is the number of inward filters and z the number of outward filters. When analysing the fully-connected layers, since there are no filters, the layer is represented by m is the number of inward node and n the number of outward nodes. We call filters-in the list of inwards filters indices, and filters-out the list of outward filters indices, from the above tunable parameters. It should be noted that if we are pruning the first convolutional layer, then the filters-in would be the colour depth of the input image, which for an RGB image would be $\langle 0, 1, 2 \rangle$. For the remaining convolutional layers, the filters-in are the filters-out from the previous layer. To find the filters-out, *Unsupervised PulseNet* clusters the outward filters using Algorithm 1, retaining only the filter nearest to the centroid of each cluster, removing the rest which are deemed to be redundant. The retained filter indices or the filters-out become the next layer's filters-in and are used to subset its inward filters. This is repeated for all the layers in the network. The filters-out are found by running the k-means algorithm with all possible k values between 1 and the number of filters or nodes in the layer. The sum of the L2 distances between each filter/node and the centre within each cluster (distortion) is calculated.

The algorithm runs until either no change, within a tolerance (10^{-3}), of the distortion occurs or the maximum number of iterations is reached (300). The *k-means* algorithm had 5 restarts to reduce the possibility of getting stuck in a local minimum. The distortion is recorded, along with its corresponding k value. By using algorithm 2 we determine the optimal number of filters/nodes to retain. Algorithm 1 shows how loops through the layers of the network, pruning each layer in an unsupervised way. The relevant filters or nodes that Unsupervised PulseNet extracts are re-used to create a smaller network, which is fine-tuned on the dataset to regain any loss in accuracy.

4   Results

Table 1. Computational results on datasets CIFAR10, CIFAR100 and Tiny-ImageNet using three CNNs; CifarNet, AlexNet and VGG16. The storage of the CNNs is measured in megabytes, the energy per image in mJoules and the time per image in milliseconds. It shows the storage space each network requires, the inference speed per image and the energy consumed per image of both the original and compressed networks using a batch size of a single image.

Dataset	CNN	Original			Unsupervised PulseNet		
		Storage	Energy	Time	Storage	Energy	Time
Cifar10	CifarNet	3.044	0.06	2.20	0.567	0.04	1.87
–	AlexNet	178.482	1.11	32.05	1.208	0.12	4.11
–	VGG16	128.32	0.98	27.68	6.068	0.12	6.12
Cifar100	CifarNet	3.11	0.08	2.43	1.234	0.06	2.24
–	AlexNet	179.889	1.14	32.01	9.853	0.27	8.14
–	VGG16	129.726	0.98	27.66	4.567	0.21	6.97
Tiny ImageNet	CifarNet	16.684	0.23	8.05	7.066	0.16	5.45
–	AlexNet	225.451	1.74	32.05	6.053	0.54	18.28
–	VGG16	155.289	1.92	50.69	8.152	0.28	12.21

To compare inference efficiency between networks, we use the common metric of the number of FLOPs needed to classify a test image. We use the difference between the number of FLOPs for the original and the *Unsupervised PulseNet* network to measure computational improvement. Although we might expect to see similar speedups in inference time and similar reduced energy consumption, in fact we do not. This is due to other layers within the network being non-tensor (batch normalization and pooling layers) as well as the overhead of reading time. To fully understand the improvements our proposed method makes on the tested networks, we shall show both the theoretical improvements and the actual improvements, with respect to inference time and consumed energy (Table 1).

Table 2. Overall accuracies and standard deviations (%) of different CNN architectures, both original and compressed using proposed method *Unsupervised PulseNet* on the CIFAR10 data set. The entries in bold show the method with the best classification for the network, while the percentage of the original network is highlighted in red.

Method	Network structure	# Parameters	# FLOPs	Accuracy
CifarNet				
Original	$64 - 64 - 384 - 192$	797962 (100%)	1594501 (100%)	85.66
PulseNet	$24 - 35 - 133 - 64$	148593 (18.62%)	296659 (18.61%)	83.20
AlexNet				
Original	$96 - 256 - 384 - 384 -$ $256 - 4096 - 4096$	46787978 (100%)	93556808 (100%)	90.50
PulseNet	$39 - 59 - 132 - 141 -$ $106 - 340 - 549$	316571 (0.68%)	631874 (0.68%)	88.79
VGG16				
Original	$64 - 64 - 128 - 128 - 256 -$ $256 - 256 - 512-$ $512 - 512 - 512 - 512 -$ $512 - 4096 - 4096$	33638218 (100%)	67251600 (100%)	91.85
PulseNet	$14 - 17 - 37 - 44 - 65 - 65 -$ $62 - 104-$ $164 - 184 - 174 - 232 -$ $157 - 25 - 6$	1590755 (4.73%)	3178806 (4.73%)	89.32

Table 2 shows that *Unsupervised PulseNet* reduces the complexity of Cifar-Net, AlexNet and VGG16 by 5.4×, 147.1× and 21.1× respectively. This can be compared to similar work on ResNet networks and the CIFAR10 dataset, where [8,9] reduced the number of FLOPs by 50% and 52.6% respectively, [4] reduced FLOPs by 34.2%, and [14] compressed the network by 50%. Although on a different network, the *Unsupervised PulseNet* reduction in number of FLOPs ranged from 81.39% on an already very small network (CifarNet) to 99.32% on AlexNet, and 95.27% on VGG16. [4] used a layer-wise pruning method on a 3-convolutional- and 2-fully-connected-layer network based on AlexNet, applied to the CIFAR10 dataset. They were able to compress it to 9% of its original size while maintaining an accuracy of 80.64%. We reduced our CifarNet to 18.62% of its original size with a classification accuracy of 83.20%. Although they achieved a higher compression ratio, it should be remembered that their network was based on AlexNet with 3 convolutional layers of sizes 96, 256, 256 with the same fully-connected layers as ours. Hence our network has far fewer parameters than theirs, with less pruning potential. If we compare our version of AlexNet on CIFAR10 we pruned to a ratio of 0.68%. [19] proposed a teacher-student network idea called FitNets, that compressed their model down to ∼ 2.5M parameters with an accuracy of 91.61% on the CIFAR10 dataset. Comparing our *Unsupervised PulseNet* version of AlexNet, we achieved a slightly worse classification accuracy of 88.79% but with only ∼ 0.6M parameters: more than 4× fewer than FitNets. In the work of [11] on SqueezeNet they compressed a network by 50× while maintaining an AlexNet accuracy. Our Unsupervised PulseNet model of

AlexNet was compressed by 147.1× with negligible loss in accuracy. The pruning method of [24] compressed the convolutional layers of VGG16 using the CIFAR10 dataset. The first 4 layers of their version of VGG16 had 30, 46, 94 and 102 filters, with the remaining convolutional layers containing 206 filters, while as can be seen in Table 2 all but one of our version of VGG16 layers were pruned much more. On the first 4 layers, our network had less than half the number of filters compared to theirs, with the rest of the convolutional layers ranges from 1.1× to 3.3× fewer filters (one of our layers retained 26 more filters), making the *Unsupervised PulseNet* network computationally more efficient. [10] pruned the filters in the convolutional layers of VGG16, and on the CIFAR10 dataset reduced FLOPs by 80.6%, while our method reduced FLOPs by 95.27%. This resulted in a speedup of their network by 63.4%, whereas our VGG16 network improved inference time by 78.8%. They had a loss in accuracy of 3.4% compared to *Unsupervised PulseNet's* loss of 2.5%. [3] used an iterative approach called Auto-Balanced Filter Pruning to compress the VGG16 network by 81.4% on the CIFAR10 dataset, whereas our proposed method pruned VGG16 by 95.3%. *Unsupervised PulseNet* lost an average of 2% accuracy while [3] lost approximately 0.5%. [13] compressed AlexNet and VGG16 on the CIFAR10 dataset by 10× and VGG16 by 19.6×, while our method reducing AlexNet by 147.1× and VGG16 by 21.1×. [23] pruned VGG16 by 3.8×, with a 2% loss in accuracy, whereas we pruned it by 21.1× with approximately the same loss in accuracy. [1] used an iterative pruning approach, that simulated the pruning of filters/nodes by using binary matrices. On the CIFAR10 dataset this compressed the CifarNet, AlexNet and VGG16 networks by 4.2×, 22.9×, and 8.2×, losing 3.6%, 2%, 0.9% accuracy, respectively. In comparison, *Unsupervised PulseNet* pruned CifarNet by 5.4×, AlexNet by 147.1× and VGG16 by 21.1×, with a classification loss of 2.46%, 1.7% and 2.5% respectively.

Unsupervised PulseNet reduced the complexity of CifarNet by 2.5×, AlexNet by 22.4× and VGG16 by 28.4×, as shown in Table 3. The reduction in the number of FLOPs ranged from 60.27% on CifarNet to 96.48% on VGG16, with 95.53% on AlexNet. [19] proposed the FitNets method, which compressed their model down to ~ 2.5M parameters with an accuracy of 64.96% on the CIFAR100 dataset. Comparing our *Unsupervised PulseNet* version of VGG16, we maintained a classification accuracy of 65.38% with ~ 2.4 M parameters, improving both accuracy and compression. [23] pruned VGG16 by 1.6× without loss in accuracy, while *Unsupervised PulseNet* compressed VGG16 by 28.4× with just over 2% classification loss. [1] on the CIFAR100 dataset compressed the CifarNet, AlexNet and VGG16 networks by 2.9×, 7.1×, and 8.1×, losing 4.5%, 2.3%, 1.1% accuracy, respectively. In contrast, *Unsupervised PulseNet* pruned CifarNet by 2.5×, AlexNet by 22.4× and VGG16 by 28.4×, with accuracy losses of 1.9%, 2.16% and 2.3%, respectively.

Table 3. Overall accuracies and standard deviations (%) of different CNN architectures, both original and compressed using *Unsupervised PulseNet* on the CIFAR100 data set. The entries in bold show the method with the best classification for the network, while the percentage of the original network is highlighted in red.

Method	Network structure	# Parameters	# FLOPs	Accuracy
CifarNet				
Original	64 − 64 − 384 − 192	815332 (100%)	1629061 (100%)	58.71
PulseNet	38 − 37 − 258 − 129	323394 (39.66%)	645669 (39.63%)	56.82
AlexNet				
Original	96 − 256 − 384 − 384 − 256 − 4096 − 4096	47156708 (100%)	94294088 (100%)	70.56
PulseNet	39 − 75 − 116 − 105 − 84 − 748 − 773	2582926 (5.48%)	5161780 (4.47%)	68.40
VGG16				
Original	64 − 64 − 128 − 128 − 256 − 256 − 256 − 512− 512 − 512 − 512 − 512 − 512 − 4096 − 4096	34006948 (100%)	67988880 (100%)	67.71
PulseNet	17 − 13 − 30 − 42 − 98 − 72 − 74 − 161− 127 − 161 − 144 − 101 − 131 − 228 − 201	1197197 (3.52%)	2391010 (3.52%)	65.38

Table 4. Overall accuracies and standard deviations (%) of different CNN architectures, both original and compressed using *Unsupervised PulseNet* on the Tiny-Imagenet data set. The entries in bold show the method with the best classification for the network, while the percentage of the original network is highlighted in red.

Method	Network Structure	# Parameters	# FLOPs	Accuracy
CifarNet				
Original	64 − 64 − 384 − 192	4373576 (100%)	8745349 (100%)	41.08
PulseNet	47 − 49 − 210 − 126	1852402 (42.35%)	3703545 (42.35%)	39.70
AlexNet				
Original	96 − 256 − 384 − 384 − 256 − 4096 − 4096	59100744 (100%)	118181960 (100%)	52.47
PulseNet	29 − 134 − 170 − 167 − 108 − 198 − 214	1586747 (2.68%)	3171062 (2.68%)	50.13
VGG16				
Original	64 − 64 − 128 − 128 − 256 − 256 − 256 − 512− 512 − 512 − 512 − 512 − 512 − 4096 − 4096	40708104 (100%)	81390992 (100%)	55.29
PulseNet	17 − 17 − 40 − 32 − 82 − 84 − 109 − 149− 176 − 188 − 244 − 215 − 186 − 25 − 14	2137115 (5.25%)	4270690 (5.25%)	52.84

The last dataset for analysis is Tiny-ImageNet, Table 4. *Unsupervised PulseNet* reduces the network complexity of PulseNet's CifarNet by 2.4×, eliminating 57.65% of the number of FLOPs. It decreases the complexity of AlexNet by 37.3× which eliminates 97.32% of the number of FLOPs. And it decreases the VGG16 complexity by 19.1×, eliminating 95.75% of FLOPs. [4] compressed both AlexNet and VGG16 on the ImageNet dataset and, although we cannot perform a direct comparison because Tiny-ImageNet is only a subset of that dataset, it is still interesting to compare the results. They were able to compress AlexNet by 17.5× and VGG16 by 13.3×, compared to *Unsupervised PulseNet* which pruned AlexNet and VGG16 by 37.3× and 19.1×, respectively, showing we can achieve better compression rates. The pruning method of [17] called ThiNet, applied to the ImageNet dataset, reduced VGG16 down to 8.34M parameters, while our compressed version of VGG16 on Tiny-ImageNet is almost 4× less with 2.1M parameters. [21] used a neuron importance score propagation (NISP) approach to prune AlexNet on the ImageNet dataset. Their NISP AlexNet had a reduction in the number of FLOPs by 67.85%, compared to *Unsupervised PulseNet* AlexNet on Tiny-ImageNet with a reduction in FLOPs of 97.32%. [12] compressed both AlexNet and VGG16 networks on the ImageNet dataset, with AlexNet being pruned by 5.5× and VGG16 by 7.4×m with 1.7% and 0.55% loss in accuracy respectively. In contrast, we pruned AlexNet by 37.3× with a accuracy loss of 2.3%, and VGG16 by 19× with a loss of 2.5%. The method of [13], called Single-Shot Network Pruning, compressed AlexNet to 10.1% and VGG16 to 20% of their original sizes, while *unsupervised PulseNet* compressed AlexNet and VGG16 to 2.7% and 5.2% of their original sizes, respectively, on the Tiny-ImageNet dataset within acceptable accuracy loss. Comparing to the results of [22] on AlexNet, where they achieved a theoretical improvement of 13×, *Unsupervised PulseNet* improved its version of the network by over 3× their compression, to 37.1× smaller. The method of [1] on the Tiny-ImageNet dataset compressed the CifarNet, AlexNet and VGG16 networks by 3.9×, 5.2×, and 6.2×, losing accuracy 2.91%, 3.75%, 2%, respectively. In contrast, *Unsupervised PulseNet* pruned CifarNet by 2.4×, AlexNet by 37.3× and VGG16 by 19.1×, with a classification loss of 1.4%, 2.3% and 2.45%, respectively.

5   Conclusion

We proposed an effective neural network pruning algorithm based on finding clusters of filters and nodes in each layer via unsupervised K-means clustering. By retaining only the filters and nodes close to cluster centroids, we achieve state-of-the-art compression with negligible loss in accuracy. Our approach does not require any additional software or hardware, is automated, and can be implemented on any type of CNN. We demonstrated our method, which we call *Unsupervised PulseNet*, on three benchmark datasets using well-established neural networks in the area of computer vision. It achieves state-of-the-art results, pruning VGG16, AlexNet and CifarNet models into 6.07MB, 1.21MB and 0.57MB respectively, with little loss in classification accuracy. For future work other types of network may be explored, along with other clustering methods, with the aim of further reducing computational cost and network compression. Finally, extensive exploration on different computer vision tasks (such as object detection and segmentation) using *Unsupervised PulseNet* would be of great interest.

References

1. Browne, D., Giering, M., Prestwich, S.: Pulse-net: dynamic compression of convolutional neural networks. In: 2019 IEEE 5th World Forum on Internet of Things (WF-IoT), pp. 346–351. IEEE (2019)
2. Courbariaux, M., Hubara, I., Soudry, D., El-Yaniv, R., Bengio, Y.: Binarized neural networks: training deep neural networks with weights and activations constrained to+ 1 or-1. arXiv preprint arXiv:1602.02830 (2016)
3. Ding, X., Ding, G., Han, J., Tang, S.: Auto-balanced filter pruning for efficient convolutional neural networks. In: 32nd AAAI Conference on AI (2018)
4. Dong, X., Chen, S., Pan, S.: Learning to prune deep neural networks via layer-wise optimal brain surgeon. In: Advances in Neural Information Processing Systems, pp. 4857–4867 (2017)
5. Girshick, R.: Fast R-CNN. In: Proceedings of the IEEE International Conference on Computer Vision, pp. 1440–1448 (2015)
6. Han, S., Mao, H., Dally, W.J.: Deep compression: compressing deep neural networks with pruning, trained quantization and huffman coding. arXiv preprint arXiv:1510.00149 (2015)
7. He, K., Zhang, X., Ren, S., Sun, J.: Deep residual learning for image recognition. In: Proceedings of the IEEE Conference on Computer Vision and Pattern Recognition, pp. 770–778 (2016)
8. He, Y., Kang, G., Dong, X., Fu, Y., Yang, Y.: Soft filter pruning for accelerating deep convolutional neural networks. arXiv preprint arXiv:1808.06866 (2018)
9. He, Y., Liu, P., Wang, Z., Hu, Z., Yang, Y.: Filter pruning via geometric median for deep convolutional neural networks acceleration. In: Proceedings of the IEEE Conference on Computer Vision and Pattern Recognition, pp. 4340–4349 (2019)
10. Huang, Q., Zhou, K., You, S., Neumann, U.: Learning to prune filters in convolutional neural networks. In: 2018 IEEE Winter Conference on Applications of Computer Vision (WACV), pp. 709–718. IEEE (2018)
11. Iandola, F.N., Han, S., Moskewicz, M.W., Ashraf, K., Dally, W.J., Keutzer, K.: Squeezenet: alexnet-level accuracy with 50x fewer parameters and < 0.5 mb model size. arXiv preprint arXiv:1602.07360 (2016)
12. Kim, Y.D., Park, E., Yoo, S., Choi, T., Yang, L., Shin, D.: Compression of deep convolutional neural networks for fast and low power mobile applications. arXiv preprint arXiv:1511.06530 (2015)
13. Lee, N., Ajanthan, T., Torr, P.H.: Snip: single-shot network pruning based on connection sensitivity. arXiv preprint arXiv:1810.02340 (2018)
14. Li, H., Kadav, A., Durdanovic, I., Samet, H., Graf, H.P.: Pruning filters for efficient convnets. arXiv preprint arXiv:1608.08710 (2016)
15. Liu, B., Wang, M., Foroosh, H., Tappen, M., Pensky, M.: Sparse convolutional neural networks. In: Proceedings of the IEEE Conference on Computer Vision and Pattern Recognition, pp. 806–814 (2015)
16. Liu, Z., Sun, M., Zhou, T., Huang, G., Darrell, T.: Rethinking the value of network pruning. arXiv preprint arXiv:1810.05270 (2018)
17. Luo, J.H., Wu, J., Lin, W.: Thinet: a filter level pruning method for deep neural network compression. In: Proceedings of the IEEE International Conference on Computer Vision, pp. 5058–5066 (2017)
18. Rastegari, M., Ordonez, V., Redmon, J., Farhadi, A.: XNOR-Net: ImageNet classification using binary convolutional neural networks. In: Leibe, B., Matas, J., Sebe, N., Welling, M. (eds.) ECCV 2016. LNCS, vol. 9908, pp. 525–542. Springer, Cham (2016). https://doi.org/10.1007/978-3-319-46493-0_32

19. Romero, A., Ballas, N., Kahou, S.E., Chassang, A., Gatta, C., Bengio, Y.: Fitnets: hints for thin deep nets. arXiv preprint arXiv:1412.6550 (2014)
20. Wen, W., Wu, C., Wang, Y., Chen, Y., Li, H.: Learning structured sparsity in deep neural networks. In: Advances in Neural Information Processing Systems, pp. 2074–2082 (2016)
21. Yu, R., et al.: Nisp: pruning networks using neuron importance score propagation. In: Proceedings of the IEEE Conference on Computer Vision and Pattern Recognition, pp. 9194–9203 (2018)
22. Zhang, X., Zhou, X., Lin, M., Sun, J.: Shufflenet: an extremely efficient convolutional neural network for mobile devices. In: Proceedings of the IEEE Conference on Computer Vision and Pattern Recognition, pp. 6848–6856 (2018)
23. Zhao, C., Ni, B., Zhang, J., Zhao, Q., Zhang, W., Tian, Q.: Variational convolutional neural network pruning. In: Proceedings of the IEEE Conference on Computer Vision and Pattern Recognition, pp. 2780–2789 (2019)
24. Zou, J., Rui, T., Zhou, Y., Yang, C., Zhang, S.: Convolutional neural network simplification via feature map pruning. Comput. Electr. Eng. **70**, 950–958 (2018)

A Noisy-Labels Approach to Detecting Uncompetitive Auctions

Natalya Goryunova(ID), Artem Baklanov(✉)(ID), and Egor Ianovski(ID)

HSE University, 3A Kantemirovskaya Street, St Petersburg 194100,
Russian Federation
apbaklanov@hse.ru

Abstract. Despite several rounds of institutional reform starting from 2005, the public procurement process in Russia remains marred by low competitiveness and inefficiency. In the years 2014–2018, almost half of the studied auctions failed to attract more than a single-bidder. But are single-bidder auctions necessarily uncompetitive? The auction format we study is a sealed-bid auction, where a bidder is unaware of who else is participating. If they were to submit a bid with the expectation of competition that fails to materialise, for all means and purposes the auction can be said to be competitive. More importantly, the presence of many bidders does not guarantee competition – we could be facing a cartel, or the restriction of competition via a corrupt procurer, such as the case of bid-leakage. We assume that bids in multi-bidder auctions are predominantly competitive while bids in single-bidder auctions are not, and apply generalized confident learning, a method for classification in the presence of noisy labels, to attempt to separate competitive and uncompetitive bids. This allows us to identify behaviour patterns resembling monopolists and cartels.

Keywords: Noisy-labels learning · Public procurement · Single-bidder auctions

1 Introduction

Russia's transition to a market economy was chaotic and troubled, marked with questionable policies and suboptimal implementation. One of these was the system of public procurement, which until 2005 gave officials almost complete freedom in how they purchase goods and services from the private sector. Moral hazard abounded – a sole trader spends his own money for his own needs, which is incentive to purchase a quality product at a low price; a public official spends the taxpayer's money for the benefit of the taxpayer: at best, we can expect a certain amount of negligence in his duties, and worse, outright embezzlement.

The study was supported by a grant from the Russian Science Foundation (project No. 20-71-00034).

Federal Law No. 94-FZ [10] put this to an end, stipulating that all purchases by a public institution had to be done through a competitive procedure, and establishing the rules on advertisement, documentation, publication, intended to ensure a transparent process. Unfortunately, one cannot simply legislate competition into existence. In the "requests for quotation" category of auction, in the years 2014–2018, 48% of auctions attracted a single bidder.

The single-bidder rate is a key indicator of the efficiency of the public procurement process, and is used by the European Commission to assess the performance of member states [7]. A "satisfactory" rating is $\leq 10\%$, "average" 10–20%, "unsatisfactory" $> 20\%$. Compared to the EU states, Russia fares better only than Poland and Czechia (51%). Even the most competitive region in Russia – Moscow Oblast – has a rate of 34%.

This is, of course, a sobering statistic – almost half of the instances of a procedure designed to guarantee a competitive process fail to generate any competition at all. And indeed, Russia's problems with corruption are well known [1, 28].

However, while the single-bidder rate is a useful proxy for problems in the procurement process, it is nevertheless a proxy. An auction could attract a single bidder due to an official concealing the auction or a bid-rotation scheme of a cartel, which are criminal acts and demand immediate regulatory attention. An auction could attract a single bidder due to the presence of a monopolist – regrettable, but not necessarily illegal; this problem can only be addressed by long-term institutional change. And an auction could attract a single bidder incidentally: in a sealed-bid auction the participants are unaware of each other, and it is conceivable that a firm makes a competitive bid in the expectation of competition that never materialises.

Moreover, we cannot assume that all is well in a multi-bidder auction: bid-leakage [2, 18, 20], and cartel activity [24] could restrict competition in an auction that looks competitive at first glance.

The purpose of this paper is to question the assumption that multi-bidder auctions are necessarily competitive, and single-bidder auctions necessarily are not. We use a noisy-labels approach [11] on a dataset of Russian public procurement to detect single-bidder auctions which nevertheless resemble competitive auctions in other respects, and multi-bidder auctions which do not appear to be competitive. Novel to our approach is the holistic approach to malfeasance in public procurement. Previous works have focused on identifying concrete forms of illicit activity, or specific markers that this activity has taken place. In our work, instead, we take the fundamental unit of the procurement data – the bid – and use a state-of-the-art classifier to separate these into bids that appear to have been placed with the expectation of competition, and those that were not. When we examine the results of this classification, we do indeed find patterns resembling cartel and monopolist activity in a subset of the uncompetitive bids.

1.1   Related Work

Illegal restriction of competition in procurement can be divided into two, possibly intersecting, categories. The first is *collusion*, a tacit or explicit agreement between firms to limit competition on tenders, i.e. a cartel. The second is *corruption*, interaction between a firm and procurer to extract rent from a government contract.

Collusion. The empirical literature on collusion began with the idea that certain statistical screens – such as higher price, lower price variance, stable market shares [15] – can allow a researcher to separate legitimate businesses from suspected cartels in the data. A seminal work in the field is [24], who detect Long Island state highway construction cartels by considering the price difference between cartel members and non-members. They discover that the "phony-bid" strategy was popular, where several members place high, uncompetitive bids close to each other, and one designated winner places a lower bid to secure the contract. In contrast, they did not detect the "bid rotation" strategy, where cartel members refrain from bidding on each other's tenders. Of interest to this paper is that such a cartel would be present only in multi-bidder auctions.

The ready availability of public data makes the application of statistical methods to cartel detection appealing, and subsequent works studied various markets such as dairy [25] and cement [17], and entire countries such as Brazil [12] and Indonesia [3].

A key difficulty in this approach is labelling the data. Since cartels are illegal, members generally do not advertise the fact. The approach in the literature generally involved using a court verdict [16,17,24] or expert assessment [12] to label a subset of the firms as cartel members, and assuming the remaining firms are not.

This necessarily introduces bias: the classifiers are taught to detect a very specific form of cartel activity, namely the one that ended up in court. This could be the reason why [16] found that classifiers trained on Okinawan data performed poorly in Switzerland, and vice versa.

Corruption. Of particular relevance to our paper is the line of work on bid leakage, also known as magic number cheating [18]. This is a form of corruption in a first-price, sealed-bid auction where the procurer either reveals the values of the other bids to a favoured firm (bid leakage) thus allowing the firm to undercut the winner close to the deadline, or doctors the value of the favoured firm's bid to be marginally lower than the lowest fair bid (magic number cheating). Magic number cheating in New York school construction was studied by [18] by measuring the distance between the three lowest bids: the argument being that in the presence of bid leakage, the winning bid would be much closer to the second lowest bid than statistically expected. In [2], the authors studied bid leakage in Russian public procurement, based on the assumption that in a fair auction the order of the bids should be independent of the winner, and if it is shown that the last bidder is statistically likely to win, there is cause for suspicion. This work was extended by [20,21], who relaxed this assumption as they felt that there are legitimate reasons that a winner should bid last – a serious contender would take more time to consider the tender and decide on a competitive bid – and instead used a positive-unlabelled approach where all runner-ups were labelled as "fair" and used the DEDPUL classifier [19] to divide the winners into "fair" and "suspicious". Their approach found signs of bid leakage in 9% of auctions with three or more participants, and 16% of auctions with two or more.

The nature of bid leakage, however, presupposes the presence of more than one participant, else there would be no bids to leak. Single-bidder auctions had to be removed from the dataset, and as a result the authors in [20,21] had to throw away 42% of their data due to single-bidder auctions. This is a huge amount – if all these failed to attract competition due to corruption or collusion, then the cost of single-bidder auctions would likely dwarf bid leakage or any other form of machination.

However, while the single-bidder rate is a common proxy of corruption [5,22,29], it is acknowledged that there could be legitimate reasons for an auction attracting only a single bid. The first work to attempt to distinguish these legitimate single-bidder auctions from those suspect of corruption was [13], who used positive-unlabelled classification on Russian procurement auctions.

1.2   Our Contribution

We train a generalized confident learning classifier (Cleanlab) [23] on a dataset of Russian procurement auctions in the period 2014–2018, under the assumption that bids in multi-bidder auctions are predominantly competitive, and in single-bidder auctions predominantly are not.[1] We find that 29% of the bids in single-bidder auctions nevertheless resemble the competitive bids, and 14% of the bids in multi-bidder auctions resemble uncompetitive bids. Within the multi-bidder, uncompetitive bids 21.14% resemble phony-bid cartel activity, and within single-bidder, uncompetitive bids 5.39% seem to have complete monopoly power.

In the context of the literature, we continue the line of work of [2,13,20,21] on statistical detection of malfeasance in Russian procurement auctions. Our dataset is the same as [13,20,21], and like [13] we take a holistic approach to the detection of uncompetitive behaviour: we do not single out a particular strategy such as bid leakage or auction concealment, but seek to divide all auctions into those that appear to be competitive and otherwise.

The work of [13] is based on a positive-unlabelled approach: all bids in multi-bidder auctions are assumed to be competitive, the rest are divided into those that appear to be competitive or uncompetitive. This approach missed suspicious multi-bidder auctions such as those involving cartels or bid leakage, which our approach, based on noisy-label classification, takes into account. Noisy-label classification has been successfully used in fields where data is plentiful but is expensive or difficult to label correctly, such as image classification [26,31,33],

---

[1] The code and data is available on https://github.com/NatalyaGoryunova/LOD-21.

sentiment analysis [30, 32], or medical diagnosis [14]. To our knowledge this is the first work to approach procurement auctions from a noisy-labels perspective.

2   Methodology

2.1   Classification with Noisy Labels

Label noise is observed when some examples in the data have class labels that do not coincide with the true values.

[11] identify four sources of noise: insufficient information for an expert to make an accurate decision, the labelling was done by a non-expert or an automated algorithm, the subjective nature of the labelling task (i.e. interexpert variability), errors due to communication or data encoding problems. Our main assumption in this paper – that bids in multi-bidder auctions are mostly competitive, and bids in single-bidder auctions mostly are not – is closest to the first source of the noise.

In contrast to the traditional setting of supervised learning (classification with correct labels), the ideal outcome of classification in the presence of label noise is not only a trained algorithm to make predictions for out-of-sample instances, but also corrected labels for the training data. In this paper it is the corrected labels that interest us – we do not run the classifier on out-of-sample instances.

Recent papers on corruption in public procurement [13, 20] used the method of positive-unlabelled (PU) learning, identifying a class of auctions that do not exhibit signs of corruption, and assuming the remaining auctions are a mix of corrupt and non-corrupt instances. The setting of PU classification can be treated as the special case of (binary) classification with noisy labels, when only true instances of one class have label noise (e.g., see [4, Sec 8.3]). Hence, many common theoretical assumptions from the PU learning literature have direct counterparts for learning with noisy labels. For example, [20] and [13] make the Selected Completely At Random (SCAR) assumption (see [6] and [4, Sec 3.1.1]) that is the basis of majority of PU learning methods. The SCAR assumption postulates that the labelled examples are sampled (from the positive distribution) independently from their features. In noisy-label learning SCAR has several names: Noisy At Random (NAR) [11], asymmetric label noise, and a class-conditional noise process [23]. In this paper we use the NAR assumption, supposing that the probability of label error depends on the true latent class only.

Confident Learning. Learning with noisy labels has great practical importance and many approaches have been explored. In this paper we apply generalized confident learning (GCL)[2], a state-of-the-art approach proposed in [23] that

---

[2] GCL implementation is available as the Python package Cleanlab (https://github.com/cgnorthcutt/cleanlab/).

generalizes techniques proposed earlier in the literature to allow estimating the joint distribution between noisy and uncorrupted labels. GCL requires only two inputs; for every observation, it requires (1) the out-of-sample predicted probabilities to belong to a specific class and (2) the (noisy) class labels themselves. This input allows GCL to estimate the joint distribution, latent distributions of true classes and rank label errors by likelihood of being an error [23].

Our choice of GCL was motivated by the following important considerations:

- it is a model-agnostic approach, meaning that many advanced machine learning algorithms can produce the input to GCL;
- it allows not only learning with label errors but finding them;
- the software is open-source, easy to install and use, and well-documented;
- the authors provide extensive reproducible benchmarks of the accuracy of GCL versus recent methods for noisy-labels learning;
- there are sufficient conditions under which GCL is guaranteed to exactly find label errors and estimate the joint distribution of noisy and uncorrupted labels.

2.2   The Data

In this paper we focus on requests for quotation (first-price sealed-bid auction, award determined by price). These are low-value auctions (the reserve price is restricted to 500,000 roubles, approximately 4,700 GBP) which are frequent and have an objective award criteria, which makes them attractive for machine learning methods.

Data on public procurement in the Russian Federation is available on the official website.[3] The dataset used in this paper was extracted by [21]. It covers the years 2014–2018 and consists of 3,081,719 bids from 1,372,307 auctions and 363,009 firms. An observation in the dataset is a bid and is labelled by the identification of the procurer, firm, auction, and region; the reserve price of the auction and the actual bid of the firm; the start and end date of the auction; the date the bid was actually placed.

After preliminary processing we removed 10.6% of the bids. About 3% were removed due to obvious errors in the data, consisting in one or more of:

1. Missing values in the bid description.
2. The start date of the auction being later than the end date.
3. The bid amount being less than zero or higher than the reserve price.
4. The reserve price being higher than the maximum allowed price of 500,000 roubles.

The rest were removed for one of three reasons:

1. The auction took place in Baikonur, which is administered by Russia but is part of Kazakhstan.

---

[3] https://zakupki.gov.ru/.

2. The reserve price was under 3,440 roubles (lowest 0.5%).
3. The firm placing the bid appears once in the dataset.

Baikonur was excluded for its peculiar status. The minimum reserve price of 3,440 (about 30 GBP) is an ad hoc approach to remove potential data errors – a price of 0 or 1 rouble should probably be classed as an error, but it is not clear where to draw the line, so we opted to drop the bottom 0.5%.

Firms that bid once were removed because one of our features is the length of time the firm is active in the system. This is a potential issue since our dataset covers the years 2014–2018 and could capture a firm that was active before this period and stopped in 2014, or a firm that began activity in 2018. We do not wish to misidentify an established firm with a long history of bids that ceased operations in 2014 with a firm that only placed one bid, ever.

This left us with 2,787,136 bids. Every bid consists of four identifiers and five values. The ranges of these values are summarised in Table 1.

2.3   Features of the Classifier

We train the classifier on the features in Table 2.

The label, `single`, is whether or not the auction attracted a single firm. Our assumption is that bids in multi-bidder auctions (`single` = 0) are predominantly competitive, while bids in single-bidder auctions (`single` = 1) are not. And indeed, in Table 3 we can see at a glance that single-bidder and multi-bidder auctions are very different affairs with respect to our features. Our hypothesis that bids in multi-bidder auctions are predominantly competitive is maintained by the lower relative price, lower ratio of firm victories with a single procurer, and a higher number of unique winners per procurer.

However we allow that there may exist bids with `single` = 1 that in other respects closely resemble multi-bidder auctions and vice versa, and the purpose of noisy-label classification is to identify these. To this end we chose the remaining features to be indicative of corruption and collusion.

The features can be divided into five groups, according to whether they relate to the bid (`bid.date`, `bid.price`), the firm (`sel.num`, `sel.period`), the procurer (`buy.unique`) a connection between the agents (`con.met`, `con.win`), or the auction (`au.reserve`, `au.duration`, `au.moscow`). We discuss these in turn.

Features of the Bid. The bid is our fundamental observation, and detecting signs of competition restriction on a bid-by-bid basis is important as we cannot assume firms are totally corrupt or totally clean: it is reasonable to assume that many firms would collude with a competitor or bribe an official if the opportunity presents itself, but participate in legitimate competition if not.

- `bid.price`: This measures the ratio of the bid to the reserve price. In the case of standardised contracts for homogeneous goods the absolute price can be used [17, 22, 25, 27], but without knowledge of what good/service is produced and in what quantity only the relative price is relevant [5, 8, 9].

Table 1. Variables in the data

Variable	Description	Min	Median	Max
reserve_price	Reserve price set by procurer (roubles)	3,440	134,637	500,000
price	Bid price set by firm (roubles)	0.01	106,500	500,000
start_date	Start date of the auction	28.01.14		26.03.18
end_date	End date of the auction	31.01.14		30.03.18
date	Time of bid	29.01.14		26.03.18
procurer_id	Identification of the procurer	1		43,311
firm_id	Identification of the firm	1		255,650
auction_id	Identification of the auction	1		1,358,369
region_id	The auction location (federal subject)	1		85

Table 2. Features of the classifier.

Variable	ID	Type	Min	Median	Max
Is the auction a single-bid auction?	single	Binary	0	0	1
Time from bid to the end date (seconds)	bid.date	Int	0	72,000	783,840
Ratio of bid to reserve price	bid.price	Float	0.00	0.90	1
Has the firm dealt with the procurer before?	con.met	Binary	0	0	1
Ratio of firm's victories with procurer to total victories	con.win	Float	0	0.06	1
How many auctions did the firm bid in?	sel.num	Int	2	27	8319
How long the firm is active in the data (days)	sel.period	Int	0	980	1,498
Ratio of reserve price to maximum (500,000)	au.reserve	Float	0.00	0.27	1
Auction duration (days)	au.duration	Int	0	7	26
Is auction in Moscow or Moscow Oblast?	au.moscow	Binary	0	0	1
Ratio of unique winners to number of auctions held by procurer	buy.unique	Float	0.02	0.5	1

Table 3. Statistics of single-bidder and multi-bidder auctions.

ID	Mean		Median		Std. Dev.	
	single = 1	single = 0	single = 1	single = 0	single = 1	single = 0
bid.date	146 910	133 815	76 800	71 220	172 297	167 765
bid.price	0.94	0.81	0.99	0.86	0.12	0.19
con.met	0.58	0.43	1	0	0.49	0.50
con.win	0.42	0.20	0.29	0.02	0.37	0.32
sel.num	288	181	22	29	1 070	683
sel.period	927	855	1064	947	422	439
au.reserve	0.30	0.38	0.20	0.30	0.29	0.31
au.duration	7.83	8.26	7	7	2.83	2.94
au.moscow	0.06	0.14	0	0	0.25	0.35
buy.unique	0.49	0.54	0.48	0.52	0.18	0.19

Bids in single-bidder auctions have a significantly higher relative price than other auctions (median of 0.99 and 0.86 respectively). This is a strong hint that firms do not expect competition.

– `bid.date`: The number of seconds to the deadline when the bid is registered. The fine granularity is necessary due to intense bid activity near the deadline [21]. In the presence of bid leakage, it makes sense for a corrupt firm to wait until the last second to either see the bids of its competitors, and for a fair firm to prevent its bid being leaked to a corrupt firm [2,21].

Features of the Connection Between Firm and Procurer. It takes two to tango, and equally to defraud the taxpayer. These features are intended to track repeated interactions between suspect firms and procurers.

– `con.win`: This measures what proportion of tenders awarded to a given firm were awarded by the same procurer.

$$\texttt{con.win} = \frac{auctions\ won\ by\ firm\ with\ this\ procurer}{auctions\ won\ by\ firm}.$$

A firm with a high `con.win` hints at a strong connection between the firm and a given procurer, and such ties could be indicative of a corrupt relationship. In the data both the median and mean are considerably higher in case of single-bidder auctions than auctions with more than one participant (0.29 compared to 0.02 for the median, 0.42 compared to 0.2 for the mean).

– `con.met`: This is a binary feature tracking whether the firm had bid in one of the procurer's auctions before. In the dataset, 58% of the bids in single-bidder auctions were made by firms who have met the procurer before, as opposed to 43% in auctions with more than one participant.

Features of the Firm. A common characteristic of corruption in Russia is the creation of "one-day firms",[4] firms that exist on paper but do not engage in any legitimate commercial activity. Instead these firms are used for criminal ends such as money laundering or, in our case, snapping up procurement auctions. These features are intended to identify such firms.

– `sel.num`: The number of auctions in which the firm participated. An established company is likely to participate in more auctions than a one-day firm.
– `sel.period`: The number of days the firm was active in the dataset, calculated as the number of days between its first bid and last bid.

Features of the Auction. The decisions made by the procurer in posting the auction – the reserve price and duration – can be indicative of intent.

---

[4] According to a Rossiyskaya Gazeta article (https://rg.ru/2016/02/15/chislo-firm-odnodnevok-rezko-snizilos.html) an estimated 45% of registered firms in 2011 were considered "one-day firms", down to 15% in 2016.

- **au.reserve:** The ratio of the reserve price to the 500,000 rouble maximum. We would expect a corrupt procurer to charge the maximum whenever he can get away with it. In the dataset we find the mean and median reserve prices in single-bidder to be lower than in multi-bidder auctions. This could be caused by honest procurers realising they are in a monopolistic market, and adjusting the reserve price down accordingly.
- **au.duration:** The number of days the auction lasted. If the procurer wishes to conceal the auction, it makes sense to make it as short as possible. This is a common feature in the literature [5,8,9]. The mean duration of single-bidder auctions is 7.8, compared to 8.3 for competitive auctions.
- **au.moscow:** Whether or not the auctions was held in Moscow or Moscow Oblast. Moscow is the heart of the Russian economy, and if there is one place where we would expect competition, it is here. Single-bidder auctions in Moscow deserve special scrutiny.

Feature of the Procurer. The procurer has a single feature, measuring the variety of firms to whom he awards contracts.

- **buy.unique:** This is the ratio of the number of unique winners in a procurer's auctions to the number of auctions. A value of 1 would be the situation where every auction was won by a different firm, while if a procurer only bought the services of a single firm the ratio would tend to 0.

$$\text{buy.unique} = \frac{number\ of\ winners\ in\ procurer's\ auctions}{number\ of\ auctions\ held\ by\ procurer}.$$

In the dataset the mean buy.unique value in single-bidder auctions is 0.49, compared to 0.54 in multi-bidder auctions. Thus procurers in single-bidder auctions are likely to work with a smaller number of firms.

3 Results

We trained the GCL classifier on our features with the assumption that multi-bidder auctions are predominantly competitive, and single-bidder auctions predominantly are not. The classifier produced the following confusion matrix, meaning that 29% of single-bidder auctions, in fact, closely resemble multi-bidder auctions:

	Competitive	Uncompetitive
single = 0	86%	14%
single = 1	29%	71%

This is significant as previous attempts to estimate the number of "legitimate" single-bidder auctions [8,9], based on market sector, came up with a figure of around 5%. In contrast, our figure is much lower than the 46% obtained by the PU-learning approach of [13].

That left us with 71% of bids in single-bidder auctions and 14% in multi-bidder auctions that do not resemble competitive behaviour. These are likely a mix of legal, yet undesirable behaviour such as monopolies, and illegal behaviour such as cartels or corruption. In the remainder of this section we discuss two classes of firms we found that resemble monopolist and cartel activity respectively.

3.1 Identifying Monopolists

While the notion of a monopolist is intuitively clear to all, identifying them in the data is challenging as the most visible feature of a monopolist – high market power – could just as well indicate corrupt ties between a firm and procurer. We decided to proceed via three criteria:

1. A monopolist should exclude other firms from its market (high rate of single-bidder auctions).
2. A monopolist should not expect to compete (high rate of uncompetitive bids).
3. A monopolist should be large (dealings with multiple procurers).

While considering how to select an appropriate cut-off point for 1) and 2), we noticed an interesting phenomenon in the distributions, which we illustrate in Fig. 1a.

The cluster in the top right consists of firms which are at exactly 1 on both axes, i.e. *every* bid was in a single-bidder auction, and *every* bid was uncompetitive. This is much stricter than we would typically demand from a monopolist – few firms in history could boast of absolute market power – but since such firms form a clear class, we decided it warranted attention.

Given the demanding choices for 1) and 2), we chose 2 procurers for 3) – a corrupt firm that absolutely never has to compete is likely to have a very close relationship with the procurer, and maintaining such relationships with even 2 procurers does not seem plausible.

We will refer to such firms as M-firms, since they represent a very particular kind of monopolist, and not necessarily the kind that first comes to mind. M-firms account for 2.65% of all firms in our dataset, and 5.39% of uncompetitive single-bidder auction bids.

To test our hypothesis that M-firms are monopolists rather than corrupt firms, we decided to observe whether the date at which M-firms place their bid differs from other uncompetitive bids. If the other bids are the result of corruption, we would expect them to bid close to the deadline [2,20], while presumably a monopolist, confident in his market power, could place a bid at any time.

In Fig. 1b we see that M-firms are, indeed, less likely to bid close to the dead-line than other uncompetitive bids.[5] The means differed from 49.95 to 41.38 h before the deadline, and medians 24 to 21.

Another curious pattern was observed by considering when exactly these bids were placed (Fig. 1c). The spikes in the graph correspond to 0, 24, 48, 72. That is to say, firms have a tendency to place their bids a fixed number of days before the deadline, but this behaviour is much less pronounced for M-firms. The behaviour of M-firms seems a lot more reasonable: we would expect a firm to place a bid when the application is ready, and not exactly twenty-four hours before the deadline. The curious behaviour of other firms could be the result of coordination between a firm and procurer – shootouts happen at noon, not 11:37.

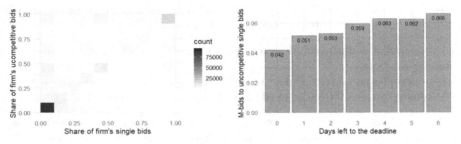

(a) Distribution of firms' proportion of uncompetitive bids and bids in single-winner auctions.

(b) Proportion of M-firm bids versus time to the deadline for auctions lasting six days.

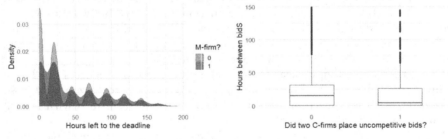

(c) Distribution of bid dates for M-firms and other uncompetitive bids for six day auctions.

(d) Time difference between the first and last bids in two-bidder auctions.

Fig. 1. Visualisation of bidding behaviour

3.2   The Search for Cartels

A cartel is a group of firms who have, explicitly or implicitly, agreed to restrict competition between themselves to raise the price for their services. This could

---

[5] Six day auctions were chosen as they are the most common length M-firms partici-pate in.

be done with a bid-rotation strategy, where firms refrain from bidding on each other's tenders, which would result in single-bidder auctions. However, the phony-bid strategy [24] involves the firms participating together, but placing bids that are not designed to win. Since this results in a multi-bidder auction, we sought to detect this behaviour in the class of uncompetitive bids in multi-bidder auctions.

We searched for collusive behaviour with the following criteria:

1. The firms participate together in at least two auctions, where both place uncompetitive bids.
2. Each such firm wins at least once with an uncompetitive bid.

The second criterion is to distinguish between cartel activity, which is intended to benefit all members, and other firms that may happen to place uncompetitive bids.[6]

We call the resulting firms C-firms. C-firms accounts for 2.18% of all bids, or 21.14% of uncompetitive bids in multi-bidder auctions. To verify that the behaviour of C-firms indeed resembles collusion, we looked at the time difference between bids in auctions where two C-firms participated versus other two-bid auctions. In Fig. 1d we see that C-firms bid much closer together than other firms, which is what we would expect if the firms coordinated between themselves. The medians in two-bidder auctions differ by 4.83 h for auctions consisting of uncompetitive bids by C-firms, to 14.45 for other auctions.

4   Conclusion

It is important to stress that the results of this, or of any statistical approach cannot be taken as proof that corruption has taken place. This can only be established by a court, on the basis of direct evidence of malfeasance such as bribery, ownership of contracted firms, or violations of procurement procedures. The purpose of such works is to guide regulators to where limited policing resources are best spent.

With that in mind, it is noteworthy that we have found that a considerable portion of single-bidder auctions in all other respects resembles multi-bidder auctions; we interpret these as incidental – firms submitted a bid with the expectation of competition that did not materialise, and no malfeasance took place. In the absence of a specific reason to examine these, a regulator's attention is best spent elsewhere.

However that left us with 71% of single-bidder auctions and 14% of multi-bidder auctions that look very different from competitive auctions, and is reasonable to suspect that collusion or corruption is at play.

Among the uncompetitive, multi-bidder instances we identified the class of C-firms, accounting for 21.14% of the class, whose behaviour resembled the phony-bid strategy of cartels – the firms did not compete against each other, shared

---

[6] For example, [21] find that 1.2% of firms are "snipers", who place high bids at the beginning of the auction, presumably in the hope that no one else will come.

their victories, and their bids were much closer in time than other firms. These are worthy of closer scrutiny.

Among the uncompetitive, single-bidder instances we identified the class of M-firms, accounting for 5.39% of the class, who seemed to have absolute market power and were a lot less inclined to bid close to the deadline than other firms. Market power, in and of itself, is not a crime, but monopolists have been known to use government ties to maintain their position. It would be interesting to investigate just who these firms are, and whether their market power is justified.

Future work should be directed to further understanding the class of uncompetitive bids. One avenue of attack could be identifying specific forms of illicit behaviour – such as bid-rotation, bid-leakage, one-day firms – and searching the data for their markers. However there will remain the problem of verification: in the absence of a reliable means to label corrupt firms in the data, there will remain a reliance on human interpretation to decide what resembles illicit activity, and what does not.

References

1. Accounts Chamber of the Russian Federation: Report on results of the analytical event «Monitoring of public and corporate procurement development in Russian Federation in 2018». https://ach.gov.ru/promo/goszakupki-2018/index.html (2018). Accessed 18 Jan 2021
2. Andreyanov, P., Davidson, A., Korovkin, V.: Detecting auctioneer corruption: evidence from Russian procurement auctions. https://www.researchgate.net/publication/333755312 (2018)
3. Arief, H.A., Saptawati, G.A.P., Asnar, Y.D.W.: Fraud detection based-on data mining on Indonesian e-procurement system (SPSE). In: ICoDSE 2016, pp. 1–6. IEEE, New York (2016)
4. Bekker, J., Davis, J.: Learning from positive and unlabeled data: a survey. Mach. Learn. **109**(4), 719–760 (2020). https://doi.org/10.1007/s10994-020-05877-5
5. Charron, N., Dahlström, C., Lapuente, V., Fazekas, M.: Careers, connections, and corruption risks: investigating the impact of bureaucratic meritocracy on public procurement processes. J. Pol. **79** (2016). https://doi.org/10.1086/687209
6. Elkan, C., Noto, K.: Learning classifiers from only positive and unlabeled data. In: Proceedings of the 14th ACM SIGKDD Conference on Knowledge Discovery and Data Mining, KDD 2008, pp. 213–220. ACM, New York (2008). https://doi.org/10.1145/1401890.1401920
7. European Commission: performance per policy area: Public procurement. https://ec.europa.eu/internal_market/scoreboard/performance_per_policy_area/public_procurement/index_en.htm (2019). Accessed 22 Jan 2021
8. Fazekas, M., János, T., King, L.: Anatomy of grand corruption: a composite corruption risk index based on objective data. SSRN Electron. J. (2013). https://doi.org/10.2139/ssrn.2331980
9. Fazekas, M., Kocsis, G.: Uncovering high-level corruption: cross-national objective corruption risk indicators using public procurement data. Br. J. Polit. Sci **50**(1), 155–164 (2020). https://doi.org/10.1017/S0007123417000461

10. Federal Antimonopoly Service of the Russian Federation: Federal Law No. 94-FZ On State and Municipal Procurement of Goods, Works and Services (as amended in 2011). http://en.fas.gov.ru/documents/documentdetails.html?id=13920 (2011). Accessed 18 Jan 2021

11. Frenay, B., Verleysen, M.: Classification in the presence of label noise: a survey. IEEE Trans. Neural Netw. Learn. Syst. **25**(5), 845–869 (2014)

12. Ghedini Ralha, C., Sarmento Silva, C.V.: A multi-agent data mining system for cartel detection in Brazilian government procurement. Expert Syst. Appl. **39**(14), 11642–11656 (2012). https://doi.org/10.1016/j.eswa.2012.04.037

13. Goryunova, N., Baklanov, A., Ianovski, E.: Detecting corruption in single-bidder auctions via positive-unlabelled learning. In: Strekalovsky, A., Kochetov, Y., Gruzdeva, T., Orlov, A. (eds.) MOTOR 2021. CCIS, vol. 1476, pp. 316–326. Springer, Cham (2021). https://doi.org/10.1007/978-3-030-86433-0_22

14. Gündel, S., et al.: Robust classification from noisy labels: integrating additional knowledge for chest radiography abnormality assessment. Med. Image Anal **72**, 102087 (2021)

15. Harrington, J.: Behavioral screening and the detection of cartels. In: Ehlermann, C.D., Atanasiu, I. (eds.) European Competition Law Annual 2006: Enforcement of Prohibition of Cartels. Hart Publishing, Oxford (2006)

16. Huber, M., Imhof, D., Ishii, R.: Transnational machine learning with screens for flagging bid-rigging cartels. Working Papers SES 519, Université de Fribourg (2020)

17. Hüschelrath, K., Veith, T.: Cartel detection in procurement markets. Manag. Decis. Econ. **35** (2011). https://doi.org/10.2139/ssrn.1983280

18. Ingraham, A.: A test for collusion between a bidder and an auctioneer in sealed-bid auctions. Contrib. Econ. Anal. Policy (4) (2005). https://doi.org/10.2202/1538-0645.1448

19. Ivanov, D.: Dedpul: difference-of-estimated-densities-based positive-unlabeled learning. In: 2020 19th IEEE International Conference on Machine Learning and Applications (ICMLA), pp. 782–790 (2020). https://doi.org/10.1109/ICMLA51294.2020.00128

20. Ivanov, D., Nesterov, A.: Identifying bid leakage in procurement auctions: machine learning approach. In: EC 2019, pp. 69–70. ACM, New York (2019)

21. Ivanov, D., Nesterov, A.S.: Stealed-bid auctions: detecting bid leakage via semi-supervised learning (2020)

22. Klasnja, M.: Corruption and the incumbency disadvantage: theory and evidence. J. Polit. 77 (2015). https://doi.org/10.1086/682913

23. Northcutt, C., Jiang, L., Chuang, I.: Confident learning: Estimating uncertainty in dataset labels. J. Artif. Intell. Res. **70**, 1373–1411 (2021)

24. Porter, R., Zona, J.: Detection of bid rigging in procurement auction. J. Polit. Econ. **101**, 518–38 (1993). https://doi.org/10.1086/261885

25. Porter, R.H., Zona, J.D.: Ohio school milk markets: an analysis of bidding. RAND J. Econ. **30**(2), 263–288 (1999)

26. Tai, X., Wang, G., Grecos, C., Ren, P.: Coastal image classification under noisy labels. J. Coast. Res. **102**(SI), 151–156 (2020)

27. Tkachenko, A., Yakovlev, A., Kuznetsova, A.: Sweet deals: state-owned enterprises, corruption and repeated contracts in public procurement. Econ. Syst. **41**, 52–67 (2017)

28. Transparency International: Transparency international corruption perceptions index. https://www.transparency.org/en/cpi (2019). Accessed 18 Jan 2021

29. Wachs, J., Fazekas, M., Kertész, J.: Corruption risk in contracting markets: a network science perspective. Int. J. Data Sci. Anal. **12**, 45–60 (2021). https://doi. org/10.1007/s41060-019-00204-1
30. Wang, H., Liu, B., Li, C., Yang, Y., Li, T.: Learning with noisy labels for sentence-level sentiment classification (2019)
31. Wang, X., Wang, S., Wang, J., Shi, H., Mei, T.: Co-mining: deep face recognition with noisy labels. In: Proceedings of the IEEE/CVF International Conference on Computer Vision (ICCV) (October 2019)
32. Wang, Y., Rao, Y., Zhan, X., Chen, H., Luo, M., Yin, J.: Sentiment and emotion classification over noisy labels. Knowl.-Based Syst. **111**, 207–216 (2016). https:// doi.org/10.1016/j.knosys.2016.08.012
33. Wu, X., He, R., Sun, Z., Tan, T.: A light CNN for deep face representation with noisy labels. IEEE Trans. Inf. Forensics Secur. **13**(11), 2884–2896 (2018). https:// doi.org/10.1109/TIFS.2018.2833032

Deep Autonomous Agents Comparison for Self-driving Cars

Alessandro Riboni[1], Antonio Candelieri[1], and Matteo Borrotti[1,2]

[1] University of Milano-Bicocca, Milano, Italy
{antonio.candelieri,matteo.borrotti}@unimib.it
[2] Institute for Applied Mathematics and Information Technology, Milano, Italy

Abstract. Autonomous driving is one of the most challenging problems of the last decades. The development in recent years is mainly due to the continuous expansion of Artificial Intelligence. Nowadays, most self-driving systems use Deep Learning techniques. In recent years, however, thanks to the successful learning demonstrations of Atari games and AlphaGo by Google DeepMind, new frameworks based on Deep Reinforcement Learning are being developed. The objective is to combine the advantages of image processing and feature extraction of convolutional networks, and the learning process through the interaction of one or multiple agents with their environment. This work aims to deepen and explore these new methodologies applied to autonomous driving cars. In particular, we developed a framework for controlling a car in a simulated environment. The agent learns to drive within a neighborhood with constant speed, variable light conditions, and avoiding collisions with external objects. The proposed techniques are based on Double Deep Q-learning and Dueling Double Deep Q-learning. We implemented two variants of the algorithms: one trained from random weights and one exploiting the concepts of Transfer Learning. After a simulation study, the Dueling Double Deep Q-learning with Transfer Learning has showed promising performance.

Keywords: Autonomous driving · Deep Q-learning · Transfer learning

1 Introduction

The development of self-driving cars is considered one of the greatest revolutions of the 21st century. In the last ten years, large investments have been made in this area, continually raising the state-of-the-art. Artificial intelligence (AI) and computer vision are the most important areas where researchers and engineers try to find solutions to the autonomous driving problem. A clear example is the Autopilot system of Tesla [14], which uses a multi-head neural network to perceive, predict, and act on the streets.

Theoretically, there are six levels of automation [13]. Most of the cars developed in the mobility history belong to level zero due to the absence of automation. In the first level, there is only a steering and acceleration/deceleration

© Springer Nature Switzerland AG 2022
G. Nicosia et al. (Eds.): LOD 2021, LNCS 13163, pp. 201–213, 2022.
https://doi.org/10.1007/978-3-030-95467-3_16

assistance system, while in the second, this task is fully automated. From level three to five, the driver has less and less responsibility. Beyond these traditional levels, there are two different strategies: human-centered autonomy and full autonomy, where AI is fully responsible. An example that emphasizes continuous innovation is the study conducted by Waymo in 2019 [1], where they combine Deep Learning (DL) with Reinforcement Learning (RL), another area of AI. These methods are called Deep Reinforcement Learning (DRL) [12], and their growth is due to the successful learning demonstrations of Atari Games and AlphaGo by Google DeepMind. Their objective is to merge the advantages of image processing and feature extraction of deep learning with the learning process of reinforcement learning.

The aim of this work is to investigate the state-of-the-art of these methods and propose an application in the context of autonomous driving. The final purpose is to understand and evaluate the potential of these combined approaches.

The typical supervised learning algorithms perform a first training phase on pre-processed and labeled data. Only after a validation process, these algorithms are deployed in the reference scenario. The reinforcement learning algorithms, instead, have a different approach. The agent has to interact with the environment iteratively. It is driven by an objective function to be maximized over time to perform the specific task in the best possible way. For this reason, it is necessary to identify a simulated environment in which reproduce the iterative system. In this work, the Microsoft AirSim simulator is chosen [9]. More precisely, we used a pre-built environment, called *Neighborhood*. This environment is an accurate reconstruction of a small city neighborhood, ideal for developing and testing an autonomous driving algorithm. The goal is to make the agent autonomous, *i.e.*, driving in the neighborhood with constant speed, variable light conditions, and avoiding collisions with external objects. A flexible framework has been implemented to handle the interaction between the agent and the environment.

The learning techniques developed are based on the Deep Q-Networks (DQN) algorithm, presented for the first time by Mnih et al. (2013) [5]. Two evolutions of this algorithm have been implemented, called Double (D2QN) DQN and Dueling Double (D3QN) DQN, respectively.

The paper is organized as follows. After a short state-of-the-art analysis (Sect. 1.1), Sect. 2 describes deep RL formulation and implementation. Section 3 briefly introduces the simulation platform. The results are shown in Sect. 4, whereas Sect. 5 provides conclusions and future work.

1.1 Related Works

The complexity of the domain and its sub-problems makes this area in continuous evolution. In the survey presented by Kiran et al. (2020) [2], a modern autonomous guidance system is represented as a pipeline composed of several modules, which can be divided into three macro areas: scene understanding, plan and decision, and control. These modules can be implemented in different ways: some examples are the different technologies to acquire information (cameras,

LiDAR, and ultrasonic sensors), localization methods, and algorithms to plan and decide what actions to take.

A complete autonomous guidance system contains several sub-tasks, such as motion planning, overtaking, lane keep, and lane change. Each of these tasks can be formalized as a DRL problem, in which it is necessary to learn a policy or specific behavior. In literature, there are several works that have achieved good results in one of these sub-problems [7,17].

This diversification of challenges and pipeline's modules makes the state-of-the-art very heterogeneous. The use of different simulators, many of them unrealistic, makes the comparison between studies very difficult. Some of the most interesting works have been implemented through The Open Racing Car Simulator (TORCS) [15]. It was released as a car game in 2000, and later, it was adapted as a research platform. Sallab et al. (2017) [8] have presented a framework for lane keep on this simulator, integrating recurrent neural networks and attention models to the DQN architecture proposed by Google DeepMind.

Another work developed on this platform is the one proposed by Wang et al. (2018) [18]. They applied a Deep Deterministic Policy Gradient (DDPG) [3] algorithm to train an agent to drive autonomously. In this case, the training was done not by raw pixels but through a series of sensors provided by the simulator, such as speed and car position.

2 Deep Reinforcement Learning Formulation and Implementation

Reinforcement learning (RL) is a subfield of Machine Learning (ML), and it is considered one of the main three paradigms together with supervised learning and unsupervised learning [12]. The basic idea behind this technique is to learn what to do from experience. An agent learns to perform a specific task by interacting with the surrounding environment. The agent maps situation to actions to achieve the goal, *i.e.*, to maximize a numerical reward over time. The RL process is done through direct interaction with the environment.

A RL process can be described through a formal framework of Markov Decision Process (MDP). In a MDP, an agent interacts with the surrounding environment. These interactions are sequential in time; in particular, at each discrete time step $t = \{0, 1, 2, ...\}$ the agent selects an action $a_t \in \mathcal{A}$, a set of actions, given a state $s_t \in \mathcal{S}$, a set of states. The state is a representation of the environment that the agent receives at every iteration. At the following time step, it will be in a new state s_{t+1}, and it will receive a numerical reward $r_{t+1} \in \mathcal{R}$, for the action taken in the previous state s_t. The sequence of this process is called *trajectory*.

2.1 Markov Decision Process Formulation

The first step is to formulate the autonomous driving problem through the MDP framework. In this study, the speed has been kept constant for simplicity, around

10 km/h, while the agent chooses the steering angle at each iteration. The action space is discretized, and, at each time-step, the vehicle can choose the action a_t from the set of possible action $\mathcal{A} = [-1, -0.5, 0, 0.5, 1]$. Collection $\mathcal{A}$ contains the steering angles that the agent can perform, measured in radiants. Figure 1 shows a schematic representation of the legal actions. The action is passed to the simulator, which modifies its internal state and computes a numerical reward.

Fig. 1. Set of legal actions.

At each time-step, the agent receives from the environment a vector of raw pixel values obtained from the front camera of the car. This image is pre-processed in order to reduce the input dimensionality. The first operation performed is the cropping of the upper and lower portion of the picture. Secondly, the size is reduced through down-sampling to 200x66 pixels. This process is performed for each frame obtained from the environment. The final output corresponds to the current state of the agent. The problem is formulated as an episodic task. Each episode begins from a starting point, which is randomly sampled from a set of 10 possible starting points of the virtual world. The standard assumption to discount the future rewards through a factor γ, defined as $G_t = R_{t+1} + \gamma R_{t+2} + \gamma^2 R_{t+3} + ... = \sum_{k=0}^{\infty} \gamma^k R_{t+k+1}$, is considered to give less importance to the uncertain future estimates.

Every episode can end with a collision with other objects or when the agent goes out of the street. To avoid infinite loops, each episode can process a maximum of 2,000 frames. Figure 2 presents a simplified representation of the interaction between the agent and the environment.

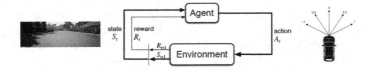

Fig. 2. Interaction between the agent and the environment.

2.2   Reward Function Definition

The reward function is defined taking inspiration from the work done by Sprtyn et al. (2018) [10], in which a distributed approach of the classic DQN is presented.

When the agent performs an action, the simulator returns to the algorithm the vehicle's new position. If the vehicle is in the middle of the roadway, it is awarded with the maximum reward equal to 1. This value decreases as the car approaches the roadsides. If the agent goes out of bounds or commits a collision, it receives a reward equal to 0. The reward function can assume values in the range $[0, 1]$. This clipping method makes the learning process of the model easier than using an unbounded function. The reward function is computed as defined by Eq. 1.

$$R(s_t, a_t, s_{t+1}) = \exp\left(-\beta * ||dist||\right), \tag{1}$$

where β is a positive constant that controls the shape of the function while $dist$ is the distance from the car position to the center of the road. In other words, β determines the decay rate of the reward from the center to the sides of the streets.

Given our simulator, it is possible to obtain the coordinates of the roads object. These points are used to calculate the distance. For each iteration, $dist$ is given by the distance between the car's position and the line connecting the two closest centers of the road. A function that determines whether an episode was terminated or not is also considered. In case the agent is in a terminal state, the reward associated with the last action is zero, and from the next iteration, a new independent episode will start.

2.3   DQN Agent Implementation

This section aims to present the application of the algorithm proposed by Mnih et al. (2015) [6] in this autonomous driving task. Concerning the original implementation, some adjustments have been made. Algorithm 1 presents the pseudo-code of the DQN Agent. This procedure is the same for all methods. The differences concern the structure of the neural network for the Q-values estimation.

Firstly, it is necessary to initialize the online network, the target network, and create an instance of *airisim_wrapper* that handles the interaction with the environment. Then an empty replay memory D is initialized. This memory works like a queue and keeps track of the last d experiences of the agent. At each iteration, the transaction [*action, state, reward, terminal*] is stored. The main purpose of this technique is to break the correlation between sequential frames, which have adverse effects during the training phase of the neural network. The optimization through stochastic gradient descent requires that the training data are independent and identically distributed. This technique also allow to limit the variance of the weights update, making the training process more stable and smoother. The memory is finite, and it can contain a maximum of 300,000 experiences. Once the full capacity is reached, the oldest information is overwritten.

The *airsim_wrapper* class resets the environment and sets the agent in a starting point sampled from a collection of 10 predefined points. The **reset()** function starts the episode, which may end due to a collision or if the maximum number of frames per episode is reached.

At each iteration, the agent chooses which action to perform according to an epsilon-greedy strategy and saves the current experience in the replay memory. This strategy lets to manage the trade-off between exploration and exploitation in a simple way. Initially, the agent does not know anything about the environment, so it needs a higher exploration level to gather knowledge through random actions. The ε value controls this trade-off: with a probability of ε, the agent performs a random action, otherwise selects the best action according to its Q-value. Initially, ε is equal to 1 and it decreases as the agent accumulates knowledge. Over the first 500,000 frames, the value is linearly reduced to 0.1. In the second half of the training, it is decreased to 0.01.

The primary network is trained every four frames. This process is performed on a minibatch of 64 experience sampled randomly from the replay memory. For simplicity, let's consider only a transition j containing the state s_j, the action performed a_j, the reward obtained r_j, the next state s_{j+1}, and a boolean value that indicates if the episode is finished. The online network estimates $Q(s_j, a; \theta)$, which determines how good each possible action is. Then the target Q-value (y_j) is calculated according to the Bellman equation. To manage possible overestimation problems, the Bellman equation is modified as suggested by van Hasselt et al. (2015) [16]. Instead of estimating the Q-values of the next state s_{j+1} only using the target network, the online network is used to estimate the best action, and then the target network is used to predict how much is the Q-value of that action. This adjustment is formalized as $y_i^{DoubleDQN} = r + \gamma Q(s', \arg\max_{a'} Q(s', a'; \theta_i), \theta^-)$, where θ_i are the weights of the online network and θ^- are the weights of the target network for the evaluation of the current greedy policy. The weights of the target network are fixed, and they are periodically copied from the online network $Q(s, a, \theta)$. Once the target Q-value is obtained, it is compared with the Q-value predicted by the online network. The loss function is computed, allowing to perform a gradient descent step. In this work, the error clipping technique has been implemented directly replacing the loss function. Instead of the quadratic cost function, the Huber loss is used. Finally, the weights of the main network are copied periodically into the target network. The update rate is every 10,000 frames. The use of two different networks is crucial as it makes the training process more stable.

Double DQN (D2QN). The first architecture implemented is a Double DQN, called D2QN. The algorithm structure follows step by step the pseudocode presented in Algorithm 1. The Q-values estimation is done through an approximation function, which is a convolutional neural network.

The input images are normalized in the range [0,1]. Three convolutional, one flatten and two fully connected layers compose the network. The first convolves 32 filters of 8 × 8 with stride 4 and applies a non-linear activation function called Rectifier Linear Unit (ReLU). This activation function is also used in the following convolutional layers. Both convolve 64 filters but of different sizes. The second has 4×4 size with stride 2, while the third has 3×3 size with stride 1. Then a flatten layer collapses the spatial dimensions of the input into the channel dimension. The head of the network is formed by two fully connected: the first is formed by 512 units while the second by 5 neurons, one for each available action. The values of the output layer neurons are the Q-values estimates of the possible actions from the state given input to the neural network.

Algorithm 1: DQN Agent

TOTAL_FRAMES = 1,000,000
MIN_REP_SIZE = 100,000
MAX_EPISODE_LENGTH = 2,000
UPDATE_RATE = 10,000
Initialize online network Q with random weights θ
Initialize target network $\hat{Q}$ with random weights $\theta^- = \theta$
Initialize an empty replay memory $\mathcal{D}$
Initialize $airsim\_wrapper$ and the agent
for $frame\_number = 1, \text{TOTAL\_FRAMES}$ **do**
　Reset $airsim\_wrapper$ from a random starting point
　for $frame = 1, \text{MAX\_EPISODE\_LENGTH}$ **do**
　　With probability ε select a random action a_t
　　otherwise select $a_t = \arg\max_a Q(s_t, a; \theta)$
　　Take action a_t, observe reward r_t and the next_state s_{t+1}
　　Add experience $[a_t, s_t, r_t, terminal]$ in the replay memory $\mathcal{D}$
　　if frame_number % 4 = 0 and replay memory > MIN_REP_SIZE
　　　Sample a random batch of experiences $[s_j, a_j, r_j, s_{j+1}]$ from $\mathcal{D}$
　　　Set $y_j = \begin{cases} r_j & \text{if } s_{j+1} \text{ is terminal} \\ r_j + \gamma Q(s_{j+1}, \arg\max_{a'} Q(s_{j+1}, a'; \theta), \theta^-) & \text{otherwise} \end{cases}$
　　　Perform a gradient descent step on $(y_i - Q(s_j, a_j; \theta))^2$
　　if frame_number % UPDATE_RATE = 0
　　　Copy weights from Q to $\hat{Q}$
　　$frame+ = 1$, $frame\_number+ = 1$
　　if $terminal$
　　　Break
　end for
end for

Dueling Double DQN (D3QN). The second architecture implemented is a Dueling Double DQN, called D3QN. Also in this case, the algorithm structure follows the previously presented pseudocode, reported in Algorithm 1. The network architecture is equal to the one proposed by Wang et al. (2016) [19].

The first four layers are the same of D2QN architecture. After the flatten layer, however, two streams are created. The first stream estimates the state value and is formed by two fully connected layers. One is composed of 512 neurons, and one has only a unit that corresponds to the scalar $V(s)$. The second stream estimates the advantage of performing an action compared to the others available. This second stream has a fully connected layer of 512 units and a final layer with as many neurons as the action space's dimension. The two streams are then combined for obtaining the Q-values related to the possible actions.

2.4 Transfer Learning

The training process of DRL algorithms requires a lot of time to obtain satisfactory results. The technique of Transfer Learning (TL) can help achieve excellent performance in a shorter overall time and increase the level of generalization of the algorithm. TL is a machine learning technique where a model transfers the knowledge acquired during the training process to a second model for a different task. For comparison reasons, the two architectures are trained both from random weights, and starting from weights pre-trained on a similar task. The chosen task aims to predict the steering angle of a car through supervised learning. The data used for training are a sub-sample of the public SullyChen dataset [11]. It contains more than 63,000 images, recorded with a dashcam around Rancho Palos Verde and San Pedro California, USA. Each frame is associated with the steering angle executed by the driver.

Before training the model, a pre-processing operations is made. The images have been normalized, cropped, and downsampled in order to obtain a size of 200×66 pixels. The subsequent step is to adapt the DQN network to the regression task to predict the steering angle. The goal is to transfer the ability of the first convolutional layers to extract the low-level features present in the images. For this reason, the convolutional block remained unchanged, while the head of the network is modified. After the flatten and the first Dense layers, two fully connected layers are added. The first has 256 units and the second one, *i.e.*, the output layer, has only one neuron. To limit the overfitting, a Dropout with a rate equal to 0.5 before the output layer is added. The network is trained for 10 epochs, with a *batch size* = 64 and the *Adam* optimizer. At the end of the training process, the weights of the three convolutional layers are transferred and used as a starting point for the DRL algorithms.

3   Simulation Platform

AirSim is an open-source, cross-platform simulator developed by Microsoft [9]. This software is created as a plugin for game engines such as Unreal Engine and Unity. The purpose of AirSim is to reduce the gap between simulation and reality to help the development of autonomous vehicles. One of its main advantages is flexibility. The modular construction of the simulator allows the development of projects with different degrees of complexity. Moreover, it is feasible to adapt or combine different approaches, increasing the scalability and robustness of the proposed architectures. This project is realized within one virtual scenario, named Neighborhood. This environment represents an area of a small city. The streets are characterized by long straights, with several cars parked on the sides, and curves at ninety degrees. Figure 3 shows some images of the chosen environment.

Fig. 3. *Neighbourhood* environment of AirSim.

4   Results

Four architectures have been compared: D2QN and D3QN starting with random weights and D2QN and D3QN exploiting Transfer Learning, D2QN_TL and D3QN_TL respectively. The final aim is to propose a DRL algorithm suitables for a vehicle completely autonomous inside an environment with constraints. In what follows, three different analyses are report. For the sake of clarity, we mention that the first comparison is done on the training data and second and third comparisons are made on the test data.

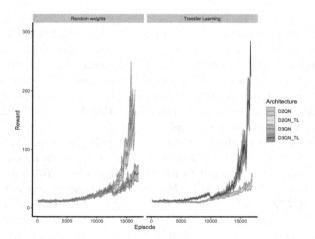

Fig. 4. Average reward during learning process with confidence interval (95%).

The first comparison regards the training phase of the models. In particular, it is considered the average of the rewards in the last 100 episodes for the whole duration of the process. Figure 4 shows two line graphs: the first one presents the average rewards with the relative confidence interval for the two architecture trained from scratch, while the second one shows the same chart for the methods with transfer learning. In the first case, it is possible to notice that the trend of D2QN is better than D3QN after about 12,000 episodes. In the second case, instead, the two architectures' trend is similar for about 14,000 episodes, after which the D3QN_TL performance improves significantly.

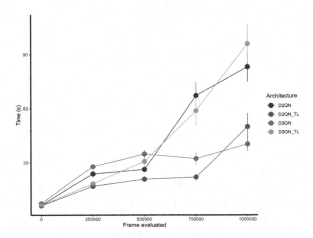

Fig. 5. Average time of autonomous driving during learning process from test starting points.

The second comparison is made on the test points. This allowed evaluating the improvement of the four methods' performance, taking into account their generalization level. For each point, 30 runs were carried out. Figure 5 shows the average time of autonomous driving with the relative 95% confidence interval on test points, especially every 250,000 frames. Even in this situation, the figure underlines that the average trends of D2QN and D3QN_TL are similar and better than the other two architectures implemented.

This consideration is also motivated by a pairwise Mann-Whitney U test performed on the time of autonomous driving of the four models on the test points. More specifically, we fail to reject the hypotesis H_0 comparing D2QN and D3QN_TL (p-value = 0.278). However, the time of autonomous driving for D2QN and D3QN_TL is significantly higher than the other two models (p-value < 0.001). D2QN_TL and D3QN are significantly similar in terms of time of autonomous driving (p-value = 0.369). This can be also notice from Fig. 5.

The third comparison is made at the end of the learning process, evaluating the performance in terms of autonomous driving time. This is carried out on

Table 1. Summary of architectures performance from test starting points.

Architecture	Mean time	Median time	1st quartile	3th quartile	Collision-free rate
D2QN	83.06	58.04	20.34	129.20	5.33%
D2QN_TL	49.89	23.04	17.29	53.67	5.33%
D3QN	40.26	21.15	15.72	59.26	0.00%
D3QN_TL	**95.89**	**59.10**	19.97	169.14	**17.33%**

the test starting points. Table 1 shows the mean time, the median time, 1st quartile, 3th quartile and the rate of episodes ended without collisions, called *collision-free rate*. The mean time, the median time, 1st quartile, 3th quartile are computed considering the time of autonomous driving counted as the time from the starting point to the potential collision. The median value of D2QN and D3QN_TL is similar, while the mean value and the interquartile range of the latter are greater, as showed in Table 1. On test data, the percentage of episodes ended without collision shows a clear advantage of D3QN_TL compared to other architectures.

The results show that D3QN_TL is the most suitable approach to perform a final learning process. The D3QN_TL is than used for a final learning process of 600,000 frames, namely D3QN_TL_FINAL. D3QN_TL_FINAL obtained an average of 106.28 s of autonomous driving, a median time of 56.99 s and a collision-free rate equal to 25%.

To guarantee replicability, our code is available at the following GitLab repository: https://gitlab.com/ub-dems-public/cs-labs/user-ariboni/csp-drive-rl.

5 Conclusion and Future Works

In this work, two variants of the DQN algorithm proposed by Google DeepMind were implemented, namely Double DQN and Dueling Double DQN, with the purpose of comparing a set of autonomous driving agents for self-driving car. The AirSim simulator was used to implement a realistic environment with some constraints in order to test and compare the approaches. The proposed methods were trained both from random weights and by means of transfer learning from a related task to evaluate the impact of this technique on performance and reliability.

Considering the limited number of frames evaluated, the results obtained are satisfactory. It is possible to notice a remarkable improvement in terms of autonomous driving time and rewards during the training process. The final architecture, Dueling Double DQN with transfer learning, can move autonomously for an average time of 106.28 s with a collision-free rate of 25%.

Thanks to the complexity of the domain and the continuous growth of the DRL field, there are many possible future developments. It would certainly be interesting to apply other DRL algorithms, such as the Deep Deterministic Policy Gradient (DDPG) [3]. Another possible improvement regards Adversarial

Learning techniques [4] in order to modify weather conditions within the simulated environment to make the model more reliable. Other possible developments can be the use of multi-environment or multi-agent systems.

As such, considering these elements for future work is surely a good prospect to improve the deep autonomous driving agent for self-driving cars.

Acknowledgements. We greatly acknowledge the DEMS Data Science Lab for supporting this work by providing computational resources.

References

1. Bansal, M., Krizhevsky, A., Ogale, A.: ChauffeurNet: learning to drive by imitating the best and synthesizing the worst. arXiv:1812.03079, pp. 1–20 (2018)
2. Kiran, B.-R., et al.: Deep reinforcement learning for autonomous driving: a survey. arXiv:2002.00444, pp. 1–18 (2020)
3. Lillicrap, T., et al.: Continuous control with deep reinforcement learning. arXiv:1509.02971, pp. 1–14 (2015)
4. Lowd, D., Meek, C.: Adversarial learning. In: Proceedings of the 11th ACM SIGKDD International Conference on Knowledge Discovery in Data Mining, KDD, pp. 641–647. ACM, Beijing China (2005)
5. Mnih, V., et al.: Playing Atari with deep reinforcement learning. arXiv:1312.5602, pp. 1–9 (2013)
6. Mnih, V., Kavukcuoglu, K., Silver, D., Rusu, A.-A., Veness, J., Bellemare, M.-G., et al.: Human-level control through deep reinforcement learning. Nature **518**(7540), 529–533 (2015)
7. Ngai, D.-C.-K., Yung, N.-H.-C.: Deep reinforcement learning for autonomous driving: a survey. IEEE Trans. Intell. Transp. Syst. **12**(2), 509–522 (2011)
8. Sallab, S.-E.-L., Abdou, M., Perot, E., Yogamani, S.: Deep reinforcement learning framework for autonomous driving. Electron. Imaging **2017**(19), 70–76 (2017)
9. Shah, S., Dey, D., Lovett, C., Kapoor, A.: AirSim: high-fidelity visual and physical Simulation for autonomous vehicles. arXiv:1705.05065, pp. 1–14 (2017)
10. Spryn, M., Sharma, A., Parkar, D., Shrimal, M.: Distributed deep reinforcement learning on the cloud for autonomous driving. In: 2018 IEEE/ACM Proceedings of the 1st International Workshop on Software Engineering for AI in Autonomous Systems, SEFAIAS, pp. 16–22. IEEE, Gothenburg, Sweden (2018)
11. SullyChen Dataset: driving dataset. https://github.com/SullyChen/driving-datasets. Accessed 19 Jan 2021
12. Sutton, R.-S-., Barto, A.-G.: Reinforcement Learning: An Introduction. The MIT Press, Massachusetts (2018)
13. Taxonomy and Definitions for Terms Related to Driving Automation Systems for On-Road Motor Vehicles. https://www.sae.org/standards/. Accessed 19 Jan 2021
14. Tesla Autopilot: Future of Driving. https://www.tesla.com/autopilot. Accessed 19 Jan 2021
15. Torcs, the open racing car simulator. http://torcs.sourceforge.net. Accessed 19 Jan 2021
16. van Hasselt, H., Guez, A., Silver, D.: Deep reinforcement learning with double q-learning. arXiv:1509.06461, pp. 1–13 (2015)

17. Wang, P., Chan, C.-Y., de La Fortelle, A.: A reinforcement learning based approach for automated lane change maneuvers. In: 2018 IEEE Intelligent Vehicles Symposium (IV), pp. 1379–1384. IEEE, Changshu, China (2018). https://doi.org/ 10.1109/IVS.2018.8500556

18. Wang, S., Jia, D., Weng, X.: Deep reinforcement learning for autonomous driving. arXiv:1811.11329, pp. 1–9 (2018)

19. Wang, Z., Schaul, T., Hessel, M., van Hasselt, H., Lanctot, M., Freitas, N.: Dueling network architectures for deep reinforcement learning. In: Proceedings of the 33rd International Conference on Machine Learning, PMLR, pp. 1–9, New York, USA, JMLR (2016)

Method for Generating Explainable Deep Learning Models in the Context of Air Traffic Management

Keith Rudd[✉], Michelle Eshow, and Mary Gibbs

Mosaic ATM Inc., Leesburg, VA, USA
{krudd,meshow,mgibbs}@mosaicatm.com,
{krudd,meshow,mgibbs}@mosaicdatascience.com

Abstract. Model explainability, interpretability, and explainable AI have become major research topics, particularly for deep neural networks where it is unclear what features the network may have used to come to a particular output. This paper presents a method for understanding these features. The method processes auto-encoder outputs to generate feature vectors and allows a user to explore these features and gain insight into the network's behavior. The method is applied to the U.S. air traffic management domain, an area rich in data and complexity, where use of deep learning is growing rapidly. In particular, the method is used to create models to predict throughput at major airports based on current and predicted weather and air traffic conditions. Models are created for two major U.S. airports of interest to NASA. For this application, the method is found to produce acceptable levels of prediction accuracy. It also produces explanations that relate input conditions to each other and to the predictions in ways that align with those of subject matter experts. Acceptance by subject matter experts is necessary if deep learning models are to be adopted in the air traffic management domain.

Keywords: Explainable AI · Deep learning · Air traffic management

1 Background

With the recent growth in machine learning capabilities and availability, there has been more emphasis placed on shedding light on black box models. The phrases "interpretability" and "explainable AI" are frequently used to refer to the extent that a model can not only give an output, but also a justification for why that output was given [14]. While this concept is easy to define at a high level, some have suggested that interpretability is a somewhat ill-defined concept that may refer to more than one idea [20].

This work was sponsored by NASA Ames Research Center under the NASA Small Business Innovative Research Program, Phase II, Contract No. 80NSSC19C0108.

Among the topics that tend to arise with the idea of interpretability are [20]:

- Generalization: A measure of how well a model can apply a learned skill to unfamiliar situations.
- Robustness: A measure of how sensitive the model is to small perturbations. Neural networks are notorious for being sensitive, particularly those with many fully connected layers. For example, convolutional neural networks (CNNs) have been seen to misclassify images that were perturbed on a scale that was imperceptible to a human [39].
- Transparency: The degree to which the mechanisms within the model can be generally understood.
- Trust: A general feeling that the model performs accurately and is appropriately interpreting the input data.

There are many benefits that come with explainable AI. Some that have been previously mentioned in [33] include verification that the model/system is working correctly, the ability to identify areas of improvement, the opportunity to learn from the system, and the ability to evaluate compliance with regulations. Other opportunities that explainable deep learning may bring include injecting human knowledge into the model, training on less data, and others [7]. For the case of airport throughput prediction in Air Traffic Management (ATM), a large potential benefit is the ability to use one approach, including data processing, modeling, and visualization software, for any number of different airports.

Deep neural networks (DNNs), in particular, have experienced a high degree of scrutiny due to their opaque nature and, despite their accuracy, have been passed over for simpler models in applications where model transparency is required [5,33].

As succinctly summarized in [33], there are perhaps two approaches to explainability: (1) to understand what a model has learned and (2) to explain individual predictions. For CNNs, examples of the former include [10,23,26], and examples of the latter include [1,16,24,37,41].

Explainability has also been explored in recurrent neural networks. For example, in [18] the authors present a method for explaining the output of a recurrent convolutional network (RCNN). Their strategy was to seek a "rationale" that was a simplified, interpretable version of the input that was able to reach nearly the same model output as one that was not interpretable. More recently, [14] proposed a method for measuring a CNN's robustness to perturbations. The authors of [28] combine a CNN with a long short-term memory (LSTM) recurrent neural network to generate short text explanations of the CNN's output.

Two important aspects of explainable machine learning are (1) the question of what constitutes an explanation and (2) the degree of human input that is required to produce the explanations. One common approach, such as [4, 13], formulates the explanation in terms of a contrasting reason. Other popular methods, such as [19,29,30,38], give the reasoning behind a model's output as a weighted value of the model's inputs. These methods require relatively little input from the user in crafting the explanations. However, this type of explanation may not be practical (helpful) if the number of relevant inputs is large, or if there are related features that may dominate the explanation.

Explainable principal component analysis (EPCA) [2] is an iterative method that uses a human in the loop to group similar features into orthogonal basis vectors that may provide a better (more intuitive and/or concise) set from which explanations can be built. This allows for greater flexibility in crafting the explanations, but also requires input from someone with domain expertise. Additionally, while EPCA works well for capturing linear relationships between the model inputs, it does not capture non-linear relationships.

The work presented in this paper builds upon that EPCA algorithm [2] and provides a general methodology for building and dissecting a generic (non-recurrent) deep learning model to convey both an understanding of what the model has learned, and an explanation for a particular output, addressing both approaches to explainability at once. The methodology is described in the following section. This is followed by a real-world example in which deep learning is applied to the problem of forecasting airport throughput, which we define as the total number of flights that will land or take off from an airport in a 15-minute window. Accurate models to predict airport throughput, based on complex air traffic and meteorological conditions and constraints, are of great value to airspace operators and users. Previous approaches have used first principles to develop such models which require specific data and software to be written for each new airport. Using our novel methodology, we developed a deep learning model that accurately predicts throughput for any major U.S. airport and provides explanations that domain experts managing air traffic operations can understand and use in decision-making. This approach saves extensive effort of building or adapting models for more than 30 individual airports and makes the model more likely to be trusted.

2   Methodology

This section presents our methodology for building and dissecting a deep learning model that conveys an understanding of what the model has learned and an explanation for a particular output. The first subsection addresses the fundamental model architecture we used, which can be adapted to build a model in an domain. The second subsection presents a method to decompose a fully trained model, which is key to providing model users with an understanding of what the model has learned as well as explanations for the model output.

2.1   The Model

In deep learning models, as the inputs are fed progressively from layer to layer, it is generally accepted that the layer outputs progress from lower-level to higher-level or more abstract features [32]. It has also been shown that using auto-encoders can provide very rich feature vectors. For example, in [17] a sparse nine-layer auto-encoder was used to perform unsupervised learning to teach a model to successfully recognize faces. Similarly, in [17] a sparse auto-encoder is used to generate feature vectors. The approach in this work is somewhat similar in that it relies on feature vectors produced by auto-encoders and uses these vectors to produce explanations for the model outputs.

Let $\{(\mathbf{x}_k, \mathbf{y}_k)\}_1^K$ be a set of K input/output training examples, where $\mathbf{x}_k \in \mathbb{R}^n$, and $\mathbf{y}_k \in \mathbb{R}^m$. The approach presented in this paper aims to be as general as possible but will be given in the context of a regression problem. In practice, the specific network structure is dictated by the type of data that is used. For data that is spatial or temporal in nature, where neighboring values within $\mathbf{x}_k$ have some relation, the hidden layers consist of a convolutional layer followed by max-pooling [27]. For data

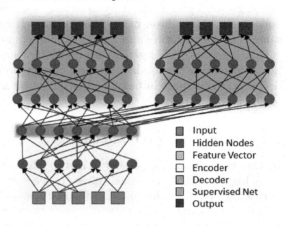

Input
Hidden Nodes
Feature Vector
Encoder
Decoder
Supervised Net
Output

Fig. 1. Diagram of the model architecture, comprising three sub-models.

that is not spatially or temporally correlated, these layers may be dense layers with dropout or batch normalization. Without much modification, this method can also be used with 'residual layers' [12], in which the output of a layer is passed both to the subsequent layer as well as added to the output of that layer.

The model chosen comprises three sub-models: an encoder, a decoder, and a supervised multi-layer perception (MLP), as shown in Fig. 1. For simplicity in notation, the following network structure is assumed, which can trivially be extended to include residual learning and many other types of network structures:

$$\phi(\mathbf{x}) = \begin{bmatrix} \mathbf{F}(\mathbf{H}(\mathbf{x})) \\ \mathbf{G}(\mathbf{H}(\mathbf{x})) \end{bmatrix} \tag{1}$$

$$\mathbf{F}(\mathbf{H}(\mathbf{x})) = f_N(f_{N-1}(f_{N-2}(...f_0(\mathbf{H}(\mathbf{x})))))$$

$$\mathbf{G}(\mathbf{H}(\mathbf{x})) = g_M(g_{M-1}(g_{M-2}(...g_0(\mathbf{H}(\mathbf{x})))))$$

$$\mathbf{H}(\mathbf{x}) = h_P(h_{P-1}(h_{P-2}(...h_0(\mathbf{x}))))$$

where the function $\mathbf{H}$ is the encoder network, $\mathbf{F}$ is the decoder network, and $\mathbf{G}$ is the supervised branch of the network. This approach to structuring deep networks is similar in nature to one of the early methods shown to be effective at overcoming the difficulties of training deep neural networks [9]. Additionally, as will be further shown below, the decoder network will allow the user to explore how information is represented within the model.

Each sub-model contains weights (parameters) that are tuned so that the output of the decoder approximates the model inputs ($\mathbf{x}_k \approx \mathbf{F}(\mathbf{H}(\mathbf{x}_k))$), and the output of the supervised network approximates the target ($\mathbf{y}_k \approx \mathbf{G}(\mathbf{H}(\mathbf{x}_k))$).

The parameter optimization with these two objectives (commonly referred to as multi-objective deep learning [35]) can be done using one of many algorithms, such as those reviewed in [31].

Although not explored in the current work, it may be possible to take an existing model and adapt it by attaching a decoder (generative) network to the output of a hidden layer of the existing model. This would, in essence, create the same network structure and may help to decrease training time. In the following subsection we provide a general approach to using the decoder network to explore how information is contained in the feature vector space. It also describes how to decompose this space into orthogonal basis vectors that will serve as explanations to the model output.

2.2 Decomposing the Model

In this subsection, we present a method to decompose a fully trained model. At a high level, the approach aims to decompose the feature vector space (or mid-point of the model) into orthogonal basis vectors that encapsulate distinct information. The decoder network can then be used to explore how these vectors relate to the original inputs. This will help the user gain a greater understanding of what information the model has learned and how it is using that information. The first step is to generate a set of feature vectors using the encoder network:

$$\boldsymbol{\xi}_k = \mathbf{H}(\mathbf{x}_k) = h_P(h_{P-1}(h_{P-2}(...h_0(\mathbf{x}_k)))), \quad k = 1, ..., K \qquad (2)$$

Once the feature vector set $\{\boldsymbol{\xi}_k\}_{k=1}^k$ is obtained, Principal Component Analysis (PCA) is performed on the feature vector space by mean-subtracting and decomposing the feature vectors into orthogonal components, represented here by the set of basis vectors $\{\hat{\mathbf{u}}_j\}_{j=1}^J$. This can be done using a standard Singular Value Decomposition (SVD) or more sophisticated method, as discussed below. Once the orthogonal basis vectors are formed, each feature vector can then be approximated as follows:

$$\boldsymbol{\xi}_k \approx \alpha_{k,0}\hat{\mathbf{u}}_0 + ...\alpha_{k,J}\hat{\mathbf{u}}_J + \bar{\boldsymbol{\xi}} \qquad (3)$$

where $\bar{\boldsymbol{\xi}}$ is the mean of the feature vectors.

There are a few motivating factors for using this approach outlined above. First, decomposing the feature vectors (the output of an encoder network) can lead to a more feature-rich space than PCA on the original input space [15]. One of the key benefits of this approach is that the researcher can use the decoding network to explore how these features are related to the original data. This can be done by feeding the principal components individually into the second half of the auto-encoder, with varying magnitudes, to get an intuitive understanding of what information that feature vector represents. The principal components are also passed through the supervised network to see what effect they have on the target outputs:

$$\tilde{\mathbf{x}} = \mathbf{F}(\beta\hat{\mathbf{u}}_j + \bar{\boldsymbol{\xi}}) = f_N(f_{N-1}(f_{N-2}(...f_0(\beta\hat{\mathbf{u}}_j + \bar{\boldsymbol{\xi}})))) \tag{4}$$
$$\tilde{\mathbf{y}} = \mathbf{G}(\beta\hat{\mathbf{u}}_j + \bar{\boldsymbol{\xi}}) = g_M(f_{M-1}(g_{M-2}(...g_0(\beta\hat{\mathbf{u}}_j + \bar{\boldsymbol{\xi}}))))$$

In the above equations, a user is able to manipulate the parameter β and see the resulting effects on $\tilde{\mathbf{x}}$. Practically speaking, this is accomplished by visualizing the output of the decoder and supervised networks across values of β that span the variance within the training data. This allows for greater model transparency because the user is able to visually observe relationships that the model has learned, both within the model inputs themselves and between the features and model outputs.

Different approaches may be used to decompose the feature space ($\{\boldsymbol{\xi}_k\}_1^K$) into orthogonal basis vectors ($\{\mathbf{u}_j\}_1^J$). For example, an analyst may use SVD or one of its variants and then use the decoder network to explore the relationship between each vector and the original inputs, to assign a label to each vector. Depending upon the specific network architecture and activation functions used, it may be that the feature vectors exhibit sparsity and may benefit from the use of robust principal component analysis (RPCA) [3,40]. However, the feature vectors should be decomposed in such a way as to maximize the understanding of the user. The explanations must be unique, concise, and intuitive. Because SVD and its variants seek to minimize variance rather than maximize intuitiveness, this decomposition may not result in good explanations. In our research, we found that an iterative approach with a human in the loop worked well in the context of a regression problem such as this one. Our approach benefited greatly from an interactive user interface (UI) that will be discussed in the subsequent section.

The process for building an Explainable Basis Vector (EBV) is as follows. The user first selects a primary input (i.e. an input that is known to be a major factor) , a target output, and whether he or she expects the input and output to have a positive or negative correlation. Without loss of generality (WLOG), suppose input feature x_l and output target y_q are chosen and believed to have a positive correlation. Let μ_{x_l} and μ_{y_q} be their respective means (estimated from the training data) and σ_{x_l} and σ_{y_q} be their respective standard deviations. One subset, $\mathbf{A}$, of the feature vectors is then found by identifying all examples in the training data for which the feature x_l and target y_q are one standard deviation above the mean, and one subset, $\mathbf{B}$ where they are one standard deviation below the mean:

$$\mathbf{A} = \{\boldsymbol{\xi}_k | \boldsymbol{\xi}_k = \mathbf{H}(\mathbf{x}_k) \wedge x_{l,k} \geq \mu_{x_l} + \sigma_{x_l} \wedge y_{q,k} \geq \mu_{y_q} + \sigma_{y_q}\} \tag{5}$$
$$\mathbf{B} = \{\boldsymbol{\xi}_k | \boldsymbol{\xi}_k = \mathbf{H}(\mathbf{x}_k) \wedge x_{l,k} \leq \mu_{x_l} - \sigma_{x_l} \wedge y_{q,k} \leq \mu_{y_q} - \sigma_{y_q}\}$$

The feature vectors within these groups are averaged, and the normalized difference between the averages is used as a potential explainable basis vector. WLOG, suppose that j explainable basis vectors have already been formed. The $j + 1$ explanation is found by projecting out the previous j, as done in the Gram-Schmidt algorithm [6]:

$$\mathbf{u} = \left(\sum_{\boldsymbol{\xi}_i \in \mathbf{A}} \boldsymbol{\xi}_i - \bar{\boldsymbol{\xi}} \right) / |\mathbf{A}| - \left(\sum_{\boldsymbol{\xi}_i \in \mathbf{B}} \boldsymbol{\xi}_i - \bar{\boldsymbol{\xi}} \right) / |\mathbf{B}| \tag{6}$$

$$\mathbf{u}_{j+1} = \mathbf{u} - \sum_{k=0}^{j} (\mathbf{u}^T \hat{\mathbf{u}}_k) \hat{\mathbf{u}}_k$$

$$\hat{\mathbf{u}}_{j+1} = \frac{\mathbf{u}_{j+1}}{||\mathbf{u}_{j+1}||}$$

The unit vector, $\hat{\mathbf{u}}_{j+1}$ is now a potential explainable basis vector. The user can use (4) to verify that this is a 'good' explanation. While the definition of what constitutes a 'good' EBV is subjective, we argue that it must accomplish three things:

– The basis vector must have a clear relationship with the model inputs (as approximated by the decoder model outputs).
– The basis vector must have a clear relationship with the targets (supervised model outputs). Ideally this would be a monotonic relationship.
– The basis vector must explain a non-trivial portion of the variance within the feature vector space. If this is not the case, then, assuming the training data does not have significant biases, the basis vector will rarely be used as an explanation.

If the basis vector meets these requirements, the user saves it for use in subsequent iterations. If not, the user discards it and starts again with a new model input/output pair. The process is repeated until one of the following criteria is met:

– The explainable basis vectors $\{\hat{\mathbf{u}}_j\}$ span the feature vector space.
– The explainable basis vectors $\{\hat{\mathbf{u}}_j\}$ span the column space of the weights of the first layer of the supervised network (assuming it is a dense layer). Anything out of the column space falls into the kernel space of the matrix and will have no effect on the output of the supervised sub-model.
– The bulk of the variance has been captured, and the user is content to use SVD or other standard PCA algorithm to capture the remaining orthogonal basis vectors.

The feature vector space likely contains more information than is used by the supervised network, because the feature vector layer should, in theory, contain enough information to reconstruct the original outputs. The supervised network, however, may only require a subset of that information to be accurate and not over-fit the data. Suppose, for example, that the output dimension of the encoder network is 128, but the first layer of the supervised network contains only 32 nodes and has weight matrix $\mathbf{W}_0^S \in \mathcal{R}^{128 \times 32}$. Then there are several dimensions within the feature vector space that are irrelevant to the supervised network. As a pre-processing step, we can construct an ortho-normal set of basis vectors that span the kernel space of $\mathbf{W}_0^S$ and use these to remove any information from the feature vector space that is part of the kernel (i.e. irrelevant to the supervised network). This pre-processing step helps to remove superfluous information and arrive at a complete set of EBVs sooner.

The full set of EBVs constitutes a global set of explanations that can be used to provide insights on a case level basis, that is, to provide explanations for a single prediction. This is done using an algorithm such as 'Local Interpretable Model-Agnostic Explanations' (LIME) [29,30] or 'SHapley Additive exPlanations' (SHAP) [22]. In this context, rather than apply these algorithms to the original model inputs, it is applied to the vector coefficients from (3): $\{\alpha_j | \alpha_j = \boldsymbol{\xi}^T \hat{\mathbf{u}}_j\}$. This approach not only provides a case-level set of explanations, but also extends linear explaination algorithms (such as LIME) in a way that goes beyond local linear explanations to global, non-linear, ones.

In the following section, we present the results of modeling and explaining airport throughput using this approach. The section includes comparisons between LIME explanations using the original inputs and LIME applied to the explainable basis vectors to assess whether the human-guided, iterative approach is more valuable than an automated one. We also include examples of SHAP applied to the EBVs. For brevity we will refer to these approaches as the LIME-EBV and SHAP-EBV methods.

3   Application

3.1   Problem

This section presents the application of the above methodology to a practical problem in the domain of ATM in the United States. Enhancement of ATM through advanced scheduling and automation systems is a decades-long focus of research at NASA Ames Research Center, which funded this work [34]. NASA Ames has a rich history of collaborative research with the Federal Aviation Administration (FAA); for example, it has performed ATM research on site at Dallas Fort

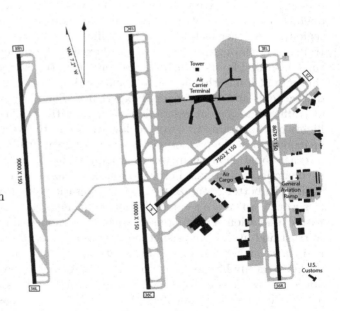

Fig. 2. A diagram of the runways at CLT.

Worth Airport (DFW) since the 1990s, and at Charlotte Douglas International

Airport (CLT) since 2016. NASA Ames has deployed prototype real-time decision support tools (DST) to both airports to help human operators optimize arrival, departure, and surface operations. These DST are in daily use by FAA and airline air traffic managers [36]. We chose to apply our explainable deep learning algorithms to forecast airport throughput at DFW and CLT to take advantage of NASA's substantial knowledge of operations at these airports, which allowed NASA researchers to assess how "explainable" our model results were. For reference, Fig. 2 shows a schematic of the CLT airport and its runways (DFW was not included for brevity).

The following definitions are useful for this discussion:

- Throughput: the sum of takeoffs and landings at an airport within each 15-min window over each hour of the day
- Capacity: the maximum throughput possible in a given 15-min window for a given airport
- Demand: the throughput that would result if every flight were to land and take off at its originally scheduled time, that is, with no capacity-induced delay

Throughput can be thought of as min(demand, capacity). When demand exceeds capacity, throughput becomes limited, and flight delays result. Capacity is not constant for an airport, as it varies depending on visibility and cloud ceiling, presence of convective weather, runway availability, the mix of aircraft types in operation, traffic constraints that are imposed on airports or related airspace regions, and other factors. The air traffic control (ATC) system operators (controllers) set throughput limits to avoid exceeding predicted capacity, with a lead time of several hours, which is considered the strategic planning timeframe. The throughput limits the air traffic managers impose are based on a variety of predictive tools and many years of experience. The limits result in the application of traffic management restrictions that slow the traffic flow in the air or keep flights on the ground to absorb delay. An accurate forecast of throughput, based on explained model predictions, would be of great utility to these controllers. The forecast could show them what throughput has been achieved in prior periods with similar conditions. Perhaps even more useful, this capability would enable airlines to better optimize their flight operations for the day. Thus, the goal of this work is to create a capability for real-time prediction of airport throughput, with explanations enabling users such as controllers and airline operations staff to trust and utilize the predictions. In the current effort, the predictions are not real-time, but work is planned in that area.

For this application, we use the NASA Ames Sherlock ATM Data Warehouse [11] as the source of model input data as well as the computing platform for training and assessment of the model. Sherlock has over 16 TB of US air traffic and weather data that is archived continuously from a variety of real-time sources. The traffic data comprises feeds provided by the FAA that contain all flight plans (intended routes) and every radar track update for commercial and private flights under the purview of FAA air traffic controllers. The FAA data also includes Traffic Flow Information, which reflects all restrictions that the FAA's System Command Center has imposed on any facility or airspace region in the U.S. The weather data includes current observations as well as forecasts, in several different formats, representing a variety of weather prediction models. On top of the raw data, Sherlock computes derived flight information that, while not in real time, is far easier to use in conducting analyses. For example, Sherlock processing examines individual flight tracks to derive metadata for each flight, such as take-off and landing times and runways, which the FAA feeds do not provide. Sherlock also has a Big Data cluster that provides a massively parallel processing capability using the Hadoop ecosystem.

We use the Big Data cluster for our DNN pre-processing, training, and evaluation. We pre-processed three years of these data sources, from January 2017 through December 2019, using a Scala/Spark program running on the Sherlock Big Data system. An important part of the pre-processing is to reorient the flight data from being flight-centered to time-bin centered. Rather than tell the model that a flight landed on a particular runway at a certain time, the pre-processing computes the data for each 15-min bin in the form of percentage of total number of flights in the bin that had a particular feature. For example, it computes percentage of flights that landed on each runway, approached from the south-east, took off to the north, had an aborted take-off, etc. In addition, the pre-processing normalizes all the features to provide similar ranges across each variable. Values such as wind speed, originally in knots, are mean subtracted and divided by the standard deviation. The pre-processing also removes inputs with a variance very close to zero. The sub-sections below describe each data source and how it is used as an input to the DNN.

From the three years of data, we have complete records for more than 50,000 fifteen-minute bins. All told, the data sources result in 123 different features for the model. They are distributed by type as follows: 66 related to flight data (Event and Summary); 31 related to current surface weather observations (METAR), 20 related to surface weather forecasts (TAF), nine related to convective weather coverage (CWAM), and six related to airspace flow constraints. More detail on each data source is given in the following subsections.

3.2   Weather Data

METAR. METAR, or Meteorological Aerodrome Reports, are hourly surface weather observations from hundreds of airports within the US, produced by the National Weather Service. These text-based reports include current wind speed and direction, observed cloud ceiling and visibility, and observed phenomena such as snow or thunderstorms. All of these parameters have an impact on flights and airport operations. Sherlock parses these reports into structured database fields [21], and we use all of them as inputs to the DNN, except those that never had non-zero values.

TAF. TAF, or Terminal Aerodrome Forecasts, are similar to METAR, but provide forecasted values rather than observations. We feed them into the DNN in a similar way to the METAR text fields. TAF reports add value by enabling the deep learning to incorporate the controllers' response to predictions of good or poor weather. In other words, while METAR may influence tactical decisions, TAF is likely to influence strategic planning decisions that are reflected in constraints placed on the system, such as traffic management restrictions. We use the six-hour forecast from each TAF report.

CWAM. CWAM, or Convective Weather Avoidance Model [8], is a highly processed representation of convective weather in probabilistic polygon form. At altitudes from 25,000 to 40,000 feet, from current observations to a two-hour forecast, CWAM processing produces sets of convex polygons representing the probability that a pilot would deviate around the enclosed convective weather. We present our DNN with only the current observation, and probability levels of 60, 70, and 80%. We create a set of these CWAM inputs for each fifteen-minute bin. We then aggregate the polygons to determine what percentage of the airport area is covered by convective weather at each altitude.

3.3 Flight Event and Flight Summary

Flight Event and Flight Summary are produced by Sherlock by applying complex algorithms to raw flight data, including flight intent and position data. They provide analysis-ready information for every flight in controlled U.S. airspace. These include summary information about the flight, such as flight plan route; type and weight class of the aircraft; take-off and landing airports, runways, and times; and any unusual events such as missed approaches and go-arounds. They also provide event data, including every airspace boundary crossing that the flight makes from origin to destination. Finally, this data provides the truth data, since from it we compute the actual throughput for each 15-minute bin.

3.4 TFM Flow Summary

Traffic Flow Management (TFM) Flow Summary records are created from the data that the FAA publishes to describe current, updated, and expected constraints in the airspace system. These constraints reduce the flow of en-route traffic by holding flights on the ground (ground stop), delaying them on the ground (ground delay program), and slowing the flow of en-route flights (airspace flow programs). Such programs may impact throughput at an airport by changing the capacity or demand into or out of the airport.

3.5   Results

Model. In this section, we give the results of the modeling and some examples of the explainable basis vector generation. The models for this problem were built in Scala using the DL4J deep learning library. The encoding consisted of three hidden layers of size 512, 256, and 128. Each layer is densely connected with batch normalization and a tanh activation function. The decoder model mirrors this and has hidden layers of size 128, 256, and 512, which are dense layers followed by batch normalization and a tanh activation function. The supervised model also has three hidden layers of size 32, 24, and 16. Overall, the models perform relatively well with the specific metrics given in Table 1, measured by the correlation coefficient (R^2). Note that we also included metrics for the DFW (Dallas Fort Worth) international airport to emphasis the applicability of the method to other airports.

Table 1. Metrics for model performance (calculated as R^2) for both the CLT and DFW airports.

Airport	Target	Training score	Validation score
CLT	Arrivals	.77	.82
	Departures	.79	.82
DFW	Arrivals	.75	.83
	Departures	.8	.86

Building Explanations. In this section we give some examples of the basis vectors that can be created using this process. To enable efficient EBV creation, we built a web-based user interface (Web UI) using Plotly Dash and Flask. The Web UI allowed us to build, view, and explore the explanations via separate tabs within the application. Iteration on EBV using the Web UI in general does not require in-depth knowledge of deep learning.

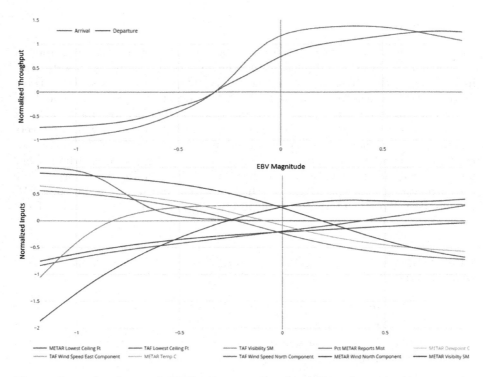

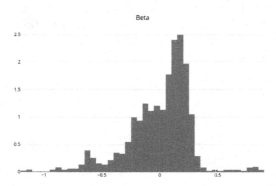

Fig. 3. Example of a good EBV. The top plot shows the relationship between the magnitude of the EBV (x-axis) and the output of the model (number of landings and departures). The bottom plot shows the relationship between the magnitude of the EBV and model inputs.

Fig. 4. This histogram shows the distribution of β within the training data for the EBV described by Fig. 3.

In our experience, EBV creation and viewing do benefit from having a data scientist and a subject matter expert working together. Exploration of the case-level explanations is meant for an ATM-oriented end-user with a minimal amount of training on how to interpret the explanations provided.

The first EBV presented was found by selecting the input 'METAR Visibility SM' (visibility as reported in METAR). The target output selected is the number of arrivals, and we expect these values to have a positive correlation (meaning we expect the number of landings to increase as the visibility improves). Figure 3 shows the relationships that are represented in this basis vector and the effect the vector has on the output of the supervised model. The top plot of the figure clearly shows an increase in the predicted number of departures and arrivals as the magnitude of the vector (measured by the x-axis) goes from negative to positive. Note that the number of departures and landings have been mean-subtracted and normalized to have standard deviation of one. So, the y-axis of this plot is showing standard deviations from the mean. The bottom plot shows the model inputs (or decoder outputs) that vary significantly with the magnitude of this vector. As expected, the value for 'METAR Visibility SM' increases as the magnitude of the vector goes from negative to positive, confirming the positive correlation with the number of landings. From the plot it can also be seen that this basis vector encapsulates information not only for this METAR input, but also the related weather values, forecasted visibility (from TAF), wind direction (the North component), the probability of mist, and flight ceiling level. That is, the model correctly associated various measures of weather with each other, and found the correct sense of the relationships: throughput increases with visibility and height of cloud cover. One important thing to note is that this vector captures the non-linear relationship between these values. Figure 4 shows the distribution of magnitudes of this vector (or variance in the direction of this EBV) within the training data; i.e. these values are the result of computing the dot product of the EBV with the feature vectors from the training data.

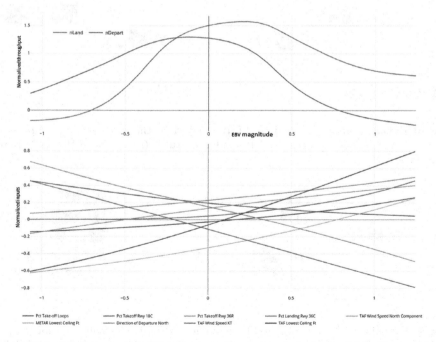

Fig. 5. Example of a bad EBV. The top plot shows the relationship of between the magnitude of the EBV (x-axis) and the output of the model (number of landings and departures). The bottom plot shows the (muddy) relationship between the magnitude of the EBV and model inputs.

As a counter example, we present the EBV described by Fig. 5. Instead of selecting a primary input to construct this EBV, this vector was found using SVD and is the vector that maximizes the amount of variance that can be explained. From the top plot one can see that the effect of this vector on the predicted number of landings and departures is not as clear as the previous example. The poorness of the EBV is more apparent in the bottom plot, where there is no discernible commonality between the inputs and, therefore, labeling this vector with a concise description is more difficult.

Explanation Comparison. In this subsection we present a brief qualitative comparison between the explanations returned by LIME applied to the original problem inputs and LIME applied to the EBVs. Due to space limitations, the number of examples is limited, but is intended to provide evidence of the utility of the method. The first case presented is for the 15-min time window starting at 2019-06-03T15:00:00.0+0000. For this time window, the model accurately predicts the number of landings (six), and Fig. 6 shows the top five explanations returned by LIME for arrivals and departures.

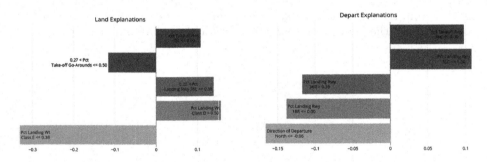

Fig. 6. Explanation as provided by LIME applied to the original model inputs for the predicted number of arrivals (left) and departures (right) for 2019-06-03T15:00:00.0+0000.

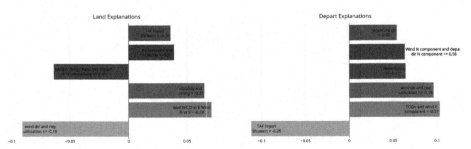

Fig. 7. Explanation as provided by LIME applied to the EBV coefficients for the predicted number of arrivals (left) and departures (right) for 2019-06-03T15:00:00.0+0000.

The LIME explanations appear to emphasize the weight class of landing aircraft, the number of take-off go-arounds, and the direction of departure. It should be noted that the mix of weight class is important because heavier aircraft (Class A, B, and C) require more space behind them, so that the following aircraft is not buffeted by wake vortices. There are also several inputs that relate to runway utilization. It is known that runway configuration is an indirect or secondary cause of a particular level of throughput. That is, weather or other conditions typically dictate runway choice, which then impacts throughput. Therefore, these particular explanations for this case are not very useful.

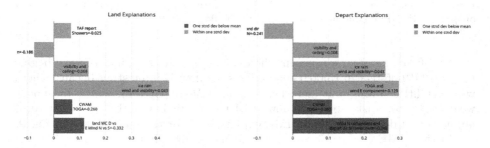

Fig. 8. Explanation as provided by SHAP applied to the EBV coefficients for the predicted number of arrivals (left) and departures (right) for 2019-06-03T15:00:00.0+0000. In this figure the color of the explanation is based on its relative extremism, i.e. how far it is from 'average'.

The LIME-EBV explanations were constructed with this in mind, so they attempt to capture the underlying conditions that drove the runway configuration. Figure 7 shows the top five explanations from LIME-EBV. The most prominent explanation shows that the number of landings was hampered primarily by wind direction. This aligns with what is known about throughput at this airport. Because of the North/South orientation of most of the runways (see Fig. 2), winds from the east become crosswinds and tend to have a dramatic effect on the throughput. The second most influential explanation shows that the number of landings was aided by the mix of aircraft. Using the same EBVs, we also applied the SHAP algorithm to this example. Figure 8 shows the top explanations returned by SHAP. Here the explanations have been colored based on how far they are from typical conditions.

Upon closer inspection of the data, it was found that, apart from runway utilization, the inputs to this model that varied significantly from their averages included the percentage of landing aircraft of weight class E, a medium size aircraft, and also the strength of the north component of the wind direction.

Fig. 9. Explanation as provided by LIME on the original problem inputs for the model output for the time window starting at 2019-05-04T20:15:00.0+0000.

As a final example, we present the explanations from a time window beginning at 2019-05-04T20:15:00.0+0000. This window is interesting because there was very little throughput (zero landings and one departure), due to inclement weather. By contrast, a busy window at CLT typically has on the order of 30 total landings and departures. The LIME explanations for these are shown in Fig. 9. Again the LIME explanations seem to focus on aircraft weight class, direction of departure, and runway utilization, which are based on percentages of aircraft that arrived/departed in these categories. Because the throughput was very low in this time window, these values do not have much meaning and so serve as poor explanations for the model output.

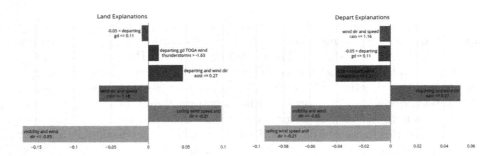

Fig. 10. Explanation as provided by LIME when applied to the EBV coefficients for the model output for the time window starting at 2019-05-04T20:15:00.0+0000.

The LIME-EBV and SHAP-EBV explanations (shown in Figs. 10 and 11) appear to shed more light on this window by attributing part of the explanation to things such as visibility, ceiling, and wind speed. These explanations are correct and relevant and were judged useful by a domain expert.

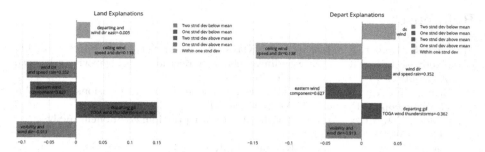

Fig. 11. Explanation as provided by SHAP when applied to the EBV coefficients for the model output for the time window starting at 2019-05-04T20:15:00.0+0000.

4   Conclusion

In this paper we have presented a novel approach to decomposing deep learning models in order to better understand what the model has learned and to build an intuitive set of explanations. The explanations, in the form of orthogonal basis vectors, can be used to provide justification for model output on a case level basis using LIME or a similar algorithm. Additionally, the method extends local, linear, explainable algorithms to be non-linear and global.

The new method was applied to busy airport throughput predictions. This is a particularly challenging problem, owing to the number of factors involved and the non-linear relationship between them. In order to demonstrate the utility of the method, we presented a qualitative comparison of our new method with the popular LIME and SHAP algorithms.

There are several areas of potential future research to improve upon the methodology presented in Sect. 2.2. For example, while it is a fairly general approach, the process for generating a potential explainable basis vector is not applicable to imagery. The equivalent approach would be to pick a particular pixel and suggest that the pixel's value has a positive or negative correlation with the supervised model's output. Future research will focus on adapting this methodology to use an approach similar to that of [17] to decompose imagery into EBVs.

Another potential avenue of research is that of uncertainty quantification in the context of specifying how confident a model is based on the data used to train the model. By evaluating how likely the value of a EBV coefficient is, one should, in theory, be able to quantify how well the model inputs were represented in the training data. Extending this further, this may also be used as a metric to identify biases within the training data distributions, such as those that have been observed in facial recognition [25].

References

1. Bach, S., Binder, A., Montavon, G., Klauschen, F., Müller, K.-R., Samek, W.: On pixel-wise explanations for non-linear classifier decisions by layer-wise relevance propagation. PloS One **10**, e0130140 (2015)
2. Brinton, C.: A framework for explanation of machine learning decisions. In: IJCAI-17 Workshop on Explainable AI (XAI), p. 14
3. Candès, E.J., Li, X., Ma, Y., Wright, J.: Robust principal component analysis? J. ACM (JACM) **58**, 11 (2011)
4. Cashmore, M., Collins, A., Krarup, B., Krivic, S., Magazzeni, D., Smith, D.: Towards explainable AI planning as a service. arXiv preprint arXiv:1908.05059 (2019)
5. Castelvecchi, D.: Can we open the black box of AI? Nat. News **538**, 20 (2016)
6. Cheney, W., Kincaid, D.: Linear algebra: theory and applications, The Australian Mathematical Society, 110 (2009)
7. Choo, J., Liu, S.: Visual analytics for explainable deep learning. IEEE Comput. Graph. Appl. **38**, 84–92 (2018)
8. DeLaura, R., Crowe, B., Ferris, R., Love, J., Chan, W.: Comparing convective weather avoidance models and aircraft-based data. In: 89th Annual Meeting of the American Meteorological Society: Aviation. Range and Aerospace Meteorology Special Symposium on Weather-Air Traffic Impacts, AMS (2009)
9. Erhan, D., Bengio, Y., Courville, A., Manzagol, P.-A., Vincent, P., Bengio, S.: Why does unsupervised pre-training help deep learning? J. Mach. Learn. Res. **11**, 625–660 (2010)
10. Erhan, D., Bengio, Y., Courville, A., Vincent, P.: Visualizing higher-layer features of a deep network. Univ. Montreal **1341**, 1 (2009)
11. Eshow, M., Lui, M., Ranjan, S.: Architecture and capabilities of a data warehouse for ATM research. In: 33rd Digital Avionics Systems Conference (DASC), AIAA and IEEE (2014)
12. He, K., Zhang, X., Ren, S., Sun, J.: Deep residual learning for image recognition. In: Proceedings of the IEEE Conference on Computer Vision and Pattern Recognition, pp. 770–778 (2016)
13. Hoffmann, J., Magazzeni, D.: Explainable AI planning (XAIP): overview and the case of contrastive explanation (extended abstract). In: Krötzsch, M., Stepanova, D. (eds.) Reasoning Web. Explainable Artificial Intelligence. LNCS, vol. 11810, pp. 277–282. Springer, Cham (2019). https://doi.org/10.1007/978-3-030-31423-1_9
14. Huang, X., Kwiatkowska, M., Wang, S., Wu, M.: Safety verification of deep neural networks. In: Majumdar, R., Kunčak, V. (eds.) CAV 2017. LNCS, vol. 10426, pp. 3–29. Springer, Cham (2017). https://doi.org/10.1007/978-3-319-63387-9_1
15. Japkowicz, N., Hanson, S.J., Gluck, M.A.: Nonlinear auto association is not equivalent to PCA. Neural Comput. **12**, 531–545 (2000)
16. Landecker, W., Thomure, M.D., Bettencourt, L.M., Mitchell, M., Kenyon, G.T., Brumby, S.P.: Interpreting individual classifications of hierarchical networks. In: IEEE Symposium on Computational Intelligence and Data Mining (CIDM), pp. 32–38. IEEE (2013)
17. Le, Q.V.: Building high-level features using large scale unsupervised learning. In: 2013 IEEE International Conference on Acoustics, Speech and Signal Processing (ICASSP), pp. 8595–8598. IEEE (2013)
18. Lei, T., Barzilay, R., Jaakkola, T.: Rationalizing neural predictions. arXiv preprint arXiv:1606.04155 (2016)

19. Lipovetsky, S., Conklin, M.: Analysis of regression in game theory approach. Appl. Stochas. Mod. Bus. Ind. **17**, 319–330 (2001)
20. Lipton, Z.C.: The mythos of model interpretability. arXiv preprint arXiv:1606.03490 (2016)
21. Lui, M.: Complete decoding and reporting of aviation routine weather reports (metars), NASA Technical Memorandum, 2014–218385 (2014)
22. Lundberg, S.M., Lee, S.-I.: A unified approach to interpreting model predictions. In: Guyon, I., et al. (eds.) Advances in Neural Information Processing Systems 30, Curran Associates Inc, pp. 4765–4774 (2017)
23. Mahendran, A., Vedaldi, A.: Understanding deep image representations by inverting them. In: Proceedings of the IEEE Conference on Computer Vision and Pattern Recognition, pp. 5188–5196 (2015)
24. Montavon, G., Lapuschkin, S., Binder, A., Samek, W., Müller, K.-R.: Explaining nonlinear classification decisions with deep Taylor decomposition. Patt. Recogn. **65**, 211–222 (2017)
25. Nagpal, S., Singh, M., Singh, R., Vatsa, M.: Deep learning for face recognition: pride or prejudiced? arXiv preprint arXiv:1904.01219 (2019)
26. Nguyen, A., Yosinski, J., Clune, J.: Multifaceted feature visualization: uncovering the different types of features learned by each neuron in deep neural networks. arXiv preprint arXiv:1602.03616 (2016)
27. O'Shea, K., Nash, R.: An introduction to convolutional neural networks. arXiv preprint arXiv:1511.08458 (2015)
28. Park, D.H., Hendricks, L.A., Akata, Z., Schiele, B., Darrell, T., Rohrbach, M.: Attentive explanations: justifying decisions and pointing to the evidence. arXiv preprint arXiv:1612.04757 (2016)
29. Ribeiro, M.T., Singh, S., Guestrin, C.: Why should I trust you? Explaining the predictions of any classifier. In: Proceedings of the 22nd ACM SIGKDD International Conference on Knowledge Discovery and Data Mining, pp. 1135–1144 (2016)
30. Ribeiro, M.T., Singh, S., Guestrin, C.: Model-agnostic interpretability of machine learning. arXiv preprint arXiv:1606.05386 (2016)
31. Ruder, S.: An overview of gradient descent optimization algorithms. arXiv preprint arXiv:1609.04747 (2016)
32. Rusk, N.: Deep learning. Nat. Methods **13**, 35 (2016)
33. Samek, W., Wiegand, T., Müller, K.-R.: Explainable artificial intelligence: understanding, visualizing and interpreting deep learning models. arXiv preprint arXiv:1708.08296 (2017)
34. Schroeder, J.: A perspective on NASA Ames air traffic management research. In: 9th AIAA Aviation Technology, Integration, and Operations Conference (ATIO). AIAA (2009)
35. Sener, O., Koltun, V.: Multi-task learning as multi-objective optimization. Adv. Neural Inf. Process. Syst. **31**, 527–538 (2018)
36. Sharma, S., Capps, A., Engelland, S., Jung, Y.: Operational impact of the baseline integrated arrival, departure, and surface system field demonstration. In: 37th Digital Avionics Systems Conference (DASC). AIAA and IEEE (2018)
37. Simonyan, K., Vedaldi, A., Zisserman, A.: Deep inside convolutional networks: visualising image classification models and saliency maps. arXiv preprint arXiv:1312.6034 (2013)
38. Štrumbelj, E., Kononenko, I.: Explaining prediction models and individual predictions with feature contributions. Knowl. Inf. Syst. **41**(3), 647–665 (2013). https://doi.org/10.1007/s10115-013-0679-x

39. Szegedy, C., Zaremba, W., Sutskever, I., Bruna, J., Erhan, D., Goodfellow, I., Fergus, R.: Intriguing properties of neural networks. arXiv preprint arXiv:1312.6199 (2013)
40. Wright, J., Ganesh, A., Rao, S., Peng, Y., Ma, Y.: Robust principal component analysis: exact recovery of corrupted low-rank matrices via convex optimization. In: Advances in Neural Information Processing Systems, pp. 2080–2088 (2009)
41. Zeiler, M.D., Fergus, R.: Visualizing and understanding convolutional networks. In: Fleet, D., Pajdla, T., Schiele, B., Tuytelaars, T. (eds.) ECCV 2014. LNCS, vol. 8689, pp. 818–833. Springer, Cham (2014). https://doi.org/10.1007/978-3-319-10590-1_53

ShufText: A Simple Black Box Approach to Evaluate the Fragility of Text Classification Models

Rutuja Taware[1]([✉]) [iD], Shraddha Varat[1] [iD], Gaurav Salunke[1] [iD],
Chaitanya Gawande[1] [iD], Geetanjali Kale[1] [iD], Rahul Khengare[1] [iD],
and Raviraj Joshi[2] [iD]

[1] Pune Institute of Computer Technology, Pune, Maharashtra, India
gvkale@pict.edu
[2] Indian Institute of Technology Madras, Chennai, Tamilnadu, India

Abstract. Text classification is the most basic Natural Language Processing (NLP) task. It has a wide range of applications ranging from sentiment analysis to topic classification. Recently, deep learning approaches based on Convolutional Neural Network (CNN), Long Short-Term Memory (LSTM), and Transformers have been widely used for text classification. In this work, we highlight a common issue associated with these approaches. We show that these systems are over-reliant on the important words present in the text that are useful for classification. With limited training data and discriminative training strategy, these approaches tend to ignore the semantic meaning of the sentence and rather just focus on keywords or important n-grams. We propose a simple black box technique ShufText to present the shortcomings of the model and identify the over-reliance of the model on keywords. This involves randomly shuffling the words in a sentence and evaluating the classification accuracy. We see that on common text classification datasets there is very little effect of shuffling and with high probability these models predict the original class. We also evaluate the effect of language model pre-training on these models and try to answer questions around model robustness to out-of-domain sentences. We show that simple models based on CNN or LSTM as well as complex models like BERT are questionable in terms of their syntactic and semantic understanding.

Keywords: Simple models · Pre-trained models · Universal Language Model Fine-tuning (ULMFiT) · Bidirectional Encoder Representations from Transformers (BERT) · CNN · LSTM · Probability · Confidence

1 Introduction

The domain of natural language processing involves multiple tasks such as text classification, language translation, text summarization, etc. With recent

Supported by L3Cube Pune.

advances in Deep Neural Networks (DNNs), neural network approaches are known to perform best on these tasks [12]. Text classification is the most fundamental task which has a variety of applications. It forms the basis of sentiment analysis, document classification, and news categorization. It is also used for intent identification in chatbot systems [17]. These techniques have also been evaluated for domains like biomedical text [23] and non-English languages [10,13].

Deep learning approaches based on CNNs and recurrent neural networks (RNNs) are the most popular techniques used for text classification [11,27]. Pretrained networks like BERT based on transformer architecture perform better than networks trained from scratch [3]. Our work is centred around text classification and these deep learning models. While these models have produced a state of the art results on text classification datasets it is difficult to interpret the classification results [26]. There has been a lot of emphasis on model interpretation in the NLP community [1,4,6,20–22,25]. We would ideally expect these models to understand the text at the syntactic level and semantic level and arrive at a conclusion. However, recent works in the area of interpretable NLP has shown these models to be n-gram detectors [9,14]. These models lookout for specific n-grams to find the target class. For example in the case of sentiment analysis words like "happy", "sad", "great", "mediocre" play an important role in sentiment detection. Moreover, a typical sentiment analysis model would predict a neural sentence "I am reading the book Happy Days" as having a positive sentiment. This is mainly because of limited non-diverse training data and discriminative training such that the model tends to learn signals that are important for classification and ignores understanding the semantics of the sentence. In this work, we highlight this limitation of text classification models using a simple black-box approach. We show that these classification techniques are over-reliant on words that are important for classification decisions. It does not take into consideration the syntax or grammar and semantic meaning of the sentence. To motivate the problem let us look at two queries fired at a banking chatbot (refer Fig. 1):

- What is my bank balance?
- What about my mental balance?

Although the second query is not related to bank balance a typical chatbot still displays options to find one's account balance. This shows that the intent detection model which is also a text classification model was not able to understand the semantics of this out of domain query. As humans, we understand the meaning at the sentence level that these natural language understanding systems are unable to capture. There are real-world examples of Twitter and LinkedIn auto-reply bots misinterpreting the context [18] and we believe it to be related to problems described in this work.

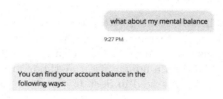

Fig. 1. Bank Chatbot

Moreover, studies in the past have discovered the vulnerabilities in DNNs by devising various adversarial attacks [19]. These attacks have shown that DNN can be easily fooled by making small perturbations in the input sample. These perturbations primarily focus on changing important keywords present in a sentence. Even though such models are deployed widely, they are still not robust enough to ensure high standards of security. Our work is not concerned with attacks on DNN but we aim to understand the ability of the model to comprehend sentence semantics.

In this work, we present a simple baseline technique - ShufText, which can be used to study the fragility of a model. The baseline acts as an indicator of the over-reliance of the model on specific keywords. We do so by creating a shuffled test set where the words in the test sentences are shuffled randomly but the labels still correspond to the original sentences. High accuracy on this test set would imply that the model has not learned the sentence structure or semantics and is relying on the keywords. Analyzing the prediction probabilities would provide further insights into the severity of the problem. Models pre-trained on large external corpus using language modelling objectives are also evaluated on this shuffled test set to check for their robustness. After observing that these models provide high accuracy on the shuffled test set, we perform a series of experiments to answer the following questions:

- Are these models capable of identifying shuffled sentences even when they are made part of training data and assigned a new label?
- What is the effect of adding a generic class that represents out of domain sentences to the original train data?

The main contributions of this work are:

- We show that text classification models are heavily reliant on keywords or n-grams and ignore understanding the meaning of sentences.
- We propose a simple black box technique- ShufText to quantize this shortcoming of the model.
- Model performance after adding shuffled sentences and generic non-shuffled sentences to the training data is evaluated. The raw(non-pretrained) models are unable to distinguish between original and shuffled sentences even after adding them to the train set.

The paper is organized as follows. We present an overview of various existing works related to the generation of adversarial text samples in Sect. 2. The experimental setup is discussed in Sect. 3. The proposed ShufText approach is elaborated in Sect. 4. The data augmentation methods are presented in Sect. 5. Finally, the findings are summarized in Sect. 6.

2   Related Work

In this section, we review literature related to the fooling of DNNs using adversarial text samples. Although our work is not directly related to fooling we share the process of creating problematic text samples to validate the target task.

Bin Liang et al. in [16] generated adversarial samples by following two different types of attacks viz. white box and a black box. In the white box attack, they used gradient computation to identify important text items, whereas, in the black box attack, they used a word occlusion technique to identify important keywords. Based on the identified keywords, three perturbation strategies viz. insertion wherein new text items were inserted, modification wherein important text items were replaced with common misspellings, and removal was undertaken to generate final adversarial samples. The samples were then fed to character and word level DNNs and the results indicated that the models were susceptible to such attacks.

Ji Gao et al. in [7] proposed a black box technique that selected important keywords based on novel scoring functions. These keywords were then converted to unknown tokens by various transformation techniques and the resultant samples were fed to character level CNN and word-level LSTM models. The resultant samples were correctly classified by humans but the models gave wrong results with high confidence. This work also indicated that the generated adversarial samples were transferable i.e. they can be used for fooling other models as well. Hence, when such samples were included in the trainset, adversarial accuracy increased for such models.

Javid Ebrahimi et al. in [5] used gradient computation, a white box technique to identify important characters, and used beam search to identify the best combination of characters for substitution. These character level modifications were effective in fooling the networks and also generated robust models when such adversarial samples were included in the trainset.

Utkarsh Desai et al. in [2] have focused on the generation of a standard test set that can be used to expose the vulnerabilities of a model. This test set consists of real-world sentences made by adding random and targeted corruptions such as misspellings, text noise, etc. in standard sentences. This paper further elaborates that the accuracy of standardized models decreases when tested on such samples.

Thus, the research work mentioned in this section greatly emphasizes the model reliance on keywords. Our work can also be viewed as a black box technique to study the fragility of a model.

3   Experimental Setup

3.1   Datasets

We use Stanford Sentiment Treebank (SST-2) [24] and Text REtrieval Conference (TREC-6) [15] datasets to evaluate the robustness of the models. These datasets were selected to cover binary and multi-class classification. The SST-2 dataset has positive and negative movie reviews with 6920 train set samples and 1821 test set samples. The TREC-6 dataset consists of questions categorized into 6 classes: Abbreviation, Description and abstract concepts, Entities, Human beings, Locations, and Numeric values. This dataset has 5452 samples in the trainset and 500 samples in the test set. The data augmentation phase makes use of the Wikipedia dataset obtained from English Wikipedia articles. It was manually ensured that the selected Wiki articles did not overlap with the domain of SST and TREC datasets.

3.2   Models

In this work, we have performed experiments on four widely used text classification models. Our first classifier is a word-level CNN network that uses a single convolutional layer followed by a MaxPooling layer. The convolutional layer has 32 1D filters with a kernel size of 8. Two linear layers are stacked upon the MaxPooling layer and a dropout layer is added after the convolutional layer and the first linear layer. We have used a uni-directional word-level LSTM network as the second classifier with two linear layers stacked on top of two LSTM layers. A dropout layer is added after the topmost LSTM layer and after the first linear layer. The LSTM has 1150 hidden units and the pre-softmax linear layer has 300 units. Our models use Adam optimizer with learning rate 10^{-3} with an exception of SST LSTM which uses RMSprop with learning rate 10^{-4}.

The third classifier is the ULMFiT with an embedding layer of 300 hidden units, followed by three LSTM layers wherein the first two layers have 1150 hidden units and the last layer has 300 hidden units. Two linear layers are stacked upon the LSTM layers and dropout is added in every layer for regularization. For each layer, the learning rate increases linearly in the initial phase, and then it decays linearly generating a slanted triangular pattern [8]. Our fourth classifier is a BERT large uncased model with 24 layers of bidirectional Transformer based encoder blocks wherein each layer has a total of 16 self-attention heads [3]. A held out validation data was used to pick the best epoch for every classification model.

4   ShufText

The proposed ShufText approach involves creating a new test set by shuffling the words of original test sentences. The model is evaluated on this test set to measure the bias of the model towards relevant keywords. The sentences in the new test set are not meaningful and at the same time grammatically incorrect. The ground truth labels of these sentences are still the original labels. For example in the context of a banking application the shuffled sentence *"bank balance my what is"* is still labelled as *get_bank_balance*. If the trained model performs well on this dataset, it is an indicator of the limitation of the model to capture semantic meaning. Although the closest thing model can predict here is *get_bank_balance* but a high prediction score is not obvious. The probability of predictions helps us quantize the severity of the problem. Since the words in the text are randomly shuffled the approach is termed as ShufText.

The following examples show how the text samples look before and after shuffling:

1. Original text: When did Hawaii become a state
   Corresponding shuffled text: Hawaii state a When did become
2. Original text: offers that rare combination of entertainment and education
   Corresponding shuffled text: that entertainment education rare and offers of combination

4.1   Method

For a given model and a dataset consisting of a train set and a test set, the following steps are followed:

1. The model is trained on the available train set.
2. The original test set is passed through the model and class labels are obtained.
3. Correctly classified samples are selected from the test set and the words of each sample are shuffled randomly.
4. Accuracy on this shuffled test set is evaluated by comparing them with the original labels.
5. The above accuracy is termed as a percentage of the same prediction i.e. the predicted label of the shuffled samples is the same as that of its original unshuffled version. A high accuracy would indicate that model is over-reliant on keywords and ignores the syntactic and semantic structure of the sentence.
6. The probability of predictions for the original test set and shuffled versions are recorded. This helped us analyze how confident a model is while making wrong predictions.

A box plot is drawn between the class labels predicted by the model and the probabilities associated with them. These plots are drawn for the newly created shuffled test set as well as the original test set. In the case of the original test set, only correctly classified sentences are chosen for drawing the plots. This is done to ensure a fair comparison of the probability scores.

The plots are used to analyze the predicted probabilities for each class. Higher median probabilities in the box plot indicate a highly confident model whereas the higher width of the box plots indicates a less confident model.

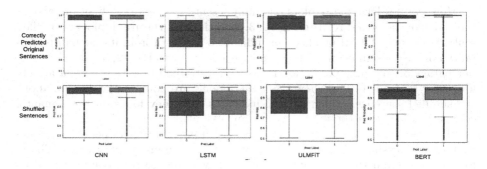

Fig. 2. ShufText SST

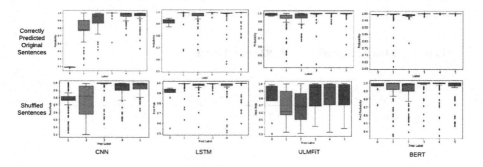

Fig. 3. ShufText TREC

Table 1. ShufText results

Model	SST-2		TREC-6	
	Original test accuracy	Percentage of same prediction	Original test accuracy	Percentage of same prediction
CNN	79.46	93.29	84.79	85.84
LSTM	80.28	92.20	82.59	94.18
ULMFiT	85.83	83.42	93.00	71.18
BERT	92.53	83.02	95.00	66.52

4.2 Result

For simple models like CNN and LSTM, the plots of the correctly classified original test set samples and shuffled test set samples are very similar to each other. No significant changes can be observed in the median probability as well as the width of the boxes. Moreover, the percentage of the same prediction for these simple models is very high in the Table 1. This indicates that shuffling the test set samples which were correctly classified by the models, does not have a major effect on their predictions. This shows that simple models are heavily dependent on keywords.

However, for BERT, the plots for shuffled sentences report a slight increase in the width of the boxes, refer to Figs. 2, 3. Additionally, the graph plots of shuffled sentences for the ULMFiT classifier indicate a major drop in its median probability and also a significant increase in its width, refer to Figs. 2, 3. Moreover, the percentage of the same prediction for these pre-trained models is comparatively low, refer to Table 1. This shows that the models are not completely sure about the shuffled sentences which in turn indicates that they focus on the semantic connections between the keywords to some extent.

However, for both the type of models i.e. simple and pre-trained, the median probability for shuffled sentences is above 0.85 in the majority of cases. Therefore, even though the pre-trained models show a decrease in confidence while classifying shuffled sentences, it is evident that this decrease is not significant enough. This shows that even complex and highly accurate models like BERT are questionable as far as robustness is concerned.

5 Data Augmentation Experiments

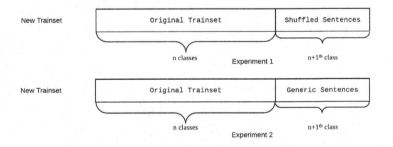

Fig. 4. Data augmentation

We have conducted a few data augmentation experiments and studied the effects that they have on the classification of standard sentences in the test set as well as their shuffled versions. The training data is augmented by adding shuffled and generic sentences. The idea is to see the effect of this addition on the test accuracy. The previous models were not capable of discriminating between shuffled and original sentences. So we experiment by explicitly adding shuffled sentences in training data. The addition of generic out of domain sentences is a more natural setup given NLP applications. So, we also experiment with the addition of generic sentences instead of shuffled sentences. The exact process and results of adding shuffled sentences are described in Experiment 1 and the experiment related to generic sentences is described in the Experiment 2 section. It is ensured that the number of samples in the new class matches the number of samples in other existing classes so that all the classes have an equal ratio of sample size, refer to Fig. 4.

5.1   Experiment 1 – Addition of Shuffled Sentences

In this experiment, the train set includes an additional class whose text samples are obtained by shuffling the sentences belonging to the original classes. The methodology and details of the experiment are outlined below.

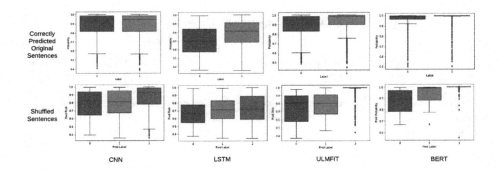

Fig. 5. Experiment 1 SST

Method: For a given model and a dataset consisting of a train set and a test set, the following steps are followed:

1. N random text samples present in the train set are shuffled where N refers to the average number of samples present in each class.
2. The shuffled samples obtained from the above step are appended to the train set and a new class label is assigned to these samples. The model is trained using the new train set.
3. The test set is passed through the model and class labels are obtained.
4. Correctly classified samples are selected from the test set and the words of each sample are shuffled randomly.
5. The shuffled test set is passed through the model and the accuracy is evaluated.

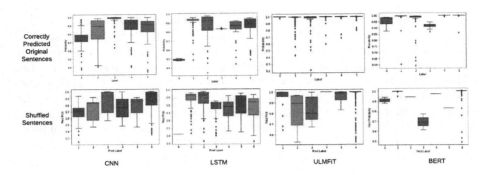

Correctly Predicted Original Sentences

Shuffled Sentences

CNN   LSTM   ULMFiT   BERT

Fig. 6. Experiment 1 TREC

6. The probability of predictions for the original test set and shuffled versions are recorded. This helped us analyze how much a model is affected when shuffled sentences are added as a new class to the train set.

Table 2. Experiment 1 results

Model	SST-2			TREC-6		
	Original test accuracy	Shuffled test accuracy	Overall test accuracy	Original test accuracy	Shuffled test accuracy	Overall test accuracy
CNN	71.77	61.28	67.39	85.0	72.23	79.13
LSTM	68.09	33.06	53.90	81.59	28.43	57.70
ULMFiT	83.80	97.77	90.17	94.0	91.91	92.98
BERT	91.87	97.96	94.79	96.2	94.59	95.41

Result: The comparison of accuracy values between simple and pre-trained models shows that the CNN and LSTM classifiers yield very low accuracy values on the shuffled testset as compared to the pre-trained models, refer to Table 2. Hence, when shuffled sentences are made a part of the training set, the pre-trained models are better at distinguishing between shuffled and non-shuffled sentences. Although the task of distinguishing between shuffled and non-shuffled sentences is a trivial task, it becomes difficult for the simple networks, given original classes are maintained and the training data is limited.

Pre-trained models yield very high values for the overall accuracy of the test set, refer to Table 2. Hence, when the plots of original and shuffled samples are compared, it can be seen that these models yield a high probability for incorrect classification, but the fraction of these errors itself is very low, refer to Figs. 5, 6. Hence, the pre-trained models can distinguish between shuffled and non-shuffled sentences with high accuracy. These pre-trained models are capable of learning syntactic structures that simple models failed to recognize. This also highlights the importance of pre-training when training data is limited.

5.2   Experiment 2 – Addition of Generic Sentences

In this experiment, the train set includes an additional class whose text samples contain generic sentences. These generic sentences are syntactically meaningful and do not contain domain-specific keywords that will aid the model in the classification task. This technique is commonly used to detect out of domain sentences in chat-bot like applications. We evaluate the effect of the addition of generic sentences on the model performance of simple and pre-trained models. The methodology and details of the experiment are outlined below.

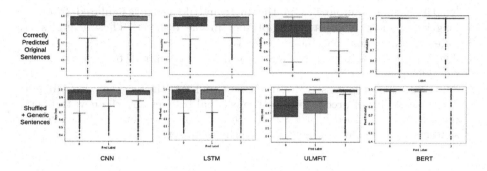

Fig. 7. Experiment 2 SST

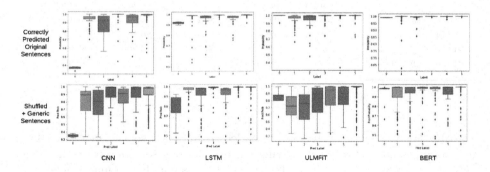

Fig. 8. Experiment 2 TREC

Method: For a given model and a dataset consisting of a train set and a test set, the following steps are followed:

1. Generic sentences are obtained from the Wikipedia dataset such that the length of each sample lies in the interquartile range calculated from the

lengths of the original samples present in the train set. N generic text samples are chosen where N refers to the average number of samples present in each class of the train set.

2. The generic samples obtained from the above step are appended to the train set and a new class label is assigned to these samples. The model is trained using the new train set.
3. The test set is passed through the model and class labels are obtained.
4. Correctly classified samples are selected from the test set and the words of each sample are shuffled randomly.
5. Generic sentences are obtained from the Wikipedia dataset such that the length of each sample lies in the interquartile range calculated from the lengths of the original samples present in the test set. These samples are different from those obtained in step 1.
6. The samples obtained from steps 4 and 5 are combined to generate a new test set.
7. The new test set is passed through the model and the accuracy is evaluated.
8. The probability of predictions for the original test set and the new test set is recorded. This helped us analyze how much a model is affected when generic sentences are added as a new class to the train set.

Table 3. Experiment 2 results

Model	SST-2			TREC-6		
	Original test accuracy	Generic sentence accuracy	Percentage of same prediction	Original test accuracy	Generic sentence accuracy	Percentage of same prediction
CNN	78.03	86.58	94.29	86.19	74.00	87.70
LSTM	77.48	92.35	92.06	82.40	86.80	72.57
ULMFiT	82.75	98.23	82.81	94.20	98.20	69.21
BERT	90.82	99.17	83.91	96.40	98.00	86.64

Result: When generic sentences are added to the train set, all models yield a very high probability while classifying the original test set. Moreover, the accuracy of the original sentences of all the models does not show a major deflection when compared to ShufText, refer to Tables 1, 3. Hence, it can be concluded that the addition of generic sentences does not hamper the confidence of simple and pre-trained models while classifying original sentences. Both types of models are equally capable of distinguishing between original sentences and out-of-domain generic sentences. This behaviour was not exhibited for shuffled sentences by simple models.

For all the models, one can observe that the plots for shuffled test set obtained from Strategy 2 and ShufText are very similar to each other, refer Figs. 2, 3, 7, 8. Hence it can be concluded that the addition of generic sentences to the trainset does not affect the models' performance on the original as well as shuffled sentences. This can again be attributed to the difference in keyword distribution seen in original sentences and generic sentences.

6 Conclusion

The NLP models are not very reliable when they are deployed and fed "real world" inputs. These models are heavily reliant on important keywords or n-grams relevant to the classification task. ShufText provides a simple approach to quantify how reliant a model is on keywords and how much the model understands the semantic or syntactic layout of the input samples. We have also performed two data augmentation experiments and analyzed model behaviour in each case. The first experiment involves the addition of shuffled samples to the training data and can be used to quantify the effect pre-training has on models. The inclusion of generic sentences to the train set as an additional class has been commonly practised in text classification tasks. The generic out of the domain sentences were added to the train set in the second experiment. We show that pre-trained models are effective in distinguishing between original and shuffled sentences whereas simple models fail to do so. Both the models are effective in distinguishing between original sentences and out of domain generic sentences.

Acknowledgements. This work was done under the L3Cube Pune mentorship program. We would like to express our gratitude towards our mentors at L3Cube for their continuous support and encouragement.

References

1. Conneau, A., Kruszewski, G., Lample, G., Barrault, L., Baroni, M.: What you can cram into a single vector: probing sentence embeddings for linguistic properties. arXiv preprint arXiv:1805.01070 (2018)
2. Desai, U., Tamilselvam, S., Kaur, J., Mani, S., Khare, S.: Benchmarking popular classification models' robustness to random and targeted corruptions (2020)
3. Devlin, J., Chang, M., Lee, K., Toutanova, K.: BERT: pre-training of deep bidirectional transformers for language understanding. CoRR abs/1810.04805 (2018). http://arxiv.org/abs/1810.04805
4. DeYoung, J., et al.: Eraser: a benchmark to evaluate rationalized NLP models. arXiv preprint arXiv:1911.03429 (2019)
5. Ebrahimi, J., Rao, A., Lowd, D., Dou, D.: HotFlip: white-box adversarial examples for text classification. In: Proceedings of the 56th Annual Meeting of the Association for Computational Linguistics (Volume 2: Short Papers), pp. 31–36. Association for Computational Linguistics, Melbourne, Australia, July 2018. https://doi.org/10.18653/v1/P18-2006, https://www.aclweb.org/anthology/P18-2006
6. Feng, S., Wallace, E., Grissom II, A., Iyyer, M., Rodriguez, P., Boyd-Graber, J.: Pathologies of neural models make interpretations difficult. arXiv preprint arXiv:1804.07781 (2018)

7. Gao, J., Lanchantin, J., Soffa, M.L., Qi, Y.: Black-box generation of adversarial text sequences to evade deep learning classifiers. CoRR abs/1801.04354 (2018). http://arxiv.org/abs/1801.04354
8. Howard, J., Ruder, S.: Fine-tuned language models for text classification. CoRR abs/1801.06146 (2018). http://arxiv.org/abs/1801.06146
9. Jacovi, A., Shalom, O.S., Goldberg, Y.: Understanding convolutional neural networks for text classification. arXiv preprint arXiv:1809.08037 (2018)
10. Joshi, R., Goel, P., Joshi, R.: Deep learning for Hindi text classification: a comparison. In: Tiwary, U.S., Chaudhury, S. (eds.) IHCI 2019. LNCS, vol. 11886, pp. 94–101. Springer, Cham (2020). https://doi.org/10.1007/978-3-030-44689-5_9
11. Kim, Y.: Convolutional neural networks for sentence classification. arXiv preprint arXiv:1408.5882 (2014)
12. Kowsari, K., Jafari Meimandi, K., Heidarysafa, M., Mendu, S., Barnes, L., Brown, D.: Text classification algorithms: a survey. Information 10(4), 150 (2019)
13. Kulkarni, A., Mandhane, M., Likhitkar, M., Kshirsagar, G., Jagdale, J., Joshi, R.: Experimental evaluation of deep learning models for Marathi text classification. arXiv preprint arXiv:2101.04899 (2021)
14. Li, J., Monroe, W., Jurafsky, D.: Understanding neural networks through representation erasure. arXiv preprint arXiv:1612.08220 (2016)
15. Li, X., Roth, D.: Learning question classifiers. In: COLING 2002: The 19th International Conference on Computational Linguistics (2002). https://www.aclweb.org/anthology/C02-1150
16. Liang, B., Li, H., Su, M., Bian, P., Li, X., Shi, W.: Deep text classification can be fooled. CoRR abs/1704.08006 (2017). http://arxiv.org/abs/1704.08006
17. Liu, B., Lane, I.: Attention-based recurrent neural network models for joint intent detection and slot filling. arXiv preprint arXiv:1609.01454 (2016)
18. NA: Amazon confuses sarcastic tweet on maharashtra turmoil for customer complaint, deletes it later. https://www.news18.com/news/buzz/amazon-help-confuses-sarcastic-tweet-on-maharashtra-political-crisis-for-customer-complaint-deletes-tweet-later-2399797.html. Accessed 31 Dec 2020
19. Nguyen, A., Yosinski, J., Clune, J.: Deep neural networks are easily fooled: high confidence predictions for unrecognizable images. In: Proceedings of the IEEE Conference on Computer Vision and Pattern Recognition, pp. 427–436 (2015)
20. Ribeiro, M.T., Singh, S., Guestrin, C.: Why should I trust you? Explaining the predictions of any classifier. In: Proceedings of the 22nd ACM SIGKDD International Conference on Knowledge Discovery and Data Mining, pp. 1135–1144 (2016)
21. Ribeiro, M.T., Singh, S., Guestrin, C.: Semantically equivalent adversarial rules for debugging NLP models. In: Proceedings of the 56th Annual Meeting of the Association for Computational Linguistics (Volume 1: Long Papers), pp. 856–865 (2018)
22. Ribeiro, M.T., Wu, T., Guestrin, C., Singh, S.: Beyond accuracy: behavioral testing of NLP models with checklist. arXiv preprint arXiv:2005.04118 (2020)
23. Rios, A., Kavuluru, R.: Convolutional neural networks for biomedical text classification: application in indexing biomedical articles. In: Proceedings of the 6th ACM Conference on Bioinformatics, Computational Biology and Health Informatics, pp. 258–267 (2015)
24. Socher, R., et al.: Recursive deep models for semantic compositionality over a sentiment treebank. In: Proceedings of the 2013 Conference on Empirical Methods in Natural Language Processing, pp. 1631–1642. Association for Computational Linguistics, Seattle, Washington, USA, October 2013. https://www.aclweb.org/anthology/D13-1170

25. Wallace, E., Tuyls, J., Wang, J., Subramanian, S., Gardner, M., Singh, S.: Allennlp interpret: a framework for explaining predictions of NLP models. arXiv preprint arXiv:1909.09251 (2019)
26. Yuan, H., Chen, Y., Hu, X., Ji, S.: Interpreting deep models for text analysis via optimization and regularization methods. In: Proceedings of the AAAI Conference on Artificial Intelligence, vol. 33, pp. 5717–5724 (2019)
27. Zhou, C., Sun, C., Liu, Z., Lau, F.: A C-LSTM neural network for text classification. arXiv preprint arXiv:1511.08630 (2015)

A Framework for Imbalanced Time-Series Forecasting

Luis P. Silvestrin(✉)[iD], Leonardos Pantiskas[iD], and Mark Hoogendoorn[iD]

Computer Science Department, Vrije Universiteit Amsterdam,
Amsterdam, Netherlands
l.p.silvestrin@vu.nl

Abstract. Time-series forecasting plays an important role in many
domains. Boosted by the advances in Deep Learning algorithms, it has
for instance been used to predict wind power for eolic energy production, stock market fluctuations, or motor overheating. In some of these
tasks, we are interested in predicting accurately some particular moments
which often are underrepresented in the dataset, resulting in a problem
known as *imbalanced regression*. In the literature, while recognized as
a challenging problem, limited attention has been devoted on how to
handle the problem in a practical setting. In this paper, we put forward
a general approach to analyze time-series forecasting problems focusing
on those underrepresented moments to reduce imbalances. Our approach
has been developed based on a case study in a large industrial company,
which we use to exemplify the approach.

Keywords: Imbalanced regression · Deep learning · Time-series
forecasting · Multivariate time-series

1 Introduction

Due to the recent advances in artificial intelligence research, the task of time-
series forecasting is being increasingly tackled with machine learning and deep
learning techniques. There has been a large number of approaches suggested,
ranging from relatively simple machine learning models [1] to a variety of deep
learning models [18]. Those approaches have been utilized in a broad spectrum
of forecasting tasks, such as wind power forecasting, stock market prediction and
motor temperature prediction [18]. In the above examples of tasks, as well as
in multiple other applied cases, some samples are more crucial from the point
of view of the user and thus would require a more accurate prediction from a
model compared to its average performance. At the same time, those data points
may be scarce in the training data. Hence, if left unattended performance might
be worse than average for that data, which is highly undesirable. This issue is
characterized as imbalanced regression, and so far has been addressed with data
pre-processing or ensemble model methods [3].

© Springer Nature Switzerland AG 2022
G. Nicosia et al. (Eds.): LOD 2021, LNCS 13163, pp. 250–264, 2022.
https://doi.org/10.1007/978-3-030-95467-3_19

Despite the existing methods to tackle imbalanced regression problems, it is still a non-trivial task for data scientists and machine learning practitioners to identify and solve them in real-life time-series forecasting contexts. In the effort of developing the best performing machine learning model and minimizing the error across all data points, some important artifacts in the data might be overlooked. Moreover, data sampling methods or ensemble model approaches [3,4] up until now focused on minimizing the prediction error in the underrepresented data samples and assume that the remaining data is negligible. That assumption is inaccurate, as in some applications, for example in stock market prediction, the cost of larger forecasting error in the more frequent cases could offset in the long run the potential benefit of a smaller error in a rare case. In order to tackle real-world applications, there is a need for a broader, balanced, flexible and iterative approach, honed through interaction with domain experts and integrating the latest research in predictive models.

In this paper, we propose such an approach that has been designed based on a case study in a large industrial company, targeted to forecast the temperature of a core component in a large production line. The approach involves three steps: first selecting a weight function which quantifies the sample importance; then applying one or more sampling methods to the data, and finally training and evaluating the model with and without sampling. In the last step, we also analyze the input importance learned by the model using SHAP [10] to gain insights into the effect of the imbalance. To exemplify our approach, we show how it is used for the aforementioned industrial task. We study the impact of choices in each of the steps, comparing different sampling techniques and deep learning models. In the end, we also combine the sampling with attention mechanisms [19] to extract insights into what is learned by a deep learning model. Furthermore, in order to verify that our conclusions hold across use cases and enable reproducibility, we apply the three main framework steps on an open industrial dataset dealing with the task of quality prediction of a mining process and present those experiment results as well.

2   Related Work

The advancements in data availability from a plethora of sources, the increasing computational capacity and the progress in artificial intelligence research have led to the usage of machine and deep learning models across a multitude of applications of time-series forecasting. Previous work [18] surveys several use-cases including wind power forecasting, stock price prediction, and estimation of remaining useful life of motors. Despite this widespread use of models, the majority of works present specific architectures for specific datasets, while works focusing on integrated frameworks in the sense of structured approaches to a more generalized problem are more scarce.

Although there has been an extensive amount of work in handling imbalanced datasets in classification tasks [3], regression with imbalanced data in the area of machine and deep learning has not been largely covered. In [4], Branco et al. study the effect of three proposed sampling methods on the predictive performance of machine learning models. In an applied example, in [17], the objective is that high water flows are predicted in a timely and accurate manner, and the problem is addressed with various sampling and ensemble methods, with an artificial neural network as a base. In the domain of extreme event prediction, a framework [5] was proposed based on a new loss function for recurrent neural networks and focusing on univariate time-series. Other works propose new neural network topologies to predict extreme events in weather data [9] and the client demand at Uber [8]. Salinas et al. [15] propose a new probabilistic autoregressive model for time-series forecasting which is trained by over-sampling the data according to its rarity. These works focus primarily on the model performance related to the extreme events while our framework focuses on finding the best performance trade-off across extreme and common events. In addition, our framework is model agnostic, which makes it possible for practitioners to adopt it without having to change the underlying machine learning method they have selected for a use case for other reasons, such as interpretability.

3 Methodology

It is common in time-series forecasting that certain data samples have more importance than others, but are also underrepresented in the dataset, resulting in an imbalanced regression problem. In this section, we present a new approach for identifying and tackling this discrepancy with respect to imbalances in the context of regression tasks. This approach uses a weight function that quantifies the importance of each sample which is combined with under-sampling methods to create a more balanced dataset. The new sampled dataset is then evaluated first visually, by making density plots of the data and then numerically, by using it for training and testing a predictive model.

3.1 Steps for Identifying and Treating Imbalanced Regression

We propose a set of general steps for approaching the imbalance on time-series forecasting problems, which has been defined based on experiences we have collected in applying machine learning in a large-scale industrial company. It consists of three steps illustrated in Fig. 1. The first step is to select or define a weight function w_i to quantify the sample importance, which allows us to identify and compare the different regions of interest in the data. The second step consists of selecting one or more sampling methods based on the weight function, applying them to the data, and comparing the resulting distribution of w_i against the original data using density plots. Finally, in the third step, a predictive model is trained and evaluated using both the sampled and the original versions of the dataset. A feedback loop can take the user from Step 3 back to Step 2 if the current combination of the selected sampling methods and models does not provide a satisfying performance after evaluation. If while applying the framework the user finds out that the weight function is not suitable, then a second feedback loop can take him back to Step 1 where it can be re-modeled. We provide more details about each step in the following sections.

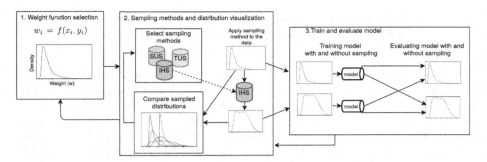

Fig. 1. Flowchart of the framework showing the three steps and how they interact with each other.

Step 1: Weight Function Definition. In the example of forecasting the temperature of a motor, there can be several days where the temperature is stable, with only small fluctuations, and only a few days where the temperature increases or decreases largely. Let us assume a use-case where the user is interested in building a model to predict accurately these rarer moments when the temperature changes more than usual. In such an example, the daily temperature variation can be computed as a function of the data, which we refer to in our framework as the weight function. In addition, we say that the data points mapped to a high variation by the weight function belong to a region of interest.

In general, the weight function can depend either only on the target variable (or a transformation of it), only on a subset of the input variables (e.g. to signify working points of interest), or on a combination of input and output variables, to express complex regions of interest. It can be written as $w_i = f(x_i, y_i)$, where x_i and y_i refer to the input (a vector for multivariate input) and the prediction target, respectively.

Equation 1 gives an example of such a function for the target variation in the context of time-series forecasting. The weight w_t models the variation of the forecast target y over the forecast horizon Δ at time step t.

$$w_t = |y(t + \Delta) - y(t)| \tag{1}$$

Step 2: Application of Sampling Method. At this step, a sampling method is applied to the dataset and its effects are analyzed. The sampling is based on the weight function previously selected and the relative proportions that the user wants to keep for the different regions of interest. We identify three scenarios for this step and we propose an under-sampling method for each one of them.

- **Threshold under-sampling:** when the user identifies which region of the weight function is not important for the forecast task and can be removed;
- **Stochastic under-sampling:** when some regions are more important than others, but none can be entirely discarded;

- **Inverse histogram under-sampling:** when all regions are equally important and the user wants to have a balanced distribution of data over all of
them.

Threshold under-sampling (TUS) consists of removing all samples that lie
below a given threshold of the weight function, and all the remaining samples
have the same chance of being selected. This method is suitable for the cases
where the user knows exactly what is the region of interest to be able to select the
best threshold, and it assumes that the samples below the threshold aren't interesting to the prediction task. Equation 2 expresses the unnormalized probability
of sampling data point t given its weight w_t.

$$\text{TUS}(w_t) = \begin{cases} 1, & \text{if } w_t > \tau \\ 0, & \text{otherwise} \end{cases} \tag{2}$$

$$\text{SUS}(w_t) = w_t^f \tag{3}$$

$$\text{IHS}(w_t) = h^{-1}(w_t) \tag{4}$$

Stochastic under-sampling (SUS) uses the weight w_t computed for each data
point as the probability of sampling it. Different from the TUS, SUS allows
every sample, even the ones with lower weight values, to be sampled to avoid
the creation of a new imbalance against those samples. Equation 3 models the
relative probability of sampling a window from the dataset at time t by using
SUS. The factor f is used to increase (or decrease) the effect of the weights, thus
emphasizing the more interesting moments which might be underrepresented in
the data.

Inverse histogram under-sampling (IHS) is an automatic method to obtain
a sample where data is approximately uniformly distributed across the selected
weight function w_t. It consists of building a histogram of the values of w_t in the
dataset and taking the inverse of the frequency of each value as the chance of
sampling it. It ensures that each w_t will be under-sampled proportionally to its
original frequency, so the most common values will have lower chance, while the
rarer values will have higher chance. In Eq. 4 we can see a formalization of the
method, where $h(w_t)$ represents the frequency of w_t in the data histogram.

A good approach to gain insight into the data and the result of the sampling method is to compare the density plot of the weight function with and
without using the sampling. Such a plot can show the regions which are over or
underrepresented in the data, and can also give insights about how to tune the
parameters of the selected method or which method should be selected.

In some real-life cases, it might not be easy to infer directly which of the
three scenarios fits the problem better. In those cases, a subset of these methods
can be selected for the next step, where we provide a heuristic to select the final
method.

Step 3: Predictive Model Training and Evaluation. Finally, at this step, we can assess how much a predictive model improves by using the selected sampling methods. For that, we train and evaluate the model with and without using the sampling method on a separate evaluation set, so we end up with different combinations of training and evaluation sets which we will use to contrast the obtained evaluation errors and determine if the model benefits from the sampling. For the cases where the goal is to have a model that performs well on the samples of higher weight without sacrificing the performance on the rest of the data, we propose a heuristic for selecting the final sampling method to train the predictive model based on the results of the different evaluation sets. It is defined as:

1. For each sampling method, sample a training set and train a model with it;
2. For each sampling method, sample a separate evaluation set and evaluate the trained model on it;
3. Make a list of highest error over all the evaluation sets of each trained model to get an upper bound on its RMSE error;
4. Select the model with the lowest error in the list.

Next to studying the impact of the sampling on the performance of the models, we also propose to study how the models themselves change by using SHAP [10], which is a model agnostic technique. SHAP gives the relative importance of each input feature to the output of the model which can be compared when the model is trained with and without the sampling.

In addition, we take advantage of deep learning models with attention mechanisms [19] to gain extra insights into what is learned. As an example of an attention-based model, TACN [12] is a deep neural network model that provides the importance of the input time-series across time steps through an attention mechanism. The change of the patterns shown by the mechanism also provides insights into the sampling effects on the model.

4   Experimental Setup

To give a real-life example of our approach, in this section we present a case to evaluate it based on a motor temperature prediction dataset. We also explain the techniques used at each step of the experiments and why they were chosen.

4.1   Motor Temperature Dataset

The dataset used in this experiment is made of sensor measurements extracted from a steel processing conveyor belt. The prediction target is the temperature of a bridle motor, which should be forecasted 5 min in advance to allow the operators to take preventive actions before a possible overheat. The rest of the data consist of properties of the steel strip (i.e. width, thickness, and yield), the speed of the line, the tension applied by the bridles, the current temperature measurements of the motor, among others. The sensors are sampled every 10 s, and there are in total about 2 million samples.

In this dataset, we identify the temperature variation as a special property regarding the prediction target. We analyze the dataset based on this property and follow the steps of our framework: selecting a weight function, then selecting the sampling methods, and visualizing the sampling result.

4.2   Instantiation of the Framework

Here we describe the choices made at each step of the framework for analyzing the imbalance of the temperature variation.

Step 1 - Temperature Variation Weight Function. The temperature variation is an important property to this forecasting task since the predictive model must predict accurately when the temperature will rise. Even if, on average, the model has a satisfying performance, it may still be inaccurate when predicting higher variation if the dataset is imbalanced. So for Step 1 of the framework, we select the temperature variation as the weight function, which is modeled by Eq. 1, using Δ as 30 time steps (5 min), which is the forecast horizon.

Step 2 - Sampling Method Choice. For Step 2, we experiment with three sampling methods: SUS with factor 1, SUS with factor 3, and IHS. Each one under-samples a different amount of low temperature variation data, creating a different balance, as shown by Fig. 2. SUS with factors 1 and 3 are chosen to compare the effect of the factor in the proportion of data samples with low and high variation. For the IHS method, we use the Freedman-Diaconis estimator [6] to compute the bin width of the histogram. 10.000 training data samples are extracted using each method.

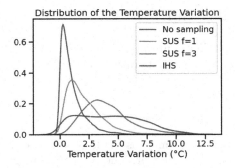

Fig. 2. Comparison of different sampling methods using the temperature variation as weight function.

Step 3 - Predictive Model Choices. In our experiments, we choose a multi-layer perceptron [14] as a deep neural network baseline which has been used in time-series forecasting [1] and three deep neural networks specialized in temporal data. These specialized architectures are the long short-term memory (LSTM) [7], a popular recurrent neural network, the temporal convolutional network (TCN) [2], a sequence-to-sequence model which has shown promise when trained on a large amount of data [16] and the temporal attention convolutional network (TACN) [12].

The TACN is an architecture that combines a TCN with an attention mechanism [19] to achieve interpretable and accurate forecasting. The per-instance interpretability comes in the form of a vector, equal to the input window size, which shows the importance of each input step to the forecasting output. The higher the value of the vector at a specific step, the higher the contribution of the input value at that step to the final output. By scaling the vector to the 0–1 range, we can estimate the relative importance among the input steps. Although this vector is produced per instance, we can draw conclusions about the generic learned behavior of the model by collecting and analyzing the vectors from a large number of instances.

For data pre-processing, we extract a window of 5 min (or 30 time steps) for each sample, which is the input for the TCN, LSTM, and TACN models. For the MLP model, we extract basic features of each sensor such as the mean, standard deviation, minimal and maximal values for each window. We also keep the last time step as an additional feature and for later analysis of the temperature variation case. All the models are evaluated using the root-mean-square error metric (RMSE).

5 Results

In this section, we describe the results obtained after applying our framework starting from Step 2. Step 1 is already defined in Sect. 4. In the last subsection, we also present the results obtained from an additional experiment conducted using an open time-series forecasting dataset.

5.1 Step 2 - Comparison of the Sampling Methods

Figure 2 shows the variation distribution after applying the sampling methods. Without any sampling, the dataset has a strong bias towards samples with variation close to zero, meaning that the temperature is stable, or varies very slowly most of the time. SUS with factor 3 give more emphasis to samples with higher variation, while significantly reducing the number of samples with lower variation. The sampling using SUS with factor 1, on the other hand, is more conservative and preserves a considerable amount of samples with low variation. Finally, IHS gives the best balance across all values and is the one that gives the highest proportion of samples in the extreme of the temperature variation spectrum (above 6 degrees in Fig. 2).

5.2   Step 3 - Analysis of the Results

The results of the four models trained and tested with the selected sampling methods based on temperature variation can be seen in Table 1, with the lower error per evaluation set highlighted. The effect of the imbalance of the original data distribution is clearly shown in the "None" rows, where the models were trained without sampling. For those lines, the RMSE is much higher in the SUS 3 column, where there is a smaller number of samples of low variation, suggesting that the models are biased towards low variation samples if trained without sampling methods.

On the other hand, these results show that there is a trade-off between favoring samples with and without temperature variation. Models trained with a more aggressive kind of sampling, such as SUS with factor 3, have a much higher error when evaluated on the unsampled data than the models trained with SUS factor 1, for example. This can be explained by the density difference between samples with low variation (below 2.5 degrees in Fig. 2), the same samples that are more common in the "no sampling" dataset. With our approach, this trade-off which exhibits non-linear behavior can be estimated, taking into account the end-user preferences, and it can lead to a re-evaluation of the sampling method in Step 2. Also, together with these metrics, using insights about the model as described later in this subsection can indicate the sampling method that leads

Table 1. RMSE results for different sampling methods based on temperature variation. "None" means that the model was trained or evaluated without using a sampling method.

Model	Trained on	Evaluated on			
		None	SUS - 1	SUS - 3	IHS
MLP	None	1.401 ± 0.181	2.270 ± 0.177	3.611 ± 0.322	2.984 ± 0.241
	SUS - 1	1.704 ± 0.289	2.085 ± 0.239	2.886 ± 0.269	2.495 ± 0.234
	SUS - 3	4.150 ± 0.635	3.089 ± 0.390	2.430 ± 0.305	2.836 ± 0.32
	IHS	3.066 ± 0.401	2.728 ± 0.228	2.539 ± 0.248	2.663 ± 0.217
LSTM	None	1.032 ± 0.091	1.857 ± 0.112	3.275 ± 0.129	3.275 ± 0.13
	SUS - 1	1.283 ± 0.153	1.469 ± 0.123	2.769 ± 0.130	2.731 ± 0.094
	SUS - 3	3.595 ± 0.268	2.549 ± 0.128	**1.464 ± 0.24**	2.415 ± 0.095
	IHS	2.728 ± 0.174	2.131 ± 0.093	1.863 ± 0.106	2.27 ± 0.093
TCN	None	**0.871 ± 0.021**	1.684 ± 0.037	3.060 ± 0.068	3.142 ± 0.05
	SUS - 1	1.007 ± 0.079	**1.462 ± 0.041**	2.686 ± 0.066	2.703 ± 0.063
	SUS - 3	3.41 ± 0.213	2.4 ± 0.091	1.592 ± 0.124	2.283 ± 0.008
	IHS	2.579 ± 0.231	2.016 ± 0.091	1.845 ± 0.062	**2.145 ± 0.039**
TACN	None	1.171 ± 0.016	2.637 ± 0.051	5.167 ± 0.1	5.064 ± 0.101
	SUS - 1	1.334 ± 0.242	2.077 ± 0.355	3.878 ± 0.675	3.183 ± 0.694
	SUS - 3	3.802 ± 0.538	2.786 ± 0.428	2.36 ± 0.758	2.883 ± 0.547
	IHS	3.093 ± 0.918	2.424 ± 0.608	2.430 ± 0.748	2.752 ± 0.623

Table 2. The maximum error obtained by the TCN model over all the evaluation sets. Each line corresponds to a training set obtained from a different sampling method.

Trained on	Max. error	Measured on
No sampling	3.142 ± 0.05	IHS
SUS - 1	2.703 ± 0.063	IHS
SUS - 3	3.41 ± 0.213	No sampling
IHS	2.579 ± 0.231	No sampling

to the most encompassing, generalizable patterns learned by the models, thus creating a balance for the performance across data samples.

Since the results show that the TCN achieves a relatively lower error in all the evaluation sets, we select it as the best model and follow the heuristic described in Sect. 3.1. Table 2 shows the maximum error obtained by it over all the evaluation samples. The two lowest RMSE values reported in that table are from the TCN model trained with SUS factor 1 and IHS, and the evaluation sets where they have the highest error are *No sampling* and IHS. By comparing the performance of the TCN trained with both methods on the evaluation set without sampling, we can clearly see that the model trained with SUS with factor 1 has a lower spreading of the error (Fig. 3a). On the other hand, the same comparison on the evaluation set with higher variation (Fig. 3b) shows that both models have similar error spreading, and the small advantage of using IHS, in this case, does not compensate for the increase in error in the low variation samples. Therefore, we can conclude that SUS with factor 1 is the sampling method with the best performance across samples with low and high temperature variation.

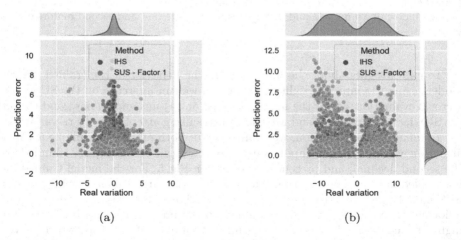

(a)   (b)

Fig. 3. (a) Prediction error for TCN model trained using IHS and SUS with factor 1 on "no sampling" evaluation set and (b) on SUS with factor 3 evaluation set.

Imbalance Effects in DL Models. In the third step of the framework, we also verify how the imbalances affect the performance and learned patterns of the predictive models, when they are trained on data with sampling versus unsampled data. To do that, we focus on the temperature variation property of the dataset, and we measure the SHAP values of the MLP model, as well as the attention importance values of the TACN.

To assess how the sampling methods influence the MLP model, we extract its SHAP values using the SUS 3 evaluation set. We compare both the MLP trained with SUS 3 and without sampling. Figure 4 shows that both models rely mostly on the last temperature measurement to make the forecast. This could be explained by the fact that the last temperature is relatively close to the predicted temperature, even when there is high variation. One hypothesis for such fact is that the MLP does not handle the time dependency of the inputs and, thus has a disadvantage in comparison to other temporal models such as the TCN or the LSTM.

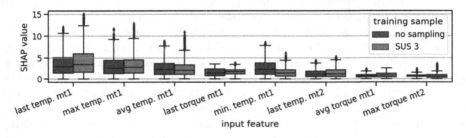

Fig. 4. Comparison of the absolute SHAP values estimated for the MLP model trained with SUS factor 3 and without sampling. The values are computed based on inputs from the evaluation set sampled using SUS factor 3. The input features are computed over a window of 5 min. *mt1* and *mt2* correspond to the first and second motors of the bridle set.

To gain insights about the differences in the behavior of the trained TACN models using the interpretability mechanism, we run inference on the SUS with factor 3 evaluation set for the models trained on (a) unsampled data and (b) on the SUS factor 3 train set, and we study the resulting attention pattern variation.

To quantify this variation, we enumerate for both models the unique learned attention values for each input time step across all test samples, rounded to the second decimal, and present the results on Fig. 5. For the model trained on unsampled data, the unique values for each position are at most 3, while for the SUS model they are between 30 and 50. The above observations lead us to the following conclusions: The model trained on the unsampled data has learned a high reliance on the last value and a limited number of patterns, which serves well in minimizing the error for the majority of the samples but results in low performance on the large variation samples. In contrast, the model trained on

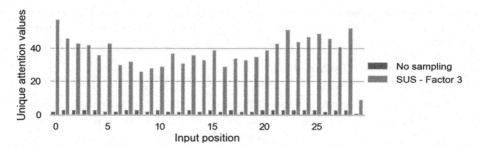

Fig. 5. Unique attention values per input step from sample TACN models trained on data with (a) no sampling and (b) SUS with factor 3

the SUS data is forced to learn a larger variety of patterns to accommodate for this target variation.

5.3   Additional Results from Mining Process Dataset

To confirm our conclusions and enable reproducibility of our methods, we apply our suggested framework on an open dataset from another real-world industrial application [11], which is the quality prediction of the output of a mining process. Specifically, the goal is to predict the impurity of the final ore product, which is measured as the percentage of silica contained in it. It is reasonable to assume that the process engineers are less interested in the majority of the cases where this percentage is low enough for the quality to be acceptable and more interested in the more rare cases, where the percentage is higher and may cross a threshold that requires the final product to be discarded. Following our framework, the steps are as follows:

Step 1 - Weight Function. Given the formulation of this task, it is clear that the prediction output is the most important property and is thus selected as the weight function.

Step 2 - Sampling Method Choice. Following the example of the motor temperature use case, we experiment with three sampling methods: SUS with factor 1, SUS with factor 3, and IHS.

Step 3 - Predictive Model Choices. Given the time series nature of this problem and its input variables, we elect to experiment with the LSTM and TCN models.

The results from our experiments with this task can be seen in Table 3 and the maximum RMSE across all evaluation sets for each model and sampling method combination in Table 4. We observe that using an appropriate sampling method in combination with the weight function reduces the error for the rarer and most important cases (high silica percentage). Moreover, the heuristic of the third framework step helps select the most appropriate sampling method for each forecasting model (SUS with factor 1 for the LSTM and IHS for the TCN). The code used to obtain these results is accessible at [13].

Table 3. RMSE results for different sampling methods based on silica percentage. "None" means that the model was trained or evaluated without using a sampling method.

	Trained on	Evaluated on			
		None	SUS - 1	SUS - 3	IHS
LSTM	None	0.620 ± 0.016	0.528 ± 0.048	0.675 ± 0.052	0.547 ± 0.048
	SUS - 1	0.594 ± 0.031	0.634 ± 0.016	0.600 ± 0.039	0.563 ± 0.036
	SUS - 3	0.731 ± 0.028	0.621 ± 0.022	0.633 ± 0.012	0.609 ± 0.031
	IHS	0.638 ± 0.032	0.587 ± 0.031	0.571 ± 0.045	0.643 ± 0.018
TCN	None	0.570 ± 0.009	0.533 ± 0.023	0.705 ± 0.031	0.578 ± 0.027
	SUS - 1	0.603 ± 0.015	0.586 ± 0.010	0.644 ± 0.026	0.606 ± 0.023
	SUS - 3	0.690 ± 0.022	0.580 ± 0.015	0.592 ± 0.009	0.561 ± 0.020
	IHS	0.617 ± 0.018	0.538 ± 0.019	0.566 ± 0.021	0.599 ± 0.013

Table 4. Maximum RMSE error across all evaluation sets for each model and sampling method.

	Trained on	Max RMSE
LSTM	None	0.675 ± 0.052
	SUS - 1	**0.634 ± 0.016**
	SUS - 3	0.731 ± 0.028
	IHS	0.643 ± 0.018
TCN	None	0.705 ± 0.031
	SUS - 1	0.644 ± 0.026
	SUS - 3	0.690 ± 0.022
	IHS	**0.617 ± 0.018**

6   Conclusion

We presented a framework to analyze imbalanced time-series forecasting problems and to train and evaluate ML models taking into account important properties. To our knowledge, this is the first framework that provides clear steps to help practitioners to select and compare different sampling methods and predictive models for such problems. It is put into practice to forecast the temperature of a motor in a steel processing conveyor belt, based on data extracted from a real-world industrial process and validated in cooperation with domain experts. The problem analysis is made through the lens of the temperature variation property. We study the dataset using three different sampling methods and train four different DL models to evaluate and compare the effectiveness of each combination of sampling and model. We also show the imbalance of the temperature variation and how it changes the models' predictions when they are trained with different proportions of samples with high temperature variation. Finally, we use

SHAP values and the TACN model's attention mechanism to show the effect of low temperature variation in the dataset on the forecast models, inducing them to rely mostly on the last observed temperature. For reproducibility purposes and verification of our conclusions, we also apply the framework to an open industrial dataset regarding the quality prediction of the output of a mining process, experimenting with three sampling methods and two DL models, and we present the results from this use case as well.

As future work, our framework could be put into practice to analyze new time-series prediction tasks, combining with more sampling techniques. The use of the input x in the weight function can be further explored to make the framework suitable for an even wider range of tasks. In addition, our results point out a possible relationship between the prediction error and the distribution of the training data which might be worth investigating.

Acknowledgements. This work has been conducted as part of the Just in Time Maintenance project funded by the European Fund for Regional Development. We also thank Tata Steel Europe for providing the data and technical expertise required for our experiments.

References

1. Ahmed, N.K., Atiya, A.F., Gayar, N.E., El-Shishiny, H.: An empirical comparison of machine learning models for time series forecasting. Econometric Rev. **29**(5–6), 594–621 (2010)
2. Bai, S., Kolter, J.Z., Koltun, V.: An empirical evaluation of generic convolutional and recurrent networks for sequence modeling. arXiv:1803.01271 [cs] (2018)
3. Branco, P., Torgo, L., Ribeiro, R.P.: A survey of predictive modeling on imbalanced domains. ACM Comput. Surveys **49**(2), 1–50 (2016)
4. Branco, P., Torgo, L., Ribeiro, R.P.: Pre-processing approaches for imbalanced distributions in regression. Neurocomputing **343**, 76–99 (2019). https://doi.org/10.1016/j.neucom.2018.11.100
5. Ding, D., Zhang, M., Pan, X., Yang, M., He, X.: Modeling extreme events in time series prediction. In: Proceedings of the 25th ACM SIGKDD International Conference on Knowledge Discovery & Data Mining, pp. 1114–1122. KDD 2019. Association for Computing Machinery, New York, NY, USA (2019). https://doi.org/10.1145/3292500.3330896
6. Freedman, D., Diaconis, P.: On the histogram as a density estimator: L 2 theory. Zeitschrift für Wahrscheinlichkeitstheorie und verwandte Gebiete **57**(4), 453–476 (1981)
7. Hochreiter, S., Schmidhuber, J.: Long short-term memory. Neural Comput. **9**(8), 1735–1780 (1997)
8. Laptev, N., Yosinski, J., Li, L., Smyl, S.: Time-series extreme event forecasting with neural networks at Uber. In: 2017 International Conference on Machine Learning Time Series Workshop (2017)
9. Liu, Y., et al.: Application of deep convolutional neural networks for detecting extreme weather in climate datasets. CoRR abs/1605.01156 (2016). http://arxiv.org/abs/1605.01156

10. Lundberg, S.M., Lee, S.I.: A unified approach to interpreting model predictions. In: Guyon, I., Luxburg, U.V., Bengio, S., Wallach, H., Fergus, R., Vishwanathan, S., Garnett, R. (eds.) Advances in Neural Information Processing Systems, vol. 30, pp. 4765–4774. Curran Associates, Inc. (2017)
11. Magalhães, E.: Quality prediction in a mining process, https://www.kaggle.com/edumagalhaes/quality-prediction-in-a-mining-process. Accessed 19 July 2021
12. Pantiskas, L., Verstoep, K., Bal, H.: Interpretable multivariate time series forecasting with temporal attention convolutional neural networks. In: 2020 IEEE Symposium Series on Computational Intelligence (SSCI), pp. 1687–1694 (2020). https://doi.org/10.1109/SSCI47803.2020.9308570
13. Pantiskas, L., Silvestrin, L.P.: Open code of the experiment using the mining process dataset (2021). https://gitlab.com/lpsilvestrin/imbalanced-time-series-forecast. Accessed 20 July 2021
14. Rosenblatt, F.: The perceptron: a probabilistic model for information storage and organization in the brain. Psychol. Rev. **65**(6), 386 (1958)
15. Salinas, D., Flunkert, V., Gasthaus, J., Januschowski, T.: DeepAR: probabilistic forecasting with autoregressive recurrent networks. Int. J. Forecasting **36**(3), 1181–1191 (2020). https://doi.org/10.1016/j.ijforecast.2019.07.001. https://www.sciencedirect.com/science/article/pii/S0169207019301888
16. Silvestrin, L.P., Hoogendoorn, M., Koole, G.: A comparative study of state-of-the-art machine learning algorithms for predictive maintenance. In: 2019 IEEE Symposium Series on Computational Intelligence (SSCI), pp. 760–767. IEEE (2019)
17. Snieder, E., Abogadil, K., Khan, U.T.: Resampling and ensemble techniques for improving ANN-based high streamflow forecast accuracy. Hydrol. Earth Syst. Sci. Discuss. **2020**, 1–35 (2020)
18. Torres, J.F., Hadjout, D., Sebaa, A., Martínez-Álvarez, F., Troncoso, A.: Deep learning for time series forecasting: a survey. Big Data **9**(1), 3–21 (2021). https://doi.org/10.1089/big.2020.0159
19. Vaswani, A., et al.: Attention is all you need. In: Advances in Neural Information Processing Systems Systems (NIPS), pp. 5998–6008 (2017)

pH-RL: A Personalization Architecture to Bring Reinforcement Learning to Health Practice

Ali el Hassouni[1,2(✉)] ⓘ, Mark Hoogendoorn[1] ⓘ, Marketa Ciharova[3] ⓘ,
Annet Kleiboer[3] ⓘ, Khadicha Amarti[3] ⓘ, Vesa Muhonen[2] ⓘ, Heleen Riper[3] ⓘ,
and A. E. Eiben[1] ⓘ

[1] Department of CS, Vrije Universiteit Amsterdam, Amsterdam, The Netherlands
{a.el.hassouni,m.hoogendoorn,g.eiben}@vu.nl
[2] Mobiquity Inc., Data Science and Analytics, Amsterdam, The Netherlands
{aelhassouni,v.muhonen}@mobiquityinc.com
[3] Department of Clinical, Neuro- and Developmental Psychology, Amsterdam Public Health
Institute, Vrije Universiteit, Amsterdam, Netherlands
{m.ciharova,a.m.kleiboer,k.amarti,h.riper}@vu.nl

Abstract. While reinforcement learning (RL) has proven to be the approach of choice for tackling many complex problems, it remains challenging to develop and deploy RL agents in real-life scenarios successfully. This paper presents pH-RL (personalization in e-Health with RL), a general RL architecture for personalization to bring RL to health practice. pH-RL allows for various levels of personalization in health applications and allows for online and batch learning. Furthermore, we provide a general-purpose implementation framework that can be integrated with various healthcare applications. We describe a step-by-step guideline for the successful deployment of RL policies in a mobile application. We implemented our open-source RL architecture and integrated it with the Mood-Buster mobile application for mental health to provide messages to increase daily adherence to the online therapeutic modules. We then performed a comprehensive study with human participants over a sustained period. Our experimental results show that the developed policies learn to select appropriate actions consistently using only a few days' worth of data. Furthermore, we empirically demonstrate the stability of the learned policies during the study.

1 Introduction

Reinforcement learning (RL) has seen tremendous successes in recent years, principally due to the many breakthroughs made in deep learning (DL) [12,15,21–23]. The field has witnessed these breakthroughs in high-dimensional control tasks, e.g., complex games Atari and Go and continuous control tasks such as MuJoCo, and openAI gym [3]. In many of these tasks e.g., Atari and board games such as Go, Chess, and Shogi, superhuman performance was achieved [14,15,21]. We can attribute these successes to the rise of deep reinforcement learning (DRL) fueled by novel algorithms such as deep Q-network (DQN), the availability of powerful computing hardware, and the nature of the problems at hand that allows one to obtain large samples from the task environment and to perform exploration as one wishes.

ⓒ Springer Nature Switzerland AG 2022
G. Nicosia et al. (Eds.): LOD 2021, LNCS 13163, pp. 265–280, 2022.
https://doi.org/10.1007/978-3-030-95467-3_20

Many practical limitations arise in societal domains such as healthcare, making these benefits listed above fade away [4, 8–10]. Such limitations are the inaccessibility to large samples of data, the unavailability of environments to train and evaluate algorithms in, the limitations on the data caused by privacy laws, and safety concerns (e.g., unsafe actions and exploration), explainability, and legal responsibility [4, 10]. As a consequence, the applicability of DRL in many practical tasks remains limited. In many practical tasks where RL has been shown to perform well such as advertisement campaign optimisation, there is ample data available, interactions with users are not costly and safety does not play a big role. In healthcare tasks, all these factors play an equally important role. Therefore, there is a need for structural solutions through standardized frameworks and architectures to overcome the abovementioned obstacles and challenges. Consequently, we pose the following research questions and try to answer them with a real-life experiment: 1) **How can we integrate RL into e-Health mobile applications? and 2) Can we learn policies quickly that provide personalized interventions?**

This paper presents a general RL architecture (pH-RL) for personalization with the goal of bringing RL to health practice. We propose an RL architecture that allows for adding a personalisation component to applications in healthcare such as mobile applications for mental health. pH-RL allows for different levels of personalisation, namely: pooled (one-fits-all approach), grouped (cluster-level personalisation) and separate (hyper-personalisation on user level). Furthermore, pH-RL allows for online and offline (batch) learning. We describe a step-by-step guideline for the successful deployment of RL policies in a mobile application.

We implement our open-source RL framework and integrate it with the MoodBuster mobile application for mental health. MoodBuster is a research platform developed to treat psychological complaints online through mobile and web applications. These applications allow for interventions through daily messages and notifications to increase adherence to the online therapeutic modules, which is assumed to increase clinical effectiveness. We employ a default control policy approach based on prior knowledge coupled with random exploration in pH-RL. Next, we apply clustering techniques on the traces of states and users' rewards to find an appropriate segmentation of the experiences. Then, we apply online batch RL coupled with exploration driven by the learned policies on each cluster of users. We then perform a comprehensive study with human participants over a sustained period. Our experimental results show that the developed policies learn to select appropriate actions consistently using only a few days' worth of data. Finally, we empirically demonstrate the stability of the learned policies during the study.

2 Related Work

RL as a solution architecture for real-world problems has seen a significant increase in the last few years ranging from games to advertising and healthcare. This learning paradigm has seen applications in various areas. In this related work section, we discuss general real-world applications architectures of RL and specific Health applications and architectures for personalization.

Reinforcement Learning Applications. Much effort is put into the use of RL for various applications. A successful application of RL in the last decade was using deep RL to play Atari games [15]. This approach relies on Q-learning with convolutional neural networks to successfully learn control policies for playing Atari games using low-level high-dimensional sensory data as input. These policies surpassed human-level performance in several cases. Also related, [21] combined deep learning with RL to develop policy and value networks that play Go at a superhuman level. These networks learn from extensive amounts of self-play made possible by a well-defined environment with comprehensive rules. In a more recent application, RL has proven to be an effective solution to a real-world autonomous control problem involving the navigation of super-pressure balloon in the stratosphere [2]. This problem is characterized by its complexity, forecast errors, sparse wind measurements, and the need for real-time decision-making. This work uses data augmentation and a self-correcting design to tackle RL issues, usually by imperfect data. As mentioned in Sect. 1, all these examples do not suffer from the many limitations one encounters with problems in healthcare.

Reinforcement Learning for Clinical Applications. A literature review has shown that the number of applications of RL has been increasing [10]. Applications in healthcare range from treating patients with Sepsis at the Intensive Care Unit to sending personalized messages in e-Health mobile applications. There is strong evidence that suggests that current practices at the ICU are not optimal while the best treatment strategy remains unknown. (Komorowski et al.) used RL to develop policies that are on average more reliable than human clinicians [12]. This approach provides individualized treatment decisions that are interpretable by clinicians. Similarly, [19] used RL to develop policies for individualized treatment strategies to correct hypotension in Sepsis. More recent work showed that these developed policies for optimizing hemodynamic treatment for critically ill patients with Sepsis are transferable across different patient populations [18]. Furthermore, this work proposes an in-depth inspection approach for clinical interpretability. In a strictly regulated area such as healthcare, these examples are considered very innovative. However, structural solutions are needed. Our pH-RL standardized architecture and the corresponding generic framework allow us to bring online and offline RL for personalization to health practice.

Reinforcement Learning for Personalization in e-Health Applications. More and more real-world applications using RL for personalization in e-Health are found in literature [10]. Work by [9] focuses on developing RL policies coupled with clustering techniques for personalizing health interventions. They show that clustering using traces of states and reward and developing policies based on these clusters leads to improved personalization levels while speeding-up the learning time of the approach. In a later work, [8] demonstrates that this approach leads to improved personalization levels when applied on state representations consisting of raw sensor data obtained from mobile apps. Similarly, k-means clustering and RL were combined to develop policies across similar users for the purpose of learning better policies [24]. Clustering methods were also used to effectively learn personalized RL policies in health and wellbeing [6].

Personalization Architectures for e-Health Mobile Applications. A wealth of mobile apps exist that support people in their daily lives. We can use these apps for mental coaching, health interventions, fitness apps, and various other purposes. Although these applications can take various types of information into account, such as location, and historical behavior, they still rely on rule-based approaches and do not achieve high effectiveness and efficaciousness of medical treatment. Reinforcement learning-driven personalization has proven to be a practical approach for many health settings, including e-health and m-health [10]. Furthermore, clinical support systems could rely on the same techniques to achieve high effectiveness and officiousness of medical treatments. Related work shows a lack of publications that propose RL architectures for personalization. [5] presents a reference architecture that enables self-adaptation of mobile apps for e-Health. Although this architecture proposed a non-rule-based approach for self-adaptation, it does not specify machine learning techniques to achieve personalization. This architecture relies on MAPE (Monitoring, Analysis, Planning and Execution) loops that operate at different levels of granularity meant for different purposes. (Hoffman et al.) proposed a research framework for distributed RL (Acme) [11]. This framework aims at simplifying the process of developing RL algorithms in academia and industry.

3   PH-RL - An RL Personalization Architecture for Health Practice

This section introduces our reinforcement learning personalization architecture for mobile applications in e-Health. We start by framing the problem definition. Then we introduce our framework for personalization with RL. Finally, we present our pH-RL framework for personalization in e-Health.

3.1   The RL Architecture for Personalisation

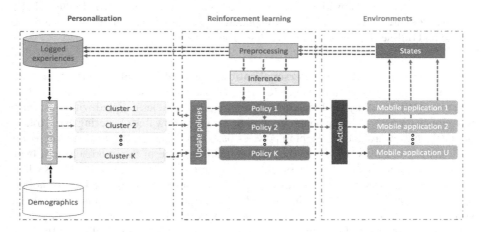

Fig. 1. pH-RL: A reinforcement learning personalization architecture for mobile applications in e-Health

Figure 1 shows the pH-RL framework for personalization of interventions in e-Health applications using RL. This section starts with a definition of the system's different components and the environment it is interacting with to learn personalized policies.

Users of the Mobile Applications. Users are the people that utilize the e-Health application to get help with achieving a specific health goal. These users own a smart device that can run the e-Health application. They install the e-Health applications and continue to sign-up to be able to use the application. We ask these users to provide information about their demographics, preferences, health issues and treatment goals to form the initial clusters. After the sign-up phase, the users start generating data used by the pH-RL framework to personalize the interventions further. The e-Health applications send these interventions to help the users achieve their treatment goals.

Smart Device. This device can be any computer that can host applications and have an interface to interact with the users. Mobile phones and smartwatches are the most natural types of smart devices used to host e-Health applications. These devices contain sensors that allow the pH-RL framework to obtain potentially very granular data about the users' behavior continuously. We can use this information to infer contextual information about the users' state without having to ask them to provide this information at all times explicitly. Additionally, smart devices contain interfaces in the form of a screen or voice that allows the users to receive interventions from the e-Health applications and provide feedback to the application.

State. In RL settings, a state contains information about the user at a certain point in time t. We capture this information through the e-Health application. Throughout this paper, we operationalize a state following the RL definition in this section. To model a real-world problem as an RL problem, one has to design a Markovian state representation. In pH-RL, a state $s \in S$ is made up of features represented by the feature vector representation $\vec{\psi}(s) = \langle \psi_1(s), \psi_2(s), \ldots, \psi_n(s) \rangle^\top$. A feature can indicate the occurrence of a certain activity, the number of times a user performed a certain activity during a specified period, or any other feature that provides useful information about the user's behavior. In pH-RL, we perform binning to transform any continuous feature into a discrete representation.

Interventions. E-Health applications running pH-RL are used by people to help them with a health-related goal. The application gathers data from the user's smart device and sends it to our pH-RL framework, which returns an action $a \in A$ presented to the user in the form of interventions. The most natural way of providing a user with an intervention is via notifications of mobile applications or smartwatches. The main goal in pH-RL is to provide users with interventions that are relevant at the right moment. This hypothesis is that personalized interventions will lead to a higher long-term adherence level to the user's goal.

Rewards. The pH-RL framework gathers data from the users through the e-Health application. Behavioral change data from the users about the effect of interventions (either direct or indirect) is used as a feedback mechanism (e.g. the reward signal) by the RL algorithm in pH-RL to learn personalized policies. For instance, the direct reward can be users providing ratings about their moods a few times per day in a mental health application. Indirect rewards can be the amount of activity measured after receiving the intervention. Rewards play an essential role in pH-RL and should be defined carefully to represent the problem at hand well.

3.2 Preliminaries and Problem Statement

Reinforcement Learning. We model a real-world problem M as a Markov Decision Process (MDP). Therefore, we consider the task M to be Markovian and therefore it can be modelled using RL algorithms. In this section we borrow the RL terminology from [9]. We define M to be $\langle S, A, T, R \rangle$ where S is a finite state space, and A the set of actions that can be selected at each time step t. There exists a probabilistic transition function $T :: S \times A \times S \rightarrow [0,1]$ over the states in S. When at time t in current state s an action a is selected, a transition is made to a next state $s' \in S$ at $t + 1$. $R :: S \times A \rightarrow \mathbb{R}$ is the reward function and outputs a scalar $r = R(s, a)$ to each combination of state $s \in S$ and action $a \in A$. The feature vector representation $\vec{\psi}(s) = \langle \psi_1(s), \psi_2(s), \ldots, \psi_n(s) \rangle^\top$ defines the features that form the states $s \in S$. Our aim when modelling task M as an RL problem is to learn a policy π. With the policy $\pi :: S \rightarrow A$ we can determine which action $a \in A$ to take in a state $s \in S$ such that the long term expected cumulative reward is maximized. Selecting action $a = \pi(s)$ will result in a transition to state s'. Here, a reward $r = R(s, a)$ will be obtained. Taking an action while in a state and transitioning to a new state forms an experience $\langle s, a, r, s' \rangle$. A trace is a sequence of experiences in a particular order. Denote a trace by $\zeta : \langle s, a, r, s', a', r', s'', a'', r'', \ldots \rangle$. Multiple transitions over time result in multiple experiences. The combination of experiences over time form a data set $Z \in \langle \zeta_1, \ldots \zeta_k \rangle$.

Reinforcement learning aims at learning the best policy π^* out of all possible policies $\Pi :: S \times A \rightarrow [0,1]$. π^* selects actions with the aim of maximizing the the sum of future rewards (at any time t). We assign a value for taking action $a \in A$ in state s of policy π $\pi(s) = a$ as follows:

$$Q^\pi(s, a) = E_\pi \{ \sum_{k=0}^{K} \gamma^k r^{t+k+1} | s^t = s, a^t = a \} \tag{1}$$

Here γ is the discount factor that gives weights to future rewards. s^t and a^t define the states and actions at time t. Denote $Q(s, a)$ as the expected long-term value of state s after taking action a. If we select the best action a in each possible state $s \in S$, a policy can be derived from the Q-function, i.e.

$$\pi'(s) = \arg\max_{a \in A} Q^\pi(s, a), \; \forall s \in S \tag{2}$$

Cluster-Based Policy Improvement. One-fits-all approaches are based on the assumption that users belong to one group, and therefore, one policy is learned across all these users. This approach has been shown to perform sub-optimally in e-Health applications because people, in general, have different preferences and are characterized by non-identical transition and reward functions [9].

In the pH-RL framework, we mitigate this issue and propose to group users with similar behavior using clustering techniques [8,9]. Clustering algorithms such as K-medoids and K-means have been shown to perform well on similar problems in e-Health [6,8,9]. We compare the behavioral traces of users consisting of states and rewards, and we use the Dynamic Time Warping (DTW) algorithm to calculate the distance between two users. Several other distance metrics, such as the Euclidean distance, have been explored in e-Health literature. Although metrics are considered valid approaches for calculating distances between two traces, DTW is more accurate because it measures the similarity between two different users' traces. It does so by finding the optimal match between two potentially similar traces that are out of phase where the Euclidean distance would have found these two traces to be very different. We define the traces of u consisting of states and rewards as: $\langle s_u, r, s'_u, r', s''_u, r'', \ldots \rangle$.

Define the group of users to be targeted by our framework as U and Σ^U as all the traces generated by these users. The experiences (excluding the actions) generated by user i during day d are defined as $\Sigma'^{u_{i,d}}$. We calculated the similarity between two users u_1 and u_2 as:

$$S_{DTW}(u_1, u_2) = \sum_{d=0}^{D} dtw(\Sigma^{u_{1,d}}, \Sigma^{u_{2,d}}). \tag{3}$$

We apply a clustering method to obtain clusters k of users based on their traces where k and $\Sigma_1^U, \ldots, \Sigma_k^U$ is a partitioning of Σ^U, and let $U_1, \ldots U_k$ be the partitioning of U [9]. In a one-fits-all approach, we would utilize all experiences of U to learn one Q-function. In pH-RL, we learn a distinct Q-function $Q_{\Sigma_i^U}$ and policy $\pi_{\Sigma_i^U}$ for each user set U_i based on all the traces in Σ_i^U. Note that these steps are done in addition to our previous setup, which allows for a comparison between a policy for U and subgroup policies.

Table 1. State features, actions and reward definitions.

Feature	Definition
Day part	A numerical encoding for part of day (0: morning, 1: afternoon, and 2: evening)
Number rating	The cumulative number of ratings inputted by the user
Highest rating	The highest rating inputted by a user during the current day
Lowest rating	The lowest rating inputted by a user during the current day
Median rating	The median rating inputted by a user during the current day
SD rating	The standard deviation of the ratings inputted by a user during the current day
Number low rating	The number of low (1 and 2) ratings inputted by a user during the current day
Number medium rating	The number of medium (3, 4, and 5) ratings inputted by a user during the current day
Number high rating	The number of high (6 and 7) ratings inputted by a user during the current day
Number message received	The number of messages received by a user during the current day
Number message read	The number of messages read by a user during the current day
Read all message	Indicator if a user reads all messages during the current day

3.3 Framework Implementation and Algorithm Setup

In this section, we discuss the framework implementation and our algorithmic setup. Furthermore, we discuss in detail our design choices for the state, actions, and rewards as can be seen in Fig. 1. Our proposed pH-RL architecture can be applied across many personalization tasks in mobile applications. In this section, we demonstrate an instance implementation of pH-RL for mental health using the MoodBuster platform.

State. We designed features (i.e. $\vec{\psi}(s_u)$) to represent the state of a user. Table 1 shows an overview of the features. These features were designed to capture the behaviour of the users on the mobile application and their mood ratings.

Action. We use four actions that the policy can select. Action 0 represents: "send no message", action 1 represents sending an action of type: "encouraging", action 2 represents sending an action of type: "informing", and action 3 represents sending an action of type: "affirming". Once the action is selected, we further decide from which sub-group of actions to select based on the user's mood. All messages and categories, including the splits based on mood, can be found in the appendix. To make sure we do not send the same message multiple times during a day, we randomly select a message from the set of possible messages that were not previously selected during the same day.

Reward. Adherence can be measured by how often users are using the Mood-Buster application. Therefore, the reward function is a combination of two components weighted equally. The first component measures the fraction of messages received during a day up until the current daypart. The second component measures the number of ratings inputted by a user during a day until the current day.

Least Squares Policy Iteration (LSPI). We perform training using (batch) online learning with the LSPI algorithm because of its ability to generalize well on relatively small datasets. Every time the policies for the different clusters of users are updated with a new batch of data, we export a policy for inference of actions. We use the exact basis function transformation of our features by first binning each of the features into four bins, increasing our features by a factor of 4. We use a policy with the LSTDQ Solver, a discount factor of 0.95, an exploration rate of 0.1, the tie-breaking strategy first wins, max iterations of 25, and stopping criterion ϵ of 0.00001. These hyper-parameters are based on various experiments from earlier work in this area [8, 9].

Technical Implementation of the pH-RL System. We utilize Amazon Web Services to run our pH-RL system. Our setup consists of an S3 bucket to store RL experiences safely and securely. pH-RL is implemented as an open-source Python package [7]. The code is deployed on an AWS EC2 instance (t2.large). The scripts for performing batch training (once a day), clustering (once during the entire experiment), inference, or sending a message (three times every day) are run with a time-based job scheduler (cronjob).

We make secure connections with the restful API of MoodBuster to make read calls to retrieve data and post calls to send messages.

4   Real-World Performance Evaluation

To evaluate the proposed pH-RL framework, we conducted a real-world experiment with a mobile application for mental health. This experiment's main aim is to demonstrate the feasibility of applying the pH-RL framework for personalization in e-Health applications and provide easy-to-follow guidelines for successful integration and deployment of RL models in real-world applications. We integrated our pH-RL framework into the MoodBuster platform to provide personalized messages and answer our first research question.

4.1   Personalized Motivational Feedback Messages

We designed a real-world experiment to improve adherence to an online course for low mood with personalized motivational feedback messages. The pH-RL framework is used to select the most appropriate messages to send to a user to maximize adherence to the course. We consider three categories of messages based on existing research [20]. Informing messages aim at providing informative messages to help the user understand the MoodBuster platform and the online course. Encouraging messages try to encourage users to perform a specific action. Affirming messages offer emotional support or encouragement. We further split the encouraging and affirming categories based on the user's mood into the following three groups: positive neutral mood, negative neutral mood, and mood unavailable.

4.2   MoodBuster

MoodBuster is a research platform that has been developed to treat or prevent psychological complaints online. Treatments on MoodBuster take place in connection with research projects. The platform gives access to three types of applications: a web application for patients, a web portal for practitioners, and a mobile and web application that can measure information such as the Ecological Momentary Assessment (mood and user state measurements) [13, 17]. The platform can be used to treat patients as part of a guided online treatment or as a prevention and self-help tool. Furthermore, MoodBuster can be used as part of guided online treatments or blended treatment (face-to-face therapy combined with online treatment). In this work, we use the cognitive behavioral therapy treatment for depression on the MoodBuster platform. This treatment consists of 6 (guided and unguided) online modules containing readable and watchable material to guide the user through the module to perform exercises and assignments. The cognitive-behavioral therapy treatment for depression helps the user better understand depression, stimulate positive thinking, stimulate behavioral change through enjoyable activities and physical exercise.

4.3 Participants

We conducted this experiment with 30 participants from our research departments at the Vrije Universiteit Amsterdam, students, and friends. All these participants were not selected based on having depression. Furthermore, we informed these users that we performed this study to test our pH-RL framework for personalization. Henceforth, they should use this application with the intent that it is part of a test case.

4.4 Setup of Runs

We train our policies using batch learning. We set the intervention moments when the application sends messages at 10:00, 14:00, and 21:00. We perform random exploration during the first week (phase 1) of the experiment by sending three random interventions a day. After week one, we perform clustering to find our clusters and train our policies using all available data from the start of the experiment. Phase 2 of the experiment runs for an additional two weeks using actions from the learned policies. We update our policies in batch at the end of every day at 23:59.

5 Results

In this section, we present the results related to the experiment laid out in Sect. 4. We experimented with 30 participants to test our integration of the pH-RL framework for personalization in e-Health with the MoodBuster mobile application for depression. We instructed the participants to use and interact with the application to generate data. We do not assume any of the participants to have any symptoms of depression, and therefore we do not expect the app to lead to any significant changes in the participants' mood. Our main aim is to present, implement and test the pH-RL architecture in an e-Health setting and demonstrate that we can learn policies quickly that provide personalized interventions.

Inactive Participants. During the experiment, a fraction of all participants were entirely dormant and showed no activity. Inactive users reflect actual real-life usage stats of mobile applications. The experiences of these users are still included in the data set provided used to develop the models. During the whole experiment, 6 participants showed barely any activity and were excluded (entered a rating or read a message at least once for maximum of two days). Furthermore, an additional eight users became inactive during weeks 2 and 3 of the experiment. During the data analysis, we reported different results that include and exclude these users. In this experiment users becoming inactive is not the results of the interaction with the application.

5.1 Exploration Phase

Developing RL policies requires a data set consisting of many experiences. At the start of our experiment, we lack such data. As a solution, we implemented a default policy to be used during the experiment's initial phase for one week. During this phase, random exploration was applied, resulting in the data presented in Fig. 2. From the figure on the right, we can see that around 70% of the messages were read throughout the first week. Furthermore, we observed that around 75% of the users rated their mood at least once per day during the first week with a drop on Friday and Saturday.

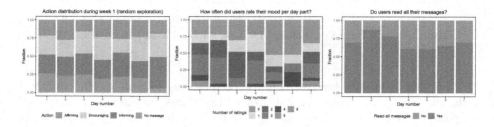

Fig. 2. Week 1 action distributions (left), number of ratings per day (middle) and fraction of messages read (right).

5.2   Learning Phase

After phase 1, we trained the first policy and started using it. We update the policy with new data at the end of every day. Here we do include data from all 8 participants that became inactive after week 1. Using the obtained results we answer the second research question in this section. Figure 3 (middle) shows how often users rated their mood per day. On average, at least 45% of the participants rated their mood at least once per day. Finally, we see from Fig. 3 (right) that around 50% of the users read all their messages per day. Figure 3 (left) shows the distribution of actions for all dayparts. We can see that the policy started favoring "Informing" messages around 50% of the time. As we move forward in time, the policy starts favoring encouraging messages more often. This is in line with what we hypothesized based on existing research [1, 20]. On day 7 of the second week, the policy decides not to send a message in around 40% of the cases. Overall the policy favors the actions in the following order: "encouraging", "informing", "affirming", and "sending no message".

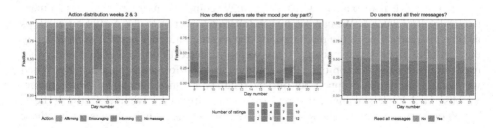

Fig. 3. Week 2 and 3 action distributions (left), number of ratings per day (middle) and fraction of messages read (right).

Table 2. The average reward per user per daypart for weeks 1, 2, and 3. Week 2* and Week 3* are with inactive users excluded.

	Week 1	Week 2	Week 2*	Week 3	Week 3*
All day parts	0.98 ± 0.79	0.83 ± 1.02	**1.20 ± 1.06**	0.77 ± 0.98	1.16 ± 1.01
Morning	0.66 ± 0.57	0.62 ± 0.78	**0.87 ± 0.81**	0.54 ± 0.64	0.81 ± 0.65
Afternoon	1.1 ± 0.80	0.87 ± 1.0	0.87 ± 0.81	0.83 ± 1.01	**1.25 ± 1.03**
Evening	1.2 ± 0.87	1.00 ± 1.19	**1.46 ± 1.22**	0.93 ± 1.16	1.40 ± 1.19

To further understand how the policy is personalizing towards specific attributes in the state space, we created the visualization that shows the action distributions of the policies per daypart in Fig. 4. In Fig. 4 (left), we can see that the policy started favoring "informing" messages in the morning but quickly changed to a strategy with "encouraging" messages. In the afternoon, we see similar behavior with more "affirming" messages. On day 14 of the experiment, the policy does not send any messages in the afternoon. Finally, the evening strategy is to mostly send "encouraging" messages during the first two days and then switch to a strategy dominated by "informing" messages in the evening. These findings are in line with existing research [20].

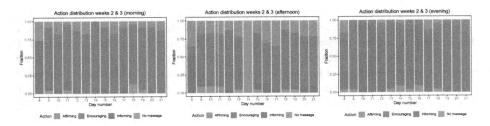

Fig. 4. Week 2 and 3 action distributions morning (left), afternoon (middle) and evening (right).

Rewards. Figure 5 and Table 2 show the observed rewards during weeks 1, 2, and 3. Furthermore, we also consider statistics and make comparisons after excluding all inactive users after week 1. We can see that the average reward per day part per user drops as time proceeds. One of the main reasons that a certain number of users stopped using the app after week 1 was because some were instructed to do so. Furthermore, other users stopped using the app once they felt they have performed enough testing. When we exclude users that dropped out, the average reward increases again. Furthermore, we observe that users obtain higher rewards consistently in the evening. Our hypothesis has to do with the fact that people have more time to check their phones during these moments of the day. From Fig. 5, we also see that the maximum reward per user per day part increased after week 1.

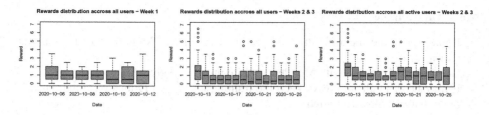

Fig. 5. The box plots of the average daily reward per day part for weeks 1, 2 and 3.

6 Discussion

This paper presented a general reinforcement learning architecture for personalization in e-Health mobile applications (pH-RL). This architecture utilizes traces of states and rewards obtained from users to form clusters with k-means and the Dynamic Time Warping distance function. We built and integrated our architecture with the Mood-Buster application for mood support. We ran an experiment with human participants for three weeks. Our results show that the pH-RL architecture can learn policies that consistently converge and provide the users with the right actions. Based on the observed reward values, we can conclude that pH-RL leads to increased adherence to the Mood-Buster application. We ran our experiment for a period of two weeks. This resulted in a significant amount of user experiences. Given the number of users, we opted for training one policy across these users. In future work, it would be of great importance to experiment with a larger number of participants to find large enough clusters. Furthermore, the experiment can be ran for a longer period of time to evaluate the behaviour of the architecture during a longer period of time. Finally, including user specific features that describe their characteristics and preferences to the state space could result in better performance of the policies.

7 Appendix

We use personalized motivational feedback messages to improve adherence to an online course for low mood. We define three groups of messages inspired by [16].

7.1 Encouraging

Positive Neutral Mood

– It seems like you're on the right track! Keep up the good work!
– Good to see that you are doing well. Good luck continuing Moodbuster Lite.
– You are making a lot of progress! You can be proud of yourself!

Negative Neutral Mood

– It is good that you take part in Moodbuster Lite. You can commend yourself for that!
– Good that you are still rating your mood on a regular basis! Keep up the good work!
– It's great that you are making time for yourself to improve your mood!

Mood Unavailable

– It may sometimes be difficult to engage in a training like Moodbuster Lite, but you can do it!
– Good that you started with Moodbuster Lite this is already a first step.
– It may be difficult to always keep the training and mood ratings on mind, but it's great that you already started.
– Don't give up if you haven't rated your mood.

7.2 Informing

– Don't forget to set a reminder in order to not forget about your scheduled pleasant activities.
– Do you know you can always review the material of sessions if you need it?
– In your calendar, you can see the activities which you planned in the past.
– It is good to track what pleasant activities you did.
– Do not forget to rate your mood three times per day.
– Did you forget what pleasant activities to do? You can always check your notes on the website.
– It is sometimes helpful to re-read the content of the training to refresh your knowledge.
– Reminders may help you to not forget about the pleasant activities.
– It's good to keep track of what pleasant activities you do and how your mood is.

7.3 Affirming

Positive Neutral Mood

– Good to see that you are doing well.
– Even if you don't rate your mood at some point, don't worry, it may be hard to always think about it.
– I am happy to see that you feel well.

Negative Neutral Mood

– It is very common to sometimes have low mood, so do not worry if that happens.
– It may be difficult to always keep the training and mood ratings on mind, but it is important for your well-being.
– Many people sometimes feel sad, this is nothing to worry about.
– It must be complicated to engage in this training, so it's completely fine if you sometimes feel that way.
– Struggling to find the time to do the scheduled pleasant activities is completely normal, so do not worry if it ever happens to you.

Mood Unavailable

- Don't get discouraged if you forget to rate your mood sometimes, it's normal.
- It is completely normal to sometimes feel demotivated.
- If you keep forgetting to do the pleasant activities? It will be ok! Don't give up!
- Do you often feel tired? That can easily happen when doing a training like this!
- It can be hard to think constantly about rating your mood.
- Struggling to find the time to do the scheduled pleasant activities is completely normal, so do not worry if it ever happens to you.
- It must be complicated to engage in this training, so it's completely fine if you sometimes feel that way.

References

1. Bailoni, T., Dragoni, M., Eccher, C., Guerini, M., Maimone, R.: Healthy lifestyle support: the PerKApp ontology. In: Dragoni, M., Poveda-Villalón, M., Jimenez-Ruiz, E. (eds.) OWLED/ORE -2016. LNCS, vol. 10161, pp. 15–23. Springer, Cham (2017). https://doi.org/10.1007/978-3-319-54627-8_2
2. Bellemare, M.G., et al.: Autonomous navigation of stratospheric balloons using reinforcement learning. Nature **588**(7836), 77–82 (2020)
3. Brockman, G., et al.: OpenAI gym. CoRR abs/1606.01540 (2016). http://arxiv.org/abs/1606.01540
4. Dulac-Arnold, G., Mankowitz, D., Hester, T.: Challenges of real-world reinforcement learning. arXiv preprint arXiv:1904.12901 (2019)
5. Grua, E.M., De Sanctis, M., Lago, P.: A reference architecture for personalized and self-adaptive e-health apps. In: Muccini, H., et al. (eds.) ECSA 2020. CCIS, vol. 1269, pp. 195–209. Springer, Cham (2020). https://doi.org/10.1007/978-3-030-59155-7_15
6. Grua, E.M., Hoogendoorn, M.: Exploring clustering techniques for effective reinforcement learning based personalization for health and wellbeing. In: 2018 IEEE Symposium Series on Computational Intelligence (SSCI), pp. 813–820. IEEE (2018)
7. el Hassouni, A.: alielhassouni/ph-rl: ph-rl, March 2021. https://doi.org/10.5281/zenodo.4628543
8. el Hassouni, A., Hoogendoorn, M., Eiben, A.E., Van Otterlo, M., Muhonen, V.: End-to-end personalization of digital health interventions using raw sensor data with deep reinforcement learning: a comparative study in digital health interventions for behavior change. In: 2019 IEEE/WIC/ACM International Conference on Web Intelligence (WI), pp. 258–264. IEEE (2019)
9. Hassouni, A., Hoogendoorn, M., van Otterlo, M., Barbaro, E.: Personalization of health interventions using cluster-based reinforcement learning. In: Miller, T., Oren, N., Sakurai, Y., Noda, I., Savarimuthu, B.T.R., Cao Son, T. (eds.) PRIMA 2018. LNCS (LNAI), vol. 11224, pp. 467–475. Springer, Cham (2018). https://doi.org/10.1007/978-3-030-03098-8_31
10. den Hengst, F., Grua, E.M., el Hassouni, A., Hoogendoorn, M.: Reinforcement learning for personalization: a systematic literature review. Data Sci. (Preprint) **3**, 107–147 (2020)
11. Hoffman, M., et al.: Acme: a research framework for distributed reinforcement learning. arXiv preprint arXiv:2006.00979 (2020)
12. Komorowski, M., Celi, L.A., Badawi, O., Gordon, A.C., Faisal, A.A.: The artificial intelligence clinician learns optimal treatment strategies for sepsis in intensive care. Nat. Med. **24**(11), 1716–1720 (2018)

13. Mikus, A., Hoogendoorn, M., Rocha, A., Gama, J., Ruwaard, J., Riper, H.: Predicting short term mood developments among depressed patients using adherence and ecological momentary assessment data. Internet Interv. **12**, 105–110 (2018)
14. Mnih, V., et al.: Human-level control through deep reinforcement learning. Nature **518**(7540), 529–533 (2015). https://doi.org/10.1038/nature14236
15. Mnih, V., et al.: Playing atari with deep reinforcement learning (2013)
16. Mol, M., Dozeman, E., Provoost, S., Van Schaik, A., Riper, H., Smit, J.H.: Behind the scenes of online therapeutic feedback in blended therapy for depression: mixed-methods observational study. J. Med. Internet Res. **20**(5), e174 (2018)
17. Provoost, S., et al.: Improving adherence to an online intervention for low mood with a virtual coach: study protocol of a pilot randomized controlled trial. Trials **21**(1), 1–12 (2020)
18. Roggeveen, L., et al.: Transatlantic transferability of a new reinforcement learning model for optimizing haemodynamic treatment for critically ill patients with sepsis. Artif. Intell. Med. **112**, 102003 (2020)
19. Saria, S.: Individualized sepsis treatment using reinforcement learning. Nat. Med. **24**(11), 1641–1642 (2018)
20. Schwebel, F.J., Larimer, M.E.: Using text message reminders in health care services: a narrative literature review. Internet Interv. **13**, 82–104 (2018)
21. Silver, D., et al.: Mastering the game of go with deep neural networks and tree search. Nature **529**(7587), 484–489 (2016)
22. Sutton, R.S., Barto, A.G.: Reinforcement Learning: An Introduction, 2nd edn. MIT Press, Cambridge (2018)
23. Vinyals, O., et al.: Grandmaster level in StarCraft II using multi-agent reinforcement learning. Nature **575**, 350–354 (2019)
24. Zhu, F., Guo, J., Xu, Z., Liao, P., Yang, L., Huang, J.: Group-driven reinforcement learning for personalized mHealth intervention. In: Frangi, A.F., Schnabel, J.A., Davatzikos, C., Alberola-López, C., Fichtinger, G. (eds.) MICCAI 2018. LNCS, vol. 11070, pp. 590–598. Springer, Cham (2018). https://doi.org/10.1007/978-3-030-00928-1_67

Predicting Worst-Case Execution Times During Multi-criterial Function Inlining

Kateryna Muts$^{(\boxtimes)}$ and Heiko Falk

Hamburg University of Technology, Hamburg, Germany
{k.muts,heiko.falk}@tuhh.de

Abstract. In the domain of hard real-time systems, the Worst-Case Execution Time (WCET) is one of the most important design criteria. Safely and accurately estimating the WCET during a static WCET analysis is computationally demanding because of the involved data flow, control flow, and microarchitecture analyses. This becomes critical in the field of multi-criterial compiler optimizations that trade the WCET with other design objectives. Evolutionary algorithms are typically exploited to solve a multi-objective optimization problem, but they require an extensive evaluation of the objectives to explore the search space of the problem. This paper proposes a method that utilizes machine learning to build a surrogate model in order to quickly predict the WCET instead of costly estimating it using static WCET analysis. We build a prediction model that is independent of the source code and assembly code features, so a compiler can utilize it to perform any compiler-based optimization. We demonstrate the effectiveness of our model on multi-criterial function inlining, where we aim to explore trade-offs between the WCET, code size, and energy consumption at compile time.

Keywords: Multi-objective optimization · Classification · Hard real-time system · Compiler-based optimization

1 Introduction

A hard real-time system is an embedded system that must satisfy its timing constraint, e.g., airplane systems. The *Worst-Case Execution Time* (WCET) represents the worst possible execution time of a program. If a hard-real time system violates the WCET limit, then the consequences might be catastrophic.

The computation of the WCET involves solving the halting problem that is undecidable [15]. Different approaches exist to estimate the WCET: measurement-based, static analysis, and hybrid approaches. Measurement-based and hybrid approaches require the hardware to perform measurements, whereas static analyzers estimate the WCET without executing it on the real hardware. We utilize a static WCET analyzer to estimate the WCET and denote its result by $WCET_{est}$. Any static analyzer aims to determine a safe and tight upper bound of the WCET, i.e., $WCET \leq WCET_{est}$ and $WCET_{est} - WCET \rightsquigarrow 0$.

© Springer Nature Switzerland AG 2022
G. Nicosia et al. (Eds.): LOD 2021, LNCS 13163, pp. 281–295, 2022.
https://doi.org/10.1007/978-3-030-95467-3_21

Lokuciejewski *et al.* [10] showed that the compiler-based optimization *function inlining* [12] can improve $WCET_{est}$. A compiler replaces a function call by the body of the callee and removes the function calls together with return instruction from the code (cf. Fig. 1). This transformation reduces the calling overhead, improves the pipeline's behavior, and enables more opportunities for subsequent optimizations such as unused path elimination or constant propagation, which simplify dataflow and path analyses.

Modern hard real-time systems have additional design restrictions such as code size and energy consumption. Function inlining becomes a multi-objective optimization problem considering $WCET_{est}$, code size, and energy consumption as objectives, because $WCET_{est}$ and energy consumption may decrease, while the code size increases. Since the objectives contradict each other, a unique solution does not exist and we aim to find a set of trade-offs between the objectives. A system designer can use the solution set, e.g., to understand the possible configurations of the hard real-time system without building the real hardware. Such a compiler-based approach has a great advantage, since it is usually very expensive to make any changes in the hardware.

An evolutionary algorithm is often used to solve a multi-objective optimization problem. The algorithm can quickly examine the search space of the problem and find the set of trade-off solutions, since it explores not only one point but a set of points from the search space at each iteration. If the evaluation of an objective is expensive in some sense, such methods become infeasible, since any evolutionary algorithm evaluates the objectives at each found point in the search space.

A static WCET analyzer performs microarchitecture, path analyses, etc. to compute $WCET_{est}$. It is a very time-consuming process for many real-world programs. Therefore, it is hard to employ an evolutionary algorithm with $WCET_{est}$ as one of the objectives. We propose a prediction model that can substitute the expensively evaluated $WCET_{est}$ with much cheaper predictions. In the paper, $WCET_{pred}$ denotes $WCET_{est}$ predicted by our proposed prediction model. $WCET_{pred}$ must be as precise as possible, but we do not require $WCET_{pred}$ to be safe in contrast to $WCET_{est}$, because

- we use the predictions only to direct an evolutionary algorithm to the best possible solution region;
- we utilize a static analyzer to compute safe $WCET_{est}$ values in order to verify the final solutions.

A compiler applies optimizations at different levels of abstraction: high level, which preserves the structure of the source code, and low level, which represents assembly code and thus is target architecture-specific. We aim to build a prediction model independent from the features that are specific for any intermediate level and that can be used performing other compiler-based optimizations, not only function inlining.

We build a prediction model for $WCET_{est}$ using machine learning. Previously proposed early stage approaches [3,7] or hybrid methods [9] to estimate the WCET also use machine learning to get the prediction model, but (i) they extract the software and hardware features of input programs to build the model and (ii) they fit the model on a set of training input programs. The approaches result in one prediction model for the specific software-hardware combination that predicts $WCET_{est}$ for any input program. In contrast, we fit the prediction model specifically for every optimization and every input program, ignoring any software and hardware features. We expect to get a more precise prediction model that can implicitly encapsulate the structure of the optimization's search space and make tighter predictions of $WCET_{est}$.

We organize the paper as follows: Sect. 2 presents related work; Sect. 3 formulates a multi-objection function inlining problem and introduces a method to solve it; Sect. 4 describes a model to predict $WCET_{est}$ at compile time; Sect. 5 presents evaluation results; Sect. 6 gives a conclusion.

2   Related Work

This section presents the related work concerning WCET-aware function inlining as well as methods that are based on machine learning to predict the WCET.

Originally, function inlining is a compiler-based optimization that aims to minimize the *Average-Case Execution Time* of a program. However, it has great potential to be combined with other optimization techniques.

Woerteler et al. [17] applied function inlining to the query language for XML database XQuery, which later became a complete functional programming language. The authors achieved a better performance combining function inlining and query optimizer techniques.

Lokuciejewski et al. [10] utilized function inlining to improve the worst-case performance. The authors presented WCET-driven inlining heuristics based on *random forests*. In the paper, the code size increase was taken into account, but not considered as the second objective. The proposed method returned one solution for the function inlining problem. In our approach, we consider WCET, code size, and energy consumption as objectives and aim to get a set of the best trade-offs between them.

Multi-objective mathematical approaches are rarely used to perform compiler-based optimizations in order to find a set of trade-offs between the objectives. Lokuciejewski et al. [11] considered a problem of finding optimal compiler optimization sequences. The authors examined two pairs of objectives (WCET, ACET) and (WCET, code size), separately making the problem bi-objective. They exploited an evolutionary algorithm to identify the set of optimal compiler optimization sequences for each pair of objectives.

Altenbernd et al. [2] presented a linear timing model to predict the execution time of an input program. They use the model to make timing estimates at the source code level. In order to identify the prediction model, the authors proposed to measure the execution time of some training programs by running them on a simulator or on real hardware. Then, the input C code was translated to an intermediate format, which consists of virtual instructions such as call and return statements, a switch statement, arithmetic and logical operations, etc. Finally, the translated code was emulated in order to record the execution counts for the different virtual instructions. The authors built the final prediction model by solving a minimization problem that aimed to minimize the overall deviation of the predicted execution time from the observed one for a given training program. The evaluation showed that for the tested benchmarks, the prediction model achieved an average deviation of 8 % considering the ARM7 target architecture.

Bonenfant *et al.* [3] introduced an approach to predict the WCET at the C source code level using static analysis of the source code as well as a machine learning technique. The prediction model relied on the worst-case event count analysis that counts certain events of the input code. The authors defined the events as either count attributes (e.g., the maximal number of function calls, arithmetic operations, global variables read accesses, etc.) or style attributes (e.g., the number of lines of code, the maximal loop nesting, etc.) Finally, a machine learning algorithm based on the extracted counts of attributes built a WCET prediction model.

Huybrechts *et al.* [9] proposed a new hybrid approach to predict the WCET based on machine learning. In the first step of the method, a set of attributes was derived from the source code by generating hybrid blocks and acquiring the features (or attributes) from them. A hybrid block was defined as a smaller entity of the input code. In the paper, 15 different code attributes were extracted with the feature selector such as a number of assign, logic and shift operations, global variable and array access, etc. Finally, the authors applied a supervised learning strategy based on the extracted features in order to fit the model and make a prediction of the WCET. 8 different regression models were compared in terms of predicting the WCET. The results showed that the support vector regression with a linear kernel achieved the best performance.

In contrast to the approaches described in [2,3,9], the prediction model presented in this paper should be universal, in the sense that both, source and assembly code level optimizations, can exploit and take advantage of it. For this reason, we focus on building a model that predicts the WCET having knowledge about the search space of optimization and avoiding an explicit description of the source or assembly code structures.

3   Function Inlining

In this section, we describe function inlining in detail and formulate it as a multi-objective optimization problem.

Performing function inlining, a compiler

1. stores input arguments of a function call in local variables;
2. substitutes the function call by the function body;
3. removes the function from the code, if there are no more calls of the function.

Removing the function call, return instructions, and parameter handling, the compiler reduces calling overhead and achieves a smoother pipeline behavior.

function DIFF(int a, int b)
   $res \leftarrow a$
   for $i \leftarrow 1, b$ **do**   ▷ Loop bound min 40 max 300.
      $res \leftarrow res - i$
   return res

res_1=DIFF(100, 40)
res_2=DIFF(500, 300)

(a) Original program.

$a_1 = 100, b_1 = 40$ ▷ The first inlined call.
$res_1 \leftarrow a_1$
for $i \leftarrow 1, b_1$ **do**   ▷ Loop bound min 40 max 40.
   $res_1 \leftarrow res_1 - i$

$a_2 = 500, b_2 = 300$ ▷ The second inlined call.
$res_2 \leftarrow a_2$
for $i \leftarrow 1, b_2$ **do**   ▷ Loop bound min 300 max 300.
   $res_2 \leftarrow res_2 - i$

(b) Program from Fig. 1a with applied function inlining.

Fig. 1. Example of function inlining.

Figure 1a shows a simple example of an input code for which the compiler can apply function inlining. Function DIFF has two input arguments, a and b. The loop bound in the function body depends on the argument b, which complicates the WCET analysis of the code. Since $WCET_{est}$ depends heavily on the loop bounds, but it is not always possible to identify them automatically, a static WCET analyzer like aiT [1] expects a user-annotation of the loop bounds. In Fig. 1a, the minimum and maximum values of the loop bounds are 40 and 300, resp. Computing $WCET_{est}$ in this case, aiT has always to assume the worst-case scenario, i.e., for all calls of DIFF, the number of loop iterations is assumed to be 300, which obviously leads to a large overestimation of the WCET.

To minimize the impact of such a phenomenon, one may apply function inlining as shown in Fig. 1b. A compiler stores the input arguments a and b in local variables, substitutes the function calls by the function body, and removes function $DIFF$ from the code. If the compiler applies constant propagation, the loop bounds are constant and the annotation is not required, because aiT can simply deduce the loop bound value.

The obvious drawbacks of function inlining are:

– code size increases, since the compiler duplicates the function body;
– the performance of the program and energy consumption may be degraded, since the compiler inserts additional variables that require more registers.

We aim to find a trade-off between $WCET_{est}$, code size, and energy consumption. In this paper, we consider function inlining to demonstrate our approach, but the presented framework is general enough to be used with other optimizations.

We mathematically formulate the multi-objective function inlining problem and present definitions of Pareto optimality [4]. The search space $X \subset \{0,1\}^d$ consists of vectors $\vec{x} \in X$ that describe which function calls shall be inlined. Every coordinate $x_i, i = \overline{1,d}$ of a vector $\vec{x}$ corresponds to a specific function call:

$$x_i = \begin{cases} 1, & \text{if the function call } i \text{ to be inlined}, \\ 0, & \text{otherwise.} \end{cases} \tag{1}$$

The objective vector $\vec{z} \in Z \subset \mathbb{R}^3$ represents the code size, $WCET_{est}$, and energy consumption corresponding to a vector $\vec{x}$. The aim is to minimize the function F that maps the search space X into the objective space Z.

Definition 1. *Let $\vec{x}_1, \vec{x}_2 \in X$, $F : X \to Z$, $F(\vec{x}) = (F_1(\vec{x}), F_2(\vec{x}), F_3(\vec{x}))$, then $\vec{x}_1$ dominates $\vec{x}_2$, if*

$$\forall t \in \{1,2,3\} \quad F_t(\vec{x}_1) \le F_t(\vec{x}_2) \tag{2}$$

and

$$\exists r \in \{1,2,3\} : \quad F_r(\vec{x}_1) < F_r(\vec{x}_2). \tag{3}$$

Definition 2. *A solution that is not dominated by any other solution is called Pareto optimal.*

Definition 3. *The Pareto front is a set $\{F(\vec{x}) | \vec{x} \text{ is Pareto optimal}\}$.*

To solve a multi-objective problem, evolutionary algorithms are often used. Their main advantage is that they produce and analyze a set of solutions at each iteration. Any evolutionary algorithm explores a search space using three operators: selection, mutation, and crossover. Selection is responsible for collecting the top-scoring points from the search space and passing them to the next iteration of the algorithm. The selection of the best solutions is done based on the concept of Pareto dominance introduced in Definition 1. During mutation and crossover, new points from the search space are created based on already known ones in order to explore the search space of the problem better. The fitness function is evaluated at new points and they are passed again to the selection phase. Selection, mutation, and crossover are repeated until a stopping criterion is satisfied.

In [13], the authors state that utilizing any evolutionary algorithm with $WCET_{est}$ as an objective is very challenging, since the WCET analysis is very time-consuming, which leads to drastically increased runtimes of the optimization. In this paper, we aim to tackle this issue by predicting the values of $WCET_{est}$. Using time-saving $WCET_{pred}$ instead of time-consuming $WCET_{est}$, we speed up the optimization and the compilation process in general. In our approach, to solve the multi-objective problem, a compiler

1. generates a set of training points, where the input space is the search space of the function inlining problem and the objective variable is $WCET_{est}$ computed by aiT;
2. fits the prediction model described in Sect. 4 utilizing the training set;
3. executes an evolutionary algorithm using $WCET_{pred}$ values returned by the prediction model instead of $WCET_{est}$, i.e., the compiler substitutes the time-consuming WCET analyses by much cheaper predictions.

4   Prediction Model

Let $X \subset \mathbb{R}^d$ be an input space of a problem and $Y \subset \mathbb{R}$ is an objective space. The coordinates of a vector $\vec{x} \in X$ are also called *features*. In the context of function inlining discussed in Sect. 3, the input space X of the prediction model coincides with the search space X of function inlining and the objective space Y represents the $WCET_{est}$ values.

We aim to predict $y \in Y$ at a given $x \in X$ as accurately as possible using a supervised machine learning technique. Any supervised machine learning task is either a regression or classification problem. Regression deals with a continuous objective space, while classification deals with a discrete objective space.

$WCET_{est}$ is a continuous variable, but Fig. 2 presents examples of the $WCET_{est}$ distribution performing function inlining. We observed two main scenarios:

- a few unique $WCET_{est}$ values with high frequency (e.g., benchmarks 3mm and cholesky);
- many unique $WCET_{est}$ values with low frequency (e.g., benchmarks fft1 and codecs_dcodrle1).

For the considered problem, we detected that in most cases, we observed the first scenario, so we decided to apply classification methods to predict $WCET_{est}$.

We compare several well-known classification methods [8]: a logistic regression, a nearest neighbors classifier, a support vector classifier (SVC) with linear and radial basis function (RBF) kernels, a Gaussian process classifier, a decision tree classifier, a random forest classifier, an AdaBoost classifier based on decision trees, a multi-layer perceptron (MLP) classifier, and a naive Bayes classifier for Bernoulli models. For more details of all algorithms and their implementation, we refer to the scientific toolbox scikit-learn [14], which provides simple and effective tools for predictive data analyses.

5   Evaluation

We used the *WCET-aware C compiler framework WCC* [6] for an ARM Cortex-M0 processor architecture. In all our evaluations, we invoked WCC with optimization level O2 in order to enable other optimizations besides function inlining like, e.g., infeasible path elimination or constant propagation.

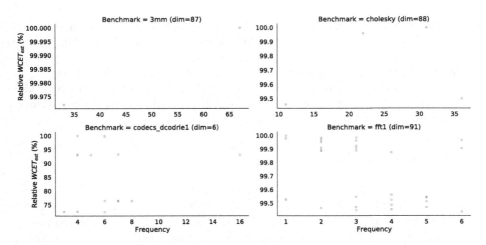

Fig. 2. Examples of the relative $WCET_{est}$ and its frequency performing function inlining. 100% corresponds to the original $WCET_{est}$. For each benchmark, the results are demonstrated for 100 random samples generated by WCC [6].

We evaluate $WCET_{est}$ and energy consumption using the static analyzer aiT [1]. Since the WCET and energy consumption analyses require the knowledge of the target architecture, aiT estimates the WCET and energy consumption based on the assembly code level representation. We used the test suites MediaBench, MRTC, PolyBench, JetBench, and StreamIt with the annotated loop bounds from the TACLeBench project [5].

We fitted the prediction model utilizing scikit-learn [14]. WCC communicates with scikit-learn through CSV files. A scikit wrapper is a stand-alone application that supports two main modes: fit a model and predict values. A procedure to fit a prediction model at compile time is the following:

1. WCC generates a training set, performs static WCET analysis in order to obtain $WCET_{est}$ and writes it to a CSV file;
2. the scikit wrapper reads the CSV file, fits the model using scikit-learn, and stores the model to a Joblib file.

A procedure to predict values using the fitted prediction model is the following:

1. WCC writes decision points from the search space to a new CSV file;
2. the scikit wrapper reads the decision points from the CSV file and the prediction model from the Joblib file, predicts the values, and writes the predicted values to another CSV file;
3. WCC reads the predicted values from the CSV file.

All classifiers from Sect. 4 are available within the scikit-learn tool. We preserved the default scikit configurations of the algorithms except for the maximum number of the iterations for the logistic regression and the multi-layer perceptron classifier. We increased it to 1,000 iterations, because otherwise, the solvers do not converge solving the optimization problems formulated within the classifiers.

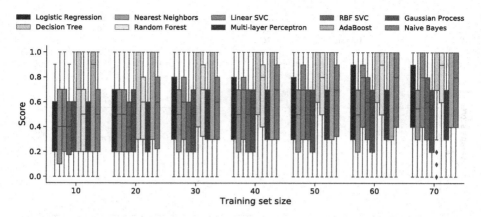

Fig. 3. Classifiers' scores over the considered benchmarks. The best score is 1.

5.1 Prediction Model

In this section, we choose the most suitable classifier for function inlining and describe an algorithm that finds a prediction model at compile time.

To evaluate the quality of classification, we use the metric *score*, which is the mean accuracy on the given test set. For each benchmark and for each classifier, we randomly generated a training set of a certain size and an independent test set of size 10, fitted the classifier using the training set, and computed the score utilizing $WCET_{est}$ and $WCET_{pred}$ of the test set. We repeated each experiment 10 times due to the randomness of the training set.

We aim to speed up the optimization process, so the goal is to build the prediction model with as few training points as possible. Figure 3 presents scores of the classifiers over all benchmarks for different sizes of the training set. The classifiers based on decision trees, namely the decision tree, random forest, and AdaBoost, achieve the highest average scores. We consider further only the AdaBoost classifier, which has the highest median value for small training sets, and the decision tree classifier, which outperforms all other classifiers, if the training set contains more than 30 points.

The score represents the quality of prediction and its acceptance rate depends on a specific problem. In our case, we accepted the score greater than 0.7, i.e., 70 % of predictions are correct on a test set. Figure 4 shows the mean over scores for the decision tree and AdaBoost classifiers. For many benchmarks, on average, both classifiers were able to find a prediction model with a score greater than 0.7, but it is not obvious which classifier is better. For the benchmark 3mm, both classifiers found the prediction model with just 20 training points; for v32mod_cnoise, the decision tree classifier achieved a higher score with 70 training points, while for fmref, vice versa. Therefore, in the next section, we consider both classifiers to make the final choice. After deciding which classifiers to use, we must fit the prediction model at compile time before utilizing it during the optimization. Since Fig. 4 suggests a different number of training points for

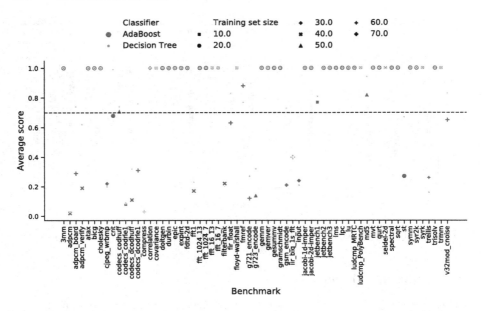

Fig. 4. The mean scores of the decision tree classifier and AdaBoost classifier based on decision trees. The best score value is 1.

Algorithm 1. Find the prediction model

1: Fix a classifier.   ▷ Decision tree or AdaBoost
2: Generate 10 test points and 10 training points ($N := 10$).
3: Compute $WCET_{est}$ for the test and training points.
4: **while** $N \leq 70$ **do**
5:     Fit the model with N training points and compute the score S.
6:     **if** $S < 0.7$ **then**
7:         Generate 10 new training points ($N = N + 10$).
8:         Compute $WCET_{est}$ for the new training points.
9:     **else**
10:         **return** The prediction model.   ▷ Model is found
11: Failed to find the model.

---

different benchmarks, we fitted the final prediction model for each benchmark as described in Algorithm 1. The algorithm might fail to find a prediction model, then one should either try another predictor or get $WCET_{est}$ from aiT.

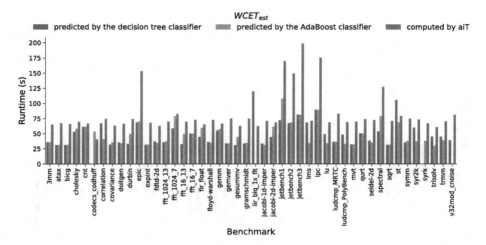

Fig. 5. The runtime computing and predicting $WCET_{est}$. Only benchmarks from Fig. 4 with a model found by Algorithm 1 are presented. The results are reported for 100 test points.

5.2 Evolutionary Algorithm

We demonstrate the advantage of the prediction model by solving multi-objective function inlining discussed in Sect. 3.

We utilize the MBPOA evolutionary algorithm [16] to solve the problem. Any evolutionary algorithm requires a predefined population size and number of generations. For every benchmark, we set the number of generations to 30 and the population size to 50. The stopping criterion for the algorithm is the maximum number of generations. MBPOA has a user-defined crossover parameter, which we set to 0.6. We generate the initial population of the algorithm randomly, therefore, we repeat every experiment 10 times for every considered benchmark.

In this section, we compare Pareto fronts produced by 3 methods:

1. $MBPOA_{est}$ – MBPOA with the WCET estimated by aiT;
2. $MBPOA_{DT}$ – MBPOA with $WCET_{est}$ predicted by the decision tree classifier;
3. $MBPOA_{AB}$ – MBPOA with $WCET_{est}$ predicted by the AdaBoost classifier based on decision trees.

Executing the evolutionary algorithm, we computed the code size exactly and estimated energy consumption by aiT. Using the prediction model, MBPOA returns an approximated Pareto front with the predicted $WCET_{est}$, but it might differ from the estimated WCET. So we estimate the WCET using aiT for the returned Pareto front and present the results for the estimated WCET. Figure 5 presents the runtime predicting $WCET_{est}$ (including runtime of Algorithm 1) and the runtime estimating the WCET by aiT for 100 random decision points. We observed a great saving in the runtime utilizing the prediction model. It

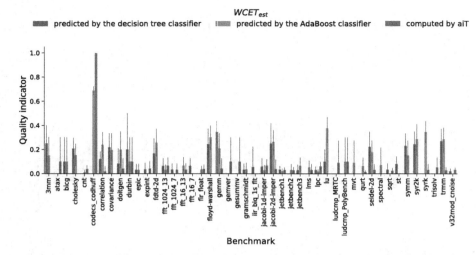

Fig. 6. Quality indicator (4) of the Pareto fronts returned by the algorithm MBPOA with computed and predicted $WCET_{est}$. The best value is 1.

motivated us to analyze the quality of the approximated Pareto fronts produced by the considered methods.

To compare the quality of the Pareto fronts returned by the three considered MBPOA methods, we used the Jaccard index:

$$Q(A) = \frac{|A \cap R|}{|A \cup R|}, \tag{4}$$

where A is an approximated Pareto front returned by the algorithm, R is the true Pareto front, and $|\cdot|$ is a size of a set. The quality indicator is to be maximized. Since in our case, the true Pareto front is unknown, for each benchmark, we pool the Pareto fronts found by all methods into a set and consider its nondominated points as the reference set.

From now on, we present the results for the benchmarks, for which the Algorithm 1 was able to find a prediction model. Figure 6 shows the mean value of the quality indicator over 10 runs of each method. In some instances, all methods result in Pareto fronts of almost the same quality, e.g., jetbench1. For such benchmarks, the predicted $WCET_{est}$ does not degrade the quality of the approximated Pareto front, while the runtime of the optimization potentially decreases. The figure also presents other instances:

- $MBPOA_{est}$ outperforms $MBPOA_{DT}$ and $MBPOA_{AB}$, e.g., benchmark atax;
- $MBPOA_{AB}$ outperforms $MBPOA_{est}$ and $MBPOA_{DT}$, e.g., benchmark correlation;
- $MBPOA_{DT}$ outperforms $MBPOA_{est}$ and $MBPOA_{AB}$, e.g., benchmark 3mm.

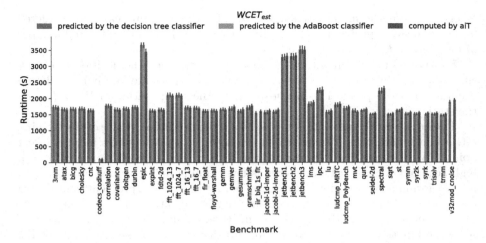

Fig. 7. The runtime of the algorithm MBPOA with computed and predicted $WCET_{est}$.

Figure 7 presents the runtime of the considered methods. The $MBPOA_{est}$ runtime summarizes

- the MBPOA runtime,
- the aiT runtime estimating the WCET during MBPOA execution.

The $MBPOA_{DT}$ and $MBPOA_{AB}$ runtime summarize

- the MBPOA runtime,
- the runtime finding the prediction model (cf. Algorithm 1),
- the runtime predicting $WCET_{est}$ during MBPOA execution.

We observe saving only around 10 % in the runtime predicting $WCET_{est}$, because we still had to run aiT analysis to get the energy consumption.

6 Conclusion

In this paper, we presented a method to predict $WCET_{est}$ (the WCET estimated by a static WCET analyzer) at compile time. The proposed prediction model is based on a machine learning technique and can be used to perform any compiler-based optimization (source and assembly code level), since it is independent of software and hardware features. To utilize the proposed prediction model, a training set of pairs $(\vec{x}, y)$ is generated, where $\vec{x}$ is a point in the search space of an optimization problem and y is the corresponding $WCET_{est}$. A compiler fits the prediction model using a chosen machine learning technique and training set for every input program.

We demonstrated the advantage of the prediction model utilizing it within the compiler-based optimization function inlining. To choose a machine learning algorithm to fit the model, we showed that function inlining can be considered as a classification problem (not a regression problem), because a limited number of unique $WCET_{est}$ was observed.

We showed that even without tuning the parameters, the decision tree classifier and AdaBoost classifier based on decision trees resulted in high prediction accuracy and the predictions are faster than the computation of $WCET_{est}$ by the static analyzer aiT.

The quality of the prediction model heavily depends on the size of the training set: a benchmark with a large search or objective space requires more training points. We presented an algorithm that tries to find a prediction model with high accuracy for a benchmark with as few training points as possible.

We formulated function inlining as a multi-objective problem considering code size, $WCET_{est}$, and energy consumption as objectives. We used the prediction model to speed up the optimization. Running an evolutionary algorithm to solve the function inlining problem, we substituted the time-consuming WCET estimations with quicker predictions. We compared the approximated Pareto fronts produced by the evolutionary algorithm with (i) expensive $WCET_{est}$, (ii) predicted $WCET_{est}$ using the decision tree classifier, and (iii) predicted $WCET_{est}$ using the AdaBoost classifier based on decision trees. The results showed that for many benchmarks, the predictions were accurate enough to find the approximated Pareto front of high quality.

The runtime of the evolutionary algorithm decreased only by around 10 % utilizing the model to predict $WCET_{est}$, because energy consumption was still estimated by the static analyzer, which is also time-consuming. The future work is to build either a multi-objective model to predict $WCET_{est}$ and energy consumption simultaneously or two models to predict $WCET_{est}$ and energy consumption separately.

For many considered benchmarks, a classification method seems to be a reasonable choice to build the prediction model. But if a benchmark has a large objective space, i.e., many unique values of $WCET_{est}$, then a classifier either results in poor predictions or requires many training points. The future task is to consider other methods to build the prediction model for benchmarks with a large objective space.

Acknowledgment. This work received funding from Deutsche Forschungsgemeinschaft (DFG) under grant FA 1017/3-2.

References

1. AbsInt Angewandte Informatik, GmbH: aiT Worst-Case Execution Time Analyzers (2020)
2. Altenbernd, P., Gustafsson, J., Lisper, B., Stappert, F.: Early execution time-estimation through automatically generated timing models. Real-Time Syst. **52**(6), 731–760 (2016). https://doi.org/10.1007/s11241-016-9250-7
3. Bonenfant, A., Claraz, D., De Michiel, M., Sotin, P.: Early WCET prediction using machine learning (2017). https://doi.org/10.4230/OASICS.WCET.2017.5

4. Ehrgott, M.: Multicriteria Optimization. Springer, Heidelberg (2006). https://doi.org/10.1007/3-540-27659-9
5. Falk, H., et al.: TACLeBench: a benchmark collection to support worst-case execution time research (2016). https://doi.org/10.4230/OASICS.WCET.2016.2
6. Falk, H., Lokuciejewski, P.: A compiler framework for the reduction of worst-case execution times. Real-Time Syst. **46**(2), 251–300 (2010). https://doi.org/10.1007/s11241-010-9101-x
7. Gustafsson, J., Altenbernd, P., Ermedahl, A., Lisper, B.: Approximate worst-case execution time analysis for early stage embedded systems development. In: Lee, S., Narasimhan, P. (eds.) SEUS 2009. LNCS, vol. 5860, pp. 308–319. Springer, Heidelberg (2009). https://doi.org/10.1007/978-3-642-10265-3_28
8. Hastie, T., Tibshirani, R., Friedman, J.: The Elements of Statistical Learning. SSS, Springer, New York (2009). https://doi.org/10.1007/978-0-387-84858-7
9. Huybrechts, T., Mercelis, S., Hellinckx, P.: A new hybrid approach on wcet analysis for real-time systems using machine learning (2018). https://doi.org/10.4230/OASICS.WCET.2018.5
10. Lokuciejewski, P., Gedikli, F., Marwedel, P., Morik, K.: Automatic WCET reduction by machine learning based heuristics for function inlining. In: Proceedings of SMART. Paphos (2009)
11. Lokuciejewski, P., Plazar, S., Falk, H., Marwedel, P., Thiele, L.: Approximating Pareto optimal compiler optimization sequences-a trade-off between WCET, ACET and code size. Softw. Pract. Exp. **41**(12), 1437–1458 (2011). https://doi.org/10.1002/spe.1079
12. Muchnick, S.S.: Advanced Compiler Design and Implementation, 1 edn., pp. 607–608, 657. Morgan Kaufmann Publishers Inc., San Francisco (1998)
13. Muts, K., Falk, H.: Multi-criteria function inlining for hard real-time systems. In: Proceedings of the 28th International Conference on Real-Time Networks and Systems. ACM, June 2020. https://doi.org/10.1145/3394810.3394819
14. Pedregosa, F., et al.: Scikit-learn: machine learning in Python. J. Mach. Learn. Res. **12**, 2825–2830 (2011)
15. Turing, A.M.: On computable numbers, with an application to the Entscheidungsproblem. Proc. London Math. Soc. **s2-42**(1), 230–265 (1937). https://doi.org/10.1112/plms/s2-42.1.230
16. Wang, L., Ni, H., Zhou, W., Pardalos, P.M., Fang, J., Fei, M.: MBPOA-based LQR controller and its application to the double-parallel inverted pendulum system. Eng. Appl. Artif. Intell. **36**, 262–268 (2014). https://doi.org/10.1016/j.engappai.2014.07.023
17. Wörteler, L., Grossniklaus, M., Grün, C., Scholl, M.H.: Function inlining in XQuery 3.0 optimization. In: Proceedings of the 15th Symposium on Database Programming Languages. ACM, October 2015. https://doi.org/10.1145/2815072.2815079

Small Geodetic Datasets and Deep Networks: Attention-Based Residual LSTM Autoencoder Stacking for Geodetic Time Series

Mostafa Kiani Shahvandi$^{(\boxtimes)}$ (iD) and Benedikt Soja (iD)

Institute of Geodesy and Photogrammetry, ETH Zürich, Zürich, Switzerland
{mkiani,soja}@ethz.ch
https://space.igp.ethz.ch

Abstract. In case only a limited amount of data is available, deep learning models often do not generalize well. We propose a novel deep learning architecture to deal with this problem and achieve high prediction accuracy. To this end, we combine four different concepts: greedy layer-wise pretraining, attention via performers, residual connections, and LSTM autoencoder stacking. We present the application of the method in geodetic data science, for the prediction of length-of-day and GNSS station position time series, two of the most important problems in the field of geodesy. In these particular cases, where we have only relatively short time series, we achieve state-of-the-art performance compared to other statistical and machine learning methods.

Keywords: Deep learning · Residual learning · Greedy layer-wise pretraining · Attention · Geodetic time series

1 Introduction

Typically, the success of deep learning is heavily dependent on the availability of large amounts of data [14]. As a result, it is used mostly for applications where plenty of data is available. This is the case for tasks like image classification using deep convolutional neural networks [22] having repositories such as ImageNet [9]. However, there are cases in which the amount of data available is small. One example would be the case of short time series in the field of geodesy. The sequential deep learning models [34] can be used for time series prediction. However, they may not present enough modelling accuracy. While in this case simpler models like linear regression may work well [24], for more complex time series methods that can better capture the dynamicity of the values are preferred. Deep learning has proven to be capable of modelling arbitrarily complex data [23]. We therefore should use deep learning to achieve this goal [18], but with a special structure for the deep learning mapping.

In short time series, extraction of meaningful information is more challenging. We suggest the following solutions to this problem based on what was mentioned.

© Springer Nature Switzerland AG 2022
G. Nicosia et al. (Eds.): LOD 2021, LNCS 13163, pp. 296–307, 2022.
https://doi.org/10.1007/978-3-030-95467-3_22

- Maximize extraction of information by exploiting deeper networks. Using residual connections is advantageous. We use Long Short Term Memory (LSTM) [16] as the base model for time series analysis and take advantage of the concept of residual learning [15] to build residual blocks around the LSTM network [21]
- Find the most important parts of the time series for prediction by exploring attention [5,25,35] and fast self attention mechanisms in the performer model [8] to achieve the best performance
- Use autoencoding structures to enable the network to learn different representations
- Pretrain the model in an unsupervised manner. We pretrain the model in an unsupervised manner to prepare it for the training phase, using so-called LSTM autoencoder stacking [33]. This improves performance, facilitates training, and helps avoid overfitting

The rest of this paper is organized as follows. In Sect. 2, we propose the architecture. In Sect. 3, we present the application for the prediction of geodetic time series. Finally, Sect. 4 is devoted to conclusions.

2 Architecture of the Model

As mentioned in the introduction, the network architecture has the LSTM model as basis and residual blocks and attention mechanism built around it. In addition, the network is pretrained in an autoencoding fashion. The architecture of the model is shown in Fig. 1. In the following, the structure is explained in more details.

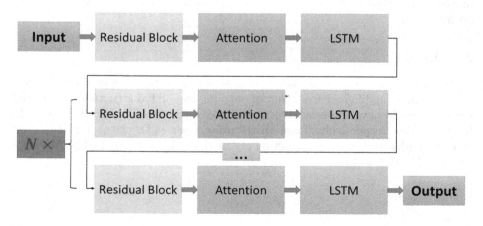

Fig. 1. Architecture of the proposed model for small dataset analysis. N is number of stacking of the residual blocks, attention and LSTM

2.1   Residual Block

The residual blocks used in the architecture are modified version of the original ones [15]. In fact, the activation function is the identity function instead of ReLu [29]. If X is the input tensor to the residual block, the output of the block, O, is computed as the following, based on Batch Normalization (BN, [26])

$$
\begin{aligned}
Y_1 &= X * W_1 \\
Y_2 &= BN(Y_1) \\
Y_3 &= Y_2 * W_2 \\
Y_4 &= BN(Y_3) \\
Y_5 &= Y_4 * W_3 \\
Y_6 &= BN(Y_5) \\
O &= X + Y_6
\end{aligned}
\tag{1}
$$

in which $W_1, W2, W3$ are the weights in the convolution window. As mentioned, residual blocks help having deeper networks by trying to learn the identity function.

2.2   Attention

The attention used in the architecture is of the self attention type [39]. In order to accelerate the computations and achieve the best performance, we use so-called Fast Attention Via Positive Orthogonal Random Features (FAVOR, [8]). In FAVOR, the softmax function in the definition of the multihead attention is approximated by other simpler functions so as to make the training faster and manageable. Note that the output of the attention layer is followed by batch normalization.

2.3   LSTM

In order to present a general case for time series prediction in which the number of inputs may be different from that of outputs, the LSTM structure used in the network should have a special structure. Three layers of LSTM with H_1, H_2, H_3 hidden nodes, respectively, Time Distribution layer (TD, [32]), and one dense layer with identity activation function are used. Figure 2 shows the LSTM structure used in the network.

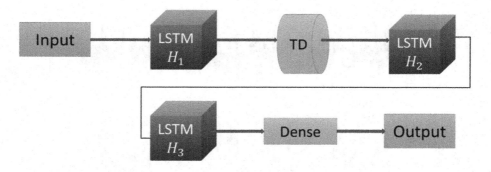

Fig. 2. LSTM part of the network architecture from Fig. 1

Remark 1. Note that the LSTM structure in Fig. 2 is an encoder-decoder structure and is proven empirically to perform well on complex time series.

2.4   Autoencoder Stacking

In order to increase the depth of the network, the same three structure-residual block, attention, LSTM-are repeated N times afterwards. The network is pretrained in an autoencoding fashion. However, this step is done through the so-called greedy layer wise approach [6], in which layers are added incrementally and the pretraining is done on the last added layer, while previously pretrained layers are excluded from retraining.

3   Experiments

We present the application of the proposed architecture in the field of geodetic science. We focus on the prediction of the so-called length of day (LOD) and Global Navigation Satellite System (GNSS) station position time series.

3.1   LOD Prediction

This geodetic parameter represents the additional length of day with respect to the nominal 86400 s, determined through space geodetic and astronomical techniques [7,28,30]. Figure 3 shows the values of this parameter collected over several years on a daily basis. The data are taken from the so-called EOP combined series (EOP 05 C04, consistent with international terrestrial reference frame 2014 [1]). The data can be accessed via [11,17].

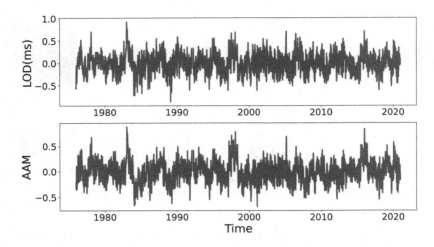

Fig. 3. LOD and AAM time series used in this study

However, the number of data is limited to 16437 values, spanning 45 years. As the prediction of LOD is important in many space and meteorology applications such as the navigation of spacecraft and weather forecasting [28], highly accurate prediction of this parameter is essential. However, it presents a challenging problem due to the high variability of the time series and the small amount of data. We use the auxiliary data called Atmospheric Angular Momentum (AAM, [12,36]) as a feature for the prediction of LOD, since they have similar variability. AAM describes to some extent the excitation in the earth's rotation due to different atmospheric phenomena and subsequently mass redistribution [10]. The data are dimensionless and like the LOD on a daily basis, The data can be accessed via [13].

We apply the proposed architecture to this problem. To this end, we use a data windowing approach in which the past 30 days are used as the input and 7 days to the future as the output. The window slides over all the values. Then the first 12000 windows (from 1976 to 2008) are used for training, the next 2000 windows (from 2008 to 2014) for the evaluation, and the remaining (2398 windows, from 2014 to 2021) as the test.

Remark 2. Note that while both LOD and AAM are used as the input features, only LOD is used as the output. In fact, AAM is the second feature in addition to LOD itself to predict next values of LOD.

Network Optimization. Based on the architecture of the model, there are 7 variables in the structure. These are size of the convolution window in residual block, number of residual blocks, reduced dimensionality and number of attention heads, and the number of hidden nodes in the 3 LSTM layers. In order to find the best structure of the network, we perform a comprehensive grid search for finding the best parmaters of the network. The accuracy measure for the network optimization is Mean Absolute Error (MAE). The Adam optimization algorithm [20] with the initial learning rate of 5×10^{-4} and 500 epochs is used. In Table 1, the optimal parameters of the network are given.

Table 1. The optimal parameters of the network found by extensive grid search

Parameter	Optimal value
Convolution window size	6
Number of attention heads	4
Reduced dimensionality	8
H_1	45
H_2	10
H_3	7
Number of residual blocks (N)	2

Figure 4 shows the 7-day predictions, and the difference between predicted and observed values (ΔLOD) over the entire test dataset.

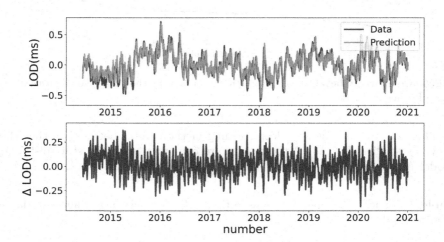

Fig. 4. Seven-day LOD predictions (upper plot) and the difference between the predicted and observed values for seven-day predictions over the entire test set

Comparison with Other Methods. There are several methods for the prediction of LOD. We use state-of-the-art results of [28] and those of the references mentioned therein, to compare our method with 15 other methods. The first five methods are based on Copulas of the type Archimedean 12, Archimedean 14, Clayton, Gumbel, Frank, and Joe, denoted respectively by AC 12, AC 14, CC,

GC, FC, and JC. The other methods are Kalman Filter (KF), Wavelet and fuzzy inference system (WFI), Least Squares Extrapolation (LSE), Least Squares combined with AutoRegression (LSAR), Adaptive Transformation (AT), AutoRegression (AR), Least Squares Collocation (LSC), Neural Networks (NN), and HE method of approximation (HE). The comparison is shown in Fig. 5.

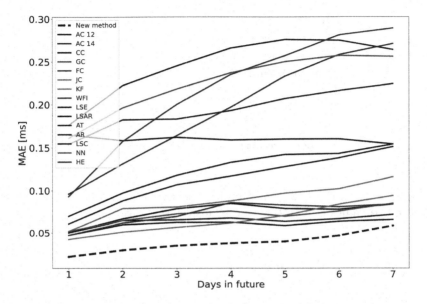

Fig. 5. Comparison between the prediction accuracy of the proposed algorithm and that of other methods

One can see that the new deep learning method works better than the other previous studies. In Table 2 the results are compared with the state-of-the-art model AC 12 in [28].

Table 2. Numerical comparison between the MAE of the new algorithm with that of other methods

Day	MAE(ms)	Improvement (%) w.r.t. [28]
1	0.021	54.3
2	0.029	51.5
3	0.035	45.2
4	0.037	40.6
5	0.039	33.0
6	0.047	27.0
7	0.059	10.7

Ablation Study for the Importance of Different Elements in the Architecture. In order to investigate the importance of the elements in the architecture, we perform an ablation study in which elements are removed individually and the prediction problem is iterated over the new architectures. We investigate effects of the following elements in the architecture mentioned in Fig. 1:

- LSTM
- Attention
- Residual Block
- Greedy layer-wise pretraining

In Table 3, the results of prediction with the ablated architecture are mentioned.

Table 3. Ablation study for the importance of different elements in the architecture, in different days using MAE metric (ms). The first row corresponds to the original architecture.

Removed element	Importance rank	Day 1	Day 2	Day 3	Day 4	Day 5	Day 6	Day 7
–	–	0.021	0.029	0.035	0.037	0.039	0.047	0.059
LSTM	1	0.131	0.271	0.355	0.564	0.712	0.868	0.931
Attention	2	0.067	0.079	0.088	0.125	0.259	0.398	0.462
Residual Block	3	0.031	0.034	0.039	0.042	0.049	0.055	0.066
Pretraining	4	0.027	0.033	0.039	0.043	0.048	0.054	0.062

From Table 3 one can observe that the most important element in the architecture is LSTM. Attention is also quite important such that without it the architecture does not work well. However, while the Residual Block is important for the general performance of the method, it is not as important as the other two. The importance of greedy layer-wise pretraining is approximately the same as of the Residual Block.

3.2 GNSS Station Position Prediction: a Comparative Large Scale Study

In this section, we investigate the predictive performance of the proposed algorithm for GNSS station position time series prediction. These time series represent the changes in the position of a station in time. There are thousands of stations across the globe which collect these data [4]. An example of this type of time series is shown in Fig. 6, in which the local upward coordinate (u) is used.

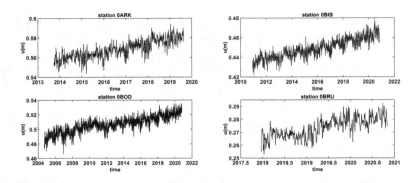

Fig. 6. Four different examples of the GNSS stations position time series

The problem of GNSS time series prediction and analysis has been investigated thoroughly in the geodetic community, using statistical methods [2,3]. Recently, however, machine learning algorithms have gained attention for this problem [19,31,37].

Remark 3. It is important to note that each time series is treated individually, which means we do not have much data for training. Therefore, unlike the problems like ImageNet classification [38], where we use a large number of images to train the model on, we define a model for each time series separately.

In [19], a comprehensive study is presented for more 18498 GNSS station position time series using different statistical and machine learning algorithms. The time series can be accessed via [4][1]. We follow the method presented there to compared our algorithm to 15 other methods, namely deep transformers, Auto-Regressive Integrated Moving Average (ARIMA), Simple Exponential Smoothing (SES), and Holtwinter statistical methods (refer to [27] and references therein for the description of these methods), Bayesian FeedForward Networks (BFFN), Bayesian inference with L_1 norm minimization (BL$_1$), CascadeForward Nets (CFN), Classification And Regression Trees (CART), Support Vector Regression Machines (SVRM), Gaussian Processes (GP), Probabilistic Neural Networks (PNN), Generalized Regression Neural Networks (GRNN), Recurrent Neural Networks (RNN), and simple Long Short-Term Memory (LSTM) (for the explanation of these methods refer for instance to [14,27,35] and references therein).

In Table 4 the results of different algorithms are mentioned and ordered based on their performance, using the same Root Mean Square Error (RMSE) metric. As one can see, the proposed approach achieves state-of-the-art performance, comparable to deep transformers.

---

[1] http://geodesy.unr.edu/.

Table 4. Comparison between the predictive performance of the proposed method and other algorithms for 18498 time series

Rank	Method	RMSE (mm)
1	Proposed method	0.335
2	Deep transformers	0.335
3	BFFN	0.344
4	GP	0.344
5	ARIMA	0.407
6	Theta	0.426
7	SES	0.491
8	BL_1	0.536
9	Holtwinter	0.589
10	GRNN	0.743
11	CART	0.896
12	RNN	1.041
13	SVRM	2.999
14	LSTM	3.328
15	CFN	6.515
16	PNN	17.952

4 Conclusions

We introduced a new deep learning architecture that is based on the greedy layer-wise pretraining of deep LSTM-based stacked autoencoders and which is augmented with self-attention via positive orthogonal random features and residual identity mapping. This method is specifically designed for small data sets of sequential data. We presented the application of the method in geodetic length of day and GNSS station position prediction, examples of highly variable time series with small amounts of data. In both cases, we compared our proposed method with a large number of other prediction methods, including machine (deep) learning and statistical ones. Although applications from the field of geodetic sciences were shown, the proposed architecture can be applied in other fields for sequential data modelling.

References

1. Altamimi, Z., Rebischung, P., Métivier, L., Collilieux, X.: ITRF2014: a new release of the International Terrestrial Reference Frame modeling nonlinear station motions. J. Geophys. Res. Solid Earth **121**(8), 6109–6131 (2016)
2. Amiri-Simkooei, A.A., Tiberius, C.C.J.M., Teunissen, P.J.G.: Assessment of noise in GPS coordinate time series: methodology and results. J. Geophys. Res. Solid Earth **117**(B7) (2007). https://doi.org/10.1029/2006JB004913

3. Amiri-Simkooei, A.R.: Noise in multivariate GPS position time-series. J. Geodesy **83**, 175–187 (2009)
4. Blewitt, G., Hammond, W.C., Kreemer, C.: Harnessing the GPS data explosion for interdisciplinary science. Eos, Science News by AGU (2018). https://doi.org/10.1029/2018EO104623
5. Bahdanau, D., Cho, K., Bengio, Y.: Neural machine translation by jointly learning to align and translate. arXiv:1409.0473 (2014)
6. Bengio, Y., Lamblin, P., Popovici, D., Larochelle, H.: Greedy layer-wise training of deep networks. In: Proceedings of the Twentieth Annual Conference on Neural Information Processing Systems, Vancouver, British Columbia, Canada (2006)
7. Bizouard, C., Lambert, S., Gattano, C., Becker, O., Richard, J.-Y.: The IERS EOP 14C04 solution for Earth orientation parameters consistent with ITRF 2014. J. Geodesy **93**(5), 621–633 (2018). https://doi.org/10.1007/s00190-018-1186-3
8. Choromanski, K., et al.: Rethinking attention with performers. In: The Ninth International Conference on Learning Representations, Virtual (2021)
9. Deng, J., Dong, W., Socher, R., Li, L.-J., Li, K., Fei-Fei, L.: ImageNet: a large-scale hierarchical image database. In: 2009 IEEE Conference on Computer Vision and Pattern Recognition, Miami, Florida, pp. 248–255. IEEE (2009)
10. Dobslaw, H., Dill, R.: Predicting earth orientation changes from global forecasts of atmosphere-hydrosphere dynamics. Adv. Space Res. **61**(4), 1047–1054 (2018)
11. Earth Orientation Center. https://hpiers.obspm.fr/eop-pc
12. Egger, J., Weickmann, K., Honika, K.-P.: Angular momentum in the global atmospheric circulation. Rev. Geophys. **45**(4007) (2007). https://doi.org/10.1029/2006RG000213
13. GFZ. ftp://ig2-dmz.gfz-potsdam.de/EAM/
14. Goodfellow, I., Bengio, Y., Courville, A.: Deep Learning. MIT Press, Cambridge (2017)
15. He, K., Zhang, X., Ren, S., Sun, J.: Deep residual learning for image recognition. In: 2016 IEEE Conference on Computer Vision and Pattern Recognition, Las Vegas, USA, pp. 770–778. IEEE (2016)
16. Hochreiter, S., Schmidhuber, J.: Long short-term memory. Neural Comput. **9**(8), 1735–1780 (1997)
17. International Earth Rotation and Reference Systems Service. https://www.iers.org/IERS/EN/DataProducts/EarthOrientationData/eop.html
18. Jiang, P., Chen, C., Liu, X.: Time series prediction for evolutions of complex systems: a deep learning approach. In: 2016 IEEE International Conference on Control and Robotics Engineering, Singapore (2016)
19. Kiani Shahvandi, M., Soja, B.: Modified deep transformers for geodetic GNSS time series prediction. In: IEEE International Geoscience and Remote Sensing Symposium, Belgium (2021)
20. Kingma, D.P., Ba, J.: Adam: a method for stochastic optimization. In: International Conference on Learning Representations, San Diego, California, USA (2015)
21. Kim, J., El-Khamy, M., Lee, J.: Residual LSTM: design of a deep recurrent architecture for distant speech recognition. In: Proceedings of the Interspeech, pp. 1591–1595 (2017)
22. Krizhevsky, A., Sutskever, I., Hinton, G.: ImageNet classification with deep convolutional neural networks. Commun. ACM **60**, 84–90 (2017)
23. LeCunn, Y., Bengio, Y., Hinton, G.: Deep learning. Nature **521**, 436–444 (2015)
24. Lin, K., Lin, Q., Zhou, C., Yao, J.: Time series prediction based on linear regression and SVR. In: Third International Conference on Natural Computation (2007)

25. Liu, J., Gong, X.: Attention mechanism enhanced LSTM with residual architecture and its application for protein-protein interaction residue pairs prediction. BMC Bioinform. **20** (2019). https://doi.org/10.1186/s12859-019-3199-1

26. Loffe, S., Szegedy, C.: Batch Normalization: accelerating deep network training by reducing internal covariate shift. In: Proceedings of the 32nd International Conference on Machine Learning, pp. 448–456 (2015)

27. Makridakis, S., Spiliotis, E., Assimakopoulos, V.: Statistical and machine learning forecasting methods: concerns and ways forward. Plos One **13**, e0194889 (2018)

28. Modiri, S., Belda, S., Hoseini, M., Heinkelmann, R., Ferrándiz, J.M., Schuh, H.: A new hybrid method to improve the ultra-short-term prediction of LOD. J. Geodesy **94**(2), 1–14 (2020). https://doi.org/10.1007/s00190-020-01354-y

29. Nair, V., Hinton, G.: Rectified linear units improve restricted Boltzmann machines. In: Proceedings of the 27th International Conference on Machine Learning, Haifa, Israel (2010)

30. Petit, G., Luzum, B.: IERS Conventions. International Earth Rotation and Reference Systems Service (2010)

31. Piccolomini, E.L., Gandolfi, S., Poluzzi, L., Tavasci, L., Cascarano, P., Pascucci, A.: Recurrent neural networks applied to GNSS time series for denoising and prediction. In: 26th International Symposium on Temporal Representation and Reasoning (2019)

32. Qiao, H., Wang, T., Wang, P., Qiao, S., Zhang, L.: A time-distributed spatiotemporal feature learning method for machine health monitoring with multi-sensor time series. Sensors **18**(9), 2932 (2018)

33. Sagheer, A., Kotb, M.: Unsupervised pre-training of a deep LSTM-based stacked autoencoder for multivariate time series forecasting problems. Nat. Sci. Rep. **9**, 19038 (2019)

34. Sutskever, I., Vinyals, O., Le, Q.-V.: Sequence to sequence learning with neural networks. In: Proceedings of the 27th International Conference on Neural Information Processing Systems, pp. 3104–3112 (2014)

35. Vaswani, A., et al.: Attention is all you need. In: 31st Conference on Neural Information Processing Systems (NIPS 2017), Long Beach, CA, USA (2017)

36. Veerman, M.-A., Heerwaarden, C.C.-v.: Trends in and closure of the atmospheric angular momentum budget in the 20th century in ERA-20C. Q. J. R. Meteorol. Soc. **145**(724), 2990–3003 (2019)

37. Wang, J., Nie, G., Gao, S., Wu, S., Li, H., Ren, X.: Landslide deformation prediction based on a GNSS time series analysis and recurrent neural network model. Remote Sens. **13**, 1055 (2021)

38. Zhai, X., Kolesnikov, A., Houlsby, N., Beyer, L.: Scaling vision transformers. arXiv (2021)

39. Zhao, H., Jia, J., Koltun, V.: Exploring self-attention for image recognition. In: Proceedings of the IEEE/CVF Conference on Computer Vision and Pattern Recognition, pp. 10076–10085, Virtual (2020)

Forecasting the IBEX-35 Stock Index Using Deep Learning and News Emotions

Sergio Consoli[1(✉)], Matteo Negri[2], Amirhossein Tebbifakhr[2], Elisa Tosetti[3], and Marco Turchi[2]

[1] European Commission, Joint Research Centre (JRC), Ispra, Italy
`sergio.consoli@ec.europa.eu`
[2] Fondazione Bruno Kessler, Via Sommarive 18, Povo, Trento, Italy
{`negri,atebbifakhr,turchi`}`@fbk.eu`
[3] Department of Management, Universitá Ca' Foscari Venezia, Cannaregio 873, Fondamenta San Giobbe, 30121 Venezia, Italy
`elisa.tosetti@unive.it`

Abstract. Measuring the informational content of text in economic and financial news is useful for market participants to adjust their perception and expectations on the dynamics of financial markets. In this work, we adopt a neural machine translation and deep learning approach to extract the emotional content of economic and financial news from Spanish journals. To this end, we exploit a dataset of over 14 million articles published in Spanish newspapers over the period from 1st of July 1996 until 31st of December 2019. We then examine the role of these news-based emotions indicators in forecasting the Spanish IBEX-35 stock market index by using DeepAR, an advanced neural forecasting method based on auto-regressive Recurrent Neural Networks operating in a probabilistic setting. The aim is to evaluate if the combination of a richer information set including the emotional content of economic and financial news with state-of-the-art machine learning can help in such a challenging prediction task. The DeepAR model is trained by adopting a rolling-window approach and employed to produce point and density forecasts. Results look promising, showing an improvement in the IBEX-35 index fitting when the emotional variables are included in the model.

Keywords: IBEX-35 stock index · Deep learning · Neural forecasting · DeepAR · Machine translation · Emotion classification · News analysis

1 Introduction

Forecasting economic and financial variables is a challenging task for several reasons including, among others, the effect of volatility, regime changes, and low signal-to-noise ratio [15]. In addition, modern economies are subject to numerous shocks that make such prediction task extremely hard, particularly during times

---

Authors listed in alphabetic order.

© The Author(s) 2022
G. Nicosia et al. (Eds.): LOD 2021, LNCS 13163, pp. 308–323, 2022.
https://doi.org/10.1007/978-3-030-95467-3_23

of economic turmoil like the ones we are currently experiencing with the Covid-19 pandemic [50]. In this context, the incorporation in forecasting models of economic and financial information coming from news media, like in particular emotions and sentiment, has already demonstrated great potentials [1, 4, 8, 23, 33, 42, 49].

Our endeavour is to explore the predictive power of news emotions for forecasting economic and financial time series by leveraging on the recent advances in the literature on deep learning [9, 31, 38, 39]. We believe that news are a promising forecasting tool since they describe recent economic events and trends, represent the updated expectations of market participants about the future, thus significantly influencing investors' perception and decisions.

In this work, we first extract sentences referring to specific economic and financial aspects from Spanish news, over a period of time ranging from July 1996 to December 2019[1]. We then use a neural machine translation (NMT) [43] approach based on deep learning for classifying sentences into groups, according to the Ekman's six basic emotions [19]: *fear, anger, joy, sadness, disgust, surprise*. The method leverages on the recent NMT approach by Tebbifakhr et al. [44] used for sentiment classification, readapting it to the massive annotation task of Spanish news with emotion labels. This approach originally adapts a NMT system, which is trained for general translation purposes, to produce translation that is easier to process by a downstream classifier in the target language. In our case, we use this methodology to adapt a Spanish-to-English NMT system targeting an emotion classifier in English, fine-tuned on the economic and financial domain. This approach allows us first to translate the Spanish news into English and then to annotate them using the English classifier. The advantage of translating before annotating is that the English classifier can be trained on a large amount of available annotated data. Although in this work we focus on the IBEX-35 index and Spanish news [14], the methodology is easily generalizable to other languages, and portable to other domains and evaluation scenarios.

We adopt this approach to extract a set of emotion indicators from Spanish economic and financial news and explore whether they provide useful predictive signals to improve the accuracy of existing forecasting models for financial variables [20]. Specifically, we focus on the Spanish IBEX-35 stock index, aiming at predicting its daily fluctuations by using as inputs the past time series values along with the daily emotion indicators.

The forecasting methodology employed for this task is *DeepAR*, a recent neural forecasting methodology proposed by Salinas et al. [39] that builds upon previous work on deep learning for time series data [9, 30, 31]. This powerful approach produces accurate probabilistic forecasts, based on training an autoregressive Recurrent Neural Network (RNN) model with feedback connections on a given number of related time series, which in our case are the emotion signals. The aim is to disentangle the improvement in the forecasting power due to the

---

[1] We focus on Spain since it gives, from our commercial provided, the largest coverage of news relative to other EU countries. The largest covered period is indeed the used one, that is from July 1996 to December 2019.

inclusion of the emotions indicators extracted from news within the DeepAR approach. Since our forecasting method calculates the probability attached to each forecast, the output can help investors in their decision making according to their individual risk tolerance.

Our results show that the emotion indicators extracted from news, used in combination with DeepAR, improve the performance of forecasting for the analysis of the IBEX-35 stock index. The method is also benchmarked against two traditional approaches (simple moving average and a naïve method for random forecasts). Overall, the obtained results look promising. We believe that the combination of the cutting-edge technologies used in our approach has high potential for the implementation of effective solutions for the prediction of other economic and financial indexes.

2   Background

Recent literature has pointed at the important role of financial investor's sentiment and emotions in anticipating interest rates dynamics [34,45]. News articles, in particular, represent a relevant data source to model economic and financial variables, and several studies have already exploited this additional source of information. A seminal work that has used a sentiment variable calculated on news articles from the Wall Street Journal is that by Tetlock [45]. The author shows that high levels of pessimism are a relevant predictor of convergence of the stock prices towards their fundamental values. Several other papers have tried to understand the role that news play in predicting, for instance, company news announcements, stock returns and volatility. Agrawal et al. [2] and Dridi et al. [17] have recently used emotions extracted from social media, financial microblogs, and news to improve predictions of the stock market. Hansen and McMahon [26] has looked at the emotional content of the Federal Reserve statements and the effects of these statements on the future evolution of monetary policy. Other papers ([46,47] and [41] among others) have classified articles in topics and extracted emotional signals that showed to have a predictive power for measures of economic activity, such as GDP, unemployment and inflation [25]. These results have shown the high potential of emotions extracted from news on monitoring and improving the forecasts of economic developments [17].

Studies adopting machine learning approaches to forecast financial indexes have also increased exponentially in recent years (see, e.g. [7,10,15,22,24,37]). Among these, several studies have successfully adopted various versions of deep learning [9,31,39]. For a survey on the use of deep learning methods for time series forecasting, the reader is referred, among others, to [9,28,30,38]. Recently, in [39] the authors proposed DeepAR, an RNN-based forecasting model using Long Short-Term Memory (LSTM) or Gated Recurrent Unit (GRU) cells, the latter being a simplification of LSTMs that does not use a separate memory cell and may result in good performance for certain applications. At each time step, DeepAR takes as input the previous time points and covariates, and estimates the distribution of the values of the next period. This is done via the estimation of the parameters of a pre-selected distribution. Training and prediction follow the general approach for auto-regressive models [39].

A common trait of the other machine learning approaches employed to forecast financial and economic time series is that they are generally constrained to a point forecasting setting [21,28,29]. Differently, the approach described in the following section focuses on the full predictive distribution, not just a single best

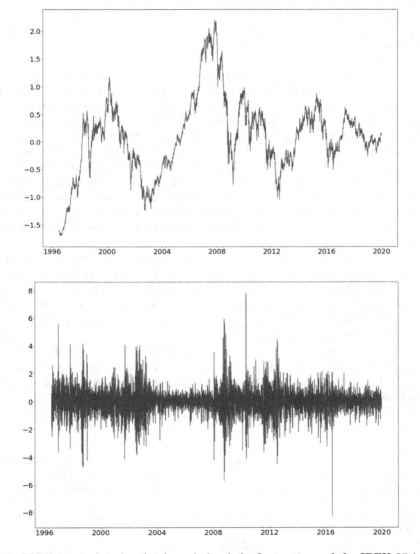

Fig. 1. IBEX-35 stock index (top), and the daily fluctuations of the IBEX-35 index defined as the log-difference between consecutive observations (bottom).

realization, making the analysis more robust and reducing uncertainty in the downstream decision-making flow. In addition, a large part of existing studies that predict stock market indices has addressed the forecasting problem as a classification task, where the goal is predicting the direction of the stock index rather than its actual variations (see e.g. [12,18,40,51]). Indeed, forecasting the variations of the stock index directly, as we aim in this work, is an extremely challenging task given that the series behaves similarly to a random walk process. All these characteristics make our approach very innovative.

3   Data

The source of economic news is obtained from a commercial provider.[2] The dataset consists of around 14 million articles, full-text, from July 1, 1996 until December 31, 2019. Their source is Spanish newspapers, selected so as to achieve a good national as well as regional coverage.[3] We extract sentences referring to specific economic and financial aspects, by using a keyword-based information extraction procedure with search keywords broadly related to the Spanish economy, monetary and fiscal policies.[4] In order to filter out only sentences referring to Spain, we also use a location detection heuristic [6] assigning the location to which a sentence is referring as its most frequent named-entity location detected in the news text, and then selecting only sentences with specific assigned location labels related to Spain. (see Footnote 4) With this procedure we obtain a total of over 4.2 million sentences.

We obtain the IBEX-35 index from Yahoo Finance.[5] This is a free-float, capitalization-weighted stock market index that tracks the performance of the 35 most liquid stocks traded on the continuous market on the Bolsa de Madrid. For our study, we consider the close price of the index, that is the price of the stock at the closing time of the market on a given day. Being the IBEX-35 a highly persistent and non-stationary index (see Fig. 1, top), we have applied a log-difference transformation to obtain a stationary series of daily changes representing our prediction target shown (Fig. 1, bottom). Missing data related to weekends have been dropped from the target time series, giving a final number of 5,950 data points for the time period of interest.

---

[2] Dow Jones Data, News and Analytics Platform: https://www.dowjones.com/dna/.

[3] *El Mundo, ABC, Expansión, La Vanguardia, Cinco Días, El País, Actualidad Económica, Agencia EFE - Servicio Económico, Alimarket, Aseguranza, El Comercio, Córdoba, El Correo, El Diario de León, Diario Montañés, El Diario Vasco, Europa Press, Hoy, Ideal, El Periódico, Las Provincias, La Rioja, Sur, La Verdad, La Voz de Galicia.*

[4] The complete list includes around 300 terms, such as *inflation, consumer prices, bankruptcy, economic volatility, housing market, competitiveness, debt, employment, bubble bust, bond market*, etc., and can be obtained upon request from the authors.

[5] https://finance.yahoo.com/quote/%5EIBEX.

4 Methods

4.1 Machine Translation

We classify the 4.2 million according to the Ekman's basic emotions [19] using a recent NMT approach [44], adapted from a sentiment to an emotion classification setting [1]. The lack of emotion-annotated data in languages different from English requires to first translate the Spanish sentences into English using NMT, and then to annotate them with an English emotion classifier.

NMT systems [43] are based on neural technology that requires large quantities of training data, from which they learn how to translate text in the source into text in the target language. The training data consists of "parallel" sentence pairs, where the source and the target sentences are one the translation of the other. During training, the NMT system iterates over the data for a number of epochs until the performance measured in terms of training loss (e.g. cross-entropy) reaches a plateau. The "MT for machines" paradigm proposed in [44] represents a variant of this general approach, which is oriented to generating automatic translations that, instead of targeting human readers, should be easy to process by NLP tools. The underlying idea is to orient NMT adaptation towards "machine-oriented" criteria (i.e. maximising the performance of a downstream NLP component fed with the NMT output) rather than the standard "human-oriented" quality criteria of output fluency and semantic adequacy. This is done by applying Reinforcement Learning techniques [15,44], in which NMT model optimization is driven by rewards collected in terms of final performance in the downstream task of interest (in our case, emotion classification).

It is known that the larger the training set, the better the capability of the model to translate and generalize to unseen inputs [43]. For our work, we first train a generic Spanish to English NMT system, built using the freely available parallel data (around 84M parallel sentences) present in the OPUS website,[6] tokenized and encoded using 32K byte-pair codes. To develop the NMT system, we use the Transformer architecture by Vaswani et al. [48] with the original parameter settings. We perform the training step until convergence, that is until we reach a plateau in the computed loss. For training the NMT system, we use the OpenNMT-tf (v2.0.1) toolkit.[7] We also embedd a pre-trained Spanish BERT model[8] inside the NMT system [13,52] to give a better representation of the source Spanish text during translation; this experimental choice has shown to be advantageous for our task.

We then adapt the generic Spanish-English NMT model to the economic domain by fine-tuning it on parallel sentences derived by the news, using two approaches:

1. *Back-translating the English in-domain data.* We automatically translate the English economic sentences back into Spanish. Doing so, we generate translation pairs in which the Spanish source side is the output of the NMT system

---

[6] OPUS, the open parallel corpus. Available at: https://opus.nlpl.eu/.

[7] https://github.com/OpenNMT/OpenNMT-tf.

[8] BETO - available at: https://github.com/dccuchile/beto.

and the English target side contain human-quality sentences. The Spanish-English sentence pairs are then used to adapt the NMT system.

2. *Selecting in-domain translation pairs from the training data.* We train a language model using the English economic sentences and use it to rank the English side of the 84M parallel sentences from OPUS. A higher rank means, for a given sentence, a higher similarity to the economic sentences. To have a fair comparison, from the top of this parallel ranked list, we select an amount of data equal to the original economic sentences in terms of number of tokens on the English side. The Spanish-English selected sentence pairs are then used to adapt the NMT system.

The fine-tuning [15, 31] is performed continuing the training of the generic model using the economic parallel data created with the two methods, considering them both together and in isolation.

4.2 Emotion Classification

The English classifier is based on a BERT language model [16] adapted to our classification problem. Recent works on sentence classification have shown that neural language models can be used to transform a textual sentence into a special token vector (CLS) that represents the input sentence. This vector can be used for any sentence-level classification task, including emotion detection. To build the classifier, the language model needs to be trained on a large unsupervised corpus, then embedded in a neural network that transforms the token vector in one of the desired categories. We use in particular one fully-connected neural layer, which maps the CLS token of the English BERT into the emotion classes. We train the resulting architecture until convergence on a freely available database with English sentences annotated with emotion labels.[9]

This general model is then further fine-tuned for our emotion detection task by re-training it using a set of 5,100 Spanish economic sentences annotated with the Ekman's six basic emotions [19] by 8 different annotators[10] and translated into English using the European Commission *eTranslation* service.[11] For the annotation task we use the commercial Amazon AWS SageMaker service.[12] In

---

[9] The annotated English corpus is taken from the *unified emotion datasets* by Bostan and Klinger [11], available at: https://github.com/sarnthil/unify-emotion-datasets. It is a large English collection of different emotion datasets [11], mapped to a unified set of emotion classes from which we select the those considered in our study. Note that, after some pre-processing, each considered emotion category contains at least 2K samples.

[10] Annotators have been also allowed to assign a "no emotion" class in the case they believe the sentence is not providing any emotion connotation.

[11] More details about the *eTranslation* service are available at: https://ec.europa.eu/info/resources-partners/machine-translation-public-administrations-etranslation_en.

[12] Amazon AWS SageMaker service, available at: https://aws.amazon.com/sagemaker/.

order to realize a unique label for each sample, the following steps are followed: (i) For each sample, we detect the label with the highest vote. In case of equal votes between classes, the priority is given to the least represented class in the dataset; (ii) We select a positive threshold equal to 3 and assign the corresponding label to all the samples with the identified vote higher than this threshold; (iii) The remaining samples are discarded. Given that the number of "Disgust" samples obtained with this procedure resulted to be very low (only 26 samples), this class has been removed from the dataset. We then split the labelled data into training, development and test sets with the following proportions: 0.6, 0.1, and 0.3. Overall, the classifier is able to reach an average F1 score on test of nearly 70%, which represents quite an acceptable classification performance for our final task.

For the final massive emotion annotation of the 4.2M sentences selected from the Spanish news, we then use the developed NMT system for translating them into English, and then the English classifier to annotate the translated sentences with the considered emotions. The final distribution of emotion labels in the annotated Spanish sentences is: *surprise* = 25%, *joy* = 19%, *sadness* = 13%, *anger* = 10%, and *fear* = 9%, overall resulting to be quite balanced between positive and negative classes.[13]

4.3   Forecasting Method

Classic techniques in economy and finance do not scale well when the dimension of the data is big, noisy, and highly volatile [15]. In these cases, we need "good", "acceptable" answers even if input data are extremely complex, working out of the box to recognize patterns among data and give improved quality predictions. Following this direction, Salinas et al. [39] proposed DeepAR, a forecasting method based on auto-regressive RNNs and leveraging on previous work on deep learning to time series data [9,28,31]. The approach is data-driven, that is, DeepAR learns a global forecasting model from historical data of all time series under consideration in the dataset. The model tailors an RNN architecture into a probabilistic forecasting setting, in which predictions are not restricted to point forecasts only, but density forecasts are also produced accordingly to a user-defined distribution (in our case a student t-distribution is experimentally selected). The outcome is more robust with respect to point forecasts alone, and uncertainty in the downstream decision making flow is reduced by minimizing expectations of the loss function (negative log-likelihood) under the forecasting distribution.

Similarly to classic RNNs, DeepAR is able to produce a mapping from input to output considering the time dimension. This mapping, however, is no longer fixed [27]. In addition to providing more accurate forecasts, DeepAR has also other advantages compared to classical approaches and other global methods

---

[13] The remaining 24% of samples are classified as "no emotion" and removed from the dataset.

[39]: (i) As the model learns seasonal behavior and dependencies on given covariates across time series, manual feature engineering is drastically minimized; (ii) DeepAR makes probabilistic forecasts in the form of Monte Carlo samples that can be used to compute consistent quantile estimates for all sub-ranges in the prediction horizon; (iii) By learning from similar items, DeepAR is able to provide forecasts for items with little history, a case where traditional single-point forecasting methods fail; (iv) DeepAR does not assume Gaussian noise, but can incorporate a wide range of likelihood functions, allowing the user to choose one that is appropriate for the statistical properties of the data.

DeepAR supports both LSTM and GRU cells. In our case we use an LSTM architecture to ensure overcoming vanishing gradients issues, typical of RNNs [31]. All the network weights and bias coefficients are estimated as usual during the training phase by back-propagating and minimizing the negative log-likelihood loss function. The DeepAR model that we use in our study has been deployed by using the implementation available in Gluon Time Series (GluonTS) [3], an open-source library for deep learning-based time series approaches[14] interfacing Apache MXNet.[15] We adopt a rolling window estimation technique for training and validation, with a window length equal to half of the full sample, that is 2,975 data points. For each window, we calculate one step-ahead forecasts. We also set a re-training step for the model equal to 7 days, meaning that every 7 consecutive data points the DeepAR model is completely retrained. Hyperparameter tuning for the model has been performed through Bayesian hyperparameter optimization using the Ax Platform [5,32] on the first estimation sample, providing the following best configuration: 1 RNN layer having 20 LSTM cells, 500 training epochs, and a learning rate equal to 0.001.

5   Results

In this section, we show our early empirical findings on the application of DeepAR to the prediction of the IBEX-35 daily changes, augmented with the emotions expressed within the Spanish economic news [14]. Note that forecasting the log-differences of the IBEX-35 index is an extremely challenging task, as the series behaves similarly to a random walk process. The goal is to assess whether news emotions contain some predictive power and might help in this difficult job.

We use standardization on training data only, a common requirement in the estimation of machine learning models. Typically, this is done by removing the mean and scaling to unit variance. However, outliers can often influence the sample mean/variance negatively, as it applies to our target variable. In such cases, the median and the inter-quartile range provide better results and, accordingly, we centere and scale each feature independently with respect to these robust statistics. Median and inter-quartile range have been computed on training only, and then stored to be used to transform later validation data.

---

[14] https://gluon-ts.mxnet.io/#gluonts-probabilistic-time-series-modeling.
[15] https://mxnet.apache.org/.

In the experiments, we consider an autoregressive-only DeepAR, that is without any covariates included in the model, referred to as *DeepAR-NoCov*. We then consider a DeepAR model with the news emotions used as covariates, referred to as *DeepAR-Emotions*. The experiments have been computed on an Intel(R) Xeon(R) E7 64-bit server having 40 cores at 2.10 GHz and overall 1TB of shared RAM. The DeepAR model training requirs to run for few computational hours in parallel on the available CPU cores.

To benchmark the forecasting power of DeepAR we can compare its performance against those of other classic models, like for example a simple moving average approach (*Seasonal-MA*) and a naïve method (*Naïve*). With the moving average method, the forecasts of all future values are equal to the average (or "mean") of the historical data. If we let the historical data be denoted by $y_1, ..., y_T$, then we can write the forecasts as $\hat{y}_{T+h|T} = \bar{y} = (y_1 + ... + y_T)/T$. The notation $\hat{y}_{T+h|T}$ is a short-hand for the estimate of y_{T+h} based on the data $y_1, ..., y_T$. In our case, we choose $T = 7$, that is we do a one-week moving average on the daily changes of the IBEX-35 index. For the naïve forecasts, instead, we simply set all forecasts to be the value of the last observation for our target (i.e. the IBEX-35 log-differences). That is, $\hat{y}_{T+h|T} = \hat{y}_T$. Since naïve forecasts are optimal when data observations follow a random walk, these are also called random walk forecasts. The naïve method works well for many economic and financial time series, as is the case with our IBEX-35 fluctuations data.

Table 1. Out-of-sample forecasting metrics of the different methods, along with loss function values obtained at 0.1, 0.3, 0.5, 0.7 and 0.9 quantiles.

Metrics	RMSE	MAPE	mQL	$QL_{0.1}$	$QL_{0.3}$	$QL_{0.5}$	$QL_{0.7}$	$QL_{0.9}$
Seasonal-MA	1.206	1.525	1.084	1.069	1.221	1.231	1.204	1.049
Naïve	1.287	1.471	1.179	1.046	1.313	1.424	1.209	0.949
DeepAR-NoCov	1.045	1.450	0.982	0.975	1.159	1.185	1.108	0.868
DeepAR-Emotions	**0.956**	**1.415**	**0.652**	**0.597**	**0.987**	**1.072**	**0.930**	**0.516**

For the evaluation, we use common time series prediction metrics, namely: root mean square error (RMSE), symmetric mean absolute percentage error (MAPE), and mean (weighted) quantile loss (mQL), that is the average quantile negative log-likelihood loss weighted with the density. Our results are shown in Table 1, along with the loss function values obtained by the methods at different quantiles. As the table shows, there is a clear superiority of the DeepAR algorithm with respect to the two other approaches. These improvements get consistently higher when the DeepAR model is combined with the news emotions. This suggests that the emotional content extracted from Spanish news contain a predictive power for our target forecasting. When these features are added to *DeepAR-NoCov*, producing the *DeepAR-Emotions* model, the results clearly improve in terms of all the metrics. These results look also consistent when we evaluate the models on the different quantiles. The best performance is obtained again by *DeepAR-Emotions*, followed by the *DeepAR-NoCov* model. We also note that the models show higher performance at high (0.9) and low (0.1) quantiles, with higher weighted quantile losses in general performing better than the lower quantiles.

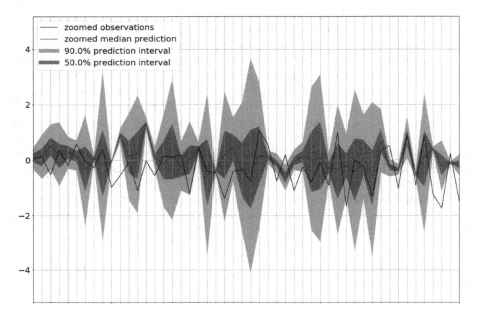

Fig. 2. Probabilistic forecasts (green) for the *DeepAR-Emotions* model and observations for the target series (blue) for the first 50 days in the forecasting period. The green continuous line shows the median of the probabilistic predictions, while the lighter green areas represents an higher confidence interval. (Color figure online)

Let's now focus more in detail on the results obtained by *DeepAR-Emotions*, that from our computational experience appears to be the best performing model for the prediction task. Figure 2 shows the observations for the target time series (blue line) in the first 50 days of the testing period, together with the median forecast (dark green line) for the *DeepAR-Emotions* model and the confidence interval (lighter green). Forecasting an interval rather than a point is an important feature of the process since it provides an estimate of the uncertainty involved in the forecast, which allows downstream decisions accounting for such uncertainty. Figure 3 illustrates the median absolute forecast error for the *DeepAR-Emotions* model for the entire forecasting period. We can qualitatively see that the model does a reasonable job at capturing the variability and volatility of the time series for such a challenging scenario, overall achieving an acceptable deviation. The performance of the model drops for periods of particular crisis, which appears to be hardly predictable even if considering the

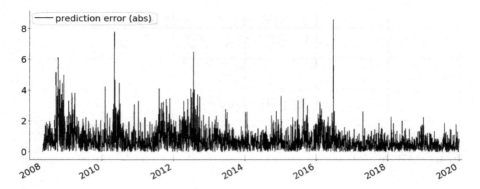

Fig. 3. Mean absolute forecast error for the *DeepAR-Emotions* model.

emotional content of news. For example, this happens in June 2016: the days after the Brexit vote. On that occasion, the IBEX-35 index drops by 12.4%, the biggest one-day drop for the benchmark index in its history, as the political and economic uncertainty unleashed by the UK referendum results hammering the shares of Spanish companies. Our model also fails at capturing this pronounced decline. The model also worsens in performance at the end of 2008 as a result of the bankruptcy of Lehman Brothers that confirmes the start of a global financial crisis. This actually corresponds to the other largest falls in the history of the IBEX-35, where the index falls by more than 9% in October 19, 2008, the day there is a crash in almost all world stock exchanges. After that black Friday, the rebound occurs but does not last: a few days later, the stock market crash is worldwide. As any prediction model would have failed on these unpredictable events, also our *DeepAR-Emotions* algorithm underperforms.

To improve interpretability and impact of the considered news emotions with respect to the DeepAR model, we also perform the computation of the Shapley values [35, 36] of the model using the SHAP library available for Python.[16] SHAP (SHapley Additive exPlanations) is a game theoretic approach to explain the output of any machine learning model [35]. It connects optimal credit allocation with local explanations using the classic Shapley values from game theory and their related extensions [36]. In our case, in particular, we use the model agnostic KernelExplainer method of SHAP, which is used to explain any function by using a specially-weighted local linear regression to estimate SHAP values for the considered model.

To get an overview of which features result to be the most important for the DeepAR model, in Fig. 4 we illustrate a standard bar plot with the mean absolute SHAP values of the top news emotions over the data samples, sorting by importance from the most impactful emotions with respect to the model output to the worst ones. As we can see, negative emotions, i.e., respectively, *fear*, *anger*, and *sadness*, result to be the features with highest impact, followed by

---

[16] https://github.com/slundberg/shap.

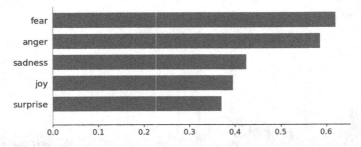

Fig. 4. SHAP bar plot: average impact of news emotions on model output magnitude.

the positive emotions of *joy* and *surprise*. This confirms the findings in previous literature that have shown media pessimism, in general, to be a relevant predictor for movements in spreads [4], bond markets interest rates [8,33], and stock prices [45].

6   Conclusions

In this paper we present an approach aimed at exploring the predictive power of news for economic and financial time series forecasting. In particular, we focus on the IBEX-35, a benchmark stock market index for Spain, and consider the log-differences of its daily close price. We then compute the emotional content of economic and financial news from Spanish outlets using neural machine translation, and use them as covariates of DeepAR, a neural forecasting method operating into a probabilistic setting, opportunely trained and validated with a rolling window approach. After providing an overview of our methodology, we report our results on this use-case application, showing satisfactory performance of the devised approach for such a challenging task. Emotions extracted from news look relevant for the forecasting exercise of the IBEX-35 fluctuations. Overall, DeepAR manages to achieve good trading results, producing better results when the news-based emotions variables are included into the model. The method is also benchmarked against two classic forecasting approaches, confirming its superiority. Results look encouraging, showing an overall validity of the employed methodology. News-based emotions appear to be good proxies for market investor's expectations and behaviour. Their combination with state-of-the-art machine learning shows to have good potential for the forecasting of other economic and financial time series.

References

1. Ackert, L., Church, B.K., Deaves, R.: Emotion and financial markets. Econ. Rev. **88**, 33–41 (2003)

2. Agrawal, S., Azar, P., Lo, A.W., Singh, T.: Momentum, mean-reversion and social media: evidence from StockTwits and Twitter. J. Portf. Manag. **44**, 85–95 (2018)
3. Alexandrov, A., et al.: GluonTS: probabilistic time series models in Python. J. Mach. Learn. Res. **21**(1), 1–6 (2020)
4. Apergis, N., Lau, M.C.K., Yarovaya, L.: Media sentiment and CDS spread spillovers: evidence from the GIIPS countries. Int. Rev. Financ. Anal. **47**(C), 50–59 (2016)
5. Bakshy, E., et al.: A domain-agnostic platform for adaptive experimentation. In: Proceedings of the Neural Information Processing Systems (NIPS), pp. 1–8 (2018)
6. Barbaglia, L., Consoli, S., Manzan, S.: Monitoring the business cycle with fine-grained, aspect-based sentiment extraction from news. In: Bitetta, V., Bordino, I., Ferretti, A., Gullo, F., Pascolutti, S., Ponti, G. (eds.) MIDAS 2019. LNCS (LNAI), vol. 11985, pp. 101–106. Springer, Cham (2020). https://doi.org/10.1007/978-3-030-37720-5_8
7. Beber, A., Brandt, M.W., Kavajecz, K.A.: Flight-to-quality or flight-to-liquidity? Evidence from the Euro-area bond market. Rev. Financ. Stud. **22**(3), 925–957 (2009)
8. Beetsma, R., Giuliodori, M., de Jong, F., Widijanto, D.: Spread the news: the impact of news on the European sovereign bond markets during the crisis. J. Int. Money Financ. **34**, 83–101 (2013)
9. Benidis, K., et al.: Neural forecasting: introduction and literature overview. CoRR, abs/2004.10240 (2020). https://arxiv.org/abs/2004.10240
10. Bernal, O., Gnabo, J.-Y., Guilmin, G.: Economic policy uncertainty and risk spillover in the Eurozone. J. Int. Money Financ. **65**(C), 24–45 (2016)
11. Bostan, L.-A.-M., Klinger, R.: An analysis of annotated corpora for emotion classification in text. In: Proceedings of the 27th International Conference on Computational Linguistics, pp. 2104–2119 (2018)
12. Carta, S.M., Consoli, S., Piras, L., Podda, A.S., Reforgiato Recupero, D.: Explainable machine learning exploiting news and domain-specific lexicon for stock market forecasting. IEEE Access **9**, 30193–30205 (2021)
13. Clinchant, S., Jung, K.W., Nikoulina, V.: On the use of BERT for neural machine translation. In: Proceedings of the 3rd Workshop on Neural Generation and Translation, pp. 108–117. Association for Computational Linguistics (2019)
14. Consoli, S., Negri, M., Tebbifakhr, A., Tosetti, E., Turchi, M.: On neural forecasting and news emotions: the case of the Spanish stock market. In: MIDAS 2021: 6th Workshop on MIning DAta for Financial ApplicationS (2021). (Extended abstract)
15. Consoli, S., Reforgiato Recupero, D., Saisana, M. (eds.): Data Science for Economics and Finance. Springer, Cham (2021). https://doi.org/10.1007/978-3-030-66891-4
16. Devlin, J., Chang, M.-W., Lee, K., Toutanova, K.: BERT: pre-training of deep bidirectional transformers for language understanding. In: Proceedings of the 2019 Conference of the North American Chapter of the Association for Computational Linguistics: Human Language Technologies, vol. 1, pp. 4171–4186 (2019)
17. Dridi, A., Atzeni, M., Reforgiato Recupero, D.: FineNews: fine-grained semantic sentiment analysis on financial microblogs and news. Int. J. Mach. Learn. Cybern. **10**(8), 2199–2207 (2018). https://doi.org/10.1007/s13042-018-0805-x
18. Dunis, C., Rosillo, R., de la Fuente, D., Pino, R.: Forecasting IBEX-35 moves using support vector machines. Neural Comput. Appl. **23**(1), 229–236 (2013)
19. Ekman, P., Cordaro, D.: What is meant by calling emotions basic. Emot. Rev. **3**(4), 364–370 (2011)

20. Fabbi, C., Righi, A., Testa, P., Valentino, L., Zardetto, D.: Social mood on economy index. In: XIII Conferenza Nazionale di Statistica (2018)
21. Faloutsos, C., Januschowski, T., Gasthaus, J., Wang, Y.: Classical and contemporary approaches to big time series forecasting. In: Proceedings of the ACM SIGMOD International Conference on Management of Data, pp. 2042–2047 (2019)
22. Favero, C., Pagano, M., von Thadden, E.-L.: How does liquidity affect government bond yields? J. Financ. Quant. Anal. 45(1), 107–134 (2010)
23. Fenton-O'Creevy, M., Soane, E., Nicholson, N., Willman, P.: Thinking, feeling and deciding: the influence of emotions on the decision making and performance of traders. J. Organ. Behav. 32(8), 1044–1061 (2011)
24. Garcia, A.J., Gimeno, R.: Flight-to-liquidity flows in the Euro area sovereign debt crisis. Technical report, Banco de Espana Working Papers (2014)
25. Gentzkow, M., Kelly, B., Taddy, M.: Text as data. J. Econ. Lit. 57, 535–574 (2019)
26. Hansen, S., McMahon, M.: Shocking language: understanding the macroeconomic effects of central bank communication. J. Int. Econ. 99, S114–S133 (2016)
27. Hochreiter, S., Schmidhuber, J.: Long short-term memory. Neural Comput. 9, 1735–1780 (1997)
28. Januschowski, T., Gasthaus, J., Wang, Y., Salinas, D., Flunkert, V., Bohlke-Schneider, M., Callot, L.: Criteria for classifying forecasting methods. Int. J. Forecast. 36(1), 167–177 (2020)
29. Kaastra, I., Boyd, M.: Designing a neural network for forecasting financial and economic time series. Neurocomputing 10(3), 215–236 (1996)
30. Lai, G., Chang, W.-C., Yang, Y., Liu, H.: Modeling long- and short-term temporal patterns with deep neural networks. In: 41st International ACM SIGIR Conference on Research and Development in Information Retrieval, SIGIR 2018, pp. 95–104 (2018)
31. Lecun, Y., Bengio, Y., Hinton, G.: Deep learning. Nature 521(7553), 436–444 (2015)
32. Letham, B., Bakshy, E.: Bayesian optimization for policy search via online-offline experimentation. J. Mach. Learn. Res. 20(145), 1–30 (2019)
33. Liu, S.: The impact of textual sentiment on sovereign bond yield spreads: evidence from the Eurozone crisis. Multinatl. Financ. J. 18(3/4), 215–248 (2014)
34. Loughran, T., McDonald, B.: When is a liability not a liability? Textual analysis, dictionaries and 10-ks. J. Financ. 66(1), 35–65 (2011)
35. Lundberg, S.M., Lee, S.-I.: A unified approach to interpreting model predictions. In: Guyon, I., et al. (eds.) Advances in Neural Information Processing Systems 30, pp. 4765–4774 (2017)
36. Lundberg, S.M., et al.: From local explanations to global understanding with explainable AI for trees. Nat. Mach. Intell. 2(1), 2522–5839 (2020)
37. Manganelli, S., Wolswijk, G.: What drives spreads in the Euro area government bond markets? Econ. Policy 24(58), 191–240 (2009)
38. Qin, Y., Song, D., Cheng, H., Cheng, W., Jiang, G., Cottrell, G.: A dual-stage attention-based recurrent neural network for time series prediction. In: IJCAI International Joint Conference on Artificial Intelligence, pp. 2627–2633 (2017)
39. Salinas, D., Flunkert, V., Gasthaus, J., Januschowski, T.: DeepAR: probabilistic forecasting with autoregressive recurrent networks. Int. J. Forecast. 36(3), 1181–1191 (2020)
40. Senol, D., Ozturan, M.: Stock price direction prediction using artificial neural network approach: the case of Turkey. J. Artif. Intell. Res. 3, 261–268 (2010)
41. Shapiro, A.H., Sudhof, M., Wilson, D.: Measuring news sentiment. Federal Reserve Bank of San Francisco Working Paper (2018)

42. Taffler, R.: Emotional finance: investment and the unconscious. Eur. J. Financ. **24**(7–8), 630–653 (2018)
43. Tang, G., Müller, M., Rios, A., Sennrich, R.: Why self-attention? A targeted evaluation of neural machine translation architectures. In: Proceedings of the 2018 Conference on Empirical Methods in Natural Language Processing, EMNLP 2018, pp. 4263–4272 (2020)
44. Tebbifakhr, A., Bentivogli, L., Negri, M., Turchi, M.: Machine translation for machines: the sentiment classification use case. In: Proceedings of the 2019 Conference on Empirical Methods in Natural Language Processing and the 9th International Joint Conference on Natural Language Processing (EMNLP-IJCNLP), Hong Kong, China, pp. 1368–1374. Association for Computational Linguistics (2019)
45. Tetlock, P.C.: Giving content to investor sentiment: the role of media in the stock market. J. Financ. **62**(3), 1139–1168 (2007)
46. Thorsrud, L.A.: Nowcasting using news topics. Big Data versus Big Bank. Norges Bank Working Paper (2016)
47. Thorsrud, L.A.: Words are the new numbers: a newsy coincident index of the business cycle. J. Bus. Econ. Stat. **38**, 393–409 (2018)
48. Vaswani, A., et al.: Attention is all you need. In: Advances in Neural Information Processing Systems, December 2017, pp. 5999–6009 (2017)
49. Yuan, H., Lau, R.Y.K., Wong, M.C.S., Li, C.: Mining emotions of the public from social media for enhancing corporate credit rating. In: Proceedings - 2018 IEEE 15th International Conference on e-Business Engineering, ICEBE 2018, pp. 25–30 (2018)
50. Zhang, D., Hu, M., Ji, Q.: Financial markets under the global pandemic of COVID-19. Financ. Res. Lett. **36**, 101528 (2020)
51. Zhou, F., Zhang, Q., Sornette, D., Jiang, L.: Cascading logistic regression onto gradient boosted decision trees for forecasting and trading stock indices. Appl. Soft Comput. J. **84**, 105747 (2019)
52. Zhu, J., et al.: Incorporating BERT into neural machine translation. In: International Conference on Learning Representations (ICLR) (2020). https://iclr.cc/virtual_2020/poster_Hyl7ygStwB.html

Action-Conditioned Frame Prediction Without Discriminator

David Valencia$^{(\boxtimes)}$, Henry Williams, Bruce MacDonald, and Ting Qiao

Centre for Automation and Robotic Engineering Science, University of Auckland,
Auckland, New Zealand
dval035@aucklanduni.ac.nz, henry.williams@auckland.ac.nz

Abstract. Predicting high-quality images that depend on past images
and external events is a challenge in computer vision. Prior proposals
have tried to solve this problem; however, their architectures are complex,
unstable, or difficult to train. This paper presents an action-conditioned
network based upon Introspective Variational Autoencoder (IntroVAE)
with a simplistic design to predict high-quality samples. The proposed
architecture combines features of Variational Autoencoders (VAEs) and
Generative Adversarial Networks (GANs) with encoding and decoding
layers that can self-evaluate the quality of predicted frames; no extra
discriminator network is needed in our framework. Experimental results
with two data sets show that the proposed architecture could be applied
to small and large images. Our predicted samples are comparable to the
state-of-the-art GAN-based networks.

Keywords: Action conditioned · Deep learning · Frame prediction ·
Generative models · Variational Autoencoders

1 Introduction

Humans have the ability to solve problems and understand the surrounding
area through visual perception, which allows them to make decisions and predict upcoming events with great precision and speed. Video frame prediction
is one way to model this human behaviour from a machine perspective. Frame
prediction has been studied for years and applied in areas such as autonomous
driving cars [32], robotic manipulation [5,20], trajectory predictions [23], or physical interaction [6]. Predicting upcoming events provides the possibility to plan
actions and an understanding of the environment; however, predicting the future
is not an easy task since it not only depends on past events but also sometimes
on external actions, input controls, or complex high dimensional features.

If we talk about image prediction, we are also talking about image generation, where deep learning approaches have shown great results in recent years.
Neural networks can be trained to generate and predict future frames, given the
current camera frame and external actions. Much research has been carried out
on generative models; the most typical and popular models based their network

© Springer Nature Switzerland AG 2022
G. Nicosia et al. (Eds.): LOD 2021, LNCS 13163, pp. 324–337, 2022.
https://doi.org/10.1007/978-3-030-95467-3_24

architectures on Variational Autoencoders (VAEs) [12], and Generative Adversarial Networks (GANs) [7]. However, these models have complex and unstable architectures with serious limitations that often result in poor predictions. This paper proposes a novel neural network architecture for action-conditioned frame prediction based upon Introspective Variational Autoencoder (IntroVAE) [10] that combines features of VAEs and GANs in a more simplistic design which can self-evaluate the quality of predicted frames. The purpose of this article is to present a network easy to train to produce highly detailed samples with minimal blurriness and increase the network's stability overcoming the VAE and GAN limitations. The proposed model can be applied in both small size images as well as large size images with high details. To the best of our knowledge, it is the first work that applies the introspective manner to action-conditioned frame prediction. This article is organized as follows: In Sect. 2, a brief background and similar projects are reviewed. In Sect. 3, the overall design of the proposed system is described. In Sect. 4, the datasets, along with the experiments and results, are analyzed. Finally, in Sect. 5, the conclusions and future works are presented.

2 Background

Recent years have seen an increase in studies related to predicting future frames based on neural networks. The current literature suggests that the frame prediction concept could be decomposed into two groups: first, an image generator, by learning a latent distribution of the original samples, new samples can be created, and second, a future frame generator, where the next frames depend not only on previous frames but also on actions or external features. Below is an analysis of related literature within these two groups.

2.1 Image Generator

Generative models have traditionally been used as anomaly detection [26], image completion, super-resolution [9,14], or as a way to learn representations of images or videos. There have been a number of promising approaches for image generation developed previous to this paper; for example, VAE is a well-known algorithm that provides an attractive solution to the image generation problem by learning a latent representation of the data. VAE architecture is comprised of two networks, an encoder and a decoder. The encoder translates from the input x (e.g., an image) to a low-dimensional representation vector z called the latent representation. The decoder takes as input a latent sample z randomly sampled from a prior distribution (e.g., normal distribution) and produces samples in the domain of the input x. VAE generally applies Kullback-Leibler divergence [16] and pixel-wise error as loss functions during the training process. VAE is stable, easy to train, and computationally inexpensive; however, it has a strong drawback; the generated images lack details and tend to have high blurriness levels. GANs comes as a viable solution to the low-quality output from VAEs. GANs consist of two networks, a generator G and a discriminator D. The generator receives as input a latent sample z and produces a sample $G(z)$. The discriminator takes as input both the generated image $G(z)$ and the input image x and tries to differentiate real data from generated samples; meanwhile, the generator tries to produce better images to fool the discriminator playing a mix-max game based upon the principle of game theory. Although GANs have notoriously bettered other alternatives in producing sharp images, training GANs is not always easy, especially when handling high-resolution images. GANs may face challenges in training stability and sampling diversity [2,11,26]. Also balancing the convergence of the discriminator and the generator could be a difficult task even with several tricks applied [2,21,25].

There are also some hybrid models such as [2,11,13,24,33] that try to reduce the instability of GANs and improving the blurring typical of VAEs. These approaches generally use an extra discriminator in their architecture to add an adversarial constraint and improve the generated images' quality. However, the majority of the current literature notes that adding a discriminator to the network may result in some challenges, such as increasing the network's complexity, high probabilities of mode collapse (i.e. produces limited varieties of samples in the output [33]), or high sensitivity to the hyper-parameters.

2.2 Frame Prediction

Trying to predict future video frames is one of the areas that has had the most interest in recent years, both recurrent and feedforward models are widely used in this area (see [3,19], and [22] for survey). Several works have been presented trying to produce a sequence of future frames, for example, [8] and [17] present a combination of VAE and recurrent neural network for frames prediction from an initial seed image. However, these approaches are implemented using small-sized images (around 64×64 pixels) where their predictions are not of the best quality as they lack detail. A Stochastic Adversarial Video Prediction (SAVP) is present in [15] which improves the prediction quality by introducing adversarial terms to the loss and models pixel motion. A Convolutional Dynamic Neural Advection (CDNA) model that can predict various futures of an object conditioned on the action of an agent is presented by Finn et al., in [6]. Walker et al., [27] combine the advantages of VAE with those of GANs for video frame forecasting of human pose, while Wang et al., present in [28] an actioned conditioned frame prediction in Atari video games where four consecutive frames are concatenated with the actions and passed as inputs to a convolutional autoencoder. In [18], a similar strategy is presented, but a recurrent encoding network is also tested as a second architecture. These proposals' predictions are accurate, but it must be considered that Atari environments are fixed tasks; in other words, the environments in Atari are the same in each game, and the size of each frame is relatively small; therefore, these methods may not be applied with more complex data. For these reasons, our main contribution is a novel model that can handle different sizes of images to predict high-quality samples without using an external discriminator that performs better than the state-of-the-art image-predictor methods.

3   Methodology

3.1   We Do Not Need a Discriminator

To predicted clear and high-quality images, we propose a model architecture as shown in Fig. 1. Our design consists of two components: an encoder E and a Generator G. No extra discriminator is needed in our proposal since the encoder here also plays the role of a discriminator. Not having an extra discriminator makes our network considerably more stable and easier to train compared to GAN or Hybrid-GAN architectures. This idea of *re-use* the encoder as a discriminator was initially proposed by Huang et al., and called IntroVAE [10]; its encoder and generator are trained in an introspective way. Inspired by this idea, we modified IntroVAE at several points. First, IntroVAE was originally conceived as an image generator/reconstructor but not as an image-predictor; consequently, the loss functions must be redefined. Second, our model is an action-conditioned image predictor where future frames also depend on external actions; therefore, an action vector needs to be added as a second input. Finally, our architecture is considerably simpler; we follow the same principle of operation of a convolutional variational autoencoder. See Fig. 1.

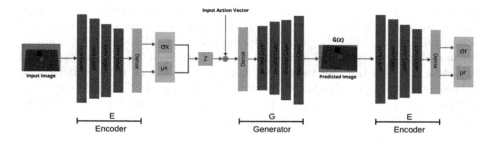

Fig. 1. Proposed network architecture.

As mentioned beforehand, our framework consists of an encoder network and a generator network (analogous to an encoder and a decoder in a VAEs). Our aim is to learn a function f capable of predicts the next frame x_{t+1}, receiving as input a previous frame x_t and an action a_t.

$$f : x_t, a_t \longmapsto x_{t+1} \tag{1}$$

Our encoder network E plays two roles: as the encoder of VAEs for real samples and as the discriminator of GANs for generated samples. On the other hand, our generator network G works the same role as a generator of GANs. We train our model following the same adversarial game idea of GANs, but in this case, the encoder learns how to distinguish between the real data from the generated samples, while the generator tries its best to produce more realistic samples to fool the encoder [9].

The encoder E takes an input image and encodes it into a smaller hidden representation, then outputs two individual vectors, one representing the mean values μ, and one denoting the standard deviations σ. Motivated by energy-based GANs [29], the encoder is trained to perform two tasks simultaneously; first, to minimize the prior regularization term $D_{KL}(q_\phi(z|x)||p(z))$ - where D_{KL} denotes Kullback-Leibler divergence - to encourage the posterior $q_\phi(z|x)$ to match the prior $p(z)$, and second, to maximize the prior regularization term to encourage the posterior $q_\phi(z|G(z))$ of the generated samples $G(z)$ to deviate from the prior $p(z)$. On the other hand, the generator G is trained to produce samples that have a small D_{KL}, such that the generated samples' posterior distribution matches the prior distribution $p(z)$ [10,31]. The input z of the generator G is generally sampled from $N(\mu, \sigma)$.

Therefore, given a real data sample x, an action vector a, the losses to train the encoder E and the generator G are designed as:

$$L_E(x, z, a) = D_{KL}(q_\phi(z|x)||p(z)) + [m - D_{KL}(q_\phi(z|G(z,a))||p(z))]^+ \qquad (2)$$

$$L_G(z, a) = D_{KL}(q_\phi(z|G(z,a))||p(z)) \qquad (3)$$

where m is a positive constant, $[.]^+ = max(0,.)$ and the prior probability is described following the original VAE notation where $p(z)$ is sampled from a know distribution, for instance $N(0,1)$. The Eq. (2) and (3) form a min-max game between the encoder network E and the generator network G aligning the generated and true distributions producing sharp samples. However, training the model in this adversarial manner is the main cause of the difficulties related to GANs, such as training instability, non-convergence, or mode collapse. As mentioned in [10], to solve these obstacles, the simpler but efficient way is to build a bridge between the encoder E and generator G, adding the reconstruction error L_{AE} to Eqs. (2) and (3) as follow:

$$L_E(x, z, a) = D_{KL}(q_\phi(z|x)||p(z)) + [m - D_{KL}(q_\phi(z|G(z,a))||p(z))]^+ + L_{AE}(x) \qquad (4)$$

$$L_G(z, a) = D_{KL}(q_\phi(z|G(z,a))||p(z)) + L_{AE}(x) \qquad (5)$$

The input z of the generator network G is sampled from $N(\mu, \sigma)$ using the method of reparameterization trick, where μ and σ are the outputs of the encoder network E. Therefore, the posterior probability could be denoted by $q_\phi(z|x) = N(z; \mu, \sigma)$. Then under these parameters and given N data samples, the $D_{KL}(q_\phi(z|x)||p(z))$ - denoted as L_{REG} for simplicity of notation - can be computed as follows:

$$L_{REG}(z; \mu, \sigma) = -\frac{1}{2} \sum_{i=1}^{N} (1 + log(\sigma_i^2) - \mu_i^2 - \sigma_i^2) \qquad (6)$$

The reconstruction error L_{AE}, which measures the difference between the target image (denoted by y) and the predicted image (denoted by x_r), is expressed by the pixel-wise mean squared error (MSE) function. Note that we measure

MSE with respect to the next ground-truth image (target image) instead of the input image x since we are not reconstructing the same image; this is the main difference from the original IntroVAE framework. The reconstruction error can be computed as below:

$$L_{AE}(x_r, y) = \frac{1}{2} \sum_{i=1}^{N} ||x_{ri} - y_i||^2 \qquad (7)$$

As proposed in VAE/GAN [13], the use of two types of fake samples, passed as input to the discrimination (in our case, the Encoder network E), helps produce better images and learn more expressive latent features [10, 30, 31]. These two types of samples are the predicted sample x_r from the posterior $q_\phi(z|x)$ and the generated sample from the prior $p(z)$ denoted by x_p. The complete architecture of the proposed model is presented in Fig. 2.

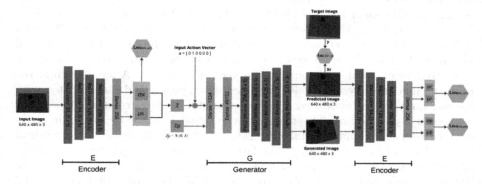

Fig. 2. Complete architecture of the proposed action-conditioned frame prediction model.

To resume, our model acts as a standard VAE for real samples and acts like a GAN when handling generated/predicted samples distinguishing the real sample x and generated samples x_r and x_p. Therefore the total loss functions for the Encoder network E and the Generator network G are redefined as:

$$L_E = L_{REG}(E(x)) + \alpha[m - L_{REG}(E(x_r))]^+ + \alpha[m - L_{REG}(E(x_p))]^+ + L_{AE}(x_r, y) \qquad (8)$$

$$L_G = \alpha L_{REG}(E(x_r)) + \alpha L_{REG}(E(x_p)) + L_{AE}(x_r, y) \qquad (9)$$

α is weighting parameter used to balance the importance of each item. Keep in mind that the encoder network E has two output variables, therefore $E(x) = (\mu_x, \sigma_x)$, $E(x_r) = (\mu_{x_r}, \sigma_{x_r})$, and finally $E(x_p) = (\mu_{x_p}, \sigma_{x_p})$. The Eqs. (8) and (9) form a min-max game between the encoder and the generator when $L_{REG}(E(x_r)), L_{REG}(E(x_p)) \leq m$.

(a) Car-Racing Dataset(64x64)   (b) Two-Cubes Dataset(640x480)

Fig. 3. Examples of frames from the two used datasets. (Color figure online)

3.2 Network Architecture

Our goal is to have a system easy to train without any special configurations that may also be applied to different image sizes. The encoder network consists of four convolutional layers with 32, 64, 128, 256 filters with a kernel size of 5 × 5, respectively. All of these convolutional layers use a stride of 2 and a *ReLU* as activation function[1]. The output of the convolutional layer is flattened and routed to a fully connected layer, which is then connected via two fully connected layers that each output the vectors μ and σ. After encoding, the resulting hidden representation is flattened into a vector and concatenated with the one-hot encoded action vector. The generator network consists of two fully connected layers, followed by five deconvolutional layers. The first four layers mirror the encoder configuration with 256, 128, 64, and 32 filters with a stride of 2, kernel size of 5 × 5 and *ReLU*. The last deconvolutional layer employs 3 filters of size 3×3 kernel with a stride of 1 and *Sigmoid* as an activation function. See Fig. 2. The pseudocode of training this network is presented in Algorithm 1.

4 Implementations

4.1 Data-Sets and Experiments

To examine the performance of our proposal, we applied our network architecture to two datasets. These datasets differ in size and features, see Fig. 3. We collected and standardized each of the images that compose these datasets.

Car-Racing Dataset. The frames for this dataset were collected using the CarRacing environment of OpenAI Gym [1]. The agent acts randomly throughout the environment during multi-role times. Each of the random actions, along with the corresponding resulting observations of the environment, were stored. Each image of this dataset is composed of 64 × 64 pixels, with 3 channels (RGB

---

[1] We have to mention that other activation functions were also tested, specifically LeakyReLU and Tanh (for the last layer of the generator). However, the results did not improve, and the computational load increased significantly.

Algorithm 1. Action-Conditioned Frame Prediction

1: Require: $\phi_{Enc}, \theta_{Gen}, \leftarrow$ Initialize network parameters
2: **while** not converged **do**
3:     $x, a \leftarrow$ random mini-batch of images and actions from training dataset
4:     $y \leftarrow$ random mini-batch of target images from training dataset
5:     $Z \leftarrow Enc(x)$
6:     $Z_p \leftarrow$ sample from $N(0, I)$
7:     $a_p \leftarrow$ vector of zeros of size of a
8:     $x_r \leftarrow Gen(Z, a)$
9:     $x_p \leftarrow Gen(Z_p, a_p)$
10:     $L_{AE} \leftarrow L_{AE}(x_r - y)$ $\triangleright$ error w.r.t. target image
11:     $Z_r \leftarrow Enc(ng(x_r))$ $\triangleright$ ng(.) back prop. of the gradient is stopped
12:     $Z_{pp} \leftarrow Enc(ng(x_p))$
13:     $L_{adv}^E \leftarrow [m - L_{reg}(Z_r)]^+ + [m - L_{reg}(Z_{pp})]^+$
14:     $\phi_{Enc} \leftarrow \phi_{Enc} - \eta \nabla_{\phi_{Enc}} (L_{REG}(Z) + \alpha L_{adv}^E + L_{AE})$ $\triangleright$ Update params. for Enc.
15:     $Z_r \leftarrow Enc(x_r)$
16:     $Z_{pp} \leftarrow Enc(x_p)$
17:     $L_{adv}^G \leftarrow L_{reg}(Z_r) + L_{reg}(Z_{pp})$
18:     $\theta_{Gen} \leftarrow \theta_{Gen} - \eta \nabla_{\theta_{Gen}} (\alpha L_{adv}^G + L_{AE})$ $\triangleright$ Update params. for Gen.
19: **end while**

---

image). In total, 30,000 images with their respective random action compose the training dataset. The validation and testing set both consist of 3,000 samples each. An example of a single frame is given in Fig. 3a. This database is a good starting point since the image size is small; Additionally, this is a 2D environment where the objects (road, car, grass, road marking) features and colours in the images are clearly defined. We train the model for 5,000 iterations with a random sample batch of size 32, using the Adam optimizer ($\beta_1 = 0.9$, $\beta_2 = 0.999$) with a learning rate of 0.00004 and a decay rate value of 1e−8. The latent dimension for this dataset is $z = 32$, the parameters $m = 2.0$, and $\alpha = 0.25$. These hyperparameters were determined empirically through the use of a small portion of the training dataset.

Two-Cubes Dataset. To examine the proposed model's performance on larger dimensional and more complex data, we use our second dataset. Each image of this dataset is composed of 640×480 pixels, with 3 channels. Each image includes two cubes with a side length of 8 cm, a red and a green one, are placed on a grey pad. An example of an image is given in Fig. 3b. The state-space is relatively simple, with only two cubes; however, it should be considered this is in a 3D environment, which increases the complexity of the prediction task. This dataset was collected in a simulated environment using Gazebo. A UR5 robot arm placed on a horizontal plane performs six possible moves with a camera mounted on its arm's gripper. After each action (randomly selected), the robot arm takes a picture of the cubes and stored it along with the respective action; The process is repeated until complete one episode. Each episode started in an initial state and consisted of 100 steps with one action per step. In total, 20,000 images, with large variations in poses, features, and angles, compose the training data, while the validation and testing set both consist of 2,000 samples each. Furthermore, the task initially seems simplistic in its design; however, the actions space with the six possible actions that move the arm in a 3D space is vastly more complex than the Car-Racing dataset, which was limited to a 2D environment. For this dataset, the latent dimension is 64, $m = 12$ and $\alpha = 0.25$. We train the model for 10,000 iterations with a random sample batch of size 32, using the Adam optimizer with a learning rate of 0.00002 and a decay rate value of $1e-8$. The source code, as well as the images dataset, could be found at https://github.com/dvalenciar/Action-Frame-Prediction.

4.2 Experiments and Results

In order to evaluate the predictions' quality of our proposal after the training process, we carry out two experiments, a single-step prediction, and a sequence-prediction. The single-step experiment consists of the prediction of one target image using one input image and one input action. On the other hand, the sequence-prediction experiment consists of predicting n sequence target images using one input image with n input actions, i.e., the model will use its own predictions as inputs during the following steps since only one input image from the dataset is available; this experiment is a complex challenge for the neural network since the predictions' quality dependent on the quality of all previous predictions. Additionally, we compare our model results against a well known convolutional VAE adapted for action-conditioned frame prediction. The results from experiment one show our system can generate and predict realistic frames. The images' quality matches the expectations in both datasets, which proves that our design allows an easy scale up the resolution of input images; in other words, the proposed architecture can be applied to small and large images. The predicted samples have enough details, the blurriness is almost imperceptible, and the predictions locate the image's objects in the right positions, see some samples results in Fig. 4. Additionally, a quantitative analysis using MSE (Mean Square Error), Peak-to-Noise Ratio (PSNR) and SSIM (Structural Similarity Index) is presented in Table 1, where the results obtained with the two data sets show our proposal is significantly superior to VAE.

Regarding the second experiment; since the model reintroduces its own predictions as inputs, high-quality in the predictions is crucial. We carry out this experiment for 100 consecutive predictions; we found that get a good performance out of the model after 30 consecutive predictions is challenging, since the model starts to generate samples where the objects (cubes or car) are located in the wrong location. However, the first 30 consecutive predictions almost exactly match the target images. From step 21 to step 30, the predicted samples show blurriness on the objects' edges; however, objects are placed in the correct position. Considering the outputs of the system are re-inserted as inputs, the results meet the expectations. A sample result with the first 15 steps of the sequence of the two data sets is presented in Fig. 5. From prediction 31, the frames get worse with each step until they reach the point where the image's objects begin to lose their geometric shape or are placed in the incorrect positions. The MSE and

Table 1. Numerical comparison between our model and VAE for the two implemented datasets. The prediction accuracy is quantified by computing the average MSE, SSIM and PSNR among all the images that compose the testing dataset.

	Car-Racing Dataset							
	Our Model				VAE			
	Avg	Std	Max	Min	Avg	Std	Max	Min
MSE	0.000662	0.00065	0.00745	0.00044	0.001098	0.00987	0.00197	0.00066
SSIM	0.972032	0.00976	0.98334	0.67765	0.900213	0.01323	0.99343	0.41654
PSNR	34.53924	0.91034	38.0232	32.3838	29.31243	1.89040	30.0012	26.5656

	Two-Cubes Dataset							
	Our Model				VAE			
	Avg	Std	Max	Min	Avg	Std	Max	Min
MSE	0.000120	0.00046	0.00117	0.00002	0.003402	0.01246	0.00763	0.00011
SSIM	0.980012	0.00132	0.98995	0.00987	0.916295	0.05321	0.93222	0.68030
PSNR	35.12535	0.45464	37.3736	31.0456	25.74028	3.00333	26.0056	21.5626

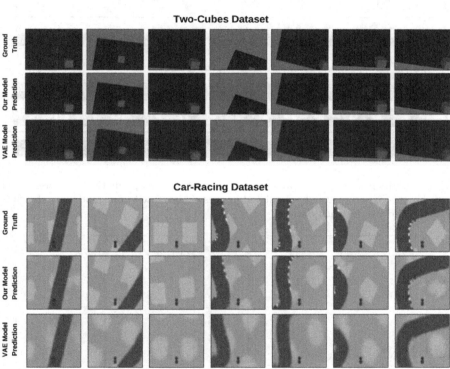

Fig. 4. Results from single-step prediction experiment. Rows one and four show the target images of the Two-cube and the Car-Racing datasets, respectively. The predicted images obtained with our model are presented in rows two and five for each data set. Rows three and six show the prediction using VAE.

SSIM achieved throughout the sequence prediction for the Two-Cubes dataset can be seen in Fig. 6. It shows that prediction errors accumulate gradually, staying below a value of 0.04, while the SSIM value in each prediction decreases slowly, reaching a minimum value of 0.71 during all 100 steps. Similar results are obtained with the Car-Racing dataset and can be analyzed in Fig. 7. The MSE rise steadily, reaching a peak of 0.023, while the SSIM value in each prediction decreases progressively, reaching a minimum value of 0.876 through all 100 predictions.

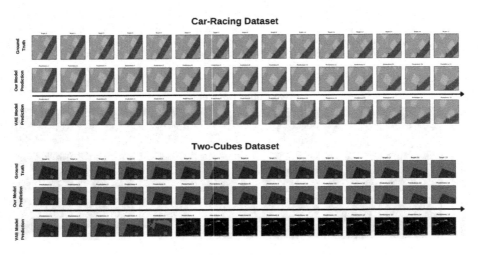

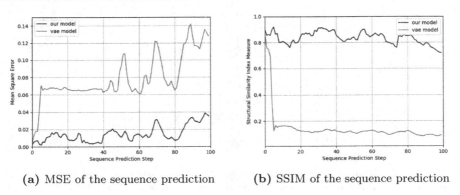

Fig. 5. Results from sequence-predictions experiment. Each prediction is re-inserted as input for this experiment. The predicted images achieved with our model are shown in rows two and five for each dataset.

(a) MSE of the sequence prediction   (b) SSIM of the sequence prediction

Fig. 6. Accuracy of sequence prediction using MSE and SSIM of Two Cubes Dataset

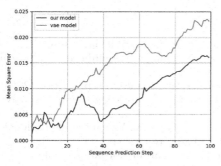 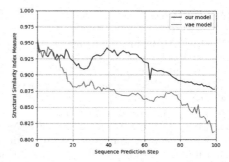

(a) MSE of the sequence prediction   (b) SSIM of the sequence prediction

Fig. 7. Accuracy of sequence prediction using MSE and SSIM of Car-Racing DataSet

5 Conclusions

In this paper, we propose an action-conditioned model for frame prediction. A model consisting of two parts is trained introspectively to predict sharp, clear, and diverse images without using an extra discriminator. The proposed architecture overcomes the limitation of VAE and GAN, especially in the stability and training process; This model can be trained easier than state-of-the-art frame prediction networks while producing equivalent results. Moreover, two action-conditioned datasets were created to test the performance of the system with different sizes of images.

We consiberer is essential to mention that directly comparing the performance of similar proposals such as soft-introVAE [4] or SRVAE [9] against our model would be unbalanced because those methods do not include external actions, and they were designed as image generators but not as image predictors; therefore, we have to modify their loss functions and part of their original architectures. That is why we compared our proposal against VAE, which is the most common and accepted algorithm for image prediction that has been previously tested with external actions.

Nevertheless, our proposed architecture still leaves much to be accomplished; even when the results were as expected, we believe that it is necessary to look for additional machine learning techniques that speed up the training process since, at the moment, our system needs to be trained for long periods to achieve acceptable results. Our future work will attempt to link this work with reinforcement learning (RL), specifically model-based RL where an accurate prediction of future events could help to learn better models of the system. Finally, we believe the model proposed in this article could bring prominent benefits in real-robot practical applications such as object detection in mobile robots, self-driven cars, or self-generation trajectories for robot arms.

References

1. Open AI: Gym toolkit. https://gym.openai.com/envs/CarRacing-v0.html
2. Berthelot, D., Schumm, T., Metz, L.: BEGAN: boundary equilibrium generative adversarial networks (2017)
3. Castelló, J.S.: A comprehensive survey on deep future frame video prediction (2018)
4. Daniel, T., Tamar, A.: Soft-introVAE: analyzing and improving the introspective variational autoencoder (2021)
5. Ebert, F., Finn, C., Dasari, S., Xie, A., Lee, A., Levine, S.: Visual foresight: model-based deep reinforcement learning for vision-based robotic control (2018)
6. Finn, C., Goodfellow, I., Levine, S.: Unsupervised learning for physical interaction through video prediction (2016)
7. Goodfellow, I.J., et al.: Generative adversarial networks (2014)
8. Ha, D., Schmidhuber, J.: World models. arXiv preprint arXiv:1803.10122 (2018)
9. Heydari, A.A., Mehmood, A.: SRVAE: super resolution using variational autoencoders. In: Pattern Recognition and Tracking XXXI, vol. 11400, p. 114000U. International Society for Optics and Photonics (2020)
10. Huang, H., Li, Z., He, R., Sun, Z., Tan, T.: IntroVAE: introspective variational autoencoders for photographic image synthesis (2018)
11. Khan, S.H., Hayat, M., Barnes, N.: Adversarial training of variational autoencoders for high fidelity image generation (2018)
12. Kingma, D.P., Welling, M.: Auto-encoding variational Bayes (2014)
13. Larsen, A.B.L., Sønderby, S.K., Larochelle, H., Winther, O.: Autoencoding beyond pixels using a learned similarity metric (2016)
14. Ledig, C., et al.: Photo-realistic single image super-resolution using a generative adversarial network (2017)
15. Lee, A.X., Zhang, R., Ebert, F., Abbeel, P., Finn, C., Levine, S.: Stochastic adversarial video prediction (2018)
16. Joyce, J.M.: Kullback-Leibler Divergence. In: Lovric, M. (eds.) International Encyclopedia of Statistical Science, pp. 720–722. Springer, Heidelberg (2011). https://doi.org/10.1007/978-3-642-04898-2_327
17. Malik, A., Troute, M., Capoor, B.: DeepGIFs: Using deep learning to understand and synthesize motion (2018)
18. Oh, J., Guo, X., Lee, H., Lewis, R., Singh, S.: Action-conditional video prediction using deep networks in atari games (2015)
19. Oprea, S., et al.: A review on deep learning techniques for video prediction (2020)
20. Paxton, C., Barnoy, Y., Katyal, K., Arora, R., Hager, G.D.: Visual robot task planning (2018)
21. Radford, A., Metz, L., Chintala, S.: Unsupervised representation learning with deep convolutional generative adversarial networks (2016)
22. Rasouli, A.: Deep learning for vision-based prediction: a survey (2020)
23. Rhinehart, N., McAllister, R., Kitani, K., Levine, S.: PRECOG: prediction conditioned on goals in visual multi-agent settings (2019)
24. Sainburg, T., Thielk, M., Theilman, B., Migliori, B., Gentner, T.: Generative adversarial interpolative autoencoding: adversarial training on latent space interpolations encourage convex latent distributions (2019)
25. Salimans, T., et al.: Improved techniques for training GANs. In: Lee, D., Sugiyama, M., Luxburg, U., Guyon, I., Garnett, R. (eds.) Advances in Neural Information Processing Systems, vol. 29, pp. 2234–2242. Curran Associates, Inc. (2016). https://proceedings.neurips.cc/paper/2016/file/8a3363abe792db2d8761d6403605aeb7-Paper.pdf

26. Vu, H.S., Ueta, D., Hashimoto, K., Maeno, K., Pranata, S., Shen, S.M.: Anomaly detection with adversarial dual autoencoders (2019)
27. Walker, J., Marino, K., Gupta, A., Hebert, M.: The pose knows: video forecasting by generating pose futures (2017)
28. Wang, E., Kosson, A., Mu, T.: Deep action conditional neural network for frame prediction in atari games. Technical report, Stanford University (2017)
29. Zhao, J., Mathieu, M., LeCun, Y.: Energy-based generative adversarial network (2017)
30. Zhao, S., Song, J., Ermon, S.: InfoVAE: information maximizing variational autoencoders (2018)
31. Zheng, K., Cheng, Y., Kang, X., Yao, H., Tian, T.: Conditional introspective variational autoencoder for image synthesis. IEEE Access **8**, 153905–153913 (2020). https://doi.org/10.1109/ACCESS.2020.3018228
32. Zhu, D., Chen, H., Yao, H., Nosrati, M., Yadmellat, P., Zhang, Y.: Practical issues of action-conditioned next image prediction (2018)
33. Zhu, J.Y., Zhang, R., Pathak, D., Darrell, T., Efros, A.A., Wang, O., Shechtman, E.: Toward multimodal image-to-image translation (2018)

Inference and De-noising of Non-gaussian Particle Distribution Functions: A Generative Modeling Approach

John Donaghy[(✉)] and Kai Germaschewski

Department of Physics, University of New Hampshire, Durham, NH 03824, USA
john.donaghy@unh.edu

Abstract. The particle-in-cell numerical method of plasma physics balances a trade-off between computational cost and intrinsic noise. Inference on data produced by these simulations generally consists of binning the data to recover the particle distribution function, from which physical processes may be investigated. In addition to containing noise, the distribution function is temporally dynamic and can be non-gaussian and multi-modal, making the task of modeling it difficult. Here we demonstrate the use of normalizing flows to learn a smooth, tractable approximation to the noisy particle distribution function. We demonstrate that the resulting data driven likelihood conserves relevant physics and may be extended to encapsulate the temporal evolution of the distribution function.

Keywords: Normalizing flow · Plasma physics · Particle-in-cell · Core-edge coupling · Likelihood free inference

1 Introduction

Studies in computational plasma physics aim to explain experimental results and confirm theory. Plasma theory generally takes either the kinetic or fluid approach to modeling plasma particles.

The first-principles description of a plasma is kinetic. Kinetic theory describes the plasma as a six dimensional phase space probability distribution for each particle species. Kinetic theory makes no assumptions regarding thermal equilibrium and thus may result in multi-modal arbitrary distributions.

In the fluid approach, it is assumed that the details of the distribution functions can be neglected and a given fluid parcel can be described by just its density, momentum and temperature. Fluid models are generally derived by marginalizing out the velocity dependence of the fully kinetic description.

Certain regimes of space and laboratory plasmas must be simulated using kinetic models, which capture all the relevant physics but are computationally more expensive. Two numerical approaches are typically used: Continuum

Partially Supported by Department of Energy Grant 17-SC-20-SC.

(Vlasov) solvers and Particle-in-Cell (PIC) methods. PIC codes are an example of a fully kinetic (six dimensional) solver. PIC codes discretize the distribution function according to the vlasov equation and then sub-sample to represent regions of plasma as macroparticles. These macroparticles are advanced by fields defined by the electromagnetic Maxwell equations. This method is computationally more tractable than a direct continuum solver, however it unfortunately introduces two sources of intrinsic noise.

The first is systemic noise inherent to the discrete plasma representation and the mapping between a discrete mesh and continuous particle positions [12]. While the particle's position is represented by continuous 3D space, it must be mapped to a 3D discrete mesh where the fields live in order to interpolate the field values and advance the particle's momentum and position.

The second source of noise is introduced in recovering the particle distribution functions from the output of the simulation. This is known as likelihood-free inference or simulation based inference. The samples, or particles in this case, are data generated by advancing the simulation through some number of timesteps. The simulation with parameters Θ, represents some implicit and unknown likelihood function $x \sim p(x|\Theta)$. Traditionally this likelihood was recovered by binning the particles into histograms. Because the simulation must make compromises on the number of particles and other numerical constants encapsulated by Θ for tractability reasons, the resulting likelihoods tend to contain noise.

For the remainder of this work we will use the terms particle distribution function and likelihood interchangeably.

A possible method of de-noising the likelihood lies in generative modeling. Generative modeling has shown great success in de-noising and super resolution tasks [1–4, 21]. Generating an accurate de-noised distribution function from PIC codes which encapsulates the underlying physics and matches the results predicted by continuum codes, would introduce a reliable method for cross-code validation as well as cut costs by allowing for inference on commodity hardware.

1.1 Contribution

In this work we aim to motivate the use of robust generative modeling techniques as a novel solution to the noise inherent to the distribution functions produced by PIC methods. We will apply techniques from generative modeling to de-noise our non-gaussian data, performing likelihood-free inference without violating the physical constraints of the fully kinetic model. We will then demonstrate that this technique may be expanded to encapsulate temporal dynamics. These experiments will be used as motivation for future core-edge coupling studies mapping distributions generated from PIC codes to distributions solved by continuum codes.

2   Background

2.1   Particle Distribution Function

The baseline particle distribution function (PDF) is seven dimensional, three spatial and three velocity components plus time per ion species,

$$f_s(x, y, z, u_x, u_y, u_z, t)$$

Normally, for analysis we look at a sub-domain region of the simulation to study plasma evolution. This amounts to marginalizing the distribution function over space and taking specific time slices resulting in a multivariate gaussian where the plasma bulk flow parameterizes the means and the temperature parameterizes the covariance. This is known as a Maxwellian distribution

$$f_s(u_x, u_y, u_z) = \left(\frac{m}{2\pi kT} \right)^{3/2} \exp \left[-\frac{m(u_x^2 + u_y^2 + u_z^2)}{2kT} \right] \tag{1}$$

It is important to note that this only holds true for an idealized plasma in thermal-equilibrium. As the domain evolves through the course of a simulation various processes will cause a departure from the Maxwellian form. The resulting PDF will be of arbitrary form and temporally dynamic, making the task of modeling density/data-driven likelihoods particularly difficult.

2.2   Generative Modeling

A generative model's aim is to represent a probability distribution in a tractable fashion such that it is capable of generating new samples. Concretely, given a datapoint $\mathbf{x} \sim p^*(\mathbf{x})$, can we learn an approximation to the true distribution $p(\mathbf{x}) \approx p^*(\mathbf{x})$ such that we may generate new samples. The likelihood of the generated samples should closely match the likelihood of the data used to train the model. We refer to likelihoods learned from data as data-driven likelihoods (DDL). Our data was produced by a simulation with predefined parameters which represents the implicit likelihood, so we can say we want to find the DDL which approximates $\mathbf{x} \sim p^*(\mathbf{x}|\Theta)$

Recent advances in machine learning have produced a wide variety of generative techniques. Chief among these are variational auto-encoders (VAE), generative adversarial networks (GAN), and expectation maximization (EM) algorithms.

The VAE is a maximum likelihood estimator that approximates the evidence by maximizing the evidence lower bound [15]. The core problem with this approach lies in the approximation of the posterior. In achieving a closed form solution, one must know a-priori the posterior's functional form. The standard approach assumes a gaussian, as such it performs poorly on multimodal or non-gaussian data. Alternative posteriors have been proposed in the literature [6], but these methods still require a-priori knowledge of the posterior's functional form.

The GAN on the other-hand, doesn't actually model the likelihood of the data. Its goal is to trick a discriminator into believing the generated samples have been drawn from the true distribution [13]. So while samples generated from the GAN may appear to be reflective of the simulation data, the possibility exists that we are not modeling the true likelihood. Relying on believable but arbitrary samples leaves no guarantee that our inference would respect the physical constraints of the domain in question.

EM algorithms performed on gaussian mixture models do well at modeling multimodal distributions, however it requires prior knowledge of the modality of the data. As we are looking to model our particle distribution functions at an arbitrary time during the evolution of the simulation, the modality is assumed to be dynamic.

2.3   Normalizing Flows

A normalizing flow describes the transformation of a probability density through a sequence of invertible mappings [7]. Given data $\mathbf{x} \in X$, a tractable prior $\mathbf{z} \sim p_z(\mathbf{z})$, and a learnable bijective transformation $f_\theta : X \to Z$ we can apply the following change of variable formula to define a distribution on X.

$$\log p_x(\mathbf{x}) = \log p_z(\mathbf{z}) + \log \left| \det \frac{d\mathbf{z}}{d\mathbf{x}} \right| \tag{2}$$

Furthermore, defining f to be a composite of a sequence of N bijective mappings, $f \equiv f_1 \circ f_2 \circ \ldots \circ f_N$ allows us to say

$$\log p_x(\mathbf{x}) = \log p_z(\mathbf{z}) + \sum_{i=1}^{N} \log \left| \det \frac{\partial \mathbf{h_i}}{\partial \mathbf{h}_{i-1}} \right| \tag{3}$$

where $\mathbf{z} = \mathbf{h}_N$ and $\mathbf{x} = \mathbf{h}_0$. Optimizing on the negative log loss gives us a maximum likelihood model that allows for efficient sampling and density estimation. What remains to be specified is the class of bijective transformation being used. To make this tractable, we would ideally pick a class which is easily invertible, flexible, and results in a Jacobian with a tractable determinant. For this work we use the Masked Autoregressive Flow (MAF).

The MAF offers a robust procedure for modeling our DDL. As an autoregressive model it aims to construct a conditional probability distribution for each feature, where the distribution is conditioned on all previous features. Assuming normal priors allows us to concisely say:

$$p(x_i | x_{1:i-1}) = \mathcal{N}(x_i | \mu_i, (\exp \alpha_i)^2) \tag{4}$$

$$\mu_i = f_\theta(x_{1:i-1}), \ \alpha = f_\phi(x_{1:i-1}) \tag{5}$$

where f_θ, f_ϕ are arbitrary functions parameterized by neural networks. We may generate new data as follows

$$x_i = z_i e^{\alpha_i} + \mu_i \tag{6}$$

To ensure robust predictions we include a permutation of the features before each layer of the flow. This class of transformation, being autoregressive, results in a lower triangular Jacobian. It also easily extends to conditional probabilities. For further details on MAF please see [18].

We can see that the normalizing flow is convenient not only because it allows us to generate samples in an interpretable manner, but gives direct access to the density, allowing us to solve the likelihood-free inference problem for the particle distribution function. For further details on normalizing flows we refer the reader to [8,14,19]

3   Experiments

The following experiments were performed with data produced by the Particle Simulation Code (PSC) [12]. Multi-modal and non-gaussian behavior manifests itself in our data due to excitation processes. Particle excitation occurs through the acquisition of energy from an outside source, usually due to magnetic reconnection or collisionless shocks. In this case, our simulation parameters are very nearly described by [16].

Shown in Fig. 1 is the temporal evolution of the data's u_z marginalized distribution function (not normalized). We see that from T-4 to T-15 an energization process occurs which drives the multi-modal behavior. Overlayed with the PDF is the normal distribution parameterized by our data's mean and variance.

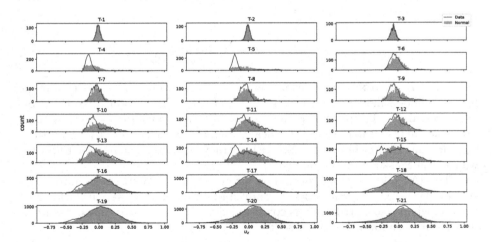

Fig. 1. Temporal evolution of single feature at the same spatial region. Inflow currents are responsible for increasing the number of particles and energization processes are responsible for driving the multi-modal evolution of the distribution. The curve represents the particle distribution function while the solid shading is a normal distribution parametrized by our data, each containing an equal number of datapoints.

3.1   Non-gaussianity

To motivate our use of the MAF we first demonstrate that our data is non-gaussian. There are several methods which may be used to demonstrate this, including the t-statistic of skewness and kurtosis, pairwise non-gaussianity of datapoints, and the Kullback-Leibler (KL) divergence. This suite of tests outlined by Diaz Rivero [20] gives us an established holistic evaluation procedure.

For brevity we focus only on the Kullback-Leibler divergence test. Taking the null hypothesis to be that the our data is gaussian, we generate a normal distribution parameterized by the mean and variance of the data. We draw two separate sample batches from the normal distribution and calculate the KL divergence between the two in order to calculate the null hypothesis. It is well established that the KL divergence between two sample sets drawn from the same distribution will be variable on both the number of samples drawn and number of bins. Taking both numbers to be very large we are able to minimize this variability and achieve the expected minimal distance for the baseline. We then calculate the KL divergence between the data and a sample batch drawn from the normal distribution for comparison. Results in Fig. 2 show that from T-4 to T-15 the KL divergence of the data is an order of magnitude greater than if the data was normally distributed, disproving the null hypothesis. This tells us that the data is non-gaussian (non-Maxwellian) and that there are excitation processes occurring.

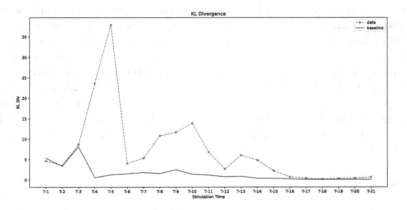

Fig. 2. The Kullback-Leibler Divergence between the particle's normalized PDF and a normal distribution along with the divergence between two samples sets drawn from the normal distribution as the null hypothesis. From T-4 to T-15 there is a departure from the null hypothesis.

3.2   Data Driven Likelihood

Having shown the non-gaussianity of the data we can confidently state that the VAE, GAN, and EM algorithm will yield poor DDL. With this in mind we select the MAF as our generative model. Nflows, built and maintained by [11], is a standardized python library built on pytorch which provides a probabilistic machine learning framework. We constructed the MAF using Nflows and trained using negative log likelihood for 1000 epochs. The specific architecture consisted of an 8 layer flow, each layer of which contained a reverse permutation transformation and a masked affine autoregressive transformation. The affine transformations themselves consist of a scale and shift parameter, each of which is represented by a single hidden layer neural network containing 32 nodes. We take our base distribution to be a multivariate normal.

Training the flow using the negative log likelihood allows us to use the Adam optimizer to iteratively update the parameters of our model in an unsupervised manner. The flow is fed simulation data which is transformed and mapped to the base distribution. Each iterative update modifies the flow's parameters so that the likelihood of the simulation data under the base distribution after transformation is maximized.

MAF hyperparameters				
Layers	Permutation	Transformation	Hidden nodes	Base distribution
8	Reverse	Masked affine autoregressive	32	Multivariate normal

Results may be seen in Fig. 3 which show the binned distribution function of both the true data and samples generated by the model, with the smooth learned likelihood. Here we see the power of using a normalizing flow as a generative model. By gaining direct access to the density function we are able to work with a smooth approximation to what would otherwise be a noisy distribution. If we were to use this data to analyze kinetic processes we would traditionally use the PDF represented in frame A of Fig. 3. This clearly contains noise at a level which could skew interpretation of the underlying physics. In frame C we see the DDL learned by the model, demonstrating a dramatic noise reduction in comparison to frame A.

3.3   Temporal Evolution

We can leverage the versatility of the normalizing flow by taking our base distribution to be a conditional normal where we condition on simulation time. This allows us to capture the underlying particle information at different times throughout the simulation and encapsulate that in our model. This is powerful in that we no longer need to store terabytes of particle data, we can compress that information into the parameters of our model and perform inference from commodity hardware.

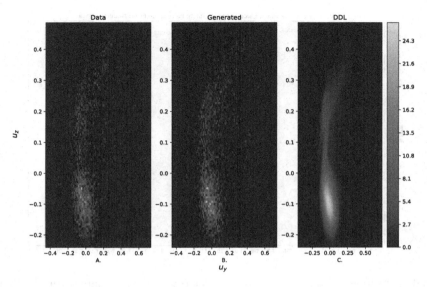

Fig. 3. A. and B. normalized 2-D histograms of u_z-u_y for particle data and generated samples respectively. C. Data driven likelihood approximating $p^*(\mathbf{x}|\varTheta)$

Here we use a single layer neural network with 8 nodes and a ReLU activation to map the simulation time to the conditional parameters of our base distribution. We repeat the same training procedure as the previous section with the exception that we now use the data produced by the simulation at each interval of 1000 time-steps.

In the framework of kinetic theory, we can use the distribution function to directly calculate the conserved physical quantities of our system. The zeroth order moment is the number density, which may be scaled to the mass or charge density. The first order moment gives us momentum and the second order moment kinetic energy.

In Fig. 4 we present the absolute percentage error of the zeroth, first, and second moment calculations directly between the raw data and the predictions of our model. As shown, the maximum error for the first 21,000 time-steps is always well below 1%, demonstrating that we have compressed the temporal evolution of our simulation into our generative model without violating the physical constraints of the system.

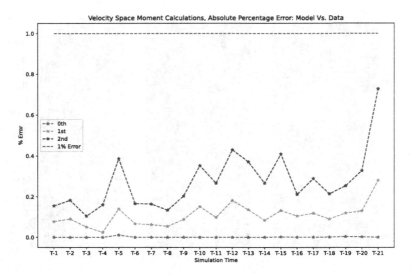

Fig. 4. Zeroth, first, and second velocity moments were calculated using both the model and the true simulation data every 1000 timesteps. The two predictions are then compared using the absolute percentage error, with results shown using 1% error as a threshold.

4   Discussion and Conclusion

We have shown our data to be non-gaussian and shown that we must be selective in which techniques we use to model it. We have shown that generative modeling with normalizing flows is flexible enough to learn our PDF. By applying the MAF to high dimensional particle data produced in PIC simulations we have successfully learned the DDL of the particles, resulting in a smooth tractable estimate of $p^*(\mathbf{x}|\Theta)$. The MAF is easily extendable to conditional distributions, which allowed us to encapsulate temporal dynamics into our model and which opens up room for further studies on adaptable sub-domains. Most importantly in modeling our data we made no assumptions as to the physical process taking place within the simulation. Our predictions align with the simulation's results implying that we have not violated physical constraints in generating new samples.

This presents exciting opportunities for the eXascale Computing Project Whole Device Modeling Application (WDMApp). WDMApp aims to model plasma within the interior of a magnetic confinement fusion device known as a tokomak. Due to the high computational cost, simulations of this nature have historically been restricted to limited volumes of the domain. WDMApp will use the continuum code GENE to model the dense core plasma and a separate, possibly PIC code, to model the less dense edge regions [5]. Domain coherence requires frequent communication of the electromagnetic fields and the particle distribution function between the two codes. The efficient transfer of this information is known as core-edge coupling and involves mapping information between the two code's disparate representations. Coupling the codes to allow information exchange in a meaningful way is an active area of research [9,10,17]. We propose using these results as motivation for further studies incorporating generative modeling into core-edge coupling schema.

References

1. Agostinelli, F., Anderson, M.R., Lee, H.: Adaptive multi-column deep neural networks with application to robust image denoising. In: Proceedings of the 26th International Conference on Neural Information Processing Systems, NIPS 2013, vol. 1, pp. 1493–1501. Curran Associates Inc., Red Hook (2013)
2. Bigdeli, S.A., Lin, G., Portenier, T., Dunbar, L.A., Zwicker, M.: Learning generative models using denoising density estimators (2020)
3. Block, A., Mroueh, Y., Rakhlin, A.: Generative modeling with denoising autoencoders and Langevin sampling (2020)
4. Cho, K.: Simple sparsification improves sparse denoising autoencoders in denoising highly noisy images. In: 30th International Conference on Machine Learning, ICML 2013, 16 June 2013–21 June 2013, pp. 1469–1477 (2013)
5. Choi, J.Y., et al.: Coupling exascale multiphysics applications: methods and lessons learned, pp. 442–452 (2018). https://doi.org/10.1109/eScience.2018.00133
6. Dilokthanakul, N., et al.: Deep unsupervised clustering with Gaussian mixture variational autoencoders (2017)
7. Dinh, L., Krueger, D., Bengio, Y.: NICE: non-linear independent components estimation (2015)
8. Dinh, L., Sohl-Dickstein, J., Bengio, S.: Density estimation using real NVP (2017)
9. Dominski, J., et al.: Spatial coupling of gyrokinetic simulations, a generalized scheme based on first-principles. Phys. Plasmas **28**(2) (2021). https://doi.org/10.1063/5.0027160
10. Dominski, J., et al.: A tight-coupling scheme sharing minimum information across a spatial interface between gyrokinetic turbulence codes. Phys. Plasmas **25**(7), 072308 (2018). https://doi.org/10.1063/1.5044707
11. Durkan, C., Bekasov, A., Murray, I., Papamakarios, G.: nflows: normalizing flows in PyTorch (November 2020). https://doi.org/10.5281/zenodo.4296287
12. Germaschewski, K., et al.: The plasma simulation code: a modern particle-in-cell code with patch-based load-balancing. J. Comput. Phys. **318**, 305–326 (2016). https://doi.org/10.1016/j.jcp.2016.05.013. https://www.sciencedirect.com/science/article/pii/S0021999116301413
13. Goodfellow, I.J., et al.: Generative adversarial networks (2014)
14. Kingma, D.P., Dhariwal, P.: Glow: generative flow with invertible 1 × 1 convolutions (2018)
15. Kingma, D.P., Welling, M.: Auto-encoding variational Bayes (2014)
16. Lezhnin, K.V., et al.: Kinetic simulations of electron pre-energization by magnetized collisionless shocks in expanding laboratory plasmas. Astrophys. J. **908**(2), L52 (2021). https://doi.org/10.3847/2041-8213/abe407
17. Merlo, G., et al.: First coupled GENE–XGC microturbulence simulations. Phys. Plasmas **28**(1), 012303 (2021). https://doi.org/10.1063/5.0026661
18. Papamakarios, G., Pavlakou, T., Murray, I.: Masked autoregressive flow for density estimation (2018)
19. Rezende, D.J., Mohamed, S.: Variational inference with normalizing flows (2016)

20. Rivero, A.D., Dvorkin, C.: Flow-based likelihoods for non-gaussian inference. Phys. Rev. D **102**(10) (2020). https://doi.org/10.1103/physrevd.102.103507
21. Xie, J., Xu, L., Chen, E.: Image denoising and inpainting with deep neural networks. In: Advances in Neural Information Processing Systems, vol. 25. Curran Associates, Inc. (2012). https://proceedings.neurips.cc/paper/2012/file/6cdd60ea0045eb7a6ec44c54d29ed402-Paper.pdf

Convolutional Neural Network for Classification of Aerial Survey Images in the Recognition System

Nguyen Van Trong[1]([✉])[iD] and Pashchenko Fedor Fedorovich[1,2][iD]

[1] Moscow Institute of Physics and Technology, Moscow, Russia
van.chong.nguen@phystech.edu
[2] V. A. Trapeznikov Institute of Control Sciences, Moscow, Russia

Abstract. In this paper, a system for recognizing aerial survey images for finding and locating objects is proposed and constructed. This system includes the following blocks: input of area information, processing of aerial survey images, installation of topography diagnostics, classification of detected objects, database, preparation of a report. The article focuses on the features of developing a convolutional neural network for classifying aerial survey images in a recognition system designed to search for and localize objects.

Keywords: Aerial survey objects recognition system · Convolutional neural network · Aerial survey images · Search and localization of objects

1 Introduction

Modern aerial survey depends on technical achievements in the field of aerial survey instrumentation and the development of aerial survey software. One of the most important tasks that engineer face is to determine the exact boundaries of objects in the aerial survey image. Computer aerial survey images are usually used to examine the area. Both methods make it possible to conduct a layer-by-layer study of the internal structure of area's structures. The result of the survey is a series of images corresponding to the selected scanning planes. By performing fairly non-trivial calculations, the software of aerial survey workstations reproduces the structural image of the scanned. Based on the obtained images, the engineer visually determines the presence of objects and their boundaries. The problem is that the presence of objects are quite easy to identify visually due to their characteristic structural features, while determining the exact boundaries between objects in urban areas or forest belts is a very difficult task, which is almost impossible to solve without performing additional measurements and calculations. The complexity of this task is due to the fact that images of objects in urban areas or forest belts can look almost identical, in terms of, for example, the color of the corresponding areas, which, in turn, makes it impossible to use visual

G. Nicosia et al. (Eds.): LOD 2021, LNCS 13163, pp. 349–356, 2022.
https://doi.org/10.1007/978-3-030-95467-3_26

image analysis methods to detect the tomographic space and borders between the specified areas. Therefore, there is a need to build a recognition system for aerial survey images to search for and locate objects in the classification of such images.

2   State-of-Art

Analysis of aerial survey images consists in choosing the algorithm that is most suitable for its segmentation for different models, such as [1–3]. In fact, its sild a software task, but it not able to using in aerial survey specialists or in aerial survey diagnostics methods. When choosing an algorithm, it is necessary to take into account both the properties of a particular aerial survey image and the features of a particular segmentation algorithm [4–6].

The authors of [4] classify segmentation methods depending on the properties based on which they are performed (similarity or similarity of low-level features); image processing strategies (sequential or parallel); image (color or grayscale); whether the method used has a built-in (internal) criterion for checking segmentation quality. In [1], segmentation methods are divided into three classes, depending on what they are based on: an edge, an area, or pixels. Classification of segmentation methods depending on the mathematical approach used this problem is considered in [2]. This feature distinguishes between threshold segmentation, morphological segmentation, and the method of increasing areas. In some works [3,7], the classification of segmentation methods is considered from the point of view of operator participation in the segmentation process: interactive, automatic, semi-automatic. Segmentation methods that are most commonly used in aerial survey image processing tasks can be classified as follows: threshold methods; edge detection methods; area selection methods; morphological watershed method; Atlas-based methods; clustering methods; artificial neural networks. To assess the effectiveness of a particular method, the following indicators are usually used [6]: sensitivity; specificity; accuracy. Practice shows that the same method can show good results on certain aerial survey images, but it can be ineffective on other images of the same type [5].

3   Results and Discussion

To search for and locate objects on aerial survey images, a system is proposed that will consist of the blocks. In the above functional structure of the proposed system, the initial stage is to receive aerial survey images, which are then sent to the area information input and aerial survey image processing units. Information about the area as a result of the introduction is included in the database along with aerial survey images. The aerial survey image processing unit with internal links has the following structure: the structure of the aerial survey image processing unit of the proposed system includes 4 subsystems that cover automatic processing or aerial survey images, as well as manual processing by an engineer.

This article presents the features of developing a convolutional neural network for classifying aerial survey images without using an open source recognition system designed for finding and localizing objects. To detect objects on aerial survey image, convolutional neural networks can be used, which will allow them to be classified and get a text output.

The idea of a short-circuit neural network is to alternate convolutional layers (convolutionlayers) and subsample layers (subsamplinglayers, subsample layers). The structure of the convolutional neural network is unidirectional (without feedbacks), fundamentally multi - layered. Standard methods are used for training, most often the error back propagation method. Neuron activation function (transfer function) - any function chosen by the researcher. In convolutional layers, hidden neurons are replaced by convolutional filters. Instead of selecting weights for neurons, you need to solve the problem of selecting weights for the filter family. Convolutional layers arrange neurons in three-dimensional mode using the height, width, and depth of the processed signal.

At the first stage, one sequence of data is taken, with the input values of each neuron set in the 0th (input) layer with a mark in the output layer. Next, the total net input signal from the previous layer to each hidden neural layer in the next layer is calculated and the total input signal is calculated using the activation function for the output in the next layer, then the process is repeated with the neurons of the output layer. This can be written as follows:

$$X(l) = Y^{(l-1)}W^{(l-1)},$$
$$W^{(l-1)} \in R\left(d(l-1) \times d(l)\right);$$
$$Y^{(l)} = \sigma\left(X^{(l)}\right), X^{(l)}iY(l) \in R\left(d(l) \times 1\right), \tag{1}$$

where $d(l)$ is the number of neurons in the l-th layer.

Then the error is propagated back in the form of:

$$W^{(l)} = W^{(l)} - \eta dW^{(l)} \tag{2}$$

Calculating the gradient dW matrix for the weights from the second to last layer $(l = n)$. The error can be calculated using the expression:

$$E = \frac{1}{2}\left(label_j^{(n)} - y_j^{(n)}\right)^2, \tag{3}$$

and the gradient value of each weight between the last layer i and its preliminary layer will be:

$$\delta^{(n)} = -\left(E - Y^{(n)}\right)\sigma'\left(X^{(n)}\right),$$
$$\delta(n) \in R\left(d(l) \times 1\right)$$
$$dW^{(n-1)} = \left(Y^{(n-1)}\right)^T \delta^{(n)}. \tag{4}$$

The gradient is calculated in the previous layers ($L = n - 1$):

$$\delta(l) = W^{(l)} \left(\delta^{(l+1)} \right);$$

$$dW^{(l-1)} = \left(Y^{(l-1)} \right)^T \delta^{(l)}. \tag{5}$$

The process is repeated until all the weights in the neural network are updated.

There must be a feedback loop for updating the weights that helps you reach a certain iteration.

The work of the convolutional neural network is based on the basic neural networks described above, and the algorithm consists of two main processes: convolution and discretization, which occur at convolutional layers and maximum pool levels.

During convolution, each neuron receives input data in the form of a matrix $n \times n$ of the previous layer, which is a local receptive field, which can be written as:

$$x_{i,j}^{(l)} = \sigma \left(b + \sum_{r=0}^{n} \sum_{c=0}^{n} w_{r,c} x_{i+r,j+c}^{(l-1)} \right). \tag{6}$$

Each local receptive field corresponds to the same weights $w_{r,c}$ and biases b, which are determined from Eq. (6) above, the parameters of which can be considered as a training filter or kernel F.

During convolution, the aerial survey image is convoluted, and the convolutional layer is the output of the previous layer. During the sampling process, it is possible to add a subsequent layer after each convolutional layer. The convolutional neural network pool layer selects small rectangular blocks from the convolutional layer and processes it. In this paper, we propose to accept the maximum of a block as one output per pool ball.

Since there are few connections in existing areas of aerial survey imaging, the use of convolutional neural network is appropriate and they are much easier to train than conventional neural networks.

In the form of activation of the output of neurons, the standard functions are applied:

$$y(x) = (1 + e - x) - 1,$$

or

$$y(x) = tanh(x),$$

where x - are the input values.

There is a vanishing gradient problem that occurs when the units of the upper layer are almost saturated at -1 or 1, resulting in the lower layers of the convolutional neural network having gradients of 0, practically 0. Such vanishing gradients cause slow convergence of optimization, and in some cases the finally trained convolutional neural network shows poor results with a new sample of images.

This can happen when using the aforementioned sigmoid function or hyperbolic tangent function. Therefore, to avoid the problem of vanishing gradient, we will use the activation function in the form:

$$y = max0, \quad b + \sum_{i=1}^{k} x_i w_i.$$

To regulate overfitting of the convolutional neural network during training, dropout neurons do not participate in forward and reverse propagation. Dropout can be considered as a discretization of a neural network within a convolutional neural network with parameter updates based on input data. This ensures that the drop-down layer is always enabled between fully connected layers. In the dropout layer, the selection of units for dropout is random and can be accepted with a fixed probability value of 0.5.

Since aerial survey images are studied-512 by 512 pixels format, the input layer of the convolutional neural network will contain 262144 (512×512) neurons (Fig. 1).

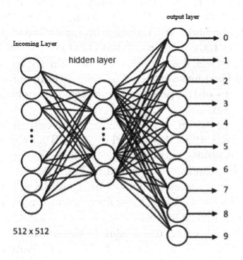

Fig. 1. General view of the layers of the convolutional neural network.

In a convolutional neural network, the second layer is hidden, and we denote this layer as to determine the optimal data from the value of this hidden layer.

In Fig. 1, the above example illustrates a small hidden layer containing only = 30 neurons. The output layer of the network contains 10 neurons that represent 10 different types of aerial survey images. The numbering of output neurons from 0 to 9 is symbolic. As a result, the neuron with the highest activation value should be selected for prediction.

Let give an example to show the advantages of the proposed method. The state of the art deep detectors like SSD, due to the limited computational resources, can be trained on high resolution images, therefore, the aerial action detection seems impossible using these types of networks. We propose a two-step framework that in the first step, a SSD network generates objects of interest or object proposals using the small-sized aerial images, separately for each frame.

In the second step, a yes and no visual question answering system determines the existence of a desired single or multiple actions. Intersection Over Union (IoU), which is defined by the area of overlap between the ground-truth and predicted bounding boxes, divided by the area of the union. Desired action(s) are converted to 13 dimensional bag-of-words representation, and next mapped to 100 dimensional multi-label features using a fully-connected layer. Image and multi-label features are concatenated and transformed into 100 dimensional imageaction common sub-space using another fullyconnected layer.

We selected 512 pixels format, the input layer of the convolutional neural network will contain 262144 (512×512) neurons.

As a result of the experiment, the training of the proposed model on fifty epochs was completed in about 2 h, which made it possible to calculate the classification accuracy and the value of functionality losses in the training data set after each epoch, where the best classification accuracy was 94%, and the values of the loss function were 0.2. The training was conducted on a personal computer with the following characteristics: an Intel Core i3 processor (2.1 GHz), 4 GB RAM, and an NVIDIA GeForce 920M GPU (954 MHz) video adapter. The training model was developed in Keras, a Python library for deep learning, using Theano Firewall and Graphics Accelerators (eng. graphic processing unit, GPU). The results of exercises of the proposed convolutional network on 32×32 color images are shown in Table 1.

All experiments for training the optimized model are implemented using the Kerns 2.0 and Tensorflow 1.0 libraries, as well as the cuDNN 5.1 library (backend) for using graphics accelerators. The experiments were performed on a GeForce 940MX GPU and are presented in Table 2.

The experiment was conducted on a GeForce 940MX graphics accelerator and an Intel I7-4930K processor. The Tensorflow optimizer uses SSE4 instructions .X, AVX, AVX2, and FMA. The results of the experiment are shown in Table 3.

Based on the obtained results of calculating the training time of the optimized convolutional network model, we can say that a significant improvement in the performance of the network itself was achieved compared to the basic model. A detailed review is described in the next paragraph.

The updated architecture of the basic model was implemented with such changes as increasing the number of input layer filters, increasing the dimension of the maximization subsample layer, and removing the bias neuron in the final layers. Removing neuron offsets in certain layers did not significantly affect the total number of parameters in the network, and applying a higher-dimensional filter reduced the number of parameters in layer 11 (Table 4), where the feature map is minimized to the smallest size and the network performs a classification task based on a set of such maps.

Table 1. Results of exercises of the proposed convolutional network on 32×32 color images.

Layer name	Cores neurons	Function activations	Channels	Weekend size	Parameters
Convolutional layer 1	3×3	ReLU	32	32×32	890
Exception layer 1 (20%)			32	32×32	0
Convolutional layer 2	3×3	ReLU	32	32×32	9230
Subsample layer 1	2×2		32	16×16	0
Convolutional layer 3	3×3	ReLU	64	16×16	18501
Exception layer 2 (20%)			64	16×16	0
Convolutional layer 4	3×3	ReLU	64	16×16	36898
Subsample layer 2	2×2		64	8×8	0
Convolutional layer 5	3×3	ReLU	128	8×8	73802
Exception layer 3 (20%)			128	8×8	0
Convolutional layer 6	3×3	ReLU	128	8×8	146765
Subsample layer 3	2×2		128	4×4	0
Branching out	2048				0
Exception layer 4 (20%)	2048				0
Fully connected layer 1	1024	ReLU			2086859
Exception layer 5 (20%)	1024				0
Fully connected layer 2	512	ReLU			534500
Exception layer 6 (20%)	512				0
Fully connected layer 3	10	Softmax			5130

Table 2. Indicator of new model recognition accuracy for different data sets.

N	Data set	Network training		Network testing	
		Accuracy	Error rate	Accuracy	Error rate
1	CIFAR-10	90.6%	a = 0.71	84.95%	a = 0.45
2	CIFAR-100	85.99%	a = 1.99	82.91%	a = 0.73
3	GTSRB	100.00%	a = 0.00	99.61%	a = 0.10
4	HASYv2	88.59%	a = 0.45	85.76%	a = 0.15
5	MNIST	99.98%	a = 0.10	99.58%	a = 0.13
6	STL-10	95.43%	a = 2.51	75.99%	a = 1.98
7	SVHN	99.08%	a = 0.07	98.88%	a = 0.12

Table 3. Training time for a new neural network model on a convolutional CPU and GPU.

Network	Tensorflow	Training time		
		1 picture	128 images	Epoch
New model	Intel i7-4930K	5 ms	432 ms	386.0 s
New model	GeForce 940MX	4 ms	205 ms	192.2 s

Table 4. Results of different method for action detection.

Method	mAP@0.5
SSD512 [4]	15.39%
SSD960 [4]	18.80%
Proposed method	28.30%

We see that the proposed method even surpasses the results of SSD960 and again this is because the proposed method exploits higher resolution (the original high resolution of proposals in original images) and multi-action information.

Results dataset show that the proposed method is more accurate compared to using only CNN for aerial action detection.

4   Conclusions

In this paper, a system for recognizing aerial survey images for finding and locating objects is proposed and constructed. This system includes the following blocks: input of area information, processing of aerial survey images, installation of diagnostics, classification of detected objects, database, preparation of a report. The article focuses on the features of developing a convolutional neural network for classifying aerial survey images in a recognition system designed to search for and localize objects. As a result, a convolutional neural network was built for classification aerial survey images in the proposed recognition system designed to search for and locate objects.

References

1. Doronicheva A.V.: Methods of aerial survey image recognition for computer-based automated diagnostics. Mod. Probl. Sci. Educ. **4** (2014)
2. Neeraj, S.: Automated aerial survey image convolution techniques. J. Aerial Surv. Phys. **35**, 3–14 (2020)
3. Roberts L.G.: Machine perception of three-dimensional solids. In: Optical and Electro-optical Information Processing, pp. 159–197. MIT Pres (1965)
4. Porshnev, S.V.: Universal classification of image convolution algorithms. J. Sci. Publ. Postgrad. Eng. Students **3**, 163–172 (2018)
5. Robinson, G.S.: Edge detection by compass gradient masks. Comput. Graph. Image Process. **5**(6), 492–502 (1977)
6. Sobel, I.E.: Camera models and machine perception. Ph.D. Dissertation. Stanford University (1970)
7. Zhuk, S.V.: Review of modern methods of convolution of raster images. Izvestiya volgogradskogo gosudarstvennogo tekhnicheskogo universiteta **6**, 115–118 (2019)

Can You Tell? SSNet - A Biologically-Inspired Neural Network Framework for Sentiment Classifiers

Apostol Vassilev$^{(\boxtimes)}$ ⓘ, Munawar Hasan ⓘ, and Honglan Jin

National Institute of Standards and Technology, Gaithersburg, USA
{apostol.vassilev,munawar.hasan,honglan.jin}@nist.gov

Abstract. When people try to understand nuanced language they typically process multiple input sensor modalities to complete this cognitive task. It turns out the human brain has even a specialized neuron formation, called sagittal stratum, to help us understand sarcasm. We use this biological formation as the inspiration for designing a neural network architecture that combines predictions of different models on the same text to construct accurate and computationally efficient classifiers for sentiment analysis and study several different realizations. Among them, we propose a systematic new approach to combining multiple predictions based on a dedicated neural network and develop mathematical analysis of it along with state-of-the-art experimental results. We also propose a heuristic-hybrid technique for combining models and back it up with experimental results on a representative benchmark dataset and comparisons to other methods (DISCLAIMER: This paper is not subject to copyright in the United States. Commercial products are identified in order to adequately specify certain procedures. In no case does such identification imply recommendation or endorsement by the National Institute of Standards and Technology, nor does it imply that the identified products are necessarily the best available for the purpose.) to show the advantages of the new approaches.

Keywords: Natural language processing · Sentiment analysis · Neural network architecture · Machine learning · Deep learning · Artificial intelligence · Bayesian decision rule combiner · Combined predictor · Heuristic-hybrid model combiner

1 Introduction

Applications of deep learning to natural language processing represent attempts to automate a highly-sophisticated human capability to read and understand text and even generate meaningful compositions. Language is the product of

We thank the NIST Information Technology Laboratory (ITL) for the research funding and support.

G. Nicosia et al. (Eds.): LOD 2021, LNCS 13163, pp. 357–382, 2022.
https://doi.org/10.1007/978-3-030-95467-3_27

human evolution over a very long period of time. Scientists now think that language and the closely related ability to generate and convey thoughts are unique human traits that set us on the high-end of the spectrum of all living creatures with varying capacity for language. Modern science describes two connected but independent systems related to language: inner thought generation and sensor modalities to express or take them in for processing [9]. For example, human sensory modalities are speaking, reading, writing, etc. This allows homo sapiens to express an infinite amount of meaning using only a finite set of symbols, e.g., the 26 letters in the English language. The result is a very powerful combination that has resulted in the vast amount of knowledge and information amassed in the form of written text today.

Over the course of the long evolutionary development and especially in the modern era, the sapiens have mastered the ability to generate and convey sophisticated and nuanced thoughts. Consequently, the texts deep learning is tasked with processing, known as natural language processing (NLP), range from the simple ones that say what they mean to those that say one thing but mean another. An example of the latter is sarcasm. To convey or comprehend sarcasm the sapiens typically invoke more than one sensory modality, e.g., combining speech with gestures or facial expressions, or adding nuances to the speech with particular voice tonalities. In written text, comprehending sarcasm amounts to what colloquially is known as reading between the lines.

With the emergence of A.M. Turing's seminal paper [38], the research in NLP kicked off. Initially, it revolved around handwritten rules, later obsoleted by statistical analysis. Until the advent of deep learning, the decision tree-based parsing techniques [26,27] were considered as the state-of-the-art methods, and linguistic performance was measured on the basis of the *Turing Test* [38].

Fast forwarding to the present day, deep learning and the enormous increase in available computational power allowed researchers to revisit the previously defined as computationally intensive family of recurrent neural networks [19,36] and produced several groundbreaking NLP results [8,20,40,42]. There are also numerous other application-specific architectures [5,10,13] for NLP problems. We refer the reader to a recent comprehensive survey [29] for a detailed review of a large number of deep learning models for text classification developed in recent years and a discussion of their technical contributions, similarities, and strengths. This survey also provides a large list of popular datasets widely used for text classification along with a quantitative analysis of the performance of different deep learning models on popular benchmarks. Still, it is a publicly-held secret that the algorithms used in machine learning, including the most advanced, are limited in the sense that all of them fail to capture *all* information contained in the data they process. Recent research even points to a systemic problem known as underspecification [12,17].

Having been faced with this reality, we asked ourselves the question: How do humans do it? How do they process ambiguous text? We all know that our human sensor abilities are limited: our vision, our hearing, our attention span, our memory are all limited. How do we then perform so well given all these limitations?

Through the evolution of their brain, sapiens have acquired a polygonal cross-road of associational fibers called sagittal stratum (SS), cf. Fig. 1[1], to cope with this complexity. Researchers have reported [34] that the bundle of nerve fibers that comprises the SS and connects several regions of the brain that help with processing of information enables people to understand sarcasm through the combination of sensory modalities, e.g., visual information, like facial expressions, and sounds, like tone of voice. Moreover, researchers have shown that the patients who had the most difficulty with comprehending sarcasm also tended to have more extensive damage in the right SS. In other words, the ability to understand sophisticated language nuances is dependent on the ability of the human brain to successfully take in and combine several different types of sensory modalities.

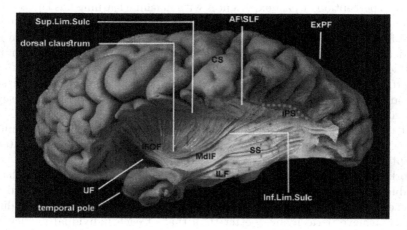

Fig. 1. This image shows the sagittal stratum (SS). The SS is situated deep on the lateral surface of the brain hemisphere, medial to the arcuate/superior longitudinal fascicle complex, and laterally to the tapetal fibers of the atrium [6]. The SS is a bundle of nerve fibers that connects many different parts of the brain and helps with processing sensory modalities (visual and sound), thus enabling people to understand nuanced language such as sarcasm.

The evolution of language and the resulting increased sophistication of expressing human thoughts has created a challenging problem for deep learning. How to capture and process the full semantics in a text is still an open problem for machine learning. This is partly manifested by the facts that (i) there are many different ways of encoding the semantics in a text, ranging from simple encoding relying on treating words as atomic units represented by their rank in a vocabulary [3] to using word embeddings or distributed representation of words [28] to using sentence embeddings and even complete language models

---

[1] Reprinted from [6] with permission by Springer Nature, order #4841991468054.

[14,18,37]; and (ii) there is no established dominant neural network type capable of successfully tackling natural language processing in most of its useful for practice applications to the extent required by each specific application domain.

Based on this observation, we explored the extent to which it is possible to utilize a simple encoding of semantics in a text and define an optimal neural network for that encoding [39] for sentiment analysis. Our study showed that although each of these encoding types and corresponding neural network architecture may yield good results, they are still limited in accuracy when taken by themselves.

The main thrust of NLP research is based on the idea of developing computationally intensive neural network architectures intended to produce better results in the form of accuracy on representative benchmark datasets. In contrast, the research on simulating the decision-making capabilities of our brain related to perception or past experiences with machine learning has lagged. Thus, the computed probability of any linguistic sample predicted by any individual model is not grounded in a state or function of a biological mind. As we mentioned above, the anatomy of the human brain allows processing of multiple input sensor modalities for making a decision. Inspired by this fact, this paper seeks to establish an approach based on integrating different methods for sentiment analysis to NLP - a strategy that has already had good results in several other scientific fields.

The primary goal of this paper is to explore the problem from a different perspective and to study ways to combine different types of encoding intended to capture better the semantics in a text along with a corresponding neural network architecture inspired by the SS in the human brain. To do this, we introduce a new architecture for neural network for sentiment analysis and draw on the experiences from using it with several different types of word encoding in order to achieve performance better than that of each individual participating encoding. The main contribution of this paper is the design of the biologically-inspired framework for neural networks for sentiment analysis in Sect. 2 and the analysis of the combiner based on a neural network in Sect. 2.1.

The authors would like to emphasize that this paper does not try to improve the metrics achieved by aforementioned papers but presents an approach to simulate certain decision-making scenarios in the human brain. Any model referenced in this section can be used as a plug-and-play module in our framework.

1.1 Limitations of Existing Standalone NLP Approaches to Machine Learning

As indicated above, there are multiple different types of encoding of semantics in text, each of varying complexity and suitability for purpose. The polarity-weighted multi-hot encoding [39], when combined with appropriately chosen neural network, is generic yet powerful enough for capturing the semantics of movie reviews for sentiment analysis. Even though the overall accuracy reported in [39] is high, the approach quickly reaches a ceiling should higher prediction accuracy be required by some application domains.

Encoding based on word embeddings or distributed representation of words [28] is widely used. For example, the approach in [32] has been influential in establishing semantic similarities between the words for a given corpus, by projecting each word of the corpus to a high dimensional vector space. While the dimension of the vector space itself becomes a hyperparameter to tweak around, the vectors can be further processed or utilized using a recurrent neural network (RNN). When tackling NLP problems, a variant of RNN, namely the long short-term memory (LSTM) variant and its bidirectional version (BLSTM) are known to perform better than other neural networks. Through our experiments on various datasets [1,21], we found that certain vocabulary provides deeper semantics to the sentence from the corpus based on the receiver's perception and context. In such situations, the idea of attention [2,16,25] plays an important role and provides the network with an additional parameter called the context vector, which can make convergence slower, but the model overall is good. It is also possible to use a learnable word embedding, where the first layer of the neural network architecture is the embedding followed by one or more RNN's.

Although intuitively one may think that word embeddings should help to increase the accuracy of the model to any desirable level because word embeddings do capture the semantics contained in the text in a way that mimics how people perceive language structure, the available empirical test evidence in terms of reported accuracy rates is inconclusive. Our own experiments with word embeddings used by themselves revealed an accuracy ceiling similar to that of the polarity-weighted multi-hot encoding. Attempts to utilize sentence embeddings have been even less successful [11].

Recently, pretrained language models have gained popularity because of their improved performance on general NLP tasks [14]. These models are trained on large corpora, and their application to specific NLP tasks typically involves some transfer learning on the corpus of interest. However, they too have limitations, which we will discuss in more detail in Sect. 3.2.

All these different types of encoding can be challenged further by varying style of writing or level of mastering the language. An example of the former is nuanced language such as sarcasm. Some reviewers choose to write a negative review using many positive words, yet an experienced reader can sense the overall negative sentiment conveyed between the lines while the polarity-weighted multi-hot encoding [39] and word embeddings [32] may struggle with it. An example of the latter is primitive use of the language by non-native speakers resulting in sentences with broken syntax and inappropriate terminology. Another difficult cases are reviews that contain a lot of narrative about the plot of the movie but very little of how the reviewer feels about the movie. Yet another problematic class are movie reviews that rate a movie excellent for one audience, e.g., children, but not good for another, e.g., adults. Careful analysis of the data in [1,21] reveals examples of all these kinds of reviews, often confusing models based on the encodings described here. Such complications represent significant challenges to each of these types of encoding when used by themselves no matter the power of the neural network.

This observation raises a question: if one is interested in obtaining a more versatile representation of the semantics of text would an approach that combines different types of encoding yield a better result than attempting to just improve each of them within their envelopes?

2   Sagittal Stratum-Inspired Neural Network

We now turn to the design of a neural network that aims to simulate the way SS in the human brain operates. Recall that the SS brings information from different parts of the brain, each responsible for processing different input sensory modalities, to enable a higher order of cognition, such as comprehension of sarcasm. Our context here is NLP, and one way to map the functioning of the SS to it is to consider combining different representations of the semantic content of a text. To do this, one first has to pick the types of representations of the text. Because we aim at computing different perspectives on the same text, it is natural to seek representations that are independent. For example, the polarity-weighted multi-hot encoding [39] is based on the bag-of-words model of the language and has nothing in common with word embeddings that rely on language structure [32] or the transformer language model [14]. But if independence of representation is adopted, how does one combine the models computed from each of them?

Unlike image processing where each model is computed over the pixel grid of the image, in NLP there is no common basis onto which to map and combine the different models. Instead, we again use a hint from how the human brain performs some cognitive tasks. When a person hears another person utter a phrase, to comprehend what the speaker is trying to convey the brain of the listener first processes the words in the phrase, then the listener assesses if the speaker rolled her eyes, for example, when uttering the words, to decide if she spoke sarcastically. The brain of the listener combines these two assessments with the help of the SS to arrive at a final conclusion if the speaker spoke sarcastically or not. This suggests we can combine the resulting assessments from each model on a particular review τ, e.g., the probability of classifying it as positive or negative, to decide on the final classification.

The neural networks based on the different language models are trained on the same corpus. In the case of transformer models, which are pre-trained on extremely large corpora, they are transfer trained on the same corpus as the remaining models to ensure proper adaptation to the problem at stake. The trained models are saved and used to compute predictions. For the sake of developing notation, we assume there are K different models.

The predictions from the K models are fed into a SS-inspired classifier. Based on our understanding for how SS works in the human brain to enable interpretation of language that can only be resolved correctly when multiple sensor modalities are used together, we construct the network shown in Fig. 2 and experiment with several different mechanisms F for combining the models.

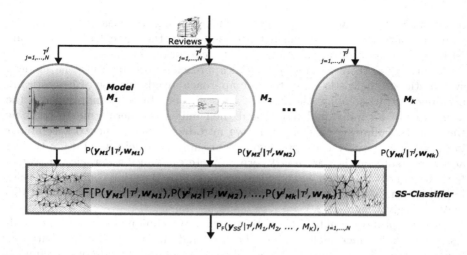

Fig. 2. The SS classifier. Here F is some appropriately defined function that combines the input from the participating models, and τ^j, $\forall j \in \{1, ..., N\}$, are the input text samples. M_1 to M_K are the K participating models, and $\mathrm{P}(\mathbf{y}^j_{M_i}|\tau^j, \mathbf{w}_{M_i})$ is the probability computed by M_i, $\forall i \in \{1, ..., K\}$, for each τ^j. Finally, $\mathrm{P}_\mathrm{F}(\mathbf{y}^j_{SS}|\tau^j, M_1, ..., M_K)$, is the resulting probability for τ^j computed by the combiner F.

In general, the computed probabilities for review classification from the participating models are combined in a way that favors identifying the most probable case, which is analogous to the way humans assess multiple sensor modalities in order to process ambiguous speech and deduce the most plausible interpretation. Our task is to combine the predictor models taking into account that they represent different views on the semantics in the same text. Recall from the observation in Sect. 2 that the only meaningful way to combine the models is through the probability assessment each of them produces for a given review and in turn the entire corpus. While the ensemble techniques [30] have been known for good performance in computer vision-related tasks [23,31,33,35], the same is not true for natural language processing-based problems. This analogy can also be backed by the fact that models using different encodings have different latent space, and, hence, merging such latent spaces may not produce an optimal solution due to the varying rate of convergence of individual models. But the major issue is the projection of one model's latent space onto another. Due to different encodings, such projections may produce inconsistent coalesced models.

One other potential concern here is that the models may be strongly correlated as they are trying to predict the same thing. We compensate for this by using fundamentally different language models. Each of the models has different limitations that are challenged by the text of the different reviews in the dataset, yielding different predictions on some of them. In addition, we apply random shuffling of the training dataset on each training epoch. These two factors alleviate this potential concern to a large extent, as confirmed by the computational results in Sect. 3. Thus, our approach is different than the classic leave-one-out training approach in [4,24] and is better suited for the current state-of-the-art NLP models and their applications on large corpora of interest.

In principle, there are two potential approaches to combining the models: systematic and heuristic. A systematic approach avoids the use of heuristics in deciding how to combine the models. Instead, one states assumptions on the properties of an individual model and then builds a general rule to combine the models. Following this principle, we introduce a neural network combiner in Sect. 2.1 and analyze its properties. This approach delivers state-of-the-art accuracy results on the benchmark corpus of interest, which we provide in Sect. 3. For a baseline comparison we consider the systematic Bayesian combination rules in [22] (**Sum, Majority Vote, Average**, and **Max**). A brief description of this method is given in Sect. 2.2.

We also propose a hybrid heuristic-systematic technique for combining models in Sect. 2.3, which makes use of the combination rules in [22] but with our heuristic way of choosing what and when to combine. This hybrid technique shows performance characteristics that are pretty close to the leading neural network combiner and outperforms the classic Bayesian rule combiners - see Sect. 3.

2.1   A Neural Network Combiner

Here we seek to define a predictor F inspired by human biology and in terms of a neural network consisting of a single dense layer and a sigmoid. The neural network computes the weights $\{w_i\}_{i=1}^{K}$ for combining the participating models M_1, ..., M_K. Let $\mathbf{y}_i(\tau^j)$ be the probability estimate computed by the i-th model on the j-th text, denoted as $P(\mathbf{y}_{M_i}|\tau^j, \mathbf{w}_{M_i})$ in Fig. 2.

We define the combined predictor as a combination of $K > 1$ individual predictors:

$$\mathbf{y}(\tau) = \sum_{i=1}^{K} w_i \mathbf{y}_i(\tau), \ \forall \tau \in \mathbb{D}, \tag{1}$$

$$w_i \geq 0, \ \forall i. \tag{2}$$

In the case of a corpus labeled for binary classification, a binary function $\mathbf{u}(\tau)$ is defined by the label assigned to each text τ in $\mathbb{D}$. Given the two classes, $\mathbf{I}^{(0)}$ and $\mathbf{I}^{(1)}$, $\mathbf{y}_i(\tau)$ is the predicted probability for the text τ to belong to $\mathbf{I}^{(1)}$. The real-valued functions $\mathbf{y}_i$ with range the interval $[0, 1]$ have values that correspond to the probability of being assigned to $\mathbf{I}^{(1)}$. Because of (1) and (2), the range of $\mathbf{y}(\tau)$ may exceed the unit interval, so typically one assigns the class by subjecting $\sigma(\mathbf{y}(\tau))$ to a threshold test with some value $t \in (0, 1)$ so that

$$\tau \in \begin{cases} \mathbf{I}^{(1)}, & \text{if } \sigma(\mathbf{y}(\tau)) \geq t, \\ \mathbf{I}^{(0)}, & \text{otherwise.} \end{cases} \tag{3}$$

Here $\sigma(x)$ is the sigmoid function given by

$$\sigma(x) = \frac{1}{1 + e^{-x}}.$$

Because $\mathbf{y}_i(\tau)$ are with ranges shifted with respect to the domain of the sigmoid, to get accurate classification one needs to shift the range of $\mathbf{y}$ to the left so it is centered with respect to zero, i.e.,

$$\sigma_b(\mathbf{y}(\tau)) = \sigma(\mathbf{y}(\tau) - b), \tag{4}$$

for some $b > 0$. Here, we assume that each predictor $\mathbf{y}_i$ is decent, i.e., it produces labels that are reasonably close to those produced by $\mathbf{u}$ over the entire $\mathbb{D}$. Mathematically, this means we assume $||\mathbf{u} - \mathbf{y}_i||$ is small, compared to $||\mathbf{u}||$. Here,

$$||\mathbf{f}||^2 = \sum_{\tau \in \mathbb{D}} \mathbf{f}^2(\tau), \tag{5}$$

where $\mathbf{f}$ is a binary function defined over $\mathbb{D}$.

For the case of a real-valued function $\mathbf{y}_i(\tau)$ we define

$$||\mathbf{y}(\tau)||_t^2 = \sum_{\tau \in \mathbb{D}} \mathbf{I}_t(\mathbf{y}(\tau))^2, \tag{6}$$

where $\mathbf{I}_t$ is the assigned class for $\mathbf{y}(\tau)$ with respect to the threshold t according to (3). Similarly, we define

$$||\mathbf{y}(\tau) - \mathbf{z}(\tau)||_t^2 = \sum_{\tau \in \mathbb{D}} (\mathbf{I}_t(\mathbf{y}(\tau)) - \mathbf{I}_t(\mathbf{z}(\tau)))^2. \tag{7}$$

Note that for a binary function $\mathbf{f}$ over $\mathbb{D}$, $||\mathbf{f}|| = ||\mathbf{f}||_t$. Note also that the definitions in (5) and (6) imply that $||\mathbf{u}||$ is large. If N is the cardinality of $\mathbb{D}$, then in fact $||\mathbf{u}||$ is close to $N/2$. Otherwise, $\mathbf{u}$ would be statistically biased to one of the classes. Also, N is large for problems of interest, otherwise the data can be processed by humans. Related to N, the number K of individual predictors is small, typically up to a half a dozen.

Analysis of the Neural Network Combiner. In this section we consider the question if the constraint in (2) is sufficient for computing reasonable weights to be used in combining the models. In the literature, people often impose the additional constraint

$$\sum_{i=1}^{K} w_i = 1. \tag{8}$$

However, we are not aware of a similar constraint imposed by the SS or another region of the brain when handling the different input modalities, based on our review of the literature. Humans seem to be making decisions when they consider all input modalities together in the proper context, not by discarding some of the input modalities upfront. So, it is reasonable to want the weights of the different inputs to our system be of the same order, i.e., there is not one input whose weight dominates the others, effectively reducing the mix to a single modality. All that without imposing artificial constraints, e.g., (8), that do not have clear backing in the biological foundations of our inspiration. Moreover, after performing extensive computations in the laboratory, we observed that imposing (8) makes computing the optimal weights much more intense and difficult without any gains in the accuracy of the combined predictor. This led us to examine the need for (8). We argue that the additional constraint in (8) is **not** necessary. To see this, let us consider the approximation error of the predictor $\mathbf{y}$ defined as $||\mathbf{u} - \mathbf{y}||_t$. Let us denote $W = \sum_{i=1}^{K} w_i$. Let

$$\hat{\mathbf{y}}(\tau) = \frac{1}{W}\mathbf{y}(\tau) = \sum_{i=1}^{K} \frac{w_i}{W}\mathbf{y}_i(\tau) \tag{9}$$

be the interpolation predictor constructed as a liner combination of $\mathbf{y}_i$ with coefficients that sum up to one. If the individual predictors are good then the interpolation predictor $\hat{\mathbf{y}}$ is also good, i.e., $||\mathbf{u} - \sigma_b(\hat{\mathbf{y}})||_t$ is small.

Let $\mathbb{L}_t(x)$ be a linear approximation of $\sigma(x)$ for some constant $t > 0$ such that $\mathbb{L}_t(x)$ minimizes $||\mathbb{L}_t(x) - \sigma(x)||_t$. Note that any straight line passing through the points $(\ln(\frac{t}{1-t}), t)$ and having the same slope as $\sigma'(\ln(\frac{t}{1-t}))$ satisfies $||\mathbb{L}_t(x) - \sigma(x)||_t = 0$. For example, for $t = \frac{1}{2}$ the straight line

$$\mathbb{L}_{\frac{1}{2}}(x) = \frac{1}{4}x + \frac{1}{2}$$

also satisfies $||\mathbb{L}_{\frac{1}{2}}(x) - \sigma(x)||_{\frac{1}{2}} = 0$. In practice, $t = \frac{1}{2}$ is the natural choice for an unbiased binary distribution $\mathbf{u}$ and an unbiased predictor $\mathbf{y}$. Note that, instead of taking the entire straight line, one may consider a piece-wise linear function but this is not necessary because the definitions in (6) and (7) can handle unbounded functions.

Then,

$$||\mathbf{u} - \sigma_b(\mathbf{y})||_t = ||\mathbf{u} - W\mathbf{u} + W\mathbf{u} - \sigma_b(\mathbf{y})||_t$$

$$= ||(1 - W)\mathbf{u} - W(\mathbf{u} - \frac{1}{W}\sigma_b(\mathbf{y}))||_t.$$

Applying the triangle inequality, we get

$$||\mathbf{u} - \sigma_b(\mathbf{y})||_t \geq |1 - W| \, ||\mathbf{u}||_t - W||\mathbf{u} - \frac{1}{W}\sigma_b(\mathbf{y}))||_t. \tag{10}$$

First, consider the case $W \leq 1$. Then from inequality (10)

$$||\mathbf{u} - \sigma_b(\mathbf{y})||_t \geq (1 - W)||\mathbf{u}||_t - W||\mathbf{u} - \frac{1}{W}\sigma_b(\mathbf{y}))||_t.$$

Let $\mathbb{L}_t$ be as defined above and

$$\mathbb{L}_{t,b}(x) = \mathbb{L}_t(x - b). \tag{11}$$

Then,

$$||\mathbf{u} - \frac{1}{W}\sigma_b(\mathbf{y}))||_t = ||\mathbf{u} - \frac{1}{W}\mathbb{L}_{t,b}(\mathbf{y}) + \frac{1}{W}\mathbb{L}_{t,b}(\mathbf{y}) - \frac{1}{W}\sigma_b(\mathbf{y}))||_t$$

Thus,

$$||\mathbf{u} - \frac{1}{W}\sigma_b(\mathbf{y}))||_t \leq ||\mathbf{u} - \mathbb{L}_{t,b}(\hat{\mathbf{y}})||_t + \frac{1}{W}||\mathbb{L}_{t,b}(\mathbf{y}) - \sigma_b(\mathbf{y}))||_t.$$

Note that

$$\frac{1}{W}||\mathbb{L}_{t,b}(\mathbf{y}) - \sigma_b(\mathbf{y}))||_t = 0.$$

From here we get,

$$||\mathbf{u} - \sigma_b(\mathbf{y})||_t \geq (1 - W)||\mathbf{u}||_t - W(||\mathbf{u} - \mathbb{L}_{t,b}(\hat{\mathbf{y}})||_t)$$

This implies that

$$W \geq \frac{||\mathbf{u}||_t - ||\mathbf{u} - \sigma_b(\mathbf{y})||_t}{||\mathbf{u}||_t + ||\mathbf{u} - \mathbb{L}_{t,b}(\hat{\mathbf{y}})||_t}.$$

Note that $||\mathbf{u} - \mathbb{L}_{t,b}(\hat{\mathbf{y}})||_t = ||\mathbf{u} - \sigma_b(\hat{\mathbf{y}})||_t$, because by construction $\mathbf{I}_t(\mathbb{L}_{t,b}(\hat{\mathbf{y}})) = \mathbf{I}_t(\sigma_b(\hat{\mathbf{y}}))$. Hence,

$$W \geq \frac{||\mathbf{u}||_t - ||\mathbf{u} - \sigma_b(\mathbf{y})||_t}{||\mathbf{u}||_t + ||\mathbf{u} - \sigma_b(\hat{\mathbf{y}})||_t}. \tag{12}$$

Note also that $||\mathbf{u} - \sigma_b(\mathbf{y})||_t$ is small, especially with respect to the size of $||\mathbf{u}||_t$. Similarly, by the definition of $\hat{\mathbf{y}}$ in (9), $||\mathbf{u} - \sigma_b(\hat{\mathbf{y}})||_t$ is small.

Next, consider the case $W > 1$. Then, inequality (10) implies

$$||\mathbf{u} - \sigma_b(\mathbf{y})||_t \geq (W - 1)||\mathbf{u}||_t - W||\mathbf{u} - \frac{1}{W}\sigma_b(\mathbf{y}))||_t. \tag{13}$$

Introducing $\mathbb{L}_{t,b}(x)$ as in the previous case, we get

$$||\mathbf{u} - \frac{1}{W}\sigma_b(\mathbf{y}))||_t = ||\mathbf{u} - \frac{1}{W}\mathbb{L}_{t,b}(\mathbf{y}) + \frac{1}{W}\mathbb{L}_{t,b}(\mathbf{y}) - \frac{1}{W}\sigma_b(\mathbf{y}))||_t$$

Thus,

$$||\mathbf{u} - \frac{1}{W}\sigma_b(\mathbf{y}))||_t \leq ||\mathbf{u} - \mathbb{L}_{t,b}(\hat{\mathbf{y}})||_t + \frac{1}{W}||\mathbb{L}_{t,b}(\mathbf{y}) - \sigma_b(\mathbf{y}))||_t.$$

As we observed above, $W^{-1}||\mathbb{L}_{t,b}(\mathbf{y}) - \sigma_b(\mathbf{y}))||_t = 0$ and $||\mathbf{u} - \mathbb{L}_{t,b}(\hat{\mathbf{y}})||_t = ||\mathbf{u} - \sigma_b(\hat{\mathbf{y}})||_t$. Hence,

$$||\mathbf{u} - \frac{1}{W}\sigma_b(\mathbf{y}))||_t \leq ||\mathbf{u} - \sigma_b(\hat{\mathbf{y}})||_t.$$

Substituting this into inequality (13) gives

$$||\mathbf{u} - \sigma_b(\mathbf{y})||_t \geq (W - 1)||\mathbf{u}||_t - W||\mathbf{u} - \sigma_b(\hat{\mathbf{y}})||_t.$$

From here we get

$$||\mathbf{u} - \sigma_b(\mathbf{y})||_t + ||\mathbf{u}||_t \geq W(||\mathbf{u}||_t - ||\mathbf{u} - \sigma_b(\hat{\mathbf{y}})||_t).$$

Note that $||\mathbf{u} - \sigma_b(\mathbf{y})||_t$ and $||\mathbf{u} - \sigma_b(\hat{\mathbf{y}})||_t$ are small relative to $||\mathbf{u}||_t$, which in turn means that $||\mathbf{u}||_t - ||\mathbf{u} - \sigma_b(\hat{\mathbf{y}})||_t > 0$ and not too far from $||\mathbf{u}||_t$. This implies that

$$W \leq \frac{||\mathbf{u}||_t + ||\mathbf{u} - \sigma_b(\mathbf{y})||_t}{||\mathbf{u}||_t - ||\mathbf{u} - \sigma_b(\hat{\mathbf{y}})||_t}. \tag{14}$$

Thus, we have proved the following theorem.

Theorem 1. *Let $\mathbf{u}$ be a binary function over $\mathbb{D}$ and $\mathbf{y}$ be the combined predictor (1) that approximates it. Let $\hat{\mathbf{y}}$ be the interpolation predictor (9). Let $t \in (0, 1)$ be the threshold (3). Then, $W = \sum_{i=1}^{K} w_i$ satisfies:*

$$\frac{||\mathbf{u}||_t - ||\mathbf{u} - \sigma_b(\mathbf{y})||_t}{||\mathbf{u}||_t + ||\mathbf{u} - \sigma_b(\hat{\mathbf{y}})||_t} \leq W \leq \frac{||\mathbf{u}||_t + ||\mathbf{u} - \sigma_b(\mathbf{y})||_t}{||\mathbf{u}||_t - ||\mathbf{u} - \sigma_b(\hat{\mathbf{y}})||_t}. \tag{15}$$

Proof. Combine (12) and (14) to obtain (15).

Note: *The theorem justifies our approach of utilizing only constraints that reflect the natural mechanisms of the SS by guaranteeing balanced and bound weights for combining the predictors, without the artificial interpolating constraint (8).*

Note: *The result of the above theorem is general and applies to binary classification problems involving predictors $\mathbf{y}_i$ in other application domains, beyond NLP sentiment analysis. This result can also be extended to multi-class classifications based on the well-known conversion of any multi-class classification problem to a binary classification problem using the **one-vs-rest** method.*

2.2   Bayesian Decision Rule Combiners

Here we consider some of the Bayesian rule combiners in [22], in particular the **Sum, Average, Majority Vote**, and **Max** rules. Kittler et al. [22] present a systematic approach to deriving the rules but acknowledge that some of the assumptions used to develop their combination rules are too restrictive for many practical applications. We present computational results from applying these rules in Sect. 3

2.3   A Heuristic-Hybrid Combiner

The idea here is to select the best model, e.g., the one with highest accuracy on the train dataset, and use it as a base model. Then use the prediction of the base model as the prediction of the combiner unless its confidence level drops below a predefined threshold value θ. In that case, use instead the predictions from the other auxiliary models and combine them using a Bayesian decision rule from [22], e.g., **Sum, Majority Vote, Average**, and **Max**.

Generally speaking, in cases where the comparison between the candidate models is inconclusive, the choice of the base and auxiliary models may be approached analogously to how humans interpret ambiguous voice: do they trust more the deciphering of the words or the evaluation of the facial expression of the speaker to decide what they mean? Some people may choose to weigh the words heavier than the voice in a given circumstance, others may opt the other way around. However, it is always important to be aware of the limitations the models may have in the context of the potential application.

3 Computational Results

In this section, we begin with an overview and performance of the individual components of the architecture. The individual components are neural network models that are built with the same corpus. Then we present the computational results obtained with our proposed architecture that combines the results from the above components.

To address the issue of accuracy fluctuation due to the stochastic nature in neural network models, we use 5-folds cross-validation in reporting individual model performance. For our proposed SSNet combiner, we reuse the 5 predictions generated from 5 folds in each participant model as input to train the combiner. The goal is to control the performance variation brought in by randomness from the models, so we use 5 different sets of inputs to train SSNet 5 times, all with the same architecture. We go even further by also training the combiner multiple times using the same input. For example, for each of the 5 predictions, we repeat the training k times, and, therefore, our total number of combiner training rounds is $5k$. In each training round we use the entire 25 000 test reviews to get a test accuracy. Then we use the mean average of accuracy computed over the $5k$ results as our final score for SSNet. We choose $k = 30$ in our experiments.

All experiments reported here are developed in Python 3.x with the TensorFlow 2.x [15] library. Research code is available at https://github.com/usnistgov/STVM_NLP_Research. The models were trained on a professional Graphics Processing Unit (GPU) cluster having 8 NVIDIA Tesla V100 (32 GB each). The inference was carried on a 2015 MacBook Pro with 2.5 GHz Intel Core i7 and 16 GB RAM *without* Graphics Processing Unit (GPU) acceleration.

3.1 Datasets

When evaluating the performance of machine learning models, one has to keep in mind that the results depend heavily not only on the model but the dataset it was trained on. The bigger and better the training dataset, the better the results. In practice, one needs to analyze the training dataset and improve its quality before commencing the benchmarking. However, in our case we are focused on evaluating the performance characteristics of the different models and their combinations. So, we benchmark the performance differences using identical data for all in order to make objective comparisons. We used the labeled Stanford Large

Movie Review dataset (SLMRD) [1] in our experiments, because it is sufficiently large, well-curated, and challenging - see the discussion in Sect. 1.

Our experiments can be divided into two parts. The first part is the training of the individual participating models. The second part combines the participating models using our proposed sagittal stratum inspired neural network (SSNet) classifier. This allows for a clear and objective assessment of the advantages the proposed architecture offers compared to individual models.

The SLMRD dataset contains 25 000 labeled train reviews and 25 000 labeled test reviews.

We split the training data following the 5-folds cross-validation mechanism: (i) split the 25 000 train reviews into 5 folds; (ii) hold out each fold of 5 000 as validation data and use the remaining 20 000 reviews to train individual models. This generates 5 sets of predictions for each model. Then, we iterate through each set from all individual models and feed them as input to SSNet combiner to train it multiple times. In each trained classifier, we apply the entire test dataset with 25 000 reviews to measure its performance based on the accuracy of prediction. Finally, we use the mean average of these runs to report the skill of SSNet. By doing this, we hope we can compensate for the randomness brought by neural network models and provide a fair result.

Please note this split size (20K/5K) between training and validation is based on conventional best practices and is heuristic in nature. When designing the models and selecting the train dataset one needs to balance the number of trainable parameters in each model and the size of the training dataset to avoid under- and over-fitting. We experimented with other split ratios using Train-Test split, e.g., 24K/1K, 23K/2K, 22K/3K, 21K/4K, 17.5K/7.5K, and the results were very similar to those presented below, hence we omitted these details. In all experiments presented in this section, we ensured that the models are trained properly.

3.2   Baseline Performance from Individual Models

The main idea behind the architecture in Sect. 2 is to incorporate separate views on the same corpus. In our experiments we used four models enumerated as M_i $\forall i \in \{1, ..., 4\}$. In this section, we present an overview of the four models and their individual performance. We use 5-folds cross-validation to measure performance, i.e., using 20 000 reviews in training and 5 000 reviews in validation in each fold. Then, we provide results using the mean average of validation accuracy and the mean average of test accuracy on the entire 25 000 reviews in the test dataset.

BowTie. We use as M_1 the model described in [39]. It is based on the well-known bag-of-words model combined with word polarity. This model produces good results on the corpora [1,21]. Here we introduced some minor tweaks to this model by incorporating few LSTM layers. This resulted in a small increase in the accuracy of the model.

We obtained a mean average of **89.55%** validation accuracy and a mean average of **88.00%** accuracy on the entire 25 000 reviews in the test dataset.

BLSTM with Attention and Glove Embeddings. In this model (M_2), we use the glove embedding [32] on the dataset. While many other researchers in this area have obtained results by simply using LSTM or BLSTM with [32]; we found that the corpora [1,21] contain reviews with nuances that are difficult to learn by simply passing the embeddings through LSTM or BLSTM. The models tend to learn the pattern of the inputs rather than the underlying meaning or semantics. This is often the cause of overfitting in a wide range of NLP problems. Further, in the case of sentiment analysis, certain words and their position in the sentence play extremely important role in determining the overall meaning. It is difficult to incorporate the positional semantics of these words using normal LSTM or BLSTM. The family of attention mechanisms [2,16,25] provides a direction to formulate such difficult semantics into the model. We revised the aforementioned attention mechanism to incorporate positional and sentimental semantics for sentences having large number of words.

Let $\overrightarrow{b}$ and $\overleftarrow{b}$ be the forward and the backward components of BLSTM and k be the sequence length, then $h = [\overrightarrow{b}, \overleftarrow{b}]$ where $dim(h) \in \mathbb{R}^{k \times (|\overrightarrow{b}| + |\overleftarrow{b}|)}$. We define the following equations to describe the attention mechanism used in this paper:

$$\begin{aligned}
h' &= tanh(h) \\
h' &= softmax(h') \\
C_v &= h \odot h' \\
M &= \sum_k C_v
\end{aligned} \tag{16}$$

The third expression in the Eq. 16 represents the context vector C_v, which we sum up in the fourth expression over the sequence to remove stochastic behavior, hence $dim(M) \in \mathbb{R}^{(|\overrightarrow{b}| + |\overleftarrow{b}|)}$. To correctly calculate the *Hadamard product*, the vector space of h' must be expanded after performing the *softmax* operation. This strategy inside the attention mechanism establishes a probabilistic vector space incorporating the positional and the sentimental semantics into M_2.

Our investigation showed that understanding nuances is not very computationally intensive but rather a logically inferential task, hence we used a low vector space, i.e., 100 of the glove embeddings with sentence length equal to 800. This resulted in a small and effective model. We would also like to emphasize that the semantic structure of the language as understood by human brain is closely related to word embeddings (rather than language modeling). Hence, we did not incorporate any language modeling techniques in this architecture.

We obtained a mean average of **90.11%** validation accuracy and a mean average of **89.78%** accuracy on the entire 25 000 reviews in the test dataset.

BERT. BERT (Bidirectional Encoder Representations from Transformers) is the well-known large pre-trained model [14]. The BERT model is pre-trained on the minimally-filtered real-world text from Wikipedia (en.wikipedia.org) and

BooksCorpus [41]. In this model (M_3), we fine-tuned BERT (https://tfhub.
dev/tensorflow/bert_en_uncased_L-12_H-768_A-12/2) using SLMRD. The
instance of BERT we used in our experiments has a maximum sequence length
of 512. Please note that the average length of SLMRD is less than 300 words,
but several go over 3000 words. This means that any text longer than 510 tokens
(two required special tokens are added by BERT) gets truncated.

We obtained a mean average of **92.87%** validation accuracy, and a mean
average of **93.10%** accuracy on the entire 25 000 reviews in the test dataset.

Universal Sentence Encoder (USE). In this model (M_4), we experimented
with the Universal Sentence Encoder [7] in embedding text. USE takes variable
length text as input and encodes text into high-dimensional vectors that can be
used for NLP tasks such as text classification, semantic similarity, etc. We use the
highest allowed dimension of 512 in embedding text using USE (https://tfhub.
dev/google/universal-sentence-encoder/4) in our training with SLMRD dataset.

We obtained a mean average of **88.98%** validation accuracy and a mean
average of **88.22%** accuracy on the entire 25 000 reviews in the test dataset.

Performance Summary of Individual Models. Table 1 summarizes individual model performance based on the training on the split dataset with 20
000 train reviews and on the validation on the rest 5 000 train reviews. The
baseline performance is the test accuracy over the entire 25 000 reviews in the
test dataset. M_3(BERT) achieves the best performance. Please note standard
deviation (stdev) is followed after each mean accuracy across 5 folds.

Table 1. Performance of individual models:

Individual models train on 20K	Mean validation accuracy (%) on 5K with stdev (SD)	Mean accuracy (%) on test (25K) with stdev (SD)
M_1 (BowTie)	89.55 (0.245)	88.00 (0.290)
M_2 (BLSTM)	90.11 (0.68)	89.78 (0.458)
M_3 (BERT)	**92.87 (0.407)**	**93.10 (0.434)**
M_4 (USE)	88.98 (0.150)	88.22 (0.155)

3.3   Performance of Model Combiners

In this section we describe our experiments and present the computational results
on proposed combiners. As discussed in previous sections, we have four models
and three approaches to combine them. We evaluate each of the combiners on the
basis of the accuracy achieved on the test dataset, consistent with the measurement criteria adopted for the performance of the individual models in Table 1.
The combiner models train optimal weights $\{w_i\}_{i=1}^4$ for combining individual
models using 20K/5K split in train dataset. First, get prediction probabilities

of 5 000 train reviews from individual models as described in Sect. 3.2. Please note these individual models are trained using 20 000 train reviews. Each prediction probability value ranges from 0 to 1. Second, feed the 5 000 probability values to the combiner architecture as input and produce trained combining weights as the output. Finally, use the trained weights to combine the prediction probabilities of 25 000 test reviews produced from the same individual models. The combined probability value is mapped to positive sentiment if it is above **0.5**; otherwise it is mapped to negative sentiment. The results of the respective combiners are shown in Tables 2, 4, and 5. Similar to Sect. 3.2, we use mean test accuracy from multiple runs to report the results. Specifically, we repeated training the combiners **30** times using predictions in each fold generated from 5-folds cross-validation. Similar to Table 1, standard deviation (stdev) is shown after each mean accuracy value across all repeated runs.

Neural Network Combiner. Table 2 shows the result obtained using the neural network combiner 2.1. Table 3 shows the trained combining weights. The neural network model is made up of a linear layer (without bias) followed by the sigmoid layer. Our combiner attained a maximum accuracy of **93.87%**. The accuracy attained from the various individual model combinations varies but in all cases the combined model delivered higher prediction accuracy than any of the underlying individual models.

Table 2. Neural Network Combiner Accuracy: A linear layer (without bias) and a sigmoid layer were used for this experiment. The maximum accuracy achieved is **93.87%**.

Combined models	Mean accuracy (%) on test (25K) with stdev (SD)
$M_{1,2}$	90.80 (0.3201)
$M_{1,3}$	93.64 (0.2453)
$M_{1,4}$	89.89 (0.0847)
$M_{2,3}$	93.68 (0.1620)
$M_{2,4}$	91.14 (0.2337)
$M_{3,4}$	93.66 (0.2721)
$M_{1,2,3}$	93.76 (0.1966)
$M_{1,2,4}$	91.29 (0.2961)
$M_{1,3,4}$	93.82 (0.2652)
$M_{2,3,4}$	93.81 (0.2286)
$\mathbf{M_{1,2,3,4}}$	**93.87 (0.1832)**

Figure 3 shows a graph of the train and test accuracy in addition to the test accuracy reported in Table 2 to illustrate that our models were trained appropriately.

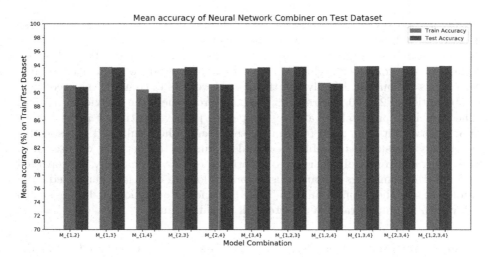

Fig. 3. Mean train accuracy vs. Mean test accuracy in Neural Network Combiner. The plot shows the comparison of mean train accuracy and mean test accuracy for all the model combinations for the neural net combiner.

Table 3. Neural network combiner mean weights:

Combined models	w_{M_1}	w_{M_2}	w_{M_3}	w_{M_4}
$M_{1,2}$	0.837 207 982	0.924 092 82	–	–
$M_{1,3}$	0.862 401 351	–	1.218 124 133	–
$M_{1,4}$	1.100 311 01	–	–	0.948 121 23
$M_{2,3}$	–	0.843 419 33	1.291 315 655	–
$M_{2,4}$	–	0.881 002 23	–	0.831 234 501
$M_{3,4}$	–	–	1.128 714 311	0.599 008 786
$M_{1,2,3}$	0.636 317 512	0.603 436 005	1.325 881 07	–
$M_{1,2,4}$	0.799 691 307	0.971 208 091	–	0.779 012 99
$M_{1,3,4}$	0.651 801 401	–	1.289 575 511	0.500 074 48
$M_{2,3,4}$	–	0.533 645 1	1.141 277 1	0.540 118 14
$M_{1,2,3,4}$	0.451 013 505	0.589 404 309	1.242 073 622	0.346 501 002

One important element of our experiments is to confirm that the computed weights of the combined predictor in Sect. 2.1 conform to the estimate in (15). The coefficients computed for the combinations in Table 2 are shown in Table 3, and they are in agreement with the estimate (15). Depending on the optimizer configured in the computational environment [15] we used for these experiments, some coefficients subject to the constraint 2 may get set to zero if they go negative in any step of the training process. This is undesirable because the training process may not be able to recover well from such an event, and this would effectively disable the contribution of the corresponding contributing model in the combination. To improve the stability of the training process one may use different optimizers from the set of available options in their computational environment. For example, the environment [15] offers several good optimizers that can greatly reduce the occurrence of such events, e.g., the adaptive momentum (ADAM) optimizer, the Nesterov adaptive momentum (NADAM) optimizer, and the Root Mean Square Propagation (RMSPRop) optimizer. In addition, one may incorporate L_2-regularization in the dense layer predictor to improve the stability and increase the accuracy of the resulting combiner. We used ADAM with a L_2-weight of **0.039** for the computations in Tables 2 and 3.

Bayesian Decision Rule Combiner. Here we present computational results from applying the Bayesian rules from [22]. The results in Table 4 are for the **Max, Avg, Sum**, and **Majority Vote** rules denoted as *max, avg, sum*, and *maj* correspondingly. We did not use the **Majority Vote** rule in the case of using two or four models, as is shown in Table 4, because of the potential tie in the vote. The different rules produced identical results when combining only two models but started to differentiate when the number of combined models increased. This is likely due to the low variance in the prediction probabilities with only a few models. Interestingly, in our case the **Max** rule tended to produce the highest accuracy unlike the results in [22] where the **Sum** rule was the best performer. This combined model performed well for the various combinations of individual models and rules.

Table 4. Accuracy of the Bayesian decision rule combiner: The indication **all** for the rule used means that all rules except *maj* produced the same result. The *maj* rule was **not** used in the case of combining an even number of models to avoid a tie in the vote. The maximum accuracy achieved is **93.63%**.

Combined models	Rule used	Mean accuracy (%) on test (25K) with stdev (SD)
$M_{1,2}$	all	90.69 (0.4052)
$M_{1,3}$	all	93.46 (0.4320)
$M_{1,4}$	all	89.86 (0.0585)
$M_{2,3}$	all	93.56 (0.2450)
$M_{2,4}$	all	91.03 (0.1974)
$M_{3,4}$	all	93.52 (0.2304)
$M_{1,2,3}$	max	93.58 (0.2829)
	avg	92.93 (0.3248)
	sum	92.93 (0.3248)
	maj	92.39 (0.2828)

(*continued*)

Table 4. (*continued*)

Combined models	Rule used	Mean accuracy (%) on test (25K) with stdev (SD)
$M_{1,2,4}$	max	91.16 (0.1707)
	avg	91.12 (0.2860)
	sum	91.12 (0.2860)
	maj	90.71 (0.2687)
$M_{1,3,4}$	max	93.50 (0.2657)
	avg	92.46 (0.2237)
	sum	92.46 (0.2237)
	maj	91.94 (0.1597)
$\mathbf{M_{2,3,4}}$	**max**	**93.63 (0.2326)**
	avg	93.06 (0.2277)
	sum	93.06 (0.2277)
	maj	92.67 (0.1875)
$M_{1,2,3,4}$	max	93.60 (0.2443)
	avg	92.89 (0.2154)
	sum	92.89 (0.2154)

Heuristic-Hybrid Combiner. Table 5 shows the results obtained using the heuristic-hybrid combiner. Each of the individual models is used as base, and when its prediction probability falls below θ, where $0.5 < \theta < 1$, then combinations of the auxiliary models are used for the prediction. We use the Bayesian decision rules from [22] to compute a prediction with the auxiliary models. The maximum accuracy achieved on the test dataset is **93.73%** with model M_3 as base and models M_1, M_2 and M_4 as auxiliary. The experimental data in Table 5 bear out the recommendation from Sect. 2.3 to use the best model as base. The results for M_3 as base show a good balance of collaboration with the auxiliary models with $\theta = 0.91$ to deliver the best accuracy result. Again, the accuracy obtained by the *max* rule tended to perform best. The maximum accuracy attained by this combiner was higher than that of the Bayesian Decision Rule combiners from [22], cf. Table 4, and in this sense our heuristic-hybrid combiner performed better.

Table 5. Heuristic Hybrid Combiner: Each model was used as a base model while *max*, *avg*, *sum*, and *maj* rules were used for predicting with the auxiliary models when the confidence of the base model fell below the threshold θ. The maximum accuracy of **93.73%** was attained with M_3 as the base model for the rule: *max*.

Combined models				Mean accuracy (%) on test
Base	Auxiliary	Rule used	Mean threshold θ	(25K) with stdev (SD)
M_1	M_2	–	0.91	90.19 (0.3709)
	M_3	–	0.97	93.09 (0.4306)
	M_4	–	0.85	89.49 (0.1617)
	$M_{2,3}$	max	0.99	93.49 (0.3107)
		avg	0.99	93.49 (0.3107)
		sum	0.99	93.49 (0.3107)
	$M_{2,4}$	max	0.96	91.06 (0.1698)
		avg	0.96	91.06 (0.1698)
		sum	0.96	91.06 (0.1698)
	$M_{3,4}$	max	0.99	93.45 (0.2848)
		avg	0.99	93.45 (0.2848)
		sum	0.99	93.45 (0.2848)
	$M_{2,3,4}$	max	0.99	93.56 (0.2872)
		avg	0.99	93.00 (0.2462)
		sum	0.99	93.00 (0.2462)
		maj	0.98	92.59 (0.1596)
M_2	M_1	–	0.82	90.49 (0.3983)
	M_3	–	0.98	93.28 (0.3105)
	M_4	–	0.81	90.76 (0.3105)
	$M_{1,3}$	max	0.99	93.47 (0.3638)
		avg	0.99	93.47 (0.3638)
		sum	0.99	93.47 (0.3638)
	$M_{1,4}$	max	0.88	91.02 (0.2680)
		avg	0.88	91.02 (0.2680)
		sum	0.88	91.02 (0.2680)
	$M_{3,4}$	max	0.98	93.53 (0.2389)
		avg	0.98	93.53 (0.2389)
		sum	0.98	93.53 (0.2389)
	$M_{1,3,4}$	max	0.99	93.50 (0.2535)
		avg	0.97	92.57 (0.1870)
		sum	0.97	92.57 (0.1870)
		maj	0.97	92.18 (0.1497)

(continued)

Table 5. (*continued*)

Combined models				Mean accuracy (%) on test
Base	Auxiliary	Rule used	Mean threshold θ	(25K) with stdev (SD)
M_3	M_1	–	0.92	93.36 (0.3938)
	M_2	–	0.85	93.47 (0.2438)
	M_4	–	0.90	93.50 (0.2670)
	$M_{1,2}$	max	0.91	93.58 (0.3228)
		avg	0.91	93.58 (0.3228)
		sum	0.91	93.58 (0.3228)
	$M_{1,4}$	max	0.91	93.60 (0.3346)
		avg	0.91	93.60 (0.3346)
		sum	0.91	93.60 (0.3346)
	$M_{2,4}$	max	0.91	93.71 (0.3039)
		avg	0.91	93.71 (0.3039)
		sum	0.91	93.71 (0.3039)
	$M_{1,2,4}$	**max**	**0.91**	**93.73 (0.3259)**
		avg	0.91	93.68 (0.3320)
		sum	0.91	93.68 (0.3320)
		maj	0.91	93.62 (0.3141)
M_4	M_1	–	0.89	89.55 (0.1175)
	M_2	–	0.96	90.72 (0.2550)
	M_3	–	0.99	93.20 (0.2550)
	$M_{1,2}$	max	0.97	90.98 (0.3637)
		avg	0.97	90.98 (0.3637)
		sum	0.97	90.98 (0.3637)
	$M_{1,3}$	max	0.99	93.30 (0.3262)
		avg	0.99	93.30 (0.3262)
		sum	0.99	93.30 (0.3262)
	$M_{2,3}$	max	0.99	93.30 (0.1960)
		avg	0.99	93.42 (0.1960)
		sum	0.99	93.42 (0.1960)
	$M_{1,2,3}$	max	0.99	93.42 (0.2397)
		avg	0.99	92.82 (0.3129)
		sum	0.99	92.82 (0.3129)
		maj	0.99	92.36 (0.2764)

4   Conclusions and Next Steps

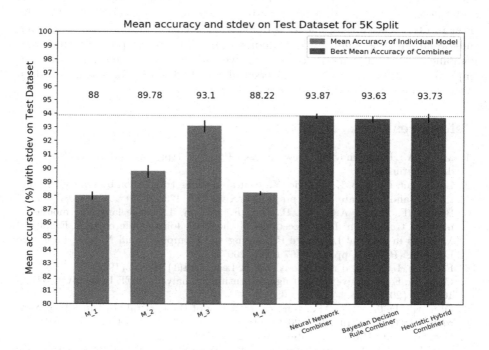

Fig. 4. Accuracy on test dataset for proposed methods. The plot shows the mean accuracy achieved by the individual models with their standard deviation and the best mean accuracy and the standard deviation for the combiner when each fold was run 30 iterations.

We successfully followed our intuition inspired by the biological underpinning of the human brain for understanding sarcasm to construct a neural network architecture for sentiment analysis. We considered novel systematic and heuristic-hybrid implementations of the framework and were able to provide theoretical justification for the state-of-the-art computational performance of the best systematic solution based on the neural network dense layer. Our heuristic-hybrid solution closely followed the intuition inspired by the biological underpinnings of our brain while at the same time relied on a systematic technique for combining the predictions of the auxiliary models using well-known Bayesian rules. This approach delivered performance results very close to those of the best combined predictor. Thus, our two novel combined models outperformed not only each individual auxiliary model in terms of accuracy and robustness but also the legacy combiner models from the literature. A graphical comparison of the three approaches is shown in Fig. 4.

The combiners we considered are built on the notion that if the combined models are sufficiently decorrelated then the combination can mitigate some of the shortcomings of the individual models. Our approach to combining models and the theoretical result for the systemic combiner are generic and may be used in other classifier application domains. Moreover, in our framework each individual model is a pluggable component, and this opens up the possibility to combine diverse multi-modal inputs to solve various machine learning tasks and improve the robustness against adversarial attacks tailored for specific models. We plan to investigate these aspects in the future.

References

1. Maas, A.: Large movie review dataset (2011). http://ai.stanford.edu/~amaas/data/sentiment/
2. Bahdanau, D., Cho, K., Bengio, Y.: Neural machine translation by jointly learning to align and translate. arXiv preprint arXiv:1409.0473 (2014)
3. Brants, T., Popat, A.C., Xu, P., Och, F.J., Dean, J.: Large language models in machine translation. In: Proceedings of the 2007 Joint Conference on Empirical Methods in Natural Language Processing and Computational Natural Language Learning (Prague), pp. 858–867 (June 2007)
4. Breiman, L.: Stacked regressions. Mach. Learn. **24**(1), 49–64 (1996)
5. Cambria, E.: Affective computing and sentiment analysis. IEEE Intell. Syst. **31**(2), 102–107 (2016)
6. Di Carlo, D.T., et al.: Microsurgical anatomy of the sagittal stratum. Acta Neurochir. **161**(11), 2319–2327 (2019). https://doi.org/10.1007/s00701-019-04019-8
7. Cer, D., et al.: Universal sentence encoder (2018)
8. Cho, K., et al.: Learning phrase representations using RNN encoder-decoder for statistical machine translation. arXiv preprint arXiv:1406.1078 (2014)
9. Chomsky, N.: Center for brains minds + machines, research meeting: language and evolution (May 2017). https://youtu.be/kFR0LW002ig
10. Collobert, R., Weston, J.: A unified architecture for natural language processing: deep neural networks with multitask learning. In: Proceedings of the 25th International Conference on Machine Learning, pp. 160–167 (2008)
11. Conneau, A., Kiela, D., Schwenk, H., Barrault, L., Bordes, A.: Supervised learning of universal sentence representations from natural language inference data. In: Proceedings of the 2017 Conference on Emprical Methods in Natural Language Processing, Copenhagen, Denmark, 7–11 September, pp. 670–680. Association of Computational Linguistics (2017). https://arxiv.org/abs/1705.02364v5
12. D'Amour, A., et al.: Underspecification presents challenges for credibility in modern machine learning. Preprint arXiv:2011.03395 (2020)
13. Deng, L., Hinton, G., Kingsbury, B.: New types of deep neural network learning for speech recognition and related applications: an overview. In: 2013 IEEE International Conference on Acoustics, Speech and Signal Processing, pp. 8599–8603 (2013)
14. Devlin, J., Chang, M.W., Lee, K., Toutanova, K.: BERT: pre-training of deep bidirectional transformers for language understanding. arXiv preprint arXiv:1810.04805v2 (2019)
15. Google Brain Team: Open source library for ML models (2020). https://www.tensorflow.org/

16. Graves, A., Wayne, G., Danihelka, I.: Neural Turing Machines. arXiv preprint arXiv:1410.5401 (2014)
17. Heaven, W.D.: The way we train AI is fundamentally flawed. MIT Technol. Rev., November 2020. https://www.technologyreview.com/2020/11/18/1012234/training-machine-learning-broken-real-world-heath-nlp-computer-vision/
18. Hoang, M., Bihorac, O.A.: Supervised learning of universal sentence representations from natural language inference data. In: Proceedings of the 22nd Nordic Conference on Computational Linguistics (NoDaLiDa), Turku, Finland, 30 September–2 October, pp. 187–196. Linköping University Electronic Press (2019)
19. Hochreiter, S., Schmidhuber, J.: Long short-term memory. Neural Comput. **9**(8), 1735–1780 (1997)
20. Howard, J., Ruder, S.: Universal language model fine-tuning for text classification. arXiv preprint arXiv:1801.06146 (2018)
21. Keras Documentation: IMDB movie reviews sentiment classification (2018). https://keras.io/datasets/
22. Kittler, J., Hatef, M., Duin, R.P., Matas, J.: On combining classifiers. IEEE Trans. Pattern Anal. Mach. Intell. **20**(3), 226–239 (1998)
23. Kumar, A., Kim, J., Lyndon, D., Fulham, M., Feng, D.: An ensemble of fine-tuned convolutional neural networks for medical image classification. IEEE J. Biomed. Health Inform. **21**(1), 31–40 (2017)
24. LeBlanc, M., Tibshirani, R.: Combining estimates in regression and classification. J. Am. Stat. Assoc. **91**(436), 1641–1650 (1996)
25. Luong, M.T., Pham, H., Manning, C.D.: Effective approaches to attention-based neural machine translation. arXiv preprint arXiv:1508.04025 (2015)
26. Magerman, D.M.: Learning grammatical structure using statistical decision-trees. In: Miclet, L., de la Higuera, C. (eds.) ICGI 1996. LNCS, vol. 1147, pp. 1–21. Springer, Heidelberg (1996). https://doi.org/10.1007/BFb0033339
27. Màrquez, L., Rodríguez, H.: Part-of-speech tagging using decision trees. In: Nédellec, C., Rouveirol, C. (eds.) ECML 1998. LNCS, vol. 1398, pp. 25–36. Springer, Heidelberg (1998). https://doi.org/10.1007/BFb0026668
28. Mikolov, T., Sutskever, I., Chen, K., Corrado, G., Dean, J.: Distributed representations of words and phrases and their compositionality. In: Advances in Neural Information Processing Systems, pp. 3111–3119 (2013). https://arxiv.org/abs/1310.4546
29. Minaee, S., Kalchbrenner, N., Cambria, E., Nikzad, N., Chenaghlu, M., Gao, J.: Deep learning based text classification: a comprehensive review (2020)
30. Opitz, D., Maclin, R.: Popular ensemble methods: an empirical study. J. Artif. Int. Res. **11**(1), 169–198 (1999)
31. Paul, R., Hall, L., Goldgof, D., Schabath, M., Gillies, R.: Predicting nodule malignancy using a CNN ensemble approach. In: 2018 International Joint Conference on Neural Networks (IJCNN), pp. 1–8. IEEE (2018)
32. Pennington, J., Socher, R., Manning, C.D.: GloVe: global vectors for word representation. In: Empirical Methods in Natural Language Processing (EMNLP), pp. 1532–1543 (2014). http://www.aclweb.org/anthology/D14-1162
33. Perez, F., Avila, S., Valle, E.: Solo or ensemble? Choosing a CNN architecture for melanoma classification. In: Proceedings of the IEEE Conference on Computer Vision and Pattern Recognition Workshops (2019)
34. Pexman, P.M.: How do we understand sarcasm? Front. Young Mind. **6**(56), 1–8 (2018). https://doi.org/10.3389/frym.2018.00056

35. Savelli, B., Bria, A., Molinara, M., Marrocco, C., Tortorella, F.: A multi-context CNN ensemble for small lesion detection. Artif. Intell. Med. **103**, 101749 (2020). https://doi.org/10.1016/j.artmed.2019.101749. http://www.sciencedirect.com/science/article/pii/S0933365719303082

36. Schuster, M., Paliwal, K.K.: Bidirectional recurrent neural networks. IEEE Trans. Sig. Process. **45**(11), 2673–2681 (1997)

37. Sun, C., Huang, L., Qiu, X.: Utilizing BERT for aspect-based sentiment analysis via constructing auxiliary sentence. In: Proceedings of the 2019 Conference of the North American Chapter of the Association for Computational Linguistics: Human Language Technologies, Volume 1 (Long and Short Papers), Minneapolis, Minnesota, pp. 380–385. Association for Computational Linguistics (June 2019). https://doi.org/10.18653/v1/N19-1035. https://www.aclweb.org/anthology/N19-1035

38. Turing, A.M.: I. - Computing machinery and intelligence. Mind **LIX**(236), 433–460 (1950). https://doi.org/10.1093/mind/LIX.236.433

39. Vassilev, A.: BowTie - a deep learning feedforward neural network for sentiment analysis. In: Nicosia, G., Pardalos, P., Umeton, R., Giuffrida, G., Sciacca, V. (eds.) LOD 2019. LNCS, vol. 11943, pp. 360–371. Springer, Cham (2019). https://doi.org/10.1007/978-3-030-37599-7_30

40. Voelker, A.R., Kajić, I., Eliasmith, C.: Legendre memory units: Continuous-time representation in recurrent neural networks. In: Advances in Neural Information Processing Systems (2019). https://papers.nips.cc/paper/9689-legendre-memory-units-continuous-time-representation-in-recurrent-neural-networks

41. Wolfram Neural Net Repository: BookCorpus dataset (2019). https://resources.wolframcloud.com/NeuralNetRepository/resources/BERT-Trained-on-BookCorpus-and-English-Wikipedia-Data

42. Yang, Z., Dai, Z., Yang, Y., Carbonell, J., Salakhutdinov, R.R., Le, Q.V.: XLNet: generalized autoregressive pretraining for language understanding. In: Advances in Neural Information Processing Systems, pp. 5753–5763 (2019)

ODIN: Pluggable Meta-annotations and Metrics for the Diagnosis of Classification and Localization

Rocio Nahime Torres[✉], Federico Milani, and Piero Fraternali

Politecnico di Milano, Piazza Leonardo da Vinci, 32, Milano, Italy
{rocionahime.torres,federico.milani,piero.fraternali}@polimi.it

Abstract. Machine Learning (ML) tasks, especially Computer Vision (CV) ones, have greatly progressed after the introduction of Deep Neural Networks. Analyzing the performance of deep models is an open issue, addressed with techniques that inspect the response of inner network layers to given inputs. A complementary approach relies on ad-hoc meta-data added to the input and used to factor the performance into indicators sensitive to specific facets of the data. We present ODIN an open source diagnosis framework for generic ML classification tasks and for CV object detection and instance segmentation tasks that lets developers add meta-annotations to their data sets, compute performance metrics split by meta-annotation values, and visualize diagnosis reports. ODIN is agnostic to the training platform and input formats and can be extended with application- and domain-specific meta-annotations and metrics with almost no coding. It integrates a rapid annotation tool for classification and object detection data sets. In this paper, we exemplify ODIN through CV tasks, but the tool can be used for generic ML classification.

Keywords: Computer vision · Metrics · Evaluation · Diagnosis

1 Introduction

In ML the availability of data sets and open challenges allows the creation of baselines essential for progress. Benchmarks rely on standard metrics to compare alternative methods. However, the metrics used for assessing the end-to-end performance with a black-box approach may not be the most adequate ones for understanding the behavior of an architecture and for optimizing it for a certain data set or task. The analysis of performance can be pursued in two ways. On one side, model interpretation techniques aim at "opening the box" to assess the relationship between the input, the inner layers and the output. For example attention models capture the essential region of the input that have most impact on the inference [31]. On the other hand, it is possible to associate the images with *meta-annotations*, i.e., annotations that do not contribute to model

© Springer Nature Switzerland AG 2022
G. Nicosia et al. (Eds.): LOD 2021, LNCS 13163, pp. 383–398, 2022.
https://doi.org/10.1007/978-3-030-95467-3_28

training but can be exploited for understanding performance. Such performance-driven meta-annotations enable the computation of task- and data set-specific metrics that may help the diagnosis. As an example of meta-annotations used to fine tune standard metrics, the MS COCO data set [15] differentiates the Average Precision (AP) metric based on the size of the detected object (small, medium or large), permitting researchers to focus their improvement on the sub-classes where they expect the most gain. The work in [9] is a pioneering effort to exploit meta-annotations in the evaluation of detectors. The described method and tool help developers evaluate the impact on performance of selected dimensions of the data (object size, aspect ratio, visibility of parts, viewpoint) or of the errors (occlusion, wrong localization, confusion with other objects and with background). In [28] we followed the line of [9] and implemented a preliminary version of ODIN, a tool supporting the diagnosis of errors in object detection and instance segmentation components allowing the plug-in of meta-annotation types and metrics. In this paper, we extend the work in [28] with novel metrics and analysis reports and expand the analysis to classification, in addition to object detection and instance segmentation. The contribution of our work can be summarized as follows:

- We present ODIN, a tool for error diagnosis applicable to generic ML classification tasks and to CV object detection and instance segmentation tasks.
- We exploit the plug&play architecture of ODIN and add a broad set of off-the-shelf metrics and reports, also for classification tasks.
- We extend the user interface supporting the editing of annotations and meta-annotations (Fig. 1) to classification tasks, in addition to localization ones. The new User Interface (UI) can be used not only for meta-annotation editing but also for the creation of classification and object detection data sets.
- We add confidence calibration [7] as a novel type of analysis.
- We showcase the use of ODIN in the diagnosis of two classification scenarios.
- We release the code publicly[1]. ODIN is developed in Python, integrates directly with the MS COCO data set and is agnostic to the training platforms.

2   Related Work

Deep learning models are typically used and evaluated as black-boxes. Performance analysis exploits standard metrics (Accuracy, Precision, Recall, F1-Score or Average Precision) implemented off-the-shelf in most evaluation frameworks. Several works [10,18,20,21] explain the standard metrics and discuss issues and best practices. The standard metrics asses a model end-to-end and thus the problem arises of how to analyse its behavior to diagnose weaknesses and improve representation power and inference accuracy. The investigation of model behavior is pursued with two complementary approaches. One line of research aims at improving model interpretability, by studying the internal representations of

---

[1] https://github.com/rnt-pmi/odin.

deep models and their relation to the input [32]. An alternative approach is to study how the properties of the input samples influence performance. The latter approaches aim at factoring out performance indicators based on the properties of the input samples and at identifying the characteristics of the inputs with greatest impact on performance.

A first step towards the diagnostic use of objects properties is found in the MS COCO data set, where the computation of mean Average Precision (mAP) is differentiated based on object size: mAP_{small}, mAP_{medium} and mAP_{big}. This distinction can help diagnose problems and apply proper techniques, e.g. multi-scale object detection [5], to improve localization ability. The work in [9] introduces a more general approach to analyse errors in object detectors. The proposed framework exploits diagnosis-oriented metadata (called *meta-annotations*, in this paper) that can affect the model accuracy. The authors employ a fixed set of such meta-annotations: occlusion, size, shape, aspect ratio, and parts visibility. They show how decomposing the standard metrics into sub-metrics associated to a meta-annotation value helps understand model failures and focus redesign where the margin of improvement is higher. In [25] the authors present a diagnostic tool tailored to the study of pose estimation errors. The tool analyzes the influences of fixed object characteristics (e.g., visibility of parts, size, aspect ratio) on the detection and pose estimation performance and enables the study of the impact of different types of pose-related False Positives. In [1] the focus is on the localization of temporal actions in videos. The diagnosis method and tool allow False Positive (FP) and False Negative (FN) analyses and the estimation of the sensitivity of mAP-based metric to six action characteristics: context size, context distance, agreement, coverage, length, and the number of instances. In [19] the authors apply the original diagnostic methodology of [9] to the case of semantic segmentation but do not provide a public implementation of their toolkit. REVISE (REvealing VIsual biaSEs) [29] is a tool that permits the investigation of bias in image data sets along three dimensions: object-based (size, context, or diversity), gender-based, and geography-based (location). The set of properties is fixed and the tool aims at revealing biases in the visual data sets rather than at supporting the diagnosis of errors by models, addressing data set curators rather than model builders. TIDE [2] is a tool for error diagnosis in object detection and instance segmentation applicable across data sets and output prediction files. The focus is on the finer classification of detection and segmentation error types and on the provision of compact error summaries and meaningful impact reports. Unlike ODIN, TIDE purposely avoids resorting to meta-annotations of the input. Finally, the most recent version of the object detection evaluation toolkit by Padilla et al. [22] generalizes the previous version: it makes the framework independent of the input formats, adds novel object detection metrics and bounding box formats, and provides a novel spatio-temporal metric for object detection in video.

In some critical ML applications, where the output of the model is used to make complex and risky decisions, the reliability of predictions is crucial. This property can be investigated by assessing the extent to which the predicted probability estimates of outcomes reflect the true correctness likelihood, a process called *confidence calibration* [7,13]. Confidence calibration is not normally employed in current neural model design and validation practices, where output confidence values are simply cut-off at a threshold to decide the output class.

ODIN aims at generalizing and integrating into a unique solution the previous approaches to error diagnosis for neural models. It supports classification, object detection and instance segmentation, allows the addition of custom meta-annotations and metrics, and includes a wide range of off-the shelf metrics and analysis reports. It combines error impact sensitivity and confidence calibration analysis. It can be used to study both model performance and data set bias. In [28], we presented a preliminary version developed along the line of [9], which featured support for instance segmentation tasks, adapting the input to the most common data set formats and providing an easy-to-use Python implementation. The version presented in this paper extends our previous work [28] by: 1) adding support for classification tasks in addition to object detection and instance segmentation thus making ODIN applicable to generic ML classification problems; 2) increasing the number of metrics available off-the-shelf; 3) integrating a novel type of analysis for confidence calibration, supporting the evaluation of the confidence error; 4) integrating a GUI for input annotation so to provide a one stop solution spanning all phases from training set preparation to model evaluation.

To the best of our knowledge no other tool offers such a complete set of functions for dissecting the performance of ML and CV models.

3   The ODIN Error Diagnosis Framework

The ODIN framework supports the development of (image and generic) classification, object detection and instance segmentation models by enabling designers to add application-specific meta-annotations to data sets, evaluate standard metrics on inputs and outputs grouped by meta-annotation values, assess custom metrics that exploit meta-annotations, evaluate the confidence calibration error, and visualize a variety of diagnostic reports.

3.1   Metrics

ODIN supports both standard metrics for (image) classification, object detection and instance segmentation assessment and their restriction to specific properties expressed by the meta-annotation values. Developers can run all metrics, or a subset thereof, for a single class or a set of classes. The values of all metrics are reported using diagrams of multiple types, which can be visualized and saved. Table 1 summarizes the implemented metrics for each task.

Normalization. The metrics that depend on the number of true positives TP (e.g., precision, average precision, accuracy, recall) can be defined in two variants: with and without normalization [9]. Normalization copes with class unbalance. The number of TP is affected by the size of a class as follows. If T_c is the fraction of objects detected with confidence of at least c and N_j is the size of class j, then

Table 1. Metrics implemented for binary/single label classification, multi label classification, object detection and instance segmentation

Metric/analysis		Binary	SL class.	ML class.	Obj. det.	Ins. seg.
Base metrics	Accuracy	X	X	X	–	–
	Precision	X	X	X	X	X
	Recall	X	X	X	X	X
	Average precision	X	X	X	X	X
	ROC AUC	X	X	X	–	–
	Precision recall AUC	X	X	X	X	X
	F1 score AUC	X	X	X	X	X
	F1 score	X	X	X	X	X
	Custom	X	X	X	X	X
Curves	Precision recall	X	X	X	X	X
	F1 score	X	X	X	X	X
	ROC	X	X	X	–	–
Confusion matrix		X	X	X	–	–
Metric per property value		X	X	X	X	X
Property distribution		X	X	X	X	X
Sensitivity and impact analysis		X	X	X	X	X
False positives analysis		–	X	X	X	X
FP, TP, FN, TN distribution		–	X	X	X	X
Calibration analysis		X	X	X	X	X
Base report	Total value	X	X	X	X	X
	Per-category value	X	X	X	X	X
	Per-property value	X	X	X	X	X

$TP = T_c \cdot N_j$. Thus, for the same detection rate, the metrics that depend on TP grow with N_j, which may be undesirable if classes are unbalanced. Normalization replaces N_j with a constant N, which represents the size that each class would have in balanced conditions ($n_{obs}/n_{classes}$). Normalization is optional and can be enabled both class-wise and for specific meta-annotation values.

Thresholding. Some of the curves supported by ODIN require computing values of the corresponding metric for different threshold values. A threshold t defines the confidence value above which a prediction is considered positive. For object detection and instance segmentation, a threshold t_{IoU} applies to the Intersection over Union (IoU) value between the proposals and ground truth objects.

Accuracy represents the fraction of correct predictions of a model (Eq. 1).

$$Accuracy = \frac{TP + TN}{TP + TN + FP + FN} \tag{1}$$

Precision, Recall, PR curve, PR AUC and Average Precision. The precision and recall metrics have the usual definition (Eq. 2). The PR curve plots the precision vs recall at different thresholds and can be computed for all classes, per class, or on a subset of the classes [23].

$$Precision = \frac{TP}{TP + FP}, Recall = \frac{TP}{TP + FN} \qquad (2)$$

Average Precision (AP) summarizes the PR curve as a single value, i.e., the precision averaged for recall values from 0 to 1, equivalent to the Area Under the PR Curve. The Interpolated AP approximation used in PASCAL VOC [6] is computed as the sum of the maximum precision values for recall greater than the current sampling value, weighted by the recall delta (Eq. 3 and 4).

$$\sum_{r=0}^{1}(r_{n+1} - r_n)\, p_{interpol}(r) \qquad (3)$$

with

$$p_{interpol}(r) = \max_{\tilde{r}:\tilde{r}\geq r_{n+1}} p(\tilde{r}) \qquad (4)$$

where $p(\tilde{r})$ is precision at recall $\tilde{r}$.

F1 Score, F1 Curve, F1 AUC. The F1 score is the harmonic mean of Precision and Recall (Eq. 5). The F1 Curve plots the F1 score over all threshold values. The area under such curve defines the F1 AUC metric [16].

$$F1Score = 2 \cdot \frac{p \cdot r}{p + r} \qquad (5)$$

ROC Curve, ROC AUC. The Receiver Operating Characteristic (ROC) Curve plots the tradeoff between True Positive Rate (TPR) and False Positive Rate (FPR) (Eq. 6). The area under the curve summarizes it into a single value (ROC AUC) [26].

$$TPR = \frac{TP}{TP + FN}, FPR = \frac{FP}{FP + TN} \qquad (6)$$

Confusion Matrix presents TN, FN, TP, FP in a matrix form where position (i, j) contains the number of samples in group i predicted as group j.

Custom metrics ODIN has a "plug&play" architecture so that adding new metrics requires extending the `Analyzer` class and providing the wrapper method that calls the code of the metrics.

3.2   Analysis Reports

ODIN supports several types of analysis based on the metrics described in Sect. 3.1. The user can restrict the analysis to a subset of the classes, to the value of a meta-annotation (henceforth called *property*) or to specific metrics. An example of property is *object size* with values *small, medium* and *large*.

Property Distribution. Data set bias can be analysed by visualizing the distribution of property values over the whole data set and over individual classes.

Metrics per Property. The values of a metric can be disaggregated by class and then by property value. For example, the metric M can be computed and visualized for the class *car* and then for the property values *small, medium* and *large*. The class mean value is reported too.

Property Sensitivity and Impact. Given a metric, its value is computed limited to the subset of the input data corresponding to each property value. The maximum and minimum values are reported. The difference between the maximum and minimum value highlights the sensitivity of the metrics w.r.t. the property. The difference between the maximum value and the overall value of the metrics suggests the impact of the property on the specific metrics.

FP, TP, FN, TN Distribution. The distribution of False Positives, True Positive, False Negatives and True Negatives by class can be reported.

False Positives Analysis. The per-class analysis of errors is supported. For detection and segmentation the FP errors are based on: confusion with background (B), poor localization (L), confusion with similar classes (S) and confusion with other objects (O) [28]. For classification we included: 1) Confusion with input samples without annotated class (W). 2) Confusion with similar classes based on a user-defined class similarity relation (S). 3) Confusion with non similar classes (G). The percentage of predictions that fall into each error type is reported along with the absolute improvement obtained by removing the FP of each type.

Calibration Analysis. It relies on the confidence histogram and on the reliability diagram [4]. Both plots have the confidence divided into buckets (e.g., 0–0.1, 0.11–0.2, ..., 0.91–1) on the abscissa. The confidence histogram shows the percentage of positive predicted samples that fall into each confidence range. The reliability diagram indicates, for each confidence range, the average accuracy of the positive samples in that range. When a classifier is well-calibrated, its probability estimates can be interpreted as correctness likelihood, i.e., of all the samples that are predicted with a probability estimate of 0.6, around 60% should belong to the positive class [7]. ODIN reports the Expected Calibration Error (ECE) (Eq. 7) and the Maximum Calibration Error (MCE) (Eq. 8)

$$ECE = \sum_{m=1}^{M} \frac{B_m}{n} acc(B_m) - conf(B_m) \tag{7}$$

$$MCE = max_{m\epsilon(1...M)} |acc(B_m) - conf(B_m)| \tag{8}$$

where n is the number of samples in the data set, M is the number of buckets (each of size $1/M$) and B_m denotes the set of indices of observations whose prediction confidence falls into the interval m.

Base Report tabulates the chosen metrics: total, per-class and per-property value. The total shows both the micro- and macro-averaged values: the first computes the value by counting the total TP, FP and FN; the latter computes the metrics for each class and then performs an unweighted mean.

3.3 Annotator

Meta-annotations can be automatically extracted (e.g., image color space) or manually provided. Meta-annotation editing is supported by a Jupyter Notebook (Fig. 1) that given the data samples (e.g., images) and the meta-annotation values allows the developer to iterate on the samples and select the appropriate value, which is saved in the chosen evaluation format. The following example shows the code needed to create, for a classification data set, a meta-annotation session for a custom property (**Evidence**). The code declares the paths to the inputs and outputs (lines 1–2), specifies the task type (line 4), instantiates the data set (line 6), creates a custom visualization (lines 8–16) and a custom validation function (lines 18–19), declares the properties to annotate (with property type, values, optional message) (line 21), creates an instance of the annotator (line 23), with an optional custom display function (if not set, the default visualization is used) and the optional validation function (useful to guide the user). Finally it starts the annotator (line 24). Similar code is used to instantiate an editor for a detection or segmentation task.

Fig. 1. Interface of the meta-annotation editor. The user can navigate between the images to: add new annotations, reset the current annotations or download the current image.

```
1 dataset_gt = '../gt.json'
2 images_path ='../images'
3
4 classific_type = TaskType.CLASSIFICATION_BINARY
5
6 my_dataset = DatasetClassification(dataset_gt, classific_type,
   ↪   observations_abs_path=images_path, for_analysis=False)
7
8 def custom_display_function(obs_record):
9     print(f"This is image {obs_record['file_name']}")
10
11    path_img = os.path.join(images_path, obs_record['file_name'])
11
12    img = Image.open(path_img) # read img from path and show it
13    plt.figure(figsize=(10, 10))
14    plt.axis('off')
15    plt.imshow(img)
16    plt.show()
17
18 def validate_function(observation_record):
19    return 'Evidence' in observation_record
20
21 properties = {"Evidence": (MetaPropertiesType.UNIQUE, ["Low",
   ↪   "Medium", "High"], "How evident is this site?")}
22
23 my_annotator = AnnotatorClassification(my_dataset, properties,
   ↪   custom_display_function=custom_display_function,
   ↪   validate_function=validate_function)
24 my_annotator.start_annotation()
```

Data Set Generation. In addition to editing meta-annotations, ODIN also supports the creation of a classification or object detection data set. The annotator can be configured to associate training labels to data samples and to draw bounding boxes over images and label them. The resulting data set is saved in a standard format and can be analysed with the illustrated diagnosis functions.

Data Set Visualizer. A GUI realized as a Jupyter Notebook enables the inspection of the data set. The visualization can be executed on all the samples, limited to the samples of a class, limited to the samples with a certain meta-annotation value, and limited to the samples of a class with a given meta-annotation value.

4   ODIN in Action

This section exemplifies the use of ODIN for the evaluation of: 1) a binary classifier of aerial images for predicting the presence of illegal landfills and 2) a multi-label classifier of painting images based on their iconography elements (e.g., Christian Saints).

Illegal Landfills. For each image the presence or absence of a suspicious site is predicted. Over 1,000 geographical coordinates of illegal waste dumps were provided by experts, each position associated with the evidence level (low, medium, high) and the extension level (low, medium, high). Other 2,000 coordinates were randomly chosen in the same region as negative samples. The evidence and extension meta-annotations are only present for the positive samples. For each location, an image was extracted with the size randomly sampled from three scales (600, 800 or 1,000 pixels) to provide a different amount of context around the center position. The scale constitutes an automatically extracted meta-annotation available for all samples. Given the application, we focus the illustration on the most relevant metric: recall. Initially, prediction was realized with ResNet-50 [8]. Figure 2 shows the distribution of the scale property among the test images (left) and plots the recall value variation with the scale value (middle). The analysis reveals sensitivity of recall to the scale. Based on this observation, a second model was trained using the same ResNet-50 as backbone augmented with Feature Pyramid Network links [14,24]. The results of such a model show that the sensitivity to the scale reduces (right).

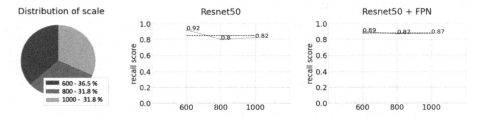

Fig. 2. Distribution of scale property and the analysis of recall for this property.

Figure 3 compares the sensitivity and impact on recall of the three meta-annotations for the ResNet-50+FPN classifier. Now the scale is the least sensitive

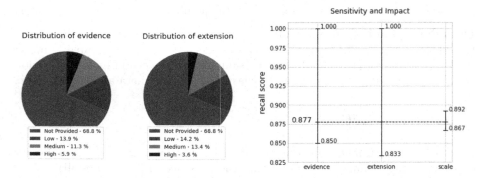

Fig. 3. Distribution of evidence and extension (left). Impact and sensitivity of meta-annotations on recall in ResNet-50+FPN architecture (right).

property whereas the extension has the largest impact; it thus becomes the focus of the next improvement cycle.

The predictions are used by local authorities to scan a large territory. Given the operational cost of field inspections, assessing the quality of the probability estimates is important. Figure 4 shows the confidence histogram and the reliability diagram. In most cases, the model is moderately more confidence than it should be, except in the 0.4–0.5 bucket, where the over-confidence is the highest, giving an MCE of 56. Yet this bin has a small effect on the ECE (7.01) given the low amount of samples in this range, as can be seen in the confidence histogram.

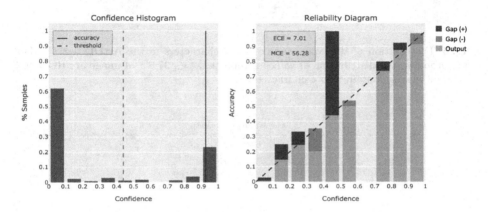

Fig. 4. Confidence histogram and reliability diagram.

ArtDL. The ArtDL data set, presented in [17], exemplifies the multi-class multi-label classification case. It comprises 42,279 painting images in 10 classes related to the iconography of Christian Saints. Predictions are made with a trained ResNet-50 model on 1,864 test images made publicly available. Three meta-annotations are used: the color space and the source collection, which determine a great variability in the image quality, and the number of characters depicted in the paintings, which describe the complexity of the scene. All properties are acquired automatically: the source collection is set during the content crawling phase, the color space is found by post-processing the images and the number of characters is counted by extracting the estimated poses from the images with OpenPose [3]. The number of characters is divided into three ranges (0–1, 2–4, 5+). Figure 5 shows the distribution of the three properties in the data set.

Figure 6 shows the analysis of the #characters property. For most classes, the F1 score deteriorates as the complexity of the scene increases. As an example, the F1-Score of Saint Jerome is ∼83% when he is the only element in a painting and it drops to ∼43% when one to three other characters are present. Saint Dominic and Saint Anthony of Padua share a similar behaviour. For other classes, such as Virgin Mary or Saint Sebastian, the performance drop is rather limited. This is explained by the fact that those two characters are associated with very distinctive visual elements, e.g., Baby Jesus for Virgin Mary or the arrows for Saint Sebastian; such strong symbols make them recognizable even when they appear in a crowded scene or in a polyptych.

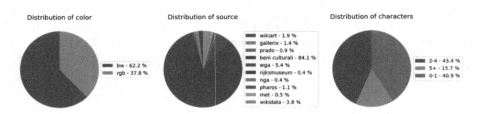

Fig. 5. Distribution of the color, source and #characters in the ArtDL test set. For each property, the distribution of values is reported, e.g., 37.8% of image are RGB and 43.4% of images contain 2 to 4 characters.

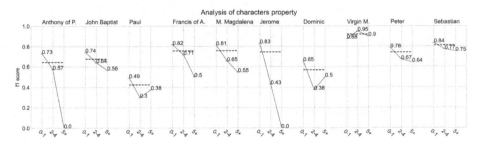

Fig. 6. Analysis of the people property on the ArtDL data set for the F1-Score metric. For each class, the performance calculated on the specific property value is reported. As expected, complex scenes, i.e. images depicting many figures, lead to a decrease of model performance.

Figure 7 shows the distribution of FP predictions over all classes and the FP analysis of two classes: Anthony of Padua and Mary Magdalene. For both classes, most errors occur when predicting images that contain similar classes (S), respectively Saint Francis of Assisi and Virgin Mary, whereas the confusion with unlabeled images (W) is irrelevant. The same analysis also shows the performance gain for the F1-score if the FP errors are mitigated, e.g., a ~7% improvement for Mary Magdalene if she is not confused with Virgin Mary.

The analysis shown in Figs. 6 and 7 suggests the application of Fine-Grained Visual Categorization (FGVC) techniques, such as attention aware data augmentation [11,12] or specific attention modules [27,30], to deal with the similarity between classes. These methods should help the model focus on the subtle iconographic symbols that make each class unique, overcoming the issues exposed by the FP analysis.

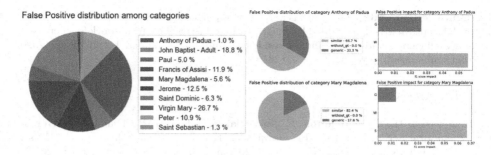

Fig. 7. FP distribution across classes (left) and FP analysis for two classes (right). In the FP analysis, the distribution and impact of the errors are reported.

5   Conclusions and Future Work

In this paper, we have described a framework for the analysis of errors and the visualization of a variety of diagnostic reports in ML and CV tasks. The illustrated work extends a previous preliminary version that focused only on object detection [28] and limited the off-the-shelf analysis to the Average Precision metric. Now ODIN supports also classification tasks, implements all the most common metrics, and assists with an automatically generated interface the association of arbitrary meta-annotations to the input data also for classification. In addition, an annotator GUI is provided to create a data set from scratch, for both object detection and classification. A new type of analysis, confidence calibration, has been added too. Performance analysis can be focused on standard or custom metrics and on arbitrary subsets of the input characterized by critical values of the meta-annotations. We have illustrated the output on two different settings, scene classification for remote sensing (illegal landfills) and multi-label image classification for cultural heritage (Christian Iconography), explaining how the analysis reports provide insight useful for improvement. For space reasons, other metrics available in ODIN (e.g., Pre/Rec curve, ROC curve, confusion matrix) were not illustrated.

ODIN is implemented in Python and released as open source. Its plug&play architecture permits the addition of novel meta-annotations and custom metrics with minimal coding effort. Our future work will concentrate on extending the library of metrics implementations with further classes for specific applications, e.g., human pose detection and temporal series analysis. In addition, we will add support for the automatic extraction of specific types of meta-annotations from images, such as the geographical coordinates, date and time of acquisition, lighting conditions, etc. We also plan to integrate the analysis of attention, by computing the position and extent of the CAM [33] w.r.t. to the object bounding box or segmentation mask, with the final goal of supporting the optimization of weakly supervised models.

Acknowledgements. This work is partially supported by the project "PRECEPT - A novel decentralized edge-enabled PREsCriptivE and ProacTive framework for increased energy efficiency and well-being in residential buildings" funded by the EU H2020 Programme, grant agreement no. 958284.

References

1. Alwassel, H., Caba Heilbron, F., Escorcia, V., Ghanem, B.: Diagnosing error in temporal action detectors. In: Ferrari, V., Hebert, M., Sminchisescu, C., Weiss, Y. (eds.) ECCV 2018. LNCS, vol. 11207, pp. 264–280. Springer, Cham (2018). https://doi.org/10.1007/978-3-030-01219-9_16
2. Bolya, D., Foley, S., Hays, J., Hoffman, J.: TIDE: a general toolbox for identifying object detection errors. arXiv preprint arXiv:2008.08115 (2020)
3. Cao, Z., Hidalgo Martinez, G., Simon, T., Wei, S., Sheikh, Y.A.: OpenPose: real-time multi-person 2d pose estimation using part affinity fields. IEEE Trans. Pattern Anal. Mach. Intell. **43**, 172–186 (2021)
4. DeGroot, M.H., Fienberg, S.E.: The comparison and evaluation of forecasters. J. R. Stat. Soc. Ser. D (Stat.) **32**(1–2), 12–22 (1983)
5. Deng, Z., Sun, H., Zhou, S., Zhao, J., Lei, L., Zou, H.: Multi-scale object detection in remote sensing imagery with convolutional neural networks. ISPRS J. Photogramm. Remote Sens. **145**, 3–22 (2018). Deep Learning RS Data. https://doi.org/10.1016/j.isprsjprs.2018.04.003. https://www.sciencedirect.com/science/article/pii/S0924271618301096
6. Everingham, M., Gool, L., Williams, C.K., Winn, J., Zisserman, A.: The PASCAL visual object classes (VOC) challenge. Int. J. Comput. Vis. **88**(2), 303–338 (2010). https://doi.org/10.1007/s11263-009-0275-4. https://doi.org/10.1007/s11263-009-0275-4
7. Guo, C., Pleiss, G., Sun, Y., Weinberger, K.Q.: On calibration of modern neural networks. In: International Conference on Machine Learning, pp. 1321–1330. PMLR (2017)
8. He, K., Zhang, X., Ren, S., Sun, J.: Deep residual learning for image recognition (2015)
9. Hoiem, D., Chodpathumwan, Y., Dai, Q.: Diagnosing error in object detectors. In: Fitzgibbon, A., Lazebnik, S., Perona, P., Sato, Y., Schmid, C. (eds.) ECCV 2012. LNCS, vol. 7574, pp. 340–353. Springer, Heidelberg (2012). https://doi.org/10.1007/978-3-642-33712-3_25
10. Hossin, M., Sulaiman, M.: A review on evaluation metrics for data classification evaluations. Int. J. Data Min. Knowl. Manage. Process **5**(2), 1–11 (2015)
11. Hu, T., Qi, H., Huang, Q., Lu, Y.: See better before looking closer: weakly supervised data augmentation network for fine-grained visual classification. arXiv preprint arXiv:1901.09891 (2019)
12. Imran, A., Athitsos, V.: Domain adaptive transfer learning on visual attention aware data augmentation for fine-grained visual categorization. In: Bebis, G., et al. (eds.) ISVC 2020. LNCS, vol. 12510, pp. 53–65. Springer, Cham (2020). https://doi.org/10.1007/978-3-030-64559-5_5
13. Kumar, A., Sarawagi, S., Jain, U.: Trainable calibration measures for neural networks from kernel mean embeddings. In: International Conference on Machine Learning, pp. 2805–2814. PMLR (2018)
14. Lin, T.Y., Dollár, P., Girshick, R., He, K., Hariharan, B., Belongie, S.: Feature pyramid networks for object detection (2017)

15. Lin, T.-Y., et al.: Microsoft COCO: common objects in context. In: Fleet, D., Pajdla, T., Schiele, B., Tuytelaars, T. (eds.) ECCV 2014. LNCS, vol. 8693, pp. 740–755. Springer, Cham (2014). https://doi.org/10.1007/978-3-319-10602-1_48
16. Lipton, Z.C., Elkan, C., Naryanaswamy, B.: Optimal thresholding of classifiers to maximize F1 measure. In: Calders, T., Esposito, F., Hüllermeier, E., Meo, R. (eds.) ECML PKDD 2014. LNCS (LNAI), vol. 8725, pp. 225–239. Springer, Heidelberg (2014). https://doi.org/10.1007/978-3-662-44851-9_15
17. Milani, F., Fraternali, P.: A data set and a convolutional model for iconography classification in paintings. J. Comput. Cult. Herit. 14, 1–18 (2020)
18. Monteiro, F.C., Campilho, A.C.: Performance evaluation of image segmentation. In: Campilho, A., Kamel, M.S. (eds.) ICIAR 2006. LNCS, vol. 4141, pp. 248–259. Springer, Heidelberg (2006). https://doi.org/10.1007/11867586_24
19. Nekrasov, V., Shen, C., Reid, I.: Diagnostics in semantic segmentation. arXiv preprint arXiv:1809.10328 (2018)
20. Novaković, J.D., Veljović, A., Ilić, S.S., Papić, Ž, Milica, T.: Evaluation of classification models in machine learning. Theor. Appl. Math. Comput. Sci. 7(1), 39–46 (2017)
21. Padilla, R., Netto, S.L., da Silva, E.A.: A survey on performance metrics for object-detection algorithms. In: 2020 International Conference on Systems, Signals and Image Processing (IWSSIP), pp. 237–242. IEEE (2020)
22. Padilla, R., Passos, W.L., Dias, T.L., Netto, S.L., da Silva, E.A.: A comparative analysis of object detection metrics with a companion open-source toolkit. Electronics 10(3), 279 (2021)
23. Raghavan, V., Bollmann, P., Jung, G.S.: A critical investigation of recall and precision as measures of retrieval system performance. ACM Trans. Inf. Syst. (TOIS) 7(3), 205–229 (1989)
24. Rahimzadeh, M., Attar, A., Sakhaei, S.M.: A fully automated deep learning-based network for detecting COVID-19 from a new and large lung CT scan dataset. medRxiv 68, 102588 (2020)
25. Redondo-Cabrera, C., López-Sastre, R.J., Xiang, Yu., Tuytelaars, T., Savarese, S.: Pose estimation errors, the ultimate diagnosis. In: Leibe, B., Matas, J., Sebe, N., Welling, M. (eds.) ECCV 2016. LNCS, vol. 9911, pp. 118–134. Springer, Cham (2016). https://doi.org/10.1007/978-3-319-46478-7_8
26. Sokolova, M., Japkowicz, N., Szpakowicz, S.: Beyond accuracy, F-score and ROC: a family of discriminant measures for performance evaluation. In: Sattar, A., Kang, B. (eds.) AI 2006. LNCS (LNAI), vol. 4304, pp. 1015–1021. Springer, Heidelberg (2006). https://doi.org/10.1007/11941439_114
27. Sun, G., Cholakkal, H., Khan, S., Khan, F., Shao, L.: Fine-grained recognition: accounting for subtle differences between similar classes. In: Proceedings of the AAAI Conference on Artificial Intelligence, vol. 34, pp. 12047–12054 (2020)
28. Torres, R.N., Fraternali, P., Romero, J.: ODIN: an object detection and instance segmentation diagnosis framework. In: Bartoli, A., Fusiello, A. (eds.) ECCV 2020. LNCS, vol. 12540, pp. 19–31. Springer, Cham (2020). https://doi.org/10.1007/978-3-030-65414-6_3
29. Wang, A., Narayanan, A., Russakovsky, O.: REVISE: a tool for measuring and mitigating bias in visual datasets. In: Vedaldi, A., Bischof, H., Brox, T., Frahm, J.-M. (eds.) ECCV 2020. LNCS, vol. 12348, pp. 733–751. Springer, Cham (2020). https://doi.org/10.1007/978-3-030-58580-8_43

30. Zhang, F., Li, M., Zhai, G., Liu, Y.: Multi-branch and multi-scale attention learning for fine-grained visual categorization. In: Lokoč, J., et al. (eds.) MMM 2021. LNCS, vol. 12572, pp. 136–147. Springer, Cham (2021). https://doi.org/10.1007/978-3-030-67832-6_12
31. Zhang, J., Bargal, S.A., Lin, Z., Brandt, J., Shen, X., Sclaroff, S.: Top-down neural attention by excitation backprop. Int. J. Comput. Vis. **126**(10), 1084–1102 (2018). https://doi.org/10.1007/s11263-017-1059-x. https://doi.org/10.1007/s11263-017-1059-x
32. Zhang, Q., Zhu, S.: Visual interpretability for deep learning: a survey. Front. Inf. Technol. Electron. Eng. **19**(1), 27–39 (2018). https://doi.org/10.1631/FITEE.1700808
33. Zhou, B., Khosla, A., Lapedriza, A., Oliva, A., Torralba, A.: Learning deep features for discriminative localization. In: CVPR (2016)

Predictable Features Elimination: An Unsupervised Approach to Feature Selection

Pietro Barbiero[1] ⓘ, Giovanni Squillero[2]([✉]) ⓘ, and Alberto Tonda[3] ⓘ

[1] Cambridge University, Cambridge, UK
pb737@cam.ac.uk
[2] Politecnico di Torino, Torino, Italy
squillero@polito.it
[3] UMR 518 MIA, INRAE, Paris, France
alberto.tonda@inrae.fr

Abstract. We propose an unsupervised, model-agnostic, wrapper method for feature selection. We assume that if a feature can be predicted using the others, it adds little information to the problem, and therefore could be removed without impairing the performance of whatever model will be eventually built. The proposed method iteratively identifies and removes predictable, or nearly-predictable, redundant features, allowing to trade-off complexity with expected quality. The approach do not rely on target labels nor values, and the model used to identify predictable features is not related to the final use of the feature set. Therefore, it can be used for supervised, unsupervised, or semi-supervised problems, or even as a safe, pre-processing step to improve the quality of the results of other feature selection techniques. Experimental results against state-of-the-art feature-selection algorithms show satisfying performance on several non-trivial benchmarks.

1 Introduction

The aim of most Machine Learning (ML) algorithms is to build a predictive model starting from the feature values of a given training set. State-of-the-art algorithms are usually quite effective at tacking problems with huge number of samples, yet they might face issues if the number of features is huge. An increase in the dimensionality of the problem, in fact, may correspond to a much steeper increase of the search space, impairing the optimization of the models, or creating other problems usually described with the vague expression "curse of dimensionality" [2].

A reduction in the number of variables may be obtained either by means of feature extraction or feature selection. Techniques in the former group, such as principal component analysis (PCA) or autoencoders, built a new, more compact set of features out of the original one. Feature selection techniques, on the other hand, aim at finding a subset of the original features, that still allows ML

© Springer Nature Switzerland AG 2022
G. Nicosia et al. (Eds.): LOD 2021, LNCS 13163, pp. 399–412, 2022.
https://doi.org/10.1007/978-3-030-95467-3_29

algorithms to build reliable predictive models. There might be practical reasons to opt for the second class of techniques, for instance, if each single feature has a cost because it needs to be physically measured. Moreover, predictive models that use tens or hundreds of features are de facto black boxes, quite hard if not completely impossible to interpret. Identifying the key features involved in a problem can make the final model more human-readable: problems involving genomic data [3] would greatly benefit from the possibility to find understandable correlations; improvement could be noticeable in the field of visualization [23]; and the general need for explainable artificial intelligence (XAI) is only but increasing in present days.

Starting from the observation that the value of a redundant feature, by definition of redundancy, can be inferred using the information contained in the other features, we propose Predictable Features Elimination (PFE). PFE is an unsupervised, model-agnostic, wrapper approach for feature selection: In a first step, each feature is scored and ranked using a statistical measure; then, starting from the lowest-ranked feature, an auxiliary ML model is trained to predict that feature using all the others; if the performance of the model exceeds a given quality (for example, $R2 > 0.95$), the information it provides is assumed to be redundant and the feature is removed. The procedure then iterates to the next feature, and once all features have been analyzed in this way, those remaining represent the final subset.

Experimental results on several non-trivial benchmarks from the OpenML repository [26] show that the proposed approach is competitive with the state of the art in the field, obtaining feature subsets that are either more informative or smaller than competing feature selection algorithms. The main contributions of this paper are:

- We describe Predictable Features Elimination, a new unsupervised, model-agnostic, wrapper approach for feature selection.
- We compare the performance of PFE against state-of-the-art feature selection algorithms, showing the advantages of using our method especially on large datasets.
- We compare PFE against other algorithms on an artificial dataset, specifically designed for assessing feature selection algorithms. Results show that the features selected by PFE include almost all meaningful information.

2 Feature Selection in Machine Learning

Feature Selection (FS) is the process of identifying the features of a data set in order to obtain a minimal, informative subset. Features may not be part of this subset for two main reasons: they might be unrelated to the underlying nature of the problem, just adding noise; they might be heavily correlated with others features, adding no relevant information for the task.

Applications range from face recognition [28] to medicine [35], while approaches can be divided into two categories [11]: filters that score features according to a criterion (often a statistical test); and recursive procedures (forward or backwards) that attempt to reduce the features to a small set of non-redundant ones [5, 16].

Several different metrics that have been proposed to assess the content of information of a given feature subset: from mutual information [15] to analysis of variance [9]. However, only some of the information content of a feature subset can be assessed through such metrics, as taking into account the contribution of non-linear combinations of features would be too computationally expensive. Recursive procedures on the other hand frequently rely on more complex measurements, usually a goodness-of-fit [11] for a model wrapped inside the feature selection, sometimes combined with regularization terms [30]. In some cases, the number of features and the quality of the fit are evaluated separately, and each candidate subset is placed on a Pareto front [32].

Literature reports FS techniques as complex as exploiting evolutionary algorithms (EAs) [6, 32], with single- or multi-objective approaches [1, 13, 31]. Anyhow, the most popular approach in literature is still probably the 20-year old Recursive Feature Elimination (RFE) [12], a supervised, wrapper methodology that iteratively removes the worst features based on the performance of the target model.

3   Predictable Feature Elimination

The Algorithm

Predictable Features Elimination, the approach we present in this work, stems from the observation that if the distribution of a feature f_r can be approximated by using the information of other features, then f_r is likely to be almost redundant and of little importance for whatever model will be eventually built. Algorithm 1 summarizes the main steps of the training process.

PFE requires the user to provide two parameters: an auxiliary machine learning model g and a threshold σ. The first is the model used to discriminate non-redundant features, the second, the acceptable loss of information. A suboptimal choice of g would cause some features to be erroneously marked as non-redundant, increasing the size of the feature set, but probably not affecting the quality of the final model. On the other hand, a low σ is likely to make PFE select a very small set of features, but also to impair the quality of the final model.

The algorithms is composed of two phases: an initialization and the main loop. In the former, features are ranked according to their mutual average linear correlation. First, the feature correlation matrix C is computed:

$$C = \Big(diag(K_{XX})\Big)^{1/2} K_{XX} \Big(diag(K_{XX})\Big)^{1/2} \tag{1}$$

where K_{XX} is the auto-covariance matrix of the input matrix X:

$$K_{XX} = E[(X - E[X])(X - E[X])^T)] \tag{2}$$

The correlation matrix C is used to estimate the amount of mutual information shared among features. By summing up the rows of C, we obtain for each feature an approximation of the amount of information which can be obtained using all the other features:

$$\kappa = \sum_i C(i, \cdot) \tag{3}$$

The more a feature is correlated with others, the lower the chances that the feature may contain exclusively useful information. Hence, by ranking features according to their mutual average linear correlation, we will obtain an ordered list of their significance:

$$\kappa_s = sort(\kappa) \tag{4}$$

Starting from the feature with the highest rank f, the ML model g is trained on the remaining features using the f-th feature as a target variable y:

$$y = X(\cdot, \kappa_s(f)) \tag{5}$$

The performance of g is assessed on a validation set X_{val} using the coefficient of determination $R2$. If the validation score is greater than the user defined threshold σ, then it means that the model g represents an accurate nonlinear association between the f-th feature and the other features. Hence, the chances that the f-th feature may contain exclusively useful information are low. Therefore, the f-th feature should be safely removed from the feature set and the process may continue using the following feature in the ranking. The algorithm stops when more than half of the features have been analyzed.

Algorithm 1: Predictable feature elimination

Input: data $X \in \mathbb{R}^{n,d}$, model g, threshold $\sigma \in [0, 1]$
Initialize $C = corr(X^T)$
Initialize $\kappa = \sum_i C(i, \cdot)$
Initialize $\kappa_s = sort(\kappa)$
for $f = 1$ **to** $\lfloor d/2 \rfloor$ **do**
    Initialize $y = X(\cdot, \kappa_s(f))$.
    Split data into train and validation sets
    Train model $g \leftarrow (X_{train}, y_{train})$
    Make validation predictions $\hat{y} = g(X_{val})$
    Evaluate predictions $score = R2(\hat{y}, y_{val})$
    if $score \geq \sigma$ **then**
        Remove current feature
    end if
end for

Theoretical Foundation

The following theorems yield a theoretical justification for the proposed approach. Besides, they show how the performance loss can be formally estimated by providing upper bounds in worst case scenarios.

Theorem 1 (Elimination for linear combinations). *Let $\mathcal{F}$ be a set of features $\mathcal{F} = \{f_1, \ldots, f_d\}$ and $\mathcal{F}'$ be a subset of $\mathcal{F}$ such that $f_i \notin \mathcal{F}'$. If the feature f_i is a linear combination of the feature set $\mathcal{F}'$, then fitting a linear model using $\mathcal{F}'$ is equivalent to fitting the same model using $\mathcal{F}' \cup \{f_i\}$.*

Proof. By definition f_i is a linear combination of $\mathcal{F}'$, hence:

$$f_i = \sum_{j \neq i} w_j f_j \tag{6}$$

which can be written as:

$$f_i = F'w \tag{7}$$

where $F' \in \mathbb{R}^{n \times d'}$ is a matrix whose columns are features in $\mathcal{F}'$ and $w \in \mathbb{R}^{d'}$ is a row vector containing the weights of the linear combination.

A linear model g trained using the matrix F' can be written as:

$$\hat{y} = g(F') = F'w^g = \sum_{j \in d'} f_j w_j^g \tag{8}$$

Let F'' be the matrix whose columns correspond to the features in $\mathcal{F}' \cup \{f_i\}$, then the model g trained on F'' can be written as:

$$
\begin{aligned}
\hat{y} = g(F'') = F''w^g &= \sum_{k \in d''} f_k w_k^g \\
&= \sum_{j \in d'} f_j w_j^g + w_i^g f_i \\
&= \sum_{j \in d'} f_j w_j^g + w_i^g \sum_{j \in d'} f_j w_j \\
&= \sum_{j \in d'} f_j w_j^g + \sum_{j \in d'} f_j w_j w_i^g \\
&= \sum_{j \in d'} f_j w_j^g w_j w_i^g \\
&= \sum_{j \in d'} f_j \omega_j^g
\end{aligned}
\tag{9}
$$

Theorem 2 (Approximate elimination for linear combinations). *Let $\mathcal{F}$ be a set of features $\mathcal{F} = \{f_1, \ldots, f_d\}$ and $\mathcal{F}'$ be a subset of $\mathcal{F}$ such that $f_i \notin \mathcal{F}'$. If the feature f_i can be written as a linear combination of the feature set $\mathcal{F}'$ with an additional term ϵ, then the upper bound of the training error obtained by fitting a linear model on $\mathcal{F}'$ instead of $\mathcal{F}' \cup \{f_i\}$ is at most ϵ.*

Proof. By definition f_i can be written as a linear combination of the feature set $\mathcal{F}'$ with an additional term ϵ, hence:

$$f_i = \sum_{j \neq i} w_j f_j + \epsilon \tag{10}$$

which can be written as:

$$f_i = F'w + \epsilon \tag{11}$$

where $F' \in \mathbb{R}^{n \times d'}$ is a matrix whose columns are features in $\mathcal{F}'$ and $w \in \mathbb{R}^{d'}$ is a row vector containing the weights of the linear combination.

A linear model g trained using the matrix F' can be written as:

$$\widehat{y} = g(F') = F'w^g = \sum_{j \in d'} f_j w_j^g \tag{12}$$

Let F'' be the matrix whose columns correspond to the features in $\mathcal{F}' \cup \{f_i\}$, then the model g trained on F'' can be written as:

$$\begin{aligned}
\widehat{y} = g(F'') = F''w^g &= \sum_{k \in d''} f_k w_k^g \\
&= \sum_{j \in d'} f_j w_j^g + w_i^g f_i \\
&= \sum_{j \in d'} f_j w_j^g + w_i^g \sum_{j \in d'} f_j w_j + \epsilon \\
&= \sum_{j \in d'} f_j w_j^g + \sum_{j \in d'} f_j w_j w_i^g + \epsilon \\
&= \sum_{j \in d'} f_j w_j^g w_j w_i^g + \epsilon \\
&= \sum_{j \in d'} f_j \omega_j^g + \epsilon
\end{aligned} \tag{13}$$

Theorem 3 (Approximate elimination). *Let $\mathcal{F}$ be a set of features $\mathcal{F} = \{f_1, \ldots, f_d\}$ and $\mathcal{F}'$ be a subset of $\mathcal{F}$ such that $f_i \notin \mathcal{F}'$. Let g and h be two nonlinear models with equivalent capacity. If the feature f_i can be written as a function of $\mathcal{F}'$ through h with an error term ϵ, then the upper bound of the training error obtained by fitting g on $\mathcal{F}'$ instead of $\mathcal{F}' \cup \{f_i\}$ is at most $\eta(g, \epsilon)$.*

Proof. By definition f_i can be written as a nonlinear function h of the feature set $\mathcal{F}'$ with an additional term ϵ, hence:

$$f_i = h(F') + \epsilon \tag{14}$$

where $F' \in \mathbb{R}^{n \times d'}$ is a matrix whose columns are features in $\mathcal{F}'$.

A nonlinear model g trained using the matrix F' can be written as:

$$\widehat{y} = g(F') \tag{15}$$

Let F'' be the matrix whose columns correspond to the features in $\mathcal{F}' \cup \{f_i\}$, then the model g trained on F'' can be written as:

$$\widehat{y} = g(F'') = g(F', f_i) = g(F', h(F') + \epsilon) \tag{16}$$

Since the information in $h(F')$ can be obtained from F' by applying the function h, then g can be fitted on F' without information loss by discarding $h(F')$:

$$\widehat{y} = g(F'') = g(F', \epsilon) = g(F') + \eta(g, \epsilon) \tag{17}$$

where η is a function of g and ϵ.

The following definition can be used to monitor in an unsupervised way the performance loss when multiple features are recursively eliminated. In some applications, this lemma may be used to derive alternative stopping conditions.

Definition 1 (Validity of feature elimination). *Let λ be an upper bound of the performance loss required for a specific application and let $\{\eta_1, \ldots, \eta_k\}$ be a sequence of training errors obtained by performing k steps of feature elimination. The sequence of k feature elimination steps is valid if and only if $\lambda \le \sum_{i=1}^{k} \eta_i$.*

4   Experimental Evaluation

The proposed approach has been implemented from scratch in Python 3, using only open-source libraries [17,19]; the source code, including all the parameter values used in the experiments, is available under the European Union Public Licence (EUPL) from GitHub[1].

All experiments have been run on the same machine equipped with an AMD EPYC 7301 16-core processor running at 2 GHz, and with 64 GiB memory.

Experimental Setup

The performance of predictable feature elimination is compared over a 10-fold cross-validation against both supervised and unsupervised feature selection algorithms [17,19]: Laplacian score for feature selection (`lap_score` [14]), spectral feature selection for unsupervised clustering (SPEC [34]), multi-cluster feature selection (MCFS [4]), non-negative spectral feature selection (NDFS [18]), regularised discriminative feature selection (UDFS [33]), and recursive feature elimination (RFE [12]).

A `Ridge` classifier has been used both as the internal estimator for RFE, and to discard redundant features in PFE. It must be noted that PFE is agnostic to the choice of the estimator g, as far it is not significantly superior to the one eventually used in the final model—the underlying assumption being that if a feature can be predicted by g, it may as well be inferred by the final model.

---

[1] https://github.com/glubbdubdrib/predictable-feature-elimination.

Ridge has been chosen both for its high train speed and its generalization ability in a variety of experimental settings.

For all the experiments the σ parameter has been set to the default 0.9, a reasonable value that leads to the removal of at most half of the original features. For the sake of comparison, all the other feature selection algorithms are set in order to provide for each fold the same number of features chosen by PFE. For each fold, each algorithm is used to select a subset of the original features.

In order to generate reproducible results, all algorithms that exploit pseudo-random elements in their training process have been set with a fixed seed. Unless differently specified, each algorithm uses its default parameters as defined in [17, 19]. Each dataset has been standardized removing the mean and scaling to unit variance (**StandardScaler** [36]).

Redundancy Detection

The MADELON dataset proposed in [10] was specifically designed to challenge feature selection algorithms in detecting redundant features. Features generated by MADELON can be informative (d_i), repeated (d_r), or redundant (d_c). The algorithm generates clusters of points normally distributed about vertices of an hypercube in a subspace of dimension d_i and assigns an equal number of clusters to each class. Then it stacks d_c linear combinations of the informative features followed by d_r duplicates, drawn randomly with replacement from the informative and redundant features. All the remaining features (d_n) are random noise ($d_n = d - d_i - d_c - d_r$). This benchmark dataset is used to assess the ability of PFE in detecting redundant features. For this experiment the number of informative features is set to 150 as well as the number of redundant and repeated features ($d_i = d_c = d_s = 150$). The total number of features is set to $d = 500$, thus $d_n = 50$ features are just random noise. The task is to detect informative, redundant, duplicate, and noisy features in order to correctly classify clusters of samples on hypercube vertices. Experimental results are shown in Fig. 1. Once feature selection algorithms are fitted on a training fold, an instance of **RidgeClassifier** and of **DecisionTreeClassifier** are used to assess the quality of the selection on the test set. The resulting $F1$ score [25] is then compared to the one obtained by training on the same fold but using all the original features. In this way, the performance of all techniques can be evaluated with respect to a fair baseline (see Fig. 1, top). Except for **lap_score**, PFE resulted as the fastest approach. The most interesting result of the simulation is represented by boxplots in Fig. 1, bottom. They show for each kind of feature (informative, redundant, duplicate, and noisy) the percentage of features retained by each algorithm. Notably, PFE and **MCFS** preserve most of the informative features while discarding most of the redundancy. However, **MCFS** is the worst technique in terms of duplicate detection, whereas PFE is the best one together with **NDFS** and **lap_score**. It should be remarked, anyway, that PFE retains all noisy features. Yet, it is not surprising at all as the approach is not designed to get rid of random noise. In authors view, PFE is not meant to be used alone but combined with other complementary feature selection approaches.

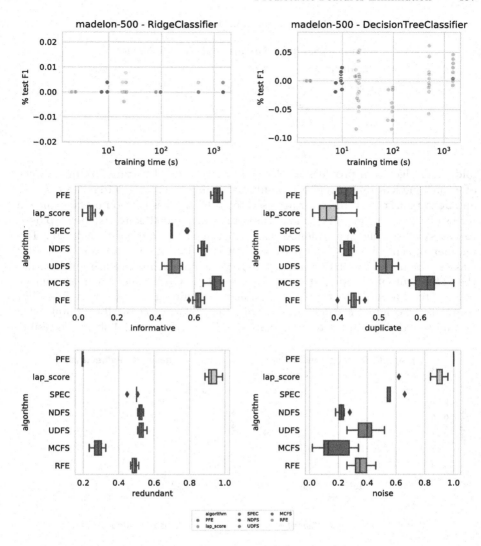

Fig. 1. Classification performances on the MADELON dataset (top two); feature selected for the MADELON dataset (bottom four).

Cross-Task Benchmarks

The ability of feature selection algorithms in tackling different kind of machine learning problems is assessed using four benchmark datasets taken from the OpenML [26]. Table 1 highlights the main characteristics of the four datasets. The first two (gas-drift and isolet) are used to test classification and clustering performances while the latters are employed for regression. The quality of the selections is assessed over a 10-fold cross-validation. Once fitted on a training

Table 1. Benchmark datasets.

Dataset	Samples	Features	Classes	Reference
Gas-drift	13,910	128	6	[27]
Isolet	7,797	617	26	[8]
Mercedes	4,209	377	–	[7]
Crime	1,994	127	–	[24]

fold, each algorithm provides a selection of the original features to an instance of a machine learning model on the filtered training set only. `RidgeClassifier` and `DecisionTreeClassifier` are used to evaluate classification performance in terms of $F1$ score. `AgglomerativeClustering` [29] and `KMeans` [22] are employed to assess clustering performances through the Silhouette coefficient [20]. The number of centroids for k-means is chosen as twice as much as the number of classes. For regression `Ridge` and `DecisionTreeRegressor` are used to measure the coefficient of determination ($R2$ score, [21]). Once collected, performance scores are compared to the ones obtained by training on the same folds but using all the original features. In this way, the performance of all techniques can be evaluated with respect to a fair baseline. Figures 2, 3, and 4 show the results

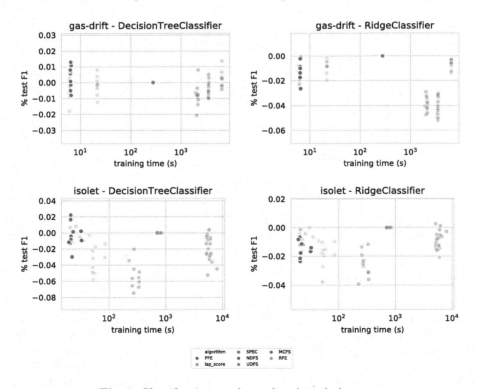

Fig. 2. Classification results on benchmark datasets.

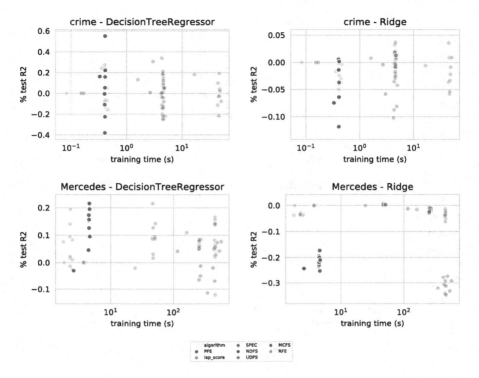

Fig. 3. Regression results on benchmark datasets.

in terms of performance metrics and training time. As mentioned before, all the other feature selection algorithms are set in order to provide for each fold the same number of features chosen by PFE, thus yielding a fair comparison.

Compared to state-of-the-art techniques, PFE is among the fastest solutions together with RFE and lap_score. Notably, RFE is not used for clustering as it is a supervised algorithm, thus it cannot be employed for unsupervised tasks. Despite its unsupervised nature, PFE often matches RFE performances and sometimes provides even better solutions (i.e., Mercedes dataset using DecisionTreeRegressor). The efficiency of PFE with respect to other unsupervised approaches is revealed on the largest dataset (gas-drift) where it is faster by a few order of magnitudes. Moreover, even when PFE performances appear to be slightly worse than others (i.e., Mercedes using Ridge), it may be sufficient to change the downstream predictor (i.e., the performance looks much better when DecisionTreeRegressor is used). Indeed, by construction, PFE performs feature selection such that the information loss is almost negligible.

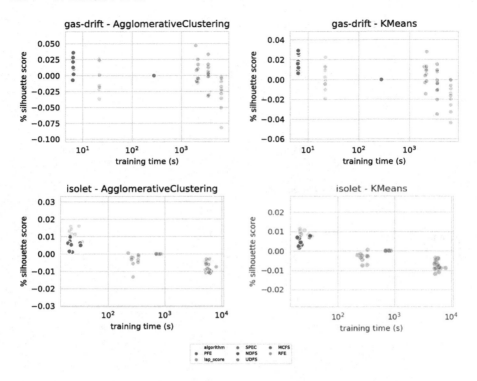

Fig. 4. Clustering results on benchmark datasets.

5   Conclusions

In this paper, a novel feature selection approach named Predictable Features Elimination has been introduced. At the heart of the methodology lies the idea that features whose value can be easily predicted based on the values of other features of the same sample, probably contain mostly redundant information. The algorithm iteratively trains a machine learning model using one of the features as a target, and if the quality of the model is above a user-defined threshold (e.g., $\overline{V} > 0.9$), the feature is removed. After all features have been treated in this way, the remaining ones will constitute the final feature set. Not relying on target labels or values, PFE can be used for supervised, unsupervised, or semi-supervised machine learning problems.

Experimental results prove PFE to be competitive with state-of-the-art feature selection algorithms, on a set of non-trivial classification, regression, and clustering benchmarks. The main drawback of the approach is the impossibility of removing uninformative, but hard-to-predict features, for example those including completely random values: In most cases, however, such features are filtered out by subsequent machine learning algorithms applied to the data, as they have no correlation with the objectives.

Future works will investigate the performance on PFE on a wider range of benchmarks, and explore the possibility of using a similar idea on samples, to uncover coresets and potentially perform dataset compression. Finally, particular focus

References

1. Barbiero, P., Lutton, E., Squillero, G., Tonda, A.: A novel outlook on feature selection as a multi-objective problem. In: Idoumghar, L., Legrand, P., Liefooghe, A., Lutton, E., Monmarché, N., Schoenauer, M. (eds.) EA 2019. LNCS, vol. 12052, pp. 68–81. Springer, Cham (2020). https://doi.org/10.1007/978-3-030-45715-0_6
2. Barbiero, P., Squillero, G., Tonda, A.: Modeling generalization in machine learning: a methodological and computational study. arXiv preprint arXiv:2006.15680 (2020)
3. Bermingham, M., et al.: Application of high-dimensional feature selection: evaluation for genomic prediction in man. Sci. Rep. **5**, 10312 (2015). https://doi.org/10.1038/srep10312
4. Cai, D., Zhang, C., He, X.: Unsupervised feature selection for multi-cluster data. In: Proceedings of the 16th ACM SIGKDD International Conference on Knowledge Discovery and Data Mining, pp. 333–342 (2010)
5. Chien, Y., Fu, K.S.: On the generalized Karhunen-Loéve expansion. IEEE Trans. Inf. Theor. **13**(3), 518–520 (1967)
6. Cilia, N.D., De Stefano, C., Fontanella, F., Scotto di Freca, A.: Variable-length representation for EC-based feature selection in high-dimensional data. In: Kaufmann, P., Castillo, P.A. (eds.) EvoApplications 2019. LNCS, vol. 11454, pp. 325–340. Springer, Cham (2019). https://doi.org/10.1007/978-3-030-16692-2_22
7. Erickson, N., et al.: AutoGluon-Tabular: robust and accurate AutoML for structured data. arXiv preprint arXiv:2003.06505 (2020)
8. Fanty, M., Cole, R.: Spoken letter recognition. In: Advances in Neural Information Processing Systems, pp. 220–226 (1991)
9. Fisher, R.A.: XV.-The correlation between relatives on the supposition of mendelian inheritance. Earth Environ. Sci. Trans. R. Soc. Edinburgh **52**(2), 399–433 (1919)
10. Guyon, I.: Design of experiments of the NIPS 2003 variable selection benchmark. In: NIPS 2003 Workshop on Feature Extraction and Feature Selection (2003)
11. Guyon, I., Elisseeff, A.: An introduction to variable and feature selection. J. Mach. Learn. Res. **3**, 1157–1182 (2003)
12. Guyon, I., Weston, J., Barnhill, S., Vapnik, V.: Gene selection for cancer classification using support vector machines. Mach. Learn. **46**(1–3), 389–422 (2002)
13. Hamdani, T.M., Won, J.-M., Alimi, A.M., Karray, F.: Multi-objective feature selection with NSGA II. In: Beliczynski, B., Dzielinski, A., Iwanowski, M., Ribeiro, B. (eds.) ICANNGA 2007. LNCS, vol. 4431, pp. 240–247. Springer, Heidelberg (2007). https://doi.org/10.1007/978-3-540-71618-1_27
14. He, X., Cai, D., Niyogi, P.: Laplacian score for feature selection. In: Advances in Neural Information Processing Systems, pp. 507–514 (2006)
15. Kozachenko, L., Leonenko, N.N.: Sample estimate of the entropy of a random vector. Problemy Peredachi Informatsii **23**(2), 9–16 (1987)
16. Lewis, P.: The characteristic selection problem in recognition systems. IRE Trans. inf. Theor. **8**(2), 171–178 (1962)

17. Li, J., et al.: Feature selection: a data perspective. ACM Comput. Surv. (CSUR) **50**(6), 94 (2018)
18. Li, Z., Yang, Y., Liu, J., Zhou, X., Lu, H.: Unsupervised feature selection using nonnegative spectral analysis. In: 26th AAAI Conference on Artificial Intelligence (2012)
19. Pedregosa, F., et al.: scikit-learn: machine learning in Python. J. Mach. Learn. Res. **12**, 2825–2830 (2011)
20. Rousseeuw, P.J.: Silhouettes: a graphical aid to the interpretation and validation of cluster analysis. J. Comput. Appl. Math. **20**, 53–65 (1987)
21. Steel, R.G.D., Torrie, J.H., et al.: Principles and Procedures of Statistics (1960)
22. Steinhaus, H.: Sur la division des corp materiels en parties. Bull. Acad. Polon. Sci. **1**(804), 801 (1956)
23. Tsai, F.S.: Dimensionality reduction for computer facial animation. Exp. Syst. Appl. **39**(5), 4965–4971 (2012). https://doi.org/10.1016/j.eswa.2011.10.018
24. Turner, M.C., Krewski, D., Pope, C.A., III., Chen, Y., Gapstur, S.M., Thun, M.J.: Long-term ambient fine particulate matter air pollution and lung cancer in a large cohort of never-smokers. Am. J. Respir. Crit. Care Med. **184**(12), 1374–1381 (2011)
25. Van Rijsbergen, C.J.: Information Retrieval. 2nd edn. Butterworth-Heinemann, Newton, MA (1979)
26. Vanschoren, J., van Rijn, J.N., Bischl, B., Torgo, L.: OpenML: networked science in machine learning. SIGKDD Explor. **15**(2), 49–60 (2013). https://doi.org/10.1145/2641190.2641198
27. Vergara, A., Vembu, S., Ayhan, T., Ryan, M.A., Homer, M.L., Huerta, R.: Chemical gas sensor drift compensation using classifier ensembles. Sens. Actuators B Chem. **166**, 320–329 (2012)
28. Vignolo, L.D., Milone, D.H., Scharcanski, J.: Feature selection for face recognition based on multi-objective evolutionary wrappers. Exp. Syst. Appl. **40**(13), 5077–5084 (2013)
29. Ward, J.H., Jr.: Hierarchical grouping to optimize an objective function. J. Am. Stat. Assoc. **58**(301), 236–244 (1963)
30. Weston, J., Mukherjee, S., Chapelle, O., Pontil, M., Poggio, T., Vapnik, V.: Feature selection for SVMs. In: Advances in Neural Information Processing Systems 13, pp. 668–674. MIT Press (2000)
31. Xue, B., Fu, W., Zhang, M.: Multi-objective feature selection in classification: a differential evolution approach. In: Dick, G., et al. (eds.) SEAL 2014. LNCS, vol. 8886, pp. 516–528. Springer, Cham (2014). https://doi.org/10.1007/978-3-319-13563-2_44
32. Xue, B., Zhang, M., Browne, W.N., Yao, X.: A survey on evolutionary computation approaches to feature selection. IEEE Trans. Evol. Comput. **20**(4), 606–626 (2015)
33. Yang, Y., Shen, H.T., Ma, Z., Huang, Z., Zhou, X.: L2, 1-norm regularized discriminative feature selection for unsupervised. In: 22nd International Joint Conference on Artificial Intelligence (2011)
34. Zhao, Z., Liu, H.: Spectral feature selection for supervised and unsupervised learning. In: Proceedings of the 24th International Conference on Machine Learning, pp. 1151–1157 (2007)
35. Zhou, Z., Li, S., Qin, G., Folkert, M., Jiang, S., Wang, J.: Multi-objective based radiomic feature selection for lesion malignancy classification. IEEE J. Biomed. Health Inform. **24**, 194–204 (2019)
36. Zill, D., Wright, W.S., Cullen, M.R.: Advanced Engineering Mathematics. Jones & Bartlett Learning (2011)

Fast ABC with Joint Generative Modelling and Subset Simulation

Eliane Maalouf[1]([✉])(iD), David Ginsbourger[2](iD), and Niklas Linde[3](iD)

[1] University of Neuchâtel, 2000 Neuchâtel, Switzerland
eliane.maalouf@unine.ch
[2] University of Bern, 3012 Bern, Switzerland
david.ginsbourger@stat.unibe.ch
[3] University of Lausanne, 1015 Lausanne, Switzerland
niklas.linde@unil.ch

Abstract. We propose a novel approach for solving inverse-problems with high-dimensional inputs and an expensive forward mapping. It leverages joint deep generative modelling to transfer the original problem spaces to a lower dimensional latent space. By jointly modelling input and output variables and endowing the latent with a prior distribution, the fitted probabilistic model indirectly gives access to the approximate conditional distributions of interest. Since model error and observational noise with unknown distributions are common in practice, we resort to likelihood-free inference with Approximate Bayesian Computation (ABC). Our method calls on ABC by Subset Simulation to explore the regions of the latent space with dissimilarities between generated and observed outputs below prescribed thresholds. We diagnose the diversity of approximate posterior solutions by monitoring the probability content of these regions as a function of the threshold. We further analyze the curvature of the resulting diagnostic curve to propose an adequate ABC threshold. When applied to a cross-borehole geophysical example, our approach delivers promising performance without using prior knowledge of the forward nor of the noise distribution.

Keywords: Inverse problems · Joint deep generative modelling · Approximate bayesian computation · Subset simulation

1 Introduction

Inverse problems encompass situations where unknown inputs are to be inferred based on given outputs, such as, inverting for physical parameters (e.g. geosciences, astrophysics, etc.) based on observations, or, in broad generality, when inferring parameters of statistical models relying on samples. Here, we focus on situations where a high-dimensional X needs to be retrieved based on observing $Y = F(X) + \eta$, for which calls to the "forward model" F are costly and with η being a noise term with an unknown distribution. Such inverse problems

© Springer Nature Switzerland AG 2022
G. Nicosia et al. (Eds.): LOD 2021, LNCS 13163, pp. 413–429, 2022.
https://doi.org/10.1007/978-3-030-95467-3_30

are generally ill-posed, rendering their solutions non-unique [6], requiring methods that recover the diversity of potential solutions. The Bayesian framework delivers a full posterior distribution of X given y, a realization of Y. It requires the specification of a prior distribution for X and a likelihood function, which relies both on F and on the noise distribution. With this problem formulation, Markov chain Monte Carlo (MCMC) algorithms are classically used to sample from posterior distributions [44].

Although MCMC approaches offer great flexibility, they still suffer from: the high cost of forward evaluations, a cost compounded by a high-dimensional X requiring a large number of explored input instances; and the distribution of η needs to be specified. MCMC methods can be accelerated by reducing the number of calls to F either by exploiting the geometry of the parameter space induced by the statistical model [46, and references therein], or by pre-screening the most promising candidate inputs based on lower-fidelity approximations of X as in two-stage MCMC [12]. While lower-fidelity approximations can be obtained by simplifying the underlying model [20, and references therein], data-driven approximations relying on statistics and machine learning have also been pursued [16,18,19]. Considerable speed-ups can be obtained by surrogating F but high input dimensionality and lack of knowledge of the noise distribution still pose notoriously hard problems.

To circumvent noise specification, Approximate Bayesian Computation (ABC) is a set of likelihood-free methods that sample from a prior distribution on the input space, running stochastic simulations emulating the forward model and the noise generating process, and accepting only candidate inputs that yield outputs close to the observed data [31]. Closeness is specified in terms of a dissimilarity measure on the output space and a tolerance level. The smaller the tolerance level is, the closer the posterior approximation gets to the true posterior while the sample acceptance rate decreases [47]. When the input is high dimensional, the cost of ABC is exacerbated by the increasing number of samples needed to cover the space and avoid missing relevant modes in the posterior. Adaptive methods for ABC aim at improving efficiency by sequentially tuning the proposal distribution in order to target promising regions in the input space [8,45, and references therein]. These methods still require calling the forward model during inference which can become a computational bottleneck.

Our proposed methodology addresses high dimensionality and costly forward models by leveraging joint Generative Neural Networks (jGNN) in combination with adaptive ABC principles. More specifically, a jGNN based on Sinkhorn Auto-Encoders (SAE) [40] parametrizes the candidate solutions by lower-dimensional latent vectors that are explored, offline, with ABC by Subset Simulation (ABC-SubSim) [8].

Our methodological contributions are:

- Development of an approximate inverse-problem-solving framework relying on jGNN based on a generalization of SAEs to joint distribution modelling,
- Efficient sampling of regions in the jGNN latent space susceptible to have generated the observed data using ABC-SubSim "offline",

- A procedure to select the ABC threshold based on monitoring the approximate posterior distribution on the latent space through its estimated prior probability content as a function of the ABC tolerance threshold.

The paper is structured as follows: Sect. 2 presents related works concerning deep generative modelling in probabilistic inference; Sect. 3 presents our methodology in detail; Sect. 4 presents an empirical investigation on a realistic test case in geophysical inversion; Sect. 5 provides a conclusion and an outlook of future works.

2   Related Works

Neural Networks (NN) have been used to estimate parameters of prescribed parametric families of distributions. *Regression ABC* and *Adaptive Gaussian Copula ABC* [5,7] train feed-forward network regressors $r(y)$ such that the posterior mean is approximated by $r(y_{obs})$, y_{obs} being the observation vector. The initial ABC sample is corrected such that the adjusted realizations correspond to a sample from the posterior. *Sequential Neural Posterior Estimation* (SNPE) [14, and references therein] sequentially approximates the posterior density where a NN takes y_{obs} as input and outputs the parameters of a Gaussian mixture over the input space. *Synthetic Neural Likelihood* (SNL) [39] applies a similar iterative idea as SNPE but to approximate the likelihood by a Masked Autoregressive Flow network. Samples from the posterior are drawn by MCMC based on the synthetic likelihood. Neural density estimators were also used to learn proposal distributions integrated in MCMC [21] or sequential Monte Carlo [15].

Variational Auto-Encoders (VAE) [23], *Generative Adversarial Networks* (GAN) [9] and *Invertible Neural Networks* (INN) [24] avoid the explicit choice of parametric families for the distributions. Instead, they are trained to sample from distributions by transforming realizations from a simple (e.g. Gaussian or uniform) latent multivariate distribution into realizations from the distribution of interest by applying a sequence of non-linear transformations. In inversion, they were used to reduce the dimension of the input space in preparation for its exploration via the latent space, by MCMC [26,27,35] or by optimization [29,43].

In the previous methods the forward F is called during training, inference or to sequentially guide the sampling from the input space. This is a limitation when F is costly or only available through a sample of realizations.

Learning direct transformations, parametrized by NN, from the observation vector into a plausible solution in the input space were investigated for inversion in geophysics [28,36] and imaging [30,32,37]. These approaches lack an inherent mechanism to quantify the variability in the proposed solutions. Conditional variants of generative NN, where a conditioning signal is provided along the latent random vector, were developed to directly sample from an approximation to the posterior distributions. cINN were demonstrated for inversion in astrophysics, medical imaging [3] and geophysics [2]. These models impose a trade-off between tractable density estimation and sampling since most implementations have difficulties to compute inverses [24]. A workaround is to train two networks: one for conditional sampling and one for density estimation [2]. Pix2pix [17] is a widely used cGAN-based [11,33] framework for inversion in computer vision. cGANs were also demonstrated in medical image reconstruction [1] and in hydrogeology [10] (as a surrogate to the forward function). cVAE [48] were also used for similar purposes in computational imaging [51]. Conditional generative NNs amortize inference by not calling the forward F yet they lack an inherent mechanism to adapt to the unknown noise and to their approximation bias.

To the best of our knowledge, our approach is the first to adapt joint generative modelling and ABC sampling on the latent space, based on Subset Simulation, to inverse problem solving. Unlike the existing methods, our novel adaptation allows to, simultaneously, surrogate F, provide sample based uncertainty quantification and avoid noise specification.

Among the available methods, we compare the performance of our method to cVAE on the experimental test case. We selected cVAE because it is conceptually close to our jGNN, it generates samples from the posterior of interest and it avoids calling F during inference. Solving inverse problems with generative neural networks is a nascent domain with limited benchmarks. Up to the time of writing, existing benchmarks [25,42] showed varying performances depending on the datasets, architectures and training adjustments. cVAE remains a relevant competitive method in this area.

3 Proposed Methodology

We assume throughout the following that (X, Y) can be expressed as a function of some latent variable Z, of moderate dimension compared to X and Y, such that $(X, Y) = G^o(Z) = (g_1^o(Z), g_2^o(Z))$. For a known G^o, uncovering the conditional distribution of X knowing $Y = y$ amounts to uncovering the distribution of $g_1^o(Z)$ knowing $g_2^o(Z)$, which follows in turn from the conditional distribution of Z knowing $g_2^o(Z)$. The goal of the following two sections is to present, first, the generative modelling framework used to estimate the map G^o, by G, from data and, second, how to approximate the conditional distribution of Z knowing $Y = y$ by relying on ABC-SubSim.

3.1 Joint Generative Modelling

The initial step is to train a joint Generative Neural Network (jGNN) to sample from the joint distribution of (X, Y), denoted P_{XY}, based on available data $(X_1, Y_1), \ldots, (X_n, Y_n)$. The jGNN is specified by a map $G : \mathbb{Z} \to \mathbb{X} \times \mathbb{Y}$ and a prior distribution P_Z on $\mathbb{Z}$, where $\mathbb{X}, \mathbb{Y}, \mathbb{Z}$ are the domains in which X, Y, Z vary, respectively.

Training of the considered jGNN consists of minimizing some prescribed distance between P_{XY} and $G_\# P_Z = P_{\tilde{X}\tilde{Y}}$, where $(\tilde{X}, \tilde{Y}) = (g_1(Z), g_2(Z))$ and $G_\# P_Z$ is the image (or *pushforward*) probability measure of P_Z by G.

In our implementation we extended the Sinkhorn Auto-Encoder (SAE) [40], a variant of the Wasserstein Auto-Encoder [50], to the joint learning case by closely applying its formalism on an augmented space $\mathbb{X} \times \mathbb{Y}$. Let $Q : \mathbb{X} \times \mathbb{Y} \to \mathbb{Z}$ represent the encoder map and $G : \mathbb{Z} \to \mathbb{X} \times \mathbb{Y}$ the decoder/generator map. The jGNN training goal is to minimize the optimal transport cost between P_{XY} and $P_{\tilde{X}\tilde{Y}}$ via the minimization over deterministic maps G, in a family $\mathcal{G}$, of:

$$W_c(P_{XY}, P_{\tilde{X}\tilde{Y}}) = \inf_{\pi \in \mathcal{P}(P_{XY}, P_{\tilde{X}\tilde{Y}})} \mathbb{E}_{(X,\tilde{X},Y,\tilde{Y}) \sim \pi}[c(X, \tilde{X}; Y, \tilde{Y})],$$

where $\mathcal{P}(P_{XY}, P_{\tilde{X}\tilde{Y}})$ is the set of all joint distributions having "marginals" (on $\mathbb{X} \times \mathbb{Y}$) P_{XY} and $P_{\tilde{X}\tilde{Y}}$ and $c(.,.,.,.)$ is a function expressing the cost of transporting a couple (X, Y) to a couple $(\tilde{X}, \tilde{Y})$. We consider $\mathbb{X}$, $\mathbb{Y}$ and $\mathbb{Z}$ to be Euclidean spaces and we set $c(X, \tilde{X}; Y, \tilde{Y}) = ||X - \tilde{X}||_p^p + ||Y - \tilde{Y}||_p^p$, a separable cost based on the L_p norms on $\mathbb{X}$ and $\mathbb{Y}$. $c(.,.,.,.)$ is an L_p norm, taken to the power p, on the product space $\mathbb{X} \times \mathbb{Y}$. Following [40], the jGNN optimization objective is to minimize over deterministic maps G and Q, in families $\mathcal{G}$ and $\mathcal{Q}$ respectively, of the quantity:

$$\mathcal{L} = \sqrt[p]{\mathbb{E}_{XY \sim P_{XY}}[||X - g_1(Q(X,Y))||_p^p + ||Y - g_2(Q(X,Y))||_p^p]} + \lambda . W_p(Q_Z, P_Z), \quad (1)$$

with λ to be greater than the Lipschitz constant of G. This loss balances between the objectives of reconstructing the training data accurately, while constraining the encoder $Q(Z|XY)$ to distribute its embeddings in $\mathbb{Z}$ such that $Q_Z = \mathbb{E}_{XY \sim P_{XY}} Q(Z|XY)$ fits a prescribed distribution P_Z.

In practice, the p-th roots are removed from (1) for computational convenience. $W_p(Q_Z, P_Z)$ is estimated based on samples using the Sinkhorn algorithm [13]. To avoid the deterioration of the Wasserstein estimation when increasing the latent space dimension we set its entropy regularization parameter to 100 and its maximum number of iterations to 40. Optimization of the loss function was done with the Adam algorithm [22] (lr $= 0.001$, $\beta_1 = 0.9$, $\beta_2 = 0.999$) with a batch size of 128. The reconstruction errors were taken as the L_2 norm normalized by the dimensions of $\mathbb{X}$ and $\mathbb{Y}$ (i.e. Mean Squared Errors). The parameter λ was set to 150 at the beginning of the training and its value was cut by half every 500 epochs. This procedure helped the training by successively adding more weight to the reconstruction part of the loss compared to the regularization part. Spectral normalization [34] was used in both the encoder and the decoder networks. In its absence we observed unstable training where one of the variables, X or Y, is not learned correctly. The network architecture and its components are shown in Fig. 1.

3.2   Inversion by Subset Simulation

We now consider that vector y_{obs}, assumed to be a realization from Y, was observed and we seek to retrieve the posterior distribution of X knowing $Y = y_{obs}$. Given the deterministic jGNN outputting $\tilde{X} = g_1(Z)$ and $\tilde{Y} = g_2(Z)$, we

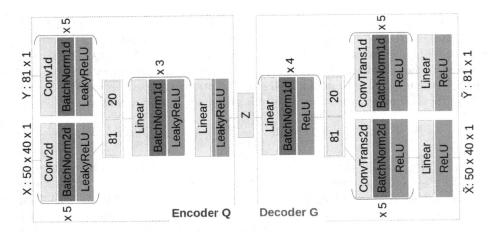

Fig. 1. Schematic of the jGNN architecture and its components. Variables X and Y are first transformed by separate sub-networks of 5 layers containing convolution-Batchnorm-LeakyReU layers. The intermediate features are then combined in 3 layers of Linear-Batchnorm-Leakyrelu. The decoder has a symmetrical architecture with Transposed Convolutions-Batchnorm-ReLU layers and ending with linear layers and ReLU activations.

can use instead the distribution of $g_1(Z)$ knowing $g_2(Z) = y_{obs}$. In other words, the posterior on X is induced by a posterior on Z and the jGNN surrogates the forward model during inversion. In practice, the equality $g_2(Z) = y_{obs}$ is seldom reached due to measurement errors on the observation vector and errors in the jGNN training, hence, we need to consider instead that $y_{obs} = g_2(Z) + \eta$, where the term η encompasses all sources of errors. To account for those errors, we introduce $\Gamma_\epsilon = \{z \in Z : d(g_2(z) - y_{obs}) \leq \epsilon\}$ with $d(.,.)$ a dissimilarity measure on Y (e.g. its L_p norm) and ϵ a tolerance parameter. Furthermore, let π_Z stand for the prior density of Z (with respect to Lebesgue or some other dominating measure on Z). We consider here a surrogate posterior density on Z (given y_{obs}) defined by $\pi_{Z|Z \in \Gamma_\epsilon}(z) \propto \mathbb{1}_{\Gamma_\epsilon}(z) \pi_Z(z)$. This posterior on Z directly leads to an approximate posterior distribution on X knowing y_{obs} by image via g_1. Depending on the choice of ϵ and other problem settings such as the dimension of Z, $\{Z \in \Gamma_\epsilon\}$ may become a rare event to simulate. We use SuS [4], a rare event sampler, as an adaptive sampler in ABC [8] to sample from $\pi_{Z|Z \in \Gamma_\epsilon}$. Our implementation of SuS is based on [52].

SuS introduces a decreasing sequence of thresholds $+\infty = t_0 > t_1 > t_2... > t_m = \epsilon$ which determines a sequence of nested subsets of Z, $\Gamma_{t_\ell} = \{z \in Z : d(g_2(z), y_{obs}) \leq t_\ell\}(\ell = 0, ..., m)$. For the sequence of events $\{Z \in \Gamma_{t_\ell}\}$ we have that : $P(Z \in \Gamma_\epsilon) = P(Z \in \Gamma_{t_0}) \prod_{\ell=1}^{m} P(Z \in \Gamma_{t_\ell} | Z \in \Gamma_{t_{\ell-1}})$ with $P(Z \in \Gamma_{t_0}) = 1$ since $\{Z \in \Gamma_{t_0}\}$ is certain. This reduces the problem of estimating the small $p_\epsilon = P(Z \in \Gamma_\epsilon)$ to estimating a sequence of larger conditional probabilities $P(Z \in \Gamma_{t_\ell} | Z \in \Gamma_{t_{\ell-1}})$.

The SuS algorithm starts with an initial sample from the prior of $\mathbb{Z}$, $\{Z_i^{(0)}\}_{i=1}^N$, with a predefined size N. The dissimilarity values $\{d(g_2(Z_i^{(0)}), y_{obs})\}_{i=1}^N$ are calculated and ordered and the first threshold t_1 is defined as the α-percentile of those values. α is prescribed and typically chosen in the range $[0.1, 0.3]$ [53]. The set Γ_{t_1} is first populated by the observations from this initial sample that yield distances below t_1. Starting from each one of those succeeding observations, sufficiently many states of a Markov chain with stationary distribution $\pi_{Z|Z \in \Gamma_{t_1}}$ are generated to complete the current elements of Γ_{t_1} up to N elements (cf. [38] for specific details on the MCMC sampling methods with SuS). At each subsequent iteration $\ell = 2, ..., m$, the sample $\{Z_i^{(\ell-1)}\}_{i=1}^N$ is used to calculate $\{d(g_2(Z_i^{(\ell-1)}), y_{obs})\}_{i=1}^N$ and to set t_ℓ as the α-percentile of those distances. New observations in Γ_{t_ℓ} are again sampled starting from the observations that yield distances below t_ℓ. This process stops when ϵ is crossed (i.e. if the proposed $t_\ell \le \epsilon$ then m is defined as ℓ and t_m is set equal to ϵ) or when a prescribed maximum number of iterations is reached. The final elements of Γ_ϵ are used to form candidate solutions in $\mathbb{X}$ via g_1. p_ϵ can be estimated via $\hat{p}_\epsilon = \alpha^{m-1} \frac{N_{m-1}}{N}$, with N_{m-1} being the number of succeeding particles at the penultimate iteration of SuS. This estimator sheds some light on the diversity/uncertainty in the proposed solutions, from the jGNN's latent space perspective.

4   Experiments

For space limitations, and to thoroughly present the methodology, we focused only on analyzing the performance for one application. We applied the method to cross-hole Ground Penetrating Radar (GPR) tomography as a realistic inversion setting. In this geophysical method, a source emits high-frequency electromagnetic waves at a given depth in one borehole, while the response is recorded by a receiver antenna at a given depth in an adjacent borehole. The first-arrival travel times of the recorded traces, for different acquisition geometries, are used to retrieve the slowness field (i.e. inverse of the velocity field) between the boreholes.

Training and test sets[1] of couples of subsurface domains and their corresponding solver output (i.e. (X, Y)) were simulated using an approximate linear forward solver (Fig. 2(b,c)). The domain (i.e. X) is discretized on a grid of size 50×40 with a cell size of $0.1\,\mathrm{m}$, leading to $\mathbb{X}$ being of dimension 2000. The boreholes are located $3.9\,\mathrm{m}$ apart (Fig. 2(a)). Nine source and receiver locations are regularly spaced between 0.5 and $4.5\,\mathrm{m}$ depth leading to a measurement vector (i.e. Y) with 81 travel times. The slowness field is described by a Gaussian prior with an isotropic exponential kernel, a length scale of $2.5\,\mathrm{m}$ and a variance at the origin of $0.16\ (\mathrm{ns/m})^2$.

The data used for training were not noise-contaminated. To validate the method, we sample solver outputs from the test set, not seen during training,

---

[1] Datasets and code scripts are available at: https://github.com/elianemaalouf/Fast-ABC.

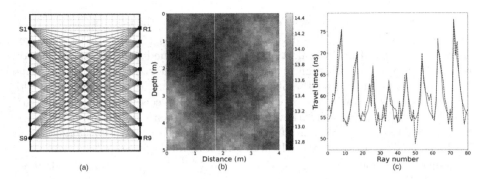

Fig. 2. (a): Cross-hole tomography setup, S1-9 GPR sources and R1-9 GPR receivers; (b): slowness field in ns/m; (c): first arrival travel time vectors in ns given by the forward solver corresponding to (b) and contaminated by Gaussian noise realizations with standard deviations of 0.54 ns (blue-solid) and 2.29 ns (black-dashed). (Color figure online)

and contaminate them with noise vectors and use the noisy vectors as the measurement vectors, y_{obs}, to invert. In the following, we present results obtained for noise vectors from the standard multivariate Gaussian with a standard deviation of 0.5 ns (referred to by "small noise") and a standard deviation of 2.5 ns (referred to by "large noise"). Furthermore, working under the unknown noise assumption, we did not contaminate the jGNN proposed travel times ($\tilde{y}$) by noise during the ABC-SubSim posterior approximation, as is done in classical ABC. This dataset, despite not being an established benchmark, allows to manipulate moderately high dimensional variables while still providing analytical solutions as basis for comparison. Indeed, when the noise is Gaussian, given the Gaussian prior on the field and the linear solver, the exact Gaussian posterior on $\mathbb{X}$ is available analytically [49]. This analytical solution is the reference against which our model and the cVAE model are compared. We present the results on forty inversions with different slowness fields and contaminate the data with different noise realizations. The metric used for comparison is the Root Mean Squared Error (RMSE)[2].

ABC-SubSim Threshold Impact: in practice, we ran the ABC-SubSim posterior approximation to retrieve solutions that guarantee $||\tilde{y} - y_{obs}||_2^2 \leq \epsilon$ with targeted threshold $\epsilon \in [0.01 \text{ ns}^2, 3000 \text{ ns}^2]$. In the following ϵ_n refers to $\sqrt{\frac{\epsilon}{81}}$ ns, the normalized value of ϵ. When the targeted value for ϵ is close or below the noise level, the SuS algorithm consumes its iterations budget before reaching the ϵ by the sequential update loop and stagnates at threshold values close to the noise level (its L_2 squared norm). At these thresholds, ABC-SubSim is trying to fit the noise very closely which leads to low diversity solutions and potential artifacts (Fig. 3(a, b) column "ϵ= 0.54 ns"). On the contrary, when the threshold is very

---

[2] For vectors V_1 and V_2, both of dimension m, $RMSE(V_1, V_2) = \sqrt{\frac{1}{m}||V_1 - V_2||_2^2}$.

large, the proposed solutions move further away from the ground truth and the posterior approximation moves closer to the prior distribution (Fig. 3(a, b) column "$\epsilon = 2.48$ ns"). Between these extremes lies a set of values for the threshold that provide an approximate posterior whose samples show comparable statistics to the analytical posterior samples (Fig. 3(a, b) column "$\epsilon = 0.7$ ns"). This set can be seen on Fig. 4 where the sample-based estimates of the Wasserstein distance between our approximate posterior and, on one hand, the ground truth Dirac, and the exact posterior on the other hand, are minimal.

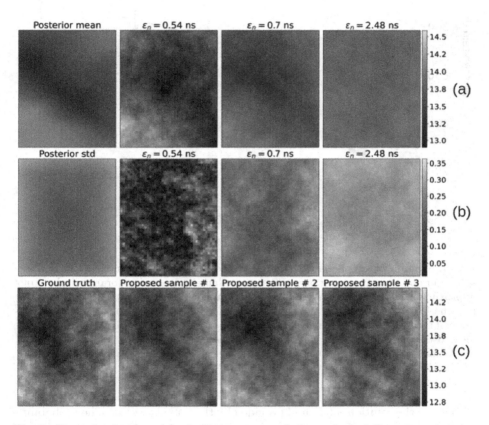

Fig. 3. Example showing: (a) pixel wise means of the analytical Gaussian posterior along pixel wise means of a sample from our approximate posterior, at different thresholds ϵ_n; (b) pixel wise standard deviations of the analytical Gaussian posterior along pixel wise standard deviations of a sample from our approximate posterior, at different thresholds ϵ_n; (c) ground truth slowness field along proposed solutions by our method at $\epsilon_n = 0.7$ ns. Gaussian noise realization with a standard deviation of 0.54 ns.

However, the plots in Fig. 4 are not available in practice and cannot be used to select a suitable threshold for ABC-SubSim. Instead, we propose to monitor the evolution of $\widehat{p}_\epsilon$, an estimate of the probability that a randomly sampled z

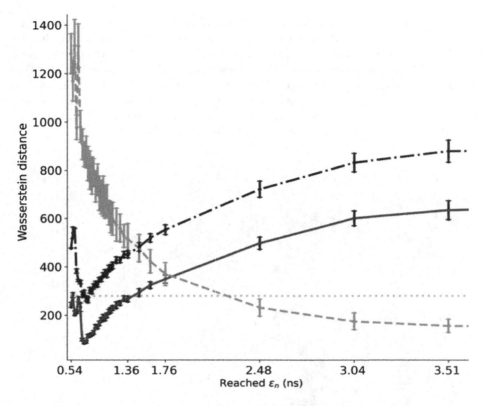

Fig. 4. Example of sample-based estimates of the Wasserstein distances between: (blue-solid) our approximate posterior and the exact Gaussian posterior; (orange-dashed) our approximate posterior and the prior on $\mathbb{X}$; (green-dot-dash) our approximate posterior and the Dirac located at the true solution. The red dotted line is a sample-based estimate of the Wasserstein distance between the exact posterior and the Dirac distribution located on the true solution. The minima of the green-dot-dashed and the blue-solid are located in the interval [0.66 ns, 0.74 ns] of ϵ_n. Gaussian noise realization with a standard deviation 0.54 ns. (Color figure online)

belongs to the solution set Γ_ϵ and provided by the SuS algorithm. The probability content curve in Fig. 5 provides two important pieces of information: the lowest value reached by ϵ_n on the horizontal axis, where the sequential update to the ABC-SubSim threshold by SuS stagnates, is informative about the (normalized) noise level; and the values of ϵ_n falling at, or in close proximity to, the point of highest curvature coincide with the region of the most suitable thresholds identified in Fig. 4. The curvature is estimated based on a smoothed estimate of the logarithm of the probability $\widehat{p}_\epsilon$ as function of ϵ.

Comparison with cVAE: We compared our methodology with a conditional distribution sampler learned by a cVAE. For space limitation, we refer the reader to

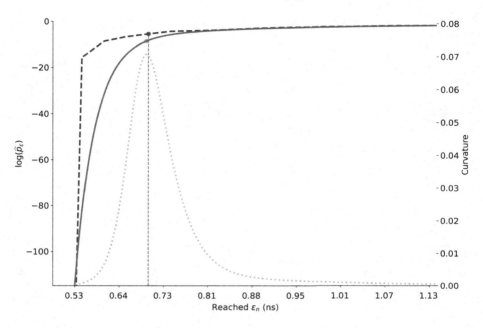

Fig. 5. Example of (blue-dashed) logarithm of the estimate $\widehat{p}_\epsilon$ of the probability that a randomly sampled z belongs to the solution set Γ_ϵ and (orange-full) its smoothed estimation used to estimate the (green-dotted) curvature. The peak of the curvature suggests an adequate threshold for the ABC-SubSim approximation. We take the closest threshold in the set of tested threshold values (grey-dashed), in this case $\epsilon_n = 0.7$ ns. Gaussian noise realization with a standard deviation 0.54 ns. (Color figure online)

[23,25,42,48] for formal and implementation details. In summary, the main differences between our jGNN and cVAE are: the jGNN is required to reconstruct both X and Y while cVAE only needs to reconstruct X given a realization of Y; and the encoder in cVAE aims to fit $Q(Z|X,Y)$ with a standard Gaussian for each couple (X,Y) while our jGNN aims to fit the aggregated $Q(Z)$ for all couples (X,Y) with the standard Gaussian.

We adapted our jGNN to the cVAE training objective in order to have models with comparable number of trainable parameters. The adaptation concerned mainly the transformation of the joint (X,Y) input-output from our jGNN into an input-output for X and a sub-network to integrate Y with the latent vector for cVAE. Both models were trained for 5000 epochs with the Adam optimizer (learning rate $= 0.001$, $\beta_1 = 0.9$, $\beta_2 = 0.999$). We monitored reconstruction statistics on a validation set and picked the best training epoch towards the end of the training. To select the regularization parameter for cVAE we tested several values in $\{0.005, 0.05, 0.585, 1\}$ and kept 0.05 which gave the best reconstruction statistics on the validation set. Under these conditions, we see in Fig. 6((a)-left column) that overall the cVAE model is able to retrieve solutions that are close to the ground truth when the noise is small. However, when looking at individual inversions results in Fig. 6(b) we see that the diversity of those solutions is very

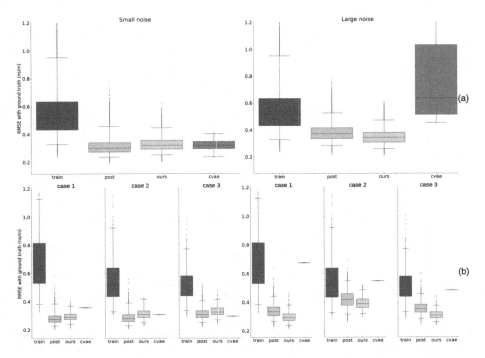

Fig. 6. (a) Distributions of the aggregated RMSE values between proposed solutions and ground truths for all forty inversion tests, with two noise scenarios: (left column) realizations from a standard Gaussian with standard deviation of 0.5 ns; (right column) realizations from a standard Gaussian with standard deviation of 2.5 ns. On the horizontal: "train" refers to RMSE values between ground truths and training data set; "post" refers to RMSE values between analytical posterior samples and ground truths; "ours" refers to RMSE values between our ABC-SubSim proposed solutions and ground truths at the threshold at maximum curvature of $\log(\widehat{p}_\epsilon)$; "cvae" refers to RMSE values between our trained cVAE proposed solutions and ground truths. These plots are at latent space size of 30 and training set size of 1000. The plots are cut off above RMSE values of 1.2 ns to reduce space. (b) Three specific inversion cases disposed as in (a) with regards to the noise and the horizontal axis.

low compared to the analytical posterior. This is an indicator of the posterior collapsing to a single mode, a behaviour similarly observed with cVAE in other contexts [25,41]. We believe that tuning the objective function could help avoid this collapse [1,41] with a better trade-off between reducing the reconstruction error and the latent space regularization. However, this trade-off is not straightforward and we restricted ourselves to the objective functions implemented in [25,42,48]. Furthermore, Fig. 6((a)-right column) shows that the cVAE model we trained is unable to retrieve meaningful solutions in the large noise situation while our methodology remains robust in such conditions at a suitable ABC-SubSim threshold.

Assessment of the Learned Forward Function: as in [25], we refer by "resimulation" to the output of the forward function F called on our proposed solutions $\tilde{X}$ and we denote them by Y_r (i.e. $Y_r = F(\tilde{X})$). RMSE between Y_r and the output of the jGNN $\tilde{Y}$, generated along the proposed solutions $\tilde{X}$, estimate the errors of the learned function F by the jGNN. For "small noise" realizations, these RMSE values had an average of 0.370 ns (median: 0.346 ns; 95% interval: [0.194 ns, 0.687 ns]) and an average of 0.424 ns (median: 0.385 ns; 95% interval: [0.204 ns, 0.834 ns]) for the "large noise" realizations. Even though no common reference for comparison is available, these values should tend to zero as the jGNN training is improved.

Furthermore, the RMSE values calculated between Y_r and y_{obs} were on average at 0.745 ns (median: 0.729 ns; 95% interval: [0.571 ns, 1.015 ns]) with the "small noise" realizations and at 2.500 ns (median: 2.489 ns; 95% interval: [2.206 ns, 2.888 ns]) with "large noise" realizations. These values should be close to the level of the noise that contaminated the observations which is often the case with the "large noise" scenario (i.e. noise standard deviation of 2.5 ns). In the "small noise" scenario we believe that the jGNN bias is having a more perceivable impact on the sampling of potential solutions explaining the discrepancy with the noise (i.e. noise standard deviation of 0.5 ns).

Latent Space Dimension and Training Set Size Impact: we trained the jGNN with dimensions of the latent space in {10, 30, 100} and with training set sizes in {1000, 4000}. For lack of space we do not detail these results here. In summary, very comparable performances across dimensions were observed for the training set size of 1000. This suggests that the inversion with ABC-SubSim is robust with regards to the latent space dimension choice. Similar observations were made with training set size of 4000 with slight deterioration for dimension 10 and 30, hinting to a potential overfit at these dimensions.

5   Conclusion and Outlook

We proposed a methodology for realistic inverse problems based on learning a joint deep generative model constructing a low dimensional latent space encoding the variables of the problem. On this latent space an approximate posterior is sampled from by ABC with the Subset Simulation algorithm locating adequate regions for the solutions. Our experiments show promising potential when compared to the analytical solution and a conditional VAE. Furthermore, the method demonstrates robustness to large levels of noise, often encountered in practice. Robustness was also observed across the latent space dimension choice. Furthermore, we proposed to monitor the evolution of the probability content in the latent space. From the resulting diagnostic curve, we retrieved an indication about the unknown noise level and we identified an empirical rule to set the ABC-SubSim threshold based on locating its maximum curvature. Finally, in our framework calling the forward solver was avoided during inference which is expected to keep the computational cost of the method relatively low across multiple inversions, after the initial training data set generation.

To improve on this work, we will extend the evaluation to inverse problems with non-linear physics and different noise distributions. Similarly, analysing the sensitivity of the approach to the norms choice in the jGNN objective and ABC-SubSim, the prior distributions of Z and X, and the network architecture is paramount to further validate the methodology. Finally, augmenting our approach with an adaptive scheme to optimally sample new training data points and integrating them on the fly can help improve its sample efficiency.

References

1. Adler, J., Öktem, O.: Deep bayesian inversion. arXiv preprint arXiv:1811.05910 (2018)
2. Anantha Padmanabha, G., Zabaras, N.: Solving inverse problems using conditional invertible neural networks. J. Comput. Phys. **433**, May 2021. https://doi.org/10.1016/j.jcp.2021.110194
3. Ardizzone, L., Kruse, J., Rother, C., Köthe, U.: Analyzing inverse problems with invertible neural networks. In: International Conference on Learning Representations, ICLR (2018)
4. Au, S.K., Beck, J.L.: Estimation of small failure probabilities in high dimensions by subset simulation. Probab. Eng. Mech. **16**(4), 263–277 (2001). https://doi.org/10.1016/S0266-8920(01)00019-4
5. Blum, M.G., François, O.: Non-linear regression models for approximate bayesian computation. Stat. Comput. **20**(1), 63–73 (2010). https://doi.org/10.1007/s11222-009-9116-0
6. Calvetti, D., Somersalo, E.: Inverse problems: from regularization to bayesian inference. Wiley Interdisc. Rev. Comput. Stat. **10**(3), e1427 (2018). https://doi.org/10.1002/wics.1427
7. Chen, Y., Gutmann, M.U.: Adaptive gaussian copula ABC. In: The 22nd International Conference on Artificial Intelligence and Statistics, pp. 1584–1592. PMLR (2019)
8. Chiachio, M., Beck, J.L., Chiachio, J., Rus, G.: Approximate bayesian computation by subset simulation. SIAM J. Sci. Comput. **36**(3), A1339–A1358 (2014). https://doi.org/10.1137/130932831
9. Creswell, A., White, T., Dumoulin, V., Arulkumaran, K., Sengupta, B., Bharath, A.A.: Generative adversarial networks: an overview. IEEE Signal Process. Mag. **35**(1), 53–65 (2018). https://doi.org/10.1016/j.jjimei.2020.100004
10. Dagasan, Y., Juda, P., Renard, P.: Using generative adversarial networks as a fast forward operator for hydrogeological inverse problems. Groundwater **58**(6), 938–950 (2020). https://doi.org/10.1111/gwat.13005
11. Ding, X., Wang, Y., Xu, Z., Welch, W.J., Wang, Z.J.: Ccgan: continuous conditional generative adversarial networks for image generation. In: International Conference on Learning Representations, ICLR (2021)
12. Efendiev, Y., Datta-Gupta, A., Ginting, V., Ma, X., Mallick, B.: An efficient two-stage Markov chain Monte Carlo method for dynamic data integration. Water Resour. Res. **41**(12) (2005). https://doi.org/10.1029/2004WR003764
13. Genevay, A., Peyre, G., Cuturi, M.: Learning generative models with sinkhorn divergences. In: International Conference on Artificial Intelligence and Statistics, pp. 1608–1617. PMLR (2018)

14. Greenberg, D., Nonnenmacher, M., Macke, J.: Automatic posterior transformation for likelihood-free inference. In: International Conference on Machine Learning, pp. 2404–2414. PMLR (2019)

15. Gu, S., Ghahramani, Z., Turner, R.: Neural adaptive sequential Monte Carlo. In: Advances in Neural Information Processing Systems, vol. 2, pp. 2629–2637 (2015)

16. Gutmann, M.U., Corander, J.: Bayesian optimization for likelihood-free inference of simulator-based statistical models. J. Mach. Learn. Res. $17(1)$, 4256–4302 (2016)

17. Isola, P., Zhu, J.Y., Zhou, T., Efros, A.A.: Image-to-image translation with conditional adversarial networks. In: Proceedings of the IEEE Conference on Computer Vision and Pattern Recognition, pp. 1125–1134 (2017)

18. Järvenpää, M., Gutmann, M., Vehtari, A., Marttinen, P.: Gaussian process modeling in approximate bayesian computation to estimate horizontal gene transfer in bacteria. stat 1050, 21 (2017)

19. Järvenpää, M., Gutmann, M.U., Vehtari, A., Marttinen, P., et al.: Parallel gaussian process surrogate bayesian inference with noisy likelihood evaluations. Bayesian Analysis (2020)

20. Josset, L., Demyanov, V., Elsheikh, A.H., Lunati, I.: Accelerating Monte Carlo Markov chains with proxy and error models. Comput. Geosci. **85**, 38–48 (2015). https://doi.org/10.1016/j.cageo.2015.07.003

21. Kim, D., Song, K., Kim, Y., Shin, Y., Moon, I.C.: Sequential likelihood-free inference with implicit surrogate proposal. arXiv preprint arXiv:2010.07604 (2020)

22. Kingma, D.P., Ba, J.: Adam: a method for stochastic optimization. arXiv preprint arXiv:1412.6980 (2014)

23. Kingma, D.P., Welling, M., et al.: An introduction to variational autoencoders. Found. Trends Mach. Learn. **12**(4), 307–392 (2019)

24. Kobyzev, I., Prince, S., Brubaker, M.: Normalizing flows: an introduction and review of current methods. IEEE Trans. Pattern Anal. Mach. Intell. (2020). https://doi.org/10.1109/TPAMI.2020.2992934

25. Kruse, J., Ardizzone, L., Rother, C., Köthe, U.: Benchmarking invertible architectures on inverse problems. arXiv preprint arXiv:2101.10763 (2021)

26. Laloy, E., Hérault, R., Jacques, D., Linde, N.: Training-image based geostatistical inversion using a spatial generative adversarial neural network. Water Resour. Res. **54**, 381–406 (2018). https://doi.org/10.1002/2017WR022148

27. Laloy, E., Hérault, R., Lee, J., Jacques, D., Linde, N.: Inversion using a new low-dimensional representation of complex binary geological media based on a deep neural network. Adv. Water Resour. **110**, 387–405 (2017). https://doi.org/10.1016/j.advwatres.2017.09.029

28. Laloy, E., Linde, N., Jacques, D.: Approaching geoscientific inverse problems with vector-to-image domain transfer networks. Adv. Water Resour. **152**, 103917 (2021). https://doi.org/10.1016/j.advwatres.2021.103917

29. Lopez-Alvis, J., Laloy, E., Nguyen, F., Hermans, T.: Deep generative models in inversion: the impact of the generator's nonlinearity and development of a new approach based on a variational autoencoder. Comput. Geosci. **152** (2021). https://doi.org/10.1016/j.cageo.2021.104762

30. Lucas, A., Iliadis, M., Molina, R., Katsaggelos, A.K.: Using deep neural networks for inverse problems in imaging: beyond analytical methods. IEEE Signal Process. Mag. **35**(1), 20–36 (2018). https://doi.org/10.1109/MSP.2017.2760358

31. Marjoram, P., Molitor, J., Plagnol, V., Tavaré, S.: Markov chain Monte Carlo without likelihoods. Proc. Natl. Acad. Sci. **100**(26), 15324–15328 (2003). https://doi.org/10.1073/pnas.0306899100

32. McCann, M.T., Jin, K.H., Unser, M.: Convolutional neural networks for inverse problems in imaging: a review. IEEE Signal Process. Mag. **34**(6), 85–95 (2017). https://doi.org/10.1109/MSP.2017.2739299
33. Mirza, M., Osindero, S.: Conditional generative adversarial nets. arXiv preprint arXiv:1411.1784 (2014)
34. Miyato, T., Kataoka, T., Koyama, M., Yoshida, Y.: Spectral normalization for generative adversarial networks. In: International Conference on Learning Representations, ICLR (2018)
35. Mosser, L., Dubrule, O., Blunt, M.J.: Stochastic seismic waveform inversion using generative adversarial networks as a geological prior. Math. Geosci. **52**(1), 53–79 (2019). https://doi.org/10.1007/s11004-019-09832-6
36. Mosser, L., Kimman, W., Dramsch, J., Purves, S., De la Fuente Briceño, A., Ganssle, G.: Rapid seismic domain transfer: seismic velocity inversion and modeling using deep generative neural networks. In: EAGE Conference and Exhibition (2018). https://doi.org/10.3997/2214-4609.201800734
37. Ongie, G., Jalal, A., Metzler, C.A., Baraniuk, R.G., Dimakis, A.G., Willett, R.: Deep learning techniques for inverse problems in imaging. IEEE J. Sel. Areas Inf. Theory **1**(1), 39–56 (2020). https://doi.org/10.1109/JSAIT.2020.2991563
38. Papaioannou, I., Betz, W., Zwirglmaier, K., Straub, D.: Mcmc algorithms for subset simulation. Probab. Eng. Mech. **41**, 89–103 (2015). https://doi.org/10.1016/j.probengmech.2015.06.006
39. Papamakarios, G., Sterratt, D., Murray, I.: Sequential neural likelihood: fast likelihood-free inference with autoregressive flows. In: The 22nd International Conference on Artificial Intelligence and Statistics, pp. 837–848. PMLR (2019)
40. Patrini, G., van den Berg, R., Forré, P., Carioni, M., Bhargav, S., Welling, M., Genewein, T., Nielsen, F.: Sinkhorn autoencoders. In: Proceedings of The 35th Uncertainty in Artificial Intelligence Conference, vol. 115, pp. 733–743. PMLR (2020)
41. Razavi, A., van den Oord, A., Poole, B., Vinyals, O.: Preventing posterior collapse with delta-VAEs. In: International Conference on Learning Representations, ICLR (2019)
42. Ren, S., Padilla, W., Malof, J.: Benchmarking deep inverse models over time and the neural-adjoint method. In: Advances in Neural Information Processing Systems, vol. 33, pp. 38–48 (2020)
43. Richardson, A.: Generative adversarial networks for model order reduction in seismic full-waveform inversion. arXiv preprint arXiv:1806.00828 (2018)
44. Robert, C., Casella, G.: Monte Carlo statistical methods. Springer Science & Business Media, New York (2013)
45. Robert, C.P., Beaumont, M.A., Marin, J.M., Cornuet, J.M.: Adaptivity for abc algorithms: the abc-pmc scheme. arXiv preprint arXiv:0805.2256 (2008)
46. Robert, C.P., Elvira, V., Tawn, N., Wu, C.: Accelerating MCMC algorithms. Wiley Interdisc. Rev. Comput. Stat. **10**(5) (2018). https://doi.org/10.1002/wics.1435
47. Sisson, S.A., Fan, Y., Beaumont, M.E.: Handbook of Approximate Bayesian Computation. CRC Press (2018). https://doi.org/10.1201/9781315117195
48. Sohn, K., Lee, H., Yan, X.: Learning structured output representation using deep conditional generative models. In: Advances in Neural Information Processing Systems, vol. 28, pp. 3483–3491 (2015)
49. Tarantola, A.: Inverse problem theory and methods for model parameter estimation, vol. 89. SIAM (2005). https://doi.org/10.1137/1.9780898717921
50. Tolstikhin, I., Bousquet, O., Gelly, S., Schölkopf, B.: Wasserstein auto-encoders. In: International Conference on Learning Representations, ICLR (2018)

51. Tonolini, F., Radford, J., Turpin, A., Faccio, D., Murray-Smith, R.: Variational inference for computational imaging inverse problems. J. Mach. Learn. Res. **21**(179), 1–46 (2020)
52. Willer, M., Uribe, F.: Subset simulation (2020). https://www.bgu.tum.de/era/software/software00/subset-simulation/. Accessed 08 April 2021
53. Zuev, K.M., Beck, J.L., Au, S.K., Katafygiotis, L.S.: Bayesian post-processor and other enhancements of subset simulation for estimating failure probabilities in high dimensions. Comput. Struct. **92**, 283–296 (2012). https://doi.org/10.1016/j.compstruc.2011.10.017

Statistical Estimation of Quantization for Probability Distributions: Best Equivariant Estimator of Principal Points

Shun Matsuura[1($\boxtimes$)] and Hiroshi Kurata[2]

[1] Keio University, 3-14-1 Hiyoshi, Kohoku-ku, Yokohama 223-8522, Kanagawa, Japan
matsuura@ae.keio.ac.jp
[2] The University of Tokyo, 3-8-1 Komaba, Meguro-ku, Tokyo 153-8902, Japan

Abstract. Quantization gives a discrete approximation (with a finite set of points called quantizer) for a probability distribution. When the approximation is optimal with respect to a loss function, it is called optimal quantization (and its set of points is called an optimal quantizer), which has been studied and applied in various areas. Especially in statistics, an optimal quantizer under a quadratic loss function (optimal quantizer of order 2) has been widely investigated and is often called a set of principal points (or simply, principal points) for a probability distribution. In practice, however, the values of the parameters of the probability distribution are sometimes unknown, and hence we have to estimate principal points based on a random sample. A common method for estimating principal points is using principal points of the empirical distribution obtained by a random sample, which can be viewed as a nonparametric estimator of principal points. Several papers discussed statistical parametric estimation of principal points based on maximum likelihood estimators of the parameters. In this paper, a class of equivariant estimators, which includes previous parametric estimators of principal points is considered, and the best equivariant estimator of principal points is derived. It turns out that, under some condition, the best equivariant estimator coincides with a previously obtained parametric estimator. However, it is also shown that, for some probability distributions not satisfying the condition, the best equivariant estimator may not be equivalent to previous estimators.

Keywords: Equivariant estimator · Principal points · Quantization

1 Introduction

Quantization gives a discrete approximation for a probability distribution, and it is called optimal quantization if the approximation is optimal with respect to a loss function. Optimal quantization has been studied and applied in various areas such as signal processing in information theory, statistical clustering in data science, pattern recognition in machine learning, and optimal location problems in operations research (Graf and Luschgy [1]). Let X be a random variable having a probability distribution F. A set $\{\delta_1, \ldots, \delta_k\}$ of k

© Springer Nature Switzerland AG 2022
G. Nicosia et al. (Eds.): LOD 2021, LNCS 13163, pp. 430–441, 2022.
https://doi.org/10.1007/978-3-030-95467-3_31

points is called a k-optimal quantizer for F of order r if this set minimizes the quantization error for F of order r:

$$Q_{k,r}(\delta_1, \ldots, \delta_k) := \mathbb{E}_F\left[\min_{1 \le j \le k}\left|X - \delta_j\right|^r\right].$$

It is well known that the 1-optimal quantizer for F of order 1 ($k = 1$ and $r = 1$) is the median of F and the 1-optimal quantizer for F of order 2 ($k = 1$ and $r = 2$) is the mean of F. Hence, k-optimal quantizers of orders 1 and 2 can be viewed as generalizations of the median and mean of the distribution from one point to k points. A k-optimal quantizer of order 2 is often called 'quadratic k-optimal quantizer' and also called 'k-principal points' (Flury [2], Tarpey et al. [3]). Graf and Luschgy [1] provided numerical examples of the values of optimal quantizers for several common probability distributions. Optimal quantization under more general loss functions has also been studied (e.g., Trushkin [4], Kieffer [5], Mease and Nair [6]).

Suppose that the distribution F belongs to a location-scale family of probability distributions, that is, F has a location parameter μ and a scale parameter σ, denoted as $F_{\mu,\sigma}$ hereafter. More specifically, suppose that the probability density function of $F_{\mu,\sigma}$ is of the form:

$$f_{\mu,\sigma}(x) = \frac{1}{\sigma}g\left(\frac{x - \mu}{\sigma}\right) \quad \text{for some } g : (-\infty, \infty) \to [0, \infty).$$

The location-scale family includes many common probability distributions such as normal distributions (Gaussian distributions), uniform distributions, and Laplace distributions (double exponential distributions). It is obvious that if a set $\{\xi_1, \ldots, \xi_k\}$ of k points is a k-optimal quantizer for $F_{0,1}$ ($\mu = 0$ and $\sigma = 1$) of order r, then the set $\{\mu + \sigma\xi_1, \ldots, \mu + \sigma\xi_k\}$ is a k-optimal quantizer for $F_{\mu,\sigma}$ of order r.

When the values of the parameters μ and σ are known, a k-optimal quantizer for $F_{\mu,\sigma}$ of order r can be obtained numerically in most cases by several algorithms (e.g., Lloyd [7], Pagès [8]). However, the values of μ and σ are sometimes unknown in practice. Let $X_1, \ldots, X_n$ be a random sample of size n drawn from $F_{\mu,\sigma}$. Then, a k-optimal quantizer for the empirical distribution $F^{(n)}$ (whose supports are $X_1, \ldots, X_n$ with probability mass $\frac{1}{n}$) of order r is a nonparametric estimator of a k-optimal quantizer for $F_{\mu,\sigma}$ of order r. Pollard [9, 10] proved the convergence of the nonparametric estimator under appropriate conditions. The convergence rate of the nonparametric estimator has been studied in many papers (e.g., Biau et al. [11], Fournier and Guillin [12], Liu and Pagès [13]).

In contrast, Flury [14], Tarpey [15, 16], Stampfer and Stadlober [17], Yamashita et al. [18], Matsuura et al. [19], and Matsuura and Tarpey [20] studied statistical parametric estimation of a k-optimal quantizer of order $r = 2$ (k-principal points) using maximum likelihood estimators of the parameters. Suppose that the maximum likelihood estimators $\hat{\mu}_{MLE}(X_1, \ldots, X_n)$ and $\hat{\sigma}_{MLE}(X_1, \ldots, X_n)$ of μ and σ exist (Note that the maximum likelihood estimators of parameters exist for normal distributions, uniform distributions, and Laplace distributions). Then, the set

$$\{\hat{\mu}_{MLE} + \hat{\sigma}_{MLE}\xi_1, \ldots, \hat{\mu}_{MLE} + \hat{\sigma}_{MLE}\xi_k\}, \tag{1}$$

where $\{\xi_1, \ldots, \xi_k\}$ is a set of k-principal points for $F_{0,1}$, is a parametric estimator of k-principal points for $F_{\mu,\sigma}$. Throughout this paper, the argument $(X_1, \ldots, X_n)$ of functions is sometimes omitted for simplicity if this does not cause any confusion. Tarpey [15, 16] reported that, for normal distributions, this parametric estimator of k-principal points is superior to the nonparametric estimator in most cases. Matsuura et al. [19] proposed another parametric estimator of k-principal points that is of the form

$$\{\widehat{\mu}_{MLE} + \widehat{\sigma}_{MLE}a_1, \ldots, \widehat{\mu}_{MLE} + \widehat{\sigma}_{MLE}a_k\} \tag{2}$$

with   the   optimal   values   of $\{a_1, \ldots, a_k\}$ minimizing $Q_{k,2}(\widehat{\mu}_{MLE} + \widehat{\sigma}_{MLE}a_1, \ldots, \widehat{\mu}_{MLE} + \widehat{\sigma}_{MLE}a_k)$. They showed that, in the case where $F_{\mu,\sigma}$ is the normal distribution $N(\mu, \sigma^2)$, although $\{\xi_1, \ldots, \xi_k\}$ is a set of k-principal points for the standard normal distribution $N(0, 1^2)$, the optimal values of $\{a_1, \ldots, a_k\}$ are given by a set of k-principal points for the t-distribution with $n + 1$ degrees of freedom. Matsuura and Tarpey [20] discussed the case of multivariate distributions. For various aspects of the theory and properties of principal points, please see, for example, Tarpey et al. [3], Tarpey [21], Yamamoto and Shinozaki [22], Tarpey and Kinateder [23], Shimizu and Mizuta [24], Kurata [25], Matsuura and Kurata [26, 27], Tarpey and Loperfido [28], Roychowdhury [29], and Qi et al. [30].

In this paper, a class of equivariant estimators of k-principal points, which includes previous parametric estimators is considered, and the best equivariant estimator minimizing $Q_{k,2}(\widehat{\delta}_1, \ldots, \widehat{\delta}_k)$ is derived. The next section defines a class of equivariant estimators of k-principal points and gives an expression for equivariant estimators. The best equivariant estimator of k-principal points is derived in Sect. 3. Section 4 shows examples for normal distributions and Laplace distributions. The final section gives concluding remarks.

2 Expression for Equivariant Estimators of Principal Points

Let $X_1, \ldots, X_n$ be a random sample of size n drawn from $F_{\mu,\sigma}$. Consider a class of equivariant estimators $\widehat{\delta}_j(X_1, \ldots, X_n), j = 1, \ldots, k$ of k-principal points with $\widehat{\delta}_1(X_1, \ldots, X_n) \leq \cdots \leq \widehat{\delta}_k(X_1, \ldots, X_n)$ that satisfy the following equivariance property with respect to location-scale changes of $X_1, \ldots, X_n$:

$$\widehat{\delta}_j(cX_1 + b, \ldots, cX_n + b) = c\widehat{\delta}_j(X_1, \ldots, X_n) + b, j = 1, \ldots, k$$

for any $c \in (0, \infty), b \in (-\infty, \infty)$.

Note that this class includes the parametric estimators (1) and (2) since the maximum likelihood estimators $\widehat{\mu}_{MLE}(X_1, \ldots, X_n)$ and $\widehat{\sigma}_{MLE}(X_1, \ldots, X_n)$ satisfy

$$\widehat{\mu}_{MLE}(cX_1 + b, \ldots, cX_n + b) = c\widehat{\mu}_{MLE}(X_1, \ldots, X_n) + b,$$

$$\widehat{\sigma}_{MLE}(cX_1 + b, \ldots, cX_n + b) = c\widehat{\sigma}_{MLE}(X_1, \ldots, X_n)$$

for any $\in (0, \infty), b \in (-\infty, \infty)$,

(see Proposition 7.11 of Eaton [31]). Hence, the class of equivariant estimators considered in this paper is wider than the one in Matsuura et al. [19]. For the general statistical theory of equivariant estimation, please see, for example, Eaton [31] and Kariya and Kurata [32].

This paper derives the best equivariant estimator of k-principal points minimizing

$$Q_{k,2}\left(\hat{\delta}_1,\ldots,\hat{\delta}_k\right) = \mathbb{E}_{F_{\mu,\sigma}}\left[\min_{1\leq j\leq k}\left(X - \hat{\delta}_j(X_1,\ldots,X_n)\right)^2\right]. \tag{3}$$

Before that, we give a characterization for equivariant estimators $\hat{\delta}_j(X_1,\ldots,X_n), j = 1,\ldots,k$, as follows.

Let $\hat{\mu}$ and $\hat{\sigma}(>0)$ be arbitrary estimators satisfying

$$\begin{cases} \hat{\mu}(cX_1+b,\ldots,cX_n+b) = c\hat{\mu}(X_1,\ldots,X_n)+b, \\ \hat{\sigma}(cX_1+b,\ldots,cX_n+b) = c\hat{\sigma}(X_1,\ldots,X_n) \end{cases} \tag{4}$$

$$\text{for any } c \in (0,\infty), b \in (-\infty,\infty).$$

The choice of $\hat{\mu}$ and $\hat{\sigma}$ is arbitrary as long as the condition (4) is satisfied. If maximum likelihood estimators of μ and σ exist and are expressed as simple functions of $X_1,\ldots,X_n$, then the maximum likelihood estimators may be a reasonable choice for $\hat{\mu}$ and $\hat{\sigma}$. However, other estimators of $\hat{\mu}$ and $\hat{\sigma}$ can also be chosen (as long as the condition (4) is satisfied). Let also

$$u_i = \frac{X_i - \hat{\mu}(X_1,\ldots,X_n)}{\hat{\sigma}(X_1,\ldots,X_n)}, \quad i = 1,\ldots,n.$$

Note that $\{u_1,\ldots,u_n\}$ is a set of maximal invariant statistics (e.g., Eaton [31], Kariya and Kurata [32]), whose distributions do not depend on the values of μ and σ. Then, a necessary and sufficient condition for estimators $\hat{\delta}_j(X_1,\ldots,X_n), j = 1,\ldots,k$ of k-principal points to be equivariant is shown below.

First, if $\hat{\delta}_j(X_1,\ldots,X_n), j = 1,\ldots,k$ are equivariant estimators, then

$$\hat{\delta}_j(u_1,\ldots,u_n) = \hat{\delta}_j\left(\frac{X_1 - \hat{\mu}(X_1,\ldots,X_n)}{\hat{\sigma}(X_1,\ldots,X_n)},\ldots,\frac{X_n - \hat{\mu}(X_1,\ldots,X_n)}{\hat{\sigma}(X_1,\ldots,X_n)}\right)$$

$$= \frac{\hat{\delta}_j(X_1,\ldots,X_n) - \hat{\mu}(X_1,\ldots,X_n)}{\hat{\sigma}(X_1,\ldots,X_n)}, \quad j = 1,\ldots,k,$$

which means that $\frac{\hat{\delta}_j(X_1,\ldots,X_n) - \hat{\mu}(X_1,\ldots,X_n)}{\hat{\sigma}(X_1,\ldots,X_n)}, j = 1,\ldots,k$ are functions of $u_1,\ldots,u_n$. Next, if

$$\hat{\delta}_j(X_1,\ldots,X_n) = \hat{\mu}(X_1,\ldots,X_n) + \hat{\sigma}(X_1,\ldots,X_n)\eta_j(u_1,\ldots,u_n), \quad j = 1,\ldots,k$$

for some functions $\eta_j : R^n \to (-\infty,\infty), j = 1,\ldots,k$, then it holds that, for $j = 1,\ldots,k$,

$$\hat{\delta}_j(cX_1+b,\ldots,cX_n+b)$$

$$
\begin{aligned}
&= \hat{\mu}(cX_1 + b, \ldots, cX_n + b) + \hat{\sigma}(cX_1 + b, \ldots, cX_n + b)\eta_j(u_1, \ldots, u_n) \\
&= c\hat{\mu}(X_1, \ldots, X_n) + b + c\hat{\sigma}(X_1, \ldots, X_n)\eta_j(u_1, \ldots, u_n) \\
&= c\{\hat{\mu}(X_1, \ldots, X_n) + \hat{\sigma}(X_1, \ldots, X_n)\eta_j(u_1, \ldots, u_n)\} + b \\
&= c\hat{\delta}_j(X_1, \ldots, X_n) + b
\end{aligned}
$$

for any $c \in (0, \infty), b \in (-\infty, \infty)$. Hence, estimators $\hat{\delta}_j(X_1, \ldots, X_n), j = 1, \ldots, k$ of k-principal points are equivariant if and only if

$$
\hat{\delta}_j(X_1, \ldots, X_n) = \hat{\mu}(X_1, \ldots, X_n) + \hat{\sigma}(X_1, \ldots, X_n)\eta_j(u_1, \ldots, u_n), \quad j = 1, \ldots, k \quad (5)
$$

hold for some functions $\eta_j : R^n \to (-\infty, \infty), j = 1, \ldots, k$.

3   Best Equivariant Estimator of Principal Points

This section derives the best equivariant estimator of k-principal points minimizing (3). Substituting the expression (5) of equivariant estimators to (3) gives

$$
Q_{k,2}(\hat{\delta}_1, \ldots, \hat{\delta}_k) = \mathbb{E}_{F_{\mu,\sigma}}\left[\min_{1 \leq j \leq k}\left(X - \hat{\delta}_j(X_1, \ldots, X_n)\right)^2\right]
$$

$$
= \mathbb{E}_{F_{\mu,\sigma}}\left[\min_{1 \leq j \leq k}\{X - \hat{\mu}(X_1, \ldots, X_n) - \hat{\sigma}(X_1, \ldots, X_n)\eta_j(u_1, \ldots, u_n)\}^2\right]. \quad (6)
$$

Hence, it is sufficient for us to derive functions $\eta_j : R^n \to (-\infty, \infty), j = 1, \ldots, k$ with $\eta_1(u_1, \ldots, u_n) \leq \cdots \leq \eta_k(u_1, \ldots, u_n)$ that minimize (6).

Noting that $\frac{X-\mu}{\sigma}, \frac{X_1-\mu}{\sigma}, \ldots, \frac{X_n-\mu}{\sigma} \sim F_{0,1}$, it holds that

$$
\mathbb{E}_{F_{\mu,\sigma}}\left[\min_{1 \leq j \leq k}\{X - \hat{\mu}(X_1, \ldots, X_n) - \hat{\sigma}(X_1, \ldots, X_n)\eta_j(u_1, \ldots, u_n)\}^2\right]
$$

$$
= \sigma^2 \mathbb{E}_{F_{\mu,\sigma}}\left[\min_{1 \leq j \leq k}\left\{\frac{X-\mu}{\sigma} - \frac{\hat{\mu}(X_1,\ldots,X_n)-\mu}{\sigma} - \frac{\hat{\sigma}(X_1,\ldots,X_n)}{\sigma}\eta_j(u_1, \ldots, u_n)\right\}^2\right]
$$

$$
= \sigma^2 \mathbb{E}_{F_{\mu,\sigma}}\left[\min_{1 \leq j \leq k}\left\{\frac{X-\mu}{\sigma} - \hat{\mu}\left(\frac{X_1-\mu}{\sigma}, \ldots, \frac{X_n-\mu}{\sigma}\right) - \hat{\sigma}\left(\frac{X_1-\mu}{\sigma}, \ldots, \frac{X_n-\mu}{\sigma}\right)\eta_j(u_1, \ldots, u_n)\right\}^2\right]
$$

$$
= \sigma^2 \mathbb{E}_{F_{0,1}}\left[\min_{1 \leq i \leq k}\{X - \hat{\mu}(X_1, \ldots, X_n) - \hat{\sigma}(X_1, \ldots, X_n)\eta_j(u_1, \ldots, u_n)\}^2\right].
$$

Hence, minimizing (6) is equivalent to minimizing

$$
\mathbb{E}_{F_{0,1}}\left[\min_{1 \leq i \leq k}\{X - \hat{\mu}(X_1, \ldots, X_n) - \hat{\sigma}(X_1, \ldots, X_n)\eta_j(u_1, \ldots, u_n)\}^2\right],
$$

which means that the functions $\eta_j : R^n \to (-\infty, \infty), j = 1, \ldots, k$ with $\eta_1(u_1, \ldots, u_n) \leq \cdots \leq \eta_k(u_1, \ldots, u_n)$ minimizing (6) do not depend on the values of μ and σ and thus can be determined even when the values of μ and σ are unknown.

Here, let $\hat{v}(X, X_1, \ldots, X_n) = X - \hat{\mu}(X_1, \ldots, X_n)$ and let also $\psi(\hat{v}|\hat{\sigma}, u_1, \ldots, u_n)$ be the probability density function of $\hat{v}$ conditioned on $\hat{\sigma}(X_1, \ldots, X_n), u_1, \ldots, u_n$ under

$X, X_1, \ldots, X_n \sim F_{0,1}$. In the discussions below, expectations are taken under distributions from $X, X_1, \ldots, X_n \sim F_{0,1}$ and denoted as $\mathbb{E}[]$ for simplicity in the remaining of this paper. It follows that

$$\mathbb{E}\left[\min_{1 \le j \le k}\left\{X - \hat{\mu} - \hat{\sigma}\eta_j(u_1, \ldots, u_n)\right\}^2\right]$$

$$= \mathbb{E}\left[\min_{1 \le j \le k}\left\{\hat{v} - \hat{\sigma}\eta_j(u_1, \ldots, u_n)\right\}^2\right]$$

$$= \mathbb{E}\left[\mathbb{E}\left[\min_{1 \le j \le k}\left\{\hat{v} - \hat{\sigma}\eta_j(u_1, \ldots, u_n)\right\}^2\Big|\hat{\sigma}, u_1, \ldots, u_n\right]\right]$$

$$= \mathbb{E}\left[\int_{-\infty}^{\infty}\min_{1 \le j \le k}\left\{y - \hat{\sigma}\eta_j(u_1, \ldots, u_n)\right\}^2\psi\left(y|\hat{\sigma}, u_1, \ldots, u_n\right)dy\right]$$

$$= \mathbb{E}\left[\hat{\sigma}^2\int_{-\infty}^{\infty}\min_{1 \le j \le k}\left\{\tfrac{y}{\hat{\sigma}} - \eta_j(u_1, \ldots, u_n)\right\}^2\psi\left(y|\hat{\sigma}, u_1, \ldots, u_n\right)dy\right].$$

The change of variable $z = \frac{y}{\hat{\sigma}}$ yields

$$\mathbb{E}\left[\hat{\sigma}^3\int_{-\infty}^{\infty}\min_{1 \le j \le k}\left\{z - \eta_j(u_1, \ldots, u_n)\right\}^2\psi\left(\hat{\sigma}z|\hat{\sigma}, u_1, \ldots, u_n\right)dz\right]$$

$$= \mathbb{E}\left[\mathbb{E}\left[\hat{\sigma}^3\int_{-\infty}^{\infty}\min_{1 \le j \le k}\left\{z - \eta_j(u_1, \ldots, u_n)\right\}^2\psi\left(\hat{\sigma}z|\hat{\sigma}, u_1, \ldots, u_n\right)dz\Big|u_1, \ldots, u_n\right]\right]$$

$$= \mathbb{E}\left[\int_{-\infty}^{\infty}\min_{1 \le j \le k}\left\{z - \eta_j(u_1, \ldots, u_n)\right\}^2\mathbb{E}\left[\hat{\sigma}^3\psi\left(\hat{\sigma}z|\hat{\sigma}, u_1, \ldots, u_n\right)\Big|u_1, \ldots, u_n\right]dz\right].$$

Let

$$h(z|u_1, \ldots, u_n) = \frac{\mathbb{E}\left[\hat{\sigma}^3\psi\left(\hat{\sigma}z|\hat{\sigma}, u_1, \ldots, u_n\right)\Big|u_1, \ldots, u_n\right]}{\mathbb{E}\left[\hat{\sigma}^2\Big|u_1, \ldots, u_n\right]}.$$

Then, $h(z|u_1, \ldots, u_n)$ is a probability density function since

$$\int_{-\infty}^{\infty} h(z|u_1, \ldots, u_n)dz = \frac{\int_{-\infty}^{\infty}\mathbb{E}\left[\hat{\sigma}^3\psi\left(\hat{\sigma}z|\hat{\sigma}, u_1, \ldots, u_n\right)\Big|u_1, \ldots, u_n\right]dz}{\mathbb{E}\left[\hat{\sigma}^2\Big|u_1, \ldots, u_n\right]}$$

$$= \frac{\mathbb{E}\left[\hat{\sigma}^3\int_{-\infty}^{\infty}\psi\left(\hat{\sigma}z|\hat{\sigma}, u_1, \ldots, u_n\right)dz\Big|u_1, \ldots, u_n\right]}{\mathbb{E}\left[\hat{\sigma}^2\Big|u_1, \ldots, u_n\right]}$$

$$= \frac{\mathbb{E}\left[\hat{\sigma}^2\int_{-\infty}^{\infty}\psi\left(y|\hat{\sigma}, u_1, \ldots, u_n\right)dy\Big|u_1, \ldots, u_n\right]}{\mathbb{E}\left[\hat{\sigma}^2\Big|u_1, \ldots, u_n\right]}$$

$$= \frac{\mathbb{E}\left[\hat{\sigma}^2\Big|u_1, \ldots, u_n\right]}{\mathbb{E}\left[\hat{\sigma}^2\Big|u_1, \ldots, u_n\right]} = 1.$$

Hence, it holds that

$$\mathbb{E}\left[\int_{-\infty}^{\infty}\min_{1\leq j\leq k}\{z-\eta_j(u_1,\ldots,u_n)\}^2\mathbb{E}\left[\hat{\sigma}^3\psi(\hat{\sigma}z|\hat{\sigma},u_1,\ldots,u_n)\Big|u_1,\ldots,u_n\right]dz\right]$$

$$=\mathbb{E}\left[\mathbb{E}\left[\hat{\sigma}^2\Big|u_1,\ldots,u_n\right]\int_{-\infty}^{\infty}\min_{1\leq j\leq k}\{z-\eta_j(u_1,\ldots,u_n)\}^2h(z|u_1,\ldots,u_n)dz\right],$$

which means that the functions $\eta_j : R^n \to (-\infty,\infty), j = 1,\ldots,k$ with $\eta_1(u_1,\ldots,u_n) \leq \cdots \leq \eta_k(u_1,\ldots,u_n)$ minimizing (6) are given by k-principal points for the probability distribution having the pdf $h(z|u_1,\ldots,u_n)$. That is, the best equivariant estimator of k-principal points minimizing (3) is given by

$$\hat{\delta}_j(X_1,\ldots,X_n) = \hat{\mu}(X_1,\ldots,X_n) + \hat{\sigma}(X_1,\ldots,X_n)\eta_j^*(u_1,\ldots,u_n), \quad j = 1,\ldots,k,$$

where $\eta_j^*(u_1,\ldots,u_n), j = 1,\ldots,k$ are k-principal points for the probability distribution having the pdf $h(z|u_1,\ldots,u_n)$.

It may be worth mentioning that if $(\hat{\mu},\hat{\sigma})$ is a sufficient statistic for (μ,σ), then $(\hat{\mu},\hat{\sigma})$ and $(u_1,\ldots,u_n)$ are independent (see Proposition 7.19 of Eaton [31]). This means that $h(z|u_1,\ldots,u_n)$ does not depend on $(u_1,\ldots,u_n)$ and thus $\eta_j^*(u_1,\ldots,u_n), j = 1,\ldots,k$ are constant functions. It follows from this fact that if the maximum likelihood estimator of (μ,σ) is a sufficient statistic for (μ,σ), then the best equivariant estimator of k-principal points minimizing (3) reduces to the estimator given by Matsuura et al. [19]. Note that a statistic (a function of $X_1,\ldots,X_n$) is called a sufficient statistic for a parameter if the conditional distribution of $X_1,\ldots,X_n$ given the statistic does not depend on the parameter (e.g., Wilks [33], Lehmann and Casella [34]). It is known that although a maximum likelihood estimator can be written as a function of some sufficient statistic in general, the maximum likelihood estimator itself is not necessarily a sufficient statistic. In the case where maximum likelihood estimators are not sufficient, the best equivariant estimator of k-principal points may be different from (and be superior to) the estimator given by Matsuura et al. [19]. The next section shows both the cases where maximum likelihood estimators are sufficient and are not sufficient.

4 Examples

Normal Distribution (Gaussian Distribution). In the first example, we consider the estimation of k-principal points for a normal distribution $N(\mu,\sigma^2)$ when the values of μ and σ are unknown. Note that the probability density function of $N(\mu,\sigma^2)$ is

$$f_{\mu,\sigma}(x) = \frac{1}{(2\pi)^{\frac{1}{2}}\sigma}e^{-\frac{1}{2\sigma^2}(x-\mu)^2}, \quad -\infty < x < \infty.$$

Let $X_1,\ldots,X_n$ be a random sample of size n drawn from $N(\mu,\sigma^2)$. The maximum likelihood estimators of μ and σ are

$$\hat{\mu} = \overline{X} = \frac{1}{n}\sum_{i=1}^n X_i \text{ and } \hat{\sigma} = \sqrt{\frac{1}{n}\sum_{i=1}^n (X_i-\overline{X})^2},$$

which obviously satisfy the condition (4). Let $u_i = \frac{X_i - \widehat{\mu}}{\widehat{\sigma}}, i = 1, \ldots, n$. Then, calculating

$$h(z|u_1, \ldots, u_n) = \frac{\mathbb{E}\left[\widehat{\sigma}^3 \psi\left(\widehat{\sigma} z | \widehat{\sigma}, u_1, \ldots, u_n\right) \middle| u_1, \ldots, u_n\right]}{\mathbb{E}\left[\widehat{\sigma}^2 \middle| u_1, \ldots, u_n\right]},$$

it holds that

$$h(z|u_1, \ldots, u_n) = \frac{\Gamma\left(\frac{n+2}{2}\right)}{\{(n+1)\pi\}^{\frac{1}{2}} \Gamma\left(\frac{n+1}{2}\right)} \left(1 + \frac{z^2}{n+1}\right)^{-\frac{n+2}{2}}, \quad -\infty < z < \infty,$$

which is the probability density function of the t-distribution with $n + 1$ degrees of freedom. Here, $h(z|u_1, \ldots, u_n)$ does not depend on $u_1, \ldots, u_n$ since $(\widehat{\mu}, \widehat{\sigma})$ is a sufficient statistic, and thus the best equivariant estimator of k-principal points is identical with the estimator given by Matsuura et al. [19]. The best equivariant estimator of k-principal points for $N(\mu, \sigma^2)$ is given by

$$\widehat{\delta}_j = \widehat{\mu} + \widehat{\sigma} \eta_j^*, \quad j = 1, \ldots, k,$$

where $\eta_j^*, j = 1, \ldots, k$ are k-principal points for the t-distribution with $n + 1$ degrees of freedom.

Laplace Distribution (Double Exponential Distribution). Consider the estimation of k-principal points for a Laplace distribution $Laplace(\mu, \sigma)$ when the values of μ and σ are unknown. The probability density function of $Laplace(\mu, \sigma)$ is

$$f_{\mu, \sigma}(x) = \frac{1}{2\sigma} e^{-\left|\frac{x-\mu}{\sigma}\right|}, \quad -\infty < x < \infty.$$

Let $X_1, \ldots, X_n$ be a random sample of size n drawn from $Laplace(\mu, \sigma)$, where we let n be an odd number. The maximum likelihood estimators of μ and σ are

$$\widehat{\mu} = \text{Median}(X_1, \ldots, X_n) \quad \text{and} \quad \widehat{\sigma} = \frac{\sum_{i=1}^n |X_i - \text{Median}(X_1, \ldots, X_n)|}{n},$$

which satisfy the condition (4). Let also $u_i = \frac{X_i - \widehat{\mu}}{\widehat{\sigma}}, i = 1, \ldots, n$. It is well known that a minimal sufficient statistic (e.g., Lehmann and Casella [34]) for (μ, σ) is the order statistic of $(X_1, \ldots, X_n)$. Hence, $(\widehat{\mu}, \widehat{\sigma})$ is not a sufficient statistic for (μ, σ) and thus $(\widehat{\mu}, \widehat{\sigma})$ and $(u_1, \ldots, u_n)$ may not be independent. In fact, to be more specific, let $n = 3$, then some lengthy but straightforward calculations for

$$h(z|u_1, u_2, u_n) = \frac{\mathbb{E}\left[\widehat{\sigma}^3 \psi\left(\widehat{\sigma} z | \widehat{\sigma}, u_1, u_2, u_n\right) \middle| u_1, u_2, u_n\right]}{\mathbb{E}\left[\widehat{\sigma}^2 \middle| u_1, u_2, u_n\right]}$$

give

$$h(z|u_1, u_2, u_3) = \frac{1}{C}\left\{ \frac{24|z| - 10|z - u_{(1)}| - 10|z - u_{(3)}| + 42}{(|z| + 3)^6} \right.$$

$$\left. - \frac{1}{\left(z + 2|z - u_{(1)}| + 3\right)^5} - \frac{1}{\left(-z + 2|z - u_{(3)}| + 3\right)^5} \right\}, \tag{7}$$

$$-\infty < z < \infty,$$

where C is a standardized constant and $u_{(1)}$ = $\text{Max}\{u_1, u_2, u_3\}, u_{(3)}$ = $\text{Min}\{u_1, u_2, u_3\}$. In this case, $h(z|u_1, u_2, u_3)$ depends on the values of u_1, u_2, u_3. Hence, the best equivariant estimator of k-principal points is not identical with the estimator given by Matsuura et al. [19] and the former gives a smaller value of (3) than the latter. Numerical examples are presented below. The best equivariant estimator

$$\hat{\delta}_j = \hat{\mu} + \hat{\sigma}\eta_j^*(u_1, u_2, u_3), \quad j = 1, \ldots, k,$$

where $\eta_j^*(u_1, u_2, u_3), j = 1, \ldots, k$ are k-principal points for the probability distribution with probability density function (7), is compared with the estimator $\hat{\delta}_j = \hat{\mu} + \hat{\sigma}a_j^*, j = 1, \ldots, k$ of Matsuura et al. [19] in terms of

$$\mathbb{E}\left[\hat{\sigma}^2 \Big| u_1, \ldots, u_n\right] \int_{-\infty}^{\infty} \min_{1 \leq j \leq k}\left\{z - \eta_j(u_1, \ldots, u_n)\right\}^2 h(z|u_1, \ldots, u_n)dz \tag{8}$$

whose expectation with respect to $u_1, \ldots, u_n$ is equivalent to the scaled quadratic quantization error $\frac{1}{\sigma^2}Q_{k,2}\left(\hat{\delta}_1, \ldots, \hat{\delta}_k\right)$. We simply set $k = 2$. Table 1 shows the values of $\eta_j^*(u_1, u_2, u_3), j = 1, 2$ (for the best equivariant estimator) and $a_j^*, j = 1, 2$ (for the estimator of Matsuura et al. [19]), and also shows the values of (8) of both the estimators for several values of $u_{(1)}$ and $u_{(3)}$. The difference between the best equivariant estimator and the estimator of Matsuura et al. [19] is that the former optimizes the values of $\eta_1^*(u_1, u_2, u_3)$ and $\eta_2^*(u_1, u_2, u_3)$ according to the values of u_1, u_2, u_3 through $u_{(1)}$ and $u_{(3)}$ while the latter uses constant values of a_1^* and a_2^* not depending on the values of u_1, u_2, u_3. The results indicate that the best equivariant estimator is superior to (gives a smaller value of (8) than) the estimator of Matsuura et al. [19] for all cases.

In addition, Fig. 1 and Fig. 2 illustrate the estimators of 2-principal points for the case of $\left(u_{(1)}, u_{(3)}\right) = (0, -3)$ and the case of $\left(u_{(1)}, u_{(3)}\right) = (2, -1)$, respectively. At a glance, although the estimators of Matsuura et al. [19] are symmetric about $\hat{\mu}$, the best equivariant estimators are located to be asymmetric about $\hat{\mu}$ according the values of maximal invariant statistics u_1, u_2, u_3, which could make further improvements over the estimators of Matsuura et al. [19]. Note that, it is well known that principal points are not necessarily symmetric about the mean even for symmetric distributions, but are proven to be symmetric for distributions having symmetric and log-concave density (e.g., Tarpey [35]). Since Laplace distributions have symmetric and log-concave densities, their principal points are always symmetric. Hence, the results for the best equivariant estimator of this paper reveal that, for the estimation of principal points even for distributions having symmetric and log-concave density, that is, even for the estimation of symmetric principal points about the mean μ, symmetric estimators about $\hat{\mu}$ are not necessarily optimal and asymmetric estimators might be the best estimators of principal points.

Table 1. Comparison of the values of (8) between the best equivariant estimator and the estimator of Matsuura et al. [19].

		$\hat{\delta}_j = \hat{\mu} + \hat{\sigma}\eta_j^*(u_1, u_2, u_3)$			$\hat{\delta}_j = \hat{\mu} + \hat{\sigma}a_j^*$		
$u_{(1)}$	$u_{(3)}$	$\eta_1^*(u_1, u_2, u_3)$	$\eta_2^*(u_1, u_2, u_3)$	(8)	a_1^*	a_2^*	(8)
0	−3	−2.4592	0.2709	**1.4619**	−1.1724	1.1724	**1.6195**
0.5	−2.5	−2.0350	0.5107	**1.4675**	−1.1724	1.1724	**1.5497**
1	−2	−1.6296	0.7753	**1.4802**	−1.1724	1.1724	**1.5035**
1.5	−1.5	−1.1607	1.1607	**1.4883**	−1.1724	1.1724	**1.4884**
2	−1	−0.7753	1.6296	**1.4802**	−1.1724	1.1724	**1.5035**
2.5	−0.5	−0.5107	2.0350	**1.4675**	−1.1724	1.1724	**1.5497**
3	0	−0.2709	2.4592	**1.4619**	−1.1724	1.1724	**1.6195**

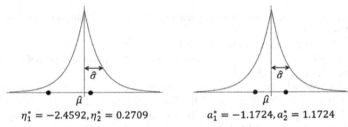

$$\eta_1^* = -2.4592, \eta_2^* = 0.2709 \qquad a_1^* = -1.1724, a_2^* = 1.1724$$

Fig. 1. Illustration of the best equivariant estimator (left) and the estimator of Matsuura et al. [19] (right) for the case of $\left(u_{(1)}, u_{(3)}\right) = (0, -3)$.

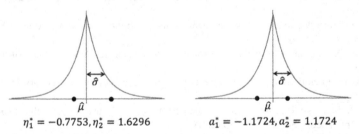

$$\eta_1^* = -0.7753, \eta_2^* = 1.6296 \qquad a_1^* = -1.1724, a_2^* = 1.1724$$

Fig. 2. Illustration of the best equivariant estimator (left) and the estimator of Matsuura et al. [19] (right) for the case of $\left(u_{(1)}, u_{(3)}\right) = (2, -1)$.

5   Conclusion

In this paper, statistical parametric estimation of k-principal points (quadratic k-optimal quantizer) has been studied for probability distributions with location and scale parameters. A class of equivariant estimators has been considered and the best equivariant estimator of k-principal points has been derived. It has been shown that the best equivariant estimator is equivalent to a previously obtained parametric estimator if a set of maximum likelihood estimators of the location and scale parameters of the underlying probability distribution is a sufficient statistic. Otherwise the best equivariant estimator may be superior to previous parametric estimators. Examples for normal distributions (Gaussian distributions) and Laplace distributions (double exponential distributions) have also been presented.

Although the best equivariant estimator of k-optimal quantizer of order $r = 2$ has been derived in this paper, a generalization of the result to any positive integer r will be an important issue for future research. Further, some extension from the class of equivariant estimators to a wider class of estimators will also be a future research topic. Finally, it is quite important to extend the results of this paper to non-linear cases and kernel spaces, which will be studied in the future.

References

1. Graf, L., Luschgy, H.: Foundations of Quantization for Probability Distributions. Springer-Verlag, Berlin (2000)
2. Flury, B.: Principal points. Biometrika **77**(1), 33–41 (1990)
3. Tarpey, T., Li, L., Flury, B.: Principal points and self-consistent points of elliptical distributions. Ann. Stat. **23**(1), 103–112 (1995)
4. Trushkin, A.: Sufficient conditions for uniqueness of a locally optimal quantizer for a class of convex error weighting functions. IEEE Trans. Inf. Theory **28**(2), 187–198 (1982)
5. Kieffer, J.C.: Uniqueness of locally optimal quantizer for log-concave density and convex error weighting function. IEEE Trans. Inf. Theory **29**(1), 42–47 (1983)
6. Mease, D., Nair, V.N.: Unique optimal partitions of distributions and connections to hazard rates and stochastic ordering. Stat. Sin. **16**(4), 1299–1312 (2006)
7. Lloyd, S.P.: Least squares quantization in PCM. IEEE Trans. Inf. Theory **28**(2), 129–137 (1982)
8. Pagès, G.: Introduction to vector quantization and its applications for numerics. ESAIM Proc. Surv. **48**, 29–79 (2015)
9. Pollard, D.: A central limit theorem for k-means clustering. Ann. Probab. **10**(4), 919–926 (1982)
10. Pollard, D.: Quantization and the method of k-means. IEEE Trans. Inf. Theory **28**(2), 199–205 (1982)
11. Biau, G., Devroye, L., Lugosi, G.: On the performance of clustering in Hilbert spaces. IEEE Trans. Inf. Theory **54**(2), 781–790 (2008)
12. Fournier, N., Guillin, A.: On the rate of convergence in Wasserstein distance of the empirical measure. Probab. Theory Relat. Fields **162**(3–4), 707–738 (2014). https://doi.org/10.1007/s00440-014-0583-7
13. Liu, Y., Pagès, G.: Convergence rate of optimal quantization and application to the clustering performance of the empirical measure. J. Mach. Learn. Res. **21**(86), 1–36 (2020)
14. Flury, B.: Estimation of principal points. J. Royal Stat. Soc. Ser. C (Appl. Stat.) **42**(1), 139–151 (1993)
15. Tarpey, T.: Estimating principal points of univariate distributions. J. Appl. Stat. **24**(5), 499–512 (1997)
16. Tarpey, T.: A parametric k-means algorithm. Comput. Stat. **22**(1), 71–89 (2007)

17. Stampfer, E., Stadlober, E.: Methods for estimating principal points. Commun. Stat. Simul. Comput. **31**(2), 261–277 (2002)
18. Yamashita, H., Matsuura, S., Suzuki, H.: Estimation of principal points for a multivariate binary distribution using a log-linear model. Commun. Stat. Simul. Comput. **46**(2), 1136–1147 (2017)
19. Matsuura, S., Kurata, H., Tarpey, T.: Optimal estimators of principal points for minimizing expected mean squared distance. J. Stat. Plan. Infer. **167**, 102–122 (2015)
20. Matsuura, S., Tarpey, T.: Optimal principal points estimators of multivariate distributions of location-scale and location-scale-rotation families. Stat. Pap. **61**(4), 1629–1643 (2020). https://doi.org/10.1007/s00362-018-0995-z
21. Tarpey, T.: Principal points and self-consistent points of symmetric multivariate distributions. J. Multivar. Anal. **53**(1), 39–51 (1995)
22. Yamamoto, W., Shinozaki, N.: On uniqueness of two principal points for univariate location mixtures. Statist. Probab. Lett. **46**(1), 33–42 (2000)
23. Tarpey, T., Kinateder, K.K.J.: Clustering functional data. J. Classif. **20**(1), 93–114 (2003)
24. Shimizu, N., Mizuta, M.: Functional clustering and functional principal points. In: Apolloni, B., Howlett, R.J., Jain, L. (eds.) International Conference on Knowledge-Based Intelligent Information and Engineering Systems 2007, LNCS, vol. 4693, pp. 501–508. Springer, Heidelberg (2007)
25. Kurata, H.: On principal points for location mixtures of spherically symmetric distributions. J. Stat. Plan. Infer. **138**(11), 3405–3418 (2008)
26. Matsuura, S., Kurata, H.: Principal points of a multivariate mixture distribution. J. Multivar. Anal. **102**(2), 213–224 (2011)
27. Matsuura, S., Kurata, H.: Principal points for an allometric extension model. Stat. Pap. **55**(3), 853–870 (2014). https://doi.org/10.1007/s00362-013-0532-z
28. Tarpey, T., Loperfido, N.: Self-consistency and a generalized principal subspace theorem. J. Multivar. Anal. **133**, 27–37 (2015)
29. Roychowdhury, M.K.: Optimal quantizers for some absolutely continuous probability measures. Real Anal. Exch. **43**(1), 105–136 (2018)
30. Qi, Z.F., Zhou, Y.D., Fang, K.T.: Representative points for location-biased datasets. Commun. Stat. Simul. Comput. **48**(2), 458–471 (2019)
31. Eaton, M.L.: Multivariate Statistics: A Vector Space Approach. Wiley, Chichester (1983)
32. Kariya, T., Kurata, H.: Generalized Least Squares. Wiley, Chichester (2004)
33. Wilks, S.S.: Mathematical Statistics. Wiley, New York (1962)
34. Lehmann, E.L., Casella, G.: Theory of Point Estimation, 2nd edn. Springer, New York (1998)
35. Tarpey, T.: Two principal points of symmetric, strongly unimodal distributions. Stat. Probab. Lett. **20**(4), 253–257 (1994)

Activity Imputation of Shared e-Bikes Travels in Urban Areas

Natalia Selini Hadjidimitriou[(✉)], Marco Lippi, and Marco Mamei

Department of Sciences and Methods for Engineering,
University of Modena and Reggio Emilia, Modena, Italy
`selini@unimore.it`

Abstract. In 2017, about 900 thousands motorbikes were registered in Europe. These types of vehicles are often selected as the only alternative when the congestion in urban areas is high, thus consistently contributing to environmental emissions. This work proposes a data-driven approach to analyse trip purposes of shared electric bikes users in urban areas. Knowing how e-bikes are used in terms of trip duration and purpose is important to integrate them in the current transportation system. The data set consists of GPS traces collected during one year and three months representing 6,705 trips performed by 91 users of the e-bike sharing service located in three South European cities (Malaga, Rome and Bari). The proposed methodology consists of computing a set of features related to the temporal (time of the day, day of the week), meteorological (e.g. weather, season) and topological (the percentage of km traveled on roads with cycleways, speed on different types of roads, proximity of arrival to the nearest Point of Interest) characteristics of the trip. Based on the identified features, logistic regression and random forest classifiers are trained to predict the purpose of the trip. The random forest performs better with an average accuracy, over the 10 random splits of the train and test set, of 82%. The overall accuracy decreases to 67% when training and test sets are split at the level of users and not at the level of trips. Finally, the travel activities are predicted for the entire data set and the features are analysed to provide a description of the behaviour of shared e-bike users.

Keywords: Trip imputation · Travel activity behaviour · e-bikes · Activity detection · GPS traces · Machine learning · Random forest · Multinomial logistic regression · Safety

1 Introduction

During the last years, the increase of electromobility and shared mobility services have created new interest for shared electric light vehicles systems. The idea is to replace private transport with less polluting transport means such as the electric ones. Especially in the countries with mild weather conditions, the use of motorbikes is very common and represents a concrete problem in terms of

© Springer Nature Switzerland AG 2022
G. Nicosia et al. (Eds.): LOD 2021, LNCS 13163, pp. 442–456, 2022.
https://doi.org/10.1007/978-3-030-95467-3_32

environmental impact and congestion. The possibility to foster the replacement of Internal Combustion Engine (ICE) vehicles or private vehicles with electric bikes is under consideration by several municipalities. Since the cost to purchase an electric bike can be high for some potential users, whereas some others do not consider the possibility to shift to this type of transport mode, one possibility is to offer shared e-bike services in order to let users test the service and be accustomed to it. Shared e-bikes systems have several advantages. According to Shuguang et al. (2014), the possibility to spread among the community the higher costs for an e-bike allows to overcome the price barriers and to promote the use of e-bikes among potential users. Furthermore, the introduction of an e-bike sharing system could help to implement several policy objectives, such as improving the efficiency of the transport system, increase safety and accessibility, reduce the impact on the environment (Rose 2012).

Since the investment by a municipality on an e-bike sharing service can be cumbersome, the main question is whether these services meet the demand. As pointed out by Campbell et al. (2016), the demand for e-bike sharing depends on several factors, such as the environment, weather conditions, or the availability of the infrastructure. For example, according to Pucher and Buehler (2006), in Canada less mild weather conditions are compensated by good cycling infrastructures, which explains the high cycling rate. Demand modeling is usually based on mobility surveys performed by face to face or phone interviews or computer-aided methods. However, these systems are subject to inaccuracies in terms of information reporting. For this reason, GPS coordinates are often deployed to fill this gap, as pointed out by Nguyen et al. (2020). One main limitation of using GPS coordinates to replace costly travel surveys is that it is not possible to infer the purpose of the trip. Tools that have been developed to collect this type information foresee that the traveler manually indicates the purpose of the trip. However, with this procedure there is a high probability of missing data especially if the GPS coordinates are collected over a long period of time.

The aim of this paper is to predict the purpose of the trip of shared e-bikes users based on temporal, meteorological and topological features. More specifically, the objective of this work is to answer the following questions:

- Is it possible to predict recurrent e-bikes travel purposes based on the characteristics of the trip?
- Do drivers typically select routes with more cycleways? Does the availability of road infrastructure affects the use of shared e-bikes?
- Does road infrastructure have an impact on shared e-bike users' behaviour?

In the following section, an overview of the existing literature is presented. Section 3 describes the data set used for the analysis and Sect. 4 how the features that describe the characteristics of the trip have been computed, and the methodology deployed to answer the research questions. Experimental results are presented in Sect. 5. Finally, Sect. 6 concludes the paper, drawing some directions for future research.

2   Related Works

In Cairns et al. (2017), an analysis of the existing literature on e-bikes use in Europe is reported together with the results of a field trial in the city of Brighton. The analysis of the trial aimed at assessing how much e-bikes are attractive for commuters by making them available. The authors found that the main effect of borrowing an e-bike consisted of a reduction of 20% of car travels and an increased use of e-bikes in the future. Another study about e-bike users in Denmark was carried out in Haustein and Møller (2016), analyzing the changes in cycling patters and car replacement with e-bikes. The authors identified three groups of e-bike users: those who had a very positive attitude towards e-bikes, regular bikers and recreational e-bikers. An analysis of how the adoption of e-bikes affects travel behaviour is proposed by Fyhri and Beate Sundfør (2020). The authors performed two travel surveys one before and another after the user had purchased an e-bike. They found that people who bought an e-bike increased their bicycle use and decreased walking, public transport and driving. With reference to the reasons that encourage bikers to select e-bikes, Cherry and Cervero (2007) analyze several types of electric bike users and the factors that may influence their choices. The study carried out in Kumming and Shanghai revealed that e-bikers travel longer distances compared to bike users and the main reason behind the choice to use e-bikes is the faster speed.

Another similar research proposed by Fyhri and Fearnley (2015) found that e-bike users increased the number of trips by bikes and the number of kilometers traveled. They also found that the impact of e-bike on travel behaviour was larger for females and similar for older and younger users. Finally, the authors found that the impact of e-bikes on leisure trips was higher compared to trips performed to commute. Yet, the main limitation of the study was that the users who participated in the survey could try the e-bike only for a few days, thus making not possible to assess the impact of the e-bikes based on long term use.

The impact of e-bikes on mode choice behaviour has been assessed in (Kroesen 2017). The authors found that e-bikes reduced the use of car, public transport and cycling. However, e-bikes do not replace car trips, they instead typically replace trips performed by bike. Stimulating the use of e-bikes is thus considered a good approach to reduce car travels although the positive effect on health might be limited for e-bikes travelers. Another interesting analysis was presented by Langford et al. (2013) who analyzed the attitudes towards the bike and e-bike sharing schemes. They conducted their study at the University of Tennessee, in North America, to determine which type of travelers chose the sharing scheme, analyzing who preferred e-bikes instead of bikes, and why they made such a choice. The authors discovered that 22% of users accounted for 81% of the trips, which means that the general users become habitual users. Speed and convenience were the factors that played major roles in users' decision to use a sharing scheme instead of another transportation mode, and also the factors that mainly influenced the selection of an e-bike instead of a bike.

For what concerns the characteristics of e-bike users, An et al. (2013) underlined that e-bikers are mainly used by middle- and low-level income groups and that the decision to buy an e-bike was mostly influenced by the lower cost compared to car and the possibility to be punctual. A study focused on the development of strategies and guidelines to attract new users for bike-sharing schemes was proposed by Morton (2018). This research was focused on the London Bicycle Sharing Scheme and it analyzed the perception of the quality of the service, the level of satisfaction, the intention of users towards renewing their membership, and their attitude to recommend the service to other people. Furthermore, the study provided a market segmentation analysis, which showed that the high price compared to bikes was important especially for low frequency users. The analysis of individual misbehavior's and predicted travel mode choice was proposed by Ding and Zhang (2016) who clustered travelers into several groups according to their personal characteristics. The travelers were divided into three different groups based on macroscopic factors (i.e., economic level, urban land use, etc.) and microscopic factors (i.e., age, income, travel time, travel cost, etc.). Results show that groups with higher income preferred comfortable modes (cars) while individuals with lower income preferred the transit modes.

A clustering of e-bikes users was proposed by Haustein and Møller (2016), who found three different groups of e-bike users: those who had a positive attitude and bought an e-bike to increase the frequency of use, travelers who use e-bikes to reduce travel time and, finally, recreational users.

Guidon et al. (2019) analyse the demand for free floating e-bikes sharing service and found that the key drivers are the quality of public transport, the availability of cycling infrastructure and social and economic activity. An analysis of the factors that influence the demand for shared bicycle and electric bicycle systems was presented by Campbell et al. (2016). They found that the use of bike share depends on the weather conditions and on the quality of air. Furthermore, according to their study the use of the e-bike sharing mainly attracts middle age males with low income and education, while, conversely, Fyhri and Fearnley (2015) found that e-bikes mainly attract females. Electric bikes are generally used for longer trips, therefore, they can be attractive for commuting.

Finally, a prediction of the demand for shared e-bikes has been performed in Guidon et al. (2020) who found that employment, bars and restaurants were the most important factors that allow to predict the demand for e-bike sharing services. As pointed out by Bourne et al. (2020), knowing how e-bikes are used in terms of frequency, trip duration and purpose of the trip is important to understand how to integrate this transport mean in the current system.

3   Data Set

In this section, we first illustrate the characteristics of the two data sets considered for the analysis. Then, we describe the data pre-processing approach, adopted to compute the features used by the classifier.

3.1 GPS Traces

A set of GPS traces have been collected in the context of *Electrified L-category Vehicles Integrated into Transport and Electricity Networks* (ELVITEN), an H2020 project that has started in November 2017 and lasted three years. The project involved six pilot cities in which different types of electric vehicles were deployed for various purposes. In the context of ELVITEN, sharing services have been organized to offer e-bikes in Rome, Bari and Malaga. Furthermore, a few electric tricycles were tested in Genoa and Trikala and electric quadricycles were offered in Trikala. All vehicles were equipped with black boxes with the objective of analyzing mobility behaviour and to create guidelines for policy makers and transport planners for a better integration of light electric vehicles in the transport and electricity network.

This work is focused on e-bikes, for which there is the highest number of observations. Therefore, data related to the other types of vehicles are not included in the analysis. For some of the trips, users have provided the information on the purpose of the trip, while for the majority of them this information is not available. This work focuses on three types of activities: *Work or education, Shopping* and *Leisure or visit*). The data set consists of 91 users who rented a shared e-bike and performed 6,705 trips during one year and three months (from April 29, 2019 to July 20, 2020) in one of the three cities of Malaga, Rome and Bari. Around 73% of these observations did not have information on the purpose of the trip. In this work, a supervised learning algorithm is deployed to predict the trip purposes based on a set of features.

3.2 Mobility Change and Attitudes Towards e-Bikes Survey

As an additional source of data, 67 respondents among 91 users of the shared e-bike service filled in a questionnaire aimed at collecting information about the experience with the shared e-bike service. The questions were mainly related to the attitude the user had with reference to the last trip performed with a shared e-bike or to the general attitudes towards this type of vehicles. All answers were ordinal. The first question was related to the frequency with which the user had travelled the same trip during the last week (*This was the first time ever, 1–3 times, 4–6 times, > 7 times*). A second question was related to the reason why the user had selected the shared e-bike service (*More friendly for the environment, Curiosity, Cheaper, More comfortable, Less time needed for the trip, My usual mode was not available, There was a lot of traffic*). The feeling of safety was assessed based on a Likert scale with four possible levels of agreement (*I strongly agree, I rather agree, I strongly disagree, I rather disagree*). The other two questions that have been considered in this work are the level of agreement with reference to the convenience of charging the vehicle (*I strongly agree, I rather agree, I strongly disagree, I rather disagree*) and the use of other transportation means in combination with the e-bike (*No, Yes with private car, Yes with public transportation*).

3.3   Data Pre-processing

The first part of the work was dedicated to data pre-processing using maps and GPS traces. Blackbox data have been imported into PostgreSQL 9.1 with Post-GIS 2.2 extension. Only the information located on the urban areas of Rome, Bari and Malaga have been selected. Furthermore, the pre-processing consisted in the selection of trips carried out with e-bikes, as some trips were carried out with other types of light electric vehicles. The association of each GPS data to the road link has been performed in PostgreSQL based on the nearest neighbour search, using spatial indexes. Once the GPS coordinates have been assigned to the road network, the second part of the pre-processing was executed in Python to correct a few mislabeled observations based on their location (e.g., some coordinates where located in urban areas different from the considered ones), to eliminate observations without the user ID and to compute the features that are described in the next section. Finally, the Point of Interests (PoI) have been downloaded from Openstreemap using osmpois, a Java framework to extract PoI from Openstreetmap data, to create additional features based on the proximity of the trip arrival to the nearest PoI. More specifically, five additional dummy variables have been created (poi_Work, poi_Education, poi_Leisure, poi_Shopping, poi_Other) which indicate the closest PoI to the arrival at destination. One main problem of this procedure was to correctly assign the right PoI to the destination.

Fig. 1. Point of interest and travel activity imputation

Figure 1 shows that the real destination of the user was Education. However, the closest PoI was the Photography Museum (Museo della Fotografia) or the University café (Bar Poliba Ladisa) that are both located inside the University campus (Politecnico di Bari). To solve this problem, one possibility that could be used in future research is to deploy PoI delimited by polygons instead of points. In this work, we use PoI although, as it will be shown later in Fig. 2, the feature poi_Education does not seem to bring highly relevant information.

4   Methodology

The proposed methodology for predicting travel activities of shared e-bike users is a supervised learning approach. It consists of a set of features, computed for each observed trip, and of a machine learning algorithm that is trained on multiple travels of shared e-bikers and users' information to predict the purpose of the trip. A subset of observations for each users and for which the purpose of the trip was available is used for training (75%) and the remaining for testing the classification results. The features are then analysed to assess if there is a relation between the topological, temporal and meteorological features and the e-bike shared trips. The next section briefly describes the Random Forest, how the features have been calculated, presents the results of the classification results and the interpretation of the features.

4.1   Random Forest

Random forest (RF) was proposed by Breiman (2001) to reduce the problem of overfitting in regression and classification trees. The main innovation of the method consists of creating several decision trees based on a sample of observations and features with replacement. Each decision tree is created by selecting a sample of n examples at random, with replacement, where n is the size of the training set. At each node in the tree, only a subset k of all K features is tested for attribute selection. From the classification results of each decision tree, a ranking of classifiers is created, based on the number of votes obtained by each class. The individual classification that obtains the most votes is selected.

4.2   Multinomial Logistic Regression

Logistic regression provides a conditional probability $P(Y|X)$ for each observation to belong to one of two classes, given N observations described by k features. The probability $P(Y|X)$ is estimated via a sigmoid function that is applied to a linear combination of input features. In case of multiclass problems the approach is called multinomial logistic regression. The main advantage of logistic regression is the possibility to estimate the coefficients of the model. The odds ratio are defined as the probability of success versus the probability of failure.

4.3   Features

A set of features have been extracted for each trip. Some of them were related to the topology of the road network, thus they are grouped under the category called *Topological*. They have been computed based on GPS traces and based on the information about the road network. For this purpose, an Openstreetmap[1] road network with information about cyclingways has been deployed. Each GPS

---

[1] https://www.openstreetmap.org/.

observation has been assigned to the closest road link using PostgreSQL, according to a nearest neighbour approach. Then, it was possible to compute a set of features such as the percentage of the trip performed on cycleways, the percentage of the trip performed on roads where the maximum speed allowed is lower than 30 km/h, included between 30 and 50 km/h, or greater than 50 km/h. Similarly, other features related to the topology of the road network and traffic conditions were the percentage of the trip performed with speed included between 10 and 15 km/h, less than 10 km/h, or more than 25 km/h. It turned out that the majority of the trips were performed on roads where the maximum speed allowed is 50 km/h and with a speed included between 10 and 25 km/h, as shown in Sect. 5.2. Finally, the last set of features associate the arrival of the shared e-bike users to the nearest PoI.

The other set of features were related to *meteorological* factors, such as precipitation, humidity and temperature. Finally, based on the GPS data it was possible to extract information on the time of departure, day of the week, season and distance.

5   Results

We describe in this section our experimental results. First, we will present the classification performance of the Random Forest predictor described in the previous section. Then, we will conduct some qualitative and quantitative analysis of the travel behaviour of our users.

5.1   Predicting Trip Purpose

This section reports the classification results of the travel purpose. In the first part of the section, we report the prediction results in terms of average precision, recall, f-score and accuracy. We then present the feature importance measure based on the Random forest. Finally, we perform an exploratory analysis of the features selected for the classification.

Prediction Results. The subset of observations that have information on the type of activity has been divided in two subgroups: 75% of the trips of each user have been used to train the algorithm and the remaining 25% as an evaluation set. Furthermore, the train and test split has been repeated randomly 10 times and the reported results are the average of the classification results of all trials. The two confusion matrices resulting from the ten trials of the logistic regression and random forest are reported in Table 1. The table shows that the majority of observations are located along the diagonal, meaning that most of the examples have been correctly classified.

Table 2 shows, for each label, the values of precision (ratio of predictions of a given class that are correct), recall (ratio of correctly detected examples of a given class), f1-score (harmonic mean of precision and recall) and support (the number of samples of the true response that lie in that class). For *Work and*

Table 1. Confusion matrix

Classification method	Activity	Work or education	Leisure or visit	Shopping	Other
Logistic regression	Work or education	207	36	4	0
	Leisure or visit	65	84	4	0
	Shopping	29	6	6	0
	Other	3	1	0	0
Random forest	Work or education	228	16	2	0
	Leisure or visit	26	121	5	1
	Shopping	17	9	15	0
	Other	0	2	0	2

education and *Leisure or visit*, the value of the indicators is above 80%, which suggests that the considered features are highly informative of the purpose of the trip. If, instead, the Random Forest is trained on 70% of the users, and tested on the remaining 30% of users (i.e., all the trips of a single users belong to either set) the overall accuracy drops to 67%. Overall, we can conclude that the selected features allow to discriminate across trip categories. However, the small number of users available in the considered dataset does not allow to easily generalize the model to novel sets of users.

Table 2. Classification report.

Classification approach	Activity	Precision	Recall	f1-score	Support
Logistic regression	Work or education	0.68	0.84	0.75	247
	Leisure or visit	0.67	0.55	0.6	153
	Shopping	0.46	0.15	0.23	41
	Other	0	0	0	4
Random forest	Work or education	0.84	0.92	0.88	247
	Leisure or visit	0.82	0.79	0.8	153
	Shopping	0.66	0.36	0.46	41
	Other	0.59	0.42	0.48	4

Features Importance. Figure 2 shows the importance of each feature according to the Random Forest classifier. The classifier was kept with the same settings used for the prediction of trip activities, that is, the entropy measure was selected. Furthermore, after several manual trials, the number of trees was set to 100 and, with reference to the max depth, we let the nodes to expand until all leaves were pure. The plot clearly shows that the distance traveled is the most important feature to predict the trip purpose: this is not surprising, because trips with the same purpose, performed by the same users, should have similar distances. Furthermore, temporal features such as the day of the week, and

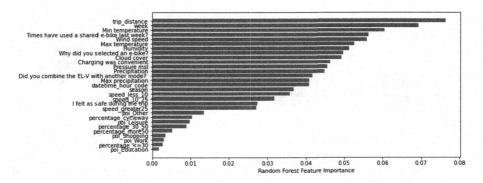

Fig. 2. Random Forest - Features importance

the weekly frequency of use of the e-bike, also contribute to predict trip activity. Especially in case of recurrent activities such as going to work, trips are performed in the same days and times of the week.

Exploratory Data Analysis. In the three urban areas, 93.4% of the trips performed for working or education purposes have been performed from Monday to Friday; while 71.7% of the trips have been done between 6am and 11am and between 3pm and 6pm. With reference to Leisure activities, 49.3% have been performed on Tuesday, Saturday and Sunday and this could be explained by the fact that this category includes leisure activities such as going to the gym but also visiting family and friends. In any case, leisure activities are almost equally distributed on the entire week. Finally, 84.4% of trips for shopping have been performed between 6am and 11am and between 3pm and 6pm and the highest percentage (23.6%) have been done on Saturday. For what concerns meteorological features, e-bikes users should prefer to travel when there are mild weather conditions. Although the three urban areas are all located in the South of Europe, in Malaga the temperature is usually higher, the weather is less humid and there are less precipitations compared to Bari and Rome.

Figure 3 shows that there is higher tolerance to precipitations when the purpose of the trip is *Work or education* (a); a similar behaviour is shown in (b) which shows that users are on average more tolerant to lower temperatures, while when the purpose of the trip is leisure or visiting a friend or family, the 75% of the users travel also with higher temperatures.

5.2   Analysis of Trip Characteristics

Based on the findings described above, we now focus on the analysis of shared e-bike travels. Using the Random Forest classifier we obtain the labels for the entire data set; then, a quantitative and qualitative analysis of shared e-bikes travel behaviour can be performed.

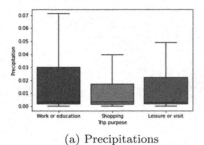

(a) Precipitations

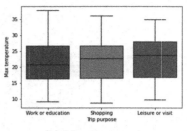

(b) Max temperature

Fig. 3. Distribution of trips by purpose with different amount of precipitations and maximum temperatures

Frequency and Duration of Shared e-Bike Travels. The analysis of the existing literature presented in (Bourne et al. 2020) revealed that, in case of e-bikes sharing schemes, the average daily distance reported by the considered works was between 2 and 10 km. While the frequency of use was included between 1.9 and 5.1 per week. According to our data set, the average distance traveled is about 4.8 km (4.1 km in Bari, 4.6 km in Malaga and 5.8 km in Rome) and the frequency is 6.4 trips per week (7.4 in Bari, 4.1 in Malaga and 7.7 in Rome). The information on the frequency and duration of the trips is important to understand the usage characteristics of the service to set up marketing campaigns that allow to promote the service.

Purpose of e-Bikes Sharing Use. According to Dill and Rose (2012), e-bikes are mainly used for commuting to work and shopping, although this information is the results of a survey filled in by only 28 participants. Furthermore, Haustein and Møller (2016) found that trips performed for leisure activities were longer than trips performed for other activities, such as commuting or shopping (Table 4).

Table 3. Average trip distance by city and trip purpose (km)

	Bari	Malaga	Rome
Work or education	3.6	4.3	5.3
Leisure or visit	6.5	7.1	6.3
Shopping	3.3	2.7	5.3
Other	2.7	-	11.7

Table 4. Percentage of trips by city and trip purpose

	Bari	Malaga	Rome
Work or education	78%	86%	50%
Leisure or visit	16%	12%	44%
Shopping	5%	2%	5%
Other	1%	0%	1%

In this work, we confirm that trips performed for leisure activities or to visit family or friends are on average longer compared to trips made for other purposes

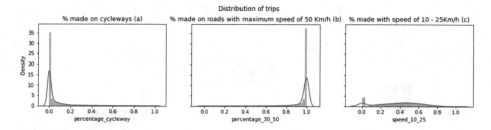

Fig. 4. Distribution of the trips as a function of the percentage of path made on cycleways, on roads with maximum speed allowed of 50 km/h and with speed included between 10 and 25 km/h

as shown in Table 3. Furthermore, the average distance traveled for shopping activities is shorter in Bari and Malaga. In Rome, which is the largest urban area, the average distance of the trips marked as *Other* is 11.7 km. These trips include activities which did not have enough observations to be analysed individually, such as *Just to try the shared EL-V*, *Charging the vehicle* and *Delivering goods*.

With reference to the types of trip performed by shared e-bikes, in all three urban areas the majority were performed for working (or education) purposes. In Rome, similar percentages of trips were performed for working and educational purposes (50%) and for leisure activities or for visiting family or friends (44%). A smaller share of the registered trips were performed for shopping activities.

Type of Infrastructures of Shared e-Bikes Trips. Overall, it can be concluded that, in the three considered cities that are located in the South of Europe, there is a lack of cycling infrastructure. Probably for this reason, the trips are mainly performed on roads where the maximum speed allowed is 50 km/h.

With reference to the type of infrastructure deployed to reach the destination, Fig. 4 shows that almost all trips in the three cities have been very rarely performed on cycleways (Fig. 4a). Moreover, Fig. 4b shows that the trips have been performed mostly by traveling on roads where the maximum allowed speed is 50 km/h. Finally, Fig. 4c shows that most of a trip (about 50%) is typically performed with a speed included between 10 and 25 km/h. Furthermore, the positive correlation of 15% between the distance of the trip and the percentage of travel made on cycleways evidences that the longer is the trip, the higher is the probability of finding a cycleway.

Safety. With reference to the purpose of the trip, a survey was carried out with the same users of the shared e-bike service for which the GPS traces are available. One of the questions was related to the feeling of safety referred to the last trip performed using shared e-bike. Since the questionnaire reported information on the purpose of the trip, it has been possible to analyse the relation between the feeling of safety with reference to the last trip. Figure 5 reports the results.

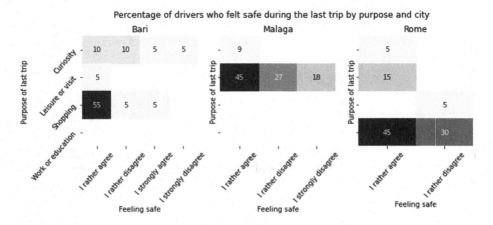

Fig. 5. Relation between feeling of safety and purpose of the trip

The majority of the respondents in the three urban areas felt rather safe during their last trip with the shared e-bike. Only in Bari and Malaga, very few users strongly disagreed on their feeling of safety while traveling but all answers are related to curiosity and recreational travel purposes since no answer concerns trips to go to work. In Rome, the 30% of the users who went to work with the shared e-bike felt rather unsafe while the 45% felt rather safe. Overall, the poor road infrastructure that characterise the urban area of Rome seem to have an impact of shared e-bike users who do not feel fully safe. It can be concluded that recreational travel activities reached by e-bike brought to a feeling of higher safety. This is probably related to the fact that users can select safer routes when they go for shopping or for recreational activities. Instead, when users have to go to work or to reach a destination for education purposes, they have to select the shortest route, which is not necessarily the safest one. Overall, 68% of the users felt rather or very safe when traveling with a shared e-bike.

6   Conclusions

This work has presented an approach to predict trip purposes of shared e-bike users based on temporal, topological and meteorological features. It was shown that, based on these features, it is possible to predict the trip purpose with over 82% of accuracy. The performance results instead to be around 67% when users, and not trips, are split between training and test sets. Furthermore, the use of topological features has allowed to make some considerations on the type of road infrastructure the users travel on by e-bike. It was found that a very small percentage of the trip is made on cycleways. On the other hand, most of the trip is performed on roads where the maximum speed allowed is 50 km/h and with a speed included between 10 and 25 km/h. Finally, thanks to the answers to a survey performed with the same users, it was shown that, in the three considered cities, e-bikes users not always feel safe while driving. Therefore, it is quite likely that the construction of new cycleways could also help to increase the use of e-bikes, or at least the feeling of safety of their users.

References

An, K., Chen, X., Xin, F., Lin, B., Wei, L.: Travel characteristics of E-bike users: survey and analysis in Shanghai. Procedia Soc. Behav. Sci. **96**, 1828–1838 (2013). International Conference of Transportation Professionals (CICTP) 2013

Bourne, J.E., et al.: The impact of e-cycling on travel behaviour: a scoping review. J. Transp. Health **19**, 100910 (2020)

Breiman, L.: Random forests. Mach. Learn. **45**(1), 5–32 (2001)

Cairns, S., Behrendt, F., Raffo, D., Beaumont, C., Kiefer, C.: Electrically-assisted bikes: potential impacts on travel behaviour. Transp. Res. Part A Policy Practice **103**, 327–342 (2017)

Campbell, A.A., Cherry, C.R., Ryerson, M.S., Yang, X.: Factors influencing the choice of shared bicycles and shared electric bikes in Beijing. Transp. Res. Part C: Emerg. Technol. **67**, 399–414 (2016)

Cherry, C., Cervero, R.: Use characteristics and mode choice behavior of electric bike users in China. Transp. Policy **14**(3), 247–257 (2007)

Dill, J., Rose, G.: Electric bikes and transportation policy: insights from early adopters. Transp. Res. Rec. **2314**(1), 1–6 (2012)

Ding, L., Zhang, N.: A travel mode choice model using individual grouping based on cluster analysis. Procedia Eng. **137**, 786–795 (2016)

Fyhri, A., Beate Sundfør, H.: Do people who buy e-bikes cycle more? Transp. Res. Part D: Transp. Environ. **86**, 102422 (2020)

Fyhri, A., Fearnley, N.: Effects of e-bikes on bicycle use and mode share. Transp. Res. Part D: Transp. Environ. **36**, 45–52 (2015)

Guidon, S., Becker, H., Dediu, H., Axhausen, K.W.: Electric bicycle-sharing: a new competitor in the urban transportation market? an empirical analysis of transaction data. Transp. Res. Rec. **2673**(4), 15–26 (2019)

Guidon, S., Reck, D.J., Axhausen, K.: Expanding a(n) (electric) bicycle-sharing system to a new city: prediction of demand with spatial regression and random forests. J. Transp. Geogr. **84**, 102692 (2020)

Haustein, S., Møller, M.: Age and attitude: changes in cycling patterns of different e-bike user segments. Int. J. Sustain. Transp. **10**(9), 836–846 (2016)

Kroesen, M.: To what extent do e-bikes substitute travel by other modes? evidence from the Netherlands. Transp. Res. Part D: Transp. Environ. **53**, 377–387 (2017)

Langford, B., Cherry, C., Yoon, T., Worley, S., Smith, D.: North America's first E-Bikeshare. Transp. Res. Rec. J. Transp. Res. Board **2387**, 120–128 (2013)

Morton, C.: Appraising the market for bicycle sharing schemes: perceived service quality, satisfaction, and behavioural intention in London. Case Stud. Transp. Policy **6**(1), 102–111 (2018)

Nguyen, M.H., Armoogum, J., Madre, J.L., Garcia, C.: Reviewing trip purpose imputation in GPS-based travel surveys. J. Traffic Transp. Eng. (English Edition) **7**(4), 395–412 (2020)

Pucher, J., Buehler, R.: Why Canadians cycle more than Americans: a comparative analysis of bicycling trends and policies. Transp. Policy **13**(3), 265–279 (2006)

Rose, G.: E-bikes and urban transportation: emerging issues and unresolved questions. Transportation **39**(1), 81–96 (2012)

Shuguang, J., Cherry, C.R., Han, L.D., Jordan, D.A.: Electric bike sharing: simulation of user demand and system availability. J. Clean. Prod. **85**, 250–257 (2014)

Machine Learning in a Policy Support System for Smart Tourism Management

Elena Bellodi$^{(\boxtimes)}$ (ID), Riccardo Zese (ID), and Francesco Bertasi

Department of Engineering, University of Ferrara, Via Saragat 1, 44122 Ferrara, Italy
{elena.bellodi,riccardo.zese,francesco.bertasi}@unife.it

Abstract. In the last few years, the Emilia-Romagna region, in Italy, has seen a significant growth in the tourism economy, due to an increasing number of Italian and foreigner visitors. This has highlighted the need of a strong synergy between tourist facilities and local administrations. In this context, Smart City solutions and Machine Learning (ML) can play an important role to analyse the amount of data generated in this sector. This paper presents part of the work done within the ongoing *POLIS-EYE* project, targeted at the development of a Policy Support System (PSS) and related intelligent services for an optimized management of the Smart City in the specific domain of tourism in this region. Several results obtained from the application of supervised and unsupervised ML techniques show the effectiveness in the prediction of the tourist flow in different scenarios, e.g., towards regional museums and big events. The integration of these results in the PSS architecture will allow a smart management of the territory on behalf of the administration and will be replicable outside the region.

Keywords: Smart City platform · Tourism · Data-driven predictive modelling · Machine Learning

1 Introduction

In 2017, according to the United Nations World Tourism Organization (UNWTO), there were 58.7 million foreign travellers in Italy, an increase of 11.8% compared to 2016, the highest growth rate among the top five international tourism destinations. According to the Bank of Italy, the tourism income reported a positive balance of 14.6 million euros in 2017 (+5.7% w.r.t. 2016). In this strong growth, where the tourism economy has exceeded 13% of the GDP, the Italian Emilia-Romagna (ER) region fits very well with an increase in tourists of 6.3% compared to 2016. Coasts, cities of art and business, the Apennines and other locations recorded a positive performance in both arrivals and attendance.

Despite these encouraging data, a request for innovation in services, which are weak in the generation of added value and require greater competitiveness and innovative capacity, has emerged. The theme of tourist flows is central to all historic cities and the integration with the commercial sector and the various

© Springer Nature Switzerland AG 2022
G. Nicosia et al. (Eds.): LOD 2021, LNCS 13163, pp. 457–472, 2022.
https://doi.org/10.1007/978-3-030-95467-3_33

impacts arising are challenges for the governance of the territory itself. In the context of *Smart Cities*, problems arise both of an organizational nature, related to the services to be made available in an integrated manner, and of security. There is the need to monitor and integrate possibly heterogeneous data sources. This opens up great opportunities for services capable of integrating and adding value to these sources and Open Data, which are often available, but little usable and used. This is a wealth of "Big Data" of which the administration is often not fully aware or capable of integrating and reprocessing through analysis tools that allow to extract information from them.

In this sense the project *POLIS-EYE*, for "POLIcy Support systEm for smart citY data governancE", was funded by the ER region in 2019 to provide the main players in the area - managers, policy makers, companies in the sector and the consultancy activities connected to them, but also public administrations and citizens - with innovative ICT tools and services from a Smart City (SC) perspective for the optimized management of tourism in the ER region. *The project aims to create a neutral platform to be potentially used by different targets in the field of tourism. However, the approach will be transferable to the various contexts relating to the innovative services of and for the city.*

The project is ongoing and involves both *academic and research laboratories* in the ER region - MechLav, the industrial Research Laboratory of the Ferrara Technopole (founded by the Department of Engineering of the University of Ferrara), the Research Laboratory on Geographical Sciences and Technologies and Smart Cities (GeoSmart Lab), the Interdepartmental Center for Industrial Research of the University of Bologna (CIRI-ICT), the research center (CROSS-TEC) of the Italian National Agency for New Technologies, Energy and Sustainable Economic Development (ENEA), active on big data, interoperability and data issues for smart cities, the Artificial Intelligence Research and Innovation Center (AIRI) of the University of Modena and Reggio-Emilia - and *companies* from very different realities, such as Gruppo TIM (one of the largest Italian telecommunications company which provides telephony services, mobile services, and DSL data services), Lepida (which deals with planning, development and management of Telecommunication infrastructures in ER), Bologna Museums Institution, the Guglielmo Marconi Bologna Airport, IF Imola Faenza Tourist Company, Eatalyworld.

POLIS-EYE aims to develop an innovative technology in the management of tourist flows, in which, in the face of unpredictable events (e.g., a large and unscheduled influx), it is possible not only to react to the emergency, but to plan them. The creation of a software platform for data management is envisaged with the following objectives: (1) reconstruction of flows of people, e.g., on the basis of data collected from the mobile phone network, for describing the attractiveness of various tourist areas of a city; (2) description of common characteristics of a tourist area; (3) correlation between events (specific and atmospheric) and people attendance, for example, based on the past trend of arrivals in a city (airport, fair, hotel, etc.), it will be possible to predict future trends. After a first phase of definition of requirements and data collection done together with the companies involved, the goal was to create *descriptive, prescriptive, and predictive analysis models. The platform and the models will then be scalable and applicable to other case studies.* This is possible thanks to the integration of technologies for Big Data management, Artificial Intelligence (AI) and Machine Learning (ML) methods, and combinatorial optimization techniques. Where possible, declarative models have been favoured, due to their high understandability by the non-expert user and the possibility to be viewable in the platform dashboards.

This paper presents the work carried out up to now by the MechLav Laboratory of the Ferrara Technopole. The laboratory has been mainly dealing with the application of ML methods for learning models from the collected data, in order to identify their salient features or for classification purposes. Thus, the objective of this paper is to show how ML techniques can be used inside a platform for smart tourism management, showing both conceptual and implementation aspects. Even though the clustering and prediction problems analysed are state-of-the-art from a computer science viewpoint, on the other hand they are interesting from the application viewpoint.

The paper describes: related work (Sect. 2), the Policy Support System (Sect. 3), the data sources (Sect. 4), the ML techniques applied (Sect. 5), the achieved results (Sect. 6). Section 7 concludes the paper.

2   Related Work

The problem of smart tourism management and tourist flows in general is of great importance, and in the last years acquired even more interest, especially from the public administration and business agents. However, to the best of our knowledge, differently from our project goal, most proposals either focus on specific aspects or describe the overall framework without giving strong and ready-to-use implementations. Interesting proposals were given in [11, 16], where the authors presented a conceptual definition on structure and communication between different agents. This framework shares several aspects with ours, especially in the division of the different levels and in the services the framework should make available. However, it lacks an implementation that can prove the feasibility of the proposal. Moreover, [16] focuses more on business agents involved in tourism.

In the larger context of SCs, many frameworks were born considering *smart grids*, i.e., the set of sensors, communications, and infrastructures that collaborate on the management of a smart electrical grid, and later extended to the problem of SCs, where the electric grid must be managed alongside other services, such as water distribution, waste management, transport, and so forth. For example, SGAM [6] (Smart Grid Architecture Model) which is expressly defined for smart grid, has been extended to Smart Cities in SCIAM [9] (Smart City Infrastructure Model), GSCAM [15] (Generic Smart City Architecture Model), and IES-City [8] (Internet of things - Enabled Smart City). They all define languages to identify interfaces for data exchange and map different architectures on a standard abstract model, by borrowing the interfaces defined by SGAM and extending them or adding new ones considering the wider scenario of a SC.

Another framework is SMArc [17] (Semantic Middleware Architecture), which adds a semantic layer composed of an ontology and inference systems to improve scalability, identification, and smart management of (new added) devices, and interoperability. U-City [2,10] is expressly tailored on the concept of SC. U-City stands for Ubiquitous City, i.e., a city were chips, computers, sensors are present in the urban element, connected to the network and always communicating with each other. The main problem in these contexts is that information comes from different sources that hardly communicate with each other. Each of these sources elaborates its own data and provides analysis results in a vertical way, forcing a framework exploiting many data sources to build an upper layer to aggregate these results. In this context, it is of foremost importance to allow each data source to access the other sources during data analysis.

Other approaches have concentrated more on the definition of platforms. FIWARE[1] is a project aimed at promoting the use of royalty-free protocols and software to particular use cases. It is a general purpose platform that considers a set of APIs and open-source references that, however, can be easily applied to SCs, as shown by many different works [1,3,12,14]. However, one of the drawbacks is that these platforms are not designed to operate with external sources.

SCIAM, SCAM, SMArc, U-City, or IES-City define abstract architectural models, but they miss usable implementations. The FIWARE framework is thought from the implementation perspective but not from the perspective of interoperability with external sources. To the best of our knowledge, the POLIS-EYE project for the first time realizes a full-stack platform for data collection and exchange, with an open interoperability-oriented implementation, AI-based Business Analytics services, and an advanced user interface, in the context of regional tourism.

As regarding the application of ML techniques to the problem, the majority of the works focuses on flow prediction, such as [13] that applies LSTM, a type of recurrent neural networks, to predict the tourist flow to the Small Wild Goose Pagoda in Xi'an, Shaanxi, China, or [5] that exploits a time series analysis approach to evaluate the relations between tourism flows and museum and monument attendance. In these cases, both shares many similarities with our work.

3   Policy Support System Architecture

The project involves the development of a Policy Support System (PSS) with a three-level architecture (Fig. 1): (1) Data level, with the task of storing and processing large amounts of information, (2) Service level, organized into Descriptive, Predictive and Prescriptive analytics services, (3) User interface. Levels with a lower degree of abstraction are associated with relatively simple operations, but performed on large amounts of data; conversely, higher abstraction levels will handle more complex operations, but on a smaller amount of data.

---

[1] https://www.fiware.org/.

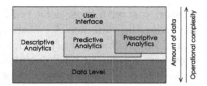

Fig. 1. 3-Level architecture of the Policy Support System.

The Service level contains a *descriptive* level, presenting information through advanced visualization techniques (e.g., dashboards) to the user; a *predictive* level providing ML models to predict future trends and highlight relationships between different data; and a *prescriptive* level to proactively provide recommendations on specific actions (e.g., budget allocation) on the basis of the results from the other levels. The different levels require radically different technologies, for example frameworks for the parallel processing of data to ensure scalability, unified databases, and meta-languages to represent information (JSON, OWL) in the Data level; Web services with REST API for the Service Level; and Web technologies such as HTML5 and JavaScript for the User Interface.

Mature, widely adopted and/or open-source tools are favoured to reduce costs and facilitate deployment and maintenance and, where possible, the software components developed in the project will be released with open-source licenses, to ensure maximum reusability and impact in an industrial and research context. The models generated at the Service level are targeted to use cases agreed with the partner companies, developed according to a data-driven approach, and validated on real data.

4   Data Sources

The data sources made available by the project partners[2] are the following: (I) data from the mobile phone network of Gruppo TIM relative to August and September 2019 (61 days) and 2020 (61 days), sampled every 15 min, and specific to each ACE ("Aree di CEnsimento" in Italian, census areas in English), sub-areas of the ER region defined by the census; data include age and gender of people connected to the network, nationality (Italians/foreigners), type of contract (business/regular), type of client (commuter/resident); (II) data from the Bologna Museums Institution relative to the months from June 2018 to February 2020; for each month, for each visitors' nationality in that month, the total number of admissions to 10 museums is available; (II) data from the Marconi Bologna Airport, relative to the months from January 2018 to February 2020, reporting the total of arrivals/departures from/to a specific country in a given month.

---

[2] Data have been provided by private Italian companies and cannot be published.

In addition, data were integrated with those collected from open sources, such as: (I) daily weather data from the "ilmeteo"[3] website: minimum, maximum and mean temperature, wind speed, humidity, pressure, rainfall, precipitation type; (II) data relative to events of different kind downloaded from municipal or regional tourist websites, described by the corresponding ACE, size (estimated attendance), category (sport, etc.), topic (football, etc.), duration (in days), and day(s) of the week in which the event took place.

5   Machine Learning for the Service Level

At the Service level, ML techniques were applied to derive valuable information from the available data sources. This activity was carried out by the MechLav research Laboratory and was focused on two aspects: (1) automatic identification of descriptive patterns, which may emerge from the data by applying unsupervised ML techniques; (2) automatic identification of predictive models of future trends, obtained by applying supervised ML techniques such as classification, in which input examples or time series labelled with a class are provided.

5.1   Learning Descriptive Models

Cluster analysis can be a powerful ML tool for any organization that needs to identify discrete groups of customers, transactions, or other types of behaviours in a descriptive manner from *unlabelled* data. K-means clustering is by far the most widely used method for discovering clusters in data. It is based on flat geometry (distance between points), even cluster size and typically discovers a reduced number of clusters. It divides a set of N samples X into K disjoint clusters, each described by the mean μ_i (called 'centroid') of the samples in the i-th cluster. The algorithm has three steps. The first step chooses the initial centroids. After initialization, K-means consists of looping between the two other steps: the first one assigns each sample to its nearest centroid; the second one creates new centroids by taking the mean value of all the samples assigned to each previous centroid. The difference between the old and the new centroids is computed, and the algorithm repeats these last two steps until this value is less than a threshold. Given enough time, K-means will always converge, however this may be to a local minimum (this is highly dependent on the initialization of the centroids). In the experiments, the *Elkan*'s implementation of the algorithm was used, an accelerated version introduced in [7] to be scalable with datasets' dimensions and number of clusters, but still computing the same result as the standard algorithm and able to use any black-box distance metric. The mean *Silhouette Coefficient* over all samples allows one to choose the best value for K: it is computed as $\frac{(b-a)}{max(a,b)}$, where a is the mean intra-cluster distance and b is the mean nearest-cluster distance for the sample and takes on a value in the range $[-1, 1]$. The best value for K is identified by a coefficient near 1; values near 0 indicate overlapping clusters, negative values generally indicate that a sample has been assigned to the wrong cluster, as a different cluster is more similar.

---

[3] https://www.ilmeteo.it/.

5.2   Learning Predictive Models

Classification requires the use of ML algorithms that, given set of *labelled* data called examples (training set), learn how to assign a class label to unseen examples from the problem domain. This assignment is called a *prediction*. Random forests (RFs) are known for their good computational performance and scalability. A RF is a meta estimator that fits a number of decision tree (DT) classifiers on various sub-samples of the data and uses averaging to improve the predictive accuracy and control overfitting. In RFs each tree is built from a sample drawn with replacement (i.e., a bootstrap sample) from the training set. Furthermore, when splitting each node during the construction of a tree, the best split is found either from all input features or a random subset (of size $max\_features$, see Subsect. 6.2). The purpose of these two sources of randomness is to decrease the variance of the forest estimator. Individual DTs typically exhibit high variance and tend to overfit; the injected randomness yields decision trees with somewhat decoupled prediction errors. By taking an average of those predictions, some errors can cancel out. In practice the variance reduction is often significant, hence yielding an overall better model. In contrast to the original publication [4], the implementation used in the experiments combines DT classifiers by averaging their probabilistic prediction, instead of letting each classifier vote for a single class. Extra Trees (ET) are similar to Random Forest but consider the whole dataset instead of using bootstrap samples, and choose the split randomly, instead of taking the best one, to add more randomness in the process.

6   Experimental Evaluation

For descriptive and predictive analytics services, the open source ML library `scikit-learn`[4], that supports supervised and unsupervised learning methods, was used.

6.1   Descriptive Models

Clustering for learning descriptive models was applied for the purpose of discovering meaningful clusters of ACE in the ER region having similar density of (1) foreigners and of (2) commuters using data from the mobile phone network of Gruppo TIM collected in a few months of 2019 combined with daily weather data (see Sect. 4). The same experiments were also replicated with data from Gruppo TIM collected in the same months of 2020 with the aim of comparing tourism before and during the Covid-19 pandemic. This is in line with a previous study where we carried on an analysis of the variation of the mobility during lockdown (spring 2020) both in the Emilia-Romagna region and at the national level considering Google[5] and Apple[6] datasets in June 2020. The results were presented

---

[4] https://scikit-learn.org/.

[5] https://www.google.com/covid19/mobility/.

[6] https://covid19.apple.com/mobility.

in the Italian magazine "Urban Design Magazine"[7]. The results showed that, as expected, the mobility of people decreased significantly during lockdown, and that the Emilia-Romagna trend mirrored the national trend.

Before learning the model, data were pre-processed. Firstly, the granularity of the data was changed from a 15-min sampling to a 1-day sampling (by summing the values for each attribute). Secondly, weather data were added to each ACE to get a 506×2013 matrix, where each row represents an ACE and columns correspond to 33 attributes for each of the 61 days.

K-Means was applied by keeping all the parameters except n_clusters to their default values: init=k-means++ (that selects initial centroids in a smart way to speed up convergence), n_init=10 (number of times the algorithm will be run with different centroid seeds), max_iter=300 (maximum number of iterations), algorithm=elkan. In order to identify the optimal number of clusters n_clusters, various values were tested in the range [2–15] by calculating the corresponding silhouette coefficients.

Results for test (1) with 2019 data are shown in Fig. 2. The highest value for the silhouette coefficient (0.82) suggested to use n_clusters=2 (Fig. 2a), which can be visualized in Fig. 2b: cluster 1 (orange) corresponds to a high density of foreigners along the coast, at the Marconi Bologna Airport and in the province of Forlì-Cesena; cluster 0 (blue) corresponds to a much lower density of foreigners in the inland. This result is in line with the distribution of foreigners in the region in the summer period; the high concentration in the Forlì-Cesena ACE could be due to the strong presence of paths and excursions towards the Bologna hills (Foreste Casentinesi National Park, Mount Falterona and Campigna).

Results for test (1) with 2020 data are shown in Fig. 3. In this case as well the highest value of the silhouette coefficient (0.906) suggests the use of n_clusters=2 (Fig. 3a), while clusters are shown in Fig. 3b. Compared to 2019, the ACE of the Marconi airport in Bologna and the more internal ACE disappear among the areas most visited by foreign visitors. This is probably due to the absence of public events and the reduction in the number of tourist flights. The presence of foreign visitors around the coast remains high.

The results of this analysis can be used for a better promotion of tourism, e.g., targeting foreigners or Italians depending on the clusters.

Results for test (2) with 2019 data are shown in Fig. 4a. The highest value for the silhouette coefficient (0.65) suggested to use n_clusters=2: cluster 1 (orange) identifies the ACE where commuters concentrated in the month of September 2019, corresponding to all the provincial capitals (plus Fidenza, famous for its mall); cluster 0 (blue) corresponds to a much lower density of commuters.

The algorithm was also applied to August 2019 data separately, identifying the same distribution pattern of cluster 1, but with much less ACE involved, due to the summer period.

Result of test (2) with 2020 data is shown in Fig. 4b. In this case the silhouette coefficient (0.633) suggested to use n_clusters = 4: in addition to cluster 0

---

[7] https://www.udmagazine.it/2020/06/30/n-13-citta-e-salute/.

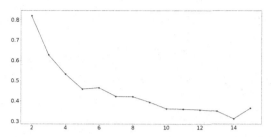

(a) Silhouette Coefficient as a function of the number of clusters.

(b) Result of K-Means w.r.t. the density of foreigners in August-September 2019: 2 clusters are identified, one including the orange ACE and the other including the blue ACE.

Fig. 2. Clustering of the ACE in ER relative to August-September 2019 w.r.t. the distribution of foreigners in the region.

(blue) which identifies a scenario with a low concentration of commuters, and cluster 1 (orange) with a high density of them, a third cluster (green) describes a medium density scenario and a fourth cluster (red) a very high density of commuters.

These results could be exploited for traffic and transportation management, for example by improving public transport in the areas where the number of commuters or tourists is higher.

In all tests, K-Means converged in less than 1 s. Besides K-Means, Affinity propagation and Mean-shift clustering algorithms were also tested. For Affinity Propagation we tried different combinations of `max_iter`, `convergence_iter`, `preference`, and `affinity` values; for Mean-shift different values for `min_bin_freq`, `max_iteration`, and `cluster_all`. However, they always achieved lower silhouette coefficients.

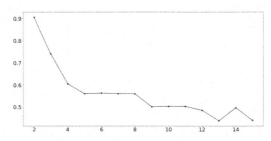

(a) Silhouette Coefficient as a function of the number of clusters.

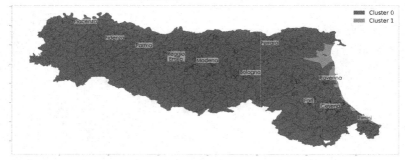

(b) Result of K-Means w.r.t. the density of foreigners in the year 2020: 2 clusters are identified, one including the orange ACE and the other including the blue ACE.

Fig. 3. Clustering of the ACE in ER relative to August-September 2020 w.r.t. the distribution of foreigners in the region.

6.2   Predictive Models

A first experiment involved building a classifier able to predict the amount of people of a certain nationality who might visit the museums in Bologna knowing the total number of arrivals at the airport.

Before learning the predictive model, data were pre-processed. A one-hot encoding scheme was applied to the 'month' and 'country' categorical attributes of the Bologna Museums Institution data in order to convert them into numerical, using the `sklearn.preprocessing.OneHotEncoder` class. Data from the two sources were then combined into a 727×13 matrix. We created a row for each combination of month and country of origin when a connection existed. Thus, each row is characterized by month, flight country of origin, total number of passengers from a specific country (Italy included) arrived in Bologna in that month, and total number of visitors to each museum in Bologna in that month from that country. The total number of visitors was then reduced to 5 classes (0–50, 51–100, 101–250, 251–500, over 500 people) in order to get a labelled dataset for *multi-class* classification purposes.

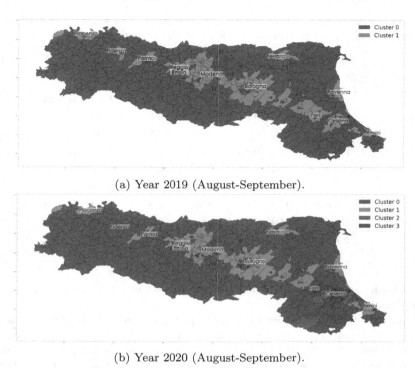

(a) Year 2019 (August-September).

(b) Year 2020 (August-September).

Fig. 4. Comparison of the results of K-Means w.r.t. the density of commuters in the years 2019 a and 2020 b.

We considered three different algorithms: Random Forest (RF), Decision Trees (DT), and Extra Trees (ET). The best values for some of the parameters of the estimators were identified through a grid search, in particular, we considered the array of values [2, 5, 10, 20] for `max_depth` (maximum depth of the trees), [1, 5, 10, 20] for `min_samples_leaf` (minimum number of samples required to be at a leaf node). For RF and ET, we also considered the values [10, 100, 250, 500] for `n_estimators` (number of trees in the forest) and [50, 100, 200] for `max_samples` (number of samples to draw from the data to train each base estimator). The grid search was carried out through a 4-fold cross-validation, where the parameters of the Random Forest were tuned 4 times, one for each of the 4 training sets, and they were validated (in terms of accuracy) on each of the corresponding test sets. The parameters producing the model with the best accuracy were chosen for training a model over 75% of the whole dataset, whose performance was tested on the remaining 25%. The training set (75%) and the test set (25%) used for learning/testing the final model did not coincide with any of the 4 training/test sets used in the previous cross-validation phase. A validation set for choosing the best parameters was not used as the datasets'

Table 1. Results of the RF, DT, and ET classifiers on the test set in terms of Precision, Recall, F1-Score for the prediction of visitors to the Bologna museums.

		Number of visitors					Acc.
		0–50	51–100	101–250	251–500	>501	
RF	Precision	0.78	0.69	0.65	0.47	0.69	**0.703**
	Recall	0.88	0.84	0.52	0.28	0.58	
	F1-score	0.83	0.76	0.58	0.35	0.63	
DT	Precision	0.86	0.53	0.57	0.50	0.79	0.670
	Recall	0.83	0.91	0.38	0.21	0.58	
	F1-score	0.84	0.67	0.46	0.29	0.67	
ET	Precision	0.79	0.63	0.63	0.46	0.74	**0.703**
	Recall	0.94	0.70	0.57	0.21	0.74	
	F1-score	0.86	0.67	0.60	0.29	0.74	

size in both experiments involving random forests was very small (727 and 77 examples).

Data were then divided into 75% as training set and 25% as test set; the distribution of the examples among the classes in the training set was: 205 examples for the [0–50] range, 86 for [51–100], 133 for [101–250], 63 for [251–500], 58 for > 500. The RF classifier was built over the training set with `max_depth=20`, `min_samples_leaf=1`, `max_samples=200`, `n_estimators=500` while keeping the default for the other parameters.

The DT classifier was built over the training set with `max_depth=10`, `min_samples_leaf=1` while keeping the default for the other parameters. The ET classifier was built over the training set with `max_depth=20`, `min_samples_leaf=1`, `max_samples=50`, `n_estimators=500` while keeping the default for the other parameters. The $predict(X)$ method was used, that returns the predicted class of the input sample X corresponding to the highest mean probability estimate across the trees in the forest. Each test example was labelled with the class achieving the highest mean probability estimate across the trees in the forest. Grid search and training took less than a minute. Overall accuracy over the test set was 0.703 for RF and ET, and 0.670 for DT classifier, while other typical ML performance metrics are reported in Table 1 for each class. As can be seen from Table 1 RF slightly overcomes ET, while DT should not be chosen for this analysis. The limited performance for class 251–500 is probably due to the reduced number of training examples belonging to that class.

Note that in RF there is no need for cross-validation during the training phase as the estimate of the test set error is done internally, during the run [4]. Given the information about the total arrivals by plane from a specific country in a month, the classifier predicts the class of people (e.g. [51–100]) who will visit the museums in Bologna.

A second experiment aimed at defining a predictive model that, given a future event for which the number of visitors is unknown, determines the expected percentage increase of people among 5 classes of increase: $+[0$–$10]\%$, $+(10$–$25]\%$, $+(25$–$50]\%$, $+(50$–$75]\%$, $+{>}75\%$. Data about different events in the region (sport competitions, exhibits, fairs, etc.) were combined with the mobile phone network and weather data. In particular, for each event the 'average peak' and the 'average peak per day' were calculated from the mobile phone data. 'Average peak' is the average, over the 61 available days, of the maximum number of people present each day in the ACE where the event takes place, while the 'average peak per day' is the average, over the 61 available days, of the maximum number of people in the ACE of the event for that specific day of the week (if the event for which we want the prediction happens on a Friday, we compute the average peak over all Fridays).

Before learning the descriptive model, data were pre-processed. A one-hot encoding scheme was applied to the 'category', 'topic', 'day of the week' and 'precipitation type' categorical attributes in order to convert them into numerical. Data from the three sources were then combined into a 77×11 matrix. Each row corresponds to an event, while the 11 columns represent: average peak, average peak per day, category, topic, duration, day of the week, size, minimum, maximum and mean temperature, and precipitation type. 44 Events registered [10,000–100,000] participants and 33 events [1,000–10,000] participants. The attribute to be predicted is the percentage increase in the number of visitors calculated as $100 \cdot \frac{max\ peak}{average\ peak\ per\ day}$, where $max\ peak$ is the maximum number of people connected to the mobile phone network inside the ACE where the event takes place on the day of the event. The percentage increase resulting from the formula above was split into the 5 classes previously described, in order to get a labelled dataset for *multi-class* classification purposes: almost half of the events (36) fall into the class of $+(25$–$50]\%$ increase.

As for the first experiment, three classifiers have been tested, namely RF, DT, and ET. To tune the hyper-parameters, we performed a grid search through a 4-fold cross-validation, as described for the first experiment. So, the best values for some of the parameters of the RF, RF, and ET estimators were identified through a grid search considering the array of values [2, 5, 10, 20] for `max_depth`, and [1, 10, 20] for `min_samples_leaf`. For RF and ET, we also considered the arrays [10, 50] for `n_estimators` and [5, 10, 20] for `max_features` (the number of attributes to consider). Data were then divided into 75% as training set and 25% as test set. The RF classifier was built over the training set with `max_depth=5`, `min_samples_leaf=1`, `max_features=20`, `n_estimators=10`. The DT classifier was built with `max_depth=2`, `min_samples_leaf=1`, while the ET classifier with `max_depth=5`, `min_samples_leaf=1`, `max_features=10`, `n_estimators=50`. All the other parameters were set to their default values. Grid search and training took less than a minute. Overall accuracy over the test set was 0.75 for RF, 0.65 for DT, and 0.7 for ET, while other ML performance metrics are reported in Table 2, demonstrating that RF has the best performance. The classifier performs

Table 2. Results of the RF, DT, and ET classifiers on the test set for predicting the class of increase of visitors to a given event.

		% Increase of visitors					Acc.
		+[0–10]	+(10–25]	+(25–50]	+(50–75]	+>75	
RF	Precision	1.00	1.00	0.69	1.00	1.00	**0.75**
	Recall	1.00	0.75	1.00	0.25	0.50	
	F1-score	1.00	0.86	0.82	0.40	0.50	
DT	Precision	0.00	1.00	0.64	0.00	0.33	0.65
	Recall	0.00	0.75	1.00	0.00	0.50	
	F1-score	0.00	0.86	0.78	0.00	0.40	
ET	Precision	1.00	1.00	0.64	0.00	0.50	0.70
	Recall	1.00	0.75	1.00	0.00	0.50	
	F1-score	1.00	0.86	0.78	0.00	0.50	

well except for the fourth class, where the low recall indicates that only a fourth of true positives are correctly recognized.

Given information about a future event and weather data, the classifier predicts the class of percentage increase in the number of visitors (e.g., +(10–25]%) on the day of the event w.r.t. the average number of people in the same ACE when no events are scheduled. In case of events lasting more than 1 day, every day of the event is treated as an independent event but is discriminated by the attribute 'duration' which is greater than 1.

Both the results on prediction of visitors to museums and specific events can be useful for a greater logistic efficiency in personnel and visitors management. In this context, DT, ET, and RF were also tested as regressors, but were discarded as we did not consider useful returning to the user a single real value.

7   Conclusions and Future Work

The paper presented some of the results achieved by applying machine learning in the context of a Smart City project, whose objective is to design a Policy Support System integrating data from heterogeneous sources to help tourism management in the ER region. In particular, clustering and classification techniques to build descriptive and predictive models were applied with good performance. The project is still ongoing, and the integration of our results with those achieved from data analysis by the other partners, new ML experiments with data collected from new sources, and the definition of *ad-hoc* dashboards are the next objectives of the project.

Acknowledgments. This research was funded by the Fondo di Sviluppo e Coesione (FSC) of Regione Emilia-Romagna within the context of the POR FESR 2014-2020 ASSE 1 AZIONE 1.2.2 (CUP E21F18000200007) project "POLIcy Support systEm for smart citY data governancE (POLIS-EYE)".

References

1. Aiello, G., Alessi, M., Marasso, L.: City enabler: a FIWARE based tool for crawling, collecting and rendering on a map valuable data at urban scale
2. Anttiroiko, A.-V.: U-cities reshaping our future: reflections on ubiquitous infrastructure as an enabler of smart urban development. AI Soc. **28**(4), 491–507 (2013). https://doi.org/10.1007/s00146-013-0443-5
3. Araujo, V., Mitra, K., Saguna, S., Åhlund, C.: Performance evaluation of FIWARE: a cloud-based IoT platform for smart cities. J. Parallel Distrib. Comput. **132**, 250–261 (2019). https://doi.org/10.1016/j.jpdc.2018.12.010
4. Breiman, L.: Random forests. Mach. Learn. **45**(1), 5–32 (2001)
5. Cellini, R., Cuccia, T.: Museum and monument attendance and tourism flow: a time series analysis approach. Appl. Econ. **45**(24), 3473–3482 (2013)
6. CEN-CENELEC-ETSI Smart Grid Coord. Group: Smart grid reference architecture. http://gridscientific.com/images/Smart_Grid_Reference_Artichtecture.pdf
7. Elkan, C.: Using the triangle inequality to accelerate k-means. In: Proceedings of the Twentieth International Conference on International Conference on Machine Learning, ICML 2003, pp. 147–153. AAAI Press (2003)
8. Frascella, A., et al.: A minimum set of common principles for enabling smart city interoperability. TECHNE-Journal of Technology for Architecture and Environment, pp. 56–61 (2018)
9. Gottschalk, M., Uslar, M., Delfs, C.: Smart city infrastructure architecture model (SCIAM). The Use Case and Smart Grid Architecture Model Approach (2017)
10. Jang, M., Suh, S.-T.: U-City: new trends of urban planning in Korea based on pervasive and ubiquitous geotechnology and geoinformation. In: Taniar, D., Gervasi, O., Murgante, B., Pardede, E., Apduhan, B.O. (eds.) ICCSA 2010. LNCS, vol. 6016, pp. 262–270. Springer, Heidelberg (2010). https://doi.org/10.1007/978-3-642-12156-2_20
11. Kazandzhieva, V., Santana, H.: E-tourism: definition, development and conceptual framework. Tourism Int. Interdisc. J. **67**(4), 332–350 (2019)
12. Latré, S., Leroux, P., Coenen, T., Braem, B., Ballon, P., Demeester, P.: City of things: An integrated and multi-technology testbed for IoT smart city experiments. In: IEEE International Smart Cities Conference, ISC2 2016, Trento, Italy, 12–15 September 2016, pp. 1–8. IEEE (2016). https://doi.org/10.1109/ISC2.2016.7580875
13. Li, Y., Cao, H.: Prediction for tourism flow based on LSTM neural network. Procedia Comput. Sci. **129**, 277–283 (2018)
14. Mehmood, Y., Ahmad, F., Yaqoob, I., Adnane, A., Imran, M., Guizani, S.: Internet-of-things-based smart cities: recent advances and challenges. IEEE Commun. Mag. **55**(9), 16–24 (2017)
15. Neureiter, C., Rohjans, S., Engel, D., Dänekas, C., Uslar, M.: Addressing the complexity of distributed smart city systems by utilization of model driven engineering concepts. In: Proceedings of the VDE-Kongress, pp. 1–6 (2014)

16. Patelis, A., Petropoulos, C., Nikolopoulos, K., Lin, B., Assimakopoulos, V.: Tourism planning decision support within an e-government framework. Electron. Gov. Int. J. **2**(2), 134–143 (2005)
17. Rodríguez-Molina, J., Martínez, J., Castillejo, P., de Diego, R.: Smarc: a proposal for a smart, semantic middleware architecture focused on smart city energy management. Int. J. Distrib. Sensor Networks **9** (2013). https://doi.org/10.1155/2013/560418

Training Artificial Neural Networks with Gradient and Coarse-Level Correction Schemes

Nadja Vater$^{(\boxtimes)}$ and Alfio Borzì

Institut für Mathematik, Universität Würzburg, Würzburg, Germany
{nadja.vater,alfio.borzi}@mathematik.uni-wuerzburg.de

Abstract. A two-level learning scheme for multi-layer neural networks is presented. This scheme combines a standard gradient scheme with a two-level correction procedure in such a way that the reduction of the value of the given loss function is improved. This construction is based on the knowledge of the Hessian of the loss function, which is used to estimate an optimal learning rate for the gradient scheme and in the construction the two-level correction procedure. The proposed two-level approach is supported by theoretical consideration in the framework of multilevel optimization schemes and by numerical investigation. Results of numerical experiments with nonlinear regression on small datasets successfully validate the proposed two-level learning scheme.

Keywords: Artificial neural networks · Gradient method · Eigendecomposition · Coarse-level correction

1 Introduction

Artificial neural networks (ANNs) are being applied to perform many different tasks, such as classification, machine translation or image and signal processing, and their growing success is supported by increasing computational power and availability of data. At the same time, the optimization problems underlying the training procedures become more large-sized in order to exploit the fact that larger networks have better approximation properties. On the other hand, as the dimensionality of the problem becomes larger, numerical optimization procedures such as gradient-based methods become increasingly inefficient with the appearance of slowdown of convergence. Moreover, due to the intrinsic nonlinearity of ANNs, the tuning of the hyperparameters involved in the learning procedure is challenging. In this field, there are several works that aim to overcome these convergence problems such as learning rate scheduling [14,24,26], second-order optimization algorithms [19], or dynamic node creation [1,9]. However, apart of specific cases, the problem of devising efficient ANNs remains wide open and motivates further research work.

Supported by the BMBF joint project on Intelligent MR Diagnosis of the Liver by Linking Model and Data-driven Processes (iDeLIVER).

A similar situation has been experienced in the field of numerical linear algebra, especially in the case of numerical solution of partial differential equations (PDEs). In this field, iterative solution procedures play a major role and the breakthrough in constructing solvers with optimal computational complexity was achieved with the formulation of multigrid (MG) methods [4,8,12]; see [27] for references. In these earlier works, the components of a MG scheme were constructed based on the underlying geometric structure of the problem and of the differential operators involved. However, soon afterwards algebraic MG (AMG) schemes were developed, where the MG components are defined based on the algebraic structure of the linear problem under consideration [27]. Moreover, in a functional context, the so-called MGOPT (or MLO) approach to solve multidimensional optimization problems has been investigated; see, e.g., [2,3,17,20]. However, while the working principle of all these multilevel schemes remains faithful to the original MG formulation, the specification of the corresponding MG components is challenging as soon as the problem at hand has no underlying geometric interpretation. This is particularly true in the context of optimization problems where the notion of multiple grids is not available and thus one needs to identify different resolution levels and to define an optimization problem at each level whose solution can be computed efficiently and can be used to accelerate the solution procedure in the next finer level where the solution is sought. Clearly, depending on the choice of the resolution spaces, this approach requires the construction of transfer operators that allow to relate the fine-level problem to the coarse-level one and to transfer the coarse-level solution to the finer space. We refer to these operators as the restriction and prolongation operators, respectively.

In the field of ANNs, the identification of different resolution levels and of the corresponding transfer operators has been considered in a number of recent works. In particular, in [11,15,18] the focus is to design learning procedures for constructing the transfer operators, in [5] a multi-level Levenberg-Marquardt method to train a neural network is discussed, and further in [10,13,16] multi-level ANNs are discussed that can be related to a geometric or algebraic MG approach. In this broad context, the purpose of our work is to contribute to the development of multilevel ANNs with a new approach that combines multilevel optimization procedures with techniques similar to that used in the AMG framework [25]. However, our approach is novel in the sense that it does not attempt to identify a 'coarse' set of weights of the ANN in order to construct a coarse space, but focuses on the Hessian of the loss function and on its eigendecomposition for the construction of a coarse level corresponding to the space spanned by a few eigenvectors of the Hessian. In this spectral framework, the restriction and prolongation operators can be defined in terms of the eigenvectors or by algebraic consideration of the Hessian operator. Moreover, the knowledge of part of the spectrum of the Hessian allows to determine the optimal learning rate for the gradient scheme applied to solve the learning problems at each level.

The result of this work is a general two-level ANN strategy with a gradient-based learning method and a coarse-level correction (CLC) scheme that outperforms the standard gradient scheme and allows to achieve a reduction of the loss function of several orders of magnitude better than in the standard approach. This new ANN framework is theoretically investigated and successfully validated by applications concerning nonlinear regression on small datasets.

This choice is driven by the need to estimate the full Hessian, which poses a limitation on the size of the ANN problems to which our methodology can be applied. However, in view of further developments, we consider variants of our approach where the transfer operators are constructed in a way that avoids the eigendecomposition of the Hessian, and also explore the possibility to partition the entire network into blocks and apply our two-level scheme separately on each block using the corresponding sub-Hessian.

In the next section, we introduce our ANN and the loss function used in our supervised learning problems. The gradient and the Hessian of this function with respect to the parameters are also given. In Sect. 3, we review the main properties of a gradient scheme and introduce the eigendecomposition of the Hessian for characterizing the convergence behaviour of the gradient scheme with respect to different eigenspaces of the Hessian. This approach allows drawing a connection with the spectral analysis of convergence of iterative schemes that is fundamental as in the classical MG framework. In Sect. 4, we build up on this latter result in order to construct a coarse-space of eigenvectors that is central for our two-level scheme. Further, we define our restriction and prolongation operators based on eigenfunctions and construct a two-level correction scheme that considerably accelerates the gradient procedure. However, we also introduce an alternative restriction-by-aggregation operator that allows to avoid the explicit eigendecomposition of the Hessian. This section is concluded with the formulation of our gradient and coarse-level correction (GCLC) scheme and its algorithmic implementation in a pseudocode. Section 5 is devoted to the experimental investigation of the performance of our GCLC scheme to learn a neural network for performing nonlinear regression on different datasets. Specifically, we consider the Spiral Data Set [23] which does not allow linear separation. Furthermore, we construct a noisy version of this dataset to show the robustness of our procedure applied to noisy data. Additionally, we consider the Concrete Compressive Strength Data Set [29] and the Forest Fire Data Set [22] that are higher-dimensional real-world data. In all cases our scheme is able to achieve a large improvement of the value of the loss function compared to the gradient descent scheme. We also use the Concrete Compressive Strength Data Set and a shallow ANN to investigate a promising block-wise implementation of our GCLC scheme that demonstrates the possibility to apply our method to large size problems. A section of conclusion completes this work.

2   An Artificial Neural Network

We define an ANN with d hidden layers by

$$
\begin{aligned}
y^{(i)} &= \sigma^{(i)}(W^{(i)}y^{(i-1)} + b^{(i)}), \quad i = 1, \dots, d-1, \\
y^{(d)} &= W^{(d)}y^{(d-1)} + b^{(d)},
\end{aligned}
\tag{1}
$$

where $\sigma^{(i)}(x) = \frac{1}{1+\exp(-x)}$ is the element-wise sigmoid function, the matrices $W^{(i)} \in \mathbb{R}^{n_i \times n_{i-1}}$ denote the weights of the network linking the ith layer with n_i nodes to the $(i-1)$th layer with n_{i-1} nodes, and the vectors $b^{(i)} \in \mathbb{R}^{n_i}$ represent the biases. The values $y^{(i)} \in \mathbb{R}^{n_i}$ are called activations of the ith layer and $y^{(0)} = x \in \mathbb{R}^{n_0}$ is the input to the neural network. The activation of the last layer $y^{(d)}$ is thus a function of x, the weights $W^{(1)}, \ldots, W^{(d)}$, and the biases $b^{(1)}, \ldots, b^{(d)}$. For this reason, we denote the output of our ANN by $y(x, \theta) = y^{(d)}$, where all weights and biases are collected in a parameter vector $\theta = (\mathrm{vec}(W^{(1)})^\top, (b^{(1)})^\top, \ldots, \mathrm{vec}(W^{(d)})^\top, (b^{(d)})^\top)^\top$. We denote the architecture of our network with $n_0 - n_1 - n_2 - \ldots - n_d$. The total number of parameters is given by $n_{param} = \sum_{i=1}^{d} n_i(n_{i-1} + 1)$.

We see that our neural network can be considered as a parametrized function $y(\cdot, \theta) : \mathbb{R}^{n_0} \to \mathbb{R}^{n_d}$. In this setting, typical applications are in approximating a function $f^* : \mathbb{R}^{n_0} \to \mathbb{R}^{n_d}$, and in regression analysis where f^* represents the dependent data.

In these cases, a loss function is defined in order to measure an approximation error. For a given set of inputs $X \subset \mathbb{R}^{n_0}$ the mean square error $J_X : \mathbb{R}^{n_{param}} \to \mathbb{R}$ is defined as

$$J_X(\theta) = \frac{1}{|X|} \sum_{x \in X} \|f^*(x) - y(x, \theta)\|^2, \tag{2}$$

where $\| \cdot \|$ denotes the norm induced by the Euclidean scalar product $(\cdot, \cdot)$. Usually, one considers a training set X_{train} to learn the parameters and another validation set X_{val} to measure the generalization of the approximation ability of a network on a different set of values. If the specification of the data set is not essential, we write $J(\theta)$ for $J_X(\theta)$. We note that J is twice continuously differentiable with respect to θ.

In order to apply gradient-based methods to minimize the loss function J, we compute the gradient as follows

$$\nabla J(\theta) = \frac{1}{|X|} \sum_{x \in X} \nabla_\theta y(x, \theta)^\top (y(x, \theta) - f^*(x)), \tag{3}$$

and the Hessian is given by

$$\nabla^2 J(\theta) = \frac{1}{|X|} \sum_{x \in X} \left(\nabla_\theta y(x, \theta) \nabla_\theta y(x, \theta)^\top - \nabla_\theta^2 y(x, \theta)(y(x, \theta) - f^*(x)) \right). \tag{4}$$

3   A Gradient-Based Learning Procedure

We consider a gradient descent (GD) method with variable step size for solving the optimization problem $\min_\theta J(\theta)$, where $J : \mathbb{R}^n \to \mathbb{R}$. This iterative scheme implements the following update step

$$\theta_{k+1} = \theta_k - \eta_k \nabla J(\theta_k), \tag{5}$$

with an arbitrarily chosen start value $\theta_0 \in \mathbb{R}^n$ and steplength $\eta_k \in (0, 1)$.

Convergence of the GD scheme is established when the steplength $\eta_k \in (0,1)$ satisfies the Armijo condition of sufficient decrease of J and the Wolfe condition; see, e.g., [21].

For the purpose of our discussion, it is convenient to consider the following quadratic optimization problem

$$\hat{J}(\theta) = \frac{1}{2}(\theta, A\theta) + (\theta, b) + c, \qquad (6)$$

with the matrix $A \in \mathbb{R}^{n \times n}$ symmetric and positive definite, $b \in \mathbb{R}^n$, and $c \in \mathbb{R}$. Notice that in this case we have the gradient $\nabla \hat{J}(\theta) = A\theta + b$ and the Hessian is given by $\nabla^2 \hat{J}(\theta) = A$.

Thus the iterates of the GD scheme (5) are given by

$$\theta_{k+1} = \theta_k - \eta_k(A\theta_k + b). \qquad (7)$$

The optimal value for η_k can be found by minimizing $\hat{J}(\theta_{k+1}) = \hat{J}(\theta_k - \eta(A\theta_k + b))$ with respect to η. The necessary condition for the minimizer $\frac{\partial}{\partial \eta}\hat{J}(\theta_k - \eta(A\theta_k + b)) = 0$ implies that the optimal step size in the kth step is given by $\eta_k = \frac{\nabla \hat{J}(\theta_k)^\top \nabla \hat{J}(\theta_k)}{\nabla \hat{J}(\theta_k)^\top A \nabla \hat{J}(\theta_k)}$. With this choice one can prove convergence of the GD method to the unique minimum $\theta^* \in \mathbb{R}^n$ of $\hat{J}$ for all $\theta_0 \in \mathbb{R}^n$; see, e.g., [21]. Notice that this term corresponds to the inverse of the Rayleigh quotient of the matrix A. Thus, it is bounded from below by $\frac{1}{\lambda_n}$, where $\lambda_n > 0$ is the largest eigenvalue of A; further, $\lambda_1 > 0$ denotes the smallest eigenvalue.

We remark that the MG strategy relies on the fact that iterative procedures like the GD scheme are efficient in solving part of the spectral components of the solution sought, and this efficiency degrades for those components in the complementary part of the spectrum. In a geometric setting, the spectral components that are well damped by a similar GD scheme correspond to high-frequency Fourier modes and the complementary part defines the low-frequency modes. In our case, we associate different modes to the different eigenspaces of the Hessian, and we call low-frequency modes those associated to the lower part of the spectrum, whereas high-frequency modes are those corresponding to the higher part of the spectrum.

In our framework, in order to characterize the low-frequency parts of the error of kth approximation θ_k to the minimizer θ^* of (6), we define the solution error at the kth iteration as $e_k = \theta^* - \theta_k$. Then the following recursive relation for the error holds:

$$e_{k+1} = \theta^* - \theta_{k+1} = e_k + \eta_k(A\theta_k + b) - \eta_k(A\theta^* + b) = (I - \eta_k A)e_k. \qquad (8)$$

Now, we consider the decomposition $A = V\Lambda V^\top$, where V corresponds to the matrix of all eigenvectors of A given by V_i, $i = 1, \ldots, n$, and Λ is the diagonal matrix of all eigenvalues λ_i, $i = 1, \ldots, n$. By using these algebraic objects in (8), we obtain $e_{k+1} = V(I - \eta_k\Lambda)V^\top e_k$. Thus, for the coefficients of the error in the basis provided by the eigenvector of A it holds

$$V_i^\top e_{k+1} = (1 - \eta_k\lambda_i)V_i^\top e_k, \quad i = 1, \ldots, n. \qquad (9)$$

We see that the magnitude of the mode $V_i^\top e_k$ is reduced by a factor $|1 - \eta_k \lambda_i|$. Therefore we can obtain the largest reduction of this value by choosing $\eta_k = \frac{1}{\lambda_i}$. Since our purpose is to apply the GD scheme to annihilate the highest-frequency mode $V_n^\top e_k$ we choose $\eta_k = 1/\lambda_n$ whenever an estimate of λ_n is available; otherwise, we consider a fixed value for η_k denoted with η_0.

4 Coarse-Level Correction

The striking efficiency of algorithms based on the MG strategy is attained by complementing iterative schemes that are efficient in solving the high-frequency modes with a method that is effective in solving the low-frequency modes. This latter method is usually called coarse-level correction (CLC) scheme, which requires to identify a coarse-level space and to construct the restriction and prolongation operators. Our approach to address these issues is based on the Hessian eigenvalue decomposition in the way illustrated below.

Let $\nabla^2 J$ be strictly positive definite, and consider the following quadratic model

$$J_f(\theta; \hat{\theta}) = J(\hat{\theta}) + \left(\nabla J(\hat{\theta}), \theta - \hat{\theta} \right) + \frac{1}{2} \left(\theta - \hat{\theta}, \nabla^2 J(\hat{\theta})(\theta - \hat{\theta}) \right), \qquad (10)$$

where $\hat{\theta}$ is sufficiently close to the minimizer θ^* of J, and f stands for 'fine'.

Next, consider the application of k steps of the GD scheme to minimize $J_f(\theta; \hat{\theta})$, starting from an arbitrary θ_0, and recall (9) with $A = \nabla^2 J(\hat{\theta})$ and eigendecomposition $\nabla^2 J(\hat{\theta}) = V \Lambda V^\top$. Thus, after k iterations of the GD scheme, we have

$$V_i^\top e_k = \prod_{l=0}^{k-1} (1 - \eta_l \lambda_i) V_i^\top e_0, \quad i = 1, \dots, n. \qquad (11)$$

In this procedure, we assume that η_l is chosen such that the solution error for the modes associated to the largest eigenvalues is reduced fast. Therefore, after the GD steps, we can approximate the error as follows

$$e_k = \theta^* - \theta_k \approx \sum_{i=1}^{m} \delta_i V_i = \left(V_1 \cdots V_m \right) \begin{pmatrix} \delta_1 \\ \vdots \\ \delta_m \end{pmatrix}, \qquad (12)$$

where $\delta_i = V_i^\top (\theta^* - \theta_k)$ and $m < n$.

This result implies that the GD scheme acting in the fine-level space $S_f = \mathrm{Span}\{V_1, \dots, V_n\}$, efficiently reduces the components of the error associated to the eigenvectors V_i, $i > m$. Thus, an effective CLC scheme should reduce the solution error in the subspace $S_c = \mathrm{Span}\{V_1, \dots, V_m\} \subset S_f$, which in turn suggests that this is the coarse-level space; the suffix c stands for 'coarse'. Therefore the restriction operator must be defined as a projection onto this space as follows

$$I_f^c := \left(V_1 \cdots V_m \right)^\top \in \mathbb{R}^{m \times n}, \qquad (13)$$

thus $I_f^c : S_f \to S_c$, such that $I_f^c(\theta^* - \theta_k) \approx \delta = (\delta_1, \ldots, \delta_m)^\top \in \mathbb{R}^m$. Furthermore, as in AMG schemes, we set the prolongation operator to $I_c^f = (I_f^c)^\top$.

At this point, we have identified our coarse level and the restriction and prolongation operators. It remains to define a coarse optimization problem whose solution allows to construct an effective CLC scheme. For this purpose, we construct a coarse loss functional as follows. We define

$$J_c(\theta^c; I_f^c \hat{\theta}) = J(\hat{\theta}) + \left(I_f^c \nabla J(\hat{\theta}), \theta^c - I_f^c \hat{\theta} \right) + \frac{1}{2} \left(\theta^c - I_f^c \hat{\theta}, I_f^c \nabla^2 J(\hat{\theta}) I_c^f (\theta^c - I_f^c \hat{\theta}) \right). \tag{14}$$

This quadratic functional is defined on S_c. Clearly, at $\theta^c = I_f^c \hat{\theta}$ we have $J_c(\theta^c; I_f^c \hat{\theta}) = J(\hat{\theta})$, and in this sense J_c approximates J near $I_f^c \hat{\theta}$. Moreover, the gradient of J_c with respect to θ^c is given by

$$\nabla J_c(\theta^c; I_f^c \hat{\theta}) = I_f^c \nabla J(\hat{\theta}) + I_f^c \nabla^2 J(\hat{\theta}) I_c^f (\theta^c - I_f^c \hat{\theta}). \tag{15}$$

Hence, the gradient of our coarse loss functional at $\theta^c = I_f^c \hat{\theta}$ is equal to the restriction of the gradient of J at $\hat{\theta}$. This fact implies that a minimizing step for $J_c(\theta^c; I_f^c \hat{\theta})$ starting at $\theta^c = I_f^c \hat{\theta}$ results in an update $\tilde{\theta}^c$ for θ^c that defines a descent direction $D^f = I_c^f (\tilde{\theta}^c - I_f^c \hat{\theta})$ for J. In particular, we can compute the minimizer for J_c based on the characterization $\nabla J_c(\theta^c; I_f^c \hat{\theta}) = 0$, which gives the solution

$$\tilde{\theta}^c = I_f^c \hat{\theta} - (I_f^c \nabla^2 J(\hat{\theta}) I_c^f)^{-1} I_f^c \nabla J(\hat{\theta}). \tag{16}$$

With this new set of parameters, we obtain an update $\tilde{\theta}$ to $\hat{\theta}$ towards the minimum of J as follows

$$\tilde{\theta} = \hat{\theta} + \mu D^f = \hat{\theta} + \mu I_c^f (\tilde{\theta}^c - I_f^c \hat{\theta}) = \hat{\theta} - \mu I_c^f (I_f^c \nabla^2 J(\hat{\theta}) I_c^f)^{-1} I_f^c \nabla J(\hat{\theta}), \tag{17}$$

where $\mu > 0$ is a step size to be determined by a linesearch procedure.

The CLC step (17) can be interpreted as the minimization of J along the descent direction D^f, since one can prove that $(\nabla J(\hat{\theta}), D^f) < 0$. Therefore, taking $\hat{\theta} = \theta_k$, our CLC scheme allows to determine a descent direction for the original loss functional at this point that is different from a gradient direction. In fact, our CLC procedure allows to determine a descent direction D^f that represents an approximation to a Newton step, while avoiding the inversion of the full Hessian. We have

$$I_c^f (I_f^c \nabla^2 J(\hat{\theta}) I_c^f)^{-1} I_f^c = \sum_{i=1}^m \frac{1}{\lambda_i} v_i v_i^\top \approx \sum_{i=1}^n \frac{1}{\lambda_i} v_i v_i^\top = (\nabla^2 J(\hat{\theta}))^{-1}. \tag{18}$$

Results of numerical experiments show that with this step much better convergence properties of the learning process are achieved.

In line with this result, in the case of a quadratic optimization problem as in (6), one coarse-level correction step with optimal stepsize η_k yields a faster convergence than with a GD scheme. We have

$$\|\theta_{k+1} - \theta^*\| \le \sqrt{\frac{\lambda_m}{\lambda_1}} \left(\frac{\lambda_m - \lambda_1}{\lambda_m + \lambda_1} \right) \|\theta_k - \theta^*\| < \sqrt{\frac{\lambda_n}{\lambda_1}} \left(\frac{\lambda_n - \lambda_1}{\lambda_n + \lambda_1} \right) \|\theta_k - \theta^*\|. \quad (19)$$

Thus, for $\lambda_m < \lambda_n$ we have faster convergence.

Our two-level iterative scheme that combines the GD method and our CLC scheme is shown in Algorithm 1. We refer to this scheme as the GCLC method.

Algorithm 1: $GCLC(\ell, m)$ method

Input: Initial guess θ_0; ℓ and m; maximum number of cycles I
        number of pre and post GD iterations ν_1, ν_2; learning rate η_0

Output: θ_I

for $i = \{0, \ldots, I - 1\}$ **do**

    Apply ν_1 GD steps with step size η_i starting with θ_i to obtain $\hat{\theta}_1$

    Compute Hessian at $\hat{\theta}_1$

    if $m > 0$ **then**

    | Compute the eigendecomposition of the Hessian.

    end

    Compute the restriction operator I_f^c from $\begin{cases} (20) & m = 0 \\ (13) & m > 0 \end{cases}$; set $I_c^f = (I_f^c)^\top$

    Set the learning rate η_{i+1} equal to $\begin{cases} \eta_0 & \ell = 0 \\ 2/(\lambda_n + \lambda_{n-\ell+1}) & \ell > 0 \end{cases}$

    Construct the CLC descent direction

$$D^f = -I_c^f (I_f^c \nabla^2 J(\hat{\theta}_1) I_c^f)^{-1} I_f^c \nabla J(\hat{\theta}_1)$$

    Perform a line search in the direction D^f to obtain μ that minimizes J. The coarse-level correction step is given by

$$\tilde{\theta} = \hat{\theta}_1 + \mu D^f$$

    Apply ν_2 GD steps with step size η_{i+1} starting with $\tilde{\theta}$ to obtain $\hat{\theta}_2$.

    Set $\theta_{i+1} = \hat{\theta}_2$

end

In this algorithm, the number m of eigenvectors defining the coarse-level space is a parameter that we choose in our experiments. Moreover, we introduce the flag $\ell \in \{0, 1, \ldots, m\}$: if $\ell = 0$ we use a fixed learning rate $\eta = \eta_0$; otherwise we set the learning rate $\eta = 2/(\lambda_n + \lambda_{n-\ell+1})$.

Based on the eigendecomposition of the Hessian, our learning procedure provides its best performance in terms of reduction of the value of the loss function. However, for a better trade-off between computational time and this reduction, it is possible to avoid the eigendecomposition step required for constructing the inter-level transfer operators. For this purpose, we also implement an alternative restriction operator that resembles the approach of restriction by aggregation considered in the AMG framework [28]. In this approach, the restriction operator takes the following form

$$I_f^c = \begin{pmatrix} 1 & 1 & 0 & & \cdots & & 0 \\ 0 & 0 & 1 & 1 & 0 & \cdots 0 \\ & & & \ddots & \ddots & \\ 0 & & \cdots & & 0 & 1 & 1 \end{pmatrix} \in \mathbb{R}^{\lceil \frac{n}{2} \rceil \times n}. \tag{20}$$

Notice that in this case we have a restriction operator of the same size of that given in (13) with $m = n/2$. In this setting we restrict the learning rate update to the choices $\ell = 0$ or $\ell = 1$ to avoid the computational effort for the eigendecomposition.

5   Numerical Investigation

In this section, we compare the proposed GCLC algorithm to the classical GD scheme for different regression problems on small datasets. It is our purpose to show that the same basic network augmented with our two-level strategy produces much better results compared to those obtained with a GD learning procedure. Details concerning the network initialization and our implementation of the GCLC scheme are given in the Appendix A and the code is provided at https://github.com/NaHenn/gclc. In the following, we describe the experimental setup and analyse the results obtained with each dataset.

For each given dataset we first determine a base learning rate η_0. The range of possible learning rates covers different orders of magnitude ($\{0.01, 0.05, 0.1, 0.5, 1\}$) and additional values around $1/\lambda_{n_{param}}$, the inverse of the largest eigenvalue of the Hessian of the loss function for a randomly initialized ANN. For each of these learning rates we apply 2500 GD iterations on 10 randomly initialized ANNs. We set the base learning rate η_0 to the value which gives the smallest value of the loss function on average.

Next, we consider 100 random initialization of our networks and learn their parameters with the proposed GCLC scheme and the GD method. For the GCLC scheme, we consider the choices $(\ell, m) \in \{(0,0), (1,0), (1,1), (4,4)\}$. This selection is based on our experience that advises the choice of $\ell = m$ for $m > 0$, and the adaptive choice of the learning rate ($\ell = 1$) for the aggregation based restriction. Further, we set the number of GCLC cycles to $I = 500$. The number of pre GD iterations is chosen to be $\nu_1 = 3$ and the number of post GD iterations to be $\nu_2 = 1$, resulting in a total of 4 GD iterations in between two CLC steps. This choice allows to benefit from the ability of GD to reduce the value of the loss function fast in the beginning, but preventing the slowdown later. For the GD scheme alone, we consider a similar equivalent of 2500 GD iterations in total.

In our first experiment, we consider the spiral data set from [23], which offers a first challenge since it cannot be linearly separated. This dataset describes a function $f : \mathbb{R}^2 \rightarrow \{-1, 1\}$ and consists of 194 data samples. It is shown in Fig. 1. We use a network with architecture 2-8-8-1 and consider the complete dataset as training data X_{train} as in [23]. Before training, we scale the data to the range $[-1, 1]$. Notice that the results are not directly comparable to the results in [23] since we use a different activation function. The base learning rate is set to $\eta_0 = 0.2$. Figure 3 (top) shows the values of the loss function after 500 cycles with different GCLC methods. The plot presents the first quartile Q_1, the median Q_2, and the third quartile Q_3 as a box as well as the positions of $Q_1 - 1.5(Q_3 - Q_1)$ and $Q_1 + 1.5(Q_3 - Q_1)$ as whiskers and outliers as circles. We restrict the range of the ordinate to $[10^{-0.5}, 10^{0.5}]$ for a better illustration. Notice that this plot shows only 68 of the GCLC(0,0) runs, 83 of the GCLC(1,0) runs, 95 of the GCLC(1,1) runs and 79 of the GCLC(4,4) runs, since in the other runs either the value of the loss function was larger than $10^{0.5}$ or the method could not complete the 500 cycles due to some computational issue such as overflow. Nevertheless, the successful runs of the GCLC methods clearly show, that with these schemes the value of the loss function can be reduced to a lower value than with GD in several runs. Notice that the values of the loss function of GD are very close after the 2500 iterations of this method, which illustrates its reliability independently of the initialization. We see, that for GCLC(1,0) and GCLC(1,1) the median values are smaller than for the other method, which implies, that half of the successful runs end up below this value. At the same time, the values are far wider spread than those of the GD scheme.

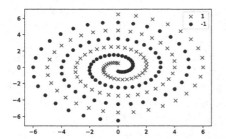 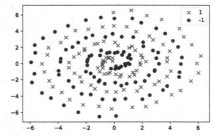

Fig. 1. Visualization of the spiral dataset.

Fig. 2. Visualization of the spiral dataset with added noise.

In order to make the spiral problem more challenging, we also construct a noisy version of the dataset, where we add uniformly distributed noise in $[-0.25, 0.25]^2$ to the training data; see Fig. 2. We use the same architecture as before, and find a base learning rate $\eta_0 = 0.1$ to be most successful. The values of the loss function after 500 GCLC cycles are shown in Fig. 3 (bottom). This plot shows the quartiles, median and outliers as described above. It covers 73 of the GCLC(0,0) runs, 88 of the GCLC(1,0) runs, 99 of the GCLC(1,1) runs and 81 of the GCLC(4,4) runs. The results are comparable to those with the dataset without noise.

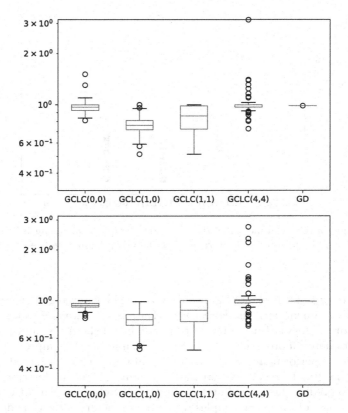

Fig. 3. Values of the loss function of the spiral dataset (top) and its variant with noise (bottom) after 500 GCLC cycles and after 2500 iterations of the GD scheme; see the text for further details.

In the following experiments, we consider datasets from the UCI Machine Learning Repository [7]. As in [23], we choose the Concrete Compressive Strength Data Set from [29]. The task is to predict the compressive strength of concrete from data describing the proportions of the ingredients and the mixing technique. The dataset contains 1030 samples of different mixtures, describing a mapping $f : \mathbb{R}^8 \rightarrow \mathbb{R}$. We consider the complete set for training and use a network with architecture 8-6-6-1 as in [23]. The base learning rate is set to $\eta_0 = 0.5$. Figure 4 presents the median, quartiles and outliers of the value of the loss function after 500 GCLC cycles on our network with 100 different initializations. It shows the results of 45 runs of GCLC(0,0), 93 runs of GCLC(1,0), and 100 runs of GCLC(1,1) and GCLC(4,4), respectively. In this setting, GCLC(0,0) produces worse results than with the other GCLC variants. Remarkably, all runs of GCLC(1,1) and GCLC(4,4) are completed and the range of the loss values at the end is quite small. Notably, 75% of these runs were able to achieve a loss function value lower than that obtained with the GD scheme.

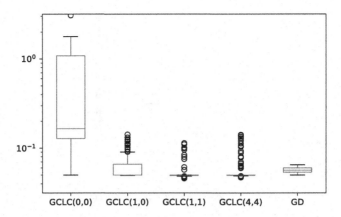

Fig. 4. Values of the loss function of the Concrete Compressive Strength Data Set after 500 GCLC cycles and after 2500 iterations of the GD scheme; see the text for further details.

While the results presented above do not consider any regularisation, in the following experiment with the Forest Fires Data Set [6], we add to the loss function a quadratic regularisation term of the weights of the ANN multiplied with a scaling parameter of order 10^{-7}. In this setting, a noticeable improvement in the computational performance of our scheme is obtained. The considered datase was ranked in the top 12 most popular datasets (June 2021). It describes a regression task to predict the burned area of forest fires from meteorological and other data. It consists of 517 data samples with 12 parameters each, thus describing a function $f : \mathbb{R}^{12} \to \mathbb{R}$. Motivated by the search for a good network architecture in [22], we use a network with architecture 12-36-1 and a base learning rate of $\eta_0 = 0.1$. Figure 5 shows the median, quartiles and outliers of different variants of the GCLC method and GD scheme applied to our network with 100 different random initializations. The plot does not include 28 outliers of GCLC(0,0). We can see the superiority of GCLC(1,0), GCLC(1,1) and GCLC(4,4) in terms of the reduction of the loss function. For these algorithms none of the initializations leads to a larger value of the loss function compared to the results with the GD scheme. As above, the variant GCLC(0,0) shows the worst performance of the four GCLC schemes, nevertheless it is still able to achieve a smaller value of the loss function compared to GD.

We remark that the results obtained in the above experiments with different datasets are representative of many other experiments indicating that: 1) using a learning rate given by the largest eigenvalue of the Hessian is advantageous in all cases (i.e. $\ell = 1$); 2) the restriction by aggregation is effective (i.e. $m = 0$), especially in combination with the learning rate update (i.e. $\ell = 1$); 3) by using a two-level strategy the reduction of the value of the loss function is greatly improved and so the ability of the given ANN to perform the given task; 4)

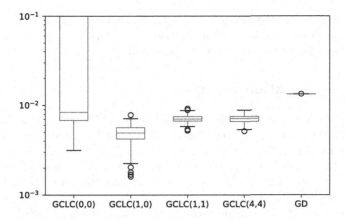

Fig. 5. Values of the loss function of the Forest Fires Data Set after 500 GCLC cycles and after 2500 iterations of the GD scheme; see the text for further details.

higher accuracy may come at the prize of reduced reliability/stability. However, improved robustness seems achievable by including a regularization term.

Our method requires to compute and store the Hessian of the loss function with respect to all parameters. This is possible for small-size ANNs but cannot be applied to very large networks. However, preliminary results with a block-wise implementation of the GCLC scheme, which involves only the part of the Hessian for the corresponding block, suggest that our methodology can be successfully extended to large-size problems. Specifically, we consider the case of a shallow network with $d = 1$, and partition the hidden nodes into groups of similar size n_p, which we consider sequentially. Then, we perform the CLC update only for the weights corresponding to the nodes in one subset at a time while considering the other weights as fixed. Thus, instead of computing the complete Hessian at once, we only need to compute a submatrix of size $n_{params} \times (n_p \cdot (n_x + n_y + 1) + 1)$ in each CLC step. We use this scheme to perform one cycle for a network of size $8 - 1000 - 1$, i.e. $n_{params} = 10001$, with $n_p = 100$ applied to the Concrete Compressive Strength Data Set. While the value of the loss function obtained with the GD scheme is 0.89, the GCLC(0,0) method with $n_p = 100$ is able to achieve a value of 0.15 and GCLC(1,1) with $n_p = 100$ reduces the loss function to 0.13. From this experiment we can see that a block-GCLC scheme is actually able to effectively reduce the loss function. At the same time we obtain in some cases larger values of the loss function, which motivates further investigation in future work.

6   Conclusion

The analysis, development and validation of a two-level learning scheme for multi-layer neural networks was presented. This scheme combines a gradient method with a two-level correction procedure defined in terms of the Hessian of the loss function and its eigenspace. Results of numerical experiments with non-linear regression problems with small datasets were presented that successfully validated the proposed two-level learning scheme.

A   Implementation Details

In our analysis, we consider different multi-layer ANNs with random initialization such that for each layer the weights $W^{(i)}$ and biases $b^{(i)}$ are chosen i.i.d. from a uniform distribution in $(-1/\sqrt{n_{i-1}}, 1/\sqrt{n_{i-1}})$.

Our GCLC algorithm is implemented in Python. The Hessian computation is realized with the help of the automatic differentiation and backpropagation methods provided by Pytorch.

The eigendecomposition is performed via `torch.symeig`, which calls the `syev` routine of the package LAPACK. This implements a tridiagonal implicitely shifted QR algorithm. If only the largest eigenvalue is needed (e.g. for GCLC(1,0)), it is computed with the method `scipy.linalg.eigh`. The line search uses functions from `scipy.optimize`. It attempts to find a step size that satisfies the strong Wolfe conditions with the routine `dcsrch` from Minpack-2. If this is not successful, it tries the algorithm from [21, pp. 59–61]. If this fails too, a GD step instead of coarse-level-correction is applied to ensure a reduction of the training loss function value.

References

1. Ash, T.: Dynamic node creation in backpropagation networks. Connection Sci. **1**(4), 365–375 (1989)
2. Borzì, A., Schulz, V.: Computational Optimization of Systems Governed by Partial Differential Equations. Society for Industrial and Applied Mathematics (2011)
3. Borzì, A.: On the convergence of the MG/OPT method. In: PAMM: Proceedings in Applied Mathematics and Mechanics, vol. 5, pp. 735–736. WILEY-VCH Verlag, Berlin (2005)
4. Brandt, A.: Multi-level adaptive technique (MLAT) for fast numerical solution to boundary value problems. In: Proceedings of the Third International Conference on Numerical Methods in Fluid Mechanics, vol. I (1972)
5. Calandra, H., Gratton, S., Riccietti, E., Vasseur, X.: On the approximation of the solution of partial differential equations by artificial neural networks trained by a multilevel Levenberg-Marquardt method. arXiv preprint arXiv:1904.04685 (2019)
6. Cortez, P., Morais, A.D.J.R.: A data mining approach to predict forest fires using meteorological data. In: Neves, J., Santos, M.F., Machado, J. (eds.) New Trends in Artificial Intelligence, Proceedings of the 13th EPIA 2007 - Portuguese Conference on Artificial Intelligence, pp. 512–523. APPIA, December 2007
7. Dua, D., Graff, C.: UCI machine learning repository (2017). http://archive.ics.uci.edu/ml
8. Fedorenko, R.P.: A relaxation method for solving elliptic difference equations. Zhurnal Vychislitel'noi Matematiki i Matematicheskoi Fiziki **1**(5), 922–927 (1961)
9. Ghaboussi, J., Sidarta, D.: New nested adaptive neural networks (NANN) for constitutive modeling. Comput. Geotech. **22**(1), 29–52 (1998)

10. Ghadai, S., Lee, X.Y., Balu, A., Sarkar, S., Krishnamurthy, A.: Multi-level 3D CNN for learning multi-scale spatial features. In: CVPR 2019 (2018)
11. Greenfeld, D., Galun, M., Basri, R., Yavneh, I., Kimmel, R.: Learning to optimize multigrid PDE solvers. In: International Conference on Machine Learning, pp. 2415–2423. PMLR (2019)
12. Hackbusch, W.: Ein iteratives Verfahren zur schnellen Auflösung elliptischer Randwertprobleme, Rep. 76–12. Institute for Applied Mathematics, University of Cologne, West Germany, Cologne (1976)
13. He, J., Xu, J.: MgNet: a unified framework of multigrid and convolutional neural network. Sci. China Math. $62(7)$, 1331–1354 (2019)
14. Jacobs, R.A.: Increased rates of convergence through learning rate adaptation. Neural Netw. $1(4)$, 295–307 (1988)
15. Katrutsa, A., Daulbaev, T., Oseledets, I.: Deep multigrid: learning prolongation and restriction matrices. arXiv preprint arXiv:1711.03825 (2017). https://github.com/amkatrutsa/dmg
16. Ke, T.W., Maire, M., Yu, S.X.: Multigrid neural architectures. In: 2017 IEEE Conference on Computer Vision and Pattern Recognition (CVPR), pp. 4067–4075 (2017)
17. Lewis, R.M., Nash, S.G.: Model problems for the multigrid optimization of systems governed by differential equations. SIAM J. Sci. Comput. $26(6)$, 1811–1837 (2005)
18. Luz, I., Galun, M., Maron, H., Basri, R., Yavneh, I.: Learning algebraic multigrid using graph neural networks. In: International Conference on Machine Learning, pp. 6489–6499. PMLR (2020)
19. Martens, J.: New insights and perspectives on the natural gradient method. J. Mach. Learn. Res. $21(146)$, 1–76 (2020). http://jmlr.org/papers/v21/17-678.html
20. Nash, S.G.: A multigrid approach to discretized optimization problems. Optim. Methods Softw. $14(1-2)$, 99–116 (2000)
21. Nocedal, J., Wright, S.: Numerical Optimization. Springer Science & Business Media, New York (2006). https://doi.org/10.1007/978-0-387-40065-5
22. Safi, Y., Bouroumi, A.: Prediction of forest fires using artificial neural networks. Appl. Math. Sci. $7(6)$, 271–286 (2013)
23. Smith, J.S., Wu, B., Wilamowski, B.M.: Neural network training with Levenberg-Marquardt and adaptable weight compression. IEEE Trans. Neural Networks Learn. Syst. $30(2)$, 580–587 (2018)
24. Smith, L.N.: Cyclical learning rates for training neural networks. In: 2017 IEEE Winter Conference on Applications of Computer Vision (WACV), pp. 464–472. IEEE (2017)
25. Stüben, K.: An introduction to algebraic multigrid. Multigrid, pp. 413–532 (2001)
26. Tan, C., Ma, S., Dai, Y.H., Qian, Y.: Barzilai-Borwein step size for stochastic gradient descent. In: Proceedings of the 30th International Conference on Neural Information Processing Systems, December 2016
27. Trottenberg, U., Oosterlee, C.W., Schuller, A.: Multigrid. Elsevier (2000)
28. Vaněk, P., Mandel, J., Brezina, M.: Algebraic multigrid by smoothed aggregation for second and fourth order elliptic problems. Computing $56(3)$, 179–196 (1996)
29. Yeh, I.C.: Modeling of strength of high-performance concrete using artificial neural networks. Cem. Concr. Res. $28(12)$, 1797–1808 (1998)

Predatory Conversation Detection Using Transfer Learning Approach

Nancy Agarwal[1], Tuğçe Ünlü[2], Mudasir Ahmad Wani[1],
and Patrick Bours[1(✉)]

[1] Norwegian University of Science and Technology, Gjøvik, Norway
{nancy.agarwal,mudasir.a.wani,patrick.bours}@ntnu.no
[2] Kadir Has University, Istanbul, Turkey

Abstract. Predatory conversation detection on social media can proactively prevent the netizens, including youngsters and children, from getting exploited by sexual predators. Earlier studies have majorly employed machine learning approaches such as Support Vector Machine (SVM) for detecting such conversations. Since deep learning frameworks have shown significant improvements in various text classification tasks, therefore, in this paper, we propose a deep learning-based classifier for detecting predatory conversations. Furthermore, instead of designing the system from the beginning, transfer learning has been proposed where the potential of the pre-trained BERT (Bidirectional Encoder Representations from Transformers) model is utilized to solve the predator detection problem. BERT is mostly used to encode the textual information of a document into its context-aware mathematical representation. The inclusion of this pre-trained model solves two major problems, i.e. feature extraction and Out of Vocabulary (OOV) terms. The proposed system comprises two components: a pre-trained BERT model and a feedforward neural network. To design the classification system with a pre-trained BERT model, two approaches (feature-based and fine-tuning) have been used. Based on these approaches two solutions are proposed, namely, BERT_frozen and BERT_tuned where the latter approach is seen performing better than the existing classifiers in terms of F_1 and $F_{0.5}$-scores.

Keywords: Child grooming · Online sexual predators · Deep learning · Language modelling · BERT

1 Introduction

With the term "online sexual predators", we refer to those criminals who leverage the internet to prey upon children, including teenagers, to abuse them sexually. Child grooming [3] is the main term used to describe the procedure whereby perpetrators establish a trustworthy and emotional relationship with the minor to

The work was supported by the European Research Consortium for Informatics and Mathematics (ERCIM) Alain Bensoussan Fellowship Program.

G. Nicosia et al. (Eds.): LOD 2021, LNCS 13163, pp. 488–499, 2022.
https://doi.org/10.1007/978-3-030-95467-3_35

deceive them into various sexual activities in terms of chatting, sending images, recording videos, etc. According to a report[1], such criminals, nowadays, seek to connect virtually with children through applications such as gaming, social networking, and chatrooms. The relative anonymity provided by these online platforms makes it easy for the predators to create fake identities [19], trick kids into chatting, and set up a digital trap for them. There are various studies [1,2] that reported that the number of cyber crimes related to child grooming is continuously rising, and thus pose serious threats to both children and their parents. Moreover, the lockdown implemented during the COVID-19 pandemic put security at greater risk as children are spending even more of their time online. Since these offenders work diligently and strategically to build a close relationship and gain the trust of the victim, child grooming often leaves a long-lasting impact on the victim with symptoms like psychological distress and trauma [20].

In recent years, online sexual predator detection has received considerable attention from the research communities [6,14]. An automated system for detecting a person with grooming intentions can proactively prevent the children from getting abused and provide a safer place on the internet. PAN 2012 competition accelerated the work in this domain by providing the dataset from the online chat logs to the researchers for the identification of predatory conversations and potential predators. The proposed work also utilizes the same dataset for the evaluation and testing of the proposed methodology. Existing studies have majorly focused on machine learning-based approaches such as Support Vector Machine (SVM), Random Forest (RF), and k-Nearest Neighbors (k-NN) to design the solution [14,16]. However, recent advancements in deep learning frameworks like Recurrent Neural Networks (RNN) and Convolutional Neural Networks (CNN) have shown significant improvements in NLP (Natural Language Processing) based problems including text classification [21]. Since the identification of sexual predators from the chat data also comes under the realm of text-classification problems, this paper present a deep learning-based system to monitor the text messages exchanged during online chat and identify if the conversation involves a sexual predator.

Moreover, instead of designing the classifier from scratch, a transfer learning approach has been proposed to address the problem. Transfer learning is a popular approach in deep learning where a pre-trained model designed to solve a problem, is re-utilized as the starting point for developing another model to solve a similar problem [11]. Transfer learning is a two-step machine learning method where a model is first trained concerning a certain task and afterward, the same (pre-trained) model is used in designing the system to solve another related task. Recently, several transfer learning approaches and models have been presented by researchers which led to remarkable enhancement in the performance of NLP-related tasks [13].

The transfer learning method is mainly employed in problems where a large training set is usually difficult to obtain. However, to have effective learning,

---

[1] https://www.nytimes.com/interactive/2019/12/07/us/video-games-child-sex-abuse.html.

the target dataset should be in correspondence to the dataset used to build the pre-trained model. BERT (Bidirectional Encoder Representations from Transformers) provided by the Google AI Language Team [5] is one of the pre-trained and powerful language models in NLP that is used to transform a text into its mathematical form. It employs the approach of bidirectional training of transformer-based neural networks to learn the contextual numeric representation of a text document. The original BERT model was designed for the English language by training it on the two huge text corpora, i.e. Wikipedia dump[2], and BooksCorpus[3]. Since the chat conversations under consideration also belong to the English language, this paper proposes the use of BERT as a language model to encode these conversations into a feature vector. These pre-trained models have shown tremendous improvement in various natural language understanding tasks including text summarizing, question answering, sentiment analysis, and grammar evaluation [7,10]. However, the application of BERT to online predator detection has not been witnessed earlier.

In this paper, a BERT-based Predatory Conversation Detector (Bert-PCD) is proposed that classifies a chat conversation as predatory or non-predatory. It has been observed that the proposed Bert-PCD provides three advantages over the existing approaches: 1) Since Bert-PCD is a deep learning classifier, feature extraction is the part of the system itself where the pre-trained language model is used to derive the feature vector from the chat conversation. 2) Existing studies have majorly relied on constructing vocabulary-based features for building the model, and so, these models may show poor performance if the testing dataset contains a high number of unseen words. Since BERT has been trained on a large corpus, the vocabulary knowledge of this model is far greater than the vocabulary knowledge built from the training dataset. 3) The chat text may contain misspelled and slang words which again increases the probability of out-of-vocabulary (OOV) problems. Since BERT has the capability of assigning the vector to the word by using its sub-word information, the OOV issue can be easily handled.

The proposed system has two components, i.e. the BERT language model and a classification model. The classification model is based on a feed-forward neural network with two fully-connected layers: a hidden layer with 560 neurons and an output layer having two neurons with a log softmax activation function. Furthermore, the BERT model has been implemented in two ways: 1) as a feature extractor by preventing the weights of its layers from getting updated during the training phase, and 2) as fine-tuned by modifying the weights of its layers according to our dataset.

The rest of the paper is structured as follows: Sect. 2 discusses the related work. Section 3 describes the dataset used for training the classifier. Section 4 explains the architecture of Bert-PCD followed by the experiments and results in Sect. 5. Finally, Sect. 6 concludes the overall work.

---

[2] https://dumps.wikimedia.org/enwiki/latest/.
[3] https://huggingface.co/datasets/bookcorpus.

2   Related Work

The research area of 'sexual predator identification' is accelerated by the PAN-2012 competition with the focus on the detection of predatory conversations and predators from the online chat logs[4]. Many studies proposed the solution by presenting two-stage classifiers where the first classifier filters the predatory conversations from the non-predatory and the second classifier distinguishes the victim and predator in the predatory conversation [8]. Machine learning approaches such as SVM, Decision Trees, k-NN, Naïve Bayes, and RF are among the popular techniques employed to design the systems [9,14,16,18]. However, since deep learning techniques have proven more successful in the NLP domain, there are a few studies that leverage their potential for addressing this problem as well. For example, in [6], the authors experimented with various combinations of machine learning (e.g. SVM) and deep learning techniques (e.g. CNN) on a different set of features including word embedding and one-hot encoding for developing a predatory conversation detector. However, all these existing methods depend on manual feature extraction for building the classifiers. In this paper, we adopt a transfer learning approach where we utilize the potential of the pre-trained BERT language model to extract the feature vector from the conversations in order to build a deep learning-based classifier.

Transfer learning has recently received considerable attention among NLP researchers [13] as it describes the methods to apply the pre-trained models for solving the cross-domain tasks. In a study [12], the authors present the deep learning-based architecture of a language model, ELMo (Embeddings from Language Models) whose vector representation reflects both semantic and syntactic aspects of a word. The performance of ELMo representations is evaluated across several cross-domain natural language understanding tasks including question-answering and sentiment analysis. In work [15], the authors apply the inductive transfer learning approach by leveraging a pre-trained model to enhance the performance of the search engines. The proposed system assists in identifying whether a search query is well formulated or not since an ill-structured query can adhere the search engine in understanding the user's intent.

Furthermore, there are several studies which have particularly used the BERT model in solving NLP tasks. For instance, in [5], the authors used BERT to design the system for web forums such as Quora, that estimates the truthfulness of submitted answers and automatically provides quality answers for the questions raised by a user on these forums. The two studies, i.e., [4] and [7] introduce a cross-domain sentiment classifier and an aspect-based sentiment model respectively by incorporating BERT as a feature extractor. In another study [10], the authors presented a BERT-based system to detect hate speech in text. And, the authors of [17] applied it for identifying whether a tweet supports or denies the claim of a news article.

---

[4] https://pan.webis.de/clef12/pan12-web/sexual-predator-identification.html.

3   Dataset

The proposed approach has been evaluated on the dataset released for the PAN-2012 competition on the sexual predator identification task. The dataset includes both predator conversations where a sexual predator is attempting to trap a minor and normal conversations where two users are just chatting. The organizers provided a separate dataset for training and testing, both in XML format. The XML files hold the chat information in the conversation tag. Each conversation tag is made up of one or more message elements where each message has further three children, i.e., author, time, and text for encoding the following three respective details: the identity of the user who is sending the message, the time at which it is sent and its actual content. Figure 1 shows the structure of the conversation tags in the XML file. Furthermore, a file is provided that lists the author identities of the sexual predators.

```
 1   <conversations>
 2     <conversation id="unique_id_of_conversation">
 3       <message line="1">
 4         <author>unique_id_of_author1</author>
 5         <time>03:20</time>
 6         <text>Hola.</text>
 7       </message>
 8       <message line="2">
 9         <author>unique_id_of_author2</author>
10         <time>03:20</time>
11         <text>hi.</text>
12       </message>
13            .
14       <message line="62">
15         <author>unique_id_of_author2</author>
16         <time>03:38</time>
17         <text>bye</text>
18       </message>
19     </conversation>
```

Fig. 1. Structure of XML file.

However, the dataset is redesigned for training and testing the Bert-PCD by parsing respective XML files. The new datasets have two columns, conversation_messages and label. The first column contains the aggregated content of text elements in a conversation, and the second column marks the conversation as predatory (1) or non-predatory (0). A conversation is marked as predatory if the identity of one of its chatters is listed as a sexual predator. Note that a conversation in the provided dataset can include messages from only one user, or from more than two users. We are calling these conversations noisy since they are not imparting much knowledge of the distinguishing behaviour between normal and predatory chatting. Sexual predators will engage in 1-on-1 conversations with their victims and not engage in multi-person chats. Therefore, for the experiments, only those conversations were used where exactly two users participated in the chatting. Furthermore, conversations that had less than 6 messages were also filtered out. Table 1 provides the statistics of filtered training and testing datasets.

Table 1. Characteristics of the datasets.

Conversation type	Training	Testing
Normal conversations	8783	20607
Predatory conversations	972	1730
Total	9755	22337

4   BERT-based Predatory Conversation Detector (Bert-PCD)

The Bert-PCD system consists of two machine learning components, i.e. a pre-trained BERT model and a classification model, connected in series as shown in Fig. 2. As mentioned in Sect. 3, each conversation in the dataset contains all the text messages exchanged between the two users. These aggregated text messages are passed as input to the BERT model which in turn returns a single vector to represent the entire conversation in a mathematical form. The output of the BERT model is used as input features for the second component, the classification model. The classifier component is a feed-forward neural network with two fully-connected layers, i.e. a hidden layer and an output layer. The hidden layer has 560 neurons with *relu* activation function, and the output layer has two neurons with *log softmax* activation function. The output layer returns a probability vector, the value at index 0 holds the probability of a conversation belonging to the predatory class, and the value at index 1 holds the probability of a conversation belonging to non-predatory class. The class with highest probability is taken as the predicted class for the conversation.

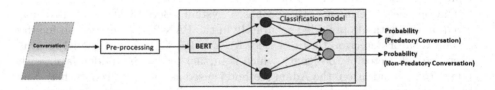

Fig. 2. Architecture of Bert-PCD.

At present, there are several pre-trained BERT models available on the Hugging site[5]. In this work, we used the *bert_base_case*[6] pre-trained model that is trained on the huge corpora of English sentences. This model is uncased in a way that it does not differentiate between upper and lower case letters (e.g. 'english' and 'English' are considered identical). Since BERT is a pre-trained model, it expects the input in a specific format. In order to convert the conversation data in the required format, we used the *batch_encode_plus* function of

---

[5] https://huggingface.co/transformers/pretrained_models.html.

[6] https://huggingface.co/bert-base-uncased.

the *BertTokenizerFast* class provided by the transformers package. The function performs the following operations on the conversation for transforming it into an appropriate representation for the model:

- It splits the conversation into a sequence of words called tokens.
- Since BERT expects equal length sequences, it applies the respective padding or truncating operations to the sequences which are either shorter or longer than the chosen maximum length.
- It encodes the tokens into their corresponding IDs. BERT has been trained on a certain corpus of English sentences. Therefore, it has a fixed vocabulary of English words where each word was assigned a unique ID. In order to use the BERT model, each token in the conversation is converted into the corresponding IDs. Furthermore, BERT is also capable of assigning IDs to the Out-Of-Vocabulary (OOV) words based on the information of the composition of their subwords.
- It designs the attention mask vector for the sequences which will assist the model in differentiating the real tokens from the padded tokens. The attention mask is a binary array to distinguish padded (0) and non-padded (1) tokens.

The *batch_encode_plus* function returns two sequences for a conversation, the input IDs and the attention mask, which are fed as input to the BERT model. The model outputs two arrays with the respective shapes, *(batch_size, sequence_length, embedding_size)* and *(batch_size, embedding_size)*. The first array contains the embedded representation for each token in the input sequence, and the second array contains the aggregated embedded representation for the input tokens. In the proposed system, we discard the first output and only pass the second output of the BERT model to the classification model as it is capable of providing the overall context of the sequence in a single vector.

During the experiments, the proposed system (Bert-PCD) is trained and tested on the datasets provided separately in the PAN-2012 competition for the sexual predator detection task (see Sect. 3). The BERT language model returns an embedded vector of 768 length which is further fed to the hidden layer with 560 neurons. In addition, the Adam method is used as the optimizer with 1e-5 as the learning rate. The batch size is kept to 1 only. Since we are dealing with the imbalanced dataset (only around 10% of conversations are predatory), weights are assigned to the two classes, predatory and non-predatory based on their number of instances. It would force the learning algorithm to give more weight to the minority class, i.e. the predatory class. The *compute_class_weight* function of *sklearn* library has been utilized to compute the values. The model uses the negative log-likelihood loss function to learn the weights of the layers. Finally, the *log softmax* function is applied at the output layer as an activation function for predicting the probabilities of an instance belonging to the respective classes. The PyTorch framework is used to implement the Bert-PCD model. The code is available in the GitHub link.

5   Experiments and Results

The pre-trained BERT model consists of a network of neural layers that have learned weights on a large corpus of English sentences in order to have a general understanding of the language. As mentioned in Sect. 4, the BERT model is integrated with a classification component for distinguishing predatory and non-predatory conversations. However, there are two ways to work with this language model in the proposed architecture. One way is to use it as a feature extractor where we freeze the weights of its layers during the training phase. It means, the weights of the first component would not change during the back-propagation of errors in training, only the classification component would learn. In the other approach, the error is back-propagated through all the layers of the architecture. This means that the weights of the pre-trained model are also updated in the training phase so as to fine-tune its layers according to the conversation data. We design two experimental setups, i.e. BERT_frozen and BERT_tuned for the respective two approaches for utilizing the model.

In order to demonstrate that BERT as a feature extractor in the proposed system is an optimal choice, we consider the two related pre-trained models, i.e., RoBERTa[7] and BertForSequenceClassification[8] for our experiments. RoBERTa (Robustly Optimized BERT Pre-training Approach) is an extension to the BERT model that has been trained on a vast dataset with a dynamic masking approach. During the experiments, the architecture and hyperparameter settings of the proposed system are kept the same. Only the BERT model is replaced with the RoBERTa. Similar to the BERT, the performance of RoBERTa is also evaluated in two configurations. In first set up, the weights of the RoBERTa are not allowed to change (RoBERTa_frozen) while in another setup, the weights are tuned according to the new labeled dataset (RoBERTa_tuned). BertForSequenceClassification is another pre-trained model that has an inbuild sequence classifier on top of the BERT. In contrast to Bert-PCD where we designed our classifier using neural layers, BertForSequenceClassification model can be used as a stand-alone for classification. The code files for developing the systems via RoBERTa and BertForSequenceClassification can be found in the GitHub link[9].

The results are compared using four evaluation metrics: precision, recall, F_1, and $F_{0.5}$-score. Precision measures the ability of a classifier to detect true predatory conversation out of total conversations detected as predatory by the classifier. On the other hand, recall tells how many predatory conversations the classifier could detect out of total predatory conversations in the dataset. F_{β}-score assists in evaluating the trade-off between precision and recall as shown in the equation below.

---

[7] https://huggingface.co/transformers/model_doc/roberta.html.

[8] https://huggingface.co/transformers/model_doc/bert.html#
bertforsequenceclassification.

[9] https://github.com/Machine-Learning-and-Data-Science/BERT-based-Predatory-Conversation-Detection-Bert-PCD-.

$$F_\beta - score = (1 + \beta^2) \cdot \frac{Precision \cdot Recall}{\beta^2 \cdot Precision + Recall} \qquad (1)$$

The F_1-score is the standard score and it assigns equal weight to both precision and recall, and estimates the balanced scores. However, the PAN-2012 competition also considered the $F_{0.5}$-score as the organizers emphasized more on the precision metric. The motivation behind prioritizing the precision is to reduce the workload on the police officers by giving the list of users who are indeed sexual predators. In other words, false positives (non-predatory conversations classified as predatory), are penalized more than false negatives (predatory conversations classified as non-predatory).

Table 2 shows the results of all experiments conducted using the three pretrained language models. It can be seen that the proposed approach with BERT as a fine-tuned model scores highest values for all four evaluation metrics (precision = 97.70%, recall = 98.68%, F_1-score = 98.19% and $F_{0.5}$-score = 97.91%). RoBERTa_tuned classifier obtains the second rank in terms of F_1 and $F_{0.5}$ scores with 93.01% and 94.72% values. It can be noted that the performance difference between the BERT and RoBERTa is significant since the former improves the F_1 and $F_{0.5}$ scores by 5.18% and 3.19% respectively. This shows that using BERT for encoding the conversations in the proposed system is an optimal decision. Also, the BertForSequenceClassification model receives the third highest values for F_1 (92.21%) and $F_{0.5}$ (91.96%) scores which confirm that the classification component of the Bert-PCD is better than the inbuilt classifier of the BertForSequenceClassification model.

Furthermore, it can also be noticed that the performance of the pre-trained models enhance when the weights of their layers are allowed to modify according to the downstream task as both BERT_tuned and RoBERTa_tuned models yield way better results than the systems where the weights were fixed. The differences between BERT_tuned and BERT_frozen for precision, recall, F_1 and $F_{0.5}$ scores are 1.14%, 31.51%, 24.06% and 14.18% respectively. In the case of RoBERTa, this difference gets further increased as RoBERTa_frozen shows 49.82%, 40.48%, 45.02%, and 47.87% increments for precision, recall, F_1 and $F_{0.5}$ scores over the respective values obtained by the RoBERTa_tuned.

The results of the best performing Bert-PCD system, i.e. BERT_tuned has further been compared with three existing studies, i.e., [6], [16], and [17]. In [6], the authors presented a CNN-based model trained on one-hot vectors as best for detecting predatory conversations. In [16] and [17], the authors proposed systems that comprised of two classifiers integrated into a sequence. The task of the first classifier is to filter the predatory conversations from the normal ones and the second classifier identifies who is the victim or predator in the predatory conversation. Since Bert-PCD focuses on identifying predatory conversation rather than the predator, we compare its performance with the first classifier only.

Table 2. Results of the pre-trained language models

Detection system	Precision	Recall	F_1-score	$F_{0.5}$-score
Bert-PCD with BERT_tuned	**97.70**	**98.68**	**98.19**	**97.91**
Bert-PCD with BERT_frozen	96.56	67.17	74.13	83.73
BertForSequenceClassification	91.80	92.64	92.21	91.96
RoBERTa_frozen	46.13	50.00	47.99	46.85
RoBERT_tuned	95.95	90.48	93.01	94.72

Table 3 shows the results obtained by the proposed system along with the results of existing systems under comparison. It can be seen that the proposed approach with fine-tuned settings obtain first rank in terms of recall (98.70%), F_1(98.19%), and $F_{0.5}$(97.91%) metrics. However, for precision, it ranks second with a 97.70% score. The classifier proposed in [9] gets the highest value in precision (99.80%). Since F_1 and $F_{0.5}$ are considered more meaningful and fruitful in evaluating the performance of the model, the proposed Bert-PCD is best for classifying suspicious conversations in online chats. The table also shows the improvement in the scores of F_1 and $F_{0.5}$ values made by proposed system over the existing classifiers.

Table 3. Comparative performance of the proposed systems.

Detection system	Precision	Recall	F_1-score	$F_{0.5}$-score	Improvement in F_1	Improvement in $F_{0.5}$
Proposed System	97.71	**98.71**	**98.20**	**97.90**	NA	NA
[6]	91.57	72.41	80.87	NA	17.33	NA
[16]	NA	NA	95.16	NA	3.04	NA
[9]	**99.80**	89.0	94.10	97.40	4.10%	0.5%

6   Conclusion and Future Work

This paper applies transfer learning via a pre-trained BERT language model in designing a novel deep learning classifier referred to as Bert-PCD for identifying the online chats which involve sexual predators. BERT has proved its potential to work in many NLP tasks, however, its application to identify the sexual predators has not been seen earlier. Employing the BERT language model solves two major problems, i.e. manual feature extraction and out-of-vocabulary (OOV) issue, and therefore, has the potential to perform better than the existing systems. The proposed system has been trained and evaluated on the dataset provided in the PAN-2012 competition.

Bert-PCD comprises two components: a *pre-trained BERT model* and a *Feed-Forward Neural Network classifier*. The classifier component is designed with two fully connected layers, i.e. hidden layer and output layer. The hidden layer contains 560 neurons with a relu activation function, and the output layer has two neurons with a log softmax activation function. The pre-trained BERT model is implemented in two configurational modes. In the first mode, BERT has been used as a feature extractor by freezing the weights of its deep neural layers during the training phase. In the second one, the BERT model is tuned according to the chat conversations by modifying the weight of its layers during the training phase.

In order to demonstrate that utilizing BERT as a language model is an optimal choice, two related pre-trained models, i.e., RoBERTa and BertForSequenceClassification are also considered for experiments. The results show that the proposed approach with BERT as a fine-tuned model scores highest values for all four evaluation metrics (precision = 97.70%, recall = 98.68%, F_1-score = 98.19% and $F_{0.5}$-score = 97.91%). Furthermore, it is also noticed that the performance of the pre-trained models is improved when they are tuned according to the chat conversations. The results also show that the best performing Bert-PCD system, i.e. BERT_tuned obtains better scores than the existing methods in terms of recall (98.70%), F_1(98.19%), and $F_{0.5}$(97.91%) metrics. In the future, we will be extending the Bert-PCD to discriminate the predators and victims involved in the predatory conversation by analysing the user behaviour as well as text messages.

References

1. Rise in online child sexual abuse cases amidst COVID-19 pandemic. https://www.humanrightspulse.com/mastercontentblog/rise-in-online-child-sexual-abuse-cases-amidst-covid-19-pandemic. Accessed 05 Feb 2021
2. Online Grooming of Children for Sexual Purposes: Model Legislation & Global Review. International Centre for Missing and Exploited Children (2017)
3. Cano, A.E., Fernandez, M., Alani, H.: Detecting child grooming behaviour patterns on social media. In: Aiello, L.M., McFarland, D. (eds.) SocInfo 2014. LNCS, vol. 8851, pp. 412–427. Springer, Cham (2014). https://doi.org/10.1007/978-3-319-13734-6_30
4. Cao, Z., Zhou, Y., Yang, A., Peng, S.: Deep transfer learning mechanism for fine-grained cross-domain sentiment classification. Connection Science, pp. 1–18 (2021)
5. Devlin, J., Chang, M.W., Lee, K., Toutanova, K.: BERT: pre-training of deep bidirectional transformers for language understanding. arXiv preprint arXiv:1810.04805 (2018)
6. Ebrahimi, M., Suen, C.Y., Ormandjieva, O.: Detecting predatory conversations in social media by deep convolutional neural networks. Digit. Investig. **18**, 33–49 (2016)
7. Gao, Z., Feng, A., Song, X., Wu, X.: Target-dependent sentiment classification with BERT. IEEE Access **7**, 154290–154299 (2019)
8. Inches, G., Crestani, F.: Overview of the international sexual predator identification competition at PAN-2012. In: CLEF (Online Working Notes/Labs/Workshop), vol. 30 (2012)

9. Kontostathis, A., Garron, A., Reynolds, K., West, W., Edwards, L.: Identifying predators using chatcoder 2.0. In: CLEF (Online Working Notes/Labs/Workshop) (2012)
10. Mozafari, M., Farahbakhsh, R., Crespi, N.: A BERT-based transfer learning approach for hate speech detection in online social media. In: Cherifi, H., Gaito, S., Mendes, J.F., Moro, E., Rocha, L.M. (eds.) COMPLEX NETWORKS 2019. SCI, vol. 881, pp. 928–940. Springer, Cham (2020). https://doi.org/10.1007/978-3-030-36687-2_77
11. Pan, S.J., Yang, Q.: A survey on transfer learning. IEEE Trans. Knowl. Data Eng. **22**(10), 1345–1359 (2009)
12. Peters, M.E., Neumann, M., Iyyer, M., Gardner, M., Clark, C., Lee, K., Zettlemoyer, L.: Deep contextualized word representations. In: Proceedings of the 2018 Conference of the North American Chapter of the Association for Computational Linguistics: Human Language Technologies, Volume 1 (Long Papers), pp. 2227–2237. Association for Computational Linguistics, New Orleans, June 2018. https://doi.org/10.18653/v1/N18-1202. https://aclanthology.org/N18-1202
13. Ruder, S., Peters, M.E., Swayamdipta, S., Wolf, T.: Transfer learning in natural language processing. In: Proceedings of the 2019 Conference of the North American Chapter of the Association for Computational Linguistics: Tutorials, pp. 15–18 (2019)
14. Seigfried-Spellar, K.C., Rogers, M.K., Rayz, J.T., Yang, S.F., Misra, K., Ringenberg, T.: Chat analysis triage tool: differentiating contact-driven vs. fantasy-driven child sex offenders. Forensic Sci. Int. **297**, e8–e10 (2019)
15. Syed, B., Indurthi, V., Gupta, M., Shrivastava, M., Varma, V.: Inductive transfer learning for detection of well-formed natural language search queries. In: Azzopardi, L., Stein, B., Fuhr, N., Mayr, P., Hauff, C., Hiemstra, D. (eds.) ECIR 2019. LNCS, vol. 11438, pp. 45–52. Springer, Cham (2019). https://doi.org/10.1007/978-3-030-15719-7_6
16. Villatoro-Tello, E., Juárez-González, A., Escalante, H.J., Montes-y Gómez, M., Pineda, L.V.: A two-step approach for effective detection of misbehaving users in chats. In: CLEF (Online Working Notes/Labs/Workshop), vol. 1178 (2012)
17. Wani, M.A., Agarwal, N., Bours, P.: Impact of unreliable content on social media users during COVID-19 and stance detection system. Electronics **10**(1), 5 (2021)
18. Wani, M.A., Agarwal, N., Bours, P.: Sexual-predator detection system based on social behavior biometric (SSB) features. Procedia Comput. Sci. **189**, 116–127 (2021). aI in Computational Linguistics
19. Wani, M.A., Jabin, S.: A sneak into the devil's colony-fake profiles in online social networks. arXiv preprint arXiv:1705.09929 (2017)
20. Whittle, H.C., Hamilton-Giachritsis, C., Beech, A.R.: Victims voices: the impact of online grooming and sexual abuse. Universal J. Psychol. **1**(2), 59–71 (2013)
21. Young, T., Hazarika, D., Poria, S., Cambria, E.: Recent trends in deep learning based natural language processing. IEEE Comput. Intell. Mag. **13**(3), 55–75 (2018)

Toward a New Approach for Tuning Regularization Hyperparameter in NMF

Nicoletta Del Buono, Flavia Esposito, and Laura Selicato$^{(\boxtimes)}$

Department of Mathematics, Members of INDAM-GNCS Research Group,
University of Bari Aldo Moro, Via E. Orabona 4, Bari, Italy
{nicoletta.delbuono,flavia.esposito,laura.selicato}@uniba.it

Abstract. Linear Dimensionality Reduction (LDR) methods has gained much attention in the last decades and has been used in the context of data mining applications to reconstruct a given data matrix. The effectiveness of low rank models in data science is justified by the fact that one can suppose that each row or column in the data matrix is associated to a bounded latent variable, and entries of the matrix are generated by applying a piece-wise analytic function to these latent variables. Formally, LDR can be mathematically formalized as optimization problems at which regularization terms can be often added to enforce particular constraints emphasizing useful properties in data. From this point of view, the tune of the regularization hyperparameters (HPs), controlling the weight of the additional constraints, represents an interesting problem to be solved automatically rather than by a trial and error approach. In this work, we focus on the role the regularization HPs act in Nonnegative Matrix Factorizations (NMF) context and how their right choice can affect further results, proposing a complete overview and new directions for a novel approach. Moreover, a novel bilevel formulation of the regularization HP selection is proposed which incorporates the HP choice directly in the unsupervised algorithm as a part of the updating process.

Keywords: Hyperparameter optimization · Regularization hyperparameter · Regularized NMF

1 Introduction

In the unsupervised learning scenario, Linear Dimensionality Reduction (LDR) methods are able to unfold the intricate information embedded in data structures using low dimensional spaces. Since entries of data matrices are often characterized by nonnegative values, related to physical meaning (e.g. pixels intensity in images), it is convenient to take this constraint into account during any data

---

N. Del Buono, F. Esposito and L. Selicato—All authors equally contribute to this work.

G. Nicosia et al. (Eds.): LOD 2021, LNCS 13163, pp. 500–511, 2022.
https://doi.org/10.1007/978-3-030-95467-3_36

analysis. According to this, a particular LDR technique, Nonnegative Matrix Factorization (NMF) emerged in literature thanks to its property of maintaining nonnegativity during data analysis process that permits to obtain better interpretation and visualization results [9].

NMF approximates a nonnegative data matrix $X \in \mathbb{R}_+^{n \times m}$ (with typically $n >> m$) as the product of two nonnegative matrices $W \in \mathbb{R}_+^{n \times r}$ and $H \in \mathbb{R}_+^{r \times m}$, namely the *basis* and the *encoding* matrix, respectively, so that $X \approx WH$. The number of columns of W or rows for H is the rank of the factorization r.

As all learning method, LDR methods require the configuration of some different Hyperparameters (HPs), that is, the variables governing the learning approach. These must be set before the running process and affect the performances of the model itself. HPs tuning usually takes a lot of effort since it is user-dependent and adjusted by hand when some domain knowledge is available. Automated HPs optimization (HPO) would bring a solution to this problem, while also providing more reproducible results and facilitating fairly comparisons between different learning models. For NMF problem the rank of the factorization (since its nature of being problem and user dependent), the learning rate (when Gradient-type algorithms are used to optimize the NMF problem), the maximum number of iteration to achieve in the minimization process or the regularization coefficient (when regularized NMF are taken into account) are HPs [6, 10]. Different empirical approaches have been proposed in literature trying a set of values and searching for the one achieving the best performances according to some defined metrics, however other more sophisticated methodologies exist [27]. Since the 1990s Grid Search and Random Search has been the main way of performing HPO. By the way, these techniques must be guided by some performance metric, typically measured by cross-validation on the training set or evaluation on a held-out validation set and for this reason they require a significant computational effort. More recently, some other methods (based on Gradient, Black-Box and Bayesian approaches) gained more attention to tackle this problem [3]. Focusing on Gradient-Based methods, the gradient respecting to the HPs (or its approximation) can be used to reduce the validation error. In this context, HPO problem can be formalized as a bilevel optimization task[1].

Particularly, let $\mathcal{A}$ be a learning model with d HPs, $\lambda \in \Lambda$[2] and n parameters, $\omega \in \Omega$[3], $X \in \mathbb{R}^{n \times m}$ a dataset with $n, m \in \mathbb{N}$, the HPO is the problem to find

$$\lambda^* = \operatorname*{argmin}_{\lambda \in \Lambda} F(\mathcal{A}(\omega(\lambda), \lambda), X) \quad \text{sbj to} \quad \omega(\lambda) = \operatorname*{argmin}_{\omega} \ell(\lambda, X), \quad (1)$$

---

[1] In bilevel programming an outer optimization problem is solved subject to the optimality of an inner optimization problem.

[2] $\Lambda = \Lambda_1 \times \cdots \times \Lambda_d$ is the HP domain, where each set Λ_i can be real-valued (e.g., learning rate, regularization coefficient), integer-valued (e.g., number of layers), binary (e.g., whether to use early stopping or not), categorical (e.g., choice of optimizer).

[3] ω can be scalar, vector or matrix. $\Omega = \Omega_1 \times \cdots \times \Omega_n$ is the parameter domain, where each set Ω_j can be real-valued or integer-valued (e.g., weights of regression and classification, factors in matrix decompositions).

where F measures the goodness of the parameter ω obtained by the algorithm $\mathcal{A}$ associated to HP λ on X. The inner problem is usually the minimization of an empirical loss ℓ while the outer problem involves HPs.

In this paper, we study the regularization coefficient as HP in particular, we include its choice as part of the algorithm to find the parameters in an alternating bilevel approach.

The bilevel optimization problem (1) is challenging to solve due to the dependency of the outer problem on λ induced by the inner problem in $\omega(\lambda)$. Recently, first-order bilevel optimization techniques have been revisited to solve these problems. These methods rely on an estimate of the Jacobian $\frac{d\omega(\lambda)}{d\lambda}$ in order to optimize λ. In [20] the Jacobian is computed by implicit differentiation. By contrast, in [7] the inner problem is seen as a dynamical system, and the Jacobian is computed by iterative differentiation. The latter approach is less sensitive to the optimality of $\omega(\lambda)$ and can also learn HPs that control the inner optimization process. Motivated by that, in this paper we decide to focus on iterative differentiation by exploring further this topic combining these recent techniques in Matrix Decompositions.

The paper is divided as follow. In Sect. 2 we provide a complete overview of NMF and the main properties of sparsity, orthogonality and smoothness constraints enforced on the matrix factors (other constrained NMF can be found in literature [10]) and we highlight the importance of the regularization HP in this context. In Sect. 3 we show how to solve this issue proposing an alternate methodology in which the bilevel approach is used and some preliminary results are shown in Sect. 4. Finally, in Sect. 5 we sketch some conclusions and new directions of future research.

2   The NMF Problem and Its Constrained Variant

We refer to the general NMF problem $\min\limits_{W \geq 0, H \geq 0} D_\beta(X, WH)$ optimization task where the cost function, evaluating how good X is fitted by its reconstruction WH, is given by the general β-divergence,

$$D_\beta(X; WH) = \sum_{i=1}^{n} \sum_{j=1}^{m} d_\beta(X_{ij}; (WH)_{ij});$$

with d_β commonly defined for each x, y as

$$d_\beta(x; y) = \begin{cases} \frac{1}{\beta(\beta-1)}(x^\beta + (\beta-1)y^\beta - \beta xy^{\beta-1}) & \beta \in \mathbb{R} - \{0, 1\}; \\ x\log(\frac{x}{y}) - x + y & \beta = 1; \\ \frac{x}{y} - \log(\frac{x}{y}) - 1 & \beta = 0. \end{cases}$$

The choice of a specific $D_\beta(\cdot, \cdot)$ is strictly related to the properties of data under study as well as the application domain data come from. The most popular chosen divergences are the squared Frobenius norm ($\beta = 2$), the generalized Kullback-Leibler (KL) divergence ($\beta = 1$) that corresponds to the maximum likelihood estimation under an independent Poisson assumption [5] and Itakura-Saito divergence ($\beta = 0$), optimal when data follow Gamma distributions.

Besides to standard NMF model introduced before, there are other variants that combine nonnegativity with additional constraints such as sparsity (used to control zero values in the factor matrices), orthogonality[4] (allows to enforce clustering capability on matrix factor) and smoothness (adopted to improve the stability of the solution, common in linear inverse problems).

These can be added as regularization terms in the original objective function for which the problem of HP tuning represents a big issue. In general, the optimization problem to be solved, is formalized in the following way:

$$\min_{W \geq 0, H \geq 0} D_\beta(X, WH) + \lambda_W R_1(W) + \lambda_H R_2(H), \tag{2}$$

being $R_1(\cdot) : \mathbb{R}^{n \times r} \to \mathbb{R}$ and $R_2(\cdot) : \mathbb{R}^{r \times m} \to \mathbb{R}$ some regularization functions which enforce particular additional constraints on W and H, respectively, while λ_W and λ_H are some real regularization HPs balancing the trade-off between the goodness of the approximation and the constraint preservation. It is worthy to note that problem (2) allows to consider either regularization functions on one or both variables, simultaneously.

Sparseness leads to several advantages in the factorization either from a computational point of view and interpretative aspect. Increasing of number of zero elements, for instance, can facilitate the storage of matrices or speed up computations; a large amount of zeros provides also a natural way to perform features extraction and to prevent over-fitting and modeling the intrinsic noise in data. Even if nonnegativity of NMF factors naturally provides sparse results, it is preferred to enforce this property with direct constraint to control the degree of sparseness in each factor [30]. A regularization function used to enforce the sparsity constraint is the ℓ_0 norm[5], defined as the number of no zeros values in a vector $x \in \mathbb{R}^n$

$$\|x\|_0 = \# \{i = 1, \ldots, n | x_i \neq 0\}. \tag{3}$$

To enforce sparsity into NMF, a method based on ℓ_0 constraints on W and H columns has been developed in [8]. Anyway, this cannot be considered a standard approach because the optimization results is a NP-hard problem and the associated objective function is difficult to be optimized because it is non-convex, non-smooth, discontinuous and globally non-differentiable.

For this reason, other norms can be considered to enforce sparsity constraint. The ℓ_1 and ℓ_2 norm of a given vector $x \in \mathbb{R}^n$ could represent some valid alternatives to the theoretical ℓ_0 norm [29] also taking into account their proprieties

---

[4] Note that the term "orthogonal" is to be understood as "soft-orthogonal" indicating the orthogonality property of the columns or rows of the matrices W or H, respectively. With this clarification, the soft-orthogonal NMF problem can be defined as
$$\min_{W \geq 0, H \geq 0} D_\beta(X, WH) \quad \text{s.t.} \quad W^\top W = I_r \quad \text{and/or} \quad HH^\top = I_r.$$
[5] ℓ_0 norm is not truly a norm since the property of positive homogeneity is not respected. Nevertheless, since it can be expressed in terms of the ℓ_p norm $\|x\|_0 = \lim_{p \to 0} \|x\|_p^p$, in literature, it is referred to as a "norm".

(ℓ_1 norm is a convex, nonsmooth, global non differentiable function, whereas ℓ_2 norm is a convex, smooth, global differentiable function). Sparsity can be also enforced adopting other choices: several examples have been proposed in [17] or by Hoyer et al. in [12], where the ℓ_1 is used in association with ℓ_2 norm on the same variable to control factors smoothness. In particular, the so called Hoyer sparse NMF model is based on the idea of quantifying vector information in few components using a normalized measure[6] which estimates sparseness. To enforce the sparsity constraint, one can also work by considering as regularization function the $\ell_{1,2}$ norm defined directly on a matrix $A \in \mathbb{R}^{n \times m}$ by summing the $\ell - 2$ norms of the column vectors of A, $A_{:i}$. This norm, firstly introduced as rotational invariant of the ℓ_1 norm [17], was used for multi-task learning [1]. In NMF context, this norm is associated to both objective and regularization functions [16].

Tuning HPs in constrained NMF problem, is usually solved by adopting static optimization mechanisms, typically based on Grid Search approaches. A well-known example in literature appears in gene expression analysis [13]. More generally, when empirical approaches for the Tikhonov regularization are considered, there exist two strategies to compute the regularization HP value: the L-curve criterion and the Discrepency Principle [11]. The L-curve method –named in this way for the shape of its representation– is a log-log plot of the regularization term vs the fitting part (with the Frobenius norm for both), measured according to different values of the solution referred to distinct HP values. Its limit cases are associated to over- and under-regularization giving an horizontal and vertical line in the $L-$ curve, respectively. The vertical part of the curve is very sensitive to the regularization. According to this, the optimal value of the regularization HP can be found in the transition between these two configurations, close to the left corner [19]. On the other hand, the Discrepency Principle finds the solution on the vertical part of the L-curve, considering the variational approach of the Tikhonov regularization and taking into account that solutions with minimum value of the regularization function naturally go lower with respect to the data fitting.

In the NMF literature panorama, other more sophisticated strategies for the tuning of regularization HPs can be applied, such as those exploiting well-known optimization and Bayesian methodologies as in the form

$$\min_{H \geq 0} \frac{1}{2} ||X - WH||_F^2 + \frac{\lambda}{2} R(H), \tag{4}$$

with $R(H) = \mathrm{Tr}\,(H^\top E H)$ and $E \in \mathbb{R}^{r \times r}$ is an all-ones matrix used to enforce sparsity on H's columns [28]. Referring to this problem, it is suggested to embed the choice of λ in the minimization problem and to update it according to the following exponential rule $\lambda^{(k)} = \lambda_0 \exp{(-\tau k)}$, where k is the number of iteration in the algorithm, λ_0 the initial value of the HP and τ another parameter controlling the results. Choosing higher initial value of λ and smaller τ can improve the results while penalizing iterations cost. By the way, τ represents another

---

[6] The Hoyer sparsity measure is computed as the normalized ratio of ℓ_1 and ℓ_2 norm.

user-dependent parameter and therefore the HP tuning problem remains still open and it was not totally solved.

Other results are related to Frobenius NMF problem with the Tikhonov regularization on the basis matrix. The problem is defined as in (4) by considering the minimization (and then the regularization with the Frobenius norm) on W and it is solved using an active-set approaches inspired by Nonnegative Least Squares (NNLS) algorithms [27]. In this work Fast Combinatorial NNLS algorithms (FC-NNLS) are presented applying the above regularized model to Raman spectra, recovering and focusing on hyperspectral unmixing and giving geometrical interpretation of the proposed approach in terms of probabilistic simplex from convex polytopes.

In all cases, the authors suggest to decrease gradually the HP starting from a large positive initial value by following the rule $\max\left(\overline{\lambda}, 2^{-k}\lambda_0\right)$ in which they set $\overline{\lambda} > 0$ the lowest value of this choice. In particular, they evidence clearly that by adopting the Singular Value Decomposition of H, a larger value of λ implies that only the largest singular vectors take part into the updating rule. In this way, higher is the value of the HP ($\lambda >> \sigma_{max}(H)$) more similar is the update rule to a gradient descent approach,

$$W \leftarrow W - \frac{1}{\lambda}((WH - X)H^{\top}), \tag{5}$$

whereas for small values of HP, $\lambda = \overline{\lambda}$ the algorithm actually correspond to the SNMF/R algortihm. Moreover, in their works, they also evidence the inverse relationship of λ with the radius Δ of the Trust Region when the equivalent problem is taken into account:

$$\min \frac{1}{2}||X - WH||_F^2, \quad \text{sbj to} \quad ||W||_F^2 \leq \Delta. \tag{6}$$

Even several approaches appeared in literature to solve this problem, a uniform theory that could be easily applicable in a more universal way to any objective and regularization functions is lacking. Our proposal is placed in the context of bilevel programming and aims at an automatic HP optimization within the matrix factorization process.

3   Proposed Approach

A novel approach to solve the general HPO issue associated to the NMF regularized model (2) can be obtained rewriting the problem as:

$$\min_{H \geq 0, W \geq 0} D_\beta(X, WH) + R_1(\lambda_W W) + R_2(\lambda_H H^{\top}). \tag{7}$$

where $\lambda_W \in \mathbb{R}^{1 \times n}$, $\lambda_H \in \mathbb{R}^{1 \times m}$ and $R_i : \mathbb{R}^r \to \mathbb{R}$ for $i = 1, 2$ are the regularization functions. The constrained optimization problem (2) is NP-hard and non convex in both the unknowns W and H, simultaneously. However, since it is convex[7] in each variable separately, alternating optimization techniques can be properly incorporated into the minimization process. Following this approach, W is fixed to totally estimate H and then H is fixed to estimate W. We consider the particular case $\lambda_H = 0_{\mathbb{R}^m}$ and $\lambda_W = \lambda$, turning our problem in:

$$\min_{H \geq 0, W \geq 0} D_\beta(X, WH) + R(\lambda W), \tag{8}$$

thanks to the fact that, in a similar way, we can extend the reasoning considering $\lambda_W = 0_{\mathbb{R}^n}$. Following the rational above, we solve the problem (8) by reformulating it as an alternate problem by including the tuning of the regularization parameter in the minimization task. Then, the problem (8) is formalized as solving the simple minimization task:

$$\min_{H \geq 0} D_\beta(X, WH), \tag{9}$$

followed by the bilevel problem applied to the row of W, adopting a row-wise writing of matrix W:

$$\min\{f(\lambda_i) : \lambda_i \in \mathbb{R}\} \tag{10}$$

$$f(\lambda_i) = \inf\{E(w_{\lambda_i}, \lambda_i) : w_{\lambda_i} \in \underset{u \in \mathbb{R}^r}{\operatorname{argmin}} L_{\lambda_i}(u)\} \tag{11}$$

where $\lambda = \{\lambda_i\}_{i=1}^n$, $w \in \mathbb{R}^r$ is the generic row of $W \in \mathbb{R}^{n \times r}$, the *Response Function f* is such that $f : \mathbb{R} \to \mathbb{R} : \lambda_i \mapsto \sum_{j=1}^m d_\beta(x_j, \sum_{a=1}^r w_a(\lambda_i)H_{aj})$. The *Error Function* $E : \mathbb{R}^r \times \mathbb{R} \to \mathbb{R}$ is the outer objective, whereas the *Loss Function* $L_\lambda : \mathbb{R}^r \to \mathbb{R}$ for every $\lambda_i \in \mathbb{R}$, is the inner objective. For simplicity let us assume that the inner objective has a unique minimizer w_{λ_i}. The Algorithm 1 shows the pseudo-code of our proposed approach.

Algorithm 1: Solve the HPO in NMF

Data: $X \in \mathbb{R}_+^{n \times m}$ and factorization rank r.
Result: $W \in \mathbb{R}_+^{n \times r}$, $H \in \mathbb{R}_+^{r \times m}$
Some initial matrices $W^{(0)} \in \mathbb{R}_+^{n \times r}$, $H^{(0)} \in \mathbb{R}_+^{m \times r}$ and initial
   regularization HP $\lambda^{(0)}$;
while *some stopping criteria are not met* **do**
   $\quad | \quad H^{(t)} = update(X, W^{(0)}, H^{(t-1)})$;
   $\quad | \quad t+=1$;
end
while *some stopping criteria not met* **do**
   $\quad | \quad (W^{(t)}, \lambda^{(t)}) = bilevelupdate(X, \lambda^{(t-1)}, W(\lambda)^{(t-1)}, H^{(T)})$;
   $\quad | \quad t+=1;$
end

To solve the optimization problem (9), different update rules have been proposed in literature satisfying some additional requirements (fast convergence

---

[7] For particular values of β and specific regularization functions.

or easy implementation mechanisms to mention few), ranging from Multiplicative Update (MU) to Additive Update (AU) rules [2]. Since they are equivalent by carrying out an appropriate rescaling, we focus on standard MU. Based on Expectation-Maximization and Richardson-Lucy algorithms [18,22], MU is founded on Multiplicative rules that iteratively scale the initialization matrices by minimizing a so called auxiliary function. The easier formulation of this function when compared to the original objective function can facilitate the minimization procedure. To find an auxiliary function, an upper-approximation of the objective function that matches it in only one point and has an easier formulation needs to be found. This auxiliary function approach was frequently adopted to minimize different NMF problems because, despite their slow convergence to local minima, they ensure nonnegativity of factors without any further manipulations. For $0 \leq \beta \leq 2$, the general β-Divergence is not increasing under the following MU rules [14]:

$$H \leftarrow H .* \frac{W^\top ((WH)^{\cdot [\beta-2]} X)}{W^\top (WH)^{\cdot [\beta-1]}}, \qquad (12)$$

where $.*$ denotes the Hadamard product and ratio and exponential operations are referred element-wise. To solve the bilevel optimization problem (10)–(11), we can rewrite it as

$$\min_{\lambda_i \in \Lambda} f(w(\lambda_i)) = E(w_{\lambda_i^*}, \lambda_i^*), \qquad w_{\lambda_i} = \operatorname*{argmin}_u L_{\lambda_i}(u); \qquad (13)$$

and assuming that the set $\Lambda \subset \mathbb{R}$ of the HP is compact, the Error Function $E : \mathbb{R}^r \times \Lambda \to \mathbb{R}$ and the map $(w, \lambda_i) \to L_{\lambda_i}(w)$ are jointly continuous, then the problem $\operatorname{argmin} L_{\lambda_i}$ is a singleton for every $\lambda_i \in \Lambda$, and $w_{\lambda_i} = \operatorname{argmin} L_{\lambda_i}$ remains bounded as λ_i varies in Λ.

The problem (13) remains challenging to solve, because in general there is no closed form expression w_{λ_i}, so it is not possible to directly optimize the outer objective function. The minimization of the inner problem can be seen as a dynamical system with a state $w^{(t)} \in \mathbb{R}^r$:

$$w^{(t)} = \Phi_t(w^{(t-1)}, \lambda_i) \quad t = 1, \dots, T; \qquad (14)$$

for every i-th row $w^{(t)}$ of W with $i = 1, \dots, n$ at time t, $\lambda_i \in \mathbb{R}$ the i-th component of λ, T is total the number of iterations, and for every $t \in \{1, ..., T\}$ the function $\Phi_t : (\mathbb{R}^r \times \Lambda) \to \mathbb{R}^r$, is a smooth mapping that represents the update performed by the t-th step of the optimization algorithm. It is worthy to note that the iterates $w^{(1)}, \dots, w^{(T)}$ implicitly depend on λ_i. Based on this approach the bilevel problem (10)–(11) can be approximated by the following constrained procedure

$$\min_{\lambda_i} f(\lambda_i) \quad \text{sbj to} \quad w^{(t)} = \Phi_t(w^{(t-1)}, \lambda_i) \quad \text{for} \quad t = 1, \dots, T; i = 1, \dots, n \qquad (15)$$

where $f(\lambda_i) = \sum_{j=1}^{m} d_\beta(x_j, \sum_{a=1}^{r} w_a^{(T)}(\lambda_i) H_{aj})$. To find the regularization HP λ suppose we want to apply a Gradient type approach on every component λ_i of λ.

According to this, the optimization result for $\lambda_i \in \Lambda$ come from the estimation of the gradient $\nabla_{\lambda_i} f$, called hypergradient. Then, since this is not directly dependent from λ_i, by the Chain Rule we have:

$$\nabla_{\lambda_i} f = \frac{\partial f}{\partial \lambda_i} + \frac{\partial f}{\partial w^{(T)}} \cdot \frac{dw^{(T)}}{d\lambda_i}, \tag{16}$$

where $\frac{\partial f}{\partial \lambda_i} \in \mathbb{R}$ and $\frac{\partial f}{\partial w^{(T)}} \in \mathbb{R}^r$ are available. Considering $w^{(T)}$ as a function of λ_i, we can handle the hypergradient estimate by focusing on the problem of computing the row-vector product $\frac{\partial f}{\partial w^{(T)}} \cdot \frac{dw^{(T)}}{d\lambda_i}$.

We focus on Iterative Differentiation approach as mentioned above. In this context, hypergradient can be computed either using Reverse-Mode Differentiation (RMD), that computes it by back-propagation, or Forward-Mode Differentiation (FMD), that uses the forward propagation. In this work, we use FMD.

Forward-Mode. FMD appeals to the chain rule for the derivative of composite functions (16). The operators Φ_t for $t = 1, \ldots, T$ depend on the regularization HP λ_i both directly by its expression and indirectly through the state $w^{(t-1)}$. By using again the chain rule, for every $t = 1, \ldots, T$, the derivative of the state according to λ_i can be formalized as follow:

$$\frac{dw^{(t)}}{d\lambda_i} = \frac{\partial \Phi_t(w^{(t-1)}, \lambda_i)}{\partial w^{(t-1)}} \frac{dw^{(t-1)}}{d\lambda_i} + \frac{\partial \Phi_t(w^{(t-1)}, \lambda_i)}{\partial \lambda_i}. \tag{17}$$

Defining $Z_t = \frac{dw^{(t)}}{d\lambda_i}$ for every $t = 1, \ldots, T$ and using A_t and B_t defined above, for $t = 1, \ldots, T$, the iterative rules FMD can be obtained in the following:

$$\begin{aligned} Z_0 &= B_0; & Z_t &= A_t Z_{t-1} + B_t \quad t = 1, \ldots, T; \\ \nabla_{\lambda_i} f &= \frac{\partial f}{\partial \lambda_i} + \frac{\partial f}{\partial w^{(T)}} \cdot Z_T, \end{aligned} \tag{18}$$

for every row of W. By initializing $Z_0 = 0$, the solution of (18) is actually the solution of the more general difference equation:

$$\nabla_{\lambda_i} f(\lambda_i) = \frac{\partial f^{(T)}(\lambda_i)}{\partial w^{(T)}} \sum_{t=1}^{T} (\prod_{s=t+1}^{T} A_s) B_t. \tag{19}$$

4   Preliminary Experiment Results and Discussions

Some preliminary numerical results showing the effectiveness of the proposed approach are here briefly reported. The proposed algorithm was implemented in R environment [21] and run on a 16 Gb RAM, I7 Octa core machine. Tests were performed on real tumor gene expression profiling data in [23] with $W^{(0)}$, $H^{(0)}$ and the initial HP $\lambda^{(0)}$ randomly initialized, as described in [4].

Figures 1 and 2 illustrate the decreasing behaviour of the *Response function* and objective *Error function E*, respectively (note the initial and final values reported in both pictures as isolated points). Table 1 reports the quantitative results (final divergence and objective function value and relative error as defined in [6]) obtained running our algorithm with random hyperparameters values of the order of 10, 10^2 and 10^3 and λ^*. As it can be observed, optimal λ^* provides the best results in terms of divergence and objective function and a good value of relative error.

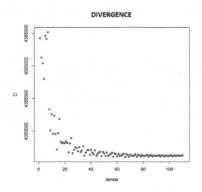

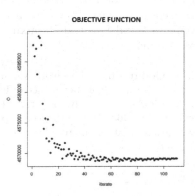

Fig. 1. *Response function* behavior   **Fig. 2.** *Error function* behavior

Table 1. Comparison with different values for λ

Metrics/λ	$\lambda_1 \sim 10^{-2}$	$\lambda_2 \sim 10$	$\lambda_3 \sim 10^3$	λ^*
Hoyer	0.7799	0.7833	0.7866	0.7975
Sparsness	0.25	0.25	0.25	0.75
Relative error	0.004	0.018	0.163	0.005

5   Conclusion and Future Works

This work proposes a method for tuning regularization HP in NMF, based on alternating the optimization the factorization and the regularization problem. The novelty of our proposal is to introduce a bilevel approach to tackle the second optimization issue. The preliminary results obtained on some test problem seem to be promising.

In the unsupervised scenario, where NMF and general LDR fall on, this topic is an innovative argument which needs massive experiments validating the theory developed in this paper. Moreover, other classes of approximate hypergradients can be investigated such as the truncated back-propagation (K-RMD) [24] that uses the intermediate variable h_{T-K} to construct an approximate gradient. Theoretical sufficient conditions has been proved to guarantying HPs converge to an approximate or exact stationary point of the upper-level objective for K-RMD, while in practice, although exact convergence appears to be uncommon,

K-RMD performances are close to full RMD in terms of application-specific metrics. These reasons encourages us to design more operative algorithms by considering $K = T - 1$. This could speed up also the computation, since NMF will advantage on its natural faster way by alternating its updates on either factors and HPs. A future research direction will focus on studying how different choices of the regularization functions (described in Sect. 2) can affect our approaches in terms of performances and computational costs, to improve applications in Blind Spectral Unmixing [15, 27], gene expression analysis [6, 25] and Text Mining [26]).

Acknowledgments. This work was supported in part by the GNCS-INDAM (Gruppo Nazionale per il Calcolo Scientifico of Istituto Nazionale di Alta Matematica) Francesco Severi, P.le Aldo Moro, Roma, Italy. The author F.E. was funded by REFIN Project, grant number 363BB1F4, Reference project idea UNIBA027 "Un modello numerico-matematico basato su metodologie di algebra lineare e multilineare per l'analisi di dati genomici".

References

1. Argyriou, A., Evgeniou, T., Pontil, M.: Multi-task feature learning. Adv. Neural Inf. Process. Syst. **19**, 41–48 (2007)
2. Berry, M.W., Browne, M., Langville, A.N., Pauca, V.P., Plemmons, R.J.: Algorithms and applications for approximate nonnegative matrix factorization. Comput. Stat. Data Anal. **52**(1), 155–173 (2007)
3. Del Buono, N., Esposito, F., Selicato, L.: Methods for hyperparameters optimization in learning approaches: an overview. In: Nicosia, G., et al. (eds.) LOD 2020. LNCS, vol. 12565, pp. 100–112. Springer, Cham (2020). https://doi.org/10.1007/978-3-030-64583-0_11
4. Esposito, F.: A review on initialization methods for nonnegative matrix factorization: towards omics data experiments. Mathematics **9**(9), 1006 (2021)
5. Esposito, F., Del Buono, N., Selicato, L.: Nonnegative matrix factorization models for knowledge extraction from biomedical and other real world data. PAMM **20**(1), e202000032 (2021)
6. Esposito, F., Gillis, N., Del Buono, N.: Orthogonal joint sparse NMF for microarray data analysis. J. Math. Biol. **79**(1), 223–247 (2019)
7. Franceschi, L., Donini, M., Frasconi, P., Pontil, M.: Forward and reverse gradient-based hyperparameter optimization. In: International Conference on Machine Learning, pp. 1165–1173. PMLR (2017)
8. Gao, T., Guo, Y., Deng, C., Wang, S., Yu, Q.: Hyperspectral unmixing based on constrained nonnegative matrix factorization via approximate L0. In: Proceedings of IEEE International Geoscience Remote Sensing Symposium, pp. 2156–2159 (2015)
9. Gillis, N.: The why and how of nonnegative matrix factorization. In: Suykens, J., Signoretto, M., Argyriou, A. (eds.) Regularization, Optimization, Kernels, and Support Vector Machines. Machine Learning and Pattern Recognition Series, pp. 257–291. Chapman & Hall/CRC, Boca Raton (2014)
10. Gillis, N.: Nonnegative Matrix Factorization. SIAM, Philadelphia (2020)
11. Hanke, M.: A Taste of Inverse Problems: Basic Theory and Examples. SIAM, Philadelphia (2017)

12. Hoyer, P.O.: Non-negative sparse coding. In: Proceedings of the 2002 12th IEEE Workshop on Neural Networks for Signal Processing, 2002, pp. 557–565. IEEE (2002)
13. Hyunsoo, K., Haesun, P.: Sparse non-negative matrix factorizations via alternating non-negativity-constrained least squares for microarray data analysis. Bioinformatics **23**(12), 1495–1502 (2007)
14. Kompass, R.: A generalized divergence measure for nonnegative matrix factorization. Neural Comput. **19**(3), 780–791 (2007)
15. Leplat, V., Gillis, N., Févotte, C.: Multi-resolution beta-divergence NMF for blind spectral unmixing. arXiv preprint arXiv:2007.03893 (2020)
16. Li, Z., Tang, Z., Ding, S.: Dictionary learning by nonnegative matrix factorization with 1/2-norm sparsity constraint. In: 2013 IEEE International Conference on Cybernetics (CYBCONF), pp. 63–67. IEEE (2013)
17. Liu, J.-X., Wang, D., Gao, Y.-L., Zheng, C.-H., Xu, Y., Yu, J.: Regularized nonnegative matrix factorization for identifying differentially expressed genes and clustering samples: a survey. IEEE/ACM Trans. Comput. Biol. Bioinf. **15**(3), 974–987 (2017)
18. Lucy, L.B.: An iterative technique for the rectification of observed distributions. Astron. J. **79**, 745 (1974)
19. Oraintara, S., Karl, W.C., Castanon, D.A., Nguyen, T.Q.: A method for choosing the regularization parameter in generalized Tikhonov regularized linear inverse problems. In: Proceedings 2000 International Conference on Image Processing (Cat. No. 00CH37101), vol. 1, pp. 93–96. IEEE (2000)
20. Pedregosa, F.: Hyperparameter optimization with approximate gradient. In: International Conference on Machine Learning, pp. 737–746. PMLR (2016)
21. R-Team, R.C.: A Language and Environment for Statistical Computing. R Foundation for Statistical Computing, Vienna, Austria (2015)
22. Richardson, W.H.: Bayesian-based iterative method of image restoration. JoSA **62**(1), 55–59 (1972)
23. Selicato, L.: A new ensemble method for detecting anomalies in gene expression matrices. Mathematics **9**(8), 882 (2021)
24. Shaban, A., Cheng, C.-A., Hatch, N., Boots, B.: Truncated back-propagation for bilevel optimization. In: The 22nd International Conference on Artificial Intelligence and Statistics, pp. 1723–1732. PMLR (2019)
25. Taslaman, L., Nilsson, B.: A framework for regularized non-negative matrix factorization, with application to the analysis of gene expression data. PloS one **7**(11), e46331 (2012)
26. Zdunek, R.: Regularized NNLS algorithms for nonnegative matrix factorization with application to text document clustering. In: Computer Recognition Systems, vol. 4, pp. 757–766. Springer, Heidelberg (2011). https://doi.org/10.1007/978-3-642-20320-6_77
27. Zdunek, R.: Regularized nonnegative matrix factorization: geometrical interpretation and application to spectral unmixing. Int. J. Appl. Math. Comput. Sci. **24**(2), 233–247 (2014)
28. Zdunek, R., Cichocki, A.: Nonnegative matrix factorization with constrained second-order optimization. Signal Process. **87**(8), 1904–1916 (2007)
29. Zhang, Z., Xu, Y., Yang, J., Li, X., Zhang, D.: A survey of sparse representation: algorithms and applications. IEEE Access **3**, 490–530 (2015)
30. Zheng, C.-H., Huang, D.-S., Zhang, L., Kong, X.-Z.: Tumor clustering using nonnegative matrix factorization with gene selection. IEEE Trans. Inf. Technol. Biomed. **13**(4), 599–607 (2009)

Malicious Website Detection Through Deep Learning Algorithms

Norma Gutiérrez, Beatriz Otero$^{(\boxtimes)}$, Eva Rodríguez, and Ramon Canal

Universitat Politècnica de Catalunya (UPC), Barcelona, Spain
{norma,botero,evar,rcanal}@ac.upc.edu

Abstract. Traditional methods that detect malicious websites, such as blacklists, do not update frequently, and they cannot detect new attackers. A system capable of detecting malicious activity using Deep Learning (DL) has been proposed to address this need. Starting from a dataset that contains both malevolent and benign websites, classification is done by extracting, parsing, analysing, and preprocessing the data. Additionally, the study proposes a Feed-Forward Neural Network (FFNN) to classify each sample. We evaluate different combinations of neurons in the model and perform in-depth research of the best performing network. The results show up to 99.88% of detection of malicious websites and 2.61% of false hits in the testing phase (i.e. malicious websites classified as benign), and 1.026% in the validation phase.

Keywords: Network attacks · Deep learning · Feed Forward Neural Network · Preprocessing

1 Introduction

Web pages may contain numerous types of attacks that target web browsers vulnerabilities. Malicious web pages have become one of the most common security threats, as stated in Abdulghani [1]. These attacks run malware in the target system, intending to take control of it. This article aims to design a system that blocks malicious website attacks by identifying possible malicious web pages. Moreover, the work parts from existing URLs and extracts relevant information from them. The big data treatment is later used to gather existing vulnerabilities and malicious websites used in real environments. It creates a DL model to detect new emerging websites even before they are listed in a blacklist database. DL techniques enable us to model complex computational architectures, such as websites features, to predict data representation.

A defensive solution is developed by implementing this mechanism, meaning that malicious software cannot penetrate the private network (i.e. blocked by a firewall). Overall, the results show high effectiveness when using only website features. The main contributions of this work are the following:

– Creation of three different datasets (training, testing and validation) parting from existing URLs and extracting data directly from the internet.

© Springer Nature Switzerland AG 2022
G. Nicosia et al. (Eds.): LOD 2021, LNCS 13163, pp. 512–526, 2022.
https://doi.org/10.1007/978-3-030-95467-3_37

- Extract and preprocess raw website data differentiating the most important attributes.
- Develop a DL NN that uses existing patterns in malicious web pages to detect malicious websites in real environments.

The system is divided into two main parts: the dataset creation and training of the model and the system's validation and detection. Firstly, the training and testing URLs are passed through feature extraction and labelling and are preprocessed, as explained later in the thesis. Furthermore, once the datasets are computed, an FFNN is created, and the data is passed to train and test the model's validity. The training process is fine tunned and repeated until a suitable NN is found. On the other hand, the second block parts from a validation set of URLs. Then, the same features as in the training and testing datasets are extracted, and the model is used to predict the sample's output. The actual label is stored in the validation dataset and compared with the predicted values to compute classification metrics. Lastly, the classification phase describes the process that an inputted URL from a user would follow. First, the user enters the URL, then the system extracts the necessary features and predicts the output from the URL (benign or malicious).

The remainder of this paper is organized as follows. Section 2 describes the related work. Section 3 and 4 illustrate the dataset and its preprocessing. Then, Sect. 5 explains the used Neural Network, and Sect. 6 describes the experiments and presents the results. We draw the main conclusions in Sect. 7.

2   Related Work

Our proposal focuses on a non-simulated dataset where features from different websites are extracted (malicious and benign). Furthermore, our data comprises the URL and characteristics associated with it, such as the related continent and its JavaScript content length. These features are simple to obtain and simpler to treat than other attributes such as the HTTP or CSS content.

Chiba et al. [2] propose a system that can detect a malicious or benign website by only analyzing the IP characteristics. They create a dataset extracting campus traffic. The article preprocesses the data separating the address by bits and applies two different Machine Learning algorithms (SVM and RBM). They achieve a maximum of 90% accuracy. In contrast, our proposal uses DL techniques, and the dataset does not use IP information. Instead, it uses the URL and the JavaScript content length. Using more features enables us to make a more precise model than the one proposed by Chiba et al.

Moreover, Xuan et al. [9] uses the URL features to extract dynamic behaviours and train them with two supervised ML algorithms (Support Vector Machine and Random Forest). The differences with the presented system are that they use far more URL features than we do, expanding the computational needs of the network. Plus, they apply ML algorithms, whereas, in our system, DL techniques are applied. Finally, their performance is less than ours, having a 3% less accuracy, 4% less precision, and 1% less recall.

Saxe et al. [5] use HTML, CSS and embedded JavaScript (JS) files; they analyze the data and create a model. First, they pass the data through an SVM and then through a DL model. The model detects up to 97% of malicious traffic and can identify content not previously caught by the vendor community. Our approach reduces the data analyzed while also achieving a higher detection rate (i.e. instead of HTML, CSS and JS content, our proposal uses URL and IP information and the JS length).

Uçar et al. [8] develop two DL models (CNN and LSTM) that add to a blacklist malicious URLs. The models detect the type of data and classify it. It achieves up to 98.86% accuracy in the CNN network. The main distinctions between our approach and this paper are: (1) the type of Neural Network used. They use a more complex Neural Network. Thus their proposal uses more resources than our proposal. (2) their dataset only contains URL information, whereas our data also contains the continent and the JS length.

Another similar approach is presented by Johnson et al. [3]. The article presents the same problem as in this project; a binary classifier detecting if the URL is malicious or benign. Nevertheless, it adds a second multi-class classification that detects the type of attack. Overall, the article adds a further step to the classification to detect the type of attack but obtain a far more complicated NN and 2% less accuracy than in our system.

Finally, Sahoo et al. [4] propose a survey that gives a structural understanding of Malicious URL detection techniques using Machine Learning. The survey separates two types of families when detecting Malicious URLs: Blacklisting/heuristic approaches or Machine Learning techniques. The survey only talks about mathematical Machine Learning algorithms that previous literature has implemented, such as SVM, Logistic Regression, Decision Trees, and online learning. We advance the state-of-the-art presented in that survey by developing DL techniques to classify previously unseen data.

Our final approach uses DL to train the NN since the quantity of data enabled us to perform a model with outstanding performance. Furthermore, the chosen model was an FFNN, which was chosen since it is the most common approach for supervised learning with binary classification datasets. Also, an FFNN needs less computation than the other DL approaches mentioned above. Consequently, the resulting NN presents outstanding results. A comparison table with the presented related works and this project can be found in Table 1.

3   Dataset

To create a DL model capable of distinguishing malicious websites, we modified the existing dataset *Visualisation of Malicious & Benign Web-pages Dataset (VoMBWeb)* [6] since the dataset was fitted to our solution but lacked consistency. Thus, the system starts from a list of URLs captured from malign and benign websites and extracts the necessary information to be later trained and correctly classified. The features were extracted from each URL crawling the

Table 1. Summary of the related works to malicious website detection using ML/DL techniques

Publication year	Work reference	Dataset	ML or/and DL	Used algorithm	Maximum accuracy
2012	[2]	From blacklists and campus information	ML	SVM and RBM	85.7%
2018	[5]	Own compilation	ML and DL	FFNN and SVM	97.2%
2019	[8]	ISCX-URL-2016 data	DL	LSTM and CNN	98.86% with CNN
2020	[9]	Own compilation	ML	SVM and RF	99.7% with RF
2020	[3]	ISCX-URL-2016 data	DL and ML	Fast.ia, Keras and Random Forest (RF)	97.55% with RF

internet. The data is extracted from three separate categories: the IP, the URL and the content. The primary group is the URL group, parsed and treated as shown in Fig. 1.

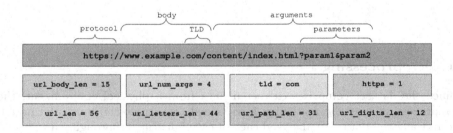

Fig. 1. Example of URL preprocessing

The first part of the URL is the protocol. The $HTTPS$ feature is extracted; in the example, we have a *https* value, so the value of the feature is 1. Secondly, the body is computed where two different features are extracted, its length (*url_body_len*) and the Top Level Domain (*tld*). The third part of the URL includes the arguments where they are quantified (*url_num_args*), and their length (*url_digits_len*) is computed. Finally, to treat the URL globally, the URL's length (*url_len*), the number of digits and symbols that it contains (*url_digits_length*), and the number of letters (*url_letters_len*) are computed.

The next group is the IP. Firstly the IP associated with the URL is extracted (*ip_addr*) as the continent where the IP address is located (*continent*). Since more than 300 countries were initially defined in the dataset, the values were grouped by continent. Furthermore, treating each country individually does not give any additional information than by doing it by continent.

Once all the IP and URL features are extracted and treated, the website's content is withdrawn. The obtained content is the one located inside the JS code. Furthermore, the content was filtered to remove spaces, code, and punctuation. Once all was computed, the cleaned JS content was saved (*content*), such as its length in KBytes (*js_len*).

The final feature inserted in the dataset is the label, which has a binary value, depending on if the website is malicious (1.0) or benign (0.0). Hence, the created dataset has a total of 15 features.

Moreover, the dataset is divided into two parts, a training dataset (containing 1200000 samples) and a testing dataset (containing 350000 samples). In the whole dataset, 27253 websites (values) are considered malicious, while 1172747 are considered benign, having far more benign websites than malign ones. In the testing dataset, the same happens with 7828 malicious samples and 342172 benign samples. Hence the dataset is mainly represented by benign websites, such as illustrated in Table 2.

Table 2. Samples and percentage of benign and malicious websites in the dataset

VoMBWeb	Benign websites	Malicious websites
Number of samples	1514919	35081
(%)	97.74%	2.26%

4   Preprocessing

Since the dataset comprises extracted data from a physical environment, the preprocessing must be meticulously designed to extract the best information from the given data. We analyzed each of the 15 features thoroughly and tested it before deciding on a particular technique.

The dataset contains eight numerical features (*entropy*, *url_len*, *url_body_len*, *url_num_args*, *url_path_len*, *url_letters_len*, *url_digits_len* and *js_len*), two binary features (*https* and *label*), and features that have categorical values or require specific treatment (*ip_addr*, *url*, *continent*, *tld* and *content*).

Firstly, the continent in which the web page is hosted is preprocessed (*continent*). The parameter was converted to a one-hot encoding. A one-hot encoding consists of passing the categorical feature into a table where each column represents a different value; hence, we created a new feature per existing continent. The column which continent corresponds to the sample will be marked as 1; otherwise, the value is marked as 0. Thus, after the *continent* preprocessing, it had six new binary features, one for each continent.

Next, the Top Level Domain (TLD) preprocessing was performed. Since more than 600 different values were computed, the preprocessing concentrated on the *.com* domain. The *.com* domain constitutes a total of 60% of the final data. Consequently, it acts as a suitable separator. Therefore, the feature was stored whether the TLD is *.com* or not.

All URL, IP and *content* features were deleted since they are thoroughly represented in other features and do not give additional information. Furthermore, the IP address was initially converted into a binary sequence, and the model was trained with the parameter. However, the results showed less performance than without this feature. Additionally, as each web page must be parsed differently, and no clear and helpful patterns were found, the *content* feature was deleted during the preprocessing. Moreover, all numerical values were normalized, and the binary parameters passed through a binary one-hot encoding. The label was transformed using a binary one-hot encoding with a 1 value if it is considered malicious (bad) and 0 if the website is deemed to be benign (good). This process is depicted in Fig. 2.

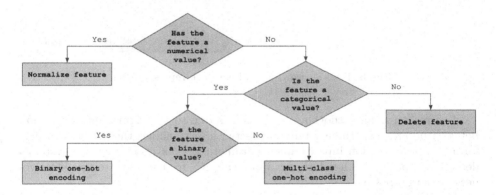

Fig. 2. Preprocessing flowchart

All the preprocessing is applied to the training, testing and validation datasets. The dataset has been divided into three sections:

- Training dataset with 1200000 samples
- Testing dataset with 350000 samples
- Validation dataset with 10000 samples

Having three distinct portions of datasets allowed to train the model with a vast amount of data. Then by testing the model, we assured the performance was the desired and that there was no over or underfitting. Once the model was trained and ready, the model was exported and saved. Next, the project validated the model by predicting the label of 10000 samples (containing 195 malicious samples). We then compared the obtained labels with the expected ones and analyzed the outputs.

5   Deep Learning Application

Given the preprocessed dataset generated, we propose the implementation of a Fully Connected Neural Network, specifically a Feed-Forward Neural Network (FFNN) depicted in Fig. 3.

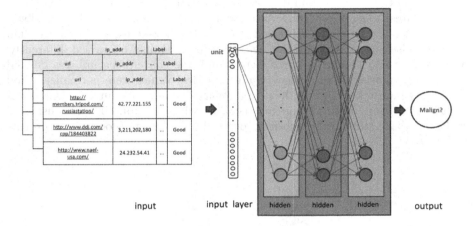

Fig. 3. Feed-Forward Neural Network representation

The reason behind choosing an FFNN is due to the significant connection between parameters. Having fully connected layers enables the network to perform complex relationships between parameters, thus improving the system's detection capability. Therefore, we apply this NN to demonstrate the effectiveness of the proposal.

An FFNN is described using several design parameters that conform a model where the training data is introduced. Additionally, the model's algorithm is run for several iterations or epochs. To avoid under or overfitting and to achieve good performance, the model parameters must be carefully chosen. Therefore, the proposed architecture has an input layer, three hidden layers and an output layer that uses the *Sigmoid* activation function. Each layer uses an activation function and has several neurons. In the model, the hidden layers use a *Rectified Linear Unit* (ReLU) activation function since they avoid saturation and do not stop to shape the sample weights. The input layer has an input size of 17 features. Furthermore, the first hidden layer has 64 neurons; the second layer contracts the values to 32 neurons. Finally, the third hidden layer has 64 neurons.

The final parameters that define the Neural Network are the loss, optimizer and epochs (or iterations). A *Binary cross-entropy loss* is used on the resulting vectors since it calculates the prediction error in a binary measure, just as we need for our output. The optimizer aims to sculpt the model into a precise form and to minimize the loss. We use *Adam* [7], which achieves good performance in few epochs. Finally, the number of epochs is set to 10, which is a good compromise between stability and over-training.

6 Experiments and Results

The correct implementation of the preprocessing was tested through the analysis of the correlation between attributes (correlation matrix). In the sample's preprocessing, it is crucial that parameters can be easily distinguishable by the network. Moreover, attributes are interconnected in the dataset. This interconnection can be seen in the feature correlation matrices. Performing these experiments, we can decide the optimal NN use, its parameters and identify non-useful attributes.

Secondly, to implement the NN depicted in the previous section, we started by implementing different combinations of FFNNs. The number of hidden layers was decided according to the dataset characteristics. In total, the dataset had an input of 17 attributes, meaning that the number of training samples considerably exceeds the number of attributes. With that in mind and the attributes dependency, we opted for medium-sized FFNN. Having less hidden layers allows the model to have a minor abstraction of the features, and having a more significant number of hidden layers allows the model to be over-complex. Additionally, to decide the number of neurons of each hidden layer, we analyzed all the possible combinations from 16 to 512 neurons (in powers of two), meaning that in total, we run 56 different FFNN ($CR_3^6 = \frac{(6+3-1)!}{3!(8-3)!} = 56$).

Furthermore, we analyzed the most frequently used metrics: accuracy, loss, Area Under the Curve (AUC), and f-score for these networks. These metrics allow us to have an extensive analysis of the network's performance.

Firstly, the accuracy is defined as the True Positives (TP) plus the True Negatives (TN) divided by the sum of TP, TN, False Positives (FP) and False Negatives (FN). The formula is represented in Eq. 1.

$$Accuracy = \frac{TP + TN}{TP + TN + FP + FN} \tag{1}$$

Secondly, the defined loss is the binary cross-entropy loss which formula is represented in Eq. 2. Note that the y value represents the real output, whereas the $\hat{y}$ represents the output estimation.

$$Loss = -[y \cdot log(\hat{y}) + (1 - y) \cdot log(1 - \hat{y})] \tag{2}$$

Next, the f-score is defined as a mixture of the precision and recall formulas to evaluate the combined performance. F-score is defined as in Eq. 3.

$$F - Score = 2 \cdot \frac{Precision \cdot Recall}{Precision + Recall} \tag{3}$$

where the precision is defined in Eq. 4, and the recall is defined in Eq. 5.

$$Precision = \frac{TP}{TP + FP} \quad (4) \qquad Recall = \frac{TP}{TP + FN} \quad (5)$$

Finally, the AUC shows the performance of a classification model. It is defined as the area that defines the ROC curve, which is the graphical representation of the True Positive Rate (TPR) vs the False Positive Rate (FPR). The TPR is defined as in Eq. 6, and the FPR is defined as in Eq. 7.

$$TPR = \frac{TP}{TP + FN} \quad (6) \qquad FPR = \frac{FP}{FP + TN} \quad (7)$$

The same metrics from the validation data was analyzed to extract further conclusions.

In the experiments, we perform 20 iterations of the three best performing FFNNs to ensure their stability. 20 iterations were chosen since it was crucial to assure the network's consistency. However, we did not want to over-charge the cloud server with redundant calculations.

Furthermore, Python was the language used to execute the system, and Keras from Tensorflow was used to create the DL blocking system. Moreover, the system has been created using a MacBook Air computer with a Dual-Core Intel Core i5 and 8 GB of RAM. The university's cluster, Sert, was used (AMD EPYC 7101p at 2.80 GHz and 128 GB of RAM) to filter the data.

6.1 Preprocessing Results

To test the data preprocessing and its relevance in the dataset, several experiments were conducted. Firstly, we parted from the VoMBWeb dataset [6] since it included some of the attributes we wanted to treat and generated in a non-simulated environment. Considering that Keras from TensorFlow needs as an input a tensor of NumPy arrays, the multi-class attributes were converted into a one-hot encoding, the IP was binarized, the webpage content was deleted, and all arguments were normalized. Once this preprocessing was performed, we observed some concerns with the dataset structure.

This dataset's main issue was that once performed the correlation matrix. The resulting values were very dispersed between the different attributes. There, it could be observed that the IP address did not give any additional information since its correlation was nearly zero. Furthermore, treating each country independently added more than 300 features and gave misguided directions to the DL model. However, the main issue was that the dataset relied exclusively on the JS obfuscated length, meaning that the FFNN only modelled its weights regarding that feature. Hence, the dataset was modified to remove this dependency and add some relevant features that enable the FFNN to train correctly. The JS obfuscated length attribute was removed from the original dataset, the country feature was grouped into continents, and the TLD was treated by distinguishing only by .com or otherwise. With this modification, the homogeneity in the features' correlation increased.

Since the URL is the only input received from the user, we decided to extract as many attributes as possible from the input. The main goal was to find the balance between extracting trainable features and having unnecessary or misguiding information inserted into the NN. The final decision was to include at least one attribute from each URL subdivision (the URL, the protocol, the body, the TLD, the arguments and the parameters) as seen in Fig. 4.

Fig. 4. URL subdivisions

Additionally, we decided to add three more attributes that gave connections between the URL attributes. Those features were the URL entropy, the URL letters length and the URL letters and digits length.

Once all the preprocessing was done and transformed into numerical values, we performed a final analysis of the dataset. First, to study the parameters' dependence and relevance, a new correlation matrix was performed with all the final preprocessed attributes. The correlation matrix can be seen in Fig. 5.

If we look at the label column, we observe the most and least interconnected parameters. The most correlated parameters are *js_len*, *https* and *who_is*, which contain a correlation between 0.24 and 0.72, meaning that these parameters are crucial for detecting malicious websites. The parameters, such as *who_is* and *https*, which have a negative correlation, indicate an inverse proportion between the label and the selected parameter. All the remaining attributes have at least some correlation with the matrix. They are highly correlated with other parameters, which improves the FFNN since it is a type of NN that relies mainly on feature interconnection and dependence.

Having performed this study, we believe that it is wise to use all the depicted parameters for evaluation in the NN. Moreover, since the parameters are correlated between them, and each column depends on other attributes, FFNNs are the best fit.

6.2   Neural Network Results

After preprocessing, we run the different combinations of the FFNNs. As commented in the previous section, we conducted two sets of experiments in the Neural Networks. The first set analyzed the performance of variations of several neurons in each layer and the network's depth. The second set consists of the repeated execution of the three best performing FFNN and the performance evaluation.

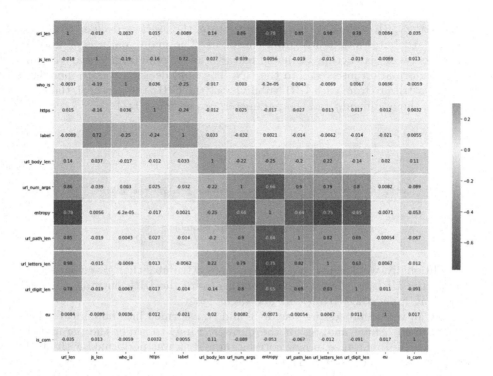

Fig. 5. Preprocessed dataset parameter correlation matrix

To finalize the network topology, we had to decide the number of layers the FFNN would have as the number of neurons in them. We conducted three different FFNNs with a low count of neurons. The reason behind having fewer neurons in each layer is that a higher neuron count adds extra complexity to the FFNN. The number of layers is directly related to the number of attributes we have (17 in total). Hence, we tried networks with 2, 3 and 4 layers. The FFNN with two layers indicated low network complexity and a lack of resources to be trained. The other two networks showed similar accuracy. Since having four layers adds complexity and computation consumption to the network, it was decided to perform the FFNN with three hidden layers. The results are shown in Table 3.

Once the number of layers was determined, we conducted 56 different combinations of FFNNs to decide the best fit. When performed the FFNNs variations, we observed certain similarities between results. First, all the networks achieved high performance in all metrics oscillating between 94.81% and 99.88%. These results indicate that the election of an FFNN with the selected loss, optimizer, activation function and epochs is ideal. The best performing networks have a minimum of 32 neurons in each layer and 64 or more neurons in -at least- one of the layers. Table 4 shows the results for the three best-performing

Table 3. Performance of three different FFNNs with different number of layers

Neurons	Loss	Accuracy	AUC	F-score
16-8	0.31%	98.98%	99.95%	97.22%
16-8-16	0.30%	99.88%	99.93%	97.30%
16-8-16-8	0.31%	99.88%	99.95%	97.34%

networks. The results of these networks are very similar. Note that the Neurons column represents the number of neurons inside each hidden layer, represented as *neurons_hidden_1* - *neurons_hidden_2* - *neurons_hidden_3*.

Table 4. Testing performance for the three best FFNNs with three layers and variation of the amount neurons per layer

Neurons	Loss	Accuracy	AUC	F-score
64-32-64	0.30%	99.88%	99.95%	97.42%
32-64-32	0.47%	99.88%	99.79%	97.22%
128-64-32	0.46%	99.87%	99.75%	97.01%

The best performing network (and the one used in the system) is the first one (64-32-64) since the loss decreases and f-score increases compared with the other two, and it is the most stable network with lesser differences between attributes than the others. Furthermore, the network is relatively small, meaning that it is a computationally efficient network.

Figure 6 shows the mean of all the different metrics used for the best network when executed a total of 20 times. The network achieves 99.88% of detection with the validation data and only ten epochs, giving a high detection rate using little resources. As for the AUC, the network achieves 99.95% in validation data. Indicating that the performance of the classification model is almost 100%, thus demonstrating its effectiveness. The loss value is less than 0.5% in all executions, meaning that the model does not have over or underfitting. Besides, the f-score achieves 97.42% with the validation data. The f-score helps us to understand the model's combined performance. A high f-score reiterates the network effectiveness showing high AUC, accuracy and performance in all studied metrics. Consequently, the proposed system is very effective in detecting malicious websites.

Finally, we compute the TP (True Positives), TN (True Negatives), FP (False Positives) and FN (False Negatives) of the selected network. The TP represents the samples that belong to a malicious website and is correctly classified. FN represents the samples that belong to malicious websites that are wrongly classified. The sum of TP and FN denote all the existing malicious websites. On the other hand, TN represents the benign samples that are correctly classified, and

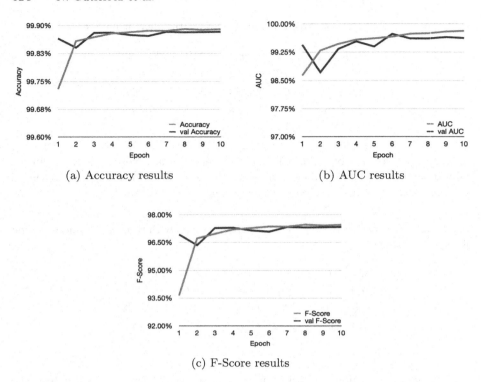

(a) Accuracy results   (b) AUC results

(c) F-Score results

Fig. 6. Mean performance for the best operating FFNN (64-32-64) in 20 iterations

FP the benign samples that are wrongly classified. Together TN and FP denote all existing benign websites. The final goal of the system is to detect all malicious websites without misclassifying any sample, which means that the network has to minimize the FN rate. Table 5 shows the training and validation results of these metrics after the tenth epoch. The results show that the FN rate in the validation data is only 2.619%. In other words, only 205 of the 8062 malicious websites are erroneously classified as benign. We can also observe that the FN rate decreases in the validation phase. This decrease indicates that there is still room for improvement in the network (i.e. adding more data and re-training the network).

As commented in the preprocessing section, the dataset was divided into three different parts. The final testing of the system consists of passing through the trained network the validation datasets (containing 10000 samples). The final analysis results show a total number of wrongly classified malicious websites (a total of 1.026%) and accuracy of 99.75%. These results show a clear identification and classification of malicious websites. Overall, these outcomes demonstrate the effectiveness of our system since almost all malicious websites will be filtered, and they will not penetrate the system.

Table 5. True Positive (TP), True Negative (TN), False Positive (FP) and False Negative (FN) for the best performing network (64-32-64) with 10 epochs

Data	TP	TN	FP	FN
Training (%)	25910 (95.070%)	1172698 (99.999%)	48 (0.001%)	1343 (4.930%)
Validation (%)	7623 (97.381%)	341977 (99.994%)	196 (0.006%)	205 (2.619%)

Furthermore, a comparison with traditional Machine Learning algorithms, such as Random Forest (RF), Logistic Regression (LR) and Gaussian Naïve Bayes (GNB), was performed. The results show a similar accuracy and f-score, but the Loss and AUC results decrease considerably. Furthermore, the use of DL is chosen due to its supremacy in performance when using large quantities of data such as in the depicted project. Hence, DL trains quickly and effectively large subsets of data, contrary to traditional ML algorithms. The results for all approaches are depicted in Fig. 6.

Table 6. Testing performance for RF, LR and GNB algorithms

Algorithm	Loss	Accuracy	AUC	F-score
RF	24%	99.88%	97.99%	97.34%
LR	16%	99.82%	96.43%	96.29%
GNB	19%	99.80%	97.27%	95.69%
FFNN (ours)	0.30%	99.88%	99.95%	97.42%

7 Conclusions

Malicious URL detection plays a critical role for many cybersecurity applications, and clearly, Machine Learning approaches are a promising direction. The importance of this detection remains in assuring the user a safe browsing, blocking the non-desired content. This work proposes a study on Malicious URL Detection using DL techniques. The proposed system evaluates the website's features, and it classifies them by preprocessing and entering them in a DL model. We evaluate a real dataset that extracts basic features of real websites (malicious and benign) to conduct the study. Furthermore, we measured the dispersion and correlation between the dataset's features to observe the label separability and the feature interconnections.

Moreover, we proposed an FFNN to compute the classification of the labels. The proposed mechanism achieves a 99.88% accuracy, 99.95% AUC and 97.42% f-score. Furthermore, the proposed NN only incorrectly classifies 2.619% of the malicious websites. This slight inaccuracy is due to the complexity of identifying all possible patterns out of malicious content. Additionally, a validation process was performed, the results showed only a 1.026% of inaccuracy in wrongly classified malicious websites, thus decreasing the error.

As future works, the system can be improved by adding more data and retraining the network. Moreover, the NN could be adapted to be automatically updated. An automatization would mean that the NN would improve with every NN search and add new features into the model.

Acknowledgments. This work was supported in part by the Catalan Government, through the program 2017-SGR-962 and the RIS3CAT DRAC project.

References

1. Abdulghani, A.: Malicious website detection: a review. J. Forensic Sci. Crim. Invest. **7** (2018). https://doi.org/10.19080/JFSCI.2018.07.555712
2. Chiba, D., Tobe, K., Mori, T., Goto, S.: Detecting malicious websites by learning IP address features. In: 2012 IEEE/IPSJ 12th International Symposium on Applications and the Internet (SAINT), pp. 29–39 (2012). https://doi.org/10.1109/SAINT.2012.14
3. Johnson, C., Basnet, B.K.R.B., Doleck, T.: Towards detecting and classifying malicious urls using deep learning. J. Wirel. Mob. Netw. Ubiq. Comput. Depend. Appl. (JoWUA) (2020). https://doi.org/10.22667/JOWUA.2020.12.31.031
4. Sahoo, D., Liu, C., Hoi, S.C.H.: Malicious url detection using machine learning: a survey (2019)
5. Saxe, J., Harang, R., Wild, C., Sanders, H.: A deep learning approach to fast, format-agnostic detection of malicious web content (2018)
6. Singh, A.K.: Dataset of malicious and benign webpages (2020). https://doi.org/10.17632/gdx3pkwp47.2, https://data.mendeley.com/datasets/gdx3pkwp47/2
7. TensorFlow: tf.keras.optimizers.adam (2020). https://www.tensorflow.org/api_docs/python/tf/keras/optimizers/Adam
8. Uçar, E., Ucar, M., İncetaş, M.: A deep learning approach for detection of malicious urls. In: International Management Information Systems Conference (2019)
9. Xuan, C., Dinh, H., Victor, T.: Malicious url detection based on machine learning. International J. Adv. Comput. Sci. Appl. **11** (2020). https://doi.org/10.14569/IJACSA.2020.0110119

Deep Learning Detection of GPS Spoofing

Olivia Jullian[1], Beatriz Otero[1(✉)], Mirjana Stojilović[2], Juan José Costa[1],
Javier Verdú[1], and Manuel Alejandro Pajuelo[1]

[1] Universitat Politècnica de Catalunya, Barcelona, Spain
{ojulian,botero,jcosta,jverdu,mpajuelo}@ac.upc.edu
[2] EPFL, Lausanne, Switzerland
mirjana.stojilovic@epfl.ch

Abstract. Unmanned aerial vehicles (UAVs) are widely deployed in air
navigation, where numerous applications use them for safety-of-life and
positioning, navigation, and timing tasks. Consequently, GPS spoofing
attacks are more and more frequent. The aim of this work is to enhance
GPS systems of UAVs, by providing the ability of detecting and preventing spoofing attacks. The proposed solution is based on a multilayer
perceptron neural network, which processes the flight parameters and
the GPS signals to generate alarms signalling GPS spoofing attacks.
The obtained accuracy lies between 83.23% for TEXBAT dataset and
99.93% for MAVLINK dataset.

Keywords: Deep learning · Intrusion detection model · Unmanned
aerial vehicles · Spoofing · Global navigation satellite system

1 Introduction

Smart devices, such as unmanned aerial vehicles (UAVs), are widely deployed
in our society. For every mission, these devices strongly rely on their communications system [11], which is typically based on the Internet of Things (IoT)
networks and GPS channels.

In the UAV world, GPS-based systems face two main threats: *jamming* and
spoofing attacks [11]. In a jamming attack, the attacker goal is a denial-of-service
(DoS), so that the UAV is unable to receive the GPS signal. In a spoofing attack,
the attacker creates a replica of the GPS signal and boosts its power, for it
to become the positioning reference of the UAV. The increased power affects
the correlation between the signals from the GPS and the navigation system.
Consequently, once the spoofed signal is sent to the UAV, the latter ignores the
real GPS signal [18] and starts drifting from the original path.

During a spoofing attack, the target UAV is unable to immediately detect
the drift because, if the attack is executed well, there are no abrupt changes
in the received GPS signal strength. Additionally, there is no knowledge of the
correct position to help the UAV notice the drift. For these reasons, the spoofing
attacks are hard to detect.

© Springer Nature Switzerland AG 2022
G. Nicosia et al. (Eds.): LOD 2021, LNCS 13163, pp. 527–540, 2022.
https://doi.org/10.1007/978-3-030-95467-3_38

Research studies on the detection and prevention of spoofing attacks are suggesting that deep neural networks (DNNs) have great potential. However, their suitability is not fully understood nor comprehensively verified on publicly-available spoofing-attack datasets.

The main contributions of this work are:

- design and software implementation of a multilayer perceptron (MLP) and a long short-term memory (LSTM) DNN for the spoofing-attack detection,
- comparison of their accuracies on MAVLINK and TEXBAT datasets,
- selection of the best DNN for the intrusion detection (ID) framework,
- retraining of the designed models for an additional function—prevention of spoofing attacks (by generating an early alarm for the UAV before the spoofing attack starts), and
- comparison to other machine-learning/deep-learning solutions proposed in the literature.

In the remainder of this paper, Sect. 2 describes the spoofing attacks. Section 3 presents the approaches proposed. Section 4 describes the related work. Section 5 presents the intrusion detection framework. Section 6 discusses the DNN model design and training. Then, Sect. 7 gives the experimental results. Finally, the conclusions are given in Sect. 8.

2   GPS Spoofing Attacks

Communication between the GPS satellites and the UAVs is needed to obtain the flight path of a UAV and for navigation. UAVs use at least four satellites to navigate. Moreover, GPS satellites provide the position reference to the UAVs [20]. Sensors such as inertial measurement units, magnetometers, and gyroscopes are often deployed, for increased precision and security [20].

During navigation, a malicious signal can become the reference for the UAV, even though it is not generated by a GPS satellite. The presence of such a signal defines a spoofing attack. Merwe et al. [9] presented a classification of spoofing attacks considering various aspects, such as synchronization between the original and the spoofed signal, the number of antennas required to attack the vehicle, or the spoofed signal generation.

In an asynchronous attack, the attacker does not monitor the reference GPS signal of the target. Creating a spoofed signal without the knowledge of the reference entails differences in signal characteristics and, simply, a different position being sent to the UAV. Thus, in an asynchronous attack, abrupt position changes are communicated to the UAV, making these attacks easier to detect than synchronous attacks [8].

In a synchronous spoofing attack [8], the attacker tracks the target UAV. Therefore, it knows the target's exact location, which allows the attacker to receive the corresponding reference GPS signal. The attacker creates a spoofed signal by replicating the reference and slightly increasing the power of this new signal. The spoofed signal, once sent back to the target, becomes the new reference, precisely because of its higher power. Additionally, the attacker becomes able to relocate the target by changing the reference signal characteristics.

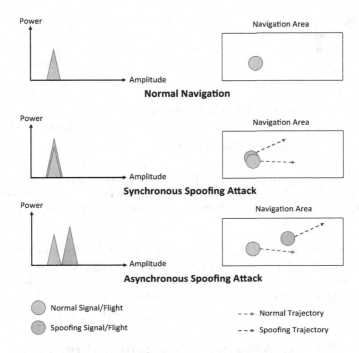

Fig. 1. Synchronous versus asynchronous spoofing attacks.

Figure 1 illustrates the differences between an asynchronous and a synchronous spoofing attack. In this figure, the synchronous spoofing signal is aligned with the reference signal, which is why the target can start drifting without being aware of the attack. On the other hand, in an asynchronous attack, the spoofing signal is not synchronized, which causes an abrupt change in the target's position and makes the attack easier to detect.

For the above mentioned and other limitations of asynchronous spoofing attacks (e.g., listed by Merwe et al. [9]), this work focuses on detection and prevention of the more serious threats: synchronous spoofing attacks [8].

3   Proposed Approaches

After presenting the threat of spoofing attacks and understanding their impact on the UAVs, we present here our strategies for the detection and prevention of synchronous spoofing attacks (illustrated in Fig. 2).

3.1   Intrusion Detection Framework for Spoofing Attack Detection

First, we propose to design an intrusion detection (ID) software framework for detecting GPS spoofing attacks. The detection will be done using only the flight

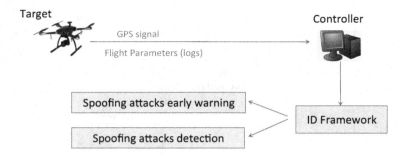

Fig. 2. Illustration of our proposed solution for synchronous spoofing attack detection and prevention; it involves a flight controller, a communication channel between the target and the controller, and a software intrusion detection framework (DNN-based).

parameters collected during one measurement cycle (e.g., one clock cycle). Communication between the flight controller and the target UAV device serves to offload the flight parameters and the GPS signal characteristics from the device. The flight controller then analyzes the received data and, with the help of the ID framework, detects the attack and signals an alarm.

3.2 Early-Warning Alarm for Spoofing Attack Prevention

In the same line of research, another approach is considered here: The ID framework described previously should also be able to generate an alarm for warning that a spoofing attack may be taking place. To that purpose, the flight parameters collected during several subsequent measurement cycles need to be processed (e.g., GPS signal power, GPS signal amplitude, changes in the UAV orientation, system status changes, etc.).

4   Related Work

4.1   Techniques for GPS Spoofing Attack Detection

In the last decade, a number of research studies focused on aircraft and navigation security problems. In the recent couple of years, UAVs have become increasingly popular and, consequently, their security vulnerabilities. Most common threats to UAVs rely on the IoT protocols or on the GPS communication.

M. P. Arthur [1] categorizes the UAV threats in three types: navigation attacks (hijacking), routing attacks (based on the IoT network), and data attacks (where data is stolen from hijacked drones). Related to navigation attacks, jamming and spoofing attacks are identified as the main threats.

Several works address detection of the spoofing attacks. Morales-Ferre et al. [10] use the Monte Carlo approach to compare two detectors: the sum of squares detector and the D^3 detector. E. Shafie et al. [18] take a more traditional approach: They test models such as a Bayesian classifier and the K-Nearest

Neighbour (K-NN) classifier, achieving accuracies of 62.31% and 77.29%, respectively, when detecting a synchronous spoofing attack.

Ranganathan et al. [16] develop SPREE, an approach for synchronous spoofing attacks detection. SPREE is a software-radio solution based on tracking the reference as well as the auxiliary GPS signals, by allocating more than one channel to the same satellite.

In the next section, we survey the use of deep learning (DL) techniques and identify the most promising candidates for our intrusion detection framework.

4.2   Deep Learning for GPS Spoofing Attack Detection

S. Semanjski et al. [17] used support vector machines (SVMs) to detect spoofed signals while lifeguard systems are flying. Despite the improvement in accuracy compared to non-ML-based techniques, in the same research [17] the authors conclude that the ML methods (in particular, SVM) are not sufficient. The reason lies in the nonlinear characteristics of the attacks. To deal with nonlinear data, the authors use kernels SVM (to transform nonlinear attack characteristics to linear ones through mathematical algorithms)—they attach many kernels to an SVM detector, achieving 94.41% accuracy.

Unsupervised DL techniques are also used to create datasets from the UAV sensor readings. It is the case of the work of M.P. Arthur et al.[1], where self-taught learning was used to develop a new dataset. An SVM model is used in the previous dataset with an accuracy of 94% with a framework installed in the UAV.

E. Shafie et al. applied an MLP model to detect spoofing attacks with a 99.3% accuracy [18]. Another DL approach [12] used convolutional neural networks (CNNs), achieving 94% to 99% accuracy.

In the research of G. Bae et al. [2], a distributed DL framework is presented, which reduces the training time per epoch from 30 to 5 s using an autoencoder-based LSTM model. In the work by K. H. Park et al. [14], an autoencoder (AE) is used to predict spoofing attacks during a flight.

In Table 1, we summarize the results of the previous studies on synchronous spoofing attack detection using deep learning techniques. The table compares MLP, C-SVM, LSTM-AE, self-taught learning, and AE-based approaches. Their accuracies range between 93.4% and 99%. An important drawback of these studies is the use of synthetic datasets and the lack of comparison to other DL models. Only one general dataset (based on simulated flight parameters) was used to test spoofing attacks detection [14], but no common metrics for comparing to other studies were considered. Hence, a comprehensive comparison of various DL techniques for detecting GPS spoofing attacks using a common dataset is still missing. In this work, we address the above issue by comparing our DNN models to SVM and random forest models, using the same datasets (Sect. 7).

The lack of a general dataset for spoofing attacks makes it difficult to choose the most suitable framework for spoofing attack detection. However, after comparing the ML and DL approaches presented in previous studies [1,15,18], we can conclude that the DL techniques are most promising. Moreover, they are proven

Table 1. Survey of synchronous attack detectors based on deep learning models.

Model	Metrics	Dataset
MLP [18]	ACC (99.3%)	Synthetic
C-SVM [17]	ACC (94.41%)	Synthetic
LSTM-AE [2]	ROC/ACC(93.4%)	Sensors data
Self-taught learning [1]	ACC (94%)	Sensors data
AE [14]	Error attack (0.25)/F1-score (94.81%)	MAVLINK

suitable not only for detection but also for prediction (and thus prevention) of an attack [14].

5   DL Models in Our Intrusion Detection Framework

5.1   MLP for GPS Spoofing Attack Detection

One of the objectives of this work is the comparison between MLP and LSTM deep-learning models, as an integral step of the design of an ID framework for spoofing attacks detection. The choice of MLP is motivated by the excellent accuracies reported in previous works, reaching 99% in the Meaconer attacks (i.e., denial-of-service attacks).

An MLP model is composed of a number of layers (some of which are hidden), in which the training flow follows one direction only (from the input towards the output layer). Additionally, MLP is a fully-connected neural network, in which the units in subsequent layers are fully interconnected, and each connection is weighted. All the weights are combined together to compute the output of a unit using activation functions. Figure 3 shows an MLP model composed by four hidden layers. The exact details of the MLP model used in this work are given in Sect. 6.3.

5.2   LSTM for GPS Spoofing Attack Detection

Besides the MLP model, we develop an LSTM model. We use flight parameters and GPS signal characteristics as time-sequential data.

As the result of the overcoming of the recurrent neural network (RNN) gradient vanishing, LSTM generates the output of a unit using recurrently the connections among hidden units. Three gates take the control of the information flow: the input, the forget, and the output gate. These three gates allow the unit to calculate its state (using the input provided by the input gate). They also allow considering previous information from other units (decided by the forget gate). Finally, in an LSTM model, after the output of the unit is computed, the output gate decides whether or not to consider the previous information and transmits its decision to the unit through the forget gate. Figure 4 illustrates an LSTM model with three hidden layers. The exact details of the LSTM model used in this work are given in Sect. 6.3.

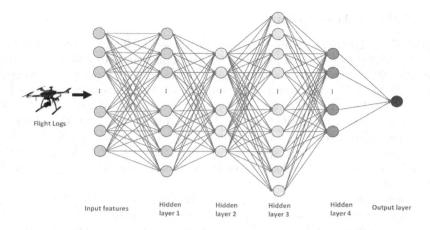

Fig. 3. An MLP for GPS spoofing attack detection.

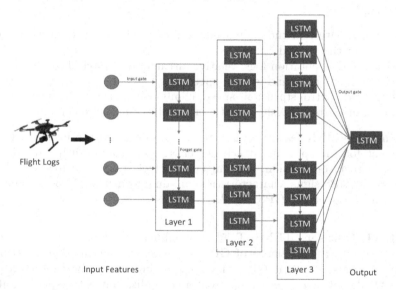

Fig. 4. An LSTM model for GPS spoofing attack detection.

6   Model Design and Training

To train and test the two DNN models presented in Sect. 5, we choose two datasets: Texas Spoofing Test Battery (i.e., TEXBAT [5]) and MAVLINK [19]. The comparison results will guide us in choosing better of the two models for the ID framework.

6.1   Datasets Description

MAVLINK Dataset. This dataset is composed of flight system parameters (also called flight logs) collected using PX4 autopilot and Gazebo robotics simulator [19]. PX4 is an open-source autopilot firmware used in many UAVs. Therefore, MAVLINK dataset contains *general* data—data corresponding to a large number of UAVs [19]. The dataset contains two groups of data samples: The first type corresponds to the parameters of a routine flight (in the absence of the attack). The second type corresponds to the parameters of a flight under a spoofing attack (also called a spoofed flight). It should be noted that the spoofing attack lasts 30 s, while the flight takes 10–30 min; in other words, this dataset is imbalanced.

A large number of features with little variance are present in the dataset. This lack of variance can make the model focus on features with no relevance for the problem at hand (even when applying the principal component analysis technique). To avoid this scenario, we consider only the flight parameters with high variance:

– GPS coordinates: latitude, longitude, military grid reference system, and the course over the ground.
– Position and orientation logs: relative altitude, roll, pitch, heading, roll rate, pitch rate, yaw rate, and ground speed.
– System and control status: air speed, climb rate, distance to home, next GPS signal transmitter to visit, throttle, and battery measurements.

Many MAVLINK features relate to the position and the location, which is convenient for the spoofing attack detection—due to the drift caused by the spoofing attack, orientation, system, and control status features are affected. Additionally, GPS signal characteristics contain information, as power and phase changes in the reference GPS signal.

TEXBAT Dataset. TEXBAT [5] is a publicly available dataset commonly used for testing the resilience of GPS receivers. It contains digital recordings of live static and dynamic GPS L1 C/A spoofing tests. The characteristics of TEXBAT allow the dataset to represent a generalisation of the spoofing attacks detection problem, where not only UAVs are considered but any vehicle with a GPS.

Among all the spoofing attacks covered by TEXBAT dataset [4,5], DS3 and DS7 scenarios have the characteristics of a synchronous spoofing attack. The DS3 scenario is based on static matched-power time push attacks. The DS7 scenario explores the same spoofing attack as DS3, while employing carrier phase alignment. Since DS7 is based on the DS3 scenario and, by introducing a new alignment the complexity of intrusion detection is increased, we focus on the DS7 scenario.

The TEXBAT dataset contains binary data. Using GRID code [6], we convert the binary into the navigation data, which we then use to train the DNN models in this work. In future work, we consider using the navigation data for real-time processing (by a digital signal processor or a field-programmable gate array).

It should be noted that, given that all the data in TEXBAT dataset corresponds to spoofed flights (i.e., the data describing regular flights is not provided), we use TEXBAT to train for and test the attack detection only (Sect. 3).

6.2   Datasets Preprocessing

This section focuses on the preprocessing of the chosen datasets. MAVLINK dataset is a set of flight parameters (i.e., flight logs) extracted from an autopilot simulator. The difference between TEXBAT and MAVLINK dataset is that the data in the TEBXAT dataset can be given to the controller without any modification, because they represent physical features of the GPS signals. On the contrary, MAVLINK data (flight logs) contain very many features (some highly correlated) and thus require preprocessing.

Dataset Balancing. The DNN models in this work will be designed with two scenarios in mind: first, for spoofing attack detection and, second, for spoofing attack prevention (early-warning alarm). In the first case, the training dataset composed of samples of a spoofed flight only is used; this dataset is imbalanced, as the attack duration is considerably shorter than the duration of the entire flight. The exact number of attack data samples in both TEXBAT and MAVLINK dataset is shown in Table 2 (80% for training and 20% for testing). In the second case, the training dataset is composed of equal number of flight logs (data samples) from a regular flight and logs from a spoofed flight. Therefore, the training dataset is balanced (because both the regular and the spoofed flights last equal time). The DNN model is built using the latter dataset, while evaluated on both.

Table 2. Dataset (im)balance.

	MAVLINK		TEXBAT	
	Train	Test	Train	Test
Attack samples	187	7	39	6
Normal flight samples	5728	1433	26149	6542

To balance the data, oversampling techniques can be used. We choose synthetic minority oversampling technique (SMOTE), which uses interpolation to create new samples. Thus, after oversampling spoofing attacks samples, we obtain the same number of attack samples and the normal flight samples and, consequently, ensure abstraction and prevent overfitting.

MAVLINK Dataset Preprocessing. Different techniques are required before training the models, to prevent overfitting problems. First, all the MAVLINK spoofing datasets originating from various UAVs are joined, to have as many samples as possible. Then, one-hot encoding is applied to treat categorical values. Finally, principal component analysis (PCA), a technique based on the correlation between the features, is used to reduce the number of input features [3]. We chose ten input features.

6.3   Models Structure

Hyperband [7] is used to tune the DNN models for both scenarios (detection and prevention) and for both datasets (MAVLINK and TEXBAT).

MAVLINK Dataset Models. The MLP model is set up and trained with four hidden layers (the first with 96 units and Sigmoid function and the remaining layers with 76, 118, and 36 units, respectively, using rectified linear unit (ReLU) activation function). A dropout rate of 0.75 is used at the end, to avoid overfitting. The output layer is a single perceptron layer with a Sigmoid activation function, which enables the output to be limited between 0 and 1. We use binary cross-entropy loss function and the Adam optimizer, with a learning rate of 0.001, running for at most 30 epochs. The batch size has 1,900 samples.

On the other hand, the LSTM model has three hidden layers with 130, 132, and 164 units, respectively. The batch size is 1,000 samples and there are at most 10 epochs. The LSTM DNN uses the same optimizer, loss function, and the learning rate as the MLP model. To improve the accuracy, when training the model in the early-warning alarm prediction, the number of epochs is increased empirically to 76 for the MLP model and to 100 for the LSTM model.

TEXBAT Dataset Models. The MLP model for spoofing attack detection based on the TEXBAT dataset is trained with three hidden layers (with 102, 78, and 70 units, respectively, using ReLU activation function). The output layer is a single perceptron unit with a Sigmoid activation function. We use binary cross-entropy loss function and the Adam optimizer, with a learning rate of 0.001, running for at most 12 epochs. The batch size has 100 samples.

The LSTM model has two hidden layers with 132 and 164 units, respectively. The batch size has 1,000 samples, running for a maximum of 12 epochs. The LSTM model uses the same optimizer, loss function and learning rate as the MLP model.

7   Results

For the intrusion detection framework design, two experiments using flight parameters (MAVLINK dataset) are considered: one for detecting the spoofing attacks and one for predicting them (raising an early-warning alarm). Table 3 summarizes the results obtained for each experiment. Similarly, Table 4 shows

Table 3. Results for attacks detection and prevention on the MAVLINK dataset.

	Attack detection		Attack prevention	
Metrics	MLP	LSTM	MLP	LSTM
ACC	99.93%	99.93%	94.43%	85.93%
Precision	99.96%	100.0%	94.94%	77.84%
Recall	85.71%	85.71%	100.0%	100.0%
F1-Score	92.29%	92.31%	97.41%	87.54%

Table 4. Results for attack detection on the TEXBAT dataset.

DL model	ACC	Precision	Recall	F1-Score
MLP	83.23%	87.07%	67.14%	82.79%
LSTM	82.1%	91.04%	75.58%	82.59%

the results of the spoofing attack detection on the TEXBAT dataset. In our experiments, 80% of the data is used for training, while the remaining 20% is used for validation. Clearly, DNNs provide excellent results, confirming the ability of MLP and LSTM to detect spoofing attacks, even though the two models consider the same scenarios in different ways: The LSTM model takes into account the past model inferences while MLP considers only the current units' inferences.

It can be observed that LSTM models have a slightly lower accuracy than MLP. This difference is linked to the very definition of a spoofing attack: If the target is considering previous flight records when a spoofing attack is taking place, then a spoofing attack will be only detected once the target is drifting to an undesired position (due to the similarities between the previous samples and the actual attack samples). For LSTM models, the fact that the spoofing attack signals are at first almost identical to the previous GPS signals has a negative impact on the model. This impact is translated into a delay of attack detection compared to MLP models. This negative impact is demonstrated in Table 3, where MLP have better F1-Score than LSTM models. Also the same behavior is observed when using MLP and LSTM models for general spoofing attacks ID (Table 4), with a difference between MLP and LSTM F1-Score of 0.2%.

On the other hand, and diving into MALVINK dataset results, it is also logical to think that raising an early alarm for spoofing attacks will be harder than detecting the threats. The results reflect this logical statement, since the accuracy reduces from 99.93% to 94.43% in MLP models and from 99.93% to 85.93% in LSTM models. Even with this difference, the same DNN has demonstrated that it has a great ability (more than 85% of the cases for the MAVLINK dataset) to not only detect spoofing attacks, but also warn if the UAV is under threats (with accuracies of 94.43% for MLP models and 85.93% for LSTM models). We can therefore conclude that MLP is a better solution for our intrusion detection framework.

Table 5. ML/DL solutions for spoofing attacks ID

Detection model	Metrics	Dataset
AE [14]	F1-score (94.81%)	MAVLINK (detection)
Random forest	F1-score (89.21%)/ACC (89.33%)	MAVLINK (detection)
SVM	F1-score (95.99%)/ACC (96%)	MAVLINK (detection)
MLP	**F1-score (92.29%)/ACC (99.93%)**	MAVLINK (detection)
Random forest	F1-score (66.68%)/ACC (68.04%)	MAVLINK (warning)
SVM	F1-score (86.18%)/ACC (86.22%)	MAVLINK (warning)
MLP	**F1-score (97.41%)/ACC (94.43%)**	MAVLINK (warning)
Random forest	F1-score (47.52%)/ACC (56.77%)	TEXBAT (detection)
SVM	F1-score (83.25%)/ACC (82.3%)	TEXBAT (detection)
MLP	**F1-score (82.79%)/ACC (83.23%)**	TEXBAT (detection)

Finally, we provide a comparison between our MLP solution and the DL techniques presented in previous studies. The comparison is performed using the same MAVLINK and TEXBAT datasets. Obtained results are summarized in Table 5. These results further confirm that the MLP solution developed in this work is not only suitable for detecting GPS spoofing attacks but also superior to a number of other approaches.

8   Conclusions

The number of applications of unmanned aerial vehicles is rapidly growing and, with it, GPS spoofing attacks are becoming a serious threat. In this work, a software-based intrusion detection framework capable of not only detecting but also predicting the attack (early-warning system) was developed. The framework is based on a DNN, trained and verified on two datasets: MAVLINK and TEXBAT. Two DNN models were compared: MLP and LSTM, with the experimental results showing that MLP is superior. On MAVLINK dataset, accuracies between 99.43% and 99.93% were achieved, while on TEXBAT dataset the accuracy reached 83.23%. Finally, the resulting MLP model was compared with two other DL-based approaches presented in the literature—random forest and SVM—and demonstrated to be better-performing.

The evolution of DNNs shows that they can significantly improve the classification accuracies in many applications [13]. However, a well-performing DNN is often large: It requires a high number of units, hidden layers, or features. This translates to a continuous increment in computational requirements, memory bandwidth, and storage needed to save the model and move the data. For UAVs, these requirements are difficult to satisfy. Hence, UAVs require a trade-off between the model complexity and the computational and storage resources. For that reason, as part of the future work, we will focus on reducing the complexity of the attack detection model and making it feasible for the model to reside and execute on the UAV.

Acknowledgments. This work was supported in part by the Catalan Government, through the program 2017-SGR-962 and the RIS3CAT DRAC project 001-P-001723, and by the EPFL, Switzerland.

References

1. Arthur, M.P.: Detecting signal spoofing and jamming attacks in UAV networks using a lightweight IDS. In: 2019 International Conference on Computer, Information and Telecommunication Systems (CITS), pp. 1–5 (2019). https://doi.org/10.1109/CITS.2019.8862148
2. Bae, G., Joe, I.: UAV anomaly detection with distributed artificial intelligence based on LSTM-AE and AE. In: Park, J.J., Yang, L.T., Jeong, Y.-S., Hao, F. (eds.) MUE/FutureTech -2019. LNEE, vol. 590, pp. 305–310. Springer, Singapore (2020). https://doi.org/10.1007/978-981-32-9244-4_43
3. Holland, S.M.: Principal components analysis (PCA). Department of Geology, University of Georgia, Athens, GA, pp. 30602–2501 (2008)
4. Humphreys, T.: TEXBAT data sets 7 and 8. The University of Texas (2016)
5. Humphreys, T.E., Bhatti, J.A., Shepard, D., Wesson, K.: The texas spoofing test battery: toward a standard for evaluating GPS signal authentication techniques. In: Radionavigation Laboratory Conference Proceedings (2012)
6. Joplin, A., Lightsey, E.G., Humphreys, T.E.: Development and testing of a miniaturized, dual-frequency GPS receiver for space applications. In: Institute of Navigation International Technical Meeting, Newport Beach, CA (2012)
7. Li, L., Jamieson, K., DeSalvo, G., Rostamizadeh, A., Talwalkar, A.: Hyperband: a novel bandit-based approach to hyperparameter optimization. J. Mach. Learn. Res. **18**(1), 1–52 (2017)
8. Mendes, D., Ivaki, N., Madeira, H.: Effects of GPS spoofing on unmanned aerial vehicles. In: 2018 IEEE 23rd Pacific Rim International Symposium on Dependable Computing (PRDC), pp. 155–160 (2018). https://doi.org/10.1109/PRDC.2018.00026
9. van der Merwe, J.R., Zubizarreta, X., Lukčin, I., Rügamer, A., Felber, W.: Classification of spoofing attack types. In: 2018 European Navigation Conference (ENC), pp. 91–99 (2018). https://doi.org/10.1109/EURONAV.2018.8433227
10. Morales-Ferre, R., Richter, P., Falletti, E., de la Fuente, A., Lohan, E.S.: A survey on coping with intentional interference in satellite navigation for manned and unmanned aircraft. IEEE Commun. Surv. Tutor. **22**(1), 249–291 (2020). https://doi.org/10.1109/COMST.2019.2949178
11. Mozaffari, M., Saad, W., Bennis, M., Debbah, M.: Unmanned aerial vehicle with underlaid device-to-device communications: Performance and tradeoffs. IEEE Trans. Wirel. Commun **15**(6), 3949–3963 (2016). https://doi.org/10.1109/TWC.2016.2531652
12. Munin, E., Blais, A., Couellan, N.: Convolutional neural network for multipath detection in gnss receivers. In: 2020 International Conference on Artificial Intelligence and Data Analytics for Air Transportation (AIDA-AT), pp. 1–10 (2020). https://doi.org/10.1109/AIDA-AT48540.2020.9049188
13. Nurvitadhi, E., et al.: Can FPGAs beat GPUs in accelerating next-generation deep neural networks? In: Proceedings of the 2017 ACM/SIGDA International Symposium on Field-Programmable Gate Arrays, FPGA '17, pp. 5–14. Association for Computing Machinery, New York (2017). https://doi.org/10.1145/3020078.3021740

14. Park, K.H., Park, E., Kim, H.K.: Unsupervised intrusion detection system for unmanned aerial vehicle with less labeling effort. In: You, I. (ed.) Information Security Applications, pp. 45–58. Springer, Heidelberg (2020). https://doi.org/10.1007/978-3-030-65299-9-4

15. Quan, Y., Lau, L., Roberts, G.W., Meng, X., Zhang, C.: Convolutional neural network based multipath detection method for static and kinematic GPS high precision positioning. Remote Sens. **10**(12) (2018). https://doi.org/10.3390/rs10122052

16. Ranganathan, A., Ólafsdóttir, H., Capkun, S.: Spree: a spoofing resistant GPS receiver. In: Proceedings of the 22nd Annual International Conference on Mobile Computing and Networking, pp. 348–360 (2016)

17. Semanjski, S., Semanjski, I., De Wilde, W., Muls, A.: Cyber-threats analytics for detection of GNSS spoofing. In: DATA ANALYTICS 2018: The Seventh International Conference on Data Analytics, pp. 136–140. IARIA (2018)

18. Shafiee, E., Mosavi, M.R., Moazedi, M.: Detection of spoofing attack using machine learning based on multi-layer neural network in single-frequency GPS receivers. J. Navig. **71**(1), 169–188 (2018). https://doi.org/10.1017/S0373463317000558

19. Whelan, J., Sangarapillai, T., Minawi, O., Almehmadi, A., El-Khatib, K.: UAV attack dataset (2020). https://doi.org/10.21227/00dg-0d12

20. Zhi, Y., Fu, Z., Sun, X., Yu, J.: Security and privacy issues of UAV: a survey. Mobile Netw. Appl **25**(1), 95–101 (2019). https://doi.org/10.1007/s11036-018-1193-x

Epicentral Region Estimation Using Convolutional Neural Networks

Leonel Cruz[1], Rubén Tous[1], Beatriz Otero[1(✉)], Leonardo Alvarado[2,3], Sergi Mus[1], and Otilio Rojas[2,4]

[1] Universitat Politécnica de Catalunya, 08034 Barcelona, Spain
{lcruz,rtous,botero,smus}@ac.upc.edu
[2] Universidad Central de Venezuela, Caracas 1070, Venezuela
[3] Fundación Venezolana de Investigaciones Sismológicas, Caracas 1070, Venezuela
[4] Barcelona Supercomputing Center, Barcelona, Spain

Abstract. Recent works have assessed the capability of deep neural networks of estimating the epicentral source region of a seismic event from a single-station three-channel signal. In all the cases, the geographical partitioning is performed by automatic tessellation algorithms such as the Voronoi decomposition. This paper evaluates the hypothesis that the source region estimation accuracy is significantly increased if the geographical partitioning is performed considering the regional geological characteristics such as the tectonic plate boundaries. Also, it raises the transformation of the training data to increase the accuracy of the predictive model based on a Projected Coordinate Reference (PCR) System. A deep convolutional neural network (CNN) is applied over the data recorded by the broadband stations of the Venezuelan Foundation of Seismological Research (FUNVISIS) in the region of 9.5 to 11.5N and 67.0 to 69.0W between April 2018 and April 2019. In order to estimate the epicentral source region of a detected event, several geographical tessellations provided by seismologists from the area are employed. These tessellations, with different number of partitions, consider the fault systems of the study region (San Sebastián, La Victoria and Morón fault systems). The results are compared to the ones obtained with automatic partitioning performed by the k-means algorithm.

Keywords: Earthquake location estimation · Supervised learning · Convolutional neural networks · Deep learning

1 Introduction and Related Works

Reliable earthquake detection and location algorithms are needed to properly catalog and analyze steadily growing seismic records. Artificial neural networks (ANN) have been employed in [5,12,15,17,18,25] to study earthquake detection and location of seismics events. In [6], ANNs are employed to pick P- and S-wave arrivals using the amplitude of three-component seismic traces, resulting successful on more of the 90% of the testing data. Same Authors in [7], later applied back

© Springer Nature Switzerland AG 2022
G. Nicosia et al. (Eds.): LOD 2021, LNCS 13163, pp. 541–552, 2022.
https://doi.org/10.1007/978-3-030-95467-3_39

propagation ANN to identify wave type, either P or S by using signal polarization, and achieved a performance near to 80% in the case of P waves, compared to 60% for S waves. Parallel efforts in [24] and [23] also developed some ANN for P and S detection, and estimate the onset times using a variety of features as input data, including STA/LTA time series [1,2], windowed spectrograms, and autoregressive coefficients. Results were highly satisfactory for both phases, and effectiveness for S detection was about 86%. Later, a ANN with a problem adaptive structure was used by [8] for P and S picking, and results compared to arrival times chosen by a trained analyst, present deviations close to 0.1 s for both phases. Recent advances of this sort for earthquake detection are ConvNetQuake [20] and networks in [12]. Using cataloged events as reference, ConvNetQuake and best candidates in [12] show a 100% accuracy detection. In addition, ConvNetQuake also detects an important amount of uncataloged earthquakes in a month of continuous data, where 94% of these events were later confirmed by autocorrelation. Such performances, along with the lower computational costs of ANN compared to established detection schemes (see again [20]), lend themselves a tremendous potential for processing large seismic datasets and real time detection.

This paper presents the outcomes of an approach, called UPC-UCV-GEO, to apply CNN over single-station 3-channel waveforms for earthquake location estimation in north-central Venezuela. The hypothesis that the source region estimation accuracy is significantly increased if the geographical partitioning is performed considering the regional geological characteristics is evaluated. The network applied is UPC-UCV, whose results for P-wave detection and basic source region estimation (with k-means based tessellation) are described in [22]. We apply our technique to seismic data collected by broadband stations at north-central Venezuela, during the time period of 2018 to 2019. The seismicity in the region results from the right-lateral strike-slip faulting experienced along the interface between the Caribbean and South American plates, as the former moves to the east with respect to the latter. An important amount of this movement seems to be accommodated along the Boconó - El Pilar fault system, that extends across Venezuela from west to east. Several geographical tessellations provided by seismologists from the area are employed. These tessellations, with different number of partitions, consider the fault systems of the study region (San Sebastián, La Victoria and Morón fault systems). The results are compared to the ones obtained with automatic partitioning performed by the k-means algorithm. A review of the seismic history and tectonic of related regions can be found in [3, 19] and [4], and references therein.

2   Methodology

2.1   Data

CARABOBO dataset is made of data provided by FUNVISIS, the official agency for monitoring and reporting seismic activity in Venezuela. The FUNVISIS network comprises 35 stations that continuously record signals on three channels

100 Hz; this is spread over the geographical area containing high seismic activity. The dataset was provisioned by data collected among April 2018 and April 2019 through 5 seismological stations (BAUV, BENV, MAPV, TACV, and TURV) in northcentral Venezuela, specifically on the region between the coordinates 9.5° to 11.5° N and 67.0° to 69.0° W and this consists of seismic data miniSEED format and includes a catalog with metadata regarding these events (hypocenter, P-wave arrival times, magnitude, etc.) in Nordic format.

The earthquakes have a magnitude ranging from 1.7 to 5.2 Mw distributed over the region shown (see Fig. 1), whose epicenters are located on the north-central states of Carabobo, Aragua and Miranda. These zones contain a set of interconnected faults such as: San Sebastián and La Victoria that make up an important seismic area, belong to a continental scale, converging to a larger fault system called Boconó. As well as El Pilar fault system that lies the Caribbean and South American plates.

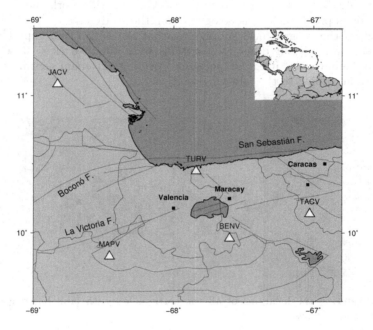

Fig. 1. Geographical distribution of the Boconó, La Victoria and San Sebastián faults, and locations of FUNVISIS stations.

2.2   Earthquake Source Region Estimation

Source region estimation is a relaxed version of the earthquake location problem that consists on, first, partitioning a study area into k geographic subdivisions and, second, attempting to determine to which one the earthquake epicenter belongs. Several works have demonstrated the possibility to estimate the source region of an earthquake from a single-station 3-channel waveform [20–22]. In this work, source region estimation is approached as a multiclass classification problem. First, the wave is divided into three-channel temporal windows of a fixed-size, and these windows will be classified into k+1 classes: one class for windows not containing a P-wave (negatives) and k classes for windows containing a P-wave (positives) but classified into the k geographic regions that we want to discriminate.

2.3   Partitioning the Study Area into Geographic Subdivisions

In order to perform source region estimation, it is first necessary to partition the study area into multiple geographic subdivisions and to define the membership criteria. Previous works, such as [21] and [22], attempted to automatically infer a relevant geographic partitioning directly from the dataset, with the help of a clustering algorithm. Contrary to those methods, in this work the geographic partitioning is provided by seismologists from the study area.

Based on the geographical subdivision that the FUNVISIS expert gave us (see Figs. 2 and 3), four different partitions were obtained (k = 3, 4, 5, 10). All these delimited by irregular polygons covering the main seismic faults of Venezuela, according to the following study [14].

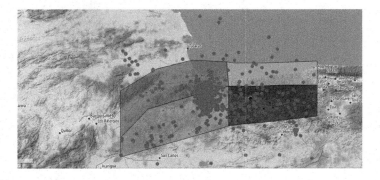

Fig. 2. Clustering the locations of all the earthquakes with fault-based geographic partitioning on 4 zones.

Seismic hazard studies carried out north and central Venezuela by FUNVISIS analyze the seismic activity in shallow seismogenic regions [10,11]. These regions were defined as polygons around each fault segment, which were chosen according to their tectonics and degree of seismicity (see Fig. 3). At first, 10 regions were delimited, which were later regrouped in new bigger regions with similar seismic-tectonic characteristics, leaving the whole study area split into the 4 regions shown in Fig. 2.

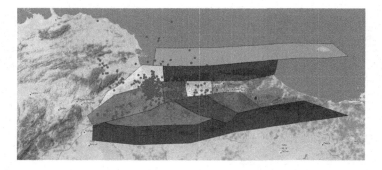

Fig. 3. Clustering the locations of all the earthquakes with fault-based geographic partitioning on 10 zones.

2.4   Data Preprocessing

For the training of the model, a filtering is carried out first, purging the most dispersed events over the study region in order to reduce overfitting.

Input waveforms are first normalized and divided into single-station streams. Each 3-channel single-station stream is split into multiple 3-channel temporal windows of a fixed size. With the events information obtained from the metadata files, we divide the windows into $k + 1$ classes: one class for windows not containing a P-wave (negatives) and k classes for windows containing a P-wave (positives) but classified into the K geographic regions that we want to discriminate. With a 50 sec./window our preprocessing stage yields $12,685$ positives and $84,911$ negatives. The classification of windows among the different K regions is done using clustering the locations of all the earthquakes with a fault-based geographic partitioning provided by a seismologist.

In Figs. 2 and 3, we can observe the several segmentations granted by FUNVISIS and the distribution of the events over the study region that will be used for the comparison of the k-means clustering method.

2.5   Spatial Data Preprocessing

In the Carabobo dataset, each of its records contains coordinates that indicate the epicenter of seismic events. To deal with this information is necessary to have a reference frame capable of making sense of these data to view and manipulate them and thus feed the CNN model. This reference frame is known as Coordinate Reference System (CRS) [13], classified in Geographical Coordinate System (GCS) and Projected Coordinate System (PCS). Figure 4 shows the representation of a specific place on earth, on the left, we have its three-dimensional visualization on the globe with a GCS, and on the right, the two-dimensional projection of this same point projected in PCS.

The first is a reference framework that defines the locations of features on a model of the earth. It's shaped like a globe-spherical. Its units are angular,

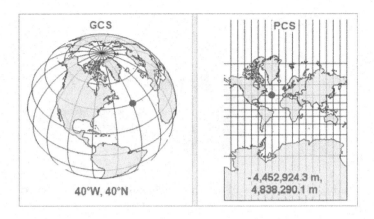

Fig. 4. Types of coordination reference system.

commonly degrees. It's the best for the location and visualization of elements, but distance measurements have a distortion when using latitude and longitude due to the earth's shape. The second is flat. It contains a GCS, but it converts that GCS into a flat surface using a projection algorithm [13] and it is excellent for performing calculations involving distance measurements over geographic areas.

For our dataset, we have selected the GCS called WGS84 to work with our initial data and its corresponding PCR named Pseudo-Mercator, which is by de facto the standard for web services such as Google Maps, Bing Maps, OpenStreet, among others. The coordinates provided generate perimeters with undefined shapes, which in Spatial Data are known as irregular polygons. In order to handle this information, it is necessary to create a JSON (See Listing 1) structure that could store an indeterminate number of points that formed these polygons.

The JSON file contains a key called clusters, whose value is composed of a list of elements that describe the n-regions of which the coordinates define each region's perimeter. An essential section of the file is the points key, because here the coordinates that delimit the boundary and shape of the area are stored; unlike other approaches here, there is no fixed number of elements when forming the list.

For instance, the list 1 shows an irregular polygon is made up of 3 points while the second zone is made up of 5. After defining the type of CRS and the JSON structure that stores the shape of the polygons, we proceeded to use Computational Geometry techniques to assign each of the events to a specific cluster and label it for use model training process. To this, we face the Point in polygon (PIP) problem in which it is decided whether or not a point is in an irregular polygon, described below:

```
1   {
2     "cluster_type": "RCPoligons",
3     "clusters":[
4
5       {
6       "id": 1,
7       "label": "Zone_01",
8       "points": [
9           {"x": 10.41413, "y": -67.90393},
10          {"x": 10.42613, "y": -66.10873},
11          {"x": 10.39413, "y": -66.90323}]
12      },
13
14      {
15      "id": 2,
16      "label": "Zone_02",
17      "points": [
18          {"x": 10.71413, "y": -66.20393},
19          {"x": 10.62613, "y": -66.40873},
20          {"x": 10.79413, "y": -67.10323},
21          {"x": 10.22763, "y": -66.30822},
22          {"x": 10.11113, "y": -67.09223}]
23      },
24
25      ...
26          ]
27  }
```

Listing 1: JSON Structure

Given a point R and a polygon P represented by n points: $P_0, P_1, ...,$ $P_{n-1}, P_n = P_0$, determine whether R is inside or outside the polygon P. When a line is drawn from R to other point S that is wagered to extend outside the polygon. If this line $\overline{RS}$ crosses the edges $e_i = \overline{P_i P_{i+1}}$ of the polygon an odd number of times, the points is inside P, otherwise it is outside.

To carry out the PIP queries, we used Shapely's binary predicates [9] that implement these algorithms to assess the topological relationship between geographic objects. It is based on the widely deployed GEOS (Geometry Engine Open Source), allowing work with three main Point, Line String, and Polygons objects. These algorithms are used to determine whether a seismic event falls within the perimeter of a given zone.

2.6 Network Architecture

Our model, called UPC-UCV, is a CNN that takes a multiple-channel single-station seismogram window as input and outputs $k + 1$ probabilities estimating if the window contains a P-wave originated at one of the k given locations (one of the outputs is the probability that the window does not contain any P-wave). Figure 5 illustrates the overall network architecture.

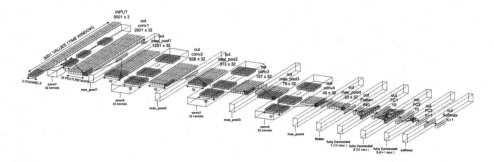

Fig. 5. Network architecture with a 3-channel input, 4 convolutional+max_pooling layers, 3 fully connected layers and a softmax layer

The network has four 32-kernels convolutional layers, each one of them with an associated max pooling layer. The convolutions are applied in a 1D fashion (only through the temporal axis), but the kernels are 2D to process the multiple input channels. Given a 2D kernel k of size $s \times c$ (width s over c channels) of a given layer l, $W^{k,l} \in \mathbb{R}^{2s+1 \times c}$:

$$
W^{(k,l)} = \begin{pmatrix}
W^{(k,l)}_{-s,1} & \cdots & & & W^{(k,l)}_{-s,c} \\
\vdots & & \vdots & & \vdots \\
W^{(k,l)}_{0,1} & \cdots & W^{(k,l)}_{0,0} & \cdots & W^{(k,l)}_{0,c} \\
\vdots & & \vdots & & \vdots \\
W^{(k,l)}_{s,1} & & \cdots & & W^{(k,l)}_{s,c}
\end{pmatrix} \tag{1}
$$

The discrete convolution of the input 2D tensor Y with filter $W^{k,l}$ at position t (the kernel only moves in 1D) is given by:

$$
(Y * W^{k,l})_t = \sum_{u=-s}^{s} \sum_{v=1}^{c} W^{k,l}_{u,v} * Y_{t+u,v} \tag{2}
$$

The output t of a convolutional layer l and kernel k is computed as:

$$
Y^{(l)}_{k,t} = \sigma(b^{(l)}_k + (Y^{(l-1)} * W^{k,l})_{t'}) \tag{3}
$$

where t' is index of the previous layer where the convolution will be applied. t' depends on t but also on the stride (2 in our case). $\sigma() = max(0,)$ is the nonlinear Rectified Linear Unit) (ReLU) activation function and $b^{(l)}_k$ is the bias term for kernel k in layer l. We employ 32 kernels with shape 5×3 in the first layer and 5×32 in the subsequent convnet layers. After each convolutional layer we apply a max-pooling layer with a pooling window of size 5 and stride 3.

After the last convolutional layer we flatten the resulting 2D tensor into a 1D tensor. This feature vector is then processed by three fully connected layers with ReLU activation functions (10 neurons the first ones, $k + 1$ neurons the last one). Finally, a softmax function is applied to the class scores to obtain a properly normalized probability distribution.

3   Experiments and Results

This work's main objective is to assess the effectiveness of source region estimation using a geographic partitioning provided by an expert and determine the impact on the prediction's improvement using a PCR transformation, compared with the approach automatically generated with k-means as in [22]. The UPC-UVC network's best configuration was taken as a basis, considering the network's parametrization and geometry to carry out this new approach.

The experiments were performed on equipment provided by the Computer Architecture Department of the UPC. The device had Intel(R) Core(TM) i7-3770 CPU running at 3.40 GHz and 8 GB in RAM. With this configuration, the training process was carried out between 3 to 4 h per model.

In the first instance, a set of experiments were performed to determine if Spatial-Data techniques within the pre-processing of the training data increased the accuracy of the model prediction results. The data in the Table 1 describe the experiment; in the first column, we partition the study area into k regions; in the second column, we have the experiment's result without using a pre-processing, taking by default a Geographical Coordinate System(GCS) as in the works [16, 22]. In the last column, we have the effect after transforming the original data and converting them into a Projected Coordinate System(PCS). As shown in the table, the post-transformation result obtains an accuracy higher than 90% in each of the cases.

Table 2 summarizes the results of UPC-UCV-GEO obtained using spatial data pre-procesing. The results of ConvNetQuake and UPC-UVC are provided for comparison. For a small number of geographic subdivisions (3-5), the obtained results don't enable to confirm the target hypothesis. The partitioning into 4 regions recommended by the expert (UPC-UCV-GEO with K = 4) provided an accuracy of 95.43%, just slightly above than the results for a k-means based partitioning (UPC-UCV) with K = 5 (93.36%) and slightly below than the results for a k-means based partitioning (UPC-UCV) with K = 3 (95.68%). However, the hypothesis seems to be confirmed for a more fine-grained partitioning (K=10), as UPC-UCV-GEO obtains an accuracy of 91.43% while the accuracy of UPC-UCV degrades to 66.10%.

Table 1. Forecasting impact of source region estimation based on Coordinate Reference System

K Zones	Accuracy GCS	Accuracy PCS
4	86.52%	95.43%
10	87.72%	91.78%
16	88.93%	91.43%

Table 2. Source region estimation results

K Zones	Model	Accuracy
3	ConvNetQuake	84.58%
	UPC-UCV	95.68%
4	UPC-UCV-GEO	95.43%
5	ConvNetQuake	82.08%
	UPC-UCV	93.36%
10	UPC-UCV-GEO	91.78%
	UPC-UCV	66.10%

4   Conclusions

In this paper, we have evaluated the hypothesis that the accuracy of methods (such as [22] and [20]) for the automated estimation of the epicentral source region of a seismic event is increased if the geographical partitioning is performed considering the regional geophysical characteristics. The UPC-UCV-GEO deep convolutional neural network is applied over the CARABOBO dataset, consisting of three-channel seismic waveforms recorded in north-central Venezuela from April 2018 to April 2019. Instead of partitioning the data with K-means, we have applied several geographical tessellations provided by seismologists from the study area.

While the obtained results for a small number of geographic subdivisions are not better than the ones obtained with k-means clustering, the good results obtained with a large number of subdivisions (91.78% with K = 10) outperform the k-means approach (66.10%). It should be noted that to obtain these results, the use of spatial-based techniques significantly improved the final model. This confirms the target hypothesis that the source region estimation accuracy is significantly increased if the geographical partitioning is performed considering the regional geophysical characteristics such as the tectonic plate boundaries.

5   Data and Resources

In order to enable the reproducibility the results, the data and the source code used in this work are publicly available on https://github.com/rtous/deepquake.

Acknowledgements. This work is partially supported by the Spanish Ministry of Economy and Competitivity under contract TIN2015-65316-P, by the Spanish Ministry of Science and Innovation under contract PID2019-107255GB-C22, and by the SGR programmes (2014-SGR-1051 and 2017-SGR-962) of the Catalan Government and has received funding from the European Union's Horizon 2020 research and innovation programme under the Marie Sklodowska-Curie grant agreement No 777778 (MATH-ROCKS). We thank FUNVISIS for providing the seismic data subject of our current studies.

References

1. Allen, R.: Automatic earthquake recognition and timing from single traces. Bull. Seismol. Soc. Am. **68**(5), 1521–1532 (1978)
2. Allen, R.: Automatic phase pickers: their present use and future prospects. Bull. Seismol. Soc. Am. **72**(6B), S225–S242 (1982)
3. Audemard, F.: Ruptura de los grandes sismos históricos venezolanos de los siglos xix y xx revelados por la sismicidad instrumental contemporánea (2002)
4. Audemard, F.: Revised seismic history of the el pilar fault, northeastern venezuela, from the cariaco 1997 earthquake and recent preliminary paleoseismic results. J. Seismolog. **11**(3), 311–326 (2007)
5. Chen, Y.: Automatic microseismic event picking via unsupervised machine learning. Geophys. J. Int. **212**(1), 88–102 (2018)
6. Dai, H., MacBeth, C.: Automatic picking of seismic arrivals in local earthquake data using an artificial neural network. Geophys. J. Int. **128**(3), 758–774 (1995)
7. Dai, H., MacBeth, C.: The application of back-propagation neural network to automatic picking seismic arrivals from single-component recordings. J. Geophys. Res. Solid Earth **102**(B7), 15105–15113 (1997)
8. Gentili, S., Michelini, A.: Automatic picking of p and s phases using a neural tree. J. Seismolog. **10**, 39–63 (2006)
9. Gillies, S., Bierbaum, A., Lautaportti, K., Tonnhofer, O.: Shapely: manipulation and analysis of geometric objects (2007). github.com/Toblerity/Shapely. Accessed 15 June 2019
10. Hernández, J.: Revisión de la sismicidad y modelo sismogénico para actualización de las evaluaciones de amenaza sísmica en la región norcentral de venezuela. In: IX Congreso Venezolano de Sismología e Ingeniería Sísmica. Caracas, May 2009
11. Hernández, J., Schmitz, M.: Modelo sismogénico de venezuela para evaluaciones de la amenaza sísmica. In: XI Congreso Venezolano de Sismología e Ingeniería Sísmica. Caracas, July 2017
12. Ibrahim, M.A., Park, J., Athens, N.: Earthquake warning system: Detecting earthquake precursor signals using deep neural networks (2018)
13. Janssen, V.: Understanding coordinate reference systems, datums and transformations. Int. J. Geoinform. **5**, 41–53 (2009)
14. Michael, S., et al.: Principales resultados y recomendaciones del proyecto de microzonificación sísmica de caracas. Revista Facultad de Ingeniería **26**, 113–127 (2011)
15. Mus, S., et al.: Long short-term memory networks for earthquake detection in venezuelan regions. In: Nicosia, G., Pardalos, P., Umeton, R., Giuffrida, G., Sciacca, V. (eds.) LOD 2019. LNCS, vol. 11943, pp. 751–754. Springer, Cham (2019). https://doi.org/10.1007/978-3-030-37599-7_62

16. Novianti, P., Setyorini, D., Rafflesia, U.: K-means cluster analysis in earthquake epicenter clustering. Int. J. Adv. Intell. Inform. **3**(2), 81–89 (2017). https://doi.org/10.26555/ijain.v3i2.100. http://ijain.org/index.php/IJAIN/article/view/100

17. Rojas, O., Otero, B., Alvarado, L., Mus, S., Tous, R.: Artificial neural networks as emerging tools for earthquake detection. Computación y Sistemas **23**(2), 335–350 (2019). https://doi.org/10.13053/CyS-23-2-3197

18. Ross, Z.E., Meier, M.A., Hauksson, E., Heaton, T.H.: Generalized seismic phase detection with deep learning. Bull. Seismol. Soc. Am. **108**, 2894–2901 (2018)

19. Suárez, G., Nábelek, J.: The 1967 caracas earthquake: fault geometry, direction of rupture propagation and seismotectonic implications. J. Geophys. Res. Solid Earth **95**(B11), 17459–17474 (1990)

20. Thibaut, P., Michaél, G., Marine, D.: Convolutional neural network for earthquake detection and location. Sci. Adv. **4**(2), e1700578 (2018)

21. Tiira, T.: Detecting teleseismic events using artificial neural networks. Comput. Geosci. **25**, 929–938 (1999). https://doi.org/10.1016/S0098-3004(99)00056-4

22. Tous, R., Alvarado, L., Otero, B., Cruz, L., Rojas, O.: Deep neural networks for earthquake detection and source region estimation in north-central venezuela. Bull. Seismol. Soc. Am. **110**(5), 2519–2529 (2020). https://doi.org/10.1785/0120190172

23. Wang, J., liang Teng, T.: Identification and picking of s phase using an artificial neural network. Bull. Seismol. Soc. Am. **87**(5), 1140–1149 (1997)

24. Wang, J., Teng, T.L.: Artificial neural network-based seismic detector. Bull. Seismol. Soc. Am. **85**(1), 308–319 (1995)

25. Zhu, W., Beroza, G.C.: Phasenet: a deep-neural-network-based seismic arrival time picking method. http://arxiv.org/abs/1803.03211v1 (2018)

Estimating Change Intensity and Duration in Human Activity Recognition Using Martingales

Jonathan Etumusei(✉) , Jorge Martinez Carracedo , and Sally McClean

Ulster University, Shore Rd, Newtownabbey, Jordanstown BT37 0QB, UK
etumusei-j@ulster.ac.uk
https://www.ulster.ac.uk

Abstract. The subject of physical activity is becoming prominent in the healthcare system for the improvement and monitoring of movement disabilities. Existing algorithms are effective in detecting changes in data streams but most of these approaches are not focused on measuring the change intensity and duration. In this paper, we improve on the geometric moving average martingale method by optimising the parameters in the weighted average using a genetic algorithm. The proposed approach enables us to estimate the intensity and duration of transitions that happen in human activity recognition scenarios. Results show that the proposed method makes some improvement over previous martingale techniques.

Keywords: Martingales · Change detection · Human activity recognition

1 Introduction

Human activity (HA) detection is getting popular in machine learning and artificial intelligence (AI) areas. Human activity studies can provide adequate and robust medical management for people with physical and movement disabilities (cerebral palsy, spina bifida, acquired brain injury, epilepsy, multiple sclerosis and arthritis) [19]. This intervention can result in allowing the vulnerable individual to live a more self-supporting lifestyle.

HA monitoring and studies can be achieved using a wearable sensor (WS) [21]. In human activity recognition (HAR), which is the process of predicting the motion of a person based on sensor data obtained from WS devices, WS has been used to gather valuable information. However, they are still limited in functionality. In the HAR area, WS are sensitive to noise, which interferes with result rendering. Consequently, this interference produces misleading information, which can affect the accuracy and precision of WS readings [21].

Physical activity intensity (PAI) [14] relates to the amount or magnitude at which an action is performed. This can also be referred to as the extent to which an activity is performed or how hard our body works while doing a specific activity. Monitoring the PAI is vital in the health care sector to assist in observing the risk associated with depressive symptoms among older adults [11]. The study of PAI enables athletes to

Supported by Ulster University.

G. Nicosia et al. (Eds.): LOD 2021, LNCS 13163, pp. 553–567, 2022.
https://doi.org/10.1007/978-3-030-95467-3_40

monitor the activity of a high-risk subgroup of the population [20]. The physical activity duration (PAD) is the time it takes to perform a selected physical activity. Measuring the PAD is essential as it enables the medical specialist to monitor the physical activity of elderly or vulnerable people with health challenges [2].

This paper presents an improvement over the previous geometric moving average of martingales (GMAM) when working with multivariate physical activity data. We called the proposed method multivariate exponential weighted moving average of the martingale sequence (MEWMS). While the previous GMAM [10] algorithm makes use of different parameters to reduce noise interference in the data stream and to discover change points, the novelty of our proposed algorithm (MEWMS) is mainly focused on improving and applying the existing GMAM to the areas of physical activities.

Based on previous works with martingales, we decided to implement MEWMS for this physical activity data as it does not make use of window size to determine its precision, unlike other change detection approaches. MEWMS is an improved version of the already published method called GMAM, that can reduce noise interference and therefore improving the change point detection. We are aware that GMAM [9] is a real univariate method and that there is no recommended parameter values for it or a fixed threshold computation. Working on these issues, our proposed method MEWMS can handle multivariate data. We added an optimization phase to obtain the optimal parameters for the type of data we work with.

Examples of optimisation techniques used in this paper are the F1 enumeration method (FEM) and genetic algorithm (GA). GA [15] is a metaheuristic procedure of natural selection that is part of a greater class of evolutionary algorithms. GA can be used to discover the optimal parameters of an algorithm. GA varies from conventional optimisation approaches (such as FEM) in four notable areas: firstly, GAs are generally implemented to produce exceptional solutions to optimisation and search issues by depending on biologically motivated operators such as crossover, mutation and selection. Secondly, GA utilises the fitness function to locate the value of the optimal parameter without any secondary information. We use FEM to maximised F1. FEM involves using a cross-validation process to iterate an algorithm given a certain parameter range to locate the optimal F1 value.

GA (further elaborated in Sect. 4) is used to maximise G-mean. We use G-mean instead of F1 as our reference metric as G-mean can measure the balance between the classification performance on the positive and negative classes [1]. G-mean can avoid to overfit the negative class and underfit the positive class [13] when compared to F1.

The paper structure is as follows: In Sect. 2, we review the latest work done on identifying changes in HAR data; in Sect. 3, we introduce our proposed approach; in Sect. 4, we show our experimental results and compare them with the existing martingale algorithm; we conclude the paper in Sect. 5 discussing the results obtained and the next steps of the research.

2 Related Work

In the last decades, many change detection techniques have been developed to identify changes or abnormalities in a time series data set. For instance, Khan et al. [8] proposed an algorithm known as the multivariate exponentially weighted moving average

(MEWMA) approach for HAR. This method uses GA to identify the optimal parameter set to discover abnormalities in wireless sensor data. Results show that the algorithm can detect changes with a G-mean value of 83.20%.

Ho and Wechsler [4] proposed a method known as randomised power martingale (RPM) to detect changes in data streams. The technique was developed to utilise the martingale framework for anomaly detection. This approach can pick out changes in a data stream by examining every arriving time point through hypothesis testing. Experimentation shows the effectiveness of the method in detecting abnormalities in time series. However, there are still issues that diminish the effectiveness of the algorithm [9], such as capturing a high number of false positives.

Kong et al. [9] proposed an algorithm using the geometric moving average martingale (GMAM) method to detect abnormalities in electromagnetic data. The GMAM method addresses the challenges of using sliding windows which needs to be selected based on the accuracy of the previous method. The technique uses the geometric moving average, which adds weight to the martingale point for better precision. The technique improves the randomised martingale method, but there are still uncertainties in choosing the suitable threshold. When the threshold is high, then significant change points are ignored and when the threshold is small, the algorithm detects many false alarms.

Etumusei et al. [3] proposed two methods known as the moving median of the martingale sequence (MMMS) and the Gaussian moving average of the martingale sequences (GMAS), respectively. These methods use the martingale framework to discover anomalies and minimise the noise effect in a terrestrial data set. Results show that the proposed approaches enhance the traditional martingale technique.

As explained above, most current approaches can detect changes in HAR. However, many of these techniques do not focus on the intensity or duration of the transition period in the HAR data set. The newly proposed MEWMA can estimate the change intensity and duration in the HAR data set using optimised parameters and a robust threshold computation. Our proposed approach can reduce noise interference, being able to better detect change points when compared to other martingale methods. The proposed approach is summarised in Fig. 1.

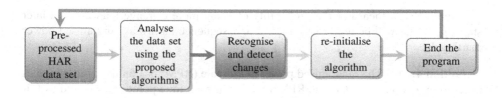

Fig. 1. Flow chart of the proposed approach

We also test our optimised approach on a HAR data set and compare the outputs of our newly developed algorithms with the original multivariate randomised power martingale (MRPM). These results are summarized in Sect. 4.

3 The HAR Model

This Section explains the proposed approach for analysing the HAR data set.

A martingale can be arbitrarily described as a succession of random variables where at a specified time, the expected value a variable is independent from the previous variables.

Definition 1: [4] A sequence of random variables $\{M_i : 0 \leq i < \infty\}$ is a martingale regarding the sequence of variables $\{X_i : 0 \leq i < \infty\}$, if for all $i \geq 0$, the following conditions hold:

– The martingale M_i is a function that is measurable of $X_0, X_1, ..., X_i$,
– $E(|M_i|) < \infty$ and
– $E(M_{n+1}|X_0, ..., X_n) = M_n$.

The foundation of the martingale structure was put forward by Ho and Wechsler [4]. This technique uses a metric called strangeness. Intuitively, it measures how much a new data points is similar to the previous data points observed. Consider an unlabelled sequence $Z = \{z_1, ..., z_{i-1}\}$, the new observed point will be named z_i. We assume that the data has been clustered into k disjoint sets $Y_1, ..., Y_k, (k <= i - 1)$ [7].

Definition 2: The strangeness of z_i is defined as:

$$s_i = s(Z, z_i) = \| z_i - C \| ,\tag{1}$$

where C is the centroid of the cluster Y_r, for any $r \in \{1, ..., k\}$ such that $z_i \in Y_r$. $\| \cdot \|$ refers to the selected distance (usually, the Euclidean distance). The strangeness of z_i is then utilise to calculate some "probability" values named as $\widehat{p}_i$. If for $j = 1, 2, ..., i$, s_j represents the strangeness of z_j and θ_i is a fixed number in $[0, 1]$. $\widehat{p}_i$ is computed as follows:

$$\widehat{p}_i(Z \cup z_i, \theta_i) = \frac{\sharp\{j : s_j > s_i\} + \theta_i \sharp\{j : s_j = s_i\}}{i}.\tag{2}$$

Intuitively, $\widehat{p}_i$ measures the probability of being more estrange than z_i. At a later stage, $\widehat{p}_i$ values will be used to compute a new sequence known as randomised power martingale.

Definition 4: [4] The randomised power martingale (RPM) is a family of martingales indexed by $\epsilon \in [0, 1]$, where the RPM function at each time point is expressed as follows:

$$M_n^{(\epsilon)} = \prod_{i=1}^{n}(\epsilon \widehat{p}_i^{\ \epsilon-1}).\tag{3}$$

This model will detect a change when

$$M_n^{(\epsilon)} > t,\tag{4}$$

where the threshold t is chosen in a probabilistic way based on Dobb's Inequality [4]. In a multidimensional data set, $M_n^{(k)}$ will be computed for each of the variables and a further processing will take place, producing an output known as the multivariate randomised power martingale (MRPM). The vector obtained using MRPM will be used later to generate our proposed method. In the following Section, we introduce a method that improves the accuracy, recall and F1 of the previously described martingale approach. The proposed method can also measure the intensity and duration of the changes that occur in the HAR data set.

3.1 Multivariate Exponential Weighted Moving Average of the Martingale Sequence (MEWMS)

To compute MEWMS, we need to use a smoothing technique on the martingale points (see [16]) called exponential weighted moving average. These martingale points have been obtained using the methods described in (3) [10]. The final equation used in our method is outlined as follow:

$$S_k = (1 - \beta)S_{k-1} + \beta M_k^{(\epsilon)}, \tag{5}$$

with $S_0 = 0$ and $k = 1, ..., n$. The coefficient β (known as the forgetting factor (FF)) is a fixed number in $[0, 1]$. β can be seen as a weight to the average of the martingale points [10]. S_k can be used to determine if an abnormal condition occurs in the data set. If S_k is greater than a chosen threshold t, then a change has occurred, and if the S_k value is lower than the chosen threshold, then no abnormal condition has taken place. We can informally write this rule as:

$$S_k > t. \tag{6}$$

Let us consider a data sequence $\{X_1, ..., X_s\}$, where each point X_i is a j vector, and j is the number of variables of the study. S_k will be computed for each of the variables at any time point. The next step will be to reduce this new multidimensional sequence into a single metric. Once S_k is computed for each variable at a given time point, the mean of all these values will be calculated. The k-th mean element is obtained using the equation:

$$Y_k = \frac{S_k(r_1^{(k)}) + S_k(r_2^{(k)}) + ... + S_k(r_j^{(k)})}{j}, \tag{7}$$

where $r_i^{(k)}$ is the i-th variable of X_k. Y_k will be the new point for analysis in the multivariate HAR data set. The next Section explains the computation of the threshold (t).

3.2 Threshold Computation

There are several ways of choosing a threshold. Ho and Weschler [4] proposed a probabilistic way of finding it while Ley et al. [3,12] proposed a method that is based on outlier detection: $\bar{x} \pm 3 * MAD$, where $\bar{x}$ denotes the mean of the data points and the MAD the mean absolute deviation. We suggest a threshold using $\bar{x} \pm \sigma$, where μ and σ denote the mean and the standard deviation of $\{Y_k \mid k = 1, ..., s\}$.

The reason why we use σ rather than the MAD is that the absolute deviation is less sensitive to large outliers compared to σ, which is more sensitive to substantial outliers [5]. The condition to detect a change is given as:

$$\bar{x} - \sigma \geq Y_k \geq \bar{x} + \sigma. \tag{8}$$

When Y_k lands out of the interval $[\bar{x} - \sigma, \bar{x} + \sigma]$, then a change has been detected. This technique can also be used to estimate the intensity and duration of the changes that occur in the HAR data set. The approach is illustrated in Fig. 2.

4   Experimental Result

The Section gives an overview of the different approaches adopted to discover changes in HAR. The Section also describes the pre-processing techniques and the implementation of optimisation approaches to enhance the performance of the previous GMAM algorithm using HAR data obtained from WS.

Algorithm 1: The proposed algorithm

Data: Input (F): HAR multivariate data set
Result: Output: MEWMS points
1 Initialise: $M(0) = 1; i = 1; F = \{\}$;
2 Set values for cluster group k, ϵ value, ;
3 **while** do
4   A new example of z_i is discovered;
5   **if** $F = \{\}$ **then**
6   Set the strangeness of $z_i := 0$
7   **else**
8   Compute the strangeness of z_i and the data points in F
9   Compute the $\hat{p}_i$ of z_i;
10   Compute the M_i using (3);
11   Compute the S_k points;
12   Translate the S_k points to a single metric Y_k;
13   Compute the threshold t
14   **end**
15   **if** $Y_k \geq t$ **then**
16   Change detected
17   Estimate the PAI
18   Estimate the PAD
19   Re-initiate $M_i = 1$
20   **else**
21   Add z_i into F ;
22   **end**
23   **if** $i = i + 1$; **then**
24 **end**

Fig. 2. Algorithm 1

4.1   Pre-processing Approach

The first step for implementing the proposed algorithm described in Sect. 3 involves obtaining accelerometry data points from the Shimmer wireless sensor platform (SWSP) platform attached to healthy participants. The SWSP has 3-axis MEMs, which are integrated into the device used to capture the acceleration of the individual. The Shimmer devices were attached to the participant right arm, left arm and right leg to enable lateral and anterior-posterior movement of the volunteer to be captured efficiently [23]. The participant performs different scenarios within a home environment

[23]. The first set of scenarios (scenario 1) involves the participant following activities that include ascending stairs, walking, and sitting down. A finite impulse response (FIR) filter is implemented to process the accelerometer data, as a low-pass filter to introduce a set of acceleration values for every specific activity and reduce the noise accumulated from such activities [23]. The labelled data (labelled by experts in the field) for the sit to stand scenario is illustrated in Figs. 3, 4 and 5. The change points occur around 30.88 to 32.68 s, equivalent to 1544 to 1634 data points. The duration of the transition is at 1.8 s.

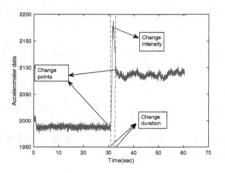

Fig. 3. Accelerometer data set-Y variable

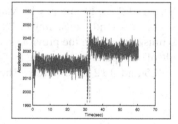

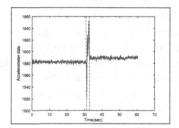

Fig. 4. Accelerometer data set-X variable   **Fig. 5.** Accelerometer data set-Z variable

Our proposed method can estimate PAI. To determine this, we first compute the threshold and then subtract it from the largest algorithm point to better measure PAI. We denote $M = max\{Y_k \mid k = 1, ..., n\}$ and T as the threshold of our algorithm. On the other hand, we can also estimate PAD by using D = seconds (TP), the time duration of change discovered by the algorithm, and A, the actual length of time the change takes place. Consequently, we define both physical activity intensity measure (PAIM) and percentage physical activity duration (PPAD) as:

$$PAIM = M - T, \qquad PPAD = \frac{D}{A} * 100.$$

The evaluation performance for the approaches is measured using robust evaluation metrics (EM) such as accuracy, precision, recall, harmonic mean $(F1)$ and G-mean. These metrics are evaluated using confusion matrix (CM) [17]. We define true negatives (TN) as the false changes that are correctly identified as false. True positives (TP) are the true changes that are correctly identified, while false positives (FP) are the false changes that are identified as true. False negatives (FN) are the actual changes that are identified as false. The following metrics are defined as:

$$Accuracy = \frac{TP+TN}{TP+FP+FN+TN}, \quad Precision = \frac{TP}{TP+FP},$$

$$Recall = \frac{TP}{TP+FN}, \quad F1score = \frac{2*Recall*Precision}{Recall+Precision},$$

$$Specificity = \frac{TN}{TN+FP}. \quad G-mean = \sqrt{Recall*Specificity}.$$

The following Section discusses ways by which we can optimise the parameter of the proposed algorithm for enhanced performance.

4.2 F1 Enumeration Method (FEM)

Note that the family of martingale we are working with depends on $\epsilon \in [0,1]$ and the FF can be any number between 0 and 1. Taking this into account, we examined each tuple of parameters for any epsilon value in the set $\{0, 0.1, 0.2, ..., 1\}$ and any FF value in the set $\{0, 0.01, 0.02, ..., 1\}$ to analyse HAR data set (sit-to-stand) consisting of 3216 data points. The epsilon and the FF values which maximised the F1 in the previous case are fixed for further analysis in a test set. The result of this parameter tuning is that the epsilon and the FF value which optimised F1 are 0.5 and 0.12 respectively. These results are illustrated in Fig. 6.

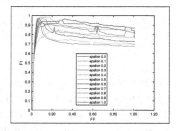
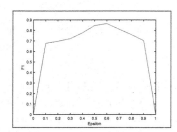

Fig. 6. F1(ϵ, FF) algorithm output values   **Fig. 7.** F1(ϵ) martingale output

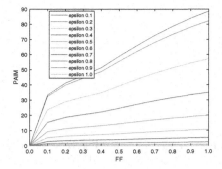

Fig. 8. PAI (FF) output

From Fig. 6, we can observe that the F1 of each epsilon value increases as the FF value move from 0 to 0.1. There are also some sharp surges and declines in F1 output for each epsilon as the FF values increase from 0.1. The MEWMS approach using FEM is represented as MEWMS (FEM). For MRPM, we compute F1 for each epsilon value $\{0, 0.1, 0.2, ..., 1\}$. In each case, the epsilon, which optimised F1, is selected and used to evaluate a test set. The epsilon that maximises F1 is 0.60. The results are shown in Fig. 7. The MRPM method using FEM is represented as MRPM (FEM). In Fig. 8, we illustrate the behaviour of physical activity intensity measure (PAIM) for varying epsilon and FF value in the set $\{0, 0.1, 0.2, ..., 1\}$. We can observe that for each epsilon value, the PAIM increases as the FF increases. The output of the proposed and baseline algorithms is plotted on a test set. Figure 9 and 11 show the algorithm output for MEWMS (FEM) and MRPM (FEM) while Fig. 10 and 12 show the test data with accompanying change-points in seconds (sec).

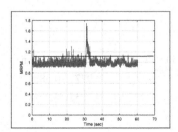

Fig. 9. MRPM (FEM) output

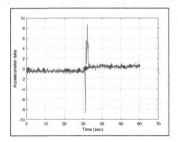

Fig. 10. Change points detected by the MRPM (FEM) method

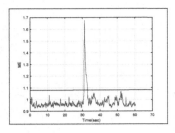

Fig. 11. MEWMS (FEM) output

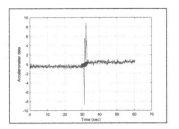

Fig. 12. Change points detected by the MEWMS (FEM) method

As discussed earlier, to evaluate the performance of the proposed and baseline algorithms, we use the standard CM: TP, TN, FP and FN. CM for MEWMS (FEM) and the original MRPM (FEM) are summarised in Table 1.

Table 1. Evaluation metrics

Approach	TN	TP	FN	FP
MEWMS (FEM)	2922(99.9%)	89(96.7%)	3(3.3%)	2(0.1%)
MRPM (FEM)	2899(99.5%)	76(73.8%)	14(0.5%)	27(26.2%)

We can notice that the new algorithms present a greater TP detection ratio and lower FN detection when compared to MRPM approach. We can also apply the evaluation metrics presented in Table 1 to compute the accuracy, recall and F1 for all the methods in the analysed data set. These metrics are presented in Table 2. In this way, we can present a comparison of the approaches performance.

Table 2. Evaluation metrics

Approach	Epsilon	FF	Accuracy	Recall	Precision	F1	G-Mean
MEWMS (FEM)	0.5	0.12	0.9983	0.9780	0.9674	0.9727	0.9884
MRPM (FEM)	0.6	–	0.9861	0.8352	0.7379	0.7835	0.9098

In Table 2, the newly proposed algorithms present a better performance than the original MRPM for every analysed metric. It is crucial to observe that while the accuracy is a bit better for the proposed method, the improvement in recall and F1 is significant. PAD is measured in Y_k units while PAI is estimated in seconds (sec) using our proposed algorithm, and the results are shown in Table 3. The MEWMS (FEM) method gives PAIM of 6 points for the sit-to-stand scenario. The approach also produces a PAD of 1.76 sec (PPAD of 97.8%). For the MRPM (FEM) method, we cannot estimate the PAD or PAIM as a result of FP as shown in Fig. 9.

Table 3. PAIM, PAD And PPAD estimation

Approach	PAIM	PAD	PPAD
MEWMS (FEM)	6 points	1.76	97.8%
MRPM (FEM)	Uncertain	Uncertain	Uncertain

The process through which we find the optimal value for the different parameters using the FEM has limitations [18]. An effective way of optimising parameters is using the genetic algorithm (GA). GA is discussed further in the next Section.

4.3 Genetic Algorithms (GA)

GAs use the fitness function to obtain the optimal parameter values of an algorithm [8]. In this case, the fitness function measures how close a given result is to the leading solution of the chosen problem. Our proposed method makes use of the following parameters (ϵ, β) as discussed in Sect. 3. Therefore, we initialise the population of vectors containing the mentioned input parameters to give the optimal G-mean value [8,22]. In this case, the fitness function is the maximum G-mean value with a specified range of parameters. It represented as follows:

$$G - Mean_{max} = max_{(\epsilon,\beta)}(G - Mean_{(MEWMS)}), \qquad (9)$$

where ϵ and β ranges from 0 to 1 for each activity [8]. In addition, the various GA parameters implemented to maximise the fitness function are shown in the Table 4.

Table 4. GA parameter values

Population size	Selection	Crossover rate	Mutation	Crossover	MaxGenerations
200	Stochastic uniform	0.8000	Gaussian	Heuristic	100*numberOfVariables

Our proposed method uses Eq. (9), which is the fitness function, to locate the maximum G-mean by initialising the lower and upper bound of the parameters [8]. The proposed algorithm using the GA is applied to a HAR data set consisting of 3216 data points. The maximal G-mean value obtained is 0.9966 and the optimal parameters are $\epsilon = 0.6939$ and $\beta == 0.1626$ respectively. The MEWMS using GA is represented as MEWMS (GA). Consecutively, we then apply these optimal parameters to a test set. We illustrate a more extensive report on the characteristics of both the training and the test set values in Tables 5 and 6. The exact process is repeated to obtain the optimal parameters for MRPM method using GA. We implement the GA on a HAR data set consisting of 3216 data points to get the maximal G-mean value of 0.9817, and the optimal parameter is $\epsilon = 0.7547$. The MRPM method using GA is represented as MRPM (GA). Subsequently, we administer the optimal parameter value on a test set. The results are shown in Table 6. The Table enables us to compare the evaluation metrics of MEWMS

(GA), and MRPM (GA) approaches to that of MEWMS (FEM), MRPM (FEM) and GMAM methods independently. The results are also indicated in Table 5 and 6.

Table 6 presents the outcome of the model performance and the best optimal parameter set (ϵ and β) for MEWMS(GA) and (ϵ) for MEWMS (FEM) method. In terms of G-mean, the proposed MEWMS (GA) method are slightly better than the proposed MEWMS (FEM). Also, the proposed MEWMS (GA) and MEWMS (FEM) approaches give preferable output in terms of recall, precision and G-mean metrics compared to that of the MRPM (GA) and MRPM (FEM) methods, respectively. Besides, our proposed methods can estimate PAI and PAD, unlike traditional approaches as illustrated in Table 6. It worthwhile to note from Table 6 that, although the objective of MEWMS (GA) is not maximized on F1 metric, the MEWMS (GA) methods can still achieve significantly better performance on HAR data sets. Finally, we note that the F1 values of both MEWMS (FEM) and MRPM (FEM) are higher than those of MEWMS (GA) and MRPM (GA) respectively. These outcomes happen because the MEWMS (FEM) and MRPM (FEM) approaches are optimised using F1 rather than G-mean.

Table 5. Training and test set summary

Approach	Training data set	Test data set	ϵ	β	G-mean (train)	G-mean (test)
MEWMS (GA)	3216	3016	0.6939	0.1626	0.9966	0.9923
MRPM (GA)	3216	3016	0.7547	–	0.9817	0.9721
MEWMS (FEM)	3016	3216	0.5	0.12	0.9902	0.9884
MRPM (FEM)	3016	3216	0.6	–	0.9134	0.9098

Table 6. Evaluation metrics (Test Set)

Approach	ϵ	β	Accuracy	Recall	Precision	F1	G-mean	PAIM	PAD	PPAD
MEWMS (GA)	0.6939	0.1626	0.9954	0.9890	0.8738	0.9278	0.9923	3 points	1.76 s	97.8
MRPM (GA)	0.7547	–	0.9768	0.9670	0.5677	0.7154	0.9721	Uncertain	Uncertain	Uncertain
MEWMS (FEM)	0.5	0.12	0.9983	0.9780	0.9674	0.9727	0.9884	6 points	1.76 s	97.8
MRPM (FEM)	0.6	–	0.9861	0.8352	0.7379	0.7835	0.9098	Uncertain	Uncertain	Uncertain
GMAM	Chosen	Chosen	Random	Random	Random	Random	Uncertain	Uncertain	Uncertain	Uncertain

The "better GA" is based on a small difference. In the first version of this work, we did not check whether or not this difference is statistically significant. The lack of this testing was due to the difficulty of checking the difference between two G-means using a statistical test. This challenge is mainly coming from the unknown distribution of the G-mean statistic. We could probably have computed its empirical distribution to create a dedicated test for this purpose. However, as we were only working with limited data, this empirical distribution might not have been useful at all. We use statistical testing in accuracy, recall and precision instead of in G-mean. These statistical tests are well known and they test the difference in proportions [6]. We set these test up with a significance level of 0.05. The equation of the statistical test is given as:

$$Z = \frac{\widehat{A_1} - \widehat{A_2}}{\sqrt{2 * \widehat{p}(1 - \widehat{p})/N}},$$

where

$$\widehat{p} = \frac{S_1 + S_2}{2N}.$$

We then state the hypothesis as: $H_0 : A_1 = A_2$ and $H_1 : A_1 < A_2$ $(Z < -z\alpha)$, $A_1 < A_2$ $(Z < -z_\alpha)$, $A_1 < A_2$ $(Z < -z\alpha)$, where z_α is acquired from a normal distribution that relates to a level of significance α. The output for this test are presented in Table 7. The outcome of the tests shows that there is no statistical difference in the precision, accuracy and recall between the tested methods. Even though we did not find a statistical difference in the improvement of these proportions, the results we got in the G-mean are still promising. These small differences that we got using our optimization methods might be vital for a more useful HAR. We also performed several runs in the two cases and presented the results in a new table in the revised paper. The run iteration time for GA is faster compared to FEM as can be observed in Table 8. This evidence shows the effectiveness of GA over FEM.

Table 7. Statistical testing outputs

Approach	Approach	Metric	S1	S2	Z	P-value	Reject H_0
MEWMS (GA)	MEWMS (FEM)	Accuracy	2996	3012	−0.00015	0.9998	NO
MEWMS (GA)	MEWMS (FEM)	Precision	2635	2918	−0.00035	0.9997	NO
MEWMS (GA)	MEWMS (FEM)	Recall	2982	2950	−0.0006	0.9995	NO

Table 8. Optimisation run time

Approach	Number of runs	Ave iteration time
GA	6.0	291.394 s
FEM	6.0	1221.656 s

5   Conclusion and Future Work

This paper briefly discusses the GMAM approach, which can detect changes in the data stream using the martingale framework. We propose a method that can enhance the performance of the GMAM method by optimising the parameters using different optimisation methods such as the F1 enumeration method and GA. From the experiment, we can conclude that optimisation using GA is faster than that of FEM techniques in computational run time. MEWMS method produces better result compared to traditional methods such as MRPM and GMAM in accuracy, recall, precision, F1, G-mean, PAIM and PPPAD respectively.

Future work will also involve validating the hypothesis in a wide range of data streams in specific populations such as the elderly and people with different health conditions and children.

Acknowledgements. This work was supported by a University of Ulster Vice-Chancellor's Research Studentship. The authors would like to thank anonymous reviewers for their constructive suggestions.

References

1. Akosa, J.: Predictive accuracy: a misleading performance measure for highly imbalanced data. In: Proceedings of the SAS Global Forum, vol. 12 (2017)
2. Brawley, L.R., Rejeski, W.J., King, A.C.: Promoting physical activity for older adults: the challenges for changing behavior. Am. J. Prev. Med. **25**(3), 172–183 (2003)
3. Etumusei, J., Martinez Carracedo, J., McClean, S.: Novel martingale approaches for change point detection. In: Abraham, A., Piuri, V., Gandhi, N., Siarry, P., Kaklauskas, A., Madureira, A. (eds.) ISDA 2020. AISC, vol. 1351, pp. 457–467. Springer, Cham (2021). https://doi.org/10.1007/978-3-030-71187-0_42
4. Ho, S.S., Wechsler, H.: A martingale framework for detecting changes in data streams by testing exchangeability. IEEE Trans. Pattern Anal. Mach. Intell. **32**(12), 2113–2127 (2010)
5. Hosseini, S.S., Noorossana, R.: Performance evaluation of ewma and cusum control charts to detect anomalies in social networks using average and standard deviation of degree measures. Qual. Reliab. Eng. Int. **34**(4), 477–500 (2018)
6. Isaac, E.: Test of hypothesis-concise formula summary
7. Kanungo, T., Mount, D.M., Netanyahu, N.S., Piatko, C.D., Silverman, R., Wu, A.Y.: An efficient k-means clustering algorithm: analysis and implementation. IEEE Trans. Pattern Anal. Mach. Intell. **24**(7), 881–892 (2002)
8. Khan, N., McClean, S., Zhang, S., Nugent, C.: Optimal parameter exploration for online change-point detection in activity monitoring using genetic algorithms. Sensors **16**(11), 1784 (2016)
9. Kong, X., Bi, Y., Glass, D.H.: Detecting seismic anomalies in outgoing long-wave radiation data. IEEE J. Sel. Top. Appl. Earth Observations Remote Sens. **8**(2), 649–660 (2014)
10. Kong, X.Z., Bi, Y.X., Glass, D.H.: A Geometric Moving Average Martingale method for detecting changes in data streams. In: Bramer, M., Petridis, M. (eds.) SGAI 2012, pp. 79–92. Springer, London (2012). https://doi.org/10.1007/978-1-4471-4739-8_6
11. Lampinen, P., Heikkinen, R.L., Ruoppila, I.: Changes in intensity of physical exercise as predictors of depressive symptoms among older adults: an eight-year follow-up. Prev. Med. **30**(5), 371–380 (2000)
12. Leys, C., Ley, C., Klein, O., Bernard, P., Licata, L.: Detecting outliers: do not use standard deviation around the mean, use absolute deviation around the median. J. Exp. Soc. Psychol. **49**(4), 764–766 (2013)
13. Lu, Y., Cheung, Y.M., Tang, Y.Y.: Goboost: G-mean optimized boosting framework for class imbalance learning. In: 2016 12th World Congress on Intelligent Control and Automation (WCICA), pp. 3149–3154. IEEE (2016)
14. Miles, L.: Physical activity and health. Nutr. Bull. **32**(4), 314–363 (2007)
15. Mirjalili, S.: Genetic algorithm. In: Evolutionary Algorithms and Neural Networks. SCI, vol. 780, pp. 43–55. Springer, Cham (2019). https://doi.org/10.1007/978-3-319-93025-1_4
16. Nau, R.: Arima models for time series forecasting (2014)
17. Nguyen, G.H., Bouzerdoum, A., Phung, S.L.: Learning pattern classification tasks with imbalanced data sets. Pattern Recogn. **36**, 193–208 (2009)
18. Roy, B.: The optimisation problem formulation: criticism and overstepping. J. Oper. Res. Soc. **32**(6), 427–436 (1981)
19. Stokes, M.: Physical management in neurological rehabilitation. Elsevier Health Sciences (2004)

20. Sugawara, J., Otsuki, T., Tanabe, T., Hayashi, K., Maeda, S., Matsuda, M.: Physical activity duration, intensity, and arterial stiffening in postmenopausal women. Am. J. Hypertens. **19**(10), 1032–1036 (2006)
21. Wang, L., Gu, T., Tao, X., Lu, J.: Sensor-based human activity recognition in a multi-user scenario. In: Tscheligi, M., de Ruyter, B., Markopoulus, P., Wichert, R., Mirlacher, T., Meschterjakov, A., Reitberger, W. (eds.) AmI 2009. LNCS, vol. 5859, pp. 78–87. Springer, Heidelberg (2009). https://doi.org/10.1007/978-3-642-05408-2_10
22. Xuan, X., Lo, D., Xia, X., Tian, Y.: Evaluating defect prediction approaches using a massive set of metrics: an empirical study. In: Proceedings of the 30th Annual ACM Symposium on Applied Computing, pp. 1644–1647 (2015)
23. Zhang, S., Galway, L., McClean, S., Scotney, B., Finlay, D., Nugent, C.D.: Deriving relationships between physiological change and activities of daily living using wearable sensors. In: Par, G., Morrow, P. (eds.) S-CUBE 2010. LNICST, vol. 57, pp. 235–250. Springer, Heidelberg (2011). https://doi.org/10.1007/978-3-642-23583-2_17

ProSPs: Protein Sites Prediction Based on Sequence Fragments

Michela Quadrini[2]([✉]) [ID], Massimo Cavallin[1], Sebastian Daberdaku[3] [ID], and Carlo Ferrari[1] [ID]

[1] Department of Information Engineering, University of Padova, Via Gradenigo 6/A, 35131 Padova, PD, Italy
massimo.cavallin.1@studenti.unipd.it, carlo.ferrari@unipd.it
[2] School of Science and Technology, University of Camerino, Via Madonna delle Carceri, 9, Camerino, MC, Italy
michela.quadrini@unicam.it
[3] Sorint.Tek, Sorint.LAB group, Via Giovanni Savelli 102, 35129 Padova, PD, Italy
sebastian.daberdaku@latek.it

Abstract. Identifying interacting sites of proteins is a relevant aspect for drug and vaccine design, and it provides clues for understanding the protein function. Although such a prediction is a problem extensively addressed in the literature, just a few approaches consider the protein sequence only. The use of the protein sequences is an important issue because the three-dimensional structure of proteins could be unknown. Moreover, such a structural determination experimentally is expensive and time-consuming, and it may contain errors due to experimentation. On the other hand, sequence based method suffers when the knowledge of sequence is incomplete.

In this work, we present ProSPs, a method for predicting the protein residues considering protein sequence fragments, which are obtained using sliding windows and become the samples for an unbalance binary classification problem. We use the Random Forest classifier for data training. Each amino acid is enriched using a selected subset of physico-chemical and biochemical amino acid characteristics from the AAIndex1 database. We test the framework on two classes of proteins, Antibody-Antigen and Antigen-Bound Antibody, extracted from the Protein-Protein Docking Benchmark 5.0. The obtained results evaluated in terms of the area under the ROC curve (AU-ROC) on these classes outperform the sequence-based algorithms in the literature and are comparable with the ones based on three-dimensional structure.

Keywords: Random forest · Sequence method · Site interaction prediction

G. Nicosia et al. (Eds.): LOD 2021, LNCS 13163, pp. 568–580, 2022.
https://doi.org/10.1007/978-3-030-95467-3_41

1   Introduction

Proteins are versatile macromolecules consisting of one or more amino acid sequences that carry out a broad range of functions in living organisms. These biological roles are fulfilled by interacting with other molecules, including RNA, other proteins, and small ligands [3]. The interactions between two proteins, known as protein-protein interactions (PPIs), are responsible for the metabolic and signaling pathways [13]. Dysfunction or malfunction of pathways and alterations in protein interactions can cause several diseases, including neurodegenerative disorders and cancer. Therefore, the protein interaction knowledge allows us to understand how proteins perform their functional roles and design new antibacterial drugs [8]. The experimental determination of three-dimensional structures of protein complexes is labor-intensive, time-consuming, and has high costs. Therefore, efficient computational methods to predict PPIs play a fundamental role. The computational approaches can be broadly divided, according to the protein representation, into sequence-based and structure-based. The former employs information derived from the amino acid sequence alone to predict the site, while the latter considers the protein three-dimensional (3D) structure. About the sequence-based methods, the representative ones include PPiPP [1], PSIVER [14], DLPred [28], and NPS-HomPP [26]. PPiPP uses the position-specific scoring matrix (PSSM) and amino acid composition, and PSIVER takes advantage of PSSM and predicted accessibility as input for a Naive Bayes classier. DLPred uses long-short term memory to learn features such as PSSM, physical properties, and hydropathy index. To improve prediction, NPS-HomPPI infers interfacial residues from the interfacial residues of homologous interacting proteins. In the literature, structure-based methods usually perform better than sequence-based ones. About the structural-based methods, several approaches have been proposed in the literature. Some of them take advantage of the molecular surface representations for describing the structure and use Zernike descriptors or geometric invariant fingerprint (GIF) descriptors to identify possible binding sites [5,7,27]. Other methods use graph representations of proteins, such as contact maps or hierarchical representations [19]. Most of these aforementioned methods employ machine learning algorithms, including support vector machines, neural networks, Bayesian networks, naive Bayes classier, and random forests. Although structure-based approaches are generally more accurate than sequence-based ones, their applicability is limited since the structure is known or contains some errors due to experimentation. As a consequence, an improvement of sequence-based methods is necessary.

In this work, we introduce ProSPs, a method for predicting the protein interaction sites taking into account protein sequence fragments. Considering sequence fragments is relevant when the entire sequence of proteins is unknown. Such fragments, obtained using sliding windows approach over the whole sequence or the known part of it, become the samples for an unbalance binary classification problem. To determine whether a single residue is part of the complex or not, we used a Machine Learning approach using a Random Forest as a classifier [23]. Although methods based on Random Forests achieve good results with unbalanced data [23], we also employed Random Sampling and a classifier combination approach, which further improved predictions made from unbalanced data. Such predictions are performed on the central residues of sliding windows, which are extracted from the entire protein sequence. Their length is computed using a normalized version of the metric introduced by Sikic et al. [23]. In other words, we select the length of the sliding windows considering the minimum difference of normalized entropy. To better represent the data, each amino acid is equipped with eight high-quality amino acid indices of physicochemical and biochemical properties extracted from the AAindex1 database [12]. We tested the framework on two classes of proteins, Antibody-Antigen and Antigen-Bound Antibody, extracted from the Protein-Protein Docking Benchmark 5.0 [25] supposing that their 3D structures are unknown. We selected these classes since antibodies recognize and bind several antigens. Such characteristic makes them the most valuable category of biopharmaceuticals for both diagnostic and therapeutic applications. To evaluate the model performance on the two data sets, we consider only the area under the receiver operating characteristic curve (AU-ROC) since the recognition of PPIs interface sites is an imbalanced classification problem. This aspect can lead to classifiers that tend to label all the samples as belonging to the majority class, thus trivially obtaining a high accuracy measure. The obtained results in terms of AU-ROC on the data set outperform the sequence-based algorithms in the literature. Moreover, they are comparable with the ones based on three-dimensional structures.

The paper is organized as follows. In Sect. 2, we describe the dataset entries, which consist of sliding windows of a predetermined number of residues In Sect. 3, we describe the used dataset and the results obtained with the model, described in Sect. 2.3. The paper ends with some conclusions and future perspective, Sect. 4.

2   Materials and Methods

2.1   Dataset Entry

Each dataset sample consists of sliding windows of a predetermined number of residues extracted from the entire length of the antibody chains sequence. The sliding window length can influence the classification of results.

Window Length Selection. To determine the sliding window length, we proposed a method based on entropy, similar to one proposed by Sikic et al. [23] and applied in Sriwastava et al. [24]. Our approach takes advantage of the normalized entropy difference between the occurrence of a particular number of interacting residues within a window length of N residues and the uniform occurrence distribution. To carry out this calculation, we define the interacting residues for all proteins in the datasets, and we compute the number of interacting residues using different length sliding windows. Finally, we consider only the windows having a central interacting residue. The normalized window entropy formula is

$$\frac{-\sum_{i=1}^{N} p_i \cdot \log_2 p_i - \log_2 N}{N} \tag{1}$$

where N is the length of a window, p_i is the frequency appearance of i interacting residues in a window of N residues, and $\log_2 N$ is the window entropy when the interacting residues number is distributed uniformly. In other words, the value $\log_2 N$ represents the maximum possible entropy of the window.

2.2 Features

In this work, we consider some physico-chemical and biochemical properties of amino acids that are published in the AAindex [12]. AAindex is a database containing numerical indices that represent various physico-chemical and biochemical properties of residues and residue pairs published in the literature. Each amino acid index is a set of 20 numerical values representing any of the different physico-chemical and biological properties of each amino acid: the AAindex1 section of the database is a collection of 566 such indices. Using a consensus fuzzy clustering method on all available indices in the AAindex1, Saha *et al.* [22] identified three high-quality subsets (HQIs) of all available indices, namely HQI8, HQI24, and HQI40. In this work, we use the features of the HQI8 amino acid index set, reported in Table 1, that are identified as the medoids (centers) of 8 clusters obtained by using the correlation coefficient between indices as a distance measure.

Table 1. HQI8 indices.

Entry name	Description
BLAM930101	Alpha helix propensity of position 44 in T4 lysozyme
BIOV880101	Information value for accessibility; average fraction 35%
MAXF760101	Normalized frequency of alpha-helix
TSAJ990101	Volumes including the crystallographic waters using the ProtOr
NAKH920108	AA composition of MEM of multi-spanning proteins
CEDJ970104	Composition of amino acids in intracellular proteins (percent)
LIFS790101	Conformational preference for all beta-strands
MIYS990104	Optimized relative partition energies - method C

2.3 Dataset Entries Definition

Each entries of the dataset is defined on a sliding window of N residues. It is a vector that consists of $N \cdot k + 2$ elements, where k is the number of selected features. The input vector shows the following scheme:

- *Features* represent the first $N \cdot k$ elements of the input vector that assigns the k selected features for each amino acids of the window.
- *interface* indicate whether the window is interfacing with a protein or not, 1 or -1 respectively. A window is defined as interfacing if its central residue interacts with another one of the other proteins.
- *group* identifies the protein that contains the sequence.

Since each residue for each chain is the possible center of an interface window, the number of windows belonging to the "interface" and "non-interface" classes in the dataset reflects exactly the number of residues previously indicated as interacting and non-interacting. There is a one-to-one correspondence between each amino acid in the antibody sequence and the windows.

2.4   Dataset Imbalance Reducing

The prediction of PPI sites can be considered a classification problem, whose objective is to assign a label, either 1 (interface) or 0 (no-interface), to each residue. This problem is extremely imbalanced. This imbalance makes it difficult for a classifier to learn significant patterns with particular reference to the samples belonging to the minority class. Therefore, a random subsampling method is used to reduce the dataset imbalance. The "Non- Interface" samples of the training set were randomly undersampled to reduce the class imbalance ratio.

2.5   Random Forest

Random Forest is an ensemble model for classification and regression. The model operates by constructing a multitude of decision trees at training time and outputting the class that is the mode (for classification problem) or mean/average prediction (for regression) of the classes output by individual trees. Developed by Breiman [4], the model combines the bagging approach with the random selection of features, introduced independently by Ho [9,10] and Amit and Geman [2], to ensure that the decision trees of the forest are uncorrelated from each other. In bagging, the decision trees depend on trees, which are created from a different bootstrap sample of the training dataset. A bootstrap sample is a sample of the training dataset with replacement, i.e., each sample may appear more than once in the sample. In details, let S be the training set containing m samples, the bagging procedure will initially realize B replicated datasets extracting by uniform sampling with replacement of m' samples from the entire dataset S. In each dataset S^i with $i \in \{1, 2, \ldots, B\}$ will therefore be possible to find samples of S repeated several times, while some may not be selected at all. The replicated datasets permit to train of decision trees, which will then make up the Random Forest so that each tree will only see different portions of the original dataset during training. This bagging approach is combined with the random selection of features, that uses only different random subsets of the entire feature space to train each tree in the random forest. This means that some features used to train a single tree may not be used to train other trees belonging to the forest. Typically, for a classification problem with p features, $\sqrt{p}$ features are used in each split.

The Random Forest classifier has several hyper-parameters that can be tuned:

- number of decision trees inside the forest
- maximum depth of each decision tree
- minimal impurity of a node for it to be converted into a leaf
- maximum number of attributes used per tree training
- minimal impurity decrease of resulting subdatasets for a node to be created

3 Experiments

3.1 Dataset

The Protein–Protein Docking Benchmark 5.0 (DB5) [25], the standard benchmark dataset for assessing docking and interface prediction methods, is the dataset in this work. The benchmark consists of 230 non-redundant, high-quality structures of protein-protein complexes, selected from the Protein Data Bank (PDB). PDB organizes the complexes according to the functional eight different classes: Antibody-Antigen (A), Antigen- Bound Antibody (AB), Enzyme-Inhibitor (EI), Enzyme-Substrate (ES), Enzyme complex with a regulatory or accessory chain, Others, G-protein containing (OG), Others, Receptor containing (OR), and Others, miscellaneous (OX). This study considers only complexes of classes A and AB. For each class, we separated the receptor proteins from the ligand ones. To easily compare our approach with other methods in the literature, we split the data into training and test sets, as shown in Table 2 and proposed in [6]. The residues of a given protein is labeled as part of the PPI interface if they had at least one heavy (non-hydrogen) atom within 5Å from any heavy atom of the other protein (the same threshold used in [6]).

Table 2. The table gives the PDB code and chain ID of each protein used in this study (the PDB code in parentheses identifies the corresponding bound complex in the DB5 database).

Dataset	Training set	Test set
$\mathbf{A}_r$	1AY1.HL (1BGX), 1BVL.BA (1BVK), 2FAT.HL (2FD6), 2I24.N (2I25), 3EO0.AB (3EO1), 3G6A.LH (3G6D), 3HMW.LH (3HMX), 3L7E.LH (3L5W), 3MXV.LH (3MXW), 3V6F.AB (3V6Z), 4GXV.HL (4GXU)	1FGN.LH (1AHW), 1DQQ.CD (1DQJ), 1QBL.HL (1WEJ), 1GIG.LH (2VIS), 2VXU.HL (2VXT), 3RVT.CD (3RVW), 4G5Z.HL (4G6J)
$\mathbf{A}_l$	1TAQ.A (1BGX), 3LZT (1BVK), 1A43 (1E6J), 1YWH.A (2FD6), 1IK0.A (3G6D), 1F45.AB (3HMX), 3M1N.A (3MXW), 3F5V.A (3RVW), 3KXS.F (3V6Z), 1DOL.A (4DN4), 4I1B.A (4G6J), 1RUZ.HIJKLM (4GXU)	1TFH.A (1AHW), 1HRC (1WEJ), 2VIU.ACE (2VIS), 1J0S.A (2VXT), 1QM1.A (2W9E), 1TGJ.AB (3EO1), 3F74.A (3EOA), 2FK0.ABCDEF (4FQI)
$\mathbf{AB}_r$	1BJ1.HL (1BJ1), 1FSK.BC (1FSK), 1I9R.HL (1I9R), 1K4C.AB (1K4C), 1KXQ.H (1KXQ), 2JEL.HL (2JEL), 1QFW.HL (9QFW)	1IQD.AB (1IQD), 1NCA.HL (1NCA), 1NSN.HL (1NSN), 1QFW.IM (1QFW), 2HMI.CD (2HMI)
$\mathbf{AB}_l$	2VPF.GH (1BJ1), 1BV1 (1FSK), 1D7P.M (1IQD), 7NN9 (1NCA), 1HRP.AB (1QFW), 1S6P.AB (2HMI), 1POH (2JEL)	1ALY.ABC (1I9R), 1JVM.ABCD (1K4C), 1PPI (1KXQ), 1KDC (1NSN)

3.2   Implementation and Results

In our work, we use a Python implementation of the Random Forest [4] classifier provided by 0.22.2 version of scikit-learn package [15]. The scheme of our approach is shown in Fig. 1, while the code used in this manuscript are available from the corresponding author upon reasonable request.

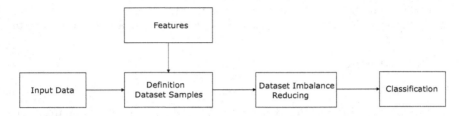

Fig. 1. The scheme of our approach

The first step in creating the dataset samples is to identify the interaction residues. Considering the PDB files of the protein-protein complexes taken from DB5 as an input, the tool extracts the sequence and the interaction residues taking advantage of Biopython package. The second step of the dataset samples creation is the identification of the number of residues to build the sliding windows. To carry out this calculation, only the windows with the central residue classified as interacting (label equal to 1) were considered. In the case of windows with the interacting central residues less than $\lfloor \frac{N}{2} \rfloor$ residues away from the edge of the chain, to keep the size of the windows fixed, a padding of 0 was used to cover the positions that would have been cut. To find the best value of N that minimizes the Eq. 1, a range of possible values from 3 to 71 with a step of 2 were tested. The results of this analysis of classes A and AB are in Figs. 2 and 3. Therefore, the dataset entries are windows composed of 28 residues for A_l class, 14 residues for A_r class, 28 residues for AB_l class, and 22 residues for AB_r class. In the entries definition, we need to introduce some padded residues when we consider the first and $N-1$ last amino acids. The padded residues are conceived as fictitious elements equipped with unnatural features. In particular, these values were obtained by increasing the maximum possible value of considered index of HIQ8 set increased by 1.

The tool reduces the dataset imbalance by a random subsampling method. In particular, it uses the RandomUnderSampler algorithm of Imbalanced-learn, an open source library relying on scikit-learn, obtaining a ratio of 60-40 of the number of samples in the "Interface" (minority) class over the number of samples in the "No-Interface" (majority) class after resampling. Finally, we tune the hyper-parameters of the Random Forest Algorithm, which is implemented with RandomForestClassifier from the sklearn-ensemble package of version 0.22.2 of Scikit-Learn.

Among the available hyper-parameters, we tune

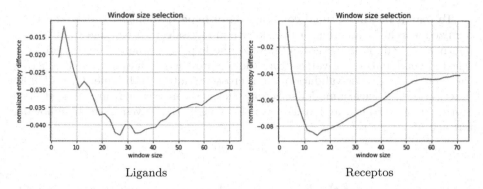

Fig. 2. Normalized Entropy difference for different windows sizes for ligands (left) and receptors (right) of class A

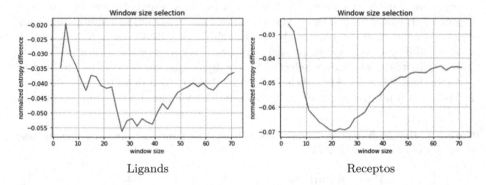

Fig. 3. Normalized Entropy difference for different windows sizes for ligands (left) and receptors (right) of class AB

- the number of decision trees in the forest, n estimators (tested value: 30)
- the criterion used to evaluate the imputiry of a split, criterion (tested Value: "gini", "entropy")
- the maximum depth of each tree, max features (tested values: 2^i, for $i \in \{2, \ldots, 6\}$)
- the maximum number of features that can be used to create a splitting rule (tested values: "sqrt", "log2")
  For example for a total of n features when "sqrt" is used for this parameter only $\sqrt{n}$ features are considered when performing each split
- the minimum number of samples in a leaf to consider further splitting (tested Values: 2^i, for $i \in \{1, \ldots, 6\}$)
- the minimum number of samples required for a leaf (tested Values: 2^i, for $i \in \{1, \ldots, 6\}$)
- bootstrap that indicates whether to use bootstrap when creating each tree during the fitting phase (tested values: True, False)

To search for the optimal combination of hyper-parameter values, the RandomizedSearchCV function of the sklearn.model selection package from Scikit-Learn was used. This method allows to tune hyper-parameters using randomly selected combinations of values from the set provided as input while also fitting the model using cross-validation. As a cross-validation technique, GroupKFold function of the sklearn.model selection package from Scikit-Learn is used. The scoring used to train Random Forest is F1 Weighted, derived from the following formula of the F1 score:

$$F_1 = 2 \cdot \frac{precision \cdot recall}{precision + recall}$$

F_1 weighted computes the F_1 score for each class separately, attributing a different weight based on the support, which is the number of true instances of each label. This metric is chosen as it takes into account the dataset's imbalance, giving more importance to the minority class. Furthermore, this score is a more expressive indicator of the classifier's real prediction capabilities compared to other metrics commonly used such as AU ROC, as it highlights the model's ability to effectively predict samples belonging to the "interface" class. Table 3 illustrates the values selected for the hyper-parameters of the final model of each class (A_r, A_l, AB_r, AB_l) following Randomized Search using Group K Fold Cross-Validation with K = 10 folds and F1 weighted as scoring function.

Table 3. Hyperparameters values chosen from Randomized Search for ligands and receptors of classes A and AB

Hyperparameters	A_r	A_l	AB_r	AB_l
n estimators	115	52	94	73
Criterion	gini	entropy	gini	entropy
Max features	log2	$log2$	log2	log2
Max depth	16	16	8	4
Min samples split	4	32	8	4
Min samples leaf	2	8	2	4
Bootstrap	False	False	True	False
F1 score	0.918	0.626	0.825	0.632

We applied our framework on ligands and receptors of classes A and AB. The performance results, evaluated in terms of AU-ROC, for the proposed methodology on the test set are presented in Tables 4 and 5.

The experiments were trained using 32 parallel threads on a HPC Server with eight 12-Core Intel Xeon Gold 5118 CPUs @2.30 GHz and 1.5 TB RAM running Fedora Linux 25.

Thanks to the appropriate division of molecules, we can compare our results with the ones obtained in [6]. The proposed methodology was also compared with

Table 4. Classification results (AU-ROC) on the test set for the proteins of class A of DB5.

	Receptors		Ligands	
	Bound	Unbound	Bound	Unbound
ProSps	0.962	0.962	0.615	0.615
Other Methods				
GCN Method with Contact Map	0.953	0.952	0.737	0.760
GCN Method with Hierarchical Representation 10	0.963	0.962	0.729	0.755
Daberdaku et al.	0.954	0.942	0.589	0.595
SPPIDER	0.773	0.754	0.630	0.575
NPS-HomPPI	0.796	0.780	0.610	0.626
PrISE	0.770	0.758	0.622	0.569

Table 5. Classification results (AU-ROC) on the test set for the proteins of class AB of DB5.

	Receptors		Ligands	
	Bound	Unbound	Bound	Unbound
ProSps	0.841	0.841	0.702	0.702
Other Methods				
GCN Method with Contact Map Å	0.904	0.899	0.711	0.778
GCN Method with Hierarchical Representation	0.905	0.903	0.749	0.800
Daberdaku et al.	0.813	0.840	0.599	0.729
SPPIDER	0.757	0.783	0.573	0.556
NPS-HomPPI	0.701	0.698	0.675	0.713
PrISE	0.776	0.789	0.683	0.649

two state-of-the-art homology-based PPI interface prediction algorithms: NPS-HomPPI [26] and PrISE [11], and with the well-known structure-based approach SPPIDER [16,17]. The results obtained with ProSPs and evaluated in terms of the AU-ROC on ligands and receptors of A and AB classes outperform HomPPI, a competitor predictors sequence-based, except for ligand of AB class. Moreover, they are comparable with the other results obtained with approaches based on the on three- dimensional structure (GCN Method with Contact Map, GCN Method with Hierarchical Representation, Daberdaku et al., SPIDER, PrISE).

4   Conclusions and Future Work

In this work, we have faced the protein interfaces prediction considering fragments of the amino acid sequence. We have proposed ProSPs, a method based on the sliding windows approach and the Random Forest technique as a residue classifier. Such a method considers the minimum difference of normalized entropy to select the length of the sliding windows. Such a sliding windows approach is a fundamental aspect when only parts of proteins are known since it allows us to consider only fragments of the amino acid sequence. We tested the ProSPs on two classes of proteins, Antibody-Antigen and Antigen-Bound Antibody, extracted from the Protein-Protein Docking Benchmark 5.0. The obtained results evaluated in terms of the AU-ROC on these classes outperform HomPPI, a sequence-based competitor. They are comparable with the ones based on three-dimensional structure (GCN Method with Contact Map, GCN Method with Hierarchical Representation, Daberdaku et al., SPIDER, PrISE). As future work, we plan to apply our framework to all classes of DB5. Moreover, we intend to investigate the role of the length of the sliding windows. Therefore, we want to consider other methods to determine the number. Feature selection is another fundamental aspect to investigate since it represents a crucial step to represent the data. Moreover, our approach achieves better classification results for receptors than ligands, so we plan to evaluate different sets of features for the various protein classes. Motivated by the obtained results, we intend to extend the framework for predicting interacting sites in Protein-RNA interaction complexes. Moreover, we want also to consider the whole 3D structure of proteins considering structural features, such as the protein secondary structure by further exploring the RNA-based methodology introduced in [18,20,21].

Funding. MQ is supported by the "GNCS - INdAM". CF has been partially supported by the University of Padua project BIRD189710/18 "Reliable identification of the PPI interface in multiunit protein complexes".

References

1. Ahmad, S., Mizuguchi, K.: Partner-aware prediction of interacting residues in protein-protein complexes from sequence data. PLoS ONE **6**(12), e29104 (2011)
2. Amit, Y., Geman, D.: Shape quantization and recognition with randomized trees. Neural Comput. **9**(7), 1545–1588 (1997)
3. Berggård, T., Linse, S., James, P.: Methods for the detection and analysis of protein-protein interactions. Proteomics **7**(16), 2833–2842 (2007)
4. Breiman, L.: Random forests. Mach. Learn. **45**(1), 5–32 (2001)
5. Daberdaku, S.: Structure-based antibody paratope prediction with 3D zernike descriptors and SVM. In: Raposo, M., Ribeiro, P., Sério, S., Staiano, A., Ciaramella, A. (eds.) CIBB 2018. LNCS, vol. 11925, pp. 27–49. Springer, Cham (2020). https://doi.org/10.1007/978-3-030-34585-3_4
6. Daberdaku, S., Ferrari, C.: Exploring the potential of 3D Zernike descriptors and SVM for protein-protein interface prediction. BMC Bioinform. **19**(1), 35 (2018)
7. Daberdaku, S., Ferrari, C.: Antibody interface prediction with 3D Zernike descriptors and SVM. Bioinformatics **35**(11), 1870–1876 (2019)
8. Fry, D.C.: Protein-protein interactions as targets for small molecule drug discovery. Peptide Sci. Original Res. Biomolecules **84**(6), 535–552 (2006)
9. Ho, T.K.: Random decision forests. In: Proceedings of 3rd International Conference on Document Analysis and Recognition, vol. 1, pp. 278–282. IEEE (1995)

10. Ho, T.K.: The random subspace method for constructing decision forests. IEEE Trans. Pattern Anal. Mach. Intell. **20**(8), 832–844 (1998)

11. Jordan, R.A., Yasser, E.M., Dobbs, D., Honavar, V.: Predicting protein-protein interface residues using local surface structural similarity. BMC Bioinform. **13**(1), 41 (2012)

12. Kawashima, S., Pokarowski, P., Pokarowska, M., Kolinski, A., Katayama, T., Kanehisa, M.: Aaindex: amino acid index database, progress report 2008. Nucleic Acids Res. **36**(suppl_1), D202–D205 (2007)

13. Keskin, O., Tuncbag, N., Gursoy, A.: Predicting protein-protein interactions from the molecular to the proteome level. Chem. Rev. **116**(8), 4884–4909 (2016)

14. Murakami, Y., Mizuguchi, K.: Applying the naïve bayes classifier with kernel density estimation to the prediction of protein-protein interaction sites. Bioinformatics **26**(15), 1841–1848 (2010)

15. Pedregosa, F., et al.: Scikit-learn: machine learning in python. J. Mach. Learn. Res. **12**, 2825–2830 (2011). http://jmlr.org/papers/v12/pedregosa11a.html

16. Porollo, A., Meller, J.: Prediction-based fingerprints of protein-protein interactions. Proteins: Struct. Funct. Bioinform. **66**(3), 630–645 (2007)

17. Porollo, A., Meller, J., Cai, W., Hong, H.: Computational methods for prediction of protein-protein interaction sites. Protein-Protein Interact. Comput. Exp. Tools **472**, 3–26 (2012)

18. Quadrini, M., Culmone, R., Merelli, E.: Topological classification of RNA structures via intersection graph. In: Martín-Vide, C., Neruda, R., Vega-Rodríguez, M.A. (eds.) TPNC 2017. LNCS, vol. 10687, pp. 203–215. Springer, Cham (2017). https://doi.org/10.1007/978-3-319-71069-3_16

19. Quadrini, M., Daberdaku, S., Ferrari, C.: Hierarchical representation and graph convolutional networks for the prediction of protein–protein interaction sites. In: Nicosia, G., Ojha, V., La Malfa, E., Jansen, G., Sciacca, V., Pardalos, P., Giuffrida, G., Umeton, R. (eds.) LOD 2020. LNCS, vol. 12566, pp. 409–420. Springer, Cham (2020). https://doi.org/10.1007/978-3-030-64580-9_34

20. Quadrini., M., Merelli., E., Piergallini., R.: Loop grammars to identify RNA structural patterns. In: Proceedings of the 12th International Joint Conference on Biomedical Engineering Systems and Technologies - Volume 3: BIOINFORMATICS, pp. 302–309. SciTePress (2019)

21. Quadrini, M., Tesei, L., Merelli, E.: ASPRAlign: a tool for the alignment of RNA secondary structures with arbitrary pseudoknots. Bioinformatics **36**(11), 3578–3579 (2020)

22. Saha, I., Maulik, U., Bandyopadhyay, S., Plewczynski, D.: Fuzzy clustering of physicochemical and biochemical properties of amino acids. Amino Acids **43**(2), 583–594 (2012)

23. Šikić, M., Tomić, S., Vlahoviček, K.: Prediction of protein-protein interaction sites in sequences and 3d structures by random forests. PLoS Comput. Biol. **5**(1), e1000278 (2009)

24. Sriwastava, B.K., Basu, S., Maulik, U.: Predicting protein-protein interaction sites with a novel membership based fuzzy SVM classifier. IEEE/ACM Trans. Comput. Biol. Bioinf. **12**(6), 1394–1404 (2015)

25. Vreven, T., et al.: Updates to the integrated protein-protein interaction benchmarks: docking benchmark version 5 and affinity benchmark version 2. J. Mol. Biol. **427**(19), 3031–3041 (2015)

26. Xue, L.C., Dobbs, D., Honavar, V.: Homppi: a class of sequence homology based protein-protein interface prediction methods. BMC Bioinform. **12**(1), 244 (2011)

27. Yin, S., Proctor, E.A., Lugovskoy, A.A., Dokholyan, N.V.: Fast screening of protein surfaces using geometric invariant fingerprints. Proc. Natl. Acad. Sci. **106**(39), 16622–16626 (2009)

28. Zhang, B., Li, J., Quan, L., Chen, Y., Lü, Q.: Sequence-based prediction of protein-protein interaction sites by simplified long short-term memory network. Neurocomputing **357**, 86–100 (2019)

The Label Recorder Method

Testing the Memorization Capacity of Machine Learning Models

Kyle Rong$^{(\boxtimes)}$, Aditya Khant$^{(\boxtimes)}$, David Flores$^{(\boxtimes)}$,
and George D. Montañez$^{(\boxtimes)}$

AMISTAD Lab, Harvey Mudd College, Claremont, CA 91711, USA
{krong,akhant,deflores,gmontanez}@hmc.edu

Abstract. Highly-parameterized deep neural networks are known to have strong data-memorization capability, but does this ability to memorize random data also extend to simple standard learning methods with few parameters? Following recent work exploring memorization in deep learning, we investigate memorization in standard non-neural learning models through the label recorder method, which uses a model's training accuracy on randomized data to estimate its memorization ability, giving a distribution- and regularization-dependent label recording score. Label recording scores can be used to measure how capacity changes in response to regularization and other hyperparameter choices. This method is fully empirical, easy to implement, and works for all black-box classification methods. The label recording score supplements existing theoretical measures of model capacity such as Rademacher complexity and Vapnik-Chervonenkis (VC) dimension, while agreeing with conventional intuitions regarding statistical learning processes. We find that memorization ability is not limited to only over-parameterized models, but instead exists as a continuum, being present (to some degree) even in simple learning models with few parameters.

Keywords: Representational capacity · Label recorder · Label recording score

1 Introduction

Representational capacity of a model captures the ability of a model to fit various distributions [3,6,10]. A low-capacity model is incapable of fitting a complex training dataset, leading to underfitting and poor generalization. A high-capacity model can memorize a training dataset and overfit [1,2]. Thus, representational capacity is central to understanding whether a model will generalize well given a training set, and is of general importance in machine learning research.

VC (Vapnik-Chervonenkis) dimension and Rademacher complexity are well-known theoretical measures of representational capacity. The VC dimension upper bounds the capacity of a model by considering the maximum size of a dataset for which the model can correctly draw decision boundaries that differentiate all possible label combinations [13]. In contrast, Rademacher complexity measures a model's capacity through its ability to fit random noise, gauging the maximum expected correlation that a model can

---

K. Rong and A. Khant—These authors contributed equally.

ⓒ Springer Nature Switzerland AG 2022
G. Nicosia et al. (Eds.): LOD 2021, LNCS 13163, pp. 581–595, 2022.
https://doi.org/10.1007/978-3-030-95467-3_42

create between its predicted labels and the true (random) labels. Rademacher complexity has been used to create algorithms for learning kernels [4] and to improve generalization performance of models trained with adversarial learning [15].

We take inspiration from these theoretical tools to present an empirical method for estimating representational capacity, called the *label recorder method*. In the spirit of Rademacher complexity, the label recorder method evaluates a learning algorithm's ability to fit noise and provides an empirical method for the same. It does this by training and evaluating a model on the same set of randomized data, hence the name *label recorder*, as this method trains the model to record labels of random data. We seek to measure the ability of a model to store and recall information from a random dataset, in which there is no exploitable regularity between features and labels to compress. In supervised learning, correct label prediction is the result of memorization, generalization, and luck, in some combination. By using data with no dependence between features and labels we remove the contribution of generalization, which allows us to probabilistically bound a method's information storage capacity for its models, a quantity that affects its generalization behavior [1, 2, 14]. We refer to the accuracy of the model in reproducing labels as its *label recording score*.

The label recorder method was first introduced by Sandoval Segura et al. [11]. They demonstrated how to directly estimate model capacity by proposing the label distribution matrix (LDM). For a model and some pre-selected datasets, the matrix computes the probabilities that the model predicts each possible labeling for each dataset and stores them in simplex vectors. It determines a probability distribution that can generate these simplex vectors and uses the entropy of the recovered distribution to infer the flexibility of a model. The more uniformly a model spreads its corresponding probability mass over the support (i.e., over the possible labelings of test examples), the more flexible the model is. To verify their method, Sandoval Segura et al. ran experiments to determine whether the LDM was a good empirical measure, but the results were inconclusive. In the paper, Sandoval Segura et al. also introduced the label recorder method. They showed that the method was promising because initial results of the method aligned with intuition about the models tested. In our paper, we provide theoretical background, continue the empirical exploration of the label recorder method, and explore its implications on model capacity with more experiments and a wider range of models.

Zhang et al. recently investigated the relationship (or lack thereof) between memorization and generalization for deep neural networks [16]. By training and testing state-of-the-art neural network models on randomized data, Zhang et al. determined that models which memorize training data perfectly can still generalize well. Smith and Le followed up on the work of Zhang et al., considering the memorization ability of logistic regression models [12]. They showed that a weakly regularized logistic regression model generalizes well, despite perfectly memorizing training data for the MNIST dataset, similar to the behavior observed by Zhang et al. Others have looked at the ability of human beings to create concepts from randomly generated data as a way of estimating human Rademacher complexity [17]. These experiments serve as inspiration for the label recorder method, and our study extends this mode of investigation to the memorization behavior of several standard non-neural learning methods.

2   Experimental Setup

We now describe our experimental setup, namely, the models, datasets, and data randomization methods used by our label recorder experiments. The standard classification methods we investigate are listed in Table 1. For Decision Trees and Random Forest, we generated groups of models by varying the tree depth regularization parameter from 1 to 21, in increments of 5. For the k-Nearest Neighbors algorithm, we do the same by varying the k regularization parameter from 6 to 21, in increments of 5. We used the default parameters in sklearn toolkit for rest of the models [8].

Table 1. List of models used, their abbreviations and hyperparameters varied.

Model name	Abbreviation	Hyperparameters
Decision Trees	DT	Depth: 1–21, Criterion: Gini Impurity
k-Nearest Neighbors	KNN	k:1–21, Weights: Uniform
Random Forest	RF	Max-Depth: 1–21, Criterion: Gini
Adaboost	AB	Learning Rate: 1.0, Algorithm: SAMME.R
Quadratic Discriminant	QD	Priors: None, Regularization Parameter: 0
Gaussian Process Classifier	GPC	Optimizer:fmin_l_bfgs_b, Max Iters: 100
Gaussian Naive Bayes	NB	Priors: None, Smoothing: 10^{-9}
Linear Support Vector Machine	LinearSVC	Penalty: l2, Loss: Square-hinged
Logistic Regression	LogReg	Penalty: l2. Tolerance: 10^{-4}

We use two variants of data for our experiments. The first variant, as in Smith and Le [12], is a randomized digits dataset. For computational efficiency, we used an abridged version of randomized digits dataset, called Digits, provided by the scikit-learn library [9]. To create a balanced binary classification problem (which facilitates our later analysis), we select the 150 samples with label 0 and 150 samples with label 1 from that dataset. To randomize this digits dataset, we shuffle the labels of the samples. Then, for each model, we train it on this shuffled dataset and measure its training accuracy (namely, testing it on the same training set). To ensure the statistical significance of the results, for each algorithm and hyperparameter configuration, we repeat the above process for 500 independent trials, and compute the average and 95% confidence intervals of the resulting accuracy values. The average of those values is the label recording score of that model for the randomized Digits dataset.

However, the Digits dataset is limited in that we cannot vary the number of features nor the number of labels without compromising the distribution (digits data) that the dataset represents. Furthermore, being a real categorical dataset, the samples of the Digits dataset cluster in Euclidean space and do not represent a uniform random sampling of that space. We therefore create an additional dataset variant through uniform random sampling. This scheme generates random features and labels using integers drawn from a uniform random distribution. To create different datasets, we vary the parameters of the randomly sampled datasets as follows. The number of features for each sample ranges between 2 and 12 dimensions. The sizes of the datasets vary between 100 and

5000 samples. Finally, to compute the label recording score for the models on each dataset, we apply the label recorder method as described in the Digits experiments.

In the following section, we organize our analysis of the results in the following ways. First, we explore how label recording scores differ between the dataset variants, demonstrating the distribution dependency of label recording scores. Then, we inspect the label recording scores for all models on the shuffled Digits dataset; this demonstrates how label recording scores differ across models. After this, we use the results of the full synthetic data experiments to investigate how dataset parameters and model hyperparameters affect the label recording score of the models. Lastly, we conduct a brief theoretical analysis of the label recorder method, showing how scores can be probabilistically mapped to memorization capacities for rote learners and other supervised classification methods. Throughout all sections, we explore how the label recording score aligns with intuition on model capacity through the lens of decision boundaries.

3   Results

3.1   Differences Between Data Distributions

First, we investigate how the distribution of our datasets affects the label recording score for our models. We observe that the label recording score for models on the shuffled Digits dataset (shown in Table 3) and those of the fully synthetic data (Table 4) are clearly different. Namely, the label recording score of each model is generally lower for the shuffled Digits dataset than for the fully synthetic dataset. We can explain this phenomenon through the consideration of decision boundaries. As embodied in the notion of VC dimension, the more difficult it is to shatter a dataset, the harder it is to memorize that dataset. We hypothesize that it is more difficult to shatter the shuffled Digits dataset, i.e., to draw decision boundaries that separate the samples of that dataset by label within the feature space, than it is for the fully synthetic data, explaining the lower label recording scores for the former dataset variant. We also hypothesize that the shuffled Digits dataset is more difficult to shatter than the real Digits dataset.

To verify this, we use t-SNE [5] to visualize the spatial distribution of the samples of the real Digits dataset, the shuffled Digits dataset, and the uniform random (fully synthetic) dataset, as shown in Fig. 1, projecting the samples onto a two-dimensional plane. In the resulting plots, we first notice the real digits dataset clusters samples of similar labels (as expected) while shuffled digits dataset clusters samples of different labels (due to randomization). In other words, shuffling the labels of the real Digits dataset preserves the clustering of samples but makes it harder to assign the same label to samples that are close to each other in feature space. Thus, it is more difficult for a model to draw a good decision boundary on the shuffled Digits dataset than on the real Digits dataset, which is expected as the former dataset has no correlation between labels and features.

We can also compare the t-SNE visualizations of the shuffled Digits and fully synthetic datasets. Note that the visualized synthetic dataset has the same number of samples and features as those of the shuffled Digits dataset. As shown in the Fig. 1, while both datasets have differently-labeled samples in close proximity, those of the shuffled Digits dataset are tightly clustered in groups while those of the fully synthetic dataset are more spread out in a spherical shape, due to the uniform random sampling. Thus, by the same logic as before, the shuffled Digits dataset is more difficult to shatter than the fully synthetic dataset, matching our hypothesis and explaining the higher label recording scores on the fully synthetic dataset.

We confirm our observations from the t-SNE visualization by quantifying the spread of differently labeled samples of the examined datasets. For each dataset, we calculate the average Euclidean distance from samples to their closest neighbors (ignoring labels), as well as to their closest differently-labeled and closest same-labeled neighbors. The results are in Table 2. As shown in the table, in both the full feature space and projected t-SNE space, the shuffled Digits dataset has smaller spread for differently labeled data points than both the real Digits dataset and the fully synthetic dataset.

While the shuffled Digits dataset has lower label recording scores than the fully synthetic dataset, we observe that their relative scores are similar. Specifically, when we rank the models by their scores in Table 3 and Table 4 respectively, all but two models (namely NB and QD) have the same rank. Also, preliminary experiments demonstrated that the label recording score trends with respect to dataset (i.e., the shape of the visualized line charts) of the two variants resembled each other. Combined with the fact that it easier to try different numbers of features and samples using the fully synthetic variant, we use the fully synthetic data to investigate the effects of dataset and model parameters on label recording score. We present these results in Sects. 3.3–3.5.

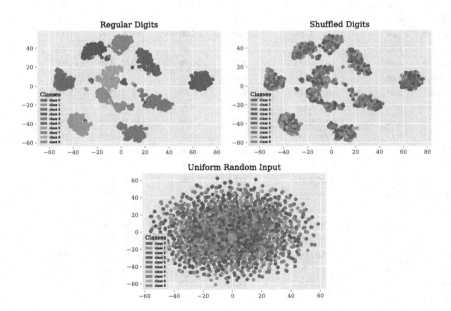

Fig. 1. The results of t-SNE for regular/true Digits dataset and Digits dataset with shuffled labels, as well as the fully synthetic uniform random dataset.

Table 2. Average Euclidean distance between a point and its nearest neighbor with specified label type in specified dataset.

Label type	Dataset	Avg. feature space distance	Avg. t-SNE space distance
Same label	Real Digits	16.47	0.728
Same label	Shuffled Digits	22.05	2.261
Same label	Fully Synthetic	41.98	3.847
Different label	Real Digits	29.50	11.54
Different label	Shuffled Digits	16.62	0.638
Different label	Fully synthetic	39.42	1.071
Any label	Real Digits	16.44	0.593
Any label	Shuffled Digits	16.44	0.593
Any label	Fully synthetic	39.32	0.977

Table 3. Label recording scores for the shuffled Digits dataset. Maximum label recording scores (corresponding to perfect memorization) are bolded.

Model	Digits input Avg. accuracy	Digits input 95% Conf. Int.
NB	0.52	(0.52, 0.52)
GPC	**1.00**	(1.00, 1.00)
AB	0.81	(0.80, 0.81)
QD	0.63	(0.61, 0.65)
KNN$_1$	**1.00**	(1.00, 1.00)
KNN$_6$	0.65	(0.65, 0.66)
KNN$_{11}$	0.62	(0.62, 0.63)
KNN$_{16}$	0.60	(0.59, 0.60)
KNN$_{21}$	0.59	(0.58, 0.59)
DT$_1$	0.56	(0.56, 0.57)
DT$_6$	0.79	(0.78, 0.81)
DT$_{11}$	0.97	(0.97, 0.98)
DT$_{16}$	**1.00**	(1.00, 1.00)
DT$_{21}$	**1.00**	(1.00, 1.00)
RF$_1$	0.62	(0.61, 0.63)
RF$_6$	0.98	(0.97, 0.98)
RF$_{11}$	**1.00**	(1.00, 1.00)
RF$_{16}$	**1.00**	(1.00, 1.00)
RF$_{21}$	**1.00**	(1.00, 1.00)
LinearSVC	0.56	(0.55, 0.57)
LogReg	0.66	(0.66, 0.67)

Table 4. Label recording scores for fully synthetic data.

Model	Rand. input avg. acc.	Random input 95% conf. int.	Random average minus digits avg.
NB	0.73	(0.72, 0.73)	0.21
GPC	**1.00**	(1.00, 1.00)	0.00
AB	0.87	(0.87, 0.88)	0.06
QD	**1.00**	(1.00, 1.00)	0.37
KNN$_1$	**1.00**	(1.00, 1.00)	0.00
KNN$_6$	0.66	(0.65, 0.66)	0.01
KNN$_{11}$	0.62	(0.61, 0.63)	0.00
KNN$_{16}$	0.60	(0.59, 0.60)	0.00
KNN$_{21}$	0.59	(0.58, 0.59)	0.00
DT$_1$	0.58	(0.58, 0.58)	0.02
DT$_6$	0.87	(0.86, 0.88)	0.08
DT$_{11}$	**1.00**	(1.00, 1.00)	0.03
DT$_{16}$	**1.00**	(1.00, 1.00)	0.00
DT$_{21}$	**1.00**	(1.00, 1.00)	0.00
RF$_1$	0.74	(0.74, 0.75)	0.12
RF$_6$	**1.00**	(1.00, 1.00)	0.02
RF$_{11}$	**1.00**	(1.00, 1.00)	0.00
RF$_{16}$	**1.00**	(1.00, 1.00)	0.00
RF$_{21}$	**1.00**	(1.00, 1.00)	0.00
LinearSVC	0.59	(0.58, 0.60)	0.03
LogReg	0.70	(0.70, 0.71)	0.04

3.2   Examining Labeled Recorder Scores

We begin by inspecting the label recording scores for the models trained on the shuffled Digits dataset. Given the randomization of labels and the balance in the distribution of the labels in the shuffled Digits dataset, one might guess that the result of training would not be much better than random guessing. However, to the contrary, we observe that many models perform significantly better than a uniform random guesser, with some achieving perfect memorization. The baseline expected accuracy for a uniform random guesser is $1/\ell$ where ℓ is the number of class labels. Table 3 gives the label recording scores for the various methods, with an average standard deviation of 0.01.

All methods perform better than 0.5, which is the baseline for a random guesser over two evenly distributed classes, and several methods achieve perfect accuracy. This demonstrates that above average labeling recording capacity is not exclusive to neural networks [16] or even limited to over-parameterized models [12]. Simple models such as depth-limited decision trees and KNN also exhibit nontrivial memorization capacity. While the dataset sizes are small for computational efficiency, our results provide evidence that standard learning methods have above uniform average memorization capacity.

One might be curious about why some methods perform better than others. This happens because of the some methods are able to carve out more complex decision boundaries than others. For example, as its name suggests, a LinearSVC model has a simple linear decision boundary. Thus it is a rigid model and no matter how the decision boundary line is drawn, on a binary classification problem on uniform random data it will perform close to a random guesser. But for tree-like classifiers (such as DT and RF) each branch allows you to encode some decision, thus making the boundary which can exclude or include points. This effectively operates as a way of storing information (namely, label mappings) from a dataset. Zhang et al.'s experiments show that neural networks can perfectly memorize random data [16]. Given many empirical instances where neural networks perform better than standard machine learning models, a difference in label recording capacity serves as one possible explanation for this performance difference.

3.3   Varying Dataset Size

To investigate the effect of dataset size on the label recording score, we conduct an additional set of uniform random data experiments, holding the number of classes, features, and feature values constant, while varying the number of samples.

As seen in Fig. 2, increasing dataset size reduces label recording score for all but the KNN models. It makes intuitive sense that most methods will have lower label recording scores as they try to memorize more random samples, since models with limited storage capacity cannot retain an unlimited number of arbitrary label assignments. Note that the feature hyperspace is finite as it consists of a finite number of dimensions and finite number of possible values for each dimension. As we increase the size of the uniform random dataset, we uniformly sample this feature space more, which makes it such that datasets of larger size are more dense in the feature space. However, the labels of these samples are random; therefore, the samples with conflicting labels of larger datasets are more likely to be in close proximity (or overlap) in the feature space. This makes it more difficult to draw decision boundaries that separate and thus correctly label the uniform random samples. Thus, for most standard machine learning models, especially those whose decision boundaries are calculated using the entire dataset, the label recording score decreases with more samples, and models with these characteristics tend to approach random guessing asymptotically.

As the size of the datasets increase, Fig. 2 shows that the average accuracies approach steady rates of decline, which is expected once models saturate their memorization capacity. Indeed, by computing the first and second pseudo-derivatives of the average accuracy using the differences in consecutive terms, we find that for all models the rates of change approach zero (results not shown).

In contrast to most models, the label recording scores of KNN models do not asymptotically decrease nor increase as the number of samples increases. Consider how KNN creates its decision boundaries as it trains on more samples: the predictions of a KNN model are only a function of the input sample's k nearest points. While other methods typically use the entire training set to generate a decision boundary, KNN draws its decision boundaries locally by labeling a sample with the most common label among the input sample's k nearest points. Thus, the decision boundary of a KNN model is a hyperdimensional polytope defined by the k closest samples to each point in the feature space. As more samples fill the feature space, the polytopes of the decision boundaries shrink.

Given that KNN predicts using local data points and the random nature of our data, we can calculate the expected accuracy or label recording score for a KNN model of a given k hyperparameter, and compare for agreement with our experimental results. For example, for KNN_2 testing on its own training data, the querying point will consider itself and its closet neighbor. Given that data points are randomly labeled, the neighboring point has equal probability of matching the querying point's label, and thus of being correct, assuming ties are broken randomly. For KNN_6, we can find the probability that two or more randomly labeled neighbors share the same label as the querying point to produce a correct classification, again assuming randomly broken ties and binary labels. There are 2^5 ways assigning binary labels to the 5 neighbors. We compute the probability of a correct classification as follows: there is 1 way to get all 5 other neighbors to have the specified label; there are $\binom{5}{4}$ ways to have 4 neighbors with the specified label; and there are $\binom{5}{3}$ ways to have 3 neighbors with the specified label. Assuming that KNN breaks ties randomly, there is a $\frac{1}{2}\binom{5}{2}/2^5$ probability of having exactly 2 neighbors with the specified label to get a plurality. The probability of getting a correct label is

$$\frac{\left[1 + \binom{5}{4} + \binom{5}{3} + \frac{1}{2}\binom{5}{2}\right]}{2^5} \approx 0.656.$$

This agrees precisely with our observed results.

Besides the geometric interpretation, we can also think about the KNN results analytically. For each new data point, KNN determines its labeling by collecting the votes from its k-nearest neighbors. From another perspective, the model takes in the k-nearest neighbors (the rest of the dataset actually does not matter) and forms a classifier; we will call this a KNN-subclassifier. The larger a dataset, the more KNN-subclassifiers there are. Hence KNN is an ensemble of n KNN-subclassifers, and this ensemble without size limitation explains why KNN has a consistent capacity across different dataset size. KNN_1 is not displayed here as it has a 100% accuracy because it uses only one data point, which is itself, and training and testing data is identical.

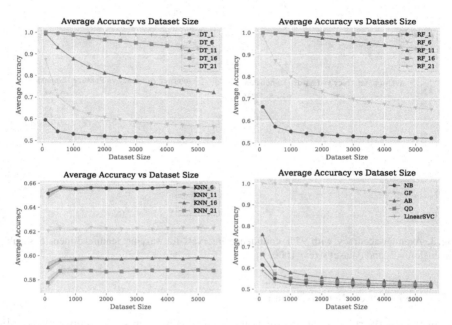

Fig. 2. Average accuracy with 95% confidence intervals for varying dataset size, label dimension = 2, and feature dimension = 5.

3.4   Varying the Number of Features

We next vary the number of feature dimensions. Here the dataset consists of data with 10 possible labels and 750 data points, drawn from a uniform distribution.

As shown in Fig. 3, in most cases the label recording score increases as the feature dimension increases. With fewer features, the feature space is smaller and we are more likely to experience collisions, namely, the same or similar samples having different labels. By the same logic, with few features each model (which maps features to labels) will have less information to work with. Conversely, increasing the number of features reduces these collisions. Note that weakly regularized tree-based models, e.g., Decision Trees and Random Forests with large tree depths, have high label recording scores irrespective of increasing feature dimension, because they are able to take advantage of these features in a better way through encoding each individual feature as a level of the tree. KNNs remain unaffected by changing feature dimensions because, as explained in Sect. 3.3, they perform inference locally and not globally.

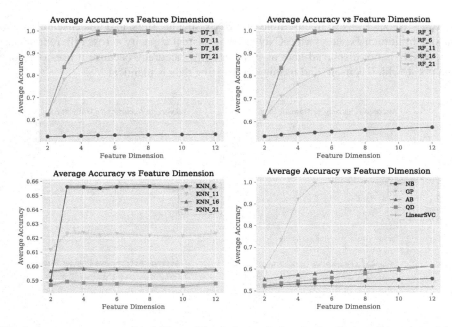

Fig. 3. Average accuracy with 95% confidence intervals for varying feature dimensions, label dimension = 2, and dataset size = 1000.

3.5 The Effect of Regularization

To investigate the regularization effect on label recording scores, we compare the results of the KNN, decision trees, and random forest models with varying regularization parameters. In particular, note that having a larger number of neighbors increases regularization for the KNN model while a lower maximum tree depth increases regularization for decision tree and random forest models.

In agreement with expectation, Fig. 4 shows that the more regularized a model is, the less it memorizes, highlighting how the label recording score is an intuitive measure of memorization capability. Because the data is random, this suggests the label recording score can be a useful empirical proxy for representational capacity.

3.6 Using the Label Recording Score to Gain Insights on New Models

From our analysis, we see that the label recorder score intuitively responds to changes in the parameters of the machine learning problem and model. For example, we've demonstrated a correspondence between the increase of data complexity and size and regularization of the model with the decrease of the label recording score—reflecting the model's memorization ability. It is a natural extension of this observation to use the label recorder score to gain insight into new models. For example, if adjusting a parameter of a model decreases the label recording score, we might speculate that the parameter regularizes the model. As another example, if a model's label recording score

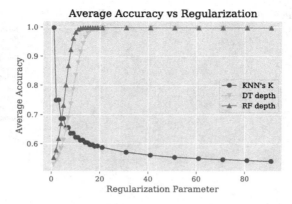

Fig. 4. Average accuracy with 95% confidence intervals for varying regularization parameters, label dimension = 2, feature dimension = 5, and dataset size = 1000.

does not change significantly as we increase the dataset size, we might surmise that the model creates local decision boundaries similar to those of KNN. This could be an area of further investigation.

As observed in the differences in label recording score between the two dataset variants (keeping dataset size and number of features fixed), the label recording score is distribution dependent. This might indicate that a model's memorization ability depends on the distribution from which the training data is sampled. From the perspective of representational capacity, this tells us that models are better at representing some types of data rather than others.

4   Theoretical Analysis

In this section we perform a preliminary theoretical analysis of some properties of the label recorder method, showing how to probabilistically relate label recording scores to model capacities, and work through an example using simple memorization models for which exact capacities are known. A fuller theoretical treatment is the subject of future work.

4.1   Rote Memorizer

As the name suggests, a *Rote Memorizer* memorizes some finite number of examples and will uniformly randomly guess the label of any example not memorized. It is implemented via a simple look-up table, with the features as keys and the labels as values. Figure 5 shows the label recording performance for rote memorizers of varying capacities, as measured in the number of examples memorized. As expected, a rote memorizer has perfect accuracy when the number of examples is fewer than its memorization capacity, and accuracy decreases once the dataset size exceeds its capacity.

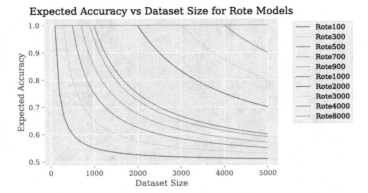

Fig. 5. Analytical plot for varying dataset size for Rote models, with varying number of examples memorized (i.e., Rote100 refers to a rote memorizer capable of storing 100 examples). The label dimension of the dataset is 2, and feature dimension is 5. These analytical plots agree with subsequent independent empirical validation (figure not shown).

Comparing Figs. 5 and 2, which demonstrate the effects of varying dataset size on the Rote Memorizer and other models, we see that both have similar asymptotic behavior of approaching 0.5, that is, they both turn into random guessers for large dataset sizes. There is a corresponding decrease in accuracy after the models are saturated, which for most models occurs with the smallest dataset tested ($n = 100$), suggesting that their capacity is smaller than needed to perfectly memorize all examples. It may additionally demonstrate a strong reliance on dependence between features and labels, or between data points themselves, suggesting a strategy of generalization rather than memorization [7]. Removing all dependence would hinder these methods accordingly. Additionally, while Rote memorizers can store feature-label pairs independently of one another, generalizing methods like Logistic Regression and Decision Trees store their information in interacting ways, such that changing the classifier to correctly label one point often affects the classification of other points. This further explains why Rote Memorizers demonstrate a sharp "phase transition" after saturation, compared to the more gradual reductions in capacity observed in the other methods.

One can qualitatively compare the curves from real models to those of Rote Memorizers of different capacities. For example, seeing that Adaboost responds to increasing dataset size in a way that closely mimics the Rote100 learner suggests that its memorization capacity is close to 100 examples. Figure 5 can thus serve as a reference guide.

4.2   Expected Label Recording Scores

Let us consider expected accuracy of a Rote Memorizer. Let m be the number of entries that can be memorized by a Rote Memorizer, d be the size of the data set and ℓ be the label dimension. Furthermore, let $m' = \min(m, d)$. The number of correct examples becomes the number of examples memorized plus the number correctly guessed. Thus,

$$\mathbb{E}\left[\text{Accuracy}\right] = \frac{m' + (d - m')\frac{1}{\ell}}{d} = \left(1 - \frac{1}{\ell}\right)\frac{m'}{d} + \frac{1}{\ell} = 1 - \left(1 - \frac{1}{\ell}\right)\left(1 - \frac{m'}{d}\right).$$

For binary classification case with $\ell = 2$, this simplifies to

$$\mathbb{E}\left[\text{Accuracy}\right] = 1 - \left(1 - \frac{1}{2}\right)\left(1 - \frac{m'}{d}\right) = 0.5 + 0.5\left(\frac{m'}{d}\right).$$

When $m' \ll d$, $\mathbb{E}\left[\text{Accuracy}\right] \approx 0.5$, explaining the observed asymptotic behavior.

Similarly, for a general algorithm $\mathcal{A}$ and a dataset D of size d, we can decompose $\mathbb{E}\left[\text{Accuracy}\right]$ into its two components: the accuracy on the memorized portion of the dataset, m'/d, and the accuracy on the remaining, unmemorized portion, $\frac{d-m'}{d}u_{\mathcal{A}}(D)$, where m' is the number of data points that $\mathcal{A}$ can memorize from the dataset D, and $u_{\mathcal{A}}(D)$ is the expected accuracy of the algorithm $\mathcal{A}$ on unmemorized data. This yields

$$\mathbb{E}\left[\text{Accuracy}\right] = \frac{m'}{d} + \frac{d - m'}{d}u_{\mathcal{A}}(D) = 1 - (1 - u_{\mathcal{A}}(D))\left(1 - \frac{m'}{d}\right).$$

For the specific case of a Rote Memorizer on random data D with ℓ labels, we have $u_{\text{rote}}(D) = 1/\ell$, since the Rote Memorizer performs uniform random guessing for all unmemorized parts of the dataset. Because completely random data has no correlation between features and responses, we conjecture $u_{\mathcal{A}}(D)$ will be approximately $1/\ell$ for all methods trained on such datasets, as no generalization is possible, leaving luck and memorization as the only paths to correct label prediction.

4.3   Relating Label Recorder Score to Memorization Capacity

Let $LR(M, D)$ denote the label recording score of model M trained on dataset D, which is the observed accuracy of the model trained and tested on that same dataset. When M is stochastic or D is random, this becomes a random variable $Z = LR(M, D)$, and considering a collection of n random datasets, the label recording score for each dataset D_i is $Z_i = LR(M, D_i)$. Because our datasets are independently and identically distributed, we have $\mathbb{E}\left[\text{Accuracy}\right] = \mathbb{E}\left[Z_i\right]$.

We can reverse the relationship between $\mathbb{E}\left[\text{Accuracy}\right]$ and m' to obtain

$$m' = d\frac{\mathbb{E}\left[\text{Accuracy}\right] - u_{\mathcal{A}}(D)}{1 - u_{\mathcal{A}}(D)}.$$

Therefore, knowing $u_{\mathcal{A}}(D)$ and having a bound on $\mathbb{E}\left[\text{Accuracy}\right]$ would allow us to bound the memorization capacity of a learner.

Consider the average label recording score over n independent trials, $\bar{Z} = \frac{1}{n}\sum_{i=1}^{n}Z_i$. By linearity of expectation, $\mathbb{E}\left[\bar{Z}\right] = \mathbb{E}\left[Z_i\right] = \mathbb{E}\left[\text{Accuracy}\right]$. Since $0 \leq Z_i \leq 1$, we apply Hoeffding's inequality to obtain

$$\mathbb{P}(|\bar{Z} - \mathbb{E}\left[\text{Accuracy}\right]| \geq \varepsilon) = \mathbb{P}(|\bar{Z} - \mathbb{E}\left[\bar{Z}\right]| \geq \varepsilon) \leq 2e^{-2n\varepsilon^2}.$$

With this inequality and the average of n independent observations of the labeling recorder score, we can obtain a probabilistic bound on $\mathbb{E}\left[\text{Accuracy}\right]$, and by extension, on the memorization capacity of a learning method.

Example. For a Rote Memorizer, assume we have computed the label recording score $n = 1000$ times, and found that average of the scores is $\bar{Z} = 0.8$. As such,

$$\mathbb{P}(|0.8 - \mathbb{E}[\text{Accuracy}]| \geq \varepsilon) \leq 2e^{-2000\varepsilon^2} := \delta.$$

For example, with probability at least $1 - \delta \approx 0.9$, we have $|0.8 - \mathbb{E}[\text{Accuracy}]| < 0.04$. For our Rote Memorizer, this implies that with probability greater than $1 - \delta = 0.89$, we have $0.76 < \mathbb{E}[\text{Accuracy}] < 0.84$, and thus,

$$d\frac{0.76 - \frac{1}{\ell}}{1 - \frac{1}{\ell}} < m' < d\frac{0.84 - \frac{1}{\ell}}{1 - \frac{1}{\ell}}.$$

More generally, we can say that for a learning method $\mathcal{A}$ with average label recorder score of $\bar{Z}$ computed from n independent trials, we have

$$\mathbb{P}\left(d\frac{(\bar{Z} - \varepsilon) - u_{\mathcal{A}}(D)}{1 - u_{\mathcal{A}}(D)} < m' < d\frac{(\bar{Z} + \varepsilon) - u_{\mathcal{A}}(D)}{1 - u_{\mathcal{A}}(D)}\right) > 1 - 2e^{-2n\varepsilon^2}. \tag{1}$$

5 Conclusion

We investigate the label recorder method, a way of empirically assessing the (data-dependent) memorization capacity of a model. To use the label recorder method, we train and evaluate a model on the same set of random data, with the evaluation accuracy (i.e., training accuracy) serving as the label recording score. We investigate how the label recording score is influenced by: the distribution of a dataset, the mechanics of a model, the size of a dataset, the number of feature of a dataset, and the regularization parameters of a model. We demonstrate that the label recording score can be explained by reasoning about the decision boundary of each model, and we observe that the relative magnitude of the label recording score matches our intuitions regarding representational capacity. The method is fully empirical and can be applied to black-box classification methods, allowing one to reason about representational and information storage capacity independently from theoretical concerns.

We further suggest that running label recording experiments on black-box models can help us to gain insights into their inner workings and hyperparameter effects on that model. Future research directions include expanding the family of models considered, using label recording scores to estimate the information storage capacity of concrete models, and using estimated capacity to derive probabilistic generalization guarantees. Estimating label recording scores directly from model hyperparameters and parameters of datasets would be useful and desirable, but cannot be done perfectly for arbitrary learning algorithms and datasets, since doing this would allow us to determine whether an arbitrary algorithm will overfit a dataset, a problem recently shown to be formally undecidable [1].

Running label recording on machine learning problems during hyperparameter optimization to compare different variations of models is another promising future application. For example, one could compare the label recording score of stopping a model at 20 epochs vs. 10 epochs. More work remains to investigate the correlations between label recording scores, regularization, and algorithm information storage capacity.

References

1. Bashir, D., Montañez, G.D., Sehra, S., Segura, P.S., Lauw, J.: An information-theoretic perspective on overfitting and underfitting. In: Gallagher, M., Moustafa, N., Lakshika, E. (eds.) AI 2020. LNCS (LNAI), vol. 12576, pp. 347–358. Springer, Cham (2020). https://doi.org/10.1007/978-3-030-64984-5_27
2. Bassily, R., Moran, S., Nachum, I., Shafer, J., Yehudayoff, A.: Learners that use little information. In: Janoos, F., Mohri, M., Sridharan, K. (eds.) Proceedings of Algorithmic Learning Theory. Proceedings of Machine Learning Research, vol. 83, pp. 25–55. PMLR, 07–09 April 2018. http://proceedings.mlr.press/v83/bassily18a.html
3. Castellini, J., Oliehoek, F.A., Savani, R., Whiteson, S.: The representational capacity of action-value networks for multi-agent reinforcement learning. In: Proceedings of the 18th International Conference on Autonomous Agents and MultiAgent Systems, pp. 1862–1864 (2019)
4. Cortes, C., Kloft, M., Mohri, M.: Learning kernels using local rademacher complexity (2013)
5. Maaten, L.V.D., Hinton, G.: Visualizing data using t-SNE. J. Mach. Learn. Res. **9**, 2579–2605 (2008)
6. Mahalunkar, A., Kelleher, J.D.: Using regular languages to explore the representational capacity of recurrent neural architectures. In: Kůrková, V., Manolopoulos, Y., Hammer, B., Iliadis, L., Maglogiannis, I. (eds.) ICANN 2018, Part III. LNCS, vol. 11141, pp. 189–198. Springer, Cham (2018). https://doi.org/10.1007/978-3-030-01424-7_19
7. Montanēz, G.D.: Why Machine Learning Works. In: Dissertation. Carnegie Mellon University (2017)
8. Pedregosa, F., et al.: Scikit-learn: machine learning in Python. J. Mach. Learn. Res. **12**, 2825–2830 (2011)
9. Pedregosa, F., et al.: Scikit-learn: mchine learning in Python. J. Mach. Learn. Rese. **12**, 2825–2830 (2011)
10. Samengo, I., Treves, A.: Representational capacity of a set of independent neurons. Phys. Rev. E **63**(1), 011910 (2000)
11. Sandoval Segura, P., et al.: The Labeling Distribution Matrix (LDM): a tool for estimating machine learning algorithm capacity. In: Rocha, A.P., Steels, L., van den Herik, H.J. (eds.) Proceedings of the 12th International Conference on Agents and Artificial Intelligence, ICAART 2020, Valletta, Malta, 22–24 February 2020, vol. 2, pp. 980–986. SCITEPRESS (2020). https://doi.org/10.5220/0009178209800986
12. Smith, S.L., Le, Q.V.: A Bayesian perspective on generalization and stochastic gradient descent. In: International Conference on Learning Representations (ICLR) (2018)
13. Vapnik, V., Levin, E., Cun, Y.L.: Measuring the VC-dimension of a learning machine. Neural Comput. **6**(5), 851–876 (1994)
14. Xu, A., Raginsky, M.: Information-theoretic analysis of generalization capability of learning algorithms. In: Proceedings of the 31st Conference on Neural Information Processing Systems (2017)
15. Yin, D., Kannan, R., Bartlett, P.: Rademacher complexity for adversarially robust generalization. In: International Conference on Machine Learning, pp. 7085–7094. PMLR (2019)
16. Zhang, C., Bengio, S., Hardt, M., Recht, B., Vinyals, O.: Understanding Deep Learning Requires Rethinking Generalization. CoRR abs/1611.03530 (2016). http://arxiv.org/abs/1611.03530
17. Zhu, J., Gibson, B., Rogers, T.T.: Human Rademacher Complexity. Adv. Neural Inf. Process. Syst. **22**, 2322–2330 (2009)

Neural Weighted A*: Learning Graph Costs and Heuristics with Differentiable Anytime A*

Alberto Archetti$^{(\boxtimes)}$, Marco Cannici , and Matteo Matteucci

Politecnico di Milano, 20133 Milan, Italy
alberto1.archetti@mail.polimi.it,
{marco.cannici,matteo.matteucci}@polimi.it

Abstract. Recently, the trend of incorporating differentiable algorithms into deep learning architectures arose in machine learning research, as the fusion of neural layers and algorithmic layers has been beneficial for handling combinatorial data, such as shortest paths on graphs. Recent works related to data-driven planning aim at learning either cost functions or heuristic functions, but not both. We propose Neural Weighted A*, a differentiable anytime planner able to produce improved representations of planar maps as graph costs and heuristics. Training occurs end-to-end on raw images with direct supervision on planning examples, thanks to a differentiable A* solver integrated into the architecture. More importantly, the user can trade off planning accuracy for efficiency at run-time, using a single, real-valued parameter. The solution suboptimality is constrained within a linear bound equal to the optimal path cost multiplied by the tradeoff parameter. We experimentally show the validity of our claims by testing Neural Weighted A* against several baselines, introducing a novel, tile-based navigation dataset. We outperform similar architectures in planning accuracy and efficiency.

Keywords: Weighted A* · Differentiable algorithms · Data-based planning

1 Introduction

A* [13] is the most famous heuristic-based planning algorithm, and it constitutes one of the essentials for the computer scientist's toolbox. It is widely used in robotic motion [27] and navigation systems [19], but its range extends to all the fields that benefit from shortest path search on graphs [24]. Differently from other shortest path algorithms, such as Dijkstra [10] or Greedy Best First [25], A* is known to be optimally efficient [25]. This means that, besides returning the optimal solution, there is no other algorithm that can be more efficient, in general, provided the same admissible heuristic. Even though optimality seems a desirable property for A*, it is often more of a burden than a virtue in practical

© Springer Nature Switzerland AG 2022
G. Nicosia et al. (Eds.): LOD 2021, LNCS 13163, pp. 596–610, 2022.
https://doi.org/10.1007/978-3-030-95467-3_43

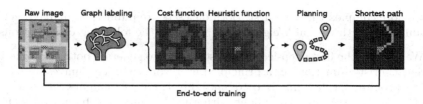

Fig. 1. Can we learn to navigate a terrain effectively by just looking at its map? Neural Weighted A* accurately predicts from the raw image of the navigation area the costs of traversing local regions and a global heuristic for reaching the destination.

applications. This is because, in the worst case, A* takes exponential time to converge to the optimal solution, and this is not affordable in large search spaces.

Another compelling issue of A* is that hand-crafting non-trivial heuristics is costly and reliant on domain knowledge. Despite the prolific research in deep-learning-based graph labeling [33], neural networks often struggle with data exhibiting combinatorial complexity, such as shortest paths [23]. For this reason, many researchers started including differentiable algorithmic layers directly into deep learning pipelines. These layers implement algorithms with combinatorial operations in the forward pass, while providing a smooth, approximated derivative in the backward pass. This approach helps the neural components to converge faster with fewer data samples, promoting the birth of hybrid architectures, trainable end-to-end, that extend the reach of deep learning to complex combinatorial problems. Many backpropagation-ready algorithmic layers have been developed, such as [1,2,6,23,30,32]. Among these, some [6,23,32] propose differentiable shortest path solvers able to learn graph costs from planning examples on raw image inputs. However, none of the previous works tackles heuristic design, which is the essential aspect that makes A* scale to complex scenarios.

With Neural Weighted A* (NWA*), we propose the first deep-learning-based differentiable planner able to predict graph costs and heuristic functions from unlabeled images of navigation areas (Fig. 1). Training occurs end-to-end on shortest-path examples, exploiting a fusion of differentiable planners from [23,32]. Also, NWA* is the first architecture that enables the user to trade off planning accuracy for convergence speed with a single, real-valued parameter, even at runtime. Balancing search accuracy and efficiency from unlabeled images is crucial in many navigation problems. Among the most notable examples, we find hierarchical planning for robotic navigation, where accuracy and efficiency assume a different priority depending on the spacial granularity at which planning is executed, and real-world pedestrian modeling, where graph labeling from raw images is not feasible by hand [32]. As a final remark, since our method arises from the Weighted A* algorithm [12], the solution cost never exceeds the optimal one by a factor proportional to the tradeoff parameter.

We extensively test Neural Weighted A* against the baselines from [23,32], and conduct experiments on two tile-based datasets. The first is adapted from [23], while the second dataset is novel, and its goal is to provide a scenario more complex than the first. Both datasets are publicly available (Sect. 5). In summary, with Neural Weighted A*, we make the following contributions:

- We develop the first deep-learning system able to generate both cost functions and heuristic functions in a principled way from raw map images.
- We propose the first method to smoothly trade off planning accuracy and efficiency at runtime, compliant with the Weighted A* bound on solution suboptimality.
- We augment an existing dataset and propose a new one for planning benchmarks on planar navigation problems.

2   Related Work

Connections between deep learning and differentiable algorithms arise from different domains. The first examples lie within the 3D rendering literature [16], composing neural-network-based encoders with differentiable renderer-like decoders to learn the constructing parameters of the input scene. Differentiable decoders spread to physics simulations [4, 26], logical reasoning [30, 31], and control [1, 11, 15]. Combinatorial optimization is also a topic of interest, from differentiable problem-specific solvers [5, 18, 30] to general-purpose ones [2, 6, 23]. Indeed, many combinatorial algorithms and their differentiable implementation have already been studied, such as Traveling Salesman [5, 9], (Conditional) Markov Random Fields [7, 17, 20, 34], and Shortest Path [32]. Each of these works shows how structured differentiable components enable deep learning architectures to learn combinatorial patterns easily from data.

A handful of works started experimenting with convexity, one of the most important properties of combinatorial optimization. The first is the neural layer by Amos et al. [3], which is constrained to learn convex functions only. Following this work, Pitis et al. [22] exploit the convex neural layer to design a trainable graph-embedding metric that respects triangle inequality. This is beneficial for learning graph costs that encode mathematically sound distances, even though the method is limited to train on a single graph.

Among search-based planning research, some studies focus on a data-driven approach where planning cues are inferred from raw image inputs [6, 23, 32]. In [23], Vlastelica et al. develop a technique to differentiate solvers for integer linear optimization problems, treating them as black-boxes. As the shortest path belongs to this set of problems [28], the authors are able to map images of navigation areas to extremely accurate graph costs, such that the paths evaluated on the cost predictions closely resembles the ground-truth ones. At its core, the technique from [23] consists of a smooth interpolation of the piecewise constant function defined by the black-box solver. This technique is well suited for learning accurate costs, but, due to its black-box nature, cannot address heuristic design, the aspect that makes the search efficient, and which we study in this work.

On the other side of the spectrum, Yonetani et al. [32], reformulate the canonical A* algorithm as a set of differentiable tensor operations. Their goal is to develop a deep-learning-based architecture able to learn improved cost functions such that the planning search avoids non-convenient regions to traverse. In order to train the architecture, the authors define a loss function that minimizes the difference between the nodes expanded by A* and the ground truth paths. Therefore, the neural network is forced to learn shortcuts and bypasses that severely accelerate the search, but may result in inaccurate path predictions.

Lastly, Berthet et al. [6] propose a general-purpose differentiable combinatorial optimizer based on stochastic perturbations with a strong theoretical insight. Despite this work being more recent and general than [23], it was outperformed by [23] in our experimental settings. Therefore, we choose to focus on [23] for the rest of the paper. In fact, our work builds on [23,32] to develop the first learning architecture that is not forced to choose to plan either accurately or efficiently, but is able to smoothly tradeoff between these opposing aspects of planning.

3   Preliminaries

Let $\mathcal{G} = (\mathcal{N}, \mathcal{E})$ be a graph where $\mathcal{N}$ is a finite set of nodes and $\mathcal{E}$ is a finite set of edges connecting the nodes. Let s and t be two distinct nodes from $\mathcal{N}$, called source and target. We define a path y on $\mathcal{G}$ connecting s to t as a sequence of adjacent nodes $(n_0, n_1, \ldots, n_k)$ such that $n_0 = s$, $n_k = t$, and each node is traversed at most once.

In this work, we always refer to the 8-GridWorld setting [6,8,23,32] but the techniques we describe can be easily applied to general graph settings, nevertheless. In 8-GridWorld, nodes are disposed in a grid-like pattern, and edges connect only the nodes belonging to neighboring cells, including the diagonal ones. Each node is paired with a non-negative, real-valued cost belonging to a cost function $\bar{W} \in \mathbb{R}_+^{\mathcal{N}}$. Paths are represented in binary form as $Y \in \{0,1\}^{\mathcal{N}}$ with ones corresponding to the traversed nodes. The total cost of a path Y, denoted as $\langle \bar{W}, Y \rangle$, is the sum of its nodes' costs. Given a graph $\mathcal{G}$ with costs $\bar{W}$, a source node s, and a target node t, the shortest path problem consists of finding the path $\bar{Y}$ having the minimal total cost among all the paths connecting s and t.

3.1   A* and Weighted A*

We focus on A* [13], a heuristic-based shortest path algorithm for graphs. A* searches for a minimum-cost path from s to t iteratively expanding nodes according to the priority measure

$$F(n) = G(n) + H(n). \tag{1}$$

$G(n)$ is the exact cumulated cost from s to n, and $H(n)$ is a heuristic function estimating the cost between n and t. A* is known to be optimally efficient when $H(n)$ is admissible [25], i.e., it never overestimates the optimal cost between n and t. An example of admissible heuristic on 8-GridWorld is

$$H_C(n) = w_{\min} \cdot D_C(n, t) \tag{2}$$

where $w_{\min} = \min_{n \in \mathcal{N}} \bar{W}(n)$ and $D_C(n, t)$ is the Chebyshev distance between n and t in the grid, i.e., $D_C(n, t) = \max\{|n_x - t_x|, |n_y - t_y|\}$.

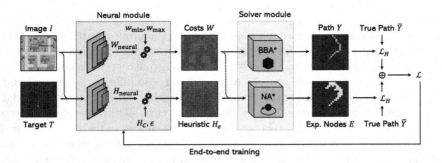

Fig. 2. Schematics of Neural Weighted A*. The neural module (blue) predicts the costs W and the heuristic function H_ϵ. The solver module (yellow) runs two A* solvers, differentiable according to the techniques described in [23,32]. The first solver computes the shortest path Y, while the second computes the nodes expanded by A*, E. (Color figure online)

For large graphs, A* may take exponential time to find the optimal solution [12]. Hence, in practical applications, it is preferable to find an approximate solution quickly, sacrificing the optimality constraint. This idea is explored by one of A*'s extensions, called Weighted A* (WA*) [21]. This algorithm is equivalent to a standard A* search, but the heuristic $H(n)$ in Eq. 1 is scaled up by a factor of $1 + \epsilon$, where $\epsilon \geq 0$. Assuming $H(n)$ to be admissible, WA* returns the optimal path for $\epsilon = 0$. Conversely, for $\epsilon > 0$, the heuristic function drives the search, leading to fewer node expansions, but influencing the path trajectory. The cost difference between the WA* solution Y and the optimal path $\bar{Y}$ is linearly bounded [12]:

$$\langle \bar{W}, Y \rangle \leq (1 + \epsilon) \cdot \langle \bar{W}, \bar{Y} \rangle. \tag{3}$$

4   Neural Weighted A*

In the A* algorithm, the nodes are expanded according to the balance between the cumulated costs $G \in \mathbb{R}_+^{\mathcal{N}}$ and the heuristic function H (Eq. 1). If $G \gg H$, A* expands nodes mostly according to G, behaving similarly to Dijkstra's algorithm. If, on the other hand, $H \gg G$, then the A* behavior is closer to a Greedy Best First search. Therefore, tuning the scale of the final cost and heuristic functions is the key to control the tradeoff between planning accuracy and efficiency. We propose to accomplish this goal with a novel, deep-learning-based architecture for graph labeling from planning examples, called Neural Weighted A* (Fig. 2). It is composed of two modules: the *neural module* (Sect. 4.1) and the *solver module* (Sect. 4.2). The neural module generates planning-ready graph costs and a heuristic function from the top view of the navigation area. The solver module executes the planning procedure in the forward pass, while providing a smooth derivative in the backward pass to enable end-to-end training.

In the following, we indicate with the "neural" subscript values directly coming out of neural networks, such as W_{neural} and H_{neural}, while we use the bar superscript, as in $\bar{W}$ and $\bar{Y}$, to indicate ground-truth values.

4.1   The Neural Module

The neural module is composed of two fully-convolutional neural networks. The first one (upper network in Fig. 2) processes a color image $I \in [0,1]^{\Gamma \times 3}$ of resolution Γ returning a cost prediction $W_{\text{neural}} \in [0,1]^{\mathcal{N}}$. The second neural network (lower network in Fig. 2) takes as input the concatenation of I and the target T, i.e., a matrix with a one corresponding to the target position scaled up to the image resolution Γ, and returns a heuristic prediction $H_{\text{neural}} \in [0,1]^{\mathcal{N}}$. This separation enforces the system to learn costs that are target-agnostic, since T is not included in the input of the first neural network.

In order to control the relative magnitude between the costs and the heuristic function, we uniformly scale the values of W_{neural} in the interval $[w_{\min}, w_{\max}]$ such that $w_{\min} > 0$. We call W the new and final cost function. Then, we compute the final heuristic function as

$$H_\epsilon = (1 + \epsilon \cdot H_{\text{neural}}) \cdot H_C \qquad (4)$$

where H_C is the Chebyshev heuristic (Eq. 2), and $\epsilon \geq 0$ is the accuracy-efficiency tradeoff parameter.

For any node $n \in \mathcal{N}$, the purpose of ϵ and $H_{\text{neural}}(n)$ is to modulate the intensity of the final heuristic $H_\epsilon(n)$ between two values, $H_C(n)$ and $(1 + \epsilon) \cdot H_C(n)$. When $\epsilon = 0$, $H_\epsilon(n)$ is equal to the admissible Chebyshev heuristic $H_C(n)$. Therefore, the solution optimality is guaranteed. Conversely, when $\epsilon > 0$, $H_\epsilon(n)$ is not admissible, in general, anymore. However, if n is a node likely to be convenient to traverse, it is mapped to a value close to $H_C(n)$, as the neural network learns to predict a value $H_{\text{neural}}(n) \approx 0$. If, on the other hand, n seems very unlikely to be traversed, its heuristic value is scaled up by a factor of $1 + \epsilon$, as $H_{\text{neural}} \approx 1$. In this way, by increasing ϵ, we increase the difference in heuristic values between nodes convenient and non-convenient to expand according to the neural prediction, forcing A* to prefer the nodes where $H_{\text{neural}} \approx 0$. Figure 3 visually illustrates the relationship between H_C, H_{neural}, and H_ϵ.

Lastly, we observe that $H_\epsilon(n) \leq (1 + \epsilon) \cdot H_C(n)$. Since H_C is an admissible heuristic function for 8-GridWorld, we are guaranteed, by the Weighted A* bounding result (Sect. 3.1, Eq. 3), to never return a path whose cost exceeds the optimal one by a factor of $1 + \epsilon$.

4.2   The Solver Module

The solver module is composed of two differentiable A* solvers. The first, called Black-Box A*, implements the A* algorithm with black-box differentiation as in [23]. It computes the shortest path Y given the costs W, the admissible Chebyshev heuristic H_C (Eq. 2) and the source-target nodes. The second solver

Fig. 3. From left to right, first: image sample from the Warcraft dataset (Sect. 5). The target node is in the bottom left region of the map. Second: Chebyshev heuristic H_C (Eq. 2). Red indicates high values; blue indicates low values. Third: neural prediction H_{neural}. Fourth: final heuristic H_ϵ (Eq. 4) for $\epsilon = 9$. (Color figure online)

implements Neural A*, as in [32]. It returns the nodes E expanded during the A* search given W, H_ϵ (Eq. 4), and the source-target nodes. The two solvers provide two separate gradient signals. As Y is computed following the black-box derivative from [23], its value is differentiable only with respect to W. Following the Neural A* approach [32], instead, the matrix of expanded nodes, E, is differentiable only with respect to H_ϵ. Within the solver module, we effectively combine the two differentiation techniques, enabling the neural module to learn both costs and heuristics with the proper gradient signal. To this end, we stop propagating the gradient of H_ϵ towards W in the computational graph while running the Neural A* solver (dashed arrow in Fig. 2). This is because H_ϵ is evaluated considering the target T, and we want to be sure that T has no influence whatsoever on the target-agnostic costs W.

In principle, having two separate solvers for the evaluation of Y and E may lead to inconsistencies, as H_ϵ, for $\epsilon > 0$, affects the trajectory of the shortest path. In such a case, Y may contain nodes not belonging to E. However, this side-effect is unavoidable during training to guarantee the correct gradient information propagation and to ensure that W does not depend on T. These theoretical reasons are confirmed by a much lower performance during the experiments when trying to include H_ϵ as heuristic function in Black-Box A*. At testing time, to guarantee the output consistency, the solver module is substituted by a standard A* algorithm with W, H_ϵ, and the source-target pair as inputs, returning Y and E in a single execution.

4.3   Loss Function

The only label required for training Neural Weighted A* is the ground-truth path $\bar{Y} \in \{0, 1\}^{\mathcal{N}}$. In the ideal case, both Y and E are equivalent to $\bar{Y}$, meaning that A* expanded only the nodes belonging to the true shortest path. In a more realistic case, Y is close to $\bar{Y}$ following the same overall course but with minor node differences, while E contains $\bar{Y}$ alongside some nodes from the surrounding area. Since all of these tensors contain binary values, we found the Hamming loss $\mathcal{L}_H$, as in [23], to be the most effective to deal with our learning problem. The final loss is

$$\mathcal{L} = \alpha \cdot \mathcal{L}_H(\bar{Y}, Y) + \beta \cdot \mathcal{L}_H(\bar{Y}, E) \tag{5}$$

Table 1. Datasets' summary statistics.

	Warcraft	Pokémon
Maps I (train, validation, test)	10000, 1000, 1000	3000, 500, 500
Map resolution Γ	96 × 96	320 × 320
Tile resolution	8 × 8	16 × 16
Grid shape $\mathcal{N}$	12 × 12	20 × 20
Cost range	[0.8, 9.2]	[1.0, 25.0]
Targets per image	2	2
Sources per target	2	2
Total number of samples	48000	16000

where α and β are positive, real-valued parameters that bring the loss components to the same order of magnitude. A possible alternative to the Hamming loss is the L1 loss, as in [32]. However, we did not find any reason to prefer it over the Hamming loss. The behavior of L1 in terms of gradient propagation is similar, but the experimental results were worse.

5 Data Generation

To experimentally test our claims about Neural Weighted A*, we use two tile-based datasets.[1] The first is a modified version of the Warcraft II dataset from [23] (Sect. 5.1). The second is a novel dataset from the FireRed-LeafGreen Pokémon tileset (Sect. 5.2). In the latter, the search space is bigger, and the tileset is richer, making the setting more complex. However, Neural Weighted A* shows similar performance in both scenarios outperforming the baselines of [23,32]. Table 1 collects the summary statistics of the two datasets.

5.1 The Warcraft Dataset

The original version of the Warcraft dataset [23] contains paths only from the top-left corner to the bottom-right corner of the image. To make the dataset more challenging, we randomly sampled the source-target pairs from $\mathcal{N}$. For each image-costs pair in the dataset, we chose two target points. The targets lie within a 3-pixel margin from the grid edges. Then, we randomly picked two source points for each target, making four source-target pairs for each map. Each source point is sampled from the quadrant opposite to its target to ensure that each path traverses a moderate portion of the map, as shown in Fig. 4.

5.2 The Pokémon Dataset

The Pokémon dataset is a novel, tile-based dataset we present in this paper. It comes with 4000 RGB images of 320 × 320 pixels generated from Cartographer [29], a random Pokémon map generation tool. Each image is composed

---

[1] https://github.com/archettialberto/tilebased_navigation_datasets.

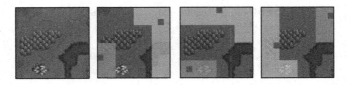

Fig. 4. From left to right, first: image sample from the Warcraft dataset. Second to fourth: examples of valid source-target pairs. Red indicates the target sampling regions, while green indicates the source sampling regions. (Color figure online)

Fig. 5. From left to right, first: image from the Pokémon dataset. Second: wall regions (black), number of steps from the target region (red-to-green gradient), and source-sampling region (green). Third and fourth: examples of valid source-target pairs. (Color figure online)

of 400 tiles, each of 16×16 pixels, arranged in a 20×20 pattern. Each tile is linked to a real-valued cost in the interval $[1, 25]$. The training set comprises 3000 image-costs pairs, while the test and validation sets contain 500 pairs each. For each image-costs pair, we sampled two target points, avoiding non-traversable regions in the original Pokémon game, i.e., where $\bar{W}(n) = 25$. We refer to these regions as walls. Then, we sampled two sources for each target, such that the number of steps separating them is at least 12 (Fig. 5).

The Pokémon dataset provides a setting more challenging than Warcraft. First, the number of rows and columns increases from 12 to 20, making the search space nearly four times bigger. Also, the tileset is richer. Warcraft is limited to only five terrain types (grass, earth, forest, water, and stone), and there is a one-to-one correspondence between terrain types and cost values. These aspects make the tile-to-cost patterns very predictable for the neural component of the architectures. Pokémon, on the other hand, has double the number of individual cost values, spread between the tilesets from four different biomes: beach, forest, tundra, and desert. Also, each image sample may contain buildings. The variability in terms of visual features is richer, and similar costs may correspond to tiles exhibiting very different patterns.

6   Experimental Validation

In the following, we describe the experiments to test the validity of our claims. Each time we refer to results obtained with Neural Weighted A*, we note the ϵ value used for the evaluation of H_ϵ.

Table 2. Metrics' definitions.

Metric	Definition
Cost ratio	$\langle \bar{W}, Y \rangle / \langle \bar{W}, \bar{Y} \rangle$
Generalized cost ratio	$\langle \bar{W}, Y^{(\text{rnd\_s})} \rangle / \langle \bar{W}, \bar{Y}^{(\text{rnd\_s})} \rangle$
Expanded nodes	$\sum_{n \in \mathcal{N}} E(n)$
Generalized expanded nodes	$\sum_{n \in \mathcal{N}} E^{(\text{rnd\_s})}(n)$

6.1 Metrics

To measure the path prediction accuracy of the compared architectures, we use the *cost ratio*, as in [23]. In order to account for cost-equivalent paths, we define the cost ratio as the ratio between the predicted path cost and the optimal path cost, according to the ground-truth costs $\bar{W}$. A cost ratio close to 1 indicates that the system produces cost functions correctly generalizing on new maps.

The cost ratio involves paths that start from the sample source and end in the sample target. Our goal, however, is to generate costs and heuristics that are source-agnostic. In principle, the cost function depends only on the image, while the heuristic also considers the target. The source point should not influence any of the two functions. To account for this behavior, we define the *generalized cost ratio* as the cost ratio measured according to $Y^{(\text{rnd\_s})}$, i.e., the path prediction from a random source point to the target. This new source is sampled uniformly from the valid sampling regions of the two datasets at each metric evaluation.

To measure the efficiency of the architectures, we simply count how many nodes have been expanded at the end of the A* execution. We refer to this metric as *expanded nodes*. Also, we provide the *generalized expanded nodes* metric to account for randomly sampled sources. Table 2 collects the metrics' definitions.

6.2 Experiments

We compare Neural Weighted A* (*NWA**) against the following baselines:

***BBA** (Black-Box A* [23]).** A fully convolutional neural network computes W from I. Then, a Black-Box A* module evaluates the shortest path Y. We follow the implementation of [23], except for the Dijkstra algorithm, substituted by A* with admissible Chebyshev heuristic (Eq. 2).
***NA** (Neural A* [32]).** A fully convolutional neural network computes W from I, using s and t as additional input channels. Then, a Neural A* module [32] evaluates the expanded nodes E. The non-admissible heuristic

$$H_{\text{NA}*}(n) = D_C(n, t) + 0.001 \cdot D_E(n, t) \tag{6}$$

is used to speed up the search, as in [32]. This heuristic is the weighted sum of the Chebyshev distance D_C and the Euclidean distance D_E between n and t in the grid. The non-admissibility arises from the fact that the scaling term $w_{\min}$ is missing, differently from Eq. 2. Despite reducing the expanded nodes, this heuristic adds a strong bias towards paths that move straight to the target, greatly penalizing the cost ratio.

ADM_NA* (**Admissible Neural A***). We propose this architecture as a clone of the original *NA** architecture [32], but we substitute the non-admissible heuristic $H_{\mathrm{NA}*}$ (Eq. 6) with the admissible Chebyshev heuristic H_C (Eq. 2). Our goal is to minimize the influence of the fixed, non-admissible heuristic $H_{\mathrm{NA}*}$ [32] on the expanded nodes E. In this way, the numerical results reflect more accurately the neural predictions, ensuring a fair comparison with *NWA**.

NS_NA* (**No-Source Neural A***). This architecture is equal to *ADM_NA**, except for the source channel, not included in the neural network input. Differently from *NA** and *ADM_NA**, by hiding the information related to the source node location, we expect *NS_NA** to exhibit no sensible performance downgrade between the cost ratio values and the generalized cost ratio values. The same holds for the expanded nodes and the generalized expanded nodes.

6.3   Implementation Details

Each architecture uses convolutional layer blocks from ResNet18 [14], as in [23], to transform tile-based images into cost or heuristic functions, encoded as single-channel tensors. We substitute the first convolution to adapt to the number of input channels, varying between 3 (*BBA**), 4 (*NS_NA**, *NWA**), and 5 (*NA**, *ADM_NA**). In *BBA**, we perform average pooling to reduce the output channels to 1. Then, to ensure that the weights are non-negative, we add a ReLU for Warcraft and a sigmoid for Pokémon. All the baselines involving Neural A* (*NA**, *ADM_NA**, and *NS_NA**), instead, include a 1×1 convolution followed by a sigmoid. Finally, in *NWA**, the channel-reduction strategy depends on the neural network. The cost-predicting ResNet18 is followed by an average operation and a normalization between $w_{\min} = 1$ and $w_{\max} = 10$. The heuristic-predicting ResNet18 is followed by a 1×1 convolution and a normalization in the range $[0, 1]$. Each architecture trains with the Adam optimizer. The learning rate is equal to 0.001. The batch size is 64 for Warcraft and 16 for Pokémon to account for GPU memory usage. The λ parameter of the black-box solvers of *BBA** and *NWA** is 20. The τ parameter of the Neural A* solvers of *NA**, *ADM_NA**, *NS_NA**, and *NWA** is set to the square root of the grid width, so 3.46 for Warcraft and 4.47 for Pokémon. In Eq. 5, we impose $\alpha = 1$ and $\beta = 0.1$ to bring the loss components to the same order of magnitude. We found that the training procedure is not affected by small deviations from the parameters described in this section. Finally, we detected sensible improvements in the efficiency when training *NWA** with random ϵ, as it expanded noticeably fewer nodes than training with fixed ϵ. Since the other metrics do not exhibit sensible differences, we always refer to the test results of *NWA** obtained after training with ϵ sampled from $[0, 9]$ at each H_ϵ evaluation. To ensure the full reproducibility of our experiments, we share the source code.[2]

---

[2] https://github.com/archettialberto/neural_weighted_a_star.

Table 3. Quantitative results on the Warcraft and Pokémon datasets.

Experiment	ϵ	Warcraft dataset				Pokímon dataset			
		CR	Gen. CR	EN	Gen. EN	CR	Gen. CR	EN	Gen. EN
*BBA**	–	**1.0**	**1.0**	69.8	69.94	1.57	1.65	79.78	79.29
*NA**	–	1.29	1.41	**9.81**	**9.82**	2.15	2.57	**15.02**	**14.64**
*ADM_NA**	–	1.04	1.17	13.12	22.48	**1.11**	1.24	26.57	37.03
*NS_NA**	–	1.12	1.11	21.19	21.19	1.16	**1.17**	39.76	39.44
*NWA**	0.0	**1.0**	**1.0**	68.42	69.04	1.06	1.05	124.06	121.2
*NWA**	1.0	1.01	1.01	49.54	50.57	**1.03**	**1.03**	80.21	78.43
*NWA**	4.0	1.03	1.03	26.61	27.15	1.08	1.06	56.4	56.21
*NWA**	9.0	1.1	1.09	14.2	14.47	1.22	1.14	31.54	31.04
*NWA**	11.0	1.13	1.11	12.74	13.0	1.22	1.24	23.37	23.06
*NWA**	14.0	1.15	1.13	**11.94**	**12.12**	1.22	1.35	**20.09**	**19.84**

6.4   Results

We collect the quantitative results of our experiments in Table 3. The table is split into four sections, two for each dataset. Each section contains either baseline experiments or *NWA**-related experiments measured on the same *NWA** architecture fixing different ϵ values at testing time. We comment on the experiments' results by answering the following three questions:

Does NWA* learn to predict cost functions correctly? By observing Table 3, *NWA** reaches a nearly perfect cost ratio on both datasets for a considerable range of ϵ values. This was expected for $\epsilon \approx 0$, but the (generalized) cost ratio remains very low for ϵ up to 4, which is an excellent result considering the corresponding expanded nodes speedup. In Warcraft, *NWA** behaves as *BBA** cost-ratio-wise, while, in Pokímon, it outperforms all the baselines. Since, by setting ϵ to low values, the path predictions do not take into account H_ϵ, the positive cost-ratio-related performance implies that *NWA** learned to predict cost functions that make A* return paths close to the ground-truth.

Does NWA* learn to predict heuristic functions correctly? By setting $\epsilon \gg 0$, H_ϵ drives the search. A* converges faster, but it may return suboptimal paths. Therefore, we expect a small penalty on cost ratios, but a noticeable decrease in the node expansions. Again, the empirical results confirm this trend on both datasets. For $\epsilon = 14$, we outperform all the baselines in terms of generalized node expansions. The only exception is *NA**, which expands fewer nodes, but exhibits an extremely higher cost ratio. *NWA** trades off few node expansions to be much more reliable than *NA** in terms of path predictions.

Can NWA* trade off planning accuracy for efficiency? By setting ϵ close to 0, *NWA** behaves accurately (low cost ratio, high expanded nodes). By increasing ϵ, *NWA** becomes more efficient (higher cost ratio, lower expanded nodes). To visually illustrate the extent of the tradeoff capabilities of *NWA**, we plot in Fig. 6 the generalized metrics (y-axis) for all the

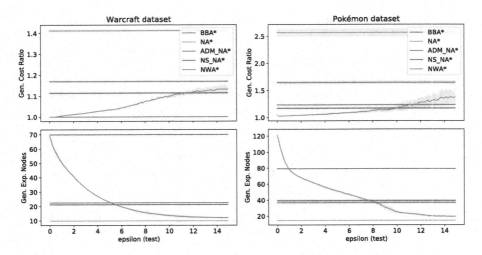

Fig. 6. Comparison between generalized cost ratio and generalized expanded nodes across the experiments for several ϵ values (mean ± std over five restarts). For low ϵ, *NWA** is the most accurate model, while for higher ϵ, it is the most efficient. The only exception is *NA**, which is barely faster but much less reliable in terms of cost ratio.

experiments with respect to several ϵ values (x-axis). Since the baseline architectures do not depend on ϵ, their behavior is plotted as a horizontal line for comparison. *NWA**, on the other hand, smoothly interpolates between the accuracy of *BBA** and the efficiency of *NA**-related architectures, offering to the user the possibility of finely tuning ϵ to the desired planning behavior, from the most accurate to the most efficient.

7   Conclusions

With Neural Weighted A*, we propose a differentiable, anytime shortest path solver able to learn graph costs and heuristics for planning on raw image inputs. The system trains with direct supervision on planning examples, making data labeling cheap. Unlike any similar data-driven planner, we can choose to return the optimal solution or to trade off accuracy for convergence speed by tuning a single, real-valued parameter, even at runtime. We guarantee the solution suboptimality to be constrained within a linear bound proportional to the tradeoff parameter. We experimentally test the validity of our claims on two tile-based datasets. By inspecting the numerical results, we see that Neural Weighted A* consistently outperforms the accuracy and the efficiency of the previous works, obtaining, in a single architecture, the best of the two worlds.

References

1. Amos, B., Jimenez, I., Sacks, J., Boots, B., Kolter, J.Z.: Differentiable mpc for end-to-end planning and control. In: Bengio, S., Wallach, H., Larochelle, H., Grauman, K., Cesa-Bianchi, N., Garnett, R. (eds.) Advances in Neural Information Processing Systems, vol. 31. Curran Associates, Inc. (2018)
2. Amos, B., Kolter, J.Z.: OptNet: differentiable optimization as a layer in neural networks. In: International Conference on Machine Learning, pp. 136–145. PMLR (2017)
3. Amos, B., Xu, L., Kolter, J.Z.: Input convex neural networks. In: International Conference on Machine Learning, pp. 146–155. PMLR (2017)
4. de Avila Belbute-Peres, F., Smith, K., Allen, K., Tenenbaum, J., Kolter, J.Z.: End-to-end differentiable physics for learning and control. In: Bengio, S., Wallach, H., Larochelle, H., Grauman, K., Cesa-Bianchi, N., Garnett, R. (eds.) Advances in Neural Information Processing Systems, vol. 31. Curran Associates, Inc. (2018)
5. Bello, I., Pham, H., Le, Q.V., Norouzi, M., Bengio, S.: Neural combinatorial optimization with reinforcement learning. In: International Conference on Learning Representations, Workshop Track (2016)
6. Berthet, Q., Blondel, M., Teboul, O., Cuturi, M., Vert, J.P., Bach, F.: Learning with differentiable pertubed optimizers. In: Larochelle, H., Ranzato, M., Hadsell, R., Balcan, M.F., Lin, H. (eds.) Advances in Neural Information Processing Systems. vol. 33, pp. 9508–9519. Curran Associates, Inc. (2020)
7. Chen, L.C., Schwing, A., Yuille, A., Urtasun, R.: Learning deep structured models. In: International Conference on Machine Learning, pp. 1785–1794. PMLR (2015)
8. Choudhury, S., Bhardwaj, M., Arora, S., Kapoor, A., Ranade, G., Scherer, S., Dey, D.: Data-driven planning via imitation learning. Int. J. Robot. Res. **37**, 1632–1672 (2018)
9. Deudon, M., Cournut, P., Lacoste, A., Adulyasak, Y., Rousseau, L.-M.: Learning heuristics for the TSP by policy gradient. In: van Hoeve, W.-J. (ed.) CPAIOR 2018. LNCS, vol. 10848, pp. 170–181. Springer, Cham (2018). https://doi.org/10.1007/978-3-319-93031-2_12
10. Dijkstra, E.W., et al.: A note on two problems in connexion with graphs. Numerische mathematik **1**(1), 269–271 (1959)
11. East, S., Gallieri, M., Masci, J., Koutnik, J., Cannon, M.: Infinite-horizon differentiable model predictive control. In: International Conference on Learning Representations (2020)
12. Hansen, E.A., Zhou, R.: Anytime heuristic search. J. Artif. Intell. Res. **28**, 267–297 (2007)
13. Hart, P.E., Nilsson, N.J., Raphael, B.: A formal basis for the heuristic determination of minimum cost paths. IEEE Trans. Syst. Sci. Cybern. **4**(2), 100–107 (1968)
14. He, K., Zhang, X., Ren, S., Sun, J.: Deep residual learning for image recognition. In: Proceedings of the IEEE Conference on Computer Vision and Pattern Recognition, pp. 770–778 (2016)
15. Karkus, P., Ma, X., Hsu, D., Kaelbling, L.P., Lee, W.S., Lozano-Perez, T.: Differentiable algorithm networks for composable robot learning. In: Robotics: Science and Systems (RSS) (2019)
16. Kato, H., et al.: Differentiable rendering: A survey. ArXiv arXiv:2006.12057
17. Liu, Z., Li, X., Luo, P., Loy, C.C., Tang, X.: Semantic image segmentation via deep parsing network. In: Proceedings of the IEEE International Conference on Computer Vision, pp. 1377–1385 (2015)

18. Nazari, M., Oroojlooy, A., Snyder, L., Takac, M.: Reinforcement learning for solving the vehicle routing problem. In: Bengio, S., Wallach, H., Larochelle, H., Grauman, K., Cesa-Bianchi, N., Garnett, R. (eds.) Advances in Neural Information Processing Systems, vol. 31. Curran Associates, Inc. (2018)
19. Paden, B., Cáp, M., Yong, S.Z., Yershov, D.S., Frazzoli, E.: A survey of motion planning and control techniques for self-driving urban vehicles. IEEE Trans. Intell. Veh. **1**, 33–55 (2016)
20. Paschalidou, D., Ulusoy, O., Schmitt, C., Van Gool, L., Geiger, A.: RayNet: learning volumetric 3D reconstruction with ray potentials. In: Proceedings of the IEEE Conference on Computer Vision and Pattern Recognition, pp. 3897–3906 (2018)
21. Pearl, J., Kim, J.H.: Studies in semi-admissible heuristics. IEEE Trans. Pattern Anal. Mach. Intell. **4**, 392–399 (1982)
22. Pitis, S., Chan, H., Jamali, K., Ba, J.: An inductive bias for distances: Neural nets that respect the triangle inequality. In: International Conference on Learning Representations (2020)
23. Pogančić, M.V., Paulus, A., Musil, V., Martius, G., Rolinek, M.: Differentiation of blackbox combinatorial solvers. In: International Conference on Learning Representations (2019)
24. Rios, L.H.O., Chaimowicz, L.: A survey and classification of A* based best-first heuristic search algorithms. In: da Rocha Costa, A.C., Vicari, R.M., Tonidandel, F. (eds.) SBIA 2010. LNCS (LNAI), vol. 6404, pp. 253–262. Springer, Heidelberg (2010). https://doi.org/10.1007/978-3-642-16138-4_26
25. Russell, S.J., Norvig, P.: Artificial Intelligence - A Modern Approach: the Intelligent Agent Book. Prentice Hall Series in Artificial Intelligence, Prentice Hall, Englewood Cliffs (1995)
26. Seo, S., Liu, Y.: Differentiable physics-informed graph networks. ArXiv abs/1902.02950 (2019)
27. Smith, C., et al.: Dual arm manipulation-a survey. Robot. Auton. Syst. **60**(10), 1340–1353 (2012)
28. Taccari, L.: Integer programming formulations for the elementary shortest path problem. Eur. J. Oper. Res. **252**(1), 122–130 (2016)
29. Unbayleefable: Cartographer (2021). https://www.pokecommunity.com/showthread.php?t=429142
30. Wang, P.W., Donti, P., Wilder, B., Kolter, Z.: SATNet: bridging deep learning and logical reasoning using a differentiable satisfiability solver. In: International Conference on Machine Learning, pp. 6545–6554. PMLR (2019)
31. Yang, F., Yang, Z., Cohen, W.W.: Differentiable learning of logical rules for knowledge base reasoning. In: Guyon, I., et al. (eds.) Advances in Neural Information Processing Systems, vol. 30. Curran Associates, Inc. (2017)
32. Yonetani, R., Taniai, T., Barekatain, M., Nishimura, M., Kanezaki, A.: Path planning using Neural A* search. ArXiv arXiv:2009.07476 (2020)
33. Zhang, Z., Cui, P., Zhu, W.: Deep learning on graphs: A survey. ArXiv arXiv:1812.04202 (2018)
34. Zheng, S., et al.: Conditional random fields as recurrent neural networks. In: Proceedings of the IEEE International Conference on Computer Vision, pp. 1529–1537 (2015)

Flexible Job-Shop Scheduling with Changeover Priorities

Holden Milne[1]([⊠]) [iD], Opeyemi Adesina[1] [iD], Russell Campbell[1] [iD],
Barbara Friesen[1] [iD], and Masud Khawaja[2] [iD]

[1] School of Computing, University of the Fraser Valley, Abbotsford, Canada
{holden.pimentel,barbara.friesen}@student.ufv.ca,
{opeyemi.adesina,russell.campbell}@ufv.ca
[2] School of Business, University of the Fraser Valley, Abbotsford, Canada
masud.khawaja@ufv.ca

Abstract. In a job shop, operators run different machines concurrently, which obviously may result in multiple jobs being completed at the same time. It becomes a concern whenever jobs with lower priorities are serviced over jobs with higher priorities. Our goal is to generate up-to-date changeover schedules that prioritize servicing high-priority jobs without jeopardizing schedule optimality in real-time. We formulate flexible job-shop scheduling with changeover priorities (FJSCP) based on the knapsack model and develop an algorithm based on greedy methodology. Results show that depending on a pairwise combinations of pivot selection modes our method could save up to 53% in idle time and up to 12% in makespan when compared with the traditional FCFS baseline.

Keywords: Optimization problem · Operations research · Job scheduling · Job-shop problem · Scheduling problem

1 Introduction

In this paper, we develop an optimization technique for a variant of the job shop problem which produces change-over schedules of jobs for operators. Our technique ensures higher priority jobs are serviced even when a lower priority job completes its cycle time in a very similar time frame as its higher priority counterpart.

Optimization problems [10,12,16] are a common area of study in Computing Science. Scheduling problems [9] seek to optimize some feature based on some set of parameters (e.g., time). The standard job shop scheduling problem [8], for example, considers a set of machines and another set of jobs, and tries to assign jobs to each machine to minimize the makespan.

This work is funded by the University of the Fraser Valley's work-study grant program.

G. Nicosia et al. (Eds.): LOD 2021, LNCS 13163, pp. 611–625, 2022.
https://doi.org/10.1007/978-3-030-95467-3_44

The problem we discuss is a variant of the FJSP but with a focus on changeover priority. Each job has its worst-case changeover time (due to operator experience) and priority value and every machine can process any job (through various configuration modes). With our variant, each job has its cycle time and will require some changeover time, where the machine needs to be serviced by some operators before a new job can be run. Our overarching goal is to minimize idle times in changing over high-priority jobs.

Various heuristics and meta-heuristics solutions have been developed for variants of FJSP. These solutions often minimize makespan. However, to the best of our knowledge, none of these solutions consider minimizing idle times during changeovers with a focus on job priorities. Therefore, our contributions include:

- the mathematical formulation of the FJSCP (i.e., Flexible Job-shop Scheduling with Changeover Priorities) problem;
- the development of a solution to the FJSCP that minimizes not only the makespan but also the idle time during changeovers while exploiting job priorities; and
- a comparative study on the impact of pivot selection modes on makespan and idle time during changeovers.

The rest of this paper is organized as follows. In Sect. 2 we discuss related literature. In Sect. 3 we provide background and the required terminologies for clarity and understanding of the topic. Section 4 presents our solution (including the proposed algorithm) to the FJSCP. In Sect. 5, we present a series of experiments and discussions of results. Section 6 presents a conclusion and our future plans for the FJSCP.

2   Related Work

The literature on the FJSP is extensive. According to Zhang et al. [18], a rich body of literature exists on the FJSP. These are not limited to heuristic approaches developed based on tabu search, simulated annealing, genetic algorithm, and game theory.

Some based on tabu search algorithm which are: [2,4,15]. Dauzère-Pérès and Paulli [4] proposed a reassignment procedure allowing the use of a neighborhood structure that is used in tabu search. The authors focused on the different classification of the neighbor solutions to solve the FJSP. Shen et al. [15] discusses FJSP with sequence-dependent setup times to minimize makespan. This results in a tabu search algorithm with specific neighborhood functions and a diversification structure. Bozek and Werner [2] implement mixed-integer linear programming, constraint programming, and graph-based models, using a tabu search and greedy constructive heuristic to solve their FJSP with priority on maximizing the sublot sizes without increasing their minimized makespan.

Solutions based on genetic algorithms include [3,11,18]. Zhang et al. [18] proposed an effective genetic algorithm (eGA) to minimize makespan time. Global selection and local selection are designed to generate a high-quality initial population while using an improved chromosome representation to represent a solution of the FJSP. Chan et al. [3] proposed a genetic algorithm-based approach for resource-constrained FJSP and solve the problem iteratively. Lou et al. [11] created an improved genetic algorithm with a single-point mutation operation that avoids illegal occurrences to minimize algorithm run time and a new generation mechanism to produce the initial population that will accelerate convergence.

Vijayalakshmi et al. [13] consider a scheduling game on parallel related machines. Jobs minimize completion time by choosing a machine on which it is to be processed, the machine then uses an individual priority list to decide the order in which the job assigned to the machine are processed. Villarrubia et al. [16] proposes the use of artificial neural networks in order to approximate the objective function in optimization problems, which will turn the function into polynomial form allowing other techniques to be able to solve for optimization. A hybrid artificial bee colony algorithm (HABCA) was used by Gong et al. [6]. The authors discuss FJSP with emphasis on worker flexibility, considering both trained and untrained. With their developed local search method, they improve the speed and exploitation ability of their algorithm.

Solutions to multi-objective FJSP's include: [7,12,19]. Panda and Pani [12] created a multi-objective SOS which handled equality and inequality constraints associated with problems in multi-objective functions, to solve optimization problems. Gong et al. [7] used a memetic algorithm to solve a multi-objective FJSP with worker flexibility. They represent the problem in non-linear integer programming model to minimize the maximum completion time and also the workloads. Zhu and Zhou [19] created an efficient evolutionary multi-objective gray wolf optimizer in order to solve the FJSP with job precedence constraints. Using an improved social hierarchy and a diverse leader strategy to enhance convergence speeds, the authors aimed to minimize the makespan, maximum machine workload, and total machine workload.

Zhu and Zhou [20] suggested a multi-micro-swarm leadership hierarchy-based optimization algorithm for their FJSP with job precedence constraints and interval gray processing time that dynamically assigns jobs to machines creating an uncertain gray schedule. Wang et al. [17] developed an improved ant colony optimization algorithm (IACO) that addressed the two deficiencies of the (ACO), which were low computational efficiency and the local optimum. With the algorithm, they minimize the makespan of the FJSP.

Andrade-Pineda et al. [1] use an iterative greedy constructive heuristic with a mixed-integer linear programming model to solve a dual resource-constrained FJSP with due date oriented criteria in order to minimize makespan and meet deadlines. Worker experience was a key factor for scheduling and time estimates in order to meet deadlines while also considering the resource availability and constraints. Fattahi et al. [5] discusses FJSP with overlapping operations, as a basis to optimize the makespan of a feasible schedule using simulated annealing methods. The solution was validated using a mixed-integer linear programming method and tested on randomly generated test problems.

In this paper, we solve a variant of the flexible job-shop scheduling problem (FJSP) but by exploiting job priorities (i.e., FJSCP), in a bid to speed up time-to-market (i.e., the time when the job is completely finished). We minimize idle times for changeovers without exacerbating the makespan. In [6], the level of expertise of workers was exploited to speed up the algorithm but in our work, while the experience of operators is critical in optimizing changeover times, with our variant – job priorities drive schedule generation for changeovers and assume that workers can operate any machine, even with diverse levels of expertise. Our work differs from [6] by their objectives. Similar to [5], we validated our work with a randomly generated test problem.

3 Background

In this section, we present relevant information we deem essential to facilitate readers' understanding of this paper. First, we introduce some terminologies, then present a motivation for the problem and its mathematical formulation.

3.1 Definition of Terms

We obtain the following terminologies as well as their definition for the Flexible Job-Shop Scheduling with Changeover Priorities (FJSCP) problem from our interaction with a domain expert. These definitions are fundamental to the understanding of the problem we address in this paper and the solution we provide.

1. **Changeover Time (COT)**: The minimum expected time it takes an operator to ready a machine to run the next job if the operator were to begin servicing as soon as the machine completed its run cycle.
2. **Cycle Time**: The total time taken to transform any job (input raw material) into the desired product on any given machine.
3. **Active Job**: A job is active whenever the job is currently running a machine.
4. **Time to Completion (TTC)**: The time remaining in an active job's cycle time.
5. **Total Time (TOT)**: The shortest time remaining before a machine can start its next job. This is simply $COT + TTC$.
6. **Priority (P)**: The job's priority. Priority is set fixed in advance, is decided by a manager, and is selected from a finite set of values. For simplicity, we will use the values 1–5 with 5 being a job with the highest priority.
7. **Idle Time**: The amount of time a machine spends idle. This occurs when a machine is waiting for the operator to service the machine and start the next job.

3.2 Motivation for the FJSCP

While in classical FJSP problems, the goal is to schedule the order and machines on which jobs are executed optimally. The FJSCP assumes there is some optimal or preferred feasible schedule for the jobs to be machined. Therefore, we are only interested in ensuring that an operator changeover the most prioritized job among other jobs whose cycle time had just been completed.

The scenario that inspired this problem was for a smaller parts manufacturing company. Scheduling of jobs was done based on what jobs need to be completed, and each job is assigned a level of priority that can change from day to day depending on deadlines, and whether the failure to meet a specific quota could bottleneck the rest of production. These priorities are not specific to the jobs themselves and are not necessarily dependent on one factor such as the size of the job, the time it takes to run each job, etc.

The manufacturing shop we worked with was not completely autonomous; they hired human operators to handle the non-autonomous parts of the job. Specifically, operators do the following: *unload completed parts, load new raw materials, reconfigure the machine if necessary, and ensure correct jobs are run.* Due to the physical size of the machine shop, there were seldom more than 3 operators on any shift operation, and more often than not only 1 or 2.

To alert the operators to a completed machine, the only signal was a 3-staged light, with *green* signifying the machine was running, *orange* signifying the machine needs to be serviced, and *red* signifying that some error had occurred. This light system meant that the machines were serviced on a first-come-first-serve basis: a machine would finish, the operator would service it, and then move to the next idle machine. Servicing, also known as changeover, can take anywhere between 30 s to 10 min leaving ample time for a higher priority job, with perhaps a short run cycle, to complete. This meant that a low priority job could hold the only operator for up to 10 min when a higher priority job would complete only a minute later - this implies that the machine with the higher priority job would sit idle for up to 9 min depending on the number of operators at the current shift operation.

Even if the feasible schedule itself is optimal, in practice that optimality can be hindered by these kinds of issues. That optimality requires that changeovers be consistently optimal, which is seldom possible in this circumstance. Thus, it was necessary to develop an algorithm that would alert the operators which machine to service next, even if a machine was already idle, and this algorithm needs to focus a great deal on each job priority.

3.3   Problem Formulation for the FJSCP

An FJSCP problem is a *sextuple* $\langle M, J, A, O, p, \prec \rangle$, where

- M is a set of m machines, $M = \{M_1, M_2, \ldots M_m\}$;
- J is a set of j jobs, $J = \{J_1, J_2, \ldots J_j\}$;
- A is a set of active jobs, $A \subseteq J$;
- O is a set of n operators, $O = \{O_1, O_2, \ldots O_n\}$ on any work schedule;
- $p : x \rightarrow \mathbb{Z}^+$, such that: $x \in \{J, M\}$, assigning a priority value to either the job or the machine on which it runs; and

- $\prec: J \to J$ or $M \to M$, defines a *successor-predecessor* completion time relationship between any pair of jobs or machines respectively.

It is worthy to note that the priority of a job and that of the machine on which it runs are synonymous and will be used interchangeably in the rest of this paper. This is because the priority of a machine would be dependent only on the active job of that machine. Machines do not themselves have a priority, but instead, inherit this from the job it is processing. This goes for TTC, COT and TOT as well. Our goal is to minimize the idle times on high-priority jobs, which means reducing time-to-market on those jobs.

For optimization purposes, we assume $n \leq m$ (indicating that the number of operators cannot exceed the number of machines) and $|A| \leq m$ (indicating that the number of active jobs cannot exceed the number of working machines). Conventionally, the best-case scenario for our method (i.e., when no optimization is required) occurs when the number of operators is the same as the number of running machines. In this case, each operator is naturally assigned to a machine. But optimization is required when the number of operators is less than the number of running machines because multiple jobs may complete their cycle time simultaneously.

In an ideal circumstance, for any pair of jobs in the operator schedule a and b, such that a is scheduled before b implies a will complete both its cycle time, and changeover time (TOT_a) before b completes its cycle time (TTC_b). Thus, a is scheduled for changeover before b. We formalize this with Eq. (1), so that if it holds for any pair of jobs then there will be *no idle time* for the active jobs. This will later be used to formulate the constraint in Eq. (4)

$$TOT_a \leq TTC_b \Longleftrightarrow a \text{ is scheduled before } b \qquad (1)$$

The constraint presented in (1) is extremely difficult to achieve because often times multiple jobs may complete their cycles at the same time or have their TTCs as close as possible – that is, their TTCs complete prior to finalizing change-over of the current job being serviced by an operator.

Our algorithm seeks to satisfy this constraint as often as possible while taking into account job priorities. To achieve this, we revise this requirement in Eq. (1) into the constraint we present in Eq. (4).

$$\min \left\{ \sum_{i=1}^{|S|} \max\left\{0, t_{i-1} - TTC_i\right\} \right\} \qquad (2)$$

where

$$t_n = t_{n-1} + COT_n + \max\left\{0, TTC_n - t_{n-1}\right\}$$
$$t_0 = 0 \qquad (3)$$

Subject to:

$$g(a,b) \leq TTC_b, \text{ where } \{a,b\} \subseteq A \qquad (4)$$

where

$$g(a,b) = \begin{cases} TOT_a, & \text{if } p(a) < p(b) \\ 0 & O/W \end{cases}$$

In Eqs. (2) and (3), i refers to the position of some job in the operator schedule S, and TTC_n and COT_n refer to the TTC and COT respectively of the jobs at position n. This should not be confused with later notation for a named job j_a in which a is a label not a position. To avoid this confusion, let s_i be the job at position i in the operator schedule. Equations (2) and (3) together formulate the total idle time calculation. Idle time results from the case where the time it takes to finish servicing all jobs prior to some job s_i exceed job s_i's TTC.

The recurrence relation t_n represents the total time it would take an operator to service the first n jobs, and thus the idle time for the job at position i is the total time it takes to service the first $i - 1$ jobs, minus the TTC for the job at position i. With this we can imagine a perfect scenario where there is no idle time and whenever the operator finishes servicing a machine they always have exactly one other machine to service immediately, meaning they never have to wait for the next job to finish. In this scenario, the total time to complete the first n jobs is $t_n = TTC_1 + \sum_{i=1}^{n} COT_n$. This results from the fact that $\max\{TTC_n - t_{n-1}, 0\}$ represents the time that an operator will have to wait for the next machine to finish its cycle.

Equation (4) implies whenever two machines have different priorities, the machine with the lower priority will be serviced before its counterpart with higher priority, only when the lower priority machine has both its cycle time and changeover time completed prior to completing the cycle time of the higher priority machine (or at the exact same time). This ensures that no machine running a 5-priority job can be held up by any job with a lesser priority, essentially ensuring that 5-priority jobs will always complete as often as possible. This constraint should be satisfied by our method in order to minimize idle times.

To tackle this problem, we will explore the famous Knapsack Problem (KP) [14]. The KP presents a situation where a list of objects has associated weights and values. It aims to optimize the value of some set of selected objects while ensuring the sum of weights of the selected object is less than or equal to the capacity of the knapsack. KP is another highly studied problem, with many variants and solutions. The general idea of the KP is used as a conceptual framework for our solution, and the solution is a novel variant of the KP, at least to the best of our knowledge.

3.4   Example Scenario

Table 1 outlines a constructed example. We will use this throughout the paper to guide explanations of different parts. This example contains the issue presented where a job with a lower priority finishes before a job with higher priority, and the changeover time of the lower priority job will cause the higher priority job to sit idle if the traditional approach is being used.

Table 1. A feasible job schedule

Machine	Active job	Priority	TTC	COT
m_1	j_1	3	12	8
m_2	j_2	4	4	4
m_3	j_3	3	5	5
m_4	j_4	1	15	5
m_5	j_5	2	20	7
m_6	j_6	5	12	3
m_7	j_7	3	3	5
m_8	j_8	4	10	8
m_9	j_9	1	6	4

The changeover schedule for the first-come-first-serve approach for this case, ignoring future jobs that may become active as a result of servicing a job on this list, would be $m_7, m_2, m_8, m_6, m_3, m_1, m_5, m_9$, and m_4. To build this list, we break all zero ties by highest priority, and then smallest COT. This approach yields an idle time over all machines of 133 min; that is, an average of 14 $min/machine$. We can notice that the highest priority machine m_6 will sit idle for 8 min. However, we could switch m_6 with the machine prior, m_8 and service a higher priority machine sooner.

Making this slight change to the order so that m_6 is serviced third and m_8 fourth not only decreases the total idle time down to 128 min but also reduces the idle time for the 5-priority job down to zero, at the expense of letting the 4-priority m_8 sit idle for longer. In some cases, doing a switch like this can worsen the total idle time, but this example shows even an optimal first-come-first-serve selection can force high-priority machines to suffer. In reality, the case is much worse, as, at least for our partner manufacturing company, there was no system to signify to an operator that a machine has higher priority than another.

4   Our Work

We observe an analog to the *The Knapsack Problem*. In our context, for some job a, we can let TTC_a be the capacity of the knapsack. For any other job b, the TOT_b becomes the weight, and $p(b)$ becomes the value for optimization. After selecting the first knapsack capacity to be TTC_a, we then look to selecting some other job b such that the $TOT_b \leq TTC_a$. b then becomes our next capacity, and we continue searching this way until no more element in the list to be serviced.

A job selected to be the knapsack in the algorithm will be referred to as the pivot job. This terminology comes from and is analogous to that of the Quicksort pivot. Each pivot job can be considered to be fixed in its scheduled position (whatever that may end up being), and other jobs will be scheduled around it. Thus we can consider the schedule to be broken into two parts around that pivot job. The first part is the jobs that come before it whose makespan is less than the TTC for the pivot job. In other words, for two sequentially selected pivot jobs $\mathfrak{p}$ and $\mathfrak{q}$ such that $\mathfrak{q}$ is scheduled before $\mathfrak{p}$ then $TTC_\mathfrak{q} \leq TOT_\mathfrak{p}$.

Ideally, for any jobs a and b in the operator schedule such that a is scheduled before b, a will finish before b needs to be changed over. Thus, the idle time for b is 0. If it were ever the case that for every pivot, a new pivot could be selected until there were no jobs left, the idle time for each of the machines would be zero. This is because the first scheduled job would finish its cycle time before the second needs to be changed over and the second job would finish its cycle before the third needs to be changed over and so on. While ideal, this is unlikely to ever occur.

The other part is the chunk of jobs that fall before $\mathfrak{p}$ and after $\mathfrak{q}$. Since the segment that falls before $\mathfrak{q}$ has at most makespan $TTC_\mathfrak{q}$, then the second part can begin to be serviced after $TOT_\mathfrak{q}$. This means that for every job to be serviced before $\mathfrak{p}$ completes, the second segment must have a makespan of at most $TTC_\mathfrak{p} - TOT_\mathfrak{q}$. Since the pivot job $\mathfrak{p}$ will have no idle time, so long as we ensure that the operator is available when the $TTC_\mathfrak{p}$ reaches zero, and likewise, for $\mathfrak{q}$, the only jobs that can introduce idle time are the ones scheduled between two pivots like this.

Table 2. Summary of the pivots tested.

Largest TOT	Find the job j with the largest priority and the **largest** TOT, such that its TTC fits in the TOT of the previous pivot
Smallest TOT	Choose the job j with the largest priority and the **smallest** TOT, such that its TTC fits in the TOT of the previous pivot
Best fit	Choose the job j with the largest priority such that its TTC is maximal while **less than** or **equal** to TOT of the previous pivot

An important observation to consider when selecting a pivot is the fact that for any pivot, when we partition the output list into 2 parts, the left and the right sides of the pivot, those to the left will contribute nothing to the idle time of the pivot, whereas those on the right may. This means after we select our first pivot, when we choose the next pivot, we want to have as many jobs possibly scheduled before the new pivot as possible. Of course, it may not be necessarily sufficient to always select the best fit. For example, if we select pivot $\mathfrak{q}$ with a large TOT that fits within the TTC of the previously selected pivot $\mathfrak{p}$, any job chosen within the $TTC_\mathfrak{q}$ that does not fit will also unlikely fit between $\mathfrak{q}$ and $\mathfrak{p}$. Naturally, this will push that job to come after $\mathfrak{q}$, in some cases drastically increasing that job's idle time.

At some point, every job will recursively be considered a pivot. Every time we select a pivot, a subset of the remaining jobs will be scheduled in front or behind that pivot. Conceptually, we can visualize this as a binary tree, where the left child of any non-leaf vertex comes before the parent which comes before the right children, in other words and in-order traversal.

As we trace recursively down through pivots starting with b we will likely come to a scenario by which some jobs have gone unscheduled. These unscheduled jobs will need to be scheduled after b, and thus the idle time the jobs

---

Algorithm 1. (Greedy Priority Scheduling)

---

function GREEDYPRIORITYSCHED-
ULER(L)
    finalList ← [ ]
    while size(L) > 0 **do**
        p ← getPivot(L)
        remove p from L
        \\ *operation invocation*
        SchedulerRecursion(p,TTC_p,L)
        append p to finalList
    end while
    return finalList
end function

function
SCHEDULERRECURSION(p, capacity, L)
    if capacity ≤ 0 or size(L) = 0 **then**
        return [ ]
    else if size(L) = 1 **then**
        if TOT_{L_0} ≤ capacity **then**
            return [L_0]
        else
            return [ ]
        end if
    end if
    outList ← [ ]
    q ← getPivot(L)
    left ← SchedulerRecursion(q,TTC_q,L)
    remove q from L
    for x in left **do**
        append x to outList
        remove x from L
    end for
    append q to outList
    right ← SchedulerRecursion(q, capacity-TTC_q, L)
    for y in right **do**
        append y to outList
        remove y from L
    end for
    return outList
end function

---

scheduled after b may have some idle time. So it is worth noting that pivots selected after the first pass will likely not have zero idle time and so it makes sense to select the highest priority value to be the first pivot.

The algorithm presented is based on a general greedy approach, that seeks to select the highest priority job that will fit inside the TOT of the pivot, while, in some cases, trying to ensure more jobs can be selected. It is broken into two different functions, that is, *GreedyPriorityScheduler* and *SchedulerRecursion*. It is worth mentioning that this algorithm will be run repeatedly at varying fixed time steps, in which all TTC's and $TOT's$ are relative to this point in time. It should also be noted that this is an offline algorithm, needing to consider the active list of jobs simultaneously.

For simplicity, we consider notations p and q denote a pivot job, capacity is the Knapsack capacity, L represents an array-like list of active jobs where L_i is the ith element of L, and TTC_a and TOT_a are the TTC and TOT of some job a, respectively. An empty array-like list will be represented with [ ] and such a list with one element e will be represented with [e].

5   Experiments and Discussion of Results

As machines get serviced, the schedule must be recalculated. In terms of implementation, it would likely be sufficient to generate the first k entries, where k is the number of operators. For the purpose of analysis, we will let the scheduler process the full list of machines and their active jobs.

A simulation program was written in Python 3.8. This program was run on randomly generated jobs based on the summarized data given to us by our partner company. This means jobs run with a TTC between 5 and 60 min, COT between 1 and 15 min, and priority between 1 and 5. These same jobs were then used to calculate the baseline (i.e., the first-come-first-serve approach). The program emulated a full 18-hour day, scheduling the list, skipping ahead to the next scheduled changeover, performing that changeover, updating the machines accordingly, and repeating. This is, again, the way in which the algorithm is intended to be used. Like the algorithm, these simulations assume there is only 1 operator. Although, our algorithm can be applied to a scenario where there are multiple operators without any changes.

The idle time is calculated by looking at the next machine needing to be serviced with the active job a and subtracting TOT_a from all other jobs. If for any job b, $TTC_b - TOT_a < 0$ then that machine will have been idle for some amount of time and the TTC_b will be set to zero. For example, if we used the first-come-first-serve approach with the example in Table 1 then m_7 would be serviced first. After processing this machine, all active jobs have their TTC reduced by j_7's TOT. This TOT for some jobs is greater than those jobs TTC, namely j_2, j_3, and j_9, which will be idle for 4, 3 and 2 min respectively. Thus TTC_2, TTC_3 and TTC_9 are all set to 0, and the total idle time is increased by 9. The resulting scenario after this changeover is presented in Table 3. For simplicity, we'll assume that the next job processed on m_7's TTC is sufficiently large to ignore.

The next machine to be serviced is j_2 (breaking ties by priority), since TTC_2 is now zero. Thus machines m_3, m_8, and m_9 are idle for 4, 2, and 4 min each, increasing the idle time at this step by 10 to give us a total of 19 min in idle time in two iterations. m_6 completes, however, since $TTC_6 = TOT_2$, it is not idle for any amount of time when m_2 is finished being serviced. This process was run until an 18 h day was simulated.

Makespan on the other hand is rather hard to calculate in this manner since the list is a rolling list over a fixed amount of time. Instead, we looked at the makespan of the first 50 jobs processed. Here the makespan is simply calculated by summing the TOT_a where a is the next job to be serviced until we have serviced 50 jobs. Naturally, 50 jobs are not likely to be serviced in an 18 h day, so the testing function continues to run until both the desired number of machines have been processed and the number of hours simulated exceeds 18. Idle time counting stops after the 18 h condition has been met, and the makespan calculation stops after the number of machines condition has been met.

Table 3. The schedule in Table 1 after the first iteration of the optimal-first-come-first-serve approach.

Machine	Active job	Priority	TTC	COT
m_1	j_1	3	4	8
m_2	j_2	4	0	4
m_3	j_3	3	0	5
m_4	j_4	1	7	5
m_5	j_5	2	12	7
m_6	j_6	5	4	3
m_7	—	—	—	—
m_8	j_8	4	2	8
m_9	j_9	1	0	4

Due to the nature of the algorithm having two opportunities for the selection of pivots it may be possible that 2 different selection methods presented in Table 2 may yield better results. Thus we have 9 possible combinations to test. For each of these combinations, the above calculations were made over 10,000 tests with randomly generated schedules.

While our goal was to minimize the idle time it was important that the makespan still be considered. That is any solution found to minimize idle time while increasing the makespan should be considered inadequate. At a minimum, we would like to see no change or an insignificant increase to the makespan but a significant decrease to the idle time. Some pivot selection approaches had varying effects. As we will see in Table 4 and Fig. 1, *Smallest TOT–Largest TOT* and *Smallest TOT–Bestfit* perform the best for our purposes.

For the results presented in Table 4, test conditions are dependent only on the pivot selections. Pivot 1 refers to the pivot selection in the *GreedyPriorityScheduler* operation of Function 1, whereas Pivot 2 refers to that of *SchedulerRecursion* operation of Function 2. Makespan and idle time are the average results of those 10,000 tests for each combination of Pivot 1 and Pivot 2 features. In Fig. 1, we visualized the results presented in Table 4. Percentage gains are computed relative to the average baseline. This becomes important for visualizing the improvements our work contributes to makespans and idle times.

From Table 4 we can see that selecting the *Smallest TOT* in the *GreedyPriorityScheduler* operation tends to yield the best improvements overall. However, selecting *Smallest TOT* in the *SchedulerRecursion* operation often leads to a larger idle time, while making small improvements to the makespan. In fact, the best makespan improvements come from this method. Because of how prevalent makespan is in similar optimization problems, this method should not be ignored. For our purposes, however, we want to minimize idle time, and if at all possible, the makespan as well.

Table 4. Simulation results by pivot selection combinations

Pivot 1	Pivot 2	Makespan	Idle time
Largest TOT	Largest TOT	344	25862
Largest TOT	Smallest TOT	250	30468
Largest TOT	Best fit	275	32995
Smallest TOT	Largest TOT	263	16862
Smallest TOT	Smallest TOT	241	30964
Smallest TOT	Best fit	265	16851
Best fit	Largest TOT	371	22516
Best fit	Smallest TOT	241	31030
Best fit	Best fit	420	15483
Average baseline[a]		**275**	**33009**

[a] The baseline was calculated alongside each test, and those results were averaged for these tests. The averages are listed here, and the standard deviations are $\sigma_{\text{makespan}} = 0.96$ and $\sigma_{\text{idle time}} = 37.13$

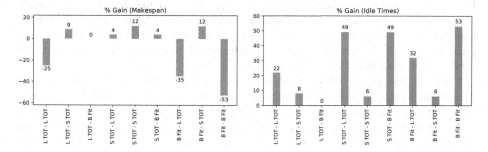

Fig. 1. Comparing gains/loss in makespan and idle times against the baseline (FCFS method). A high percent gain in makespan or idle time means that those values are decreased.

In Table 4, we can see that there are some specific cases with a drastic reduction to the idle time, but a significant increase of the makespan, such as with *best fit–best fit*. According to Fig. 1, it was 53% improvement for idle time but 53% loss for makespan. It is also interesting to see that the mode involving *largest TOT–best fit* behaves just like the baseline. In fact, it is clear that for each of the combinations of the three pivot selection methods, they all make at least some minor improvements to idle time. Again, it is imperative that we do not bring down the makespan and ideally that we improve it.

For that reason, *Smallest TOT–Largest TOT* and *Smallest TOT–Bestfit* serve to minimize idle time substantially, while making some improvement to makespan. While *Bestfit–Smallest TOT* and *Smallest TOT–Smallest TOT* tend to have the best makespan improvement, there is an insignificant change in idle time which leads us to conclude that those methods are insufficient.

6 Conclusion and Future Plan

The FJSCP is an understudied problem. While many existing literatures look at either scheduling with operators or scheduling with priority, none of them consider the two simultaneously, to the best of our knowledge. The effect of operators on schedule efficiency should not be overlooked. As mentioned in Sect. 3, the optimal schedule is dependent on the execution and maintenance of that schedule by the operators. We guide the operators through their shifts to ensure the schedule is optimal. The approach used was constructed by considering each subproblem as a Knapsack problem, and exploring this greedily. With this, it may be possible to apply other solution designs for the Knapsack problem to the FJSCP problem to get further improved results.

These preliminary results illustrate the powerful effect that operators can have on a schedule. It also reveals that operators must act efficiently when performing these tasks. Our algorithm showed significant improvements to idle time but slight improvements to the makespan over the first-come-first-serve approach for some pivot selection modes. Further research should be performed to ensure the effectiveness of this algorithm, looking at different initial machine schedules gathered from different scheduling algorithms and comparing the pivot selection methods over an iteratively increasing size of machines.

Further research would also involve exploring this technique as a secondary processing method. With some modification, the algorithm could be extended to make slight improvements upon existing approaches for schedule optimization. Since many existing optimization solutions are imperfect, a variant of this algorithm could be used to take the results generated by these optimization techniques and make explicit improvements to obtain a slightly better schedule.

References

1. Andrade-Pineda, J.L., Canca, D., Gonzalez-R, P.L., Calle, M.: Scheduling a dual-resource flexible job shop with makespan and due date-related criteria. Ann. Oper. Res. **291**(1), 5–35 (2020). https://doi.org/10.1007/s10479-019-03196-0
2. Bożek, A., Werner, F.: Flexible job shop scheduling with lot streaming and sublot size optimisation. Int. J. Prod. Res. **56**(19), 6391–6411 (2018)
3. Chan, F., Wong, T., Chan, L.: Flexible job-shop scheduling problem under resource constraints. Int. J. Prod. Res. **44**(11), 2071–2089 (2006)
4. Dauzère-Pérès, S., Paulli, J.: An integrated approach for modeling and solving the general multiprocessor job-shop scheduling problem using Tabu search. Ann. Oper. Res. **70**, 281–306 (1997)
5. Fattahi, P., Jolai, F., Arkat, J.: Flexible job shop scheduling with overlapping in operations. Appl. Math. Model. **33**(7), 3076–3087 (2009)
6. Gong, G., Chiong, R., Deng, Q., Gong, X.: A hybrid artificial bee colony algorithm for flexible job shop scheduling with worker flexibility. Int. J. Prod. Res. **58**(14), 4406–4420 (2020)

7. Gong, X., Deng, Q., Gong, G., Liu, W., Ren, Q.: A memetic algorithm for multiobjective flexible job-shop problem with worker flexibility. Int. J. Prod. Res. **56**(7), 2506–2522 (2018)
8. Graham, R.L.: Bounds for certain multiprocessing anomalies. Bell Syst. Tech. J. **45**(9), 1563–1581 (1966)
9. Kletzander, L., Musliu, N.: Solving the general employee scheduling problem. Comput. Oper. Res. **113**, 104794 (2020)
10. Krause, J., Cordeiro, J., Parpinelli, R.S., Lopes, H.S.: A survey of swarm algorithms applied to discrete optimization problems. In: Yang, X.S., Cui, Z., Xiao, R., Gandomi, A.H., Karamanoglu, M. (eds.) Swarm Intelligence and Bio-inspired Computation, pp. 169–191. Elsevier, Oxford (2013)
11. Luo, X., Qian, Q., Fu, Y.F.: Improved genetic algorithm for solving flexible job shop scheduling problem. Procedia Comput. Sci. **166**, 480–485 (2020)
12. Panda, A., Pani, S.: A symbiotic organisms search algorithm with adaptive penalty function to solve multi-objective constrained optimization problems. Appl. Soft Comput. **46**, 344–360 (2016)
13. Ravindran Vijayalakshmi, V., Schröder, M., Tamir, T.: Scheduling games with machine-dependent priority lists. Theor. Comput. Sci. **855**, 90–103 (2021)
14. Salkin, H.M., De Kluyver, C.A.: The knapsack problem: a survey. Naval Res. Logist. Q. **22**(1), 127–144 (1975)
15. Shen, L., Dauzère-Pérès, S., Neufeld, J.S.: Solving the flexible job shop scheduling problem with sequence-dependent setup times. Eur. J. Oper. Res. **265**(2), 503–516 (2018)
16. Villarrubia, G., De Paz, J.F., Chamoso, P., la Prieta, F.D.: Artificial neural networks used in optimization problems. Neurocomputing **272**, 10–16 (2018)
17. Wang, L., Cai, J., Li, M., Liu, Z.: Flexible job shop scheduling problem using an improved ant colony optimization. Sci. Program. **2017**, 9016303 (2017)
18. Zhang, G., Gao, L., Shi, Y.: An effective genetic algorithm for the flexible job-shop scheduling problem. Expert Syst. Appl. **38**(4), 3563–3573 (2011)
19. Zhu, Z., Zhou, X.: An efficient evolutionary grey wolf optimizer for multi-objective flexible job shop scheduling problem with hierarchical job precedence constraints. Comput. Ind. Eng. **140**, 106280 (2020)
20. Zhu, Z., Zhou, X.: Flexible job-shop scheduling problem with job precedence constraints and interval grey processing time. Comput. Ind. Eng. **149**, 106781 (2020)

The Sea Exploration Problem Revisited

João Dionísio[1(✉)], Davi dos Santos[2], and João Pedro Pedroso[1]

[1] INESC TEC, Faculdade de Ciências, Universidade do Porto,
Rua do Campo Alegre s/n, 4169-007 Porto, Portugal
`up201606210@up.pt`
[2] Universidade de São Paulo, Porto, Portugal

Abstract. Sea exploration is important for countries with large areas in the ocean under their control, since in the future it may be possible to exploit some of the resources in the seafloor. The sea exploration problem was presented by Pedroso et al. [13] (unpublished); we maintain most of the paper's structure, to provide the needed theoretical background and context.

In the sea exploration problem, the aim is to schedule the expedition of a ship for collecting information about the resources on the seafloor. The goal is to collect data by probing on a set of carefully chosen locations, so that the information available is optimally enriched. This problem has similarities with the orienteering problem, where the aim is to plan a time-limited trip for visiting a set of vertices, collecting a prize at each of them, in such a way that the total value collected is maximum. In our problem, the score at each vertex is associated with an estimation of the level of the resource on the given surface, which is done by regression using Gaussian processes. Hence, there is a correlation among scores on the selected vertices; this is the first difference with respect to the standard orienteering problem. The second difference is the location of each vertex, which in our problem is a freely chosen point on a given surface. Results on a benchmark test set are presented and analyzed, confirming the merit of the approach proposed. In this paper, additional methods are presented, along with a small topological result and subsequent proof of the convergence of these same methods to the optimal solution, when we have instant access to the ground truth and the underlying function is piecewise continuous.

Keywords: Active learning · Surface exploration · Orienteering · Gaussian processes · Recognition problems · Tour planning · Stochastic optimization

1 Introduction

As an example of sea exploration in a real-world context, we mention the "Solwara 1 Project", where mining of high grade copper and gold in the waters of Papua New Guinea has been considered [14]. However, seafloor contents are largely unknown; for characterizing them, a preliminary step is to fetch information about its composition. This is currently being done by sending a ship in an

© Springer Nature Switzerland AG 2022
G. Nicosia et al. (Eds.): LOD 2021, LNCS 13163, pp. 626–640, 2022.
https://doi.org/10.1007/978-3-030-95467-3_45

expedition where an underwater robot, or other equipment, collects samples at selected points. Such expeditions are typically very costly; additionally, the ship must be available for other commitments at a predetermined port within a rigid and tight time limit. Due to its costs, expeditions are relatively rare; in the applications that we are aware of, there is typically a trip to a given area in the period of several years [1]. Nowadays, planning is usually done by experts, based on previously collected information and on intuition; because of the importance of the trips for inventorying seafloor resources, a method for helping decision makers carrying out the ship's schedule is desirable. The aim of this paper is to provide a step in this direction. To our knowledge, this is the first attempt to address this problem. Even though this paper describes the problem in the context of sea exploration, similar problems arise in other contexts (e.g., fire detection by drones on a forest). More formally, the aim is to schedule the journey of a ship for collecting information about the resources of the seafloor (e.g., its composition in certain materials). The surface being considered here is represented as a given (bounded) surface $S \subset R^2$. For the sake of simplicity, we consider that the actual resource level at any point $(x, y) \in S$ can be conveyed by a real number, denoted by $v(x, y)$. This true value is unknown, except for a limited number N of points in S for which there is previous empirical information. Optimal expedition planning involves three subproblems, each corresponding to a different phase on the process. The first one is **assessment**, which consists of the following: given a finite set of points for which the contents are known, build a function $h(x, y)$ that associates to each point $(x, y) \in S$ the "attractiveness" (a real number) for exploring it, in terms of information that can be gathered in case that point is selected for probing. The second subproblem is **planning**, i.e., deciding on the position of a certain number n of points to probe in the next expedition so as to maximize the overall informational reward; the duration of the trip includes time for probing the chosen points and traveling between them, and is limited to a known bound which implicitly limits n. The third subproblem, **estimation**, is related to the final aim of the problem, which is to have an evaluation $w(x, y)$ of the resource level available at any point on the surface S, based on all the information available at the end of the trip.

This paper's contributions fall on subproblem 2, planning, by introducing new algorithms for the selection of the point to be probed. It does so with randomness, by drawing random samples on the surface S, while favouring points with higher variance. We prove the convergence of the algorithms to the optimal solution, when we have instant access to the ground truth, and apply our algorithms to more general functions than those of the previous paper, here they are piecewise continuous.

This paper is organized as follows. In Sect. 2 we put this problem in the context of the literature. Section 3 describes the methods of the previous paper and the ones we developed. The proof is presented in Sect. 4. The benchmark instances are described in Sect. 5. The results we obtained are in Sect. 6. We discuss these results and provide some concluding remarks in Sect. 7.

2   Related Work

Our problem involves multiple research areas. Subproblem 2, planning, is studied in artificial intelligence and operational research; see, e.g., [7] for planning in the setting of artificial intelligence and [2] for related integer optimization models. Subproblems 1 and 3, assessment and estimation, belong to the areas of machine learning and data mining (see, e.g., [17] and [10]). In particular, our problem's context can be seen as a particular case of active learning, where arbitrary points on the relevant surface can be selected for probing in such a way that the pattern to be discovered-resource content values allover the surface-is optimally enhanced. Typical applications of active learning for data acquisition involve a discrete set of entities, for which additional information may be gathered if required. For example, in [23] models for customer behavior are built, and data is acquired for selected customers in order improve the corresponding model. Mentioned examples are the classification of customers into those who do transactions or not; the data acquisition problem is determining how many and which customers from which data should be acquired. As our space for sampling is continuous and the model that we want to build involves all the samples, our setting is substantially different. It is closer to active learning via query synthesis [21], where, in a classification context, the focus is on the synthesis of (unlabeled) instances close to the decision boundary, which are chosen for annotation, so that at the end a small labeled set can be used without compromising the solution quality. In the regression context, the method presented in [5] selects the most informative unlabeled samples for expanding a small initial training set, in the context of ε-insensitive support vector regression. This method is based on the evaluation of three criteria for the selection of samples to be labeled: relevance, diversity and density. A two step procedure based on clustering identifies the most relevant unlabeled samples, assuming that training samples in the same cluster of support vectors are the most relevant; among these, the most "diverse" samples-lying on different clusters in another clustering process-are chosen. As this method relies on clustering of unlabeled samples, it is not obvious how it could be adapted to our setting.

The following subsection presents a literature review for the subproblem that will be more focused on this paper, planning, as well as for the evaluation and comparison of solution methods. For a more comprehensive literature review, see the original paper in [13], where equal attention is paid to each of the three subproblems.

2.1   Planning

The optimization problem addressed in this work is a routing problem with similarities to the orienteering problem (OP). The orienteering problem was initially introduced by [9], and its roots are in an outdoor sport with the same name, where there is a set of "control points", each with an associated score, in a given area. Competitors use a compass and a map for assisting in a journey where they visit a subset of control points, starting and ending at given nodes, with the objective of maximizing their total score. They must reach the end point within a predefined amount of time. The input to the standard OP consists of a vertex- and edge-weighted graph $G = (V, E)$, a source and a target vertices $s, t \in V$, and a time limit T; V is the set of vertices and E is the set of edges. The goal is to find an $s - t$ walk of total length at most T so as to maximize the sum of weights at vertices visited through the walk. It can be shown that the OP is NP-hard via a straightforward reduction from the traveling salesman problem. It is also known to be APXhard to approximate. The literature describes an unweighted version (i.e., with a unit score at each vertex), for which a $(2 + \varepsilon)$ approximation is presented in [4]; for the weighted version, the approximation ratio has a loss with factor $(1 + o(1))$. An essential difference between the OP and our problem is that in the OP a finite set of vertices is given, from which the walk must be selected. In our problem, only the surface where some locations may be chosen for sampling is given. To the best of our knowledge, the closest related work can be found in [22]. The authors propose a non-linear extension to the orienteering problem (OP), called the correlated orienteering problem (COP). They use the COP to model the planning of informative tours for persistent monitoring, through a single or multiple robots, of a spatiotemporal field with time-invariant spatial correlations. The tours are constrained to have a fixed length time budget. Their approach is discrete, as they focus on a quadratic COP formulation that only looks at correlations between neighboring nodes in a network. Another problem related to ours is tour recommendation for groups, introduced in [2], where the authors deal with estimating the best tour that a group could perform together in a city, in such a way that the overall utility for whole group is maximized. They use several measures to estimate this utility, such as the sum of the utilities of members in the group, or the utility of the least 4 satisfied member. In our case, we estimate this utility (the attractiveness of a point) using a Gaussian process regression.

2.2   Related Problems

Methods for deciding data points whose unknown label should be determined are relatively common for classification tasks; see, e.g., [16] for a comparison. However, to the best of our knowledge, no equivalent study has been done for regression problems. A method for high-dimensional regression models, when the annotation of the samples is expensive, has been proposed in [20]. There, the authors present a fast active learning algorithm for regression, tailored for neural network models; the stochastic output of the neural network model, performed using different dropout masks at the prediction stage, is used to rank unlabeled samples and to choose among them the ones with the highest uncertainty. Even though the setting is somehow similar to ours, the pool of unlabeled points is considered a finite set; these points are ranked at each iteration according to the respective value of the acquisition function, and those with the best value are chosen. Hence, data sets from standard machine learning can be used in their context. In our context, any point in the surface could potentially be selected for annotation; hence, common data sets for regression problems, where labels only exist for a discrete subset of points in the domain, are not applicable. Besides, in our context data available is supposed to be scarce; otherwise regression without acquisition of new points would probably be satisfactory since the beginning, and hence the interest of an expedition for collecting new data would be limited. In the context of exploration problems, methods for using novelty in robotic exploration have been studied in [19], where an algorithm based on density estimation and adaptive threshold detection is proposed to characterize novelty, taking into account a prior model of novel data. It has been used with images from a particular mission, where the algorithm identifies interesting cases among a variety of images. On a different perspective, a discussion on the usage of machine learning techniques in exploration of unknown places-rovers on Mars surface has been made in [8]. The usage of quantitative measurements that can match the algorithms to the priorities of experts is proposed. Applications include the situation where image-based novelty can be used, e.g., for prioritizing images to be transmitted, or to provide the rover with the capability of changing its course or stopping when a key factor is detected, in order to improve the "science return" of the mission. The main difference between these works and our setting is that prior information about the surface being explored is not taken into account for scheduling the expedition. Besides, in these previous works it is assumed to have a continuous flow of information, while in our case probing must be made on a discrete set of points; in other words, if we consider an underlying graph, these works collect information on arcs, while in the sea exploration problem information is collected on vertices. The position of these vertices and the corresponding order of visit are the variables at stake. Another related problem is that of searching environments in rescue operations. This problem is dealt with in [3], which presents a multi-criteria method for searching an environment without any a priori information about structure and target locations. There, the authors combine a set of criteria (amount of anticipated free area, probability of a robot being able to send back information, distance between the current position and the place to explore) in order to produce an assessment of the global utility for a candidate point for exploration; the point which maximizes this utility is visited next (see also [15] for a survey on related problems). Contrasting to this problem, in our setting the aim is to use previously available information and improve it in an optimal way.

3 Method

This section provides a detailed description of each of the steps present in the algorithm.

3.1 Assessment and Estimation

The first and the third subproblems, assessment and estimation, are strongly related, in the sense that the aim of the assessment phase is to have a measure of the interest of having empirical information on new points in S for improving the estimation. Assessment evaluates how much a given point, if probed, is expected to improve the quality of the estimation done at the third subproblem. The estimation phase is a regression problem: given the known resource levels at the N previously observed points and at n points to be observed in the expedition, what is the best estimate for the resource level at a new point in S? A first step for answering this question is to make an assumption on the nature of the underlying function $v(x, y)$. Our assumption is that it can be conveniently estimated by a Gaussian process. In this approach, the model attempts to describe the conditional distribution $p(z|(x, y))$ based on a set of empirical observations of z on input (x, y), conveyed as a set of triplets $D = \{(\overline{z}_i, \overline{x}_i, \overline{y}_i)\}_{i=1}^{m}, S$, where m is the number of samples (in our case, N before the trip and $N + n$ after the trip). This conditional distribution describes the dependency of the observable z on the input $(x, y) \in S$, assuming that this relation can be decomposed into a systematic and a random component. The systematic dependency is given by a latent function $w : S \to \mathbb{R}$, which is to be identified based on data D. Hence, the prior is on function values associated with the set of inputs, whose joint distribution is assumed to be multivariate normal. We use the posteriors inferred through the Gaussian process model in two ways. In the assessment phase, we use the standard deviation of the model at each point $(x, y) \in S$ directly as an indicator of attractiveness for probing at that point. Later, in the estimation phase, the Gaussian process (now with an enlarged data set) is used as a regression for the resource level at any point in S.

3.2 Planning

The second subproblem is the selection of points in S for probing, so as to allow a subsequent estimation as accurate as possible. Points are to be probed in a trip whose maximum duration is known beforehand. We are thus in the presence of an orienteering problem. A standard orienteering problem consists of the following: given a graph with edge lengths and a prize that may be collected at each vertex, determine a path of length at most T, starting and ending at given vertices, that maximizes the total prize value of the vertices visited. Our problem is rather particular for several reasons. The first reason is that besides edge lengths (in our case, edge traversal duration), we have to take into account the time spent in probing at each vertex (which is a parameter of our problem). The second reason is that the graph may consist of any discrete subset of points $V \subset S$, as long as the duration of the tour—the time spent on probing and on traveling from a point to the next—is not larger than the upper bound T. An additional difficulty is related to the correlation between the prizes obtained in visited vertices; indeed, as the "prize" is a measure of the improvement on information obtained by probing, after probing at a given location, probing other locations in this neighborhood is expected to provide less information than distant points (other factors being equal).

3.3 Tackling the Problem

An instance of this problem must specify the area S being studied, an upper bound T for the trip duration (including traveling and probing), the duration t required for each probing (here considered independent of the location), and the traveling speed s, which allows computing the traveling time between two given points as d/s, where d is the Euclidean distance between those points. Without loss of generality, we are assuming that the initial and end points of the trip to be planned are the same. Among the instance's data, it must also be provided the previously known data $D = (\overline{z_i}, \overline{x_i}, \overline{y_i})_{i=1}^{N}$, corresponding to a set of points $(\overline{x_i}, \overline{y_i}) \in S$ and the corresponding resource level $\overline{z_i}$, for $i = 1, \ldots, N$. In order to evaluate an algorithm for this problem, another set of K points $E = (\tilde{x_k}, \tilde{y_k})_{k=1}^{K}$ at which the level of information predicted by the model is requested, should also be specified. For these points, the true value of the resource level $v(\tilde{x_k}, \tilde{y_k})$ must be known at the end (for computing the error with respect to its estimated value); notice, however, that these values cannot be used by the algorithm. The main course of action, making use of a set of auxiliary functions, is provided in Algorithm 1. A general view of its steps is the following. In line 1 the relevant data necessary for the algorithm to generate a solution is input: previously available data D, time budget T, probing time t, ship's speed s, and surface under study S. In order to highlight that only previously available data D can be used by the method, the "true function" v and the points E at which the error will be evaluated are only input after computing the solution, in lines 3 and 6, respectively. Then, the solution is computed in line 2 by means of Algorithm 2 described below. This algorithm returns the list of points to probe, in the order of visit, so that the time limit T is not exceeded. The true function is then evaluated at these points (line 4), and the updated set of points D is then used to train a Gaussian process (line 5) whose mean evaluation at each point $(x, y) \in E$ is compared to function v (line 7), where E is the set of points used for error evaluation.

The main heuristic concept behind Algorithm 2 is that adding to the data set D points where the variance (and hence the uncertainty) is large improves the outcome of the function that approximates reality (or v, in the case of benchmark tests). Hence, an estimation of the variance (or, equivalently, of the standard deviation) is necessary; this is obtained in Algorithm 3 by fitting a Gaussian process to the (growing) set of points D (line 2) and computing its standard deviation at a set of points G covering the relevant surface S. In this auxiliary algorithm, these points are then sorted and returned (lines 6 and 7); in the original algorithm, the best of them (i.e., the last in their ordered set) will be selected, on line 6. The new algorithms (4, 5 and 6) developed in this paper will replace this choice. Instead of choosing the point with highest variance, they will each make a more complex choice, that will be described afterwards. One difficulty mentioned earlier in this section concerns the correlation between variances observed at points in the surface. This is noticeable in the ordered set returned by Algorithm 3: its tail is likely to be composed of points which have a similar high variance, but which lie next to each other in the surface S. Hence, upon selection of one (the best) of them for including in the solution, the Gaussian process model used to compute attractiveness becomes unusable; a new model must be fitted to the data, including that last point added. These concerns have been addressed in Algorithm 2, described next. Algorithm 2 uses the assessment of the attractiveness on a grid of points in the surface S to determine a trip, i.e., a list of points to visit and probe. That list is constructed in a greedy way, by determining which is currently the most attractive point-by calling Algorithm 3 in line 4-and attempting to add it to the trip, in lines 6 to 10. This is done by checking if a traveling salesman tour including it and the previous points can still be completed within the time limit. We use an implementation of the algorithm described in [12] for quickly finding a tour; if its length is feasible, the solution is immediately returned, otherwise the exact model available in [11] is used to find the optimal solution with a general-purpose mixed integer programming solver.

Notice that in the length of the tour one must include the travel time between successive points and the time for probing at each point.

After a new point (x, y) is added to the tour, it is conjectured (for the purposes of the algorithm) that a simulation using the latest available Gaussian process provides the "true" evaluation $z = v(x, y)$; based on the new speculative datum (z, x, y) the attractiveness allover S will be recomputed in next call to Algorithm 3.

Algorithm 1: Main Procedure

Result: List a of points for probing
1 read instance's data D,T,t,s,S ;
2 a ← **Orienteering**(D,T,t,s,S);
3 input instance's "true function" evaluator v;
4 update D with probings on all points a;
5 w ← GP regression trained with data D;
6 input points for error evaluation E;
7 output $\Delta \leftarrow \sum_{(x,y) \in E} |v(x, y) - w(x, y)|$;

Algorithm 2: Orienteering

Result: List a of points for probing
Data: D = $\{(\overline{z}_i, \overline{x}_i, \overline{y}_i)\}_{i=1}^{m}$, S
1   **procedure Orienteering**(D,T,t,s,S);
2   a ← [];
3   **while** *True* **do**
4   │   V ← GPstdev(D,S);
5   │ (σ, x, y) ← V.pop();
6   │   r ← TSP solution visiting (x,y) and all the positions in a;
7   │   **if** *length(r)* < T **then**
8   │   │   a ← r;
9   │   **else**
10 │   │   break;
11 │   **end**
12 │   R ← GP regression trained with data D;
13 │   z ← R(x,y) ;
14 │   D.append((z,x,y));
15 **end**
16 **return** a;

Algorithm 3: "Attractiveness" of points for probing

Result: Assessment of standard deviation on grid G, $\{\sigma_i, x_i, y_i)\}_{i \in G}$
Data: D = $\{(\overline{z}_i, \overline{x}_i, \overline{y}_i)\}_{i=1}^{m}$, S;
1   **procedure GPstdev**(D,S):
2   G ← $\{(x_0 + \delta k, y_0 + \delta l), k = 0, ..., K, l = 0, ..., L\}$;
3   R ← GP regression trained with data D;
4   s ← standard deviation function, as evaluated by R;
5   V ← $\{(s(x_i, y_i), x_i, y_i\}_{i \in G}$;
6   sort(V);
7   **return** V;

The other algorithms (presented below) will try to improve the planning part. The original algorithm picks the point on a grid whose variance is highest. The variations introduce randomness to the choice of this highest variation point, in hopes of finding one that is more valuable.

The first variation picks the point with highest variance, given by the grid search, and samples n points from a normal distribution centered on it with a low variance. From these n points, it picks the one with highest variance and repeats the process until no improvement can be found. It essentially performs local search and so converges towards local maxima.

On line 2 and 3 we get the best point provided by the traditional grid search. We then sample n points from a normal distribution centered on this point in line 7 and choose the one with the highest variance. If there is an improvement, we ressample from a normal distribution, this time centered on the new best point. We do this until no improvement is found. Our second algorithm came from the realization that there were plenty of points that had the same highest variance, at the grid search level, and we had no real reason to pick one over another. So instead of choosing which point we would "attach" a normal distribution to, we decided to attach one to every single point, and choose a point randomly, with weights proportional to each point's variance. This is an attempt to simulate a multimodal normal distribution. In line 2 we get all the points in the grid along with their variance (according to the most recent gaussian process). In line 3 we get the probability distribution from the weights of each points' variance, in relation to the sum. We then sample a point P in line 4, from these probabilities, and sample another set of points from a normal distribution centered on P. Our third and last algorithm, is a conjunction of these last two. We sample n points from a multimodal distribution, keep the best, and then do a local search around this point. The entirety of the code can be found in [6].

Algorithm 4: Local Search

```
   Result: Most promising point for probing
 1 procedure local_search(D,S,n)
 2    V ← GPstdev(D,S);
 3    ((x,y),(z,z_std)) ← V.pop() ;
 4    best_point ← ((x,y),(z,z_std));
 5    improvement ← True ;
 6    while improvement do
 7       random_points ← n Samples from N((x,y), 0.01) ;
 8       chosen_point ← point with highest variance from random_points ;
 9       if variance of chosen_point > variance of best_point then
10          improvement ← True;
11          best_point ← chosen_point;
12       else
13          break;
14       end
15    end
16    return best_point;
```

Algorithm 5: Multimodal Distribution

```
   Result: Most promising point for probing
 1 procedure multimodal(D,S):
 2    {(z̄_i, x̄_i, ȳ_i)}_{i=1}^{m} ← GPstdev(D,S);
 3    probabilities ← [ z̄_i / (Σ_{i∈[m]} z̄_i) ]_{i∈[m]} ;
 4    I ← sample from probabilities ;
 5    points ← sampled from N((x_I, y_I), z_I) ;
 6    return point with highest variance from points
```

4   Proof of Convergence

In order to prove our algorithm's pseudo convergence, we will require some definitions and results from Topology. We assume that the reader is familiar with the mathematical notions of topology, closure, basis of a topology, boundary, metric spaces and (strictly positive) measures.

Definition 1. *Let T be a topological space. Let $A \subseteq T$. Then A is **regular closed** in T if and only if:*

$$A = \overline{A^{\circ}} \tag{1}$$

That is, if and only if A equals the closure of its interior. Note that this implies that $\overline{A} = \overline{A^{\circ}}$.

Lemma 1. *Let S be a non-empty regular closed subset of a metric space (X, d) and μ a strictly positive measure defined on X. Then,*

$$\forall x \in S, \forall \varepsilon > 0, \mu(B(x, \varepsilon) \cap S) > 0 \tag{2}$$

Proof. From the definition of regular closed, we have that $S = \overline{S^{\circ}}$. We already know that the points in S° trivially satisfy this property (since open balls form a basis for the usual metric topology), so we only need to prove the lemma for the points in the boundary. The boundary of S can be defined as $\overline{S} \setminus S^{\circ}$. By manipulating the definitions of regular closed and boundary, we come to a crucial conclusion.

$$\overline{S} \setminus S^{\circ} = \overline{\overline{S^{\circ}}} \setminus S^{\circ} = \overline{S^{\circ}} \setminus S^{\circ \, \circ} \tag{3}$$

This means that the boundary of S is actually the boundary of S° as well. Let then $x \in \delta S$ and $\varepsilon > 0$. Since $\delta S = \delta S^{\circ}$, the open ball will have to intersect S° at a point x' different from x (because $S^{\circ} \cap \delta S = \emptyset$). Since (X, d) is a metric space, this makes it so $d(x, x') > 0$. So we have that $B(\frac{x+x'}{2}, \frac{d(x,x')}{3})$ is an open ball contained in $B(x, \varepsilon) \cap S$, meaning that $\mu(B(x, \varepsilon) \cap S) > 0$ as was required. Hence, our proof is complete. □

Definition 2. *A function defined in a region $S \subseteq \mathbb{R}^2$ is called **piecewise continuous** if S can be partitioned into a finite number of $2-$dimensional regions of strictly positive area in each of which the function is continuous and has finite limits everywhere. (Adapted from [18].)*

However, we can only prove convergence for a particular kind of piecewise continuous functions. So we define good partitions and say that good piecewise continuous functions are those where the underlying partition is good.

Definition 3. *A partition of a region $S \subseteq \mathbb{R}^2$ is called a **good partition** if the closure of each of its elements is regular closed.*

Definition 4. *Given a partition $\{s_j\}_{j \in J}$ of a set S and a point x on S, we define PART: $S \to \{s_j\}_{j \in J}$, where $PART(x)$ returns the partition's subset that x belongs to.*

We will prove the convergence for the special case of local search where the number n of sampled points is equal to 1. We do this to make the proof less cumbersome, but it could be adapted and generalized to each of our algorithms. When we talk about optimal solution, we mean the set of points that should be probed in order to minimize the prediction error, with the possibility of these points not being probable, but instead being the limit of a sequence of probable points.

Theorem 1. *Let S be a compact space in $\mathbb{R}^2$ and f a good piecewise continuous function on S. If we have access to the ground truth, Algorithm A converges to the optimal solution of The Sea Exploration Problem, if we run it enough times, keeping the best solution found so far, assuming a time limit $T \in \mathbb{N}$ and a probing time $t > 0$.*

Proof. Let $k \in \mathbb{N}$ and $\{s_j\}_{j \in J}$ be a good partition of S such that $f|_{s_j}$ is continuous $\forall j \in J$. We'll call C^* to the optimal solution to this problem, when it exists. We want to prove that the solution $\overline{C}$ provided by our algorithm converges to C^*, when the number of restarts of our algorithm approaches infinity. Suppose that C^* is comprised of n points and let us look at what happens when our algorithm picks a point.

On a given iteration, our algorithm initially chooses a point, P_0, and let P^* be the optimal choice. Our algorithm will, given P_0, return a point $\overline{P}$ by sampling from a normal distribution. Hence, we have that $P(\overline{P} \in B(P^*, \varepsilon)) > c > 0$, for a given constant c, because it is the result of integrating a positive function defined in $\mathbb{R}^2$ over a bounded region. For the proof, we'll also require that P_0 belongs to the same subset s_j that P^* belongs to. Again, since the normal distribution is strictly positive everywhere, and because the subsets are regular closed, we have that $P(\overline{P} \in B(P^*, \varepsilon) \wedge PART(\overline{P}) = PART(P^*))) > c' > 0$ from Lemma 1. Of course that $c > c'$, so we will work with the special case where every point in the optimal path is in the boundary of the subset it belongs to.

Looking back at the paths C^* and $\overline{C}$, we can pair every point of these paths according to the iteration that the point is chosen. For a given iteration i, we pair the point $\overline{P}(i)$ from $\overline{C}$ and the optimal point $P^*(i)$ from C^*.

Looking at the entire path, our initial probability becomes

$$P(\forall i \in [n], \overline{P}(i) \in B(P(i)^*, \varepsilon) \wedge PART(\overline{P}(i)) = PART(P(i)^*)) > \prod_{i=1}^{n} c'(i) > 0 \tag{4}$$

At this point, this simply becomes a formulation of the infinite monkey theorem. We look at the complement of this event:

$$P(\exists i \mid (\overline{P}(i) \notin B(P(i)^*, \varepsilon) \vee PART(\overline{P}(i)) \neq PART(P^*)) \tag{5}$$

And we know that it is smaller than 1. Let r be the number of restarts to our algorithm and let us keep the best solution we have found so far, throughout our restarts. Because these are independent events, the probability of all solutions not being ε close to the optimal solution is given by

$$P(\exists i \mid (\overline{P}(i) \notin B(P(i)*, \varepsilon) \vee PART(\overline{P}(i)) \neq PART(P^*))^r \qquad (6)$$

This approaches 0 as r approaches infinity, and since f is piecewise continuous, the error also approaches 0 and hence the proof is complete.   □

A result that can be analogously proven is that, without access to the ground truth, we can always achieve a solution that is ε close to the optimal, we just will not be able to know which one it is. As the error measure used involves an assessment of the ground truth allover the relevant surface, it is probably difficult to make this proof stronger.

5   Benchmark Instances Used

We decided to go with more complicated functions than in the previous paper, functions that we felt better represent the seabed. Instead of working with continuous functions we worked with piecewise continuous functions, and we did this by randomly gluing continuous functions together (see Fig. 1 for an example). Complete descriptions of the continuous functions used for the gluing are publicly available[1].

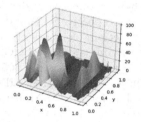

Fig. 1. Seabed function example

Notice that our algorithm decides the position on the relevant surface of a set of points for probing; hence, testing the quality of an algorithm is only possible if the "ground truth" is known on a continuum. As a replacement for this "ground truth", we devised a test set consisting of 10 functions of varying complexity. In each benchmark, an initial small set of points on the surface and the corresponding value of the function are given; these are used in the assessment step. Further points, chosen by the algorithm at the planning step, are probed at the end of this step—i.e., their ground truth value is calculated. These two sets are joined at the estimation step for building the function that will approximate the ground truth. Finally, differences between these two functions, evaluated at another set of points over the surface, will be summed and used to determine the error of the algorithm. With this setting we can establish the quality of an

---

[1] http://www.dcc.fc.up.pt/~jpp/code/CORAL.

algorithm, and use it to compare different algorithms. A solution to our problem consists of two parts: a sequence of locations $a = [(\dot{x}_1, \dot{y}_1), \ldots, ((\dot{x}_n, \dot{y}_n)]$, where to collect samples (aiming at having maximum information collected), such that the total probing and travel time does not exceed T; and an estimation $\tilde{z}_k$ of the level of information predicted by the model on each of the K requested points $E = \{(x_k, y_k)\}_{k=1}^{K}$ The evaluation of a method for solving this problem is firstly based on feasibility: the orienteering tour is checked by verifying that the duration of tour $[(\dot{x}_1, \dot{y}_1), \ldots, ((\dot{x}_n, \dot{y}_n), ((\dot{x}_1, \dot{y}_1)]$ does not exceed T. Then, the final solution quality is measured by $\Sigma_{k=1}^{K} |v(x_k, y_k) - w(x_k, y_k)|$, as an approximation for $\iint |v(x, y) - w(x, y)| dx dy$.

6   Results Obtained

For kernel selection, we manually selected a kernel that would give the best result for the original method, Orienteering, so that if overfitting were to occur, then it would be in detriment of the new methods. We ended up using sklearn's Rational Quadratic with alpha = 0.4 and length_scale = 4. This selection was done using a simple grid search.

Table 1 presents the average of the results obtained over all 10 functions, for every method, and for 16, 49 and 100 initial probings. These probings are either placed on top of a grid, or they are uniformly distributed, and these cases are denoted as Grid and Random, respectively. Table 2 compares every algorithm against each other for every function; elements of each tuple are the number of wins for the line and for the column, respectively. Given an algorithm A and an algorithm B, the first will get a point if its score is 5% lower than the other, for one function. For example, on Table 2, for the grid case, in the Local Search x Multimodal cell, we can see that for N = 4 Multimodal won 5 times vs 3, for N = 7, Multimodal won 3 times vs 1, and for N = 10, Multimodal won 3 times and Local Search won 4.

Table 1. Average error using each of the algorithms.

	Grid			Random		
	N = 4	N = 7	N = 10	N = 4	N = 7	N = 10
Orienteering	13754.29	13933.17	9276.161	15700.96	13170.22	10974.04
Local Search	14230.23	13272.47	9341.03	18112.77	13231.55	10923.35
Multimodal	13275.73	12812.27	9244.21	15653.18	12087.29	10382.21
M + LS	13858.45	12039.93	8785.06	16484.65	12972.35	10424.77

Table 2. Algorithms' comparison.

	Grid			Random		
	Local Search	M	M+LS	Local Search	M	M+LS
Orienteering	[4,4], [0,2], [5,1]	[4,6], [2,3], [4,2]	[3,5], [0,3], [4,4]	[4,1], [1,0], [2,2]	[2,4], [0,5], [3,4]	[3,4], [2,2], [2,4]
Local Search	–	[3,5], [1,3], [4,3]	[1,6], [0,2], [2,5]	–	[2,6], [1,5], [2,4]	[2,4], [2,2], [1,2]
M	–	–	[3,3], [1,2], [3,6]	–	–	[4,3], [6,1], [3,4]

7   Discussion of the Results and Concluding Remarks

Looking at the average error, we see that Normal Local Search performs poorly, compared to most other methods and both Multimodal and Multimodal+Local Search outperform the original algorithm, the original points being on a grid or randomly distributed. If we add up every win, with Grid and Random respectively, we have Local Search with 18 and 13 wins, Orienteering with 26 and 19, Multimodal with 29 and 41 and finally M+LS with 36 and 26. The Multimodal+Local Search algorithm seems to come out on top in the first case, but dropping the Local Search seems to be the best option on the second. Here in this setting, Multimodal was the best algorithm, and only Local Search performed comparatively worse to the original algorithm. As expected, having the initial probings on random locations worsened the overall solutions. As we can see, the methods we developed performed generally better than what was being done previously. Furthermore, these methods have the added benefit of randomness and as we proved previously, can get arbitrarily close to the optimal solution, if we repeat the algorithms often enough.

There are variants of this problem that may provide interesting research. For example, having a variable probing time and ship's speed (related to ocean depth and currents) will probably be more realistic. Additionally, planning the tour dynamically, allowing for changes while the ship is already travelling, may also provide good results. Right now, the tour is being planned entirely in the beginning, without doing more probings, which will rely more on the predictions of the Gaussian Processes, that may be inaccurate. On the other hand, changing the tour after every probing will make it more difficult to plan a good tour, so a balance between these two variants might be the way to go.

The Sea Exploration Problem is one that deserves attention from the scientific community, since from it arise several technical and scientific problems that are both interesting and are able to generate great value, if solved. The methods presented in this paper perform generally better that the previous approaches, for the functions we used. We also provide a proof of the convergence of these algorithms to the optimal solution, with some important caveats, along with a lemma from topology.

References

1. Expedition Schedules expedition schedules. https://www.iodp.org/expeditions/expeditions-schedule. Accessed 4 Dec 2020

2. Anagnostopoulos, A., Atassi, R., Becchetti, L., Fazzone, A., Silvestri, F.: Tour recommendation for groups. Data Min. Knowl. Disc. **31**(5), 1157–1188 (2016). https://doi.org/10.1007/s10618-016-0477-7

3. Basilico, N., Amigoni, F.: Exploration strategies based on multi-criteria decision making for searching environments in rescue operations. Auton. Robots **31**, 401–417 (2011). https://doi.org/10.1007/s10514-011-9249-9

4. Chekuri, C., Korula, N., Pál, M.: Improved algorithms for orienteering and related problems. ACM Trans. Algorithms **8**(3), 1–27 (2012). https://doi.org/10.1145/2229163.2229167

5. Demir, B., Bruzzone, L.: A multiple criteria active learning method for support vector regression. Pattern Recognit. **47**, 2558–2567 (2014). https://doi.org/10.1016/j.patcog.2014.02.001

6. Dionísio, J., Santos, D., Pedroso, J.: Sea exploration problem (2021). https://github.com/Joao-Dionisio/Sea-Exploration-Problem

7. Ghallab, M., Nau, D., Traverso, P.: Automated planning and acting, February 2016

8. Gilmore, M., et al.: Strategies for autonomous rovers at mars. J. Geophys. Res. Atmos. **105**, 29223–29237 (2002). https://doi.org/10.1029/2000JE001275

9. Golden, B., Levy, L., Dahl, R.: Two generalizations of the traveling salesman problem. Omega **9**(4), 439–441 (1981). https://doi.org/10.1016/0305-0483(81)90087-6

10. Han, J., Kamber, M., Pei, J.: Data Mining: Concepts and Techniques. Elsevier, Amsterdam (2012)

11. Kubo, M., Pedroso, J.P., Muramatsu, M., Rais, A.: Mathematical Optimization: Solving Problems Using Gurobi and Python. Kindaikagakusha, Tokyo (2012)

12. Lin, S., Kernighan, B.W.: An effective heuristic algorithm for the traveling-salesman problem (1973). https://doi.org/10.1287/opre.21.2.498

13. Pedroso, J.P., Kramer, A.V., Zhang, K.: The sea exploration problem: Data-driven orienteering on a continuous surface (2019). http://arxiv.org/abs/1802.01482

14. Phillips, H.: A Sea of Voices: Deep sea mining and the Solwara 1 Project in Papua New Guinea. PhD thesis, January 2019

15. Li, A.Q.: Study, design, and evaluation of exploration strategies for autonomous mobile robots. AI Matters **1**, 23–28 (2015). https://doi.org/10.1145/2757001.2757005

16. Ramirez-Loaiza, M.E., Sharma, M., Kumar, G., Bilgic, M.: Active learning: an empirical study of common baselines. Data Min. Knowl. Discov. **31**(2), 287–313 (2016). https://doi.org/10.1007/s10618-016-0469-7

17. Robert, C.: Machine learning, a probabilistic perspective (2014)

18. Spiegel, M.R.: Schaum's Outline of Theory and Problems of Laplace Transforms. Mcgraw-Hill, New York (1965)

19. Thompson, D.: Predictive exploration for autonomous science, pp.1953–1954, January 2007

20. Tsymbalov, E., Panov, M., Shapeev, A.: Dropout-based active learning for regression. In: van der Aalst, W.M.P., et al. (eds.) AIST 2018. LNCS, vol. 11179, pp. 247–258. Springer, Cham (2018). https://doi.org/10.1007/978-3-030-11027-7_24

21. Wang, L., Hu, X., Yuan, B., Lu, J.: Active learning via query synthesis and nearest neighbour search. Neurocomputing **147**, 426–434 (2015). https://doi.org/10.1016/j.neucom.2014.06.042

22. Jingjin, Yu., Schwager, M., Rus, D.: Correlated orienteering problem and its application to persistent monitoring tasks. IEEE Trans. Robot. **32**(5), 1106–1118 (2016). https://doi.org/10.1109/TRO.2016.2593450

23. Zheng, Z., Padmanabhan, B.: On active learning for data acquisition, pp. 562–569, February 2002. https://doi.org/10.1109/ICDM.2002.1184002

Author Index

Printed in the United States
by Baker & Taylor Publisher Services